The hated Protector

THE STORY OF CHARLES WIGHTMAN SIEVWRIGHT,
PROTECTOR OF ABORIGINES
1839-42

by Lindsey Arkley

First published 2000

**Published by Orbit Press, PO Box 373,
Mentone, Victoria, Australia, 3194**
Ph: (03) 9584 6571; Fax: (03) 9585 5580
Website: www.orbitpress.com.au
Email: lindsark@ozemail.com.au

National Library of Australia Cataloguing-in-Publication entry:

Arkley, Lindsey.

The hated Protector: the story of Charles Wightman
Sievwright, protector of Aborigines 1839-42

Bibliography.
Includes index.
ISBN 0 646 40421 0

1. Sievwright, Charles Wightman. 2. Aborigines, Australian
- Victoria - Government relations. 3. Aborigines,
Australian -Victoria - History. I. Title

994.50049915

Printed in Australia by Shannon Books Pty Ltd for Orbit Press

ACKNOWLEDGEMENTS

The author wishes to acknowledge the advice and assistance of the staff of the following: the State Library of Victoria; the Mitchell and Dixson Libraries in Sydney; the Public Record Offices in Melbourne and London; the State Records Authority of New South Wales; the Archives Office of Tasmania; the Guildhall Library in London; the National Archives of Scotland; and the National Library of Scotland.

Deserving of particular thanks for advice and encouragement are Ian MacFarlane, at the the PRO in Melbourne, and Lindsay Smith, of the Western Victorian Association of Historical Societies.

Grateful acknowledgement is also made to the Victorian government, which provided part-funding for this publication through the PRO, the Community Support Fund and Arts Victoria.

Numerous people have provided invaluable support over the years this project has taken to complete. But special thanks is due to Peter and Geeta Goldie (notably for research and transport assistance in Edinburgh); to Gregg Borschmann (especially for advice on publishing); and to my late father, Norm, who was the first to read the completed draft manuscript and to suggest amendments.

Thanks also to Joan Bognuda for the cover and inside illustrations; to Nicola Rusciano for the maps; and to Alyssa and Brittany Rusciano, of Orbit Press, for their production and design assistance.

Finally, I must thank my partner, Villy, who much more than anyone else has shared the frustrations and the joys of bringing this project to completion.

Public Record Office Victoria

COMMUNITY SUPPORT FUND

VICTORIA

ARTS VICTORIA

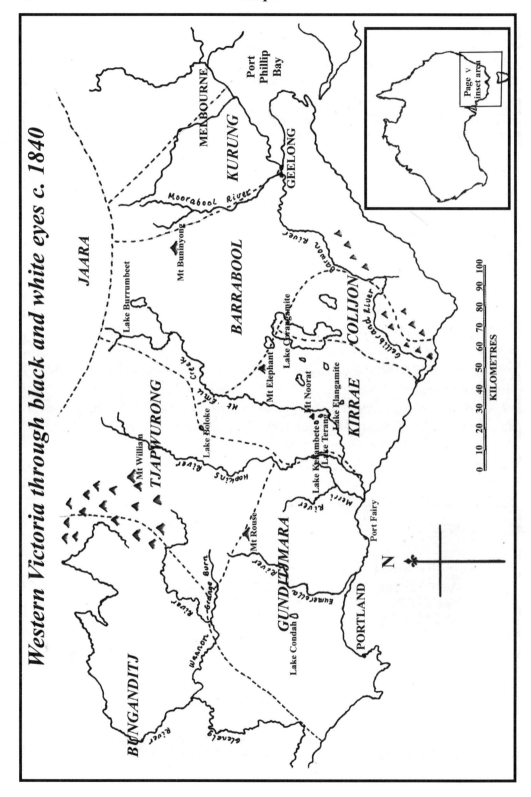

Western Victoria through black and white eyes c. 1840

Map2 v

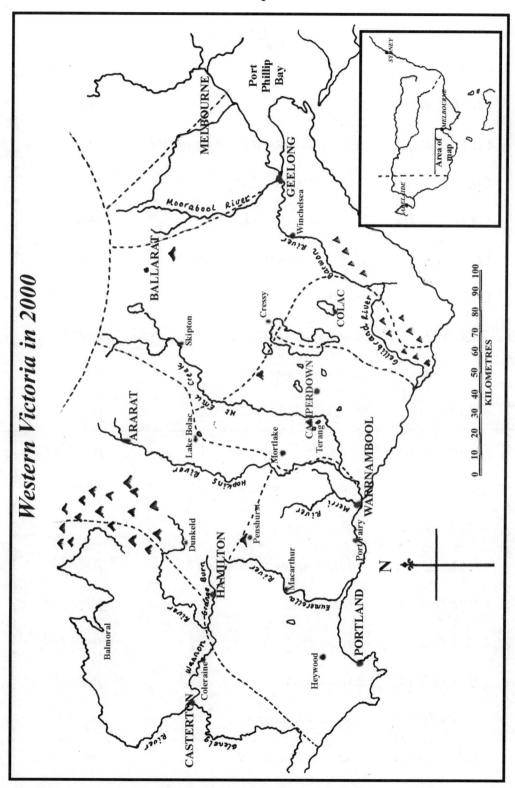

Western Victoria in 2000

<u>*Contents*</u>

<u>Illustrations</u>

FOREWORD

Essentially, this story about Charles Wightman Sievwright and the Aborigines of the Western District of Victoria is a work of non-fiction, based largely on official archival and private manuscript sources, as well as contemporary published reports, newspaper accounts, and some oral history. Nevertheless, gaps in the available information have made it necessary to make a few assumptions. Notably, unless otherwise stated, it has been assumed that events involving particular Aboriginal groups all occurred within their tribal territory.

Identifying tribal territory -- and indeed naming tribes -- has presented a major problem. There is no universally recognised authority on this issue, and it will be a matter of academic debate for years to come. For the sake of a consistent narrative, one widely respected source has been used for defining the names of tribes and their territory: Professor Norman B. Tindale's 1974 work *Aboriginal Tribes of Australia*.

The main exception to this is the "Barrabool" tribe. According to Tindale, this was an alternative term for the Kurung tribe. But Sievwright certainly regarded the Barrabool and the Waddaro (Tindale's Wathaurung) tribes to be one and the same. Sievwright's more commonly-used term was Barrabool, so this has been used for both. Unless specifically stated otherwise, other references to events in the "Wathaurung" territory defined by Tindale are stated as involving Barrabool people.

The maps on pages *iv* and *v* outline the Aboriginal territorial boundaries as described by Tindale (with the Wathaurung territory named Barrabool). Readers should take these boundaries as merely indicative, and bear in mind that other detailed academic studies have already produced a number of respected alternatives.

Some adjustments have been made to original spellings of place names which remain in usage and for which pronunciations remain the same or similar. For example, Sievwright's "Lake Tarang" has been made "Lake Terang", as it refers to the place where the township of Terang now stands. In other cases, place names with various spellings have been standardised. An example is Lake Boloke (today's Lake Bolac). Place names such as The Grange (today's Hamilton) have been left in their original form.

This book contains the names of numerous deceased Aboriginal and white people, and in some cases, information concerning the circumstances of their deaths. This information has been taken from official records or published accounts at the time. The author's intention has been to provide frank evidence of what was often a brutal period in Australian history. Readers should be aware that the details of some deaths, and perhaps particularly what happened to bodies after death, could be distressing to some people.

"When Sievwright sat down in a dingy, damp tent to write his first official report..."

CHAPTER 1
In the bush

MOST of the inhabitants of the south-western part of the British colony of New South Wales had still never heard of Queen Victoria, or the Empire over which she ruled. In the name of that Empire, and private enterprise, they were about to suffer an upheaval as severe as any experienced by any race in the history of mankind. Charles Wightman Sievwright was responsible for helping them cope. When Sievwright sat down in a dingy, damp tent to write his first official report in his new job, it had been almost three years since he'd last worn the tall bearskin cap of a Royal Fusilier, his career in the British army at an abrupt end. The respectability among his peers he craved so much to re-establish seemed even further away than when he'd taken up his appointment on the other side of the world. He set burning a new tallow candle, lit a cheroot from it, dipped his quill into the ink bottle, and began: "The Bush, Ist September, 1839, Upon the River Barwon..."

Close to Sievwright's tent, in and around their bark and sapling shelters, were dozens of members of the Barrabool tribe of Aborigines. Also nearby, in a larger, bell-shaped tent, were his wife, Christina, and their four daughters and three sons. But their presence did little to alleviate his acute loneliness, or his frustration. As an "Assistant Protector of Aborigines", Sievwright's duty was to represent the wants, wishes and grievances of the Barrabool people and thousands of other Aborigines in an area of about 40,000 square kilometres -- more than half the size of his homeland, Scotland. He was the first man to hold the post, though his fellow whites had been gradually moving into the area for almost three years. In the Port Phillip District of New South Wales, he was the equal ninth highest-paid colonial government official. He was receiving 250 pounds a year -- plus a daily allowance of 10 shillings and sixpence to feed his family, two prisoners of the Crown assigned to him as servants, one horse, and one bullock. For this, Sievwright was supposed to protect the Aborigines "from cruelty, oppression and injustice" and "from encroachments upon their property".[1] He fully appreciated the absurdity of his duty statement. Despite British government declarations to the contrary, in reality the Aborigines had virtually no rights, and were constantly being subjected to cruelty and injustice...which he'd so far been unable to stop. And they were being gradually driven from the land on which they and their ancestors had depended both economically and spiritually for tens-of-thousands of years, to make way for strange hairy animals and their white owners.

"Their wants, their grievances, their protracted sufferings, and lingering death, have been reiterated for months, and I am still in the midst of the same scenes, and have not a blanket to screen them from the storm, nor an ounce of food to save them from starvation," Sievwright wrote. "I am surrounded by them in the bush, where my family are hourly importuned for the pittance we have it not in our power to grant. I have neither the means of employing the industrious, nor of relieving the wretched."[2] Sievwright put down his quill and reflected on the irony of the largesse shown by the Aboriginal Protectorate five months earlier, when he and his three fellow Assistants, and the Chief Protector, George Augustus Robinson, had hosted a party about 70 kilometres away in the young township of Melbourne. The idea had been to explain to the Aborigines, and the colonists, the philosophies and objectives of the experimental department. Aboriginal messengers had been sent in all directions to invite their people, while one of the town's two newspapers had urged "respectable" white residents to attend the event, hailing it as "the proper manner whereby to command (the blacks') respect and obedience".[3]

With the assistance of his two convict servants who'd acted as waiters, Sievwright had been in charge of providing alcoholic refreshments to the white guests in a large marquee borrowed from the Survey Department. Outside, several whole sheep and quarters of beef had been roasted on iron spits, then portions given with generous amounts of bread and rice to the several hundred blacks who'd attended. Tea brewed in large boilers, and sweetened with liberal doses of sugar, had been served in tin pannikins. For the amusement of the whites, the Aborigines had competed for various prizes such as tomahawks and blankets. Among the games had been running races, splitting boards with spears, throwing spears at hats thrown in the air, wrestling, climbing slippery poles, and boomerang throwing. It had been the best party yet in the two-year-old town, and a good time was had by all -- even by Sievwright's waiters, who'd been flogged the next day during their hangovers for getting themselves helplessly drunk. At the end of the party, the Aborigines had carried away both the leftover food, and the message that the arrival of the Protectors was an event of exceedingly good fortune. The message was soon to sound very hollow.[4]

The Barrabool tribe was thus far among the worst affected in Sievwright's district by the white invasion, much of their land having already been claimed by squatters for sheep and cattle "runs". And as the size of the whites' flocks and herds increased, the kangaroos and other game on which the tribe depended for both food and clothing was being scared even further away, often beyond the limits of their tribal territory. As well, the hooves of the white men's animals were destroying many daisy yam plants, a staple Aboriginal food across the vast plain to the west. "In thus being obliged to quit their own district in search of that food with which it was most abundantly to supply them, their local attachments for which they are so noted, which confines the different tribes within their own immediate boundary, are hence destroyed...," Sievwright wrote. "They are moreover obliged to intrude upon the hunting grounds and localities of strange tribes, and so...hostilities amongst themselves...unless checked...must end with the extermination of the whole race."[5]

Instructions from the British government to the Governor of the colony in Sydney in January 1838, had stated the Protectors should be enabled "to supply

By permission of the National Library of Australia
"Natives oppossum hunting on the Barwon, Geelong".
by H. Friend (lithographer), S T Gill (artist)

the natives occasionally with moderate quantities of food and clothing".[6] This Sievwright had conveyed to the Barrabool people when he'd moved from Melbourne in June 1839, to live with them near the tiny white settlement called Geelong. They'd agreed to perform whatever tasks he might deem necessary in return for the supplies he'd issue. But to their astonishment, and his dismay, no such supplies had arrived at the camp, despite urgent appeals to the Chief Protector. Governor George Gipps had given Robinson discretionary power to spend up to 300 pounds a year on provisions for the Aborigines. Gipps acknowledged that this was not a large sum. He'd purposely fixed it low because he wanted to avoid "the bad practice of giving presents to the Aborigines which, in general, instead of exciting in them a desire to earn money by labour, or by making themselves useful, tends to confirm them in their habits of idleness". Gipps was prepared to consider increasing the size of the fund if he "found it to be well expended".[7]

However, for a long time Robinson jealously kept the fund to himself, not even making his assistants aware of its existence.   Robinson had become widely regarded as a "conciliator" and "civiliser" of the Aborigines in the sister colony of Van Diemen's Land -- largely through a process of bluff and manipulation of the truth.   Notwithstanding an undoubted deep concern for the future of the Aborigines, Robinson had long been more anxious to preserve his reputation as an "expert" on how to deal with them than to preserve the race. In Van Diemen's Land, he'd won the favour of some Aborigines by handing out presents when-ever touring the countryside. Intending to do the same in his new domain in the Port Phillip District, Robinson was reluctant to squander opportunities for self-aggrandisement by giving his assistants access to the fund authorised for their use.

Initially, Sievwright had won a degree of confidence in his friendly intentions through gifts from his own resources to some individual Barrabool tribe mem-bers, and promises of food and clothing for the rest. But as his charges suffered from new diseases introduced by the white men, and shivered and starved to

Reproduced courtesy of La Trobe Picture Collection, State Library of Victoria
A depiction of George Augustus Robinson in Van Diemen's Land, where he won a reputation that would lead to his appointment as Chief Protector of Aborigines in New South Wales. This image is taken from a postcard featuring a painting by Benjamin Duterrau (1836) entitled "The Conciliation".

death through the 1839 winter, his credibility had been severely damaged. He felt that confidence in him had plummeted to a level lower than when he'd first arrived in Geelong. Many of the Barrabools had given up waiting for the promised aid, and had left Sievwright's camp to again try to fend for themselves in the less-settled parts of their territory. Before leaving, some had offered to return in the spring with some kangaroo skins, retailing for about one pound per dozen in Melbourne, and some of the beautiful long tail feathers of the male lyre bird, popular among the whites as ornaments. They'd suggested trading the pelts and feathers for blankets. Not knowing when Robinson would finally send some supplies, Sievwright had been forced to decline the offer. Such was the plight of the Aborigines in his district, he reported, that they must soon "cease to be either objects of solicitude or solicitation to this Department, of fear to the Squatter, or Philanthropy to Her Majesty's Government". The delay in relieving their suffering made a mockery of the proclaimed intentions of the Protectorate "and must moreover give, even to its supporters, but a faint promise of its ultimate success, if the result is to be judged by what has already been (or is likely to be) accomplished by the present arrangement".[8]

To show he was not exaggerating the seriousness of the situation, Sievwright had recently called for a report from Dr Jonathan Clerke, the Assistant Colonial Surgeon at Geelong, who'd just attended to a Barrabool man whose condition, even after treatment, was "awful to behold". According to Clerke, the man was "dangerously ill" with pleurisy, as a result of exposure to cold. "I bled and prescribed for him accordingly," the doctor had written, "but fear that medicine can produce little effect on him or any of the Aborigines whilst they are suffered to continue in their present exposed, helpless, and miserable state, destitute (when sickness attacks them) both of shelter and clothing and other necessaries for their comforts. It cannot under these circumstances be supposed that medicine can do much good." Clerke concluded by saying that Sievwright must be aware of the urgent need to represent the deplorable state of the Aborigines to the government, "and entreating that proper means might be speedily adopted to ameliorate their sufferings".[9] Sievwright's tactic of seeking Clerke's support had driven Robinson to fraud. Fearing that his failure to respond to Sievwright's appeals might be exposed by the involvement of another branch of the bureaucracy, Robinson had immediately written a report falsely claiming that each of his assistants had issued to the blacks under their care 25 rugs or blankets, as well as 90 kilograms of flour and 45 kilograms of meat -- officially regarded as enough food for 100 people for one day. In fact, Robinson had only just requisitioned for this food, and none had yet been delivered to his assistants.[10]

It was not the first time that the Barrabools had had a white man living with them. In an experience unique in Australian history, former English soldier

William Buckley had in fact lived among them for more than 30 years. Buckley, transported for life to Australia for receiving a roll of stolen cloth, had been one of about 300 convicts sent with Lieutenant-Colonel David Collins to help establish a penal colony in the Port Phillip District in 1803. A number of the convicts would escape before the settlement at Sorrento was abandoned the following year -- young Buckley being the only one believed to have stayed free and survived. He ended up on the other side of Port Phillip Bay in Barrabool territory. Reportedly because they believed he was a reincarnated tribal leader, the Barrabools befriended Buckley and he would live safely among them until 1835, when he surrendered to a party of whites who arrived from Van Diemen's Land to assess the District's pastoral prospects. When he first rejoined white society, Buckley had forgotten English, but it gradually came back to him and for a time he was used with limited success as an interpreter. By the time Sievwright arrived in New South Wales, however, the "wild white man" had recently left the colony.[11]

Buckley had had no choice but to quickly adopt the lifestyle of the Barrabools -- and he obviously owed his life to his ability to do so. But Sievwright had neither the need nor the desire to live like his charges. Despite the misery he could see it causing, Sievwright was by no means opposed to white settlement. He suffered from a limitation to rational thought common among people the world over: the blind and unshakeable belief that they were among a minority fortunate enough to have inherited the "true" religion. White settlement, he believed, provided the opportunity to lead the Aborigines out of a state of "mental chaos" with "the beacon of civilisation" and "the blessed light of Christianity". In support of his assertion that the Aborigines were intelligent, and therefore capable of "improvement" -- a view not widely shared by his fellow whites -- Sievwright cited the case of a boy from the Colijon tribe, abducted by a group of white men two years earlier as a three or four-year-old. Although his people wanted him returned, the boy was being kept with government sanction by Dr Clerke, who'd named him Billy.[12] "He reads readily from any book given to him, and is not checked by words of three or four syllables," Sievwright wrote. "He repeats from memory hymns, and portions of scripture, and answers questions put to him, upon the subjects he has been instructed in, so as to prove that the time and care which have been devoted to his education, have not been lost."[13]

Similar claims had been made in Sydney almost a year earlier by George Robinson, at a public meeting called to establish an Aborigines' Protection Society in New South Wales. Robinson, who'd been in Sydney to discuss plans for the Protectorate and to meet his assistants, found an audience eager to hear of his exploits among what remained of the Van Diemen's Land Aborigines. He'd been in his element. There was a theatre full of credulous people with great admiration for his tales of bravery. But of most interest was his claim to have proved that the Aborigines were "capable of high moral attainments". And Robinson did not need to produce an iota of independent evidence to prove any of his wild claims about his "civilisation" achievements. Those attending the meeting believed what he said because they passionately wanted to believe it.

In another speech to the meeting, a London-born Baptist minister, John Saunders, would fuel a debate then raging in the white community of New South Wales. The debate centred on the impending trial in Sydney of 11 white men, charged with murder over a massacre of 28 Aborigines at Myall Creek in the north of the colony. There was a deep division in the white community over whether the trial was necessary -- many of those with pastoral interests arguing that whoever committed the massacre had done their fellow whites a favour. But Saunders would take on the voice of the pastoralists, the *Sydney Herald*, virtually accusing it of incitement to murder. The *Herald* was vociferous in its defence, describing Saunders as "vermin" and "a malicious propagator of untruth". It strongly denied his "foul assertion" that it was helping to promote "a murderous spirit" among the white settlers. At the same time, it advised any white men who spotted would-be Aboriginal thieves or murderers to "shoot them dead if you can".14

This advice from the *Herald* would be published the day Sievwright arrived with his family in Sydney, after a five-month voyage from London through the Atlantic, Indian and Southern Oceans. The same article would make some comments about the Protectorate. The office of Sievwright and his colleagues, it argued, would be a farce unless the white settlers were induced to assist them. One way in which the Protectors would need help, the *Herald* suggested, was in protecting themselves from the blacks. "Their lives will not be of the value of a kangaroo, for any hostile tribe would, at any moment, exterminate them, just as readily as they would the stockmen or their masters," the article claimed. But, it suggested, the settlers would not assist "such useless officials".

Nor should the white settlers have to pay for the salaries of the Protectors, the *Herald* declared. The salaries should be paid directly by the British government, unless it was through a "bold-faced robbery" by using funds raised from land sales. Certainly, the nominees representing the settlers on the Legislative Council of New South Wales should not vote to pay for the Protectors. The Aborigines should not be given any support from the revenue derived from the labour of the whites, unless some means could be devised to extract labour in return. "Place them, too, in a position where they cannot evade justice -- that when murders are committed they may be found and hanged, as white men are when they murder," the *Herald* added. "And then we might, perhaps, throw them in the salaries of the Protectors."15

The Myall Creek murder trial would go ahead while all the Assistant Protectors were still in Sydney awaiting guidance on what they should be doing. To make the case manageable, the 11 defendants were charged only with the wilful murder of one black man named Daddy, and one other black man, whose name was unknown. Hired for the defence were three leading lawyers, their fees being covered by a special "Aboriginal Association" set up by graziers in the Hunter River region, north of Sydney, some of them magistrates. Evidence would be given that the murder victims had been among a group of 28 blacks -- including women and infants -- tied together with a long rope, and led away a short distance from the hut at a sheep station at which they'd hitherto been frequent visitors. Two shots had been fired, but most of the 28 blacks had been hacked to death with swords, many of them being decapitated, before their bodies had been burned.

The defence argued that the prosecution had failed to establish that the charred remains sworn to by witnesses were those of Daddy or any other black man. The evidence against the defendants, their lawyers said, was entirely circumstantial. After retiring for just 15 minutes, the jury agreed, and the men were acquitted. "It was with exertion that the Chief Justice could prevent the audience from cheering, such was their delight," reported the *Sydney Monitor* in disgust. "The aristocracy of the colony, for once, joined heart and hand with the prison population, in expressions of joy at the acquittal of these men. We tremble to remain in a country where such feelings and principles prevail."[16] One of the jurors would later be quoted as having said he regarded the Aborigines "as a set of monkeys", and that he'd like to see their quick extermination. "I knew well they were guilty of the murder, but I for one, would never see a white man suffer for shooting a black," he reportedly stated.[17]

According to another Sydney paper, the *Gazette*, it had probably been one of the most horrible massacres ever to have occurred in a British colony. When news of it reached Britain, it was bound to arouse such a sensation that it could affect the stability of the colonial administration headed by George Gipps.[18] The Governor and his officials were well aware of the potential damage the case could do to their careers. The Irish Attorney-General, John Hubert Plunkett, had already taken the extraordinary step of ordering another trial for seven of the 11 men acquitted. This time, the seven were charged with murdering a black man named Charley, and one black boy and one black girl, both unidentified. The *Sydney Herald* was outraged. How many times, it asked, could the Attorney-General place the same men on trial for what was effectively the same crime? The evidence of a murder having been committed was the same -- some skeletal remains. Could acquitted men be put back on trial for a capital offence "for every jaw-bone, finger or toe which the scouts of the Attorney-General may ferret out?"[19]

The "Aboriginal Association" would hire the same defence lawyers on behalf of the defendants, but this time they were not successful in defending their clients. Found guilty, they were given a mandatory death sentence. As pleas for clemency were being considered by the Governor, the *Herald* would publish details of the murders of 15 white men in New South Wales in the previous six years. All of these remained unavenged, it alleged. The white settlers were demanding both equal justice, and protection from the blacks. If the hangings took place, the *Herald* warned, it would "incite an actual war of extermination". But Gipps decided that the sentences should be carried out. The morning after the Assistant Protectors set off for Melbourne aboard a barque, ironically named the *Hope*, the seven condemned men were led to a scaffold at the Sydney jail. After embracing one another and shaking hands, the bolt would be withdrawn, and the seven white men would drop to their deaths at the end of ropes.[20]

The hangings had no obvious impact on dissuading violence against the Aborigines in New South Wales. Only a few months later, in April 1839, Sievwright would report that on the south-western frontier of the colony at least, there was a "hostile spirit" towards the blacks.[21] Another four months on, at the time of writing his first official report, Sievwright estimated that he'd ridden almost 1600 kilometres investigating cases involving the Aborigines. He'd visited the stations of 45 different squatters, and believed he had a good idea of the attitude of the whites of his district towards its original inhabitants. Vicious rumours and extravagant accusations had misled the public "in regard to the natural character, disposition and conduct of the much-maligned Aborigines". Prejudice against the blacks was being perpetuated by those who came into most immediate contact with them -- the shepherds and stockmen. Whites new to the district were as credulous as children listening to fairy tales when they heard reports of alleged Aboriginal cruelty and cannibalism, and they reacted with the same dread. Promulgation of these reports by the shepherds and stockmen was "a matter of policy, as well of amusement", for it made it easy to blame a foraging party of Aborigines for any stock that went missing.

"With the more experienced stockmen, a tone of absolute authority and tyranny is assumed towards (and submitted to by) the Aborigines, although in many instances I have detected through the sullen deportment, and otherwise impertunable features of the natives, the quick and intelligent glance to each other which, while it bespoke of their outraged feeling, strongly indicated their contempt and defiance of their aggressors," Sievwright wrote. From having witnessed such scenes, he was surprised that more bloodshed had not occurred as a result of Aboriginal retaliation, since he'd daily seen examples of "feelings of attachment and warm affection" among the Aborigines that were sometimes

Sievwright's "Summary of Journies made, number of cases inquired into, number of days in travelling, and number of stations visited, from March to August, 1839". In the "distance travelled" column, he estimated that he'd ridden 720 miles (1160 kms) on "Daily incidental excursions in the Bush since 1st June returning to my Tents at night, average 12 miles per diem". In the note added later, bottom left, Port Phillip's Superintendent Charles Joseph La Trobe (CJL) deemed Sievwright couldn't claim a forage allowance for these trips, declaring: "This last item of the account is surely inadmissable!".

lacking in fellow Britishers with what he regarded as the benefits of "civilisation" and Christianity. The Protector looked forward to the arrival of an "uncon-
taminated class of labourers" to follow the example of those "respectable" settlers who had adopted an attitude towards the blacks that was beneficial to both
races. Meanwhile, there should be "a speedy and wholesome exercise of the
laws" against any aggressors among the "degraded and lawless outcasts" cur-
rently employed by the squatters.[22]

On the assumption that the tribes of Sievwright's district spoke a single language, he'd been instructed to learn it. But each tribe had its own language, and
there were dialectal variations in particular areas. So great were the differences
between the languages, even in the way words were pronounced, that conversations between members of non-neighbouring tribes could be impossible. Telling
Sievwright to learn the language was like sending a man to the middle of Europe
and telling him to simultaneously learn French, Greek, Italian, and several other
languages -- with neither bilingual teachers, nor learning aids.

It was clear that the Barrabools and the other Western District Aborigines still
by far outnumbered the whites in their territory. But neither Sievwright nor any
other white man knew by how much, or even how many tribes there were.
Sievwright had rough estimates of the size of the Barrabool tribe and two others: the Colijon and the Mainmait (Kirrae). He believed there were about 260
Barrabool members (60 men, 80 women, and 120 children), about 350 in the
Colijon tribe, and about 300 in the Mainmait. He referred to another tribe,
which he called the Nelang-guin, apparently meaning either the Jaara or
Tjapwurong people. Their numbers were uncertain, he stated, but they were
more numerous than any of the other tribes. Further west, there were other
major tribes of which he was not yet aware.

Despite his scant knowledge of the tribes and their territories, Sievwright felt
confident enough to recommend a reserve for each of them. On these reserves,
the Aborigines "might have every facility afforded them of learning, or improving those habits of industry which would ultimately and speedily tend to eman-
cipate them from their barbarous condition, and at the same time they would be
reserved from the general imputation of moral incapability for improvement
which has hitherto doomed them to neglect", he wrote. At each reserve, the sick,
the aged, and the infirm could be given adequate food and clothing by the government. The able-bodied would be given supplies as well, but only in return
for work performed in establishing agricultural operations, for which he felt at
least the young were well-suited.

"This would ensure to the peaceable and industrious a retreat, and security from
wants, which they at present so much require and, in thus being enabled to congregate the families, the seeds of instruction and civilisation might be profitably,

and at once, sown amongst the children -- to whom we must look for the result and reward of a matured and disciplined institution -- for wholly and at once to overcome the habits, prejudices and erratic propensities of the adults would be as unprofitable in the attempt as chimerical in the design," Sievwright wrote. He also believed that each reserve should have its own hospital, which was as important for the welfare of the white inhabitants of the district as it was for the treatment of Aborigines suffering from various white diseases such as syphilis and influenza. And many of the Aborigines were bearing the scars of a small-pox epidemic that had started near Sydney hundreds of kilometres away some years earlier, and spread quickly through inter-tribal contact to the southern coast of the continent. The Protector asked for vaccine against smallpox for his charges most in contact with the whites, as a precautionary measure against another devastating outbreak.

The system of reserves he was proposing would of course involve an initial increase in the funds allocated to his department. However, he envisaged that in such a fertile area, profits made from the reserves' excess produce would soon cover the department's entire budget.[23]   To propose such a scheme when the Protectorate was already being condemned as a waste of public money by many of the colonists was indicative of Sievwright's brash and at times naive nature. But there was another reason why he was unlikely to win much support for any-thing he proposed in his district. He and his wife were already the subject of many a drunken joke, most of them lewd. The disharmonious state of his mar-riage to Christina was the talk of all levels of white society, especially since an incident a few weeks earlier, so hot a story it had parched the throats of the scan-dal-mongers.

The wife of the Protector had run away to Melbourne with their eldest daugh-ter, 17-year-old Frances. Christina had been forced to borrow money from one of the convict servants for the fares on the mail coach. Sievwright had been away at the time, investigating a reported sheep theft by some Aborigines. The runaways had stayed at a public inn before being put up for several days by the most senior government official in Melbourne at the time, the Police Magistrate, Captain William Lonsdale. Christina had complained to Lonsdale about Sievwright's behaviour, alleging that she and the children were suffering from gross neglect. When she and Frances had returned to Geelong a few days later, they'd been accompanied by an English solicitor, William Meek, who'd volun-teered to try to mediate. But there'd been an ugly scene, with her repeating her allegations of neglect, and Sievwright counter-accusing her of extravagance.[24]

While still in London, Sievwright had seen the possibility of his appointment helping to repair his strained marriage -- by working with Christina. He'd asked the Colonial Office whether the wives of the Protectors could help with the religious instruction of the Aborigines, particularly the women, to help with their "redemption" from "their present state of moral degradation". The idea had been endorsed as "highly useful".[25]   Unfortunately, however, Christina had never wanted to accompany Sievwright into the bush, partly because of the state of their marriage, and partly because of the privations it would entail. Except when Sievwright had been between jobs, she'd been used to living comfortably, and when she'd agreed to go with him to the colony, she'd expected to live in Sydney, or at least Melbourne. She certainly hadn't imagined having to live in a tent surrounded by Aborigines, with the only nearby white settlement comprising two stores and an inn constructed of split logs and sheets of bark.

   Well before they'd moved to Geelong, Christina had asked the Chief Protector to make arrangements so she and the children could stay in Melbourne, complaining of Sievwright's "cold selfishness" and "outrageous behaviour". But Robinson had declined to intervene, she'd been forced to make the move, and the marriage had continued to deteriorate.[26] Sievwright of course knew that his marital problems were no secret. What he didn't yet realise was the extent to which they were known throughout the colonial bureaucracy, and that even Governor Gipps had been informed of such details as the fact that he and Christina did not sleep together, even on cold nights.[27] Nor did he realise the seriousness of the charges that had been made against his moral character, as he stubbed out his cheroot, wrapped his first report in an oilskin, and laid down to sleep to the soothing sound of the water bubbling over the falls just upstream.

Reproduced courtesy of the Archives Office of Tasmania
Frances Anna (Fanny) Sievwright

CHAPTER 2
"Equal and indiscriminate justice"

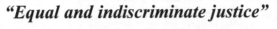

LIFE on the Australian frontier for British squatters and the men they employed was harsh and lonely. The winters were milder than those which most had previously experienced, but in summer the temperatures would soar to heights that would bake their anaemic bodies. There were other strains as well, such as the fear resulting from ignorance of which of a range of new reptiles and insects could cause irritation, pain, or even death. At the same time, there were very few comforts or amusements beyond a bottle of rum, or an occasional kangaroo hunt. For a shepherd on an outstation, it could be many days between conversations. The shortage of white women caused some white men to use each other, or their animals, to satisfy their carnal desires. More commonly, though, Aboriginal women or girls were used. When this was done with the approval of the Aboriginal men, in exchange for food or trinkets, at least both male parties were usually satisfied. But in many cases the black women were taken by force, throwing into disarray tribal mores governing sexual relations -- and resulting in great insult to pride, and bloodshed.

In May 1839, Governor Gipps issued a notice referring to an Act recently passed by the government-nominated Legislative Council of the colony, designed "further to Restrain the unauthorised Occupation of Crown Lands, and to provide the means of defraying the Expense of a Border Police". The notice declared that one of the main reasons the Council had passed the Act was to stop "the atrocities which have of late been so extensively committed" both by the Aborigines, and on them. Her Majesty's government had instructed Gipps to ensure that inquests were held in every case in which an Aborigine "may have come to a violent death in consequence of a collision with white men". In such cases, the Governor was determined to make no distinction "whether the aggressors or parties injured be one or the other race or colour, but to bring all, as far as may be in his power, to equal and indiscriminate justice". The notice added that the government officials designated "Commissioners of Crown Land", whose main responsibility was to supervise the allocation and use of 10 pound squatting licences, had been directed to help Aborigines "in obtaining redress for any wrong to which they may have been exposed". In particular, the Commissioners had been told "to prevent any interference on the part of white men with their women".[1] Gipps directed on the same day the republication of a notice issued 20 months earlier by his predecessor, Sir Richard Bourke. This notice was devoted exclusively to reports that squatters and their employees in remote districts were "not infrequently guilty of detaining by force, in their huts, and as their companions abroad, black women of the native tribes resorting to their neighbourhood". This practice was both "most heinous and revolting" and "abominable and unchristian", and had led to violence, including murder. Squatters found to be in any way connected with such behaviour faced cancellation of their annual licences, and prosecution as "illegal occupiers of Crown lands, or otherwise, as the law directs".[2]

By permission of the National Library of Australia
"Turning out the sheep from the hurdle yard, early sunrise, shepherd leaving the hut"
by S. T. Gill

   The re-issuing of Bourke's notice had as much effect as the original, and sexual liaisons between the races on the frontier, both voluntary and involuntary, continued to be commonplace. After the first few months in his district, Charles Sievwright was convinced that seduction of black women -- not white occupation per se -- was the main cause of inter-racial violence. Venereal disease was rampant among both races, and was killing many of his charges. He wanted the government to enact a law giving all public servants with any legal authority, such as the Assistant Protectors, the power to deal summary justice to any white man found with a black woman in his dwelling under any pretext. The only exception should be when the Protectors authorised certain squatters to engage black women as domestic servants.[3]

Within days of having made this recommendation, Sievwright was confronted by a group of Barrabool men, complaining for the second time in a week that some of their women had been abducted and were being held in a hut by two convicts employed at a nearby sheep station. The Aborigines were threatening to set fire to the hut, and spear the white men as they came out, if their women were not immediately released. Sievwright accompanied the enraged blacks to the hut, where he found a shepherd, John Cooke, a bullock driver, William Edwards, and a soldier, Private Thomas Lambourne. They denied there were any Aboriginal women about, but a search was made and three Barrabool women were found hiding under a bed. Their kinsmen wanted to take revenge on the spot, but the Protector ushered them back to the camp, promising that the whites would not escape punishment.

Cooke and Edwards -- convicts respectively for four years and 16 years -- appeared two days later in the small wooden building in Geelong recently erected to serve as a court, charged with having harboured the women. They appeared before the only other senior government official in the western part of the Port Phillip district at the time, the Geelong Police Magistrate, Captain Foster Fyans. A guilty verdict was quickly reached. The sentence: 50 lashes each, the prisoners to be forwarded to Melbourne to receive their punishment from the government scourger.[4] The sentence was not unusual. Fyans had given the same sentence the month before to John Blainey, one of the two convict servants assigned to Sievwright, for "disobedience of orders and extreme insolence of conduct".[5] Sievwright, who as a Justice of the Peace sometimes sat on the court bench with Fyans, and sometimes alone, had reciprocated a few days later. He ruled that William Cox, one of Fyans' convict servants, should also receive 50 lashes, for "neglect of duty, general disrespect, and idleness", before being sent to work for 12 months in irons on a road gang for trying to abscond.[6]

Although Sievwright and Fyans were fellow senior officials in the colonial administration -- Fyans being slightly more highly-paid -- were former brother officers in the British Army, and were now sometimes fellow magistrates sitting in joint judgement, their alliance was far from amiable. Fyans, an Irishman, had served the British Empire in Spain, India, Burma and Mauritius before joining a regiment in New South Wales early in 1833. He'd spent the next four-and-a-half years at two of the special settlements established to punish the prisoners regarded as the least controllable in the penal colony -- those at Norfolk Island and Moreton Bay. Norfolk Island's notoriety for brutality was maintained by the sadistic actions of "Flogger" Fyans as captain of the guard and acting commandant. One night, for instance, he ordered prisoners to receive 100 lashes by candlelight for talking in their cells.[7] Then, after a stint as commandant at Moreton Bay, Fyans had resigned from the army and left Sydney for the Port Phillip district in September 1837, to become Geelong's first Police Magistrate -- a post

Reproduced courtesy of the Royal Historical Society of Victoria
Foster "Flogger" Fyans

created in response to a complaint to the Sydney authorities from 44 squatters about "the increasing annoyances and inroads" being made by the Aborigines. The squatters had warned that further violent clashes between the blacks and whites in the district were looming, suggesting that a small body of mounted police might prevent these clashes, or at least limit their severity.[8]

Governor Bourke had acknowledged that Police Magistrate Lonsdale in Melbourne could not exercise any effective control over the situation around Geelong and beyond, and in approving Fyans' appointment had given him the assistance of a clerk, three police constables, and eight convict servants. Fyans had been reminded that the main reason for the creation of his post was the danger of inter-racial violence, and he was instructed to pay particular attention to the cultivation of racial harmony.[9] It was an objective he'd been unable to achieve, and the inevitable clashes had intensified. Within nine months, Bourke had decided that Fyans needed the help of a military force, comprising a corporal and 12 privates, to act as Mounted Police. But they were hardly ideal men for such a sensitive mission. Most were former soldiers in the British army who'd been Crown prisoners since being transported for life for desertion during the war against the United States more than 25 years earlier. In a private letter to the Governor's secretary, Edward Deas Thomson, Fyans lamented that he'd found them to be "perfect ruffians barely to be spoken to". They were so useless to him that he'd rather they be immediately sent back to Melbourne, to be under the immediate control of their commanding officer, if he could have a horse for his non-convict constables.[10]

When Sievwright arrived, Fyans had been officially responsible for the welfare of the Aborigines in what became known as the Western District for almost two years, a task he'd not tackled with zeal. He'd told Thomson that he had no faith in the Aborigines, believing there was "nothing to be done with them". Those in the interior who had so far had little or no contact with Europeans were "as wild as wild can be", and they "would eat a man (while still) half-clothed." Fyans added that he believed the Protectorate system was "humbug".[11] The Police Magistrate resented Sievwright taking over some of his theoretical responsibilities, believing it undermined his status. Relations between the two arrogant men were thus fraught with the likelihood of discord from the outset, especially when there was an apparent overlap in their vaguely-worded duty instructions.

The first major dispute between them occurred only a month after Sievwright moved to Geelong from Melbourne. The Assistant Protector had been doing what he could with his scant resources to help the Barrabool tribe members living with him who were worst affected by the winter cold and lack of food, but several deaths had already occurred. The dispute arose after an old man named

Murradone, weak from starvation, died from a pulmonary infection, or some similar disorder. Sievwright, who'd been attending Murradone when he died, watched as other Barrabool people silently and solemnly wrapped his body in possum skin cloaks and prepared to carry it into the bush for burial. But the preparations were suddenly interrupted by the arrival at the scene of Patrick McKeever, formerly batman to Fyans in the army, and now his senior constable. McKeever informed Sievwright that Fyans, as Coroner for the district, had heard of the death, and had ordered him to locate the body so an inquest could be held. Sievwright allowed the constable to unwrap the body and examine it. But see-ing how adversely Murradone's relatives reacted, he then told McKeever to report to Fyans that in accordance with their wishes, the burial was going ahead immediately. In his first few weeks with them, Sievwright had won the confi-dence of members of the Barrabool tribe to the extent that they allowed him to witness their funeral ceremonies, though they strongly objected to the presence of any other strangers. Once again, he accompanied the funeral party into the bush so he could warn off any inquisitive white men that might come near while the burial was taking place.

Fyans was furious with what he regarded as the insubordination of Sievwright's actions. He sent McKeever back with a note pointing out that the Governor had appointed him acting Coroner in the district, and that in this case the only way of carrying out his duty properly would be by disinterring Murradone's body. He declined to do this, but demanded that in future the Protector allow him to make "such investigation as required" prior to burial. Sievwright replied that he believed such cases had nothing to do with Fyans. However, he'd seek the Chief Protector's guidance. In a letter to Robinson, Sievwright suggested that inter-ference by Fyans in cases in which the cause of death was obvious would be an unjustified violation of the sacred rites of the Aborigines. At least at this early stage of contact between the races, he argued, the Aborigines could never be convinced of the value of post mortems. In their grief, they would be outraged by the mutilation of the body which these examinations required because such practice was more in accordance with their idea of how to treat the body of a conquered foe, certainly not that of a loved one.

British law, Sievwright believed, paid respect to the feelings of the relatives of a deceased person if they objected to the body being subjected to a post mortem. If this was so, with Robinson's sanction he wanted to claim the same right of objection on behalf of the Aborigines. Finally, he pointed out that during trips into the remote parts of his district he would no doubt come across many deaths that would be impossible to even tell Fyans about until well after the funeral cer-emony had taken place, let alone wait for a coronial inquiry. The arguments impressed Robinson, who told his assistant he believed he'd taken the right action. Furthermore, he shared Sievwright's sentiments that white interference in such cases would have "the most mischievous results". However, the Chief Protector thought he should refer the matter to the Governor. Fyans, meanwhile, had already written to Gipps, complaining about Sievwright's behaviour. A few weeks later, Gipps made his ruling: the appointment of Sievwright and his colleagues had altered the circumstances under which Fyans had been appointed acting Coroner. Whenever possible it would now be more appropriate for inquiries into Aboriginal deaths to be conducted by the Protectors.[12]

Even before this ruling arrived from Sydney, Sievwright and Fyans had their second major dispute over who should perform what duties. A one-handed squatter, Charles Hugh Blackney, had made the difficult ride to Fyans' office to complain about the theft of sheep from the station of which he was co-proprietor near Buninyong, about 70 kilometres north-west of Geelong. Blackney said that over the past two weeks, seven Barrabool members had been living on the station and he'd fed them and given them shoes, shirts, waistcoats and trousers. Despite his kindness, the previous Sunday night they'd stolen 20 sheep. On many other occasions, Blackney claimed, he and his partner, retired naval lieutenant Charles Ayrey, had lost sheep one or two at a time, and the total now amounted to "a vast number". He added that he believed the section of the Barrabool tribe who frequented the area around nearby Lake Burrumbeet had acquired a large number of white weapons, including at least four double-barrelled guns and two muskets. He stated a shepherd could identify two of the thieves, and asked Fyans to issue a warrant for their arrest.

This time, Fyans was delighted to pass the buck. Forcing the Protector to supervise the arrest of a couple of Aboriginal sheep thieves would put him back in his inferior place. And with a bit of luck it would hasten the end of what he regarded as the useless department he represented, by destroying some of the feeling the Aborigines might have that he was on their side. Fyans sent Blackney to Sievwright, with the message that previously he'd immediately visited the scene of any alleged Aboriginal depredations, but he now considered this to be the Protector's duty. In the exchange of letters that ensued, Sievwright testily thanked the Police Magistrate for his "gratuitous opinion" on what the duties of a Protector should be. Sievwright added that although he believed it really was a police matter, if Fyans was refusing to take responsibility he would investigate.[13]

As it turned out, when Sievwright arrived at Blackney's station with a police trooper whose services Fyans had agreed to lend, he found that most of the sheep reported stolen had been found. They'd been in an adjoining flock which the squatter hadn't bother to count before riding off to lodge his complaint. The shepherd who'd reported the earlier losses to his master had absconded when

Blackney told him Sievwright was on his way to take evidence. Sievwright concluded that the shepherd had adopted the common practice of blaming the Aborigines for any losses resulting from his own negligence. On his return to Geelong, Sievwright wrote to Robinson, asking how he should act in such cases in the future. He pointed out that he'd felt obliged to take on what he regarded as a police duty, lest the squatters should believe the Protectorate was abetting Aboriginal plunder for which they could obtain no redress. Again, Robinson and Fyans referred the matter to the Governor, who ruled that cases would arise when the Protectors in their magisterial capacity would have to act against the Aborigines, as well as for them. However, Gipps advised this should be avoided as much as possible, otherwise the Aborigines would stop looking on the Protectors as their friends. It was another rare victory for Sievwright, and marked a significant deterioration in his already poor relations with Fyans.[14]

Meanwhile, Sievwright had had his first experience with the operation of what Gipps had declared would be "equal and indiscriminate" justice, in a case too serious to be dealt with in the Geelong court. It arose from a clash between two convict shepherds and a group of men from the Jaara tribe, about 120 kilometres north-west of Geelong. Some of the squatters in the district were prepared to tolerate Aborigines on their stations, and a few even employed them on a casual basis as shepherds and stockmen. But not William Allen, who managed the station on which the clash occurred on behalf of Henry Boucher Bowerman, a Sydney-based businessman. Allen's abhorrence of the Aborigines was well-known. To intimidate the Jaara people, he'd placed a human skull over the door of his hut. Sievwright believed it was the skull of a recalcitrant black, though there was speculation it might have been that of one of two white men who disappeared in the district in 1837. Either way, Allen's message was clear.[15]

The rough bark hut of Allen's shepherds, John Davis and Abraham Brackbrook, was on a creek that ran through a small plain, bounded on two sides by forested hills. Because of the remote location, and the distance to their master's slightly more elaborate dwelling, they felt particularly vulnerable to Aboriginal attack, and were keen to establish peaceful relations with the Jaara people. Allen, however, had given them strict instructions to inform him as soon as they saw blacks in the area. On one occasion early in 1839, a group of Jaara tribe members came up to the hut, and although they were friendly the shepherds felt they had to follow Allen's orders. Davis rode off to inform him of their presence, while Brackbrook nervously guarded the hut. By the time Allen armed himself and rode back to the hut, the Aborigines had moved on and were several kilometres away. Nevertheless, he went after them and ordered them at gunpoint not to return.

The shepherds were dismayed, believing Allen's behaviour had unnecessarily placed them in even greater jeopardy. Davis and Brackbrook were particularly interested in good relations with the Jaara women, and despite the incident managed to lure one of them into their hut one afternoon only a few weeks later. As they took turns for romps with her on a straw mattress, the sheep they were supposed to be watching, and Allen's orders, were far from their minds. Then Davis suddenly spotted through the open door a group of Jaara men approaching. He and Brackbrook panicked, pulled on their trousers, grabbed their guns, and began firing. Two of the blacks fell dead as the woman rushed past and fled with her tribesmen. The shepherds quickly locked the hut and galloped off to report the clash to their master. The three men waited until the following morning before returning to the scene, where they found the blowflies fighting the sun for the last drops of moisture on the wounds of the dead Aborigines. Allen ordered his servants to light a fire and burn the bodies.[16]

Realising that the Jaara people would no doubt report what had occurred, Allen decided it would be better to give his version to the authorities before they learned of it from elsewhere. He rode to Melbourne and called at Lonsdale's office, telling him that Davis and Brackbrook had been attacked by a group of Aborigines attempting to steal flour and blankets. In self-defence, his shepherds had shot dead two of their attackers. Lonsdale told Allen to report the matter to Robinson, and the Police Magistrate believed he was on his way to do so when he left the office. Allen, however, thought there was a chance the matter

Reproduced courtesy of the La Trobe Picture Collection, State Library of Victoira
Collins Street, Melbourne, in 1839

would go no further if he made no other reports of it. And he may have been right, had he not foolishly mentioned the clash to several people while he attended to other business in Melbourne over the following week. Robinson heard rumours of what had happened, and ordered Sievwright to investigate.

When Sievwright discovered that Allen had ignored Lonsdale's instruction to report the clash to Robinson, he recommended that he should leave immediately for the station with a police trooper. The Chief Protector decided to send both Sievwright and one of his colleagues, Edward Stone Parker, because Allen's station was near the border between their districts. Robinson thought the two assistants were on friendly terms, and was not yet aware of an altercation between them a few days earlier, over Sievwright allegedly having tried to seduce Parker's wife. Sievwright set out for Allen's station with the trooper, leaving Parker behind, and when he arrived there a week later he learned what had really happened. He ordered the trooper to take Davis and Brackbrook into custody, charging them with murder. Allen was placed on a bond of 100 pounds, to appear as a witness when required.[17]

All serious criminal cases had to be referred to the authorities in Sydney before prosecution could proceed. Murder trials had to be held there, because no Supreme Court had yet been established in Melbourne. Sievwright's recommendation that Davis and Brackbrook be tried for murder was not well received

By permission of the National Library of Australia
"Lake Borambeet" (Burrumbeet) by Duncan Cooper.
Sievwright had to pass close by here to reach the station of William Allen.

by an administration still feeling the wrath of the squatters and the press over the hanging of the seven white men the previous December for the Myall Creek massacre. The Attorney-General, John Plunkett, decided he could not risk inflaming passions even more by accepting Sievwright's recommendation. He ruled that there was not enough evidence to warrant a murder trial: Davis and Brackbrook had pleaded self-defence, and there was no evidence to the contrary. However, Plunkett came up with a sop. The burning of the bodies might be a criminal act, he asserted, if it was calculated to prevent the cause of death being ascertained, and therefore an obstruction to the process of British justice. Referring the matter to Lonsdale for final decision, the Attorney-General added that William Allen was "much to blame in ordering the bodies to be burned".[18] Lonsdale decided that Davis and Brackbrook should be charged only with the misdemeanour of burning the bodies before any legal investigation took place. He told Plunkett he agreed that the illegality of such action should be made known throughout the colony. The Police Magistrate also agreed that Allen was equally guilty, but he left it up to the Crown Prosecutor in Melbourne, Horatio Nelson Carrington, to decide whether to summons him as a witness "or as may be thought proper".[19]

In the week of the trial, both of Melbourne's two newspapers ran leading articles on the Aboriginal issue. The *Port Phillip Patriot and Melbourne Advertiser* began by quoting from a *Sydney Herald* item the previous month which warned that colonists would take the administration of justice into their own hands if Gipps and his "overpaid Whiggish lawyers" dared "to punish another white man for alleged outrages on blacks, till those blacks who have murdered whites, shall have been tried, and if convicted, executed". The *Patriot*, a supporter of the Aborigines and the Protectorate, said the editor of the *Herald* must either be insane, or regard the rest of the white inhabitants of the colony as so. It described the tone of the *Herald* item as base, destructive, mean, cowardly, and contemptible, saying that "the wretch who avows such language...should be driven out from society, and placed where he truly belongs, where he would feel at home; that is, in the wilds of the desert amongst his fellow beasts of prey". The *Patriot* added that the *Herald* and other newspapers made a great fuss about the murder of white men, but showed no such concern about the murder of blacks, who had "very, very seldom been the aggressors".[20]

Melbourne's other newspaper, the *Port Phillip Gazette* had no such sympathy for the Aborigines. According to its teenage English editor, George Arden, they could "only be placed in the great animal family as one degree above the brute creation". In Arden's view, the Aborigines could at times be "tractable, generous and peaceable", with a surprising aptitude for acquiring knowledge. But they also had "restless, treacherous, and vindictive feelings" that marked a "savage disposition". Furthermore, Arden believed the Aboriginal women were ugly. "The men are far more comely than the females, who, except at a very tender age and in few examples, are withered and decrepid to a disgusting degree, presenting as close a resemblance to a she baboon or ourang outang as it is possible for a human being to assume, either in the course of nature, or by imitation."[21]

The day before the trial of Davis and Brackbrook, Arden's *Gazette* published the second part of a two-part commentary on the Protectorate. The article claimed that Sievwright, who was to be the main prosecution witness, and his fellow Protectors were "undoubtedly the best paid servants of the Colony". But so far they had failed to "purchase the value of their wages and good men's opinions by honest exertion". The *Gazette* described the choice of Protectors as "the first and principal stroke of mismanagement" of the department, saying they should have been "young, unencumbered with the cares of domestic life, of colonial experience, and suited both from inherent desire and personal abilities, to lead the stirring yet self denying, the exciting yet difficult life, of an Australian Settler".[22]

When the trial came before the Court of Quarter Sessions on 8 August 1839, the tiny court room was packed. Ironically, elected chairman of a 12-man jury was John Pascoe Fawkner, one of the earliest white inhabitants of the town, owner of its first hotel, and now proprietor of the *Patriot*. Crown prosecutor

From "The Chronicles of Early Melbourne"
In 1839, the Melbourne Police Office served as the Court of Quarter Sessions

Carrington had decided that the shepherds should face two counts: burning the bodies of the Jaara men with a view to defeating the ends of justice; and indecently burning the bodies "contrary to civilised usage". The chairman of the court, Irish barrister Edward James Brewster asked Davis and Brackbrook how they pleaded. Both answered "guilty". Extraordinarily, Carrington the *prosecutor* objected, advised them to plead "not guilty". This was allowed by Brewster. Sievwright was then called to give evidence, and he related how the accused had admitted shooting the Jaara men, and burning the bodies on Allen's orders. The circumstances which led to the shooting were deemed irrelevant to the case, the purpose of which, Brewster ruled, was to determine whether the bodies had been illegally burned.

Allen, whom Carrington had decided should appear as the other *prosecution* witness, confirmed in his evidence that the shepherds had burned the bodies. In their defence, Davis and Brackbrook reiterated the story that they'd shot the blacks while defending their lives and property, and that they'd burned the bodies on Allen's instructions. Summing up the case, Brewster told the jury that the mere act of burning the bodies was not illegal, unless done with the intention of defeating the ends of justice. If the jury was not convinced that there'd been a criminal intent to that effect, the shepherds would have to be acquitted. There being no special room for the jury attached to the court, it went outside the building to consider its verdict. Judging by the article in his newspaper before the trial, Fawkner might have been expected to use whatever influence he had over the rest of the jury to try to gain a conviction. But he was himself a former Crown prisoner, and according to the evidence submitted, Davis and Brackbrook had only been acting on Allen's orders when they burned the bodies. When the jury returned a few minutes later, Fawkner announced a verdict of "not guilty". There was thunderous applause. Carrington then suggested that Davis and Brackbrook be returned to the Public Works Department, adding that he'd be recommending the withdrawal of all other Crown prisoners from Allen's station as well.[23]

In a commentary on the case, Fawkner's newspaper fully agreed with Carrington's recommendation, on two grounds. The first, the *Patriot* remarked, was the lack of proper management shown by Allen. The second was the fact that almost all the clashes between whites and Aborigines involved Crown prisoners assigned to sheep stations as servants, who were subjected to "every indignity from their masters and overseers". In response, these prisoners tyrannised over and frequently murdered blacks: slaves were almost always cruel tyrants if given the opportunity. The commentary concluded: "Sir George Gipps, if you wish this colony to prosper, and at the same time prevent the utter destruction of the rightful lords or the soil, you will act upon the orders of the

Home Government and withdraw all Crown Servants, alias White Slaves, from this fertile district: thus you will place all parties on an equality. Some Wool Kings have 30 or more of these slaves, whilst the majority have not ONE."[24] The *Patriot* was referring to instructions from London to Governor Bourke in 1837, directing him to inform the colonists that the British government intended stopping the practice of assigning convicts to private employment, and that settlers instead should look to the employment of free immigrants.[25]

The *Gazette* did not comment directly on the outcome of the case. It did, however, have a few words to say about Carrington's behaviour before the court, accusing him of "petty ebullitions of temper" and of an insulting and intimidating attitude towards juries. If such misconduct continued, he should be dismissed as Crown Prosecutor.[26] In its following edition, the *Gazette* reported that Brewster and Carrington were business partners.[27] A few weeks later it went further, alleging that until very recently "any scoundrel who wished to escape punishment at the hands of the Magistrate had nothing to do but to fee Mr Carrington, who forthwith cleared him by a little blustering of the accusation laid against him".[28] It was not long before Carrington had resigned, and his recommendation about Davis and Brackbrook was never implemented. They returned to Sievwright's district to work as shepherds, though for a new master.[29] Allen, too, had to find a new employer. Henry Bowerman, who visited Melbourne to check how his interests had been affected by the arrest and trial of his two employees, was one of six people who went missing, never to be found, after a brig broke up soon after leaving Port Phillip Bay on a voyage back to Sydney.[30]

CHAPTER 3
"A few doses of lead"

AS the all-important spring wool clip of 1839 approached, the whites' ill-feeling towards the Aborigines of the Western District of Port Phillip became frenzied. Every sheep that went missing was assumed to have been stolen by the blacks. Embellished reports of Aboriginal attacks and theft -- real and fictitious -- were rife, and were seriously limiting the number of men prepared to work in the district as shepherds. There was increasing antagonism towards the Protectorate and its agent among the squatters, some of whom believed that annihilation of the Aboriginal race should be actively pursued. The *Port Phillip Gazette* helped whip up the hysteria, referring to the very strong feeling against the government which had arisen "from the shamefully neglected state in which life and property is left to the ravages of the native tribes".

Fear of exaggeration, the *Gazette* claimed, had made it loath to publicise the reports of Aboriginal depredations which had lately become so prevalent in the Western District, but it now believed them to be true. "Sheep to the amount of seven or eight hundred head, valued by the increased price of stock at fifteen or sixteen hundred pounds, have been carried off or destroyed; the Aborigines are met with in every part collected in large bodies and armed with European weapons, they evince the greatest treachery and hostility, commit daily the most daring acts of robbery, and leave the country in a state of the greatest excitement and alarm," it alleged. The squatters had asked Sievwright to issue warrants for the arrest of "the most conspicuous among the savages", but he'd refused on the ground that the names of the offenders could not be obtained. "By this imbecile policy, these hordes are left to work their will to the ruin of individuals and the loss of the whole community."

There was little doubt that the squatters would be justified in doing everything in their power to defend their property if they caught Aborigines committing a robbery, the *Gazette* argued. There was still less doubt of the legality of resisting personal attack "even to the destruction of the black marauders". But, it lamented, the recent hanging of the seven white men for murder in the Myall Creek case seemed to have unnerved the squatters, and paralysed their efforts to protect their property and lives. The whites in the district were now undoubtedly the greater objects of pity and commiseration, and evidently the ones needing protection, not the Aborigines. There had been a "dilatory and vexatious delay" in bringing the Border Police into active operation, and the squatters were left with only one course of action: to send a petition to the Governor outlining their plight. This important document should give full details of the number and the value of stock destroyed by the blacks. It should also refer to the distance to the nearest court, the inadequacy of the district's police force, and Sievwright's "inutility".[1]

The following day Fawkner's *Patriot* took the *Gazette* to task, querying the figures it had published on the stock losses allegedly suffered in the Western District. "Per contra, many, very many of the Aborigines have been MERCI-LESSLY slaughtered by the Flock-holders and their servants," the *Patriot* cried, "and how many tribes have been starved almost to death by the Whites taking forcible possession of all the lands, which these people possessed, and upon which they lived very happily, before the whites drove them from their homes and possessions. And now the Press of the Colony, which is bound to instil proper feelings into the people, what does it do? Why, labours in its vile pandering to the base purposes of the nefarious bloodsucking Wool-kings of the Colony, earnestly labours to excite the people to utterly exterminate the poor wretched (made so by us) Aborigines -- the only REAL LORDS of this soil..." The *Patriot* expressed the view shared by Sievwright that the Aborigines were frequently being wrongly blamed for sheep losses. Whenever a shepherd lost a few sheep, or gave a few away to an acquaintance, "the loss is instantly laid upon the natives, and armed parties are sent in pursuit, and in most cases, such is the thirst for blood -- blood of the unresisting -- that they seldom return until they are satisfied with human gore". The article concluded: "Would these

To the Settlers of the Western District of Port Phillip,

THE Settlers of this District are requested to attend at the Station of Mr. Murray, Lake Colac, on Thursday the 22d instant, for the purpose of taking into consideration the necessity of petitioning His Excellency Sir George Gipps, to adopt some measures for the prevention of the alarming outrages committed upon them by the Aborigines.

Geelong, August 1, 1839.

MELBOURNE

A front-page advertisement in the "Port Phillip Gazette" in August, 1839, calling for Western District squatters to meet at the Lake Colac station of Hugh Murray to "adopt some measures for the prevention of the alarming outrages committed upon them by the Aborigines".

Menhunters show so much eagerness for the chase, if the Blacks were really as cunning, cruel, and cannibalistic as the *Gazette* represents? We say, decidedly -- No. But the voice of that blood shall ascend and be heard. This statement we know to be fact, and if the Wool-kings, the Exterminators, wish it, we can name times, places, and people, so let them beware."[2]

Not to be deterred, the *Gazette* in its next edition published a lengthy letter to the editor, allegedly from a subscriber calling himself *Aliquis*. The letter continued the theme of the article of the previous edition, criticising Sievwright and his colleagues for failing to arrest and bring to trial Aborigines known to have been involved in robberies, and accusing him of being more interested in trying to teach his charges Christian values. *Aliquis* suggested this was a waste of time. "Gentleness or Religion to beings who have scarce a sense beyond the brute is but as 'pearls to swine'; and whilst this charitable doctrine is being preached to them, whilst their Protectors are instilling into them new senses and new feelings (or attempting to do so, for it must be a very long time ere it takes effect) they may with impunity rob and murder us, and we are to be told, these are the acts of savages who have not yet 'the fear of God before their eyes'." Aliquis referred specifically to the losses being suffered by the squatters around Lake Colac, about 60 kilometres south-west of Geelong, where he claimed the blacks were sneaking up to the sheep folds at night, and quietly lifting sheep out one by one by slipping a noose around their necks. He believed that from eight to 10 sheep had been stolen from a fold in one night in this manner: one squatter had lost more than 60 sheep, another even more. The letter appealed to the Western District squatters to unanimously petition the Governor for supportive action "in defence of what is sacred to us -- our pockets".[3]

Advertisements had already appeared in the *Gazette* inviting the squatters of the district to a meeting to draft a petition to Gipps, asking him "to adopt some measures for the prevention of the alarming outrages committed upon them by the Aborigines".[4] A large group was to attend the meeting later that month at the Lake Colac station of the young Edinburgh-born squatter, Hugh Murray, one of the first to occupy the area two years earlier. According to the petition drawn up at the meeting, Aboriginal outrages had recently increased to such an extent that most of the district's squatters had had a portion of their flocks driven off, their huts plundered, and the lives of their servants endangered. Despite these continued aggressions, it bemoaned, no efficient steps had been taken by the authorities to bring the black offenders to justice. The appointment of Sievwright to mediate between the black and white inhabitants of the district had been a complete failure. An opinion had become prevalent among the Aborigines that they could destroy the settlers' property with impunity "supposing that it is the sole office of the Protectors to shield them from retributive justice". The squatters were concerned about Gipps' declaration of "equal and indiscriminate" application of the law, "being convinced of the impracticable nature of applying a law which shall be equal in its operation alike to the civilized and uncivilized occupiers of the land". As well, the situation of Sievwright being able to sit as a Magistrate in the Geelong court in cases involving Europeans and Aborigines appeared to be "dangerous in its tendency, and calculated to impede the course of justice". A committee of 10 squatters was appointed to seek further signatures before the document was taken to Flogger Fyans, with a request that he forward it to Sydney.[5]

 The relatively mild wording of the petition hid the intense anger and impatience of some of its signatories. One of them, Scottish physician David Henry Wilsone, was initially pleased to hear that Sievwright -- a former acquaintance in Britain -- would be operating in the area, believing he would be useful in suppressing black depredation. But he had soon given up any such hope. "I expect we will have a regular fight with the natives as they are becoming very troublesome and bold," Wilsone wrote to his brother in Glasgow. "The fools of protectors have informed them that we dare not meddle with them, or if we did we would be hanged. They stole from us five fine ewe lambs, and since then all our servants are armed and are desired to shoot anyone they see attempt it again or touch them. We are well off by many (whites) around us, and soon a regular affair will settle the business and clear out our part of the country of these *regular cannibals*."[6]

 Such was the widespread attitude towards the Aborigines and their Protector among the leading members of the Western District's white community when 36 men, women and children of the Jarcoort section of the Kirrae tribe went to sleep one night in October 1839, about 110 kilometres west of Geelong. The Aborigines had camped in a gully they called Puuroyuup on a stream called Tarnpirr, near a spot notable for small black stones which they believed could cure a toothache, or induce one in an enemy. Tarnpirr snaked its way down from the north of Barrabool territory and into Kirrae country, passing on its way to the sea between the waterhole called Kuurong Killing, where the man-devouring bunyip lived, and an extinct volcano called Djerinallum. Known to the whites as Mt Elephant because of its shape, Djerinallum rose majestically almost 400 metres above the centre of the third largest basalt plains in the world, carpeted again that spring with the yellow flowers of the murnong, or daisy yam -- one of the most important Kirrae foods.

 To the whites, Tarnpirr was known as Taylor's River -- named after Frederick Taylor, another of the first whites in the area, and now manager of a sheep station near where the Jarcoort members had camped. Back in 1836, Taylor had been suspected of encouraging one of his convict shepherds, John Whitehead, to execute an Aborigine who'd been tied to a tree. Taylor had been obliged to report the murder, and Whitehead had been committed for trial before the Supreme Court in Sydney. But when he'd been subpoenaed as a witness, Taylor had secretly taken a boat back to Van Diemen's Land to lay low for a while. The move had saved Whitehead. When he'd come up for trial, there'd been no witness and he'd been discharged.[7] Taylor had then quietly returned to the Western District and had since, through his own boasting, become renowned as a murderer of blacks himself. When he heard of the party of the Jarcoort camp nearby, he decided to enhance his reputation.[8]

Taylor assembled a group of his own men, and some from neighbouring stations, to attack the Aborigines. He waited until well after dark before slowly leading the group in an extended line, himself in the middle, to the top of one side of the gully. The blacks did not wake before Taylor began the barrage, and many died where they'd been sleeping. Only one young man who managed to scurry into some long grass and hide lived to tell the tale. The stunned survivor, blood oozing from several buckshot wounds, took until the following morning to find other members of his tribe, camped further south. Never before had they heard such devastating news. According to legend, Djerinallum itself had resulted from violence, having once been a man killed in a fight. But even in legend,

Reproduced courtesy of the La Trobe picture collection, State Library of Victoria
A slightly exaggerated depiction of Mt Elephant by Robert Bruce, engraver.

such a massacre had never taken place. Some of the Jarcoort warriors wanted to seek immediate revenge. But the anguished elders knew their spears and other weapons were no match for the white men's guns. They decided to send a messenger to seek Sievwright's help, while the tribe retreated further south. It proved a wise decision. A party of whites came after the remaining Jarcoort members to complete their slaughter. One woman, Bareetch Chuurneen, straggling behind the rest, only just managed to escape from the pursuing horsemen by sliding down the steep bank of a deep fresh-water lake, then swimming across with her child clinging to her back.[9]

By the time the messenger reached Sievwright's camp at Geelong, the bodies of the dead Aborigines were already starting to rot in the waterhole into which they'd been thrown by Taylor and his men. Sievwright was shaken by the messenger's tragic news. But at the same time he was inspired with a sense of hope and enthusiasm. He couldn't help but feel that perhaps the deaths which had occurred might be the sacrifice that was needed to at last establish the authority and value of his office which his fellow whites were refusing to accept. Hitherto, with the exception of the case involving William Allen's two servants, he'd been unable to obtain any firm evidence linking a white name to any of the atrocities that had been reported to him. This time, his Aboriginal informant had provided Taylor's name, and two others -- Hamilton and Bromfield, both squatters in the area.

Without the means to carry his tent or supplies, Sievwright had so far travelled alone on the long journeys he'd made throughout his district to investigate claims of Aboriginal depredations, or of alleged mistreatment of Aborigines. He'd often been in the ludicrous situation of having to rely on the hospitality of the very parties into whose actions he was inquiring. This time, he was determined to be self-sufficient, so he didn't have to seek statements from Taylor and the other whites involved, and then ask them for food and accommodation. There was also another good reason why he should take his own supplies. Much of the country through which he'd have to travel to reach the Mt Elephant area was at the best of times swampy, but heavy Spring rains had swollen the streams and rivers of the district, and flooding was extensive. There was no way of telling how long the journey might take, and certainly no guarantee of reaching somewhere each day where he could obtain food and shelter. With somewhat excessive optimism, Sievwright wrote to Robinson, requesting to be supplied with enough horses or bullocks to take his tent and provisions to the scene of the massacre on his small travelling cart.[10]

Amazingly, the Chief Protector waited for another letter from Sievwright almost a fortnight later before he acted. He referred the matter to the Englishman who'd taken over from Lonsdale as head of the civil administration in Melbourne, Charles Joseph La Trobe. But Port Phillip's new Superintendent had only been in the job for six weeks, and had plenty on his plate. He, also, felt no urgency in dealing with Sievwright's request. It was not until Sievwright rode to Melbourne another week later to plead for a decision before one was made. La Trobe, eager to show his superior in Sydney he realised the need for austerity, ruled that the best he could do was to authorise the Assistant Protector to hire one draught horse to pull his cart, for this investigation only, and to request the assistance of the Border Police commanded by Port Phillip's first Crown Lands Commissioner, Henry Fysche Gisborne. La Trobe told Sievwright the hire charge of 21 shillings a day for a horse in Melbourne was far too high, and ordered him to immediately return to his district to try to obtain a horse there for a lower fee.[11]

Before leaving Melbourne, however, Sievwright wanted to obtain supplies for the five Barrabool men he'd just appointed constables in the newly-formed Native Police Corps, and whom he wanted to take on his imminent journey. A spate of letter-writing over the next few days finally resulted in him being authorised to obtain supplies -- and a second limited batch of food for the constables' starving tribesmen, including some which Robinson had falsely claimed to have already been distributed to them more than three months earlier. For the policemen he would receive five grey and green jackets, five caps, two haversacks, five spoons, five knives, five forks, five old plates, two combs, two old pannikins, one greatcoat, five muskets, and five cartridge boxes. He would also be given small quantities of flour, meat, sugar, tea, salt and soap, to issue daily rations in return for their services.[12]

On his return to Geelong, Sievwright found that there was no draught horse or bullock to pull his cart available in the settlement for a low enough fee, so he began riding around making personal appeals to the settlers in the area. It took more than a week before he'd exhausted all possibilities. He'd even asked Fyans to lend him a horse, but the Police Magistrate had refused. Crown Lands Commissioner Gisborne, meanwhile, had given up waiting for Sievwright, and had set off towards Mt Elephant with a small detachment of Border Police, carrying their supplies on a pack horse. Sievwright again wrote to Robinson, saying he was still unable to go to investigate the massacre, five weeks after first reporting it. When La Trobe was informed of Sievwright's predicament, he ordered that the Protector be rebuked for not having asked for further advice sooner, and for not having tried to carry out the investigation despite his transportation problems. In desperation, Sievwright bought a horse with 50 pounds of his own money, a fifth of his annual salary. To minimise the load on the cart, he decided to leave his Native Policemen behind, and take only one of his convict servants.[13]

The trip was to take a month. The two men had travelled only about 30 kilometres when they came across the first flooded ford they had to cross. It took three days. Sievwright and his servant had to unload the cart and carefully carry everything across the river on their shoulders. When the cart was reloaded on the other side, they then had great difficulty drawing the horse up the soft bank. After this experience, Sievwright decided he would have to abort his mission if he couldn't obtain another horse to help pull the cart. Luckily, a nearby settler agreed to hire a horse, and he was able to proceed. A few days later, he was within about 50 kilometres of Mt Elephant when he was checked by a marsh. In attempting to cross it, the horses were almost drowned, and the cart again had to be emptied, then reloaded on the other side. Sievwright was forced to take a completely different route to his destination. This involved going around Lake Corangamite, a salt lake of about 140 square kilometres.

Some of the ground he covered had never before been travelled by a white man, and he would never have been able to make it through, had it not been for the Jarcoort men who guided him across firm ground between the bogs. By the time he reached his destination, Gisborne and his Border Police had already returned to Melbourne, claiming to have been "unable to obtain any further information on the subject, after having made every inquiry after the alleged authors of the massacre".[14] The Protector was no more successful. Taylor had had second thoughts about the wisdom of his actions and fled from the district. And none of the other white men at the station would admit to knowing anything about the

By permission of the National Library of Australia
"Basin Banks, about 20 miles south of Mount Elephant", Rex Nan Kivell Collection. In 1839, few white men had passed through this area, near the southern end of Lake Corangamite.

killing of the Jarcoort people.[15]

The inability of the Protector to obtain information on the massacre was not surprising. Many men in the bush "bounced", or bragged, about their mistreatment of the blacks. As one squatter in the area, Scotsman Niel Black, recorded: "This they can only do by hints and slang phrases, as the Protectors of Aborigines are always on the lookout for information against the whites, and anything plainly said would subject them to a prosecution." However, Black was convinced that when it came to actual large-scale killings of Aborigines, not even vague references were openly made. Even as Sievwright was on his way to investigate the Mt Elephant massacre, Black wrote in his journal: "I believe they, poor creatures, are slaughtered in great numbers and never a word said about it." Less than a month later, Black had come to the conclusion that the odds of being able to take up a new "run" without murdering blacks were 50 to one. "But after they have got the first taming by means of a few doses of lead effectually administered, it seldom happens that they occasion much trouble afterwards," he recorded.[16]

CHAPTER 4
"A curse to the land"

BACK in Scotland, from where well over half of the first Western District squatters came, most land ownership was governed by what remained of a centuries-old system of feudal tenure. The ultimate ownership of almost all land was vested in the British monarch, but heritable tenure was held by a class of nobles who had the right to grant "feu" contracts which amounted to perpetual and heritable leases over parts of the land. The lessees, or vassals, could in turn enter feu contracts with sub-vassals. Scottish law stipulated that in all cases, transfers of tenure must be marked by ancient rituals. Details of the ceremony would depend on the land involved. If it was unimproved land, the transfer would be marked by the symbolic handover of small quantities of earth and stone to the lessee at the site. If there was an adjoining fishery, the new owner would also receive a length of net, and a flat-bottomed rowing boat known as a coble.

A feu contract would usually provide for an initial cash sum to be paid by the vassal or sub-vassal, then an annual "feu duty" payable in cash or kind. As well, it would outline special conditions, including any obligatory services which the vassal must perform for the noble who had leased the land -- such as helping to carry peat for the fires in his castle. Vassals or sub-vassals who wanted to lease their land without losing their heritable rights would enter "tack agreements" for specified periods, usually with tenant farmers. Charles Sievwright's paternal grandmother, for instance, had entered a 15-year tack agreement after the death of her husband to lease some valuable land known as The Hillock in Rattray, near Blairgowrie. The agreement specified that as rent, farmer Thomas Scott would pay 34 pounds a year in cash, and a proportion of the grindable corn produced on the land. Scott also agreed to cover part of the feu duty payable on the land to Thomas Robert, the 11th Earl of Kinnoul, who had just inherited the title and the wealth that came with it. Annual payments which had to be made to the Earl included six poultry -- the value of which amounted to several days' wages for a common labourer at the time -- about 12 sheaves of oats, and about 12 sheaves of straw for thatching the roofs of the noble's residences. At least two days a year, Scott was also required to provide his labour and cart to help the Earl move the grain he was collecting from The Hillock and other extensive properties. As well, Scott was responsible for performing whatever the Earl deemed to be The Hillock's share of the building or repairs needed at the local church, manse yard, dykes, school, and school-master's house.[1]

In Australia, the Scots and other Britishers whose usage of land had been governed by the remnants of feudalism found themselves in an entirely different situation. Here there were vast tracts of land with no nobility who could claim ownership of it; only groups of Aborigines who were not interested in money or even cultivation of any kind. Nevertheless, the Port Phillip Association -- a company formed by a group of Hobart residents to use the as yet unexploited southern part of New South Wales across Bass Strait to grow wool -- hoped that its claim to a large part of the land could be reinforced by making payments to some of its Aboriginal occupants. The Association's first expedition to Port Phillip in 1835 drew up farcical "treaties" under which, despite the language barrier, eight supposed Aboriginal "chiefs" were purported to have given the expedition leader, John Batman, the perpetual right to occupy and graze sheep and cattle on 240,000 hectares of land around Port Phillip Bay. According to the documents, there was to be an annual rent of 150 pairs of blankets, 150 knives, 150 tomahawks, 100 pairs of scissors, 100 glass mirrors, 70 suits of clothing, and seven tonnes of flour. Quantities of these items had already been supplied, plus 18 shirts, 250 handkerchiefs, and four flannel jackets. Governor Bourke in Sydney had declared the "treaties" to be void, and reminded Batman and his colleagues that unauthorised occupation of "vacant lands of the Crown" was illegal. But he had no means to stop Batman and other whites eager to expand their grazing land from shipping stock across Bass Strait, and the new settlement of Melbourne was born.

One of the signatories to the Port Phillip "treaties" on behalf of the Port Phillip Association was Scotsman Alexander Thomson. An adventurous man who'd been a surgeon on ships that took convicts to New South Wales before becoming a farmer and steam boat operator in Van Diemen's Land, Thomson had become involved with the Association as its surgeon and catechist, and 50 of his Herefords were the first cattle sent to the Port Phillip District.[2] By early 1840, Thomson was involved in a wide range of Port Phillip's commercial and civic activities. He was, for instance, a director of the newly-formed equivalent of the Highland and Agricultural Society of Scotland. He was also a co-director with Foster Fyans of the Port Phillip Bank, and a director of the Melbourne Fire and Marine Insurance Company. One of Thomson's other duties indirectly involved him in attempts to Christianise the Aborigines, through the Wesleyan Missionary Society, of which two of Sievwright's colleagues -- Edward Parker and James Dredge -- had become committee members. Thomson was the Geelong secretary of the Society, which had established a mission station at a place it called Buntingdale, about 50 kilometres south-west of the township, near the border between Barrabool and Colijon territory. As well, the doctor had an interest in the customs and practices of the Port Phillip blacks, having sent to a museum in Edinburgh "a perfect specimen of a baked child" which he'd found in an Aboriginal fire near Melbourne. To him and others, it was evidence that the blacks were cannibals.[3]

Thomson and many of the other more pious squatters would have liked to have been able to quickly teach the Aborigines to be good Christians and cherish British values, to stop them being trampled into extinction. But the basic guiding principle of all the squatters -- which had to take precedence over any Christianisation attempts -- was that hard work and careful investment of capital deserved its rewards. While attempts were being made to convince the Aborigines of their inferior way of life, they had to be made to realise that they could not stand in the way of free enterprise in a land so ripe with opportunity. On 7 February 1840, Thomson invited three of his fellow squatters for roast duck dinner at his humble home, which he'd named *Kardinia*, reportedly an Aboriginal word for sunrise. One of the dinner guests was a contemporary, David Fisher, who'd arrived in Melbourne from Van Diemen's Land on the same boat four years earlier. A fellow Scot, Fisher now lived on an adjoining property as partner in and manager for the Derwent Company, which had taken over the interests of the Port Phillip Association near Geelong. The other two guests were a generation younger, in their early twenties. John Norman McLeod, also a Scot, had been only four years old when his father, a retired British army major, had brought the family to the sister colony, and 21 when he'd moved with sheep to Port Phillip in 1837. The other guest, George Frederick Read, junior, the son of a wealthy English businessman, had been born in Van Diemen's Land, and had crossed the Strait in 1838.[4]

The topic of conversation over dinner was of course how best to make one's fortune out of wool-growing. Details were not yet known of the first sale of Port Phillip wool in London the previous October, so it remained unclear just how lucrative the district's new industry may be. But it was obvious that potential profits were being limited by the damned Aborigines and their damned Protector. Nothing had been achieved by the petition to Gipps drawn up at the meeting at Hugh Murray's a few months earlier, which none of the four had attended. Another attempt was needed to convince the Governor to act. Over sips of brandy, the four agreed on the wording of a newspaper advertisement inviting their fellow squatters to a meeting in Geelong the following month "for the purpose of considering the best means of remedying the evils arising from the aggressions of the Aborigines".[5]

Squatters such as Thomson and his friends who remained in a relatively closely-settled area near Geelong could expect help from each other, and the troopers based there, if they came under Aboriginal attack. But squatters in increasing numbers were now moving towards the westernmost part of the district, lured by the laudatory reports of its suitability for grazing. Copies had been available for some months in the colony of a book by the Scottish Surveyor-General, Major Thomas Livingstone Mitchell, who'd been so impressed he'd called it *Australia Felix*, meaning lucky or fortunate Australia. Despite numerous references to Aborigines in the area, Mitchell liked to think of it as "without inhabitants". He recorded his prophetic reaction to first sighting the area in 1836 thus: "As I stood, the first European intruder on the sublime solitude of these verdant plains, as yet untouched by flocks or herds, I felt conscious of being the harbinger of mighty changes, and that our steps would soon be followed by the men and the animals for which it seemed to have been prepared."[6]

Among the first to make the move to the new frontier were three English brothers -- Charles, Henry and Richard Wedge, nephews of John Helder Wedge, surveyor for the Port Phillip Association after Batman signed his "treaties", before becoming a squatter himself. After his return to England in 1838, Wedge had won the interest of the Colonial Office in plans to "reclaim" the Aborigines, and improve race relations. Under the plans, the government would provide food and clothing for white settlers to pay black labourers. Grants of land would be made to the settlers for each Aborigine they managed to "civilise".[7] Back in Australia, though, Wedge's nephews had adopted quicker and easier means of dealing with the blacks: outside the main hut at their head station, they'd mounted a gun on a waist-high swivel, loaded with musket balls to fire at any Aborigines who dared to wander within range.

The Wedge brothers had settled on a stream that flowed through a picturesque little valley into a river, more than 200 kilometres from Geelong. Mitchell had called the stream the Grange, and the river the Wannon. The government surveyor, Charles Tyers, had since named the Grange as a most eligible site for a future township. But the Tjapwurong people, who called the stream Mardong after the type of clay found on its banks, did not share the whites' enthusiasm for the pastoral future of the south-west corner of their territory. They and the neighbouring Bunganditj, whose land was still further from Geelong, extending into the newly-declared British province of South Australia, were alarmed about reports they'd heard of the treatment of other tribes to the east -- and were quickly realising that violent resistance to the white invaders was their only chance of survival.

With the squatters' meeting at Geelong still more than a week away, Sievwright arrived at the Wedges' station to investigate rumours of clashes between the brothers and the Tjapwurong warriors. He found the Wedges away, and the head station in charge of their Irish overseer, Patrick Codd. According to Codd, the station had been frequently raided by Aborigines in the eight months since it had been established. Losses had been heavy: about 300 sheep, a cow, a calf, and a horse worth 120 pounds. Despite the extent of the losses, Codd deposed, the Wedges and their employees -- including himself -- had shown remarkable restraint. He admitted the use of the swivel gun on only one occasion. A group of about 18 blacks had approached the head station, demanding flour from the store. When their demand had been refused, they'd attacked, throwing between 30 and 40 spears. The gun had been fired to disperse the attackers and they'd fled, driving some cattle before them. Codd claimed the gun had been most ineffective: none of the Aborigines had even been wounded.[8]

The day after Codd made his statement, another group of English brothers, with the ironic surname of Whyte, took up a new frontier run about 50 kilometres north-west of the Wedges, on another tributary of the Wannon River, which the Bunganditj called Konongwootong. George, James, John, Pringle and William were delighted with their discovery. A fire had recently swept through the area, followed by heavy rains, leaving a rich covering of grass excellent for grazing. The Whytes had only been at Konongwootong for three days, however, when the convicts they employed as shepherds reported that about 50 of their sheep had gone missing. Some of the brothers had been squatting north of Geelong for almost two years, and their limited success had been partly due to the number of sheep stolen by the blacks. They were determined not to tolerate any further

By permission of the National Library of Australia
"View on Briant's (i.e. Bryan) Creek, head of Glenelg River" by Duncan Cooper.
The Whyte brothers formed their station in this area.

thefts, especially now that the prospects of making a good profit looked so promising. The brothers stayed up late that night, preparing cartridges for their double-barrelled guns.

Early the next morning, the Whytes set off with three of their shepherds -- Daniel Turner, William Gillespie and Benjamin Wardle -- following the tracks of their sheep to some low hills covered with tea-tree about 10 kilometres away. They tied up their horses, and crept slowly into the trees. Hearing Aboriginal voices, they crawled up to the edge of a clearing on the edge of a creek, where a meal of mutton was being prepared by a large group of Bunganditj. Some sheep were already being cooked in holes dug in the ground, some had been skinned ready for cooking, while those still alive had been enclosed by a crude brush fence. As the white men moved to surround the camp, they were spotted. An alarm was screamed, and the women and children fled, as the men rushed to grab their weapons. The brush fence was broken, and the sheep scattered. A spear was thrown, and the whites started firing. Daniel Turner was speared through the thigh, and one of the squatter brothers received an accidental gun-shot wound on the cheek, prompting the other gunmen to become "savage to desperation". The Bunganditj tried valiantly to withstand the onslaught, one of them being shot nine times before he finally fell. Dozens more spears were thrown in a battle that lasted more than an hour, but no more were to hit their targets. The whites were much more successful with their guns. When the firing stopped, the two black survivors lay trembling behind some bushes, splattered with the blood of their tribesmen.

Initially, Sievwright had made the long ride to the area from Geelong to inquire into a report that a white shepherd had been murdered by the blacks. This had proved false. However, he'd heard various reports of other inter-racial clashes, including those he'd gone to investigate at the Wedges'. Not believing Patrick Codd's account of what had occurred there, Sievwright waited at the Wedges' for the brothers' imminent return to hear whether they concurred. But before they arrived, a trooper arrived with orders from La Trobe to investigate a clash five months earlier between some Bunganditj and some whites at a station about 40 kilometres further from Geelong, occupied by three Irish brothers -- George, Samuel and Trevor Winter. One of the brothers had just reported the incident to Fyans, saying five Aborigines had been killed. Sievwright was on his way to the Winters' when he heard of the massacre at the Whytes', and diverted there instead. To his surprise, the Whytes and their shepherds freely admitted what had happened. There was little variation in their accounts of the slaughter, except in their estimates of the number killed -- between 30 and 80. He used what he believed were his powers as a Justice of the Peace to record statements from each man, struggling to hide his enthusiasm. Here at last was the evidence of murder for which he'd been waiting...with sworn confessions![9]

But when Sievwright returned to Geelong with what he thought was the basis for a trial that might change the course of black-white relations in the district, if not the whole colony, he would realise he faced an uphill battle. In his absence, Sievwright and the Protectorate had come under severe public ridicule. Most scathing had been an extraordinary two-part commentary in the *Port Phillip Gazette* entitled "Relative Position of the White and Black Population", which decried "the fashion to support the principles of black philanthropy" that had resulted in the appointment of Sievwright and his colleagues. It observed that one of the main arguments put forward to justify the establishment of the Protectorate was "the natural injustice of the settler in taking possession of the hunting grounds of a people whose means of subsistence are thus destroyed or rendered more precarious". It would be difficult to explain the objections to this argument, the *Gazette* commented, "without falling into a long and profitless disquisition upon the natural and social rights of mankind, did not the very actions of the opposite party afford us a ready weapon of refutation". It was undeniable that the British government had originally claimed, and had since retained, possession of New South Wales "without the slightest reference to the prior demands of the natives". But whatever acknowledgement there had since been of the natural rights of the Aborigines had only been at the expense of their white brethren.

White settlers had been encouraged to occupy the colony, and to use the land for cultivation and grazing. With the increase in population, formerly "waste" lands had assumed a certain monetary value. The government had then sold this land, with the promise that the proceeds would be used to promote emigration from Britain of enough working class people "to strengthen and extend the oper-ations of the first (white) occupiers". Instead, the philanthropists in London had managed to convince the government of the justice of using a large portion of the funds raised from the sale of the Aborigines' land for "ameliorating their con-dition". Through this barefaced fraud, money which virtually represented the personal industry and enterprise of the settlers had been used to impose on them a costly and unnecessary Protectorate system devised by "distant and ignorant men". In theory "this measure of an insane visionary" was untenable. In prac-tice it was *"a curse to the land"*. The gross injustice being inflicted on the over-taxed settlers through the Protectorate was one of the factors that were hurrying the colony "to that desperate point, when its inhabitants must either sink in ruin or flourish in rebellion".

Another major reason put forward to justify the Protectorate, the *Gazette* noted, was "the immorality of the white population, especially the lower classes, and the frequent collisions excited by this unhappy state of relationship". The commentary scoffed at the widely-held view that much inter-racial conflict arose from "the immoral connection of the black and white population". This was a groundless attack "upon the spirit of the white man". Rather, it declared, aggression had always emanated in the natural ferocity of the blacks, whose predatory dispositions were "positively fostered by the mismanagement of the Protectors". True, there were "momentary outbreaks" of violence against the blacks by former Crown prisoners whose treatment in the colony had left them "but little in advance of the black population". But with these exceptions, the white settlers and their servants always treated the Aborigines well.

"At every third station," the commentary claimed, "may be found children, destitute orphans, who would otherwise have fallen victim to the tomahawk of the unfeeling savage, brought up with care, and often affection, an amicable relation existing between the stock-keepers and the members of the neighbouring tribes, whose *gins* receive frequent presents of flour and milk, and whose old men and children are often under the protection of the whites, during the hunting or warlike expeditions of the young men and the warriors. In many instances this expression of good feeling on the part of the white man, has been checked by the annoyance which the pilfering habits of their coloured brethren occasion; it has been found necessary to keep the men of the tribes away from the huts, and most frequented parts of the run, while the harmlessness of the women enables them at all times to find food and kindness. With regard to the particular degree of intercourse between shepherds or stock-keepers, and the black females, so pointedly marked by the philanthropists, we aver that the first overtures are invariably made by the *gins* or *loobras*, for this simple reason, they find their white friends look upon them as companions, not as beasts of burden; they find themselves fed and clothed by the white man with whom they live, whereas, had they remained in the power of their black lords, hourly fatigue and daily harshness would have been their lot."[10]

While Sievwright was in the far west of his district, the meeting in Geelong called by Alexander Thomson and his friends also took place...and he came under personal attack. According to the petition drawn up by the 38 squatters who attended, Sievwright's presence had encouraged acts of aggression by the blacks. At the same time, he had not rendered any service "in defending their rights, or protecting them from the lower classes of the white population". The way the squatters saw it, Sievwright should be facilitating white settlement by modifying the behaviour of the Aborigines, but this was not occurring. Each day sheep were being stolen, driven away or destroyed, the white servants were so frightened they could not discharge their duties and, they falsely alleged, "many" white men had been murdered. The squatters complained they had "no protection or safeguard against the repetition of such outrages". The petition appealed to the Governor to allow those squatters who had been made Justices of the Peace to punish Aborigines on the spot for the many offences which they were "in the habit of committing". These summary trials would be more effective as a deterrent than the present system, under which many offences had to be brought before the Supreme Court in Sydney, hundreds of kilometres away.

The squatters assured Gipps that they were not insensible to the claims of the unfortunate Aboriginal race "to humane and kindly treatment" and that they were "most anxious to see proper measures adopted for the amelioration of their condition". They suggested that the government set aside suitable portions of land within the territorial limits of each tribe "with the view of weaning them from their erratic habits, forming thereon depots for supplying them with provisions and clothing, under the charge of individuals of exemplary moral character, taking at the same time an interest in their welfare, and who would endeavour to instruct them in agricultural and other useful arts". Such a system to "raise" the Aborigines "to the rank of Christian and civilised men" could be funded from squatting licence fees, and land sales. In summary, the petition called for the speedy adoption of appropriate measures "to protect the colonists from native outrage, to prevent the utter extermination of the aboriginal race, and to impart to their condition every improvement of which it is susceptible".[11]

At least six of the signatories to the petition had been involved in recent clash-

By permission of the National Library of Australia
"Wool drays" by S. T. Gill

es in which Aborigines had been shot -- Edward Deane Freeman Hamilton, William Carter, John Davenport Bromfield, Hugh Murray, Joseph Stephen Pollock, and Arthur Lloyd. Port Phillip's new Crown Prosecutor, Irish barrister James Croke, agreed that the circumstances under which one black known as Boljo Jack had died were "very suspicious". Nevertheless, the evidence gathered by Sievwright, he decided, was "not sufficiently strong to ensure a conviction" -- so no charges would be laid against any of the squatters reportedly involved.[12] The ruling by Croke came as depositions were on their way to Melbourne from Sievwright relating to a Bunganditj named Woolonwong being shot by a shepherd employed by Englishman John Henty -- whose family was the first to settle in the district. For almost two months, Woolonwong had been unable to move. He'd been shot through the back of both knees as he ran away from the hut used by Henty's shepherd, named Blood. A doctor called in by Sievwright had concluded that nothing but the immediate amputation of Woolonwong's left leg could save his life. "To this the native would not submit, and the limb is now in a state of mortification," Sievwright reported. The Assistant Protector told Robinson he'd issued a warrant for Blood's arrest, but the shepherd had long since absconded.[13]

Before returning to Geelong, Sievwright would visit the Whyte brothers' station again, to investigate another clash they'd had with the Bunganditj.[14] He would also inquire into the deaths of three Bunganditj at the station of John Henty's brother, Francis -- the man responsible for bringing the first merino sheep to the district back in 1834. One of the blacks killed was known as Lanky Bill, who at the time Sievwright believed was the sole survivor of the recent massacre by the Whytes. He'd been shot dead by a shepherd named George McNamara only a week after the slaughter of his tribesmen. Francis Henty and another brother, Stephen, tried to conceal the three deaths from Sievwright -- later claiming they'd assumed he'd known about them. In the case of Lanky Bill's death, Sievwright reported, the efforts at concealment had resulted in him having to retrace his steps on a round trip of about 220 kilometres. And McNamara had been able to abscond, along with two fellow shepherds whose actions had also come under investigation.[15] Meanwhile, the barque *Alice Brook*, with a cargo of 1200 bales, had become the first wool ship to set sail for London direct from Geelong.[16]

CHAPTER 5
"The most unpopular man"

FOR many years, a high proportion of the whites in New South Wales were convicts -- some hardened criminals, but others who had committed relatively minor crimes for survival in the severe economic times that followed the Industrial Revolution, and Britain's expensive wars against France. But the first decades of white settlement of the Australian colonies also included many members of a wealthy British and Irish elite, who sailed to the Australian colonies by choice, hoping to expand their riches. These men, more than any of the other free settlers, were determined to perpetuate the pre-occupation with class and "respectability" common to many nationalities, but with which the British were obsessed. In a convict-dominated society, the obsession became more intense, as those who by birth or good fortune were regarded as "gentlemen" sought to distinguish themselves from the rabble, and stop others inveigling their way into the ranks.

At home at least, Charles Sievwright had been well-entrenched in the "gentleman" class. He'd been born in Edinburgh in March, 1800 -- the third of seven children of Andrew Sievwright and Ann Robertson, whose clergyman first husband had left her a fresh-faced young widow. At the time of Charles' birth, Edinburgh abounded in "persons of title and rank", many of whom had moved from other parts of Britain to take advantage of the city's reputation as a centre of intellectual and educational excellence -- and its robust social life. The most fashionable place to be seen was the Theatre Royal, where some of the wealthier patrons would arrive after having their hair greased with the fat of a newly-slain bear at one of the perfumers' shops that kept the unfortunate animals for the purpose. Notable among those who helped ensure that stars like the great English actress, Sarah Siddons, would always play to packed houses at the Theatre Royal were young men practising law, Edinburgh's leading profession. They included Andrew Sievwright -- one of the elite group known as "writers", or solicitors. A few, like Walter Scott, would successfully extend their writing skills beyond writs, into literature. Andrew, however, would gradually start using his legal training for entrepreneurial activities.

Charles Wightman Sievwright was named after a friend and occasional business partner of his father, who was one of two witnesses to the baptism at St Cuthbert's church, below the extinct volcano on which Edinburgh Castle stood.

Charles Wightman was a trader based on the French-held island of Tobago, who'd just come back to Edinburgh to get married to the daughter of a fellow trader also based in the West Indies. The other witness to the baptism was another friend of Andrew Sievwright, Ninian Richard Cheyne, a "bookseller" or publisher. Along with stationery items that included gilt-edged visiting cards, Cheyne sold collections of works by the great Scottish poets, Robert Burns and Allan Ramsay, and books of sermons and essays by distinguished Scottish and English Protestant clergymen and theologians. He and Andrew Sievwright would both be powerful merchant burgesses of Edinburgh.[1]

At the time of Charles Sievwright's birth, the family still lived in the Old Town of Edinburgh. Not far from the Sievwrights' home was the Palace of Holyroodhouse, where Charles-Philippe, the Comte d'Artois, and future King Charles X of France, had been living in exile with his entourage, courtesy of the British government, following the French Revolution. Uphill, at the other end of the cobble-stoned Royal Mile that ran through the Old Town, was Edinburgh Castle. Life in the Old Town was vibrant and exciting, but crowded and unsanitary, and while Charles was still an infant, Andrew and Ann would decide to move to the fashionable New Town being developed to the north. One of Ann's relatives, Elizabeth Anne Hay, and her retired merchant husband, John Turnbull, were opening a new thoroughfare called Tower Street through the middle of property they owned in the New Town, and were selling off the subdivided land adjoining it. Andrew and Ann were offered a house site on a perpetual lease, for the irresistibly generous price of two shillings and sixpence a year. Under the strange terms of the contract, the "feu duty" payable was to double with the birth of each heir and successor after Charles. In accordance with ancient Scottish law, the handover of the land was marked by the ceremonial delivery of earth and stone from the site, along with handfuls of grass and corn to symbolise a commitment to pay the tithe deemed payable by the Sievwrights to support the local church and clergy.[2]

At about the same time, Andrew would start reducing his work as a solicitor, and increasing his involvement in various other business activities. By the time his fourth child, Andrew Graham, was born in 1802, Andrew senior would no longer be describing himself as a "writer". He was by then an insurance broker and a merchant, trading mainly in goods shipped in from Russia and other countries with Baltic Sea shores: timber, flax, tallow, hemp, tar and iron. One of his neighbours in Tower Street would be his insurance company and lottery office partner, accountant John Greig. Between them lived Andrew's bookseller friend, Ninian Cheyne. Andrew would acquire some of Cheyne's excess stock, and other books from his brother Francis, whose father-in-law Peter Hill, operated a rambling bookshop in the High Street that formed part of the Old Town's Royal

Andrew Sievwright

Mile. As well, Andrew and Francis would share a sizeable book collection they inherited from their father, Francis senior, who'd been a writing master in Dundee.[3] So it was that Charles would have access to an extensive range of reading material to back up his classic education which would include, for instance, a liberal dose of Latin.

But neither the law nor commerce would be chosen for Charles' career. Like his uncle Francis, a surgeon in the British Royal Navy, and his eldest brother Francis, a surgeon in the Army Medical Service, Charles was destined for military service. In fact, he would become a junior officer in the British army in 1816, at the ludicrous age of 15. In line with the purchase-of-commission system then operating, Sievwright's parents would give a London agent the sizeable sum of 400 pounds to buy him an ensigncy in a Scottish infantry regiment, the 25th Foot. Originally known as The Edinburgh Regiment, then as The King's Own Borderers, the 25th had the exclusive privilege of being able to march through the Scottish capital with bayonets fixed, drums beating, and the regimental colours flying.[4]

Had Sievwright been able to join the army just a little earlier, he could soon have found himself fighting on some distant battlefield. Barely six months earlier, Britain's 95th Regiment had led the victory parade into Paris of allied troops which had defeated Napoleon's forces in the Battle of Waterloo. Less than two years later, Sievwright would join the elite 95th, re-named the Rifle Brigade, as a second lieutenant. The 25th Foot, and in particular the Rifle Brigade, had been awarded special honours to mark their roles in particular battles on numerous occasions. But with the wars against France and America over, the opportunities for expanding their tally of battle honours in the years after Sievwright joined the army were limited to conflicts such as those in Burma, Ceylon, and India -- to which they were not sent while he was with them.

Only 13 months after joining the Rifle Brigade, Sievwright was reduced to half-pay, amid a cost-cutting exercise that involved his battalion being completely disbanded. The regiment's other two battalions would spend more than two years in Ireland, helping to suppress dissent among mainly Roman Catholic nationalists opposed to the Union then in place with England. But Sievwright would remain on half-pay for most of his time in the Rifle Brigade, including in 1822 when he went to Stirling in Scotland to marry Christina. After Frances was born in Edinburgh just over nine months later, he managed to raise the funds to buy himself an ensigncy in another infantry regiment, the 55th Foot. He would remain in the 55th for only four months before being accepted as a lieutenant without purchase in the 7th Foot, the Royal Fusiliers. It was another prestigious regiment, and whenever marching through London to or from its quarters at The Tower, it had a similar ancient privilege to do so in style as the 25th had in

Reproduced courtesy of the Public Record Office, London

On 10 January 1816, Charles Sievwright applied to join the 25th Foot regiment in the British Army by purchasing an ensigncy "vacant by the promotion of Ensign Keough". The payment of 400 pounds was made through a firm of London solicitors, Nathaniel and George Collyer. At the time, Sievwright was aged just 15. The regiment's commanding officer was Lieutenant-General Charles FitzRoy, a son of whom would later play a brief but crucial role in Sievwright's life.

Edinburgh.

At the time Sievwright joined the Fusiliers in 1825, the regiment was stationed at Winchester in southern England. It was hardly the place for the young officer to gain battle experience. But then just a little over two months later, it appeared that he may see some active service, when six companies of the regiment set sail for the Ionian Islands in the Mediterranean, then a British Protectorate. At the time, to the south-east of the Ionians, Egyptian troops were advancing up through the mountainous Peloponnisos region, helping Turkish troops to suppress what would become an eight-year war for Greek independence. The Fusiliers landed at Corfu in July 1825, and remained in the Ionians as a deterrent force for more than three years. In 1827, Britain, France and Russia decided to intervene militarily on behalf of the Greeks. When fighting broke out between Russia and Turkey, Britain redeployed its forces in the region, and the Fusiliers were sent from the Ionians to the British colony of Malta instead.[5] At no stage did the Fusiliers become involved in fighting at that time, and during 20 years in the army -- half in Britain, and half in the Mediterranean -- Sievwright would avoid any combat duty. Even during his seven years in the Rifle Brigade, the only people he saw killed with British bullets were fellow officers who'd settled quarrels by duelling. His relatively undemanding duties, however, had given him time to develop a passion for one of the subsidiary obsessions of the British gentleman -- gambling. And it was to end his military career.

Operating a lottery office had been one of the main activities of Sievwright's father until lotteries had been outlawed. Thus, gambling had been introduced to him at a very young age. And he would be reminded of it whenever he visited London, where two of his cousins had also been lottery office operators, though they were both "freemen" of the City of London and members of one of the city's politically-powerful livery companies, the Worshipful Company of Spectacle Makers. To a man often struggling to make ends meet on half-pay, the tales Sievwright heard in his family of people making fortunes for relatively small outlays were impressive. But it was mainly card games, not lotteries, which interested him and other gentlemen at the time. And it was games of *kaxxa*, or Blackjack, with his fellow officers while stationed with the Fusiliers in Malta which would be his downfall.

Accumulated debts reached a level at which Sievwright could no longer play on credit, and his only option had been to sell his commission as a senior lieutenant to pay them off. He'd had to return to London, bankrupt, to look for a new job, where he found the friends he'd acquired in British ruling circles willing to lend both financial and moral support. His main supporters had included members of the House of Lords, and of the Privy Council -- the main advisory

The Buildings called the ADELPHI.

By permission of the Guildhall Library Print Room, Corporation of London

An engraving by Benjamin Green of The Adelphi on the edge of the River Thames, where Charles Sievwright and Charles Dickens would spend many hours.

body to the eccentric King William IV. One was Lord Frederick Fitzclarence, the King's second eldest surviving bastard son by the famous Irish comic actress, Dorothy Bland -- commonly known as Mrs Jordan. Sievwright met Fitzclarence when as a Lieutenant-Colonel he'd taken command of the Fusiliers while the regiment was stationed in the Ionians. The friendship was consolidated when Fitzclarence remained in command for a time after the Fusiliers were redeployed to Malta.

For a while after returning to London, Sievwright stayed at the Adelphi Hotel on the edge of the Thames, near The Strand. The hotel had originally been opened in 1777 as the Adelphi New Tavern and Coffee House, "completely fitted up in the most elegant and convenient manner for the entertainment of noblemen and gentleman". It had certainly had its share of distinguished residents over the years before it became Sievwright's temporary home. They included, for instance, the English historian and politician, Edward Gibbon, famous for his work on the *Decline and Fall* of the Roman Empire. The writer Isaac Disraeli, father of the statesman and novelist, Benjamin Disraeli, was another former resident. And King Kamehameha II of the Sandwich Islands and his favourite wife, Kamamalu, had both died in the hotel after contracting measles during a visit to London.

When Sievwright took up residence there, the Adelphi Hotel was about to become even more well-known, featuring in an important scene in *The Pickwick Papers*, which in monthly instalments would be the novel that would launch Charles Dickens to fame. Dickens had a special fascination with the hotel, and the adjoining complex of houses and professional chambers, also known collectively as the Adelphi. An ambitious project by the Scottish architects, Robert and James Adam, the Adelphi complex sat on top of a series of large arches. Under the residential area, and behind the arches were entrances to a system of storage vaults linked to the Thames by a number of streets. During his unhappy childhood, Dickens would play at the Adelphi, using slippery wooden stairs to reach the river's edge to watch watermen's wherries and coal lighters go past. To him, it was "a mysterious place" which he would mention in many of his novels. Like Dickens, Sievwright would spend many hours at the Adelphi, lamenting his situation and wondering how and when fate would deal him a better hand.

Fitzclarence welcomed Sievwright back to London, inviting him to Royal Fusilier reunion dinners, and trying to help him find employment -- in the meantime backing up his claim to be a "true friend" by sending him a letter with 50 pounds enclosed. But probably Sievwright's main supporter was Lucius Bentinck, whom Sievwright had also met in the army years before, and who was married to another of the King's bastard children by Mrs Jordan, Amelia

Fitzclarence. Bentinck had the title of the 10th Viscount Falkland, and it was after him that Sievwright had named his new-born son. Falkland was not only close to the Fitzclarences, but also to their father, having served for a while as one of the Lords of the Bedchamber -- a position that dated back to the Middle Ages, meaning he'd helped supervise the King's ablutions. Before Sievwright's royal connection helped secure him a job, the King would die, and be succeeded by the Fitzclarences' young cousin, Victoria. She was next in line for the throne because her parents were not only married, but both regarded to be of appropriate aristocratic blood. Nevertheless, Frederick Fitzclarence and Falkland remained influential, and helped urged others to lobby on his behalf. Among his other patrons were a former Lieutenant-Governor of Malta, Major-General Sir Frederick Ponsonby, and Ponsonby's elder brother, Lord Duncannon. Appeals for a job for Sievwright were made to prominent members of the ruling Whig Party, including Lord John Russell, Home Secretary and leader of the House of Commons. But Sievwright was one of many former army officers seeking a well-paid position. For a while, it seemed that Ponsonby had arranged a job for him as a sub-inspector in the Irish Police, but this had fallen through when Ponsonby suddenly died.[6]

The break for Sievwright had finally come about 18 months after he'd returned to London from Malta, when a select committee of the House of Commons published its final report from a two-year inquiry into the original inhabitants of all parts of the Empire. The report specifically recommended the employment of men to "protect" what it called "probably the least-instructed portion of the human race in all the arts of social life" -- the Aborigines in coastal areas of the Australian continent. "Such, indeed, is the barbarous state of these people, and so entirely destitute are they even of the rudest forms of civil polity, that their claims, whether as sovereigns or proprietors of the soil, have been utterly disregarded," it observed. "The land has been taken from them without the assertion of any other title than that of superior force..."[7] The government felt compelled to act quickly on the report's recommendation, and decided to establish the Port Phillip Protectorate on an experimental basis. Such a plan had been promoted by Sir George Arthur, racked with guilt by the fact that the extermination of the thousands of Aborigines of Van Diemen's Land had been almost completed during his recently-ended 12-year term as that colony's Lieutenant-Governor. Arthur, who said he lamented he'd not thought of the idea sooner, was asked to suggest suitable men to be Protectors.[8]

It was under Arthur's autocratic administration in Van Diemen's Land that George Robinson had won his much overrated reputation as an expert on the Aborigines. Like Sievwright, Robinson had become involved with the blacks purely through financial necessity. The business he'd established in Hobart as a builder after migrating from London was not generating enough income to keep a wife and six children, and he'd taken up a job in 1829 as a storekeeper on Bruny Island, near Hobart, where Arthur had begun a conciliation experiment with some Aborigines. Robinson later convinced Arthur he should be appointed an official conciliator to contact the remnants of the "wild" tribes in the interior who were still hampering white settlement of the colony, and entice them to move to small islands in Bass Strait. The government would ensure that their basic needs were met, and they could live in safety from white attack. It had taken Robinson almost five years to achieve his objective, and at times he underwent great hardship in the bush. The colonial authorities and the settlers had shown their gratitude financially, and when Arthur had returned to London in 1836, he'd left Robinson a relatively wealthy man, in charge of a settlement on Flinders Island with the last 130 or so of the Van Diemen's Land blacks.

Arthur's glowing reports of Robinson's handling of the Aborigines to the Secretary of State for the Colonies, Lord Glenelg, along with Robinson's own fraudulent reports about the success he'd had in "civilising" those at Flinders Island, guaranteed that he be offered the job of Chief Protector at Port Phillip, for 500 pounds a year. Arthur told Glenelg he could not immediately recommend anyone suitable to be appointed an Assistant Protector, but sustained lobbying by Sievwright's friends over the next few weeks had paid off. When Arthur had suggested 11 candidates, Sievwright's name was placed first, being "strongly recommended" by Lords Duncannon and Falkland, and with "strong testimonials" from Lord Fitzclarence. Arthur reported that Sievwright appeared to be "a very intelligent person" who had described himself "to enjoy good health, and to be able to undergo much fatigue". He could confidently be expected to be "a most valuable officer", and if Robinson declined to be Chief Protector, Arthur believed Sievwright would discharge the duties of that office "in a very superior manner". Arthur had concluded: "From the high character Mr Sievwright bears, and from his standing in society, he might most advantageously be put in the Commission of the Peace, which might prove beneficial to the mission."[9] A few days later, Glenelg had approved the appointment as Assistant Protectors of Sievwright and three other men on Arthur's list -- all schoolmasters with religious leanings -- for half of Robinson's salary. They'd been told to start preparing to leave for New South Wales. At last, it seemed, Sievwright had gained a good job, and could again start providing for himself and family. His transition back into employment, however, was not to be smooth. There'd been one more embarrassing hurdle to overcome, just as Christina and the children were on their way back from Malta to rejoin him.

Glenelg had received a private letter from the Governor of Malta, Major-General Sir Henry Bouverie, and was shocked by its contents. Bouverie alleged

that Sievwright had left his family destitute on the island when he'd returned to
London, and that they'd since been depending on charity to survive. Bouverie
himself had given Christina a total of more than 40 pounds when she'd appealed
to him for help on several occasions.[10] Glenelg ordered that Sievwright be told
to suspend his preparations for departure, and to respond to the allegation. His
appointment in jeopardy, Sievwright had been saved by yet another friend he'd
made in Malta, Sir Frederick Hankey, a former Chief Secretary to the British
government. Hankey confirmed that he'd paid for Sievwright's passage back to
London, and had voluntarily provided for his family for most of the time he was
away, after the "unfortunate man" had missed out on the job of Adjutant of
Police in Malta, promised to him by Sir Frederick Ponsonby before his sudden
death. Hankey added that while Sievwright could not "maintain a character for
prudence" in his financial affairs, his abilities were "decidedly good", rendering
him "fit for further employ". After Sievwright promised to pay back the money
Bouverie had given Christina "as a debt of honour" as soon as possible, Glenelg
had allowed his appointment to stand.[11]

Within a few months of his arrival in New South Wales, Sievwright was beginning to miss the friends who'd been so supportive, and by the time he'd moved
to Geelong his loneliness had become acute. He'd expected that as a highly-paid
government official, working for a humanitarian cause, he would soon be well-
respected among the gentlemen of the colony. Nothing could be further from
the truth. He was soon well on the way to becoming, as one Western District
squatter would describe him, "the most unpopular man that ever breathed".[12]
Opportunities for Sievwright to cultivate "gentlemen" friends in colonial society were extremely limited. None of the squatters -- gentlemen or otherwise --
could afford to be seen to be befriending him, for fear of being ostracised by
their colleagues. The *Port Phillip Gazette* reported that Sievwright was soon "in
very bad odour" with the squatters in his district. "These gentlemen, it appears,
cut him upon all occasions, and will not suffer him to enter their houses," it stated.[13]

Under the circumstances, a strong bond with his wife may have provided all
the solace he needed to strengthen his determination to carry on against the odds,
as it apparently did with other Protectors facing similar problems. But relations
with Christina were strained almost to the point of estrangement. Sievwright
gained great enjoyment from their children, particularly their two eldest sons --
Marcus, 13, and Charles, 11 -- who could occasionally share some of the pleasure he found in learning aspects of Aboriginal bushcraft and culture. But they
were far too young to understand his feeling of isolation: he desperately needed
an adult with whom he could easily converse, to share his frustrations and aspirations. By early 1840, it seemed to Sievwright the friend he wanted would have

to be a fellow government employee.

Robinson was nouveau riche, and hardly the calibre of person he sought to befriend. Besides, their relations on an official level were not conducive to friendship. Robinson, jealously guarding his officially-recognised and lucrative status as the foremost Aboriginal "expert" in the colony, never communicated well with his subordinates. And Sievwright, used to taking orders from his commanding officer, was constantly annoyed by the Chief Protector's indecision and lack of leadership. It seemed at times they were working at cross purposes. Edward Parker, the fellow Assistant Protector whose area of operations adjoined Sievwright's, would have been a possible friend. For a time after their arrival in Melbourne, he and Parker had been on good terms, drinking together in the military officers' mess, and accompanying each other on shooting expeditions. But they had fallen out over Parker's belief that Sievwright had attempted to seduce his wife. Then there was Flogger Fyans, but he and Sievwright had been at loggerheads from the start. And to top off all the disputes related to their official duties, Fyans had been drawn into the scene that had occurred when Christina and Frances had returned to Geelong after running away to Melbourne. He'd witnessed the serious claims she'd made against her husband, and had vowed never again to become involved in their affairs. Since then, both men had treated each other with disdain, and neither had attempted to improve relations by arranging a social meeting.[14]

With the tide so much against him, Sievwright was on the verge of abandoning hope of any friendship beyond whatever he might gain from his Aboriginal companions. In desperation, he wrote to his younger brother, John, urging him to quit his job as the Edinburgh agent of a London brewing company, and take the earliest possible ship to the colony. He suggested they could jointly take out a squatting licence, buy some sheep and cattle, and start their own farming operation near his camp. By taking a higher proportion of the profits made, John could gradually recoup the money he'd lent to support the family during his brother's period of unemployment in London.[15] Sievwright could not expect a reply to his letter for many months. He resolved that in the meantime he would vigorously pursue his thankless duties, in defiance of his many detractors, though he was likely to make himself even more unpopular.

But when he read Gipps' reply to the petition drawn up at the squatters' meeting in Geelong, Sievwright had an inspiration. Contrary to his expectations, the Governor had not given the squatters any comfort at all. Gipps had observed it was far too early to judge the Protectorate a failure, and if it did fail it would "only be from the want of that support and co-operation of the settlers themselves", which the government had a right to expect. Furthermore, La Trobe would be authorised to spare no reasonable expense in giving the Protectorate a full and fair trial.[16]   The thought crossed Sievwright's mind that with the Governor publicly professing such support for the Protectorate, La Trobe would find it difficult to continue to shun him, as he had apparently done on the few occasions on which they'd met so far at public functions.   And there was just a chance that he could strike up a friendship with the Superintendent, thus thwarting those who were attempting to malign him to his superiors.   Sievwright decided to seek a private audience with La Trobe.

It was with considerable optimism that Sievwright arrived at La Trobe's home in Melbourne for an appointment on 16 May 1840.   The Protector began by saying that as all their previous meetings had been on an official level, he felt he should pay his respects on an unofficial basis.   But in the long conversation that ensued, La Trobe informed Sievwright frankly that he'd only reluctantly agreed

From "The Chronicles of Early Melbourne"
Superintendent Charles La Trobe's cottage in Melbourne

to the meeting.   Not only did he wish to limit official contact, but he wanted no unofficial contact whatsoever.   The reason: that "rumours had been busy with (Sievwright's) character".   So serious were these rumours, La Trobe declared, that he would advise the Assistant Protector to resign.   Sievwright angrily demanded to know the nature and source of what had been said about him, but La Trobe did not want to give details, intimating only that they related to Christina and Fanny running away to Melbourne the previous year.   He was finding it difficult enough just discussing the matter in vague terms with a man "possessing the outward manners and demeanour of a gentleman". He rejected Sievwright's demand for a strict investigation into the rumours, saying they were not appropriate for him to inquire into now, either officially or privately. Any investigation should have been carried out by Robinson when they had first surfaced. Whether they were true had no bearing on his determination not to have any unofficial dealings with Sievwright. The fact that the rumours were in circulation was enough, and he wished to end the conversation.[17] Crestfallen, Sievwright rode back to Geelong feeling even more alone. His anger with Christina over her running away was perpetuated, although he still didn't know the extent to which he'd been vilified by her alcohol-loosened tongue when she'd stayed at Lonsdale's home for a few nights.

Meanwhile, the Aborigines of Sievwright's district were stepping up their guerilla attacks, in line with their tradition of taking revenge for wrongs committed against them -- especially the murder of a tribe member. On the chilly morning three days after he met La Trobe, a group of 18 Tjapwurong men set out to avenge the deaths of some of their tribe, including that of their most revered elder, Tuurap Warneen, whose healing and supernatural powers had been renowned throughout the district.[18] The target for the Tjapwurong revenge was Patrick Codd, the Irishman whom Sievwright believed had lied to him about the use of the swivel gun at the Wedge brothers' station, and who'd since become another white man who delighted in boasting of the number of Aborigines he'd killed.[19] Codd had left the Wedges the previous week, and was about to become the new overseer for a squatter named John Cox, a former whaler and storekeeper on the coast who'd recently decided to try squatting near an extinct volcano about 180 kilometres west of Geelong. This crater was called Kolor by the Aborigines, their name for lava, and marked part of the border between Tjapwurong and Gunditjmara territory.

When the party of Tjapwurong warriors reached Cox's station, Codd was warming himself next to a fire, listening to the bugle-playing of the overseer he was replacing, James Brock. Suspicious of the intent of the fully-armed Aborigines, Brock attempted to amuse them by continuing to play for a while. He also gave them a large piece of damper to eat, before agreeing to a suggestion from one of his shepherds, Patrick Rooney, to try to enduce them to carry some firewood back from the bush nearby, in payment for their entertainment and breakfast. Rooney walked into the bush with five of the Aborigines, and they soon returned carrying some of the wood he'd cut. But when the six men went into the bush a second time, the Aborigines suddenly attacked. As Rooney screamed, Codd was struck down, and Brock fled to his hut, dodging spears and wooden clubs on the way. When Brock nervously returned to the spot a few minutes later armed with a musket, Codd lay dead, his brains oozing from his smashed skull. Stripped naked, both his arms had been broken. Rooney, who had also been stripped of his clothing and severely beaten, had crawled from the bush and collapsed next to Codd. His lower jaw was badly broken in two places, and his right arm was broken above the wrist, but he was still alive. The Tjapwurong men had fled, their mission accomplished.[20]

A police trooper who happened to pass by on his way to Melbourne the following day took news of the attack to Sievwright, and to La Trobe, in the form of a statement from Brock.[21] La Trobe immediately ordered Sievwright to go to Mt Rouse, as the whites called Kolor, to investigate. "If you find upon examination upon the spot that (Brock's) account is fully substantiated, it really appears to me that measures should be taken to mark and secure either at this time or any other favourable time, the perpetrators of such an unprovoked murder," he instructed.[22] By the time Sievwright reached the scene, four weeks after the incident, some members of the Tjapwurong tribe had already died in punitive raids by settlers in the area.[23] Brock had gone ahead with plans to return to Van Diemen's Land for a while. A statement from Rooney, who had not actually witnessed Codd's murder, differed in some respects to Brock's, but Sievwright attributed this to "the present confused state of his memory" resulting from his head injuries. Rooney was also "wholly ignorant" of who had attacked him. Sievwright could do nothing with the two Mounted Police La Trobe had made available to help apprehend the murderers.[24]

Soon after Sievwright returned to Geelong from Mt Rouse, Robinson wrote to the Assistant Protectors, informing them that Gipps had at last sanctioned the formation of the Aboriginal reserves for which they'd been calling for months. The Governor envisaged that each Protector would have one reserve, which would ultimately comprise only about 260 hectares, with his residence in the middle. Initially, however, squatters would be banned from all land within a radius of about eight kilometres. This outer area would be used by the Aborigines for hunting, and would be gradually reduced as they provided for their own food needs through agriculture.[25] Many months earlier, Sievwright had told Robinson he believed each tribe should have its own reserve, in its own territory. He'd questioned the practicality of trying to unite people with different customs and languages, and who hitherto may have had hostile relations. Such a practice, he'd argued, would "but increase those difficulties which present themselves where no *foreign* cause of discord exists" and "might render abortive, or at least impede, any attempt to civilise the aborigines, and to uphold a well disciplined establishment".[26]

Nevertheless, Sievwright believed that the government's offer of only one reserve per protector was better than none at all. He wrote to Robinson, recommending that his reserve be established in Kirrae territory, on the edge of a volcanic crater holding a salt lake the Kirrae people called Keilambete. This lake, about two kilometres in diameter, was in the middle of his district, and was just outside the apex of a roughly triangular forest that extended to the coast about 90 kilometres in one direction, and 50 in another. Squatters had taken up most of the land adjoining it, but the forest itself was regarded as too dense for grazing, and was still a haven for kangaroos and other game. There were also other reasons why Keilambete was a good site for a reserve. About three kilometres away was a smaller, fresh water lake known in the Kirrae language as Terang, which abounded in fish and other edible wildlife such as swans. And sometimes in summer, when thick sheets of salt formed around the banks of Keilambete, hundreds of members of the Kirrae and neighbouring tribes would gather at the nearby hill of Noorat. The Noorat meetings were used to settle political disputes, and to exchange goods that might come from as far as 100 kilometres away, across several tribal boundaries...such as saplings for making quality spears, red clay for ceremonial paint, and special gum for fixing the handles of stone axes.[27]

The land around Keilambete had been first recommended by Sievwright as one of his district's reserves five months earlier, after the Jarcoort Kirrae massacre by Frederick Taylor and his men. The remaining Jarcoort Kirrae people had pointed it out to him as their favourite haunt, with a request that he live with them there.[28] Within days of this recommendation being made, an Edinburgh-born squatter named John Thomson had arrived with his flocks and settled on the banks of the salt lake. Despite a warning from Sievwright that the site might be wanted for a reserve, Thomson had proceeded to form his station. He'd erected one hut for his residence on the edge of the lake, and another for his shepherds on the outskirts of the 10,500 hectares to which he'd laid claim. Around midday, five days after Sievwright had again recommended Keilambete, two of Thomson's shepherds -- Thomas Hayes and James Abbott -- were at the out-station, preparing boiled mutton for lunch. Abbott asked Hayes to keep an eye on the pot while he took a bucket to bring water from a nearby spring to make tea. He'd walked only a short distance when their dogs began barking furiously. Abbott turned to see Hayes laying on the ground outside their hut, being severely beaten by six Kirrae men with clubs and heavy wooden leanguils. The Aborigines started towards Abbott with their weapons raised. He dropped the bucket and dashed back towards the hut around a fence that formed part of the sheep fold at night. A leanguil was thrown, hitting him on the head. He fell to his knees, but staggered up and continued running. As he reached the hut door, he received another blow to the head, but made it inside and grabbed a carbine in each hand. As he was about to fire, the Kirrae men gave a loud yell, and ran off into the nearby trees. Abbott stood trembling for a few moments before checking on Hayes' condition. He was dead, with his neck disjointed, and two deep cuts in his skull. Abbott quickly rounded up the sheep into the fold, locked the hut door, and galloped off to his master's hut on the lake.[29]

Thomson, who would later describe Hayes as having been "an honest and inoffensive person", decided to enlist the support of his neighbours before reporting the murder to the authorities. When he went to Geelong a few days later he had with him a large group of angry squatters thirsting for revenge. An urgent meeting of these and other settlers in the area was called to discuss what action to take. The 36 squatters who attended decided to send a petition to La Trobe accusing the government of an "undeserved indifference" to their right to protection from the increasingly frequent attacks on their stations. Hayes' "unprovoked and premeditated" murder was the latest example of the "merciless disposition" of the Aborigines, and the government should recognise the absolute necessity of a permanent police force of sufficient size to suppress the guerillas. The petition added that the squatters were not waiting for a reply before seeking redress for Hayes' murder. They were taking up an offer from Fyans -- recently appointed the first Crown Lands Commissioner specifically for the Western District -- to accompany them to the scene with the police at his disposal.[30]

Four of the squatters were nominated to personally deliver the petition to La Trobe in Melbourne, and it was agreed that as many as possible would meet four days later at Keilambete. On the appointed day, 17 heavily-armed squatters turned up at Thomson's station. Fyans brought with him the two Mounted Police based in Geelong, and one of the six not yet fully-equipped members of the Border Police. The Crown Lands Commissioner was asked to swear in all of the squatters as special constables for the duration of the operation. However, Fyans agreed to swear in only a few, and before the group set off he pointed out that James Abbott, who was riding with them, was sure he could identify the guilty blacks. They were in sufficient numbers, he declared, to ensure that when this occurred, excessive force should not be necessary to capture them.[31]

The posse was a fearsome sight to those Kirrae people who watched it from hiding as it passed. They had of course all seen white horsemen by now, but never in such a large group, and never in the form of a war party, led by a man with the apparent status of one of their own elders. Three days of stormy weather later, the posse finally found its first Aborigines, about 20 kilometres southeast of Keilambete. Searching for frogs in the middle of a swampy clearing were three women of the section of the tribe which frequented the country around a fresh water lake known as Elangamite. The horses of the white men plodded up to the terrified women transfixed in the mud. With the smattering of Kirrae words known to members of the party, the whites menacingly demanded to know the whereabouts of the Elangamite men. The women hesitated, but fearing they would be shot if they didn't co-operate, pointed the posse to a group of trees on the edge of the swamp a few hundred kilometres away.

Two elderly brothers, named Kowcanmarning and Wawarparneen, who'd been hiding behind a fallen tree, tried to flee. But the whites leapt from their horses and seized them. The brothers had daubed their naked bodies with animal fat for warmth, and were difficult to hold as they struggled violently to escape, but were soon handcuffed and tied. Then a young Elangamite man named Burguidningnang was spotted trying to hide high in the branches of a tree. He brandished his spear defiantly in response to Fyans' demand that he come down, though with so many guns pointed at him he didn't attempt to use his weapon. One of the squatters, Arthur Lloyd, volunteered to bring him down, and with a pistol in one hand, carefully started climbing. As he came closer, Burguidningnang tried to block his ascent with his spear, but Lloyd suddenly

The Elangamite women wept in horror as their husbands were taken away...

grabbed it. There was a brief struggle, the spear snapped, and both men lost balance and fell several metres to the ground. Burguidningnang was handcuffed and tied even before he had his wind back.

Abbott assured Fyans the posse had had miraculous luck. Although these were the first Aborigines to be encountered in three days of searching, he claimed he recognised Kowcanmarning and Wawarparneen as having been among the group he'd seen bludgeoning Hayes to death. He stated he didn't recognise Burguidningnang, but Fyans decided he should be arrested as well, and ordered the police to take all three to Thomson's home station for the night, and then to jail in Geelong. The Elangamite women wept in horror as their husbands were taken away, each with a length of rope around his neck, the other end tied to the saddle of a police horse. Corporal William Brack rode behind, urging them on with flicks of a stock whip on their bare backs and buttocks. At Thomson's station, one of Abbott's fellow shepherds, Edward Pickering, gave Fyans a justification for Burguidningnang's arrest. He swore he recognised Burguidningnang as one of a group who'd robbed him and another shepherd of four blankets and some food and clothing while they'd been in the bush splitting logs for Thomson's hut about nine months earlier.[32]

One of the members of Fyans' posse told Sievwright of the capture of the three Elangamite men the day after they'd been brought to Geelong. Sievwright was appalled that Fyans had accepted the help of the squatters to apprehend them, believing such duties should be performed exclusively by the police. He feared the incident would be used by other squatters as a precedent for similar forays against the blacks and, worse still, that their servants would jump at the chance of following their masters' example. When Sievwright visited the prisoners in the Geelong jail, he found them in a miserable state, heavily chained and ironed. While being dragged about 140 kilometres from Elangamite, they'd developed large sores from the chafing of the ropes around their necks, and the manacles around their wrists. He insisted that medical treatment be arranged by Nicholas Fenwick, who'd replaced Fyans as the Geelong Police Magistrate. The Assistant Protector was unable to converse with the prisoners, but conveyed his sympathy by bringing clothing and some extra food. Corporal Brack, one of the two police troopers who'd brought the blacks to Geelong, told him their wounds were in part due to their efforts to break free from their shackles, it having been with "great difficulty" that they'd been brought in.[33] Sievwright resolved to visit Keilambete as soon as possible to interview Thomson's men, believing he could organise the release of the three Elangamite men by showing that their capture had been illegal...and in the process, humiliate Fyans. The squatters, meanwhile, had begun taking up a collection to reward James Abbott for his willingness to testify that two of the Elangamite captives had killed Thomas Hayes: he was to receive a fine new double-barrelled gun, with a brass plate inlaid in the stock lauding "his bravery in beating off a tribe of natives".[34]

CHAPTER 6
Retaliation

B ETWEEN puffs on cigars and sips of port in the clubs of the ruling elite
in London in the late 1830s, the plight of the people whose land had been
seized around the world to become part of the British Empire was occasionally the topic of conversation. Spurred on by their recent successful campaign to have slavery abolished throughout the Empire, humanitarian organisa-
tions were raising the subject with annoying frequency. Among the concerns of
these pioneer conservationists was the Australian Aborigines' lack of legal
rights. The influential British and Foreign Aborigines Protection Society lobbied strongly in London and Sydney against one aspect of the operations of the
legal system in New South Wales which made a mockery of Governor Gipps'
declaration that Aborigines and whites, as fellow subjects of Queen Victoria,
were entitled to "equal and indiscriminate" justice: the fact that Aboriginal evidence had been deemed inadmissible in the colonial courts.

A statement from the Society in July, 1839, did not question the justice of trying to impose a foreign legal system on a people who had their own complex set
of laws, based on different concepts of what was right and wrong. But the statement argued that by not being able to give evidence in the white man's courts,
the New South Wales Aborigines were rendered "virtually outlaws in the Native
Land which they have never alienated or forfeited". It added: "It seems to be a
moral impossibility that their existence can be maintained when in the state of
weakness and degradation, which their want of civilisation necessarily implies;
they have to cope with some of the most cruel and atrocious of our species, who
carry on their system of oppression with almost perfect impunity so long as the
Evidence of Native Witnesses is excluded...".[1]

The Colonial Office decided to seek the views of one of the three judges of the
Supreme Court of New South Wales, William Westbrooke Burton, who happened to be in London on leave the month after the Society issued its statement.
Burton advised that the Court had ruled that Aboriginal evidence was inadmissible for two reasons. The first was the language barrier. There had been numerous cases in which it had been impossible to communicate with a proposed
Aboriginal witness because he could not speak English. Attempts had been
made to use white interpreters, but these had been largely futile. The second
reason for not allowing the testimony of Aborigines was their lack of belief in

the white man's god, and therefore their inability to swear on the Bible to tell the truth, with the fear of divine retribution should they lie. Burton drew the attention of the new Secretary of State for the Colonies, the Marquis of Normanby, Sir Constantine Henry Phipps, to a Bill he'd drafted the previous year, under which Aboriginal evidence would be admitted in cases where the matter at issue was "of minor importance". Burton had sent the draft Bill to Gipps, with the hope that he'd present it to the colony's Legislative Council. Gipps had declined, he presumed on the ground that such legislation should not be of colonial origin.[2]

However, Phipps -- a former Governor of the colony of Jamaica -- did not agree. After hearing Burton's arguments, he wrote to Gipps instructing him to submit to the Legislative Council "some well digested plan for obviating such impediments as prevent the admission of the testimony of the Aborigines...". Phipps acknowledged that the language problem could not be tackled with legislation alone. He suggested that the impediments would also have to be tackled by teaching the Aborigines the English language "or by engaging some competent person to study theirs" -- displaying the supercilious blindness of the British government and its colonial administrators to the fact that there were many and vastly different Aboriginal languages...a blindness which was somehow to persist for years, and result in countless court-room charades with alleged "interpreters" acting on behalf of people whose languages they could not have known. Phipps also told Gipps that he should unceasingly seek to relieve the Aborigines from their "want of religious knowledge" through "an improved system of moral and religious instruction". However, the Secretary of State added that the absolute rejection of their evidence because of their "barbarous ignorance" of Christianity "would appear to be injurious to the interests of Justice".[3]

As it happened, even as Phipps' instructions were on their way to Gipps across the oceans, the Legislative Council passed an Act to allow Aborigines to be witnesses in criminal cases. Gipps' administration had had second thoughts on the matter, though not for humanitarian reasons. Rather, Attorney-General Plunkett had become increasingly exasperated about the difficulty of gaining convictions in cases involving Aborigines -- both as the accused, and as the injured parties. Under the Act drawn up by Plunkett, the evidence of an Aborigine, or a half-caste who lived as one, could be admitted in criminal proceedings. But it hardly provided for equal and indiscriminate justice. Aboriginal evidence would be "of so much weight only as corroborating circumstances may entitle it to". As well, a clause was added at the request of the Chief Justice, Sir James Dowling, preventing the Act taking effect until it had received the approval of Queen Victoria. In a covering letter to the Colonial Office, Gipps explained that without royal assent, Dowling -- and probably his fellow judges -- would have felt "compelled to remonstrate against the Act as repugnant to the Laws of England".[4] The week Burguidningnang, Kowcanmarning and Wawarparneen were arrested by Fyans' posse, more than nine months after the Act was sent to London, the British Attorney-General, John Campbell, and Solicitor-General, Thomas Wilde, would recommend to Phipps' successor, Lord John Russell, that he advise the Queen to disallow it. This was because "to admit in a criminal case the evidence of a witness acknowledged to be ignorant of the existence of God or a future state would be contrary to the principles of British jurisprudence". Their advice was accepted.[5]

It was only a few days later that Sievwright received a bundle of documents from Robinson relating to the clashes involving the Whyte brothers earlier that year. The documents included the opinion on the cases of Irish barrister James Croke, who'd replaced Horatio Carrington as Port Phillip's Crown Prosecutor. Sievwright was astonished by what he read. He'd expected the first case to result in the Whytes being charged with mass murder. But the Crown Prosecutor made no such recommendation. Instead, he opined that in both cases the blacks appeared "to have been the aggressors", and the conduct of the Aborigines would make the conviction of the Whytes "very uncertain". In the first case -- in which at least 30 Aborigines had died -- the brothers had stated they'd only start-ed firing after spears had been thrown at them. The subsequent clash -- in which a hut-keeper had received spear wounds, but Aboriginal casualties were unknown -- had also resulted from black provocation. Croke also believed that the sworn statements taken by Sievwright, in which they admitted committing the massacre, could not be used as evidence against them. As principals in the case, the Whytes "should have been permitted to make a free and voluntary dis-closure and not a confession under the sanction of an oath". This was because of a bizarre British legal rule, with its origins in the Middle Ages, which pre-vented sworn statements by accused people being used as evidence. Croke's explanation: "The reason...is because the dread of perjury coupled with the apprehension of additional penalties may create an influence on their minds which the law is particularly careful in avoiding." The Crown Prosecutor decid-ed to lay no charges.[6]

As a soldier for most of his working life, Sievwright had had little incentive to expand the rudimentary knowledge of British law which he'd picked up from his father as a child. He'd been given a briefing on relevant aspects of it when he'd become a magistrate by virtue of his office as an Assistant Protector, but readi-ly admitted he was still baffled by its intricacies. The issue of taking depositions in the correct manner had already been drawn to his attention several weeks before he received Croke's opinion on the Whyte cases. He'd received a letter

S. Mossman 1840

By permission of the National Library of Australia
"Geelong in 1840" by S. Mossman, engraver. Until La Trobe decided to ban them from the town, the Barrabool Aborigines had been employed to carry goods from ships in the bay up the steep cliffs to the town's stores and inns. Sievwright would appeal for lifting of the ban, but Gipps would endorse it.

from the Attorney-General in relation to the depositions he'd taken from the Whytes' neighbours, the Winter brothers, about the incident in which they'd killed five Bunganditj. In this case, Croke had been quite satisfied with Sievwright's depositions. In fact, after studying them he'd told La Trobe he believed the Winters had -- on their own admission -- made "a strong case of homicide" against themselves. But Plunkett did not agree with the Crown Prosecutor. The Attorney-General had told Sievwright the depositions were "incomplete", adding that if he thought the Winters had committed homicide other than in self-defence, he should commit them for trial. Sievwright had been puzzled by the letter, believing he'd followed the proper procedures. He'd immediately written back, asking for more detailed instructions.[7]

On reading Croke's opinion on the Whyte cases, Sievwright was even more confused. What was he supposed to have done? There was one Aboriginal survivor, but the law stipulated that he could not give evidence. Sievwright had the white men who'd been at the scene to deny any involvement in killings. But, no! They'd all admitted what had happened without coercion, and he'd recorded their statements. Yet Croke would do nothing, merely because he'd taken the statements on oath. Was he supposed to have asked each of the Whyte brothers to write down their own statements, to prove they were genuine? And what of their illiterate servants? Surely his taking of statements in an apparently incorrect manner didn't mean that the Whytes could not now be charged? Surely he could, if necessary, return to the Whytes' station to take fresh depositions in a form acceptable to the authorities? Sievwright wrote to Robinson, curtly pointing out that the detailed instructions he was still awaiting from Plunkett were now even more indispensable to him, especially as his own opinion on the Whyte cases was "so dissimilar to that which I have just been allowed the benefit of". He'd take no further action on the Whyte or Winter cases, he stated, until he received the Attorney-General's advice.[8]

That same day in August 1840, Gipps was to make a ruling on another matter which Sievwright regarded as a further example of the way in which his superiors were hampering rather than helping him in the performance of his supposed duties. For more than a year, whenever he'd been with the Barrabools in Geelong, he'd encouraged them to visit the township to obtain casual work such as unloading vessels in the bay and carrying the goods up the steep rise to the town's stores and inns. The storekeepers had been eagerly using their services because white men willing to perform such back-breaking work, particularly in the summer heat, were extremely hard to find. The Aborigines had also been trading animal skins and food in season excess such as fish and oysters at the stores, and with individual inhabitants of the settlement. In return, they'd received blankets and tomahawks, and quantities of the European food to which they'd taken a liking, especially flour and sugar. Sievwright believed that in the absence of the reserves he'd been recommending for each tribe, or government assistance in the form of food and clothing, visits to Geelong were the only way the Barrabool people could provide for themselves without resorting to theft from the squatters.[9]

However, La Trobe was concerned that in Melbourne and Geelong the Aborigines were obtaining the whites' main means of dealing with black resistance -- firearms. A proposed law against selling firearms to the Aborigines had not yet been introduced, and some were beginning to believe that guns would be their only chance of survival. As the local Aborigines entered another winter of serious food shortages, Police Magistrate Fenwick in Geelong received orders from the Superintendent to use "firm but gentle means" to keep them from the settlement.[10] Fenwick, eager to act on La Trobe's instruction, threatened the storekeepers with jail if they were found trading with the blacks.[11] La Trobe neither bothered to consult Sievwright before issuing his directive, nor even inform him of it. The Protector was surprised by reports from some of the Barrabool people that they'd been driven away by the police when approaching the town. Then a squatter passing Sievwright's camp complained that he'd had to personally intervene to gain access to Geelong for a Colijon whom he'd been employing for some months, and who'd been accompanying one of his white employees taking a bullock cart in for provisions. Sievwright rode to Fenwick's office, and was enraged to hear of the ban. He wrote to Robinson requesting that it be immediately rescinded, arguing that the squatters would be all too happy to use it as an official precedent to justify driving Aborigines from their runs. Sievwright agreed that the police should keep the blacks away from the places selling liquor, but not from the whole settlement. He cynically added the suggestion that La Trobe inform the Protectorate of any future instructions to other departments affecting the Aborigines, lest the Superintendent's objectives be undermined through ignorance of them.[12]

La Trobe was prepared to compromise only slightly. He believed that although an Aborigine could obtain food and clothing in the township, either as charity or as payment for work performed, he carried away with him "vice, disease, and the means of injury to both himself and his neighbours". If the Aborigines had any skins or baskets to sell, Sievwright should appoint a white man to act as their agent. The Superintendent told Robinson he was prepared to allow individual Aborigines to work in Geelong, if this was done with Sievwright's knowledge. However, as few as possible should be granted this exemption, until the proposed law forbidding the sale of firearms to the Aborigines was in full force. In a fawning letter in reply, the Chief Protector stated his views on the matter were "in perfect accordance" with La Trobe's. Unbeknown to Sievwright, Gipps many months earlier had issued unexplained orders that the Aborigines should be discouraged from raising funds for food and clothing by selling lyre bird feathers in Melbourne. Not surprisingly, he also endorsed La Trobe's ban.[13]

Introduction of the ban coincided with an upsurge in inter-racial clashes to the west, which Sievwright had predicted in his second official report, dated June 1, 1840. He'd warned of the urgent need for the government to implement its expressed intention to set aside land for the exclusive use of the blacks, saying that their raids were no longer confined to petty thefts to relieve hunger, but were assuming "the character of retaliation and revenge which must be a natural consequence of the rapid occupation of their country without either Asylum or assistance being afforded in return".[14] In the winter of 1840, more than 2300 sheep were reported stolen in Sievwright's district -- most in parts of the Tjapwurong and Bunganditj territory, between 200 and 350 kilometres from Geelong. Roughly two-thirds of the sheep were recovered by their owners, but not without further substantial loss of Aboriginal lives.

In the winter of 1840, more than 2300 sheep were reported stolen...

In one incident, a group of Tjapwurong warriors attacked a shepherd and drove off about 500 sheep from the station of a newly-arrived English squatter, Peter Charles Aylward, not far from where Patrick Codd had been murdered the month before. To try to recover his sheep, Aylward formed a party of eight whites. They included two of his neighbours, squatter Robert William Tulloh and station manager R. W. Knowles, and some of their men. On the first day of searching, Aylward and his party found about 30 ewes and 150 lambs which had wandered off from the flock being driven towards some nearby hills. Leaving the sheep in charge of a shepherd, the party continued and a little further on they caught up with the thieves, who thought they'd travelled far enough from the scene of the crime to safely settle down for a feast. The Tjapwurong people fled into the bush as they saw the white men approach, leaving behind about 100 sheep which had either been killed, or had had their hind legs broken so they could not stray. It was almost dark, so Aylward and his party rode back to the tent which was his residence, taking with them the sheep they'd recovered. The following day they set out again, and found a few more ewes and a large number of lambs. After taking these back to Aylward's station, they decided to pay another visit at dusk to the spot where they'd discovered the Tjapwurong camp the day before. The thieves had returned, bringing with them the rest of their section of the tribe to share the sheep they'd killed or maimed.

Reproduced courtesy of the Mitchell Library, State Library of New South Wales
"The avengers" by S. T. Gill.

There were more than 150 Aborigines camped around about 70 fires, arranged in a semi-circle. This time, they did not flee, but quickly formed themselves into two lines: the young men in front, and the women, old men and children behind. As the whites dismounted, tied up their horses, and walked slowly towards the camp, guns in each hand, the Tjapwurong warriors taunted them with abuse. One young man shouted in English: "Come on, white bastards, we fight you!" and threw a spear. The whites opened fire, retreated a short distance to reload, then fired again. This process was repeated twice more over the next 15 minutes before the Aborigines gave up trying to defend the camp and ran off. Aylward, who later told Sievwright that "several" of the blacks had been killed and "a great many" wounded, asked his friends to stay the night with him at the camp. The following morning, they gathered together several hundred spears, and every other painstakingly-crafted and valuable Tjapwurong possession had been left behind -- such as possum skin cloaks, bark water and food containers, stone and bone tools, and mussel shell knives. There were also about 50 woven baskets into which the Tjapwurong women had stuffed chunks of smoked mutton on top of their usual contents of fire-making implements and small treasured objects they believed to have magical powers. The white men made a bonfire of everything combustible, while all other items were thrown into a deep waterhole. Aylward's total losses: about 230 sheep.[15]

The high price paid by the Tjapwurong people for their raid on Aylward's station did not deter them from continuing to create havoc. Only a fortnight later, they struck against another of Aylward's neighbour's, a fellow Englishman named John Muston, who had fled to the Western District from Van Diemen's Land to escape from a nagging wife. A party of about 18 Tjapwurong men drove off almost 200 sheep from one of Muston's outstations. On this occasion, there was no punitive expedition against them, and by keeping the sheep alive until wanted inside a brush wood fence at their camp in the bush, the thieves and their families were well fed for some weeks.[16] During and beyond the 1840 winter, groups of Tjapwurong attackers also staged other raids, including two on the flocks of the Wedge brothers. In one, a whole flock of 1294 sheep was driven off. The Wedges and their men, never averse to killing blacks, shot dead five Tjapwurong blacks -- one for each day it took to recover all but 164 of the sheep -- and wounded others.[17]

In another Tjapwurong attack, not vigorously brought to official attention lest it lead to an inquiry into what had provoked it, a shepherd named John Collicoat was killed. Collicoat, described as "a great blackguard" by one squatter, had been responsible for the deaths of a number of Tjapwurong people. Implicated in some of the killings was Collicoat's employer, Horatio Spencer Howe Wills, the Sydney-born son of a man transported for life to New South Wales for highway robbery. In acting against the blacks, Wills was not only seeking to protect his 5000 sheep and 500 cattle, but also his wife and three-year-old son, who he'd brought with him to live in a tent. Collicoat's murder would provoke a wave of revenge killings like the one that had occurred after Patrick Codd's murder at Mt Rouse. The victims would include two Aboriginal nursing mothers whose infants were left without milk.[18]

Further west, the Bunganditj people were also attacking the white men's flocks. In one incident -- reported to Fyans, but not to Sievwright -- another English squatter, Robert Savage, discovered a group of Bunganditj taking away 30 of his sheep. Savage claimed the sheep had been recovered without a shot being fired. But that afternoon, he'd been forced to open fire when the same group of blacks had attacked with "a great number of spears". He saw one of the attackers fall dead, though the blacks later claimed two had been killed.[19] At about the same time, arguments over the use of Bunganditj women for sex resulted in a daylight raid on one of the neighbouring outstations of Thomas William McCulloch, in which 55 ewes and a number of lambs were driven off. McCulloch led a party of fellow squatters and shepherds in the search for his sheep, eventually coming across the Bunganditj who'd stolen them camped on a creek. The whites charged at the camp, shooting dead one black man and one woman, reportedly McCulloch's favourite member of the "harem" through which he and his men had been sharing syphilis with the Bunganditj. McCulloch wrote to La Trobe appealing for protection from the "outrageous" and "mischievous" attacks by the numerous Aborigines in his district, pointing out that all but two of his stolen sheep had been "wantonly and brutally murdered". As well, he protested, a large group of blacks had returned to his outstation three days later, rushed his shepherds' hut, and "carried off every article of value". The squatter failed to mention what had provoked his differences with the Bunganditj -- or that two of them had been killed.[20]

Closer to Geelong, the Kirrae, Colijon and Kurung Aborigines also staged numerous winter raids, and some resulted in the shedding of blood other than that of sheep. One clash occurred after a group of Jarcoort Kirrae blacks stole 17 sheep from Englishman Henry Gibb. He traced the tracks of his sheep to a Jarcoort camp near Lake Corangamite, and a youth threw a spear as he threatened to arrest them for the theft. William Brack, the Mounted Police corporal, happened to be passing through the area with Burguidningnang and his other two Elangamite prisoners, and Fyans authorised him to help try to capture the youth. Brack, Gibb, his brother, and three of their shepherds were attacked with showers of spears, and large rocks rolled towards them down the side of a rocky outcrop where the Jarcoort Aborigines had taken refuge. One of Gibb's shepherds was hit in the shoulder by a spear before the Jarcoort blacks made their escape. When Brack moved on with the Elangamites the following day, Gibb called on some of the squatters who'd been members of Fyans' posse to help him capture the youth. This time, he was successful. The boy was caught nearby, and tied up in a woolshed at the station of Niel Black, which had also come under recent attack, while his captors debated what to do with him. That night, however, he escaped and rejoined his people.[21]

The Jarcoort Aborigines continued their raids, stealing 84 sheep from other original squatters in the area, John and Peter Manifold, only a few weeks later. At about the same time, not far across the tribal boundary, a party of Colijon men stole about 100 sheep from the station of Arthur Lloyd, the squatter who'd climbed the tree to bring down Burguidningnang. Lloyd and the Manifold brothers joined forces to try to recover their sheep. Lloyd's they found first: all dead. Then they came across a large group of Jarcoort blacks holding 56 of the Manifolds' sheep inside a crude fence. In a statement to Fenwick later, Lloyd reported that as he and the brothers approached, the Jarcoort people had "presented their spears, and showed signs of resistance", so they'd opened fire. "I have no doubt that some of them were wounded. There were between 40 and 50 natives," he stated.[22]

In the north-eastern corner of Sievwright's district as well, near where the borders of Barrabool, Jaara and Kurung territory met, there were attacks at about the same time on a number of stations. Wealthy Scottish brothers Thomas and Somerville Learmonth were forced to vacate one of their runs after an attack. They spent the whole of the next day searching for blacks on whom they could take revenge, but could not find any.[23] Kurung warriors also staged a series of raids on the huts of David Henry Wilsone and his fellow Scot partner, John Campbell. The attackers carried off food, firearms, clothing and bedding. The station hands, under orders to shoot black thieves, gave chase but according to Wilsone did not manage to carry their orders into effect. Nevertheless, Wilsone took heart in the fact that he and his partner had been joined by 34 other squatters at the Geelong meeting called to discuss the murder of John Thomson's shepherd, Thomas Hayes. "We have all united to defend to the utmost our properties and woe betide the blasted race when they are caught injuring us," he wrote to his brother, George. "A considerable number of murders have been committed by them on our shepherds, hutmen and several stockholders also, and they will have it dearly paid back to them without any mistake." Wilsone urged George not to believe newspaper reports about harm allegedly suffered by the Aborigines. Such reports were completely false, designed only to arouse "a false sympathy" for the blacks -- and for "a most expensive, pernicious and useless" protectorate system.[24]

After returning to his camp in late June from his trip to investigate Patrick

ACCOUNT of PROVISIONS issued to Sick, Aged, &c., Aborogines, at Geelong District from the 1st to the 30 September 1840

Days of Month.	Aged and Infirm.	Sick.	Boys.	Girls.	Pounds Flour.	Pounds Beef.	Pounds Mutton.	Pounds Tea.	Pounds Sugar.	Pounds Tobacco.	Pounds Soap.	Pounds Salt.	
1													
2													
3													
4													
5													
6	4	3		1	12	"	"	4	1.4				
7	4	3		1	12			4	1.4				
8	4	3		1	12			4	1.4				
9	4	3		1	12			4	1.4				
10	5	3		1	13½			4½	1.6½				
11	5	3		1	13½			4½	1.6½				
12	5	3		1	13½			4½	1.6½				
13	5	3		1	13½			4½	1.6½				
14	5	3		1	13½			4½	1.6½				
15	5	3		1	13½			4½	1.6½				
16	5	3		1	13½			4½	1.6½		2		
17	5	3		1	13½			4½	1.6½				
18	5	3		1	13½			4½	1.6½				
19	5	3		1	13½			4½	1.6½				
20	5	3		1	13½			4½	1.6½				
21	5	3		1	13½			4½	1.6½				
22	5	3		1	13½			4½	1.6½				
23	5	3		1	13½			4½	1.6½				
24	5	3		1	13½			4½	1.6½				
25	5	3		1	13½			4½	1.6½				
26	5	3		1	13½			4½	1.6½				
27	[illegible]	3		1	[illegible]			4½	1.6½				
28	5	3		1	13½			4½	1.6½				
29	5	3		1	13½			4½	1.6½				
30	5	3		1	13½			4½	1.6½				
31													
In Store					568½		600	23	165½	25	23	25	

I CERTIFY that the numbers of Sick and Infirm Aboriginals in the above Return, have received Provisions from me, from those under my charge, amounting to the quantities stated on the other side.

C W Sievwright Assistant Protector.

Reproduced courtesy of the Public Record Office of Victoria

After a delivery of supplies from Melbourne to his empty store early in September 1840, Sievwright was able to issue small quantities of flour, tea and sugar to a few aged and sick Barrabool people, and one female child, under his care. At the end of the month, 568 lb (258 kg) of flour; 600 lb of mutton; 23 lb of tea; 165 lb of sugar; 25 lb of tobacco; 23 lb of soap; and 25 lb of salt, comprised the scant supplies still in the store. A system of strict rationing had to continue.

Codd's murder at Mt Rouse, Sievwright spent most of the rest of the 1840 winter with the Barrabool blacks, attempting to learn their language, and helping them cope with the effects of La Trobe's order banning them from Geelong. Although he was able to help by shooting some kangaroos and other game, still there was not enough food to go around. Robinson ignored his pleas for enough food to make up for what the Barrabool people would have been able to obtain had they been allowed to continue performing casual work in the town. The Chief Protector would only authorise small amounts of food for the "sick, aged and infirm". Over 19 days of August, Sievwright had only 40 kilograms of mutton to distribute. On one day, for instance, he issued half kilogram rations to two old blacks, three sick ones, and one young girl who was particularly malnourished. It was not until after he issued yet another appeal for food, just before he left to investigate the recent spate of clashes to the west, that some further supplies arrived to stock the empty store: 410 kilograms of flour, 270 kilograms of mutton, 90 kilograms of sugar, 14 kilograms of tea, and 11 kilograms each of tobacco, salt, and soap. If the food had been distributed to all the hungry Aborigines camped with Sievwright, it would have lasted only a few days. The ration system for only the most desperate continued.[25]

Partly because many of the whites involved did their utmost to screen the facts from the authorities, La Trobe had only limited awareness of the severity of the clashes that had occurred in the Western District. Soon after Sievwright left on what would be a seven-week journey to investigate them, the Superintendent wrote to Robinson enclosing a document saying that three Aborigines had been killed at the Wedge brothers' station. No doubt, he admitted, the blood "of one party or the other" had also been shed as a result of recent Aboriginal attacks elsewhere.[26] In response to the squatters' plea for protection after Thomas Hayes' murder, La Trobe had just ordered that a small detachment of soldiers be sent to Keilambete from Geelong.[27] The Superintendent told Robinson that the squatters, with some reason, could expect the government to use force to suppress what had become the "frequent unprovoked aggressions" of the Aborigines. But he could not sanction the use of force until the Protectorate had tried to establish friendly relations and "proper influence" over the offending tribes. According to La Trobe, Sievwright had not yet attempted to achieve this objective. Although Sievwright had outlined numerous and extensive trips in his reports, the fact that he'd made them had somehow escaped La Trobe's attention. Apparently, the Superintendent remarked, Robinson's assistant had confined himself to the immediate neighbourhood of Geelong. La Trobe suggested that perhaps Sievwright was still awaiting Robinson's "promised assistance". The Chief Protector should therefore lose no time in going ahead with his planned visit to the Western District.[28]

Ten days later, La Trobe also wrote to Fyans, requesting a detailed report on the state of inter-racial relations in the district.[29] Fyans was quick to reply, saying he'd received complaints of "numerous outrages" by the Aborigines at almost every station. Many settlers, he declared, had suffered serious property losses, specifically mentioning the names Wedge, Gibb, Winter and Whyte. In Fyans' opinion, the Aborigines' "habits of idleness, extreme cunning, vice and villainy" meant that it was "out of the power of all exertion...to do any good by them". Furthermore, he could "plainly see the general conduct of the Aborigines growing worse and, if possible, more useless, and daily more daring". In an apparent reference to Sievwright, Fyans asserted the idea that no punishment awaited them had lately been instilled in the minds of the blacks with, he thought, considerable pains. They'd also come to believe that white men should be punished "for the least offence". Under such circumstances, the settlers' property was being destroyed without redress, their employees dreaded to act even when an attack was made upon their lives, and then left the station as soon as possible. "On many occasions," Fyans reported, "they have been compelled to join their flocks, making one out of three or four, for safety and protection, which is ruinous to the owner."[30]

The Crown Lands Commissioner also drew La Trobe's attention to his arrest in June 1838 "at considerable risk" of an Aborigine named Nannymoon for the tomahawk murder of a white hutkeeper called Terence McMannis north-east of Geelong.[31] Nannymoon had been sent to Sydney for trial, but had been discharged and sent back to the district more than a year later a free man, after the Attorney-General decided that the depositions on which Fyans had committed him did not amount to "legal evidence".[32] Fyans, who'd been convinced of Nannymoon's guilt, told La Trobe he had now apprehended two Aborigines for the murder at Keilambete of Thomas Hayes. He did not expect Kowcanmarning and Wawarparneen to escape punishment for their "horrid deed", pointing out that the Elangamite brothers had been identified by Hayes' fellow servant, James Abbott. Fyans stressed the difficulty of arresting Aborigines, saying it involved "great risk of life on both sides". In many parts of the district, such as that in which the Wedges had settled, "it would be impossible to take them". He suggested that the only way to bring the district's Aborigines "to a fit and proper state" was "to insist on the gentlemen in the country to protect their property, and to deal with such useless savages on the spot".[33]

Fyans failed to mention that the Elangamite brothers were the first black men sighted by his posse in three days of searching for Hayes' murderers. He added, however, that he expected his own depositions in the case to be the ones to be relied upon, rather than those taken by Sievwright. In matters involving the Aborigines, he suggested, magistrates had to be very responsible, "particularly at the present time". In the case of Hayes' murder, he'd taken inquest papers which would prove fully to La Trobe's satisfaction. However, after he'd committed Kowcanmarning and Wawarparneen for trial, Sievwright had visited Thomson's station and taken his own depositions. "I need not say how very illegal this is, and evincing a great want of common respect to me, so many years his senior as a magistrate in the colony," he wrote.[34]

Fyans also referred to a confrontation that had occurred when Sievwright had tried to take a deposition from John Thomson a few days after he'd taken statements from his shepherds. Regretting that he'd been away from his station when Sievwright had arrived, and had forgotten to instruct his men not to make further statements, Thomson had angrily refused to give one to Sievwright himself.[35] As far as he and his fellow squatters were concerned, the Crown Lands Commissioner had obtained a deposition from a white witness strong enough to convict the two men arrested. Whether they were the murderers was immaterial. As long as two blacks went to the gallows, as a warning to the rest of their race in the district, the law had served its purpose. Fyans told La Trobe that when Thomson had objected to Sievwright taking fresh depositions, Sievwright had threatened to "commit him to the common jail". Fyans presumed that La Trobe was well-acquainted with the fact that Thomson was a "worthy and moral man", and he could only suppose that the Protector's motive had been "to lower the gentleman". Sievwright's "want of decorum" warranted the Superintendent ordering him from the district, to be under Robinson's immediate supervision in Melbourne.[36]

It was not only Sievwright's actions which made Fyans particularly defensive about the depositions he'd taken in the Hayes case. He'd also just received annoying letters in relation to his depositions from Crown Prosecutor Croke, who believed they might not have been taken "in strict accordance with the rules". It appeared to Croke that the principal witness, James Abbott, had not been formally examined, and had only sworn to the general accuracy of a written statement read to him. As well, the depositions had apparently not been taken in the presence of the alleged murderers -- and them given the opportunity of cross-examining their accusers, which the law at the time stipulated was their right. Croke had instructed Fyans and Police Magistrate Fenwick to take new depositions. "There should be some person present conversant with the language of the natives who could partly by signs and partly by words communicate to them the object of the examination directed by me," he optimistically told them.[37]

In a letter to Attorney-General Plunkett in Sydney forwarding the depositions that were subsequently re-submitted, Croke would say they were still unsatisfactory. Despite an offer from a group of squatters to help find interpreters,

Fyans and Fenwick had not been able to arrange for one to allow the Elangamite men to cross-examine Abbott. "A man may say this would be idle as the natives do not understand the proceedings, but that is no objection, as the law does not distinguish between black and white people, and we should do as the law directs," Croke wrote. The Crown Prosecutor added that the difficulties he'd had with Fyans over the case were not unusual. "I have got so many irregular and informal convictions and depositions from this Magistrate that it is necessary to watch scrupulously any proceedings conducted by him," he told the Attorney-General. "He may be well-meaning now but he is being ignorant." Croke added that he'd lost a recent Quarter Sessions case because of the way in which Fyans had taken depositions. The Crown Lands Commissioner had seemed "quite offensed" when the depositions had been sent back to him with a request that they be modified. Fyans had merely returned them "without having taken any step to rectify the mistake".[38]

The way in which Sievwright had handled the Hayes case also led to a rebuke from Croke. When Thomson had refused to make another statement on the ground that he'd already made one to Fyans, Sievwright had indeed officially summonsed him to attend his tent in Geelong to give one -- under threat of jail if he refused. When Thomson had ignored the threat, Sievwright told Croke he wanted to take action against the squatter as an example "in order to curb the contempt that exists for all legal interference" in his district.[39] The Crown Prosecutor responded by telling him that it had been "a work of supererogation" to have taken fresh depositions on the murder of Thomson's shepherd when Fyans had already taken some, and forwarded them to Melbourne. As well, serving a summons on Thomson to try to force him to make a statement had been "an irregularity". Croke concluded by saying that if possible, Sievwright, should try to use "some mode of interpretation" to make Kowcanmarning and Wawarparneen understand what was happening to them.[40]

CHAPTER 7
A hostage debacle

VIOLENT clashes between Aborigines and white settlers were by no means confined to the western part of the Port Phillip District. Simultaneously, much inter-racial violence occurred from the time white settlement began in other parts of the district. The biggest massacre ever of white men in the colony took place in April 1838, as thousands of sheep and cattle were being hastily driven overland into the fine new grazing land in the north-east of Port Phillip. A group of about 150 blacks attacked a party of men in charge of a large flock belonging to brothers George and William Pitt Faithfull, about 170 kilometres from Melbourne. Seven of the whites were killed. Many other lives were to be lost -- most of them black -- in later clashes in Port Phillip's northern and central areas. Crown Lands Commissioner Frederic Armand Powlett, whose operations covered these areas, reported two-and-a-half years after the massacre of the Faithfulls' men that the Aborigines' behaviour was still "decidedly hostile and treacherous". Two white shepherds had recently been killed by the blacks: another two had gone missing, presumed murdered.[1]

In August 1840, Governor Gipps decided to send a detachment of police troopers under the command of Major Samuel Lettsom overland from Sydney on what was supposed to initially be a secret mission to Port Phillip's north-east to investigate the "great atrocities" he feared were taking place there. Lettsom was ordered in particular to inquire into an Aboriginal attack three months earlier on the property of former ship surgeon, George Edward Mackay, in which a hut-keeper had been killed. Information received by Gipps indicated that the attack had been "a preconcerted measure of revenge or retaliation", timed to take place while the doctor was away.[2] Mackay, who bitterly denied reports that the raid had been provoked by illtreatment of black women by his shepherds, would later allege that the 20 or so attackers had also killed almost 3000 head of cattle, and four horses. They'd also set ablaze a field of wheat, and huts containing valuable supplies of tea and flour. However, the doctor's brother, John Scobie Anderson Mackay -- who'd been present -- would mention the loss of only three horses, a bullock, a calf, and some poultry.[3]

Gipps rejected Mackay's claim for compensation for lack of police protection, but was prepared to punish the Aborigines responsible if they could be caught.

By permission of the National Library of Australia
Melbourne in 1840, by Robert Bruce, engraver.

In outlining guidelines for Lettsom, the Governor referred back to the principle espoused by Lord Glenelg three years earlier that the Aborigines were "in every respect to be considered as subjects of the Queen, and not as aliens against whom the Queen's troops may exercise belligerent rights". He emphasised that Lettsom was to act as a civil magistrate, and not in a military capacity. No action could be taken against blacks which English law would not allow to be taken against white men. Nevertheless, if the "actual perpetrators of any outrage" could not be apprehended, the major could take the *illegal* action of detaining "a reasonable number" of hostages from the tribes to which they belonged, in a bid to force their surrender. Gipps suggested that these hostages should be "some of the chiefs of the tribes, or the sons of the chiefs".[4] In a private letter to La Trobe, Gipps stated that he would have sent Robinson on the mission, if he'd had full confidence in "the ability and activity" of the Chief Protector. However, he had "reasons for thinking Lettsom a more fitting man for it". The Governor added that should the major uncover any "very atrocious occurrences" and ask for assistance, La Trobe should give it.[5]

After interviewing Mackay and other squatters, Lettsom arrived in Melbourne with the names of several Aborigines whom he was "particularly desirous of apprehending". La Trobe told Robinson they were generally known to be "amongst the more troublesome" of the blacks, and it was time an example was made of them. Robinson and his assistants must assist Lettsom, and their role as Protectors could not be used as a ground for refusing to co-operate.[6] Later that day, however, Assistant Protector William Thomas cited his instructions from the British government as the reason why he could not comply with Lettsom's request for help in arresting two Aborigines whom the major believed were camped with him outside the town. Thomas told Lettsom that the blacks of his district, extending east and south-east of Melbourne, were peaceable and had "conducted themselves well" for months. The others on the major's list, he said, were from areas north of the town. At least two were members of what had become known to the whites as the Goulburn River tribe, which was reported to be on its way to Melbourne. Thomas added that he was appalled by Gipps having authorised Lettsom to take hostages. Such a measure, he believed, had not been taken in a British colony since 1792, when the Governor-General of India, the Marquis of Cornwallis, had as a last resort found it necessary to help defeat the powerful Sultan of Mysore, Tipu Sahib.[7]

In a letter to Robinson explaining his stand, Thomas pointed out that he felt a duty both as a public servant and a private citizen to facilitate the ends of justice. In the early part of his "unprofitable services" among the Aborigines, for instance, he'd twice almost been murdered after he'd successfully traced the blacks responsible for killing one of their own race. He'd also often recovered property stolen from whites, and had urged the pressing of charges to stress to those under his care that even petty theft was punishable. But Lettsom's request for him to arrange for the two Aborigines "to be apprehended and lodged in safe custody in Melbourne" amounted to an order not supported by warrants or any information against them. He'd thus acted according to his instructions as a protector of the liberties of the Aborigines. "Had I as a magistrate in my own country under such circumstances have taken two individuals into custody and committed them to jail, I should have laid myself open to heavy damages by the parties, and have drawn down the reprobation of Government, and been justly expelled from the Magistracy," he argued. In line with Gipps' proposal to take hostages, the two may have been held in chains for years in an attempt to guarantee the good behaviour of the rest of their tribe. The taking of hostages from tribes involved in disturbances, Thomas predicted, "may ere long put the whole Aborigines of Australia Felix under Martial Law, and bring this fair Province into perhaps a far greater Theatre of Carnage than our sister colony a few years since...".[8]

A few days later, Thomas reported that two blacks from Sievwright's district had brought news of "a plot to assault the authorities" by a combined force of the tribes that visited Melbourne. The report came as a large group of blacks arrived, swelling the number of Aborigines camped near the town to almost 400. Thomas believed they comprised mostly members of the Goulburn tribe, but also others, including Barrabool people.[9] In a meeting with La Trobe and Lettsom, Robinson agreed that if the major was correct in his belief that the blacks he sought were among the group, they should be arrested. The Chief Protector also agreed it would be desirable to recover any guns or ammunition from the blacks' camp. However, he could not immediately suggest any way of achieving these aims, and he would not condone the use of force. La Trobe stated that under ordinary circumstances, he would hesitate to sanction the use of force. But it was evident that the Aborigines were becoming "more and more decidedly hostile" and more difficult to deal with.[10]

"That the control of the Authorities is altogether rejected and that the impunity with which this resistance to the arm of civil power, whenever employed, has been attended, has led them to set our power almost at defiance," the Superintendent declared. "Forbearance is a virtue which few savage nations either practise or comprehend. In this state of things I should decidedly say that the lesson of the necessity of yielding to rules and regulations which are after all for their ultimate good, as well as for that of the District, ought to be taught." La Trobe told Lettsom he should use all available soldiers and police "to overawe opposition" and quickly seize the blacks he wanted. At Robinson's request, he advised he was not authorising the major to also take the white weapons being held by the blacks. Responsibility for this decision would rest with the Chief Protector. La Trobe added that Lettsom should remember that "nothing but extreme and imperative necessity" could justify bloodshed.[11]

At dawn the following day, Lettsom led 45 soldiers and police in a surprise raid on the Aboriginal camp. The blacks were surrounded and ordered to lay down their weapons. Some, however, did not immediately comply. One young man named Winberri -- who'd become reputed among the whites as a leading trou-blemaker, and who was specifically being sought by Lettsom -- was spotted hiding among a group of women. As he was dragged from his hiding place, he struck and broke a soldier's gun with his waddy. Several other soldiers and police tried to grab him, but he slipped away with the help of some of his tribe. As a lieutenant named Francis David Vignolles rode up, Winberri made another swipe with his waddy, but missed his target. Then as he started to run off, Sergeant Dennis Leary of the Mounted Police rode over and fired a shot. The ball entered Winberri's body just below the ceremonial scars that ran across his back between his shoulders, and passed through the base of his skull, killing him instantly. Bayonets and truncheons were then used to force the rest of the blacks to march into Melbourne. There, the captives were herded into a stockade and a search was conducted. A total of 33 men, many found to be hiding guns under their animal skin cloaks, were taken to the already cramped jail, and placed in double irons. On La Trobe's orders, the dogs the blacks used to guard their camps and to help in hunting, which had faithfully followed them into the town, were killed. Their bodies were carted off with Winberri's for burial.[12]

Severe damage had already been caused to any prospects for peaceful black-white relations in Port Phillip by the event. But La Trobe was to aggravate the situation even further. Instead of allowing all the other blacks in the stockade to go free, the Superintendent ordered that more than 100 of them, including many women and children, be imprisoned in a store being built for the Public Works Department. The brick building had strong iron bars across its small windows, but no door to keep in the prisoners, who were "excited and under trepidation". Fearing further bloodshed in a mass escape bid, Robinson asked Clerk of Works James Rattenbury to barricade the doorway. This was partly done, but the Chief Protector was not satisfied -- especially when he discovered at nightfall that the soldiers who'd been guarding the building had been replaced by only two con-stables, one of them a convict on parole hired just for the purpose by Melbourne's Chief Constable, William Wright. Robinson expressed alarm to both La Trobe and to the commander of the military detachment in the town, Captain Charles Hamilton Smith, warning of "serious results" unless the store was placed under strong military guard. La Trobe left it up to Smith to deal with the Chief Protector's concerns. In fact, all Smith did was to give orders for the

"Windberry" (Winberri) by Assistant Protector William Thomas, who regarded him as one of the "noblest" blacks he ever met. "He had saved the lives of many shepherds and travellers on the Goulburn River and deserved a much better fate," wrote Thomas, after Winberri was shot dead by Mounted Police Sergeant Dennis Leary, during the operation near Melbourne led by Major Lettsom.

doorway to be properly barricaded, and three carpenters assigned as government labourers were taken from their barracks by lamplight to imperfectly complete the job Rattenbury was supposed to have organised.

  Assistant Protector Edward Parker happened to be in Melbourne at the time and separately raised concerns about the inadequacy of the security arrangements at the store with Chief Constable Wright. But Wright had only been ordered by Police Magistrate James Simpson to put constables on duty to relieve the soldiers -- and he did not consider himself to be responsible for the safe custody of the prisoners. Wright gave the "ticket-of-leave" constable he hired for the job, William Holland, and the ordinary constable, Samuel Mann, loaded guns with bayonets, and ordered them to fire to raise an alarm if there was any trouble. In the early hours of the morning, Mann wandered off to the nearby constables' hut to smoke his pipe. The Aborigines had been quietly digging tunnels under opposite walls of the store in preparation for a mass escape. Through gaps between the wooden boards nailed across the doorway, they could see that Holland had been left in sole charge, and decided the time had come to seek their freedom -- even though only one tunnel was ready. Dozens had managed to slip through before Rattenbury, whose house adjoined the store, was awoken and ran out to alert Holland. As Rattenbury rushed off to the military guard room to get the soldiers out of bed, some of the Aborigines pulled enough of the boards across the door down to scamble through. Holland opened fire at one group, but another man jumped out and threw a piece of board at him. The acting constable opened fire again, again apparently missing his target.

  Holland and the soldiers who arrived at the scene would later give conflicting accounts of what happened next, amid reports that one Aborigine attempting to escape had been cut by a soldier's sword before being shot dead in the store. According to Holland, one of the soldiers opened fire into the store as soon as he arrived there. He'd since heard that a black had died, but had not seen the body. Corporal William Jennings would admit shooting into the store, but some time after he arrived -- and only when the blacks inside rushed together towards the doorway while he was alone there. A few hours after the incident, a shocked La Trobe ordered the release of the prisoners who'd not escaped from the store. They left behind the body of one of their tribesmen named Narrokemulluc, called Tommy by some of the whites, who according to Robinson had been "a quiet and peacable person". Colonial Surgeon Patrick Cussen found that Narrokemulluc had died instantly from a gunshot wound to the head. But he also found that his left wrist was "horribly mutilated". It was as if the wrist had been crushed by a mill on the under side, but on the upper side there were two or three recent cuts which were "apparently sabre wounds".[13]

  The Melbourne press reflected strong support in the white community for the capture and continued detention of the 33 suspects placed in jail when Lettsom's posse first brought the Goulburn and other Aborigines into the town. But there was widespread fear over the possible repercussions of La Trobe's order to illegally detain scores of the other Aborigines in the store. "The savages who escaped were most probably under the idea that they were to be punished with severity by the whites, although they might not have been participators in any of the crimes committed by their sable brethren now in custody," remarked a *Patriot* commentary. "The consequence will be that their savage disposition will be awakened, and the settlers will be the sufferers, unless the Protectors have recourse to the most vigorous and active measures." The *Port Phillip Herald* voiced similar alarm. It undoubtedly would have had beneficial results if punishment had been inflicted on the blacks such as Winberri who'd been responsible for attacks on the settlers. But the detention of all the blacks who'd been camped near Melbourne had been unnecessary, and the manner in which they'd been guarded deserved "the severest reprehension". The result would be that "many a poor bushman will have to pay the penalty for this bungled attempt at intimidation".[14]

To the disappointment of the authorities, George Mackay's men could not identify any of the blacks still being held in the jail as having been involved in the attack on his station. Frantic efforts were made over the next few weeks to find someone to give evidence against them, to justify their patently illegal capture and detention. Mounted Police were sent out to encourage squatters and their employees around the Goulburn and Ovens Rivers to come to Melbourne to try to identify any who'd been involved in other raids.[15] As the search for witnesses continued, Lettsom arrived back in Sydney to report with some trepidation on his mission. He feared Gipps may be "displeased" with him for having "in some degree" disobeyed the Governor's orders not to act against the Aborigines in a military capacity. But, he pointed out, the blacks he'd been seeking were in a large and well-armed group, and he'd needed the soldiers and police to help capture them. He'd given orders to those under his command "not to fire till the last extremity", and he hoped it would appear to Gipps that there'd been no unnecessary bloodshed. "Should what I have stated not prove satisfactory to his Excellency," Lettsom concluded, "it remains for me to express to him my deep regret for acting as I have done, which was solely attributable to the peculiar position in which I was then placed."[16]

Lettsom need not have worried: Gipps told the major he approved of his actions, which he hoped would have "good results". In a letter to La Trobe, however, the Governor warned that "the utmost circumspection" would be needed in passing on to London any reports on the matter by the Chief Protector or his assistants. "Their representations we know in England will be credited (I do not mean by the Government -- but by Persons perhaps more powerful than the Government) whilst the reports of all persons filling official stations here, will be received with suspicion -- or entirely disbelieved," he wrote. Gipps added that "the only safe course" to be taken with the blacks in custody would be "to treat them as White men would be treated under similar circumstances". Should any of them be brought to trial and convicted, he believed the best punishment would be imprisonment on Cockatoo Island in Sydney harbour, where some wayward blacks were already being detained. He hoped "that some of them may receive instruction there that may ultimately be advantageous to them".[17]

The same day La Trobe received the Governor's letter, the Superintendent would receive another one on the same subject which made him realise that the Lettsom affair was far from over. The second letter was from Robinson, concerning an inquiry he and Parker had conducted into the two black deaths that had resulted from Lettsom's raid. Robinson told La Trobe he agreed with Parker's summary of the findings of the inquiry, already passed on. The Chief Protector and his assistant believed that Winberri's death must be regarded as justifiable homicide: a white man resisting authorities charged with his apprehension for a felony could also have been shot. But the case of Narrokemulluc was different. "I must unhesitatingly declare that the person or persons who fired into the store and caused the death of the man, and the person or persons who ordered such firing, have been guilty of manslaughter," Parker had reported. "The Aborigines confined in the store were British subjects, and as they were charged with no offence their detention was illegal...and they therefore were not in the commission of any crime in endeavouring to make their escape." Furthermore, it was apparent that the authorities could be accused of "culpable remissness" by having taken no further steps to secure the store after having been warned that the blacks feared further violence against them and could try to escape. "It also appears from the evidence that fortuitous circumstances alone prevented a greater sacrifice of life," he concluded. "Women and children were fired at indiscriminately."[18]

In his initial comments on the Lettsom affair, Gipps did not reply to La Trobe's request for instructions on what to do with the Aborigines still being held illegally in the Melbourne jail. Police Magistrate Simpson had told him that no offence of a capital nature had been obtained against any of them. When Robinson suggested that the detainees should either be charged or released, La Trobe agreed, believing that continuing to hold hostages would not achieve the aim of having "a proper influence" over the future conduct of the Port Phillip blacks.[19] Besides, he'd just been informed that the jail was too crowded to receive any further people liable to imprisonment for non-payment of fines.[20] The Superintendent instructed Robinson to consult the bench of Melbourne magistrates, led by Simpson, on what should be done about the 33 Aborigines "without entering into the justice or injustice, the policy or impolicy, of the measures that have been adopted". La Trobe added that in their dealings with the detainees and their brethren, the Chief Protector and his assistants should take advantage of what had occurred "to inculcate some wholesome lessons upon their minds, and as far as possible to advance the common interest of the whole population of the District, whether Black or White".[21]

What had become a major headache for La Trobe was still to worsen. The magistrates, Robinson told him, were unwilling to act on the matter until further advice had been received from Sydney, because Lettsom had been operating under special orders from there -- with magisterial powers -- and his actions had "involved in some particulars a departure from the course ordinarily pursued and prescribed by law". After consulting Crown Prosecutor Croke, however, La Trobe insisted that he be told which Aborigines captured by Lettsom could be charged.[22] More than a week later, Simpson advised that only 10 of the captives faced charges "of sufficient magnitude" to warrant continued detention, so La Trobe ordered the immediate release of the rest.[23] Those kept in the Melbourne jail, Simpson believed, had been identified in statements made before him and Robinson by three employees on sheep and cattle stations in the Goulburn district. The stations were operated by Scottish squatter Peter Snodgrass, a hot-headed former Crown Lands Commissioner whose father, Kenneth, was a former Lieutenant-Governor of Van Diemen's Land, and had been acting Governor of New South Wales before Gipps' arrival.[24]

Already jittery over the possible repercussions of the whole Lettsom affair, the Superintendent was then appalled to receive a scathing report from Sievwright accusing him of encouraging white hostility towards the Aborigines in the Western District. A large part of the report was devoted to La Trobe's "arbitrary" and "unwarrantable" order banning the Aborigines from Geelong. The blacks, who'd gained much benefit from their visits to the township, had been most distressed by the ban. As a result of his first complaint about the ban, La Trobe had ruled a few "individuals who could be trusted" would be allowed to work in Geelong, but only with Sievwright's sanction. "This restriction amounts to a continuance of the order," the Protector wrote, "as during the last ten months I have been but two in that neighbourhood, and for the future, my duties are likely to call me wholly from that place. Thus, if it is only with my knowledge that they are to be allowed ingress into the Township, during my absence they must be altogether excluded."

Such a harsh measure was not justified, Sievwright protested. Only two complaints had been made to him about the behaviour of the Aborigines in Geelong in the previous 12 months -- both involving Barrabool blacks. One, which he did not attempt to refute, had been reported by Police Magistrate Fenwick, who'd so exuberantly implemented La Trobe's order: a sack of flour left on the beach had been torn open, and some of it stolen. The second complaint had come from Fyans, who'd claimed that the local Aborigines had destroyed a stack of wheat belonging to him worth more than 20 pounds.[25] Fyans had complained direct to La Trobe that the incident had been carried out by blacks camped on the opposite side of the Barwon River with Sievwright, who should have prevented "so gross an outrage".[26] But according to Sievwright's inquiries, some

Reproduced courtesy of the Mitchell Library, State Library of New South Wales
From the "Illustrated Melbourne Post", 20 Oct. 1864.

Barrabool children had stolen about six sheaves of wheat, and Fyans' stack had been "otherwise uninjured".[27]

La Trobe's order banning the Barrabool people from Geelong, Sievwright argued, amounted to "oppression" and "injustice", from which he was supposed to be protecting the Aborigines, and it should be rescinded. The "mischief" the Aborigines were likely to suffer from this arbitrary example being followed by the settlers would be as difficult to remedy as it had been easy to establish. "Moreover," he wrote, "I would respectfully add that since the Aborigines are declared to be under the protection of the same laws which we enjoy, I am ignorant that any law permits the indiscriminate punishment of a community for the delinquencies of a few of its individual members...". As well, he urged the greatest caution in issuing orders concerning the Aborigines in which the police "or any subordinate authority" were likely to be brought into contact with them. The actions of the Geelong police had shown that such orders were likely to be exceeded. This placed both black and white communities in much danger as the servants of the settlers were "too ready to take the tone from anyone acting under authority, which may apparently also authorise them to act harshly towards the Aborigines, and it is a precedent they readily plead, when their own conduct is the subject of investigation".

The next subject of Sievwright's vitriol was Fyans. La Trobe's order had been partly responsible for the renewal of "a spirit of antipathy and hostility to the Aborigines" in his district. But Fyans had contributed even more to this regrettable development, by joining the posse of squatters in the recent search for the murderers of Thomas Hayes at Keilambete. Without giving details, Sievwright described the way in which the alleged murderers had been apprehended as "an indiscriminate attack". The British government and the Parliament of England had decided on the Protectorate's conciliatory measures as the only system to be pursued. But these would be rendered impracticable "if the settler instead of being won by example to co-operate with this department in its endeavours, is not only instigated to renew bad feeling, but is urged by the presence and sanction of an Officer in the Government employ to go forth for days and nights to scour the country for the purpose, as it appeared, of apprehending the first natives they fell in with".

"To lead the squatters into collision with the natives was a reckless act, for the result of which no-one could have answered," Sievwright wrote. "Had the tribe been fallen in with, amounting to, as we have lately had evidence to show, from 300 to 500 natives, consequences might have ensued involving the future tranquillity of the province. Such a proceeding was directly opposed to the only chance of success which exists for the mutual welfare of the settler and savage namely, that all strife and animosity between them be discouraged -- and that on no account shall they be suffered to come into collision. If the Commissioner with the Police force at his disposal, and which I presume is deemed by the Government sufficient for the duties he has to perform, cannot with it succeed in carrying his orders regarding the natives into effect, I most earnestly beg that he may be instructed on no account...to accept the aid of the settler, to assist him in the discharge of his functions...".

In his previous report five months earlier, Sievwright pointed out, he'd urged the government to immediately implement its proposal to set aside land for the exclusive use of the Aborigines. But even the preliminary step had yet to be made of deciding a location for the reserve authorised for his district -- either at Keilambete, as he'd recommended, or elsewhere. The delay meant that another season had been missed for the planting of crops which could at least have part-ly provided for the Aborigines' food needs, and reduced their hunger-induced attacks on the white settlers' flocks. He could only reiterate his warning that while this situation was allowed to continue, inter-racial clashes must daily increase.

The final barb in Sievwright's report was directed at Crown Prosecutor Croke in Melbourne and Attorney-General Plunkett in Sydney. The Assistant Protector pointed out that in the case of the murder of Patrick Codd at Mt Rouse, the opin-ion he'd had at the time of the motive for the killing had since been confirmed by "a gentleman" on whose report he could rely: shortly before his death, Codd had admitted shooting dead a number of Aborigines. He'd been killed in revenge, the two other whites in his company at the time having almost shared his fate. But the white community heard nothing of the reasons for such mur-ders, judging them "by what is alone held up to their notice and indignation -- the result". At the same time, there'd been an "appalling sacrifice" of black lives, but Croke and Plunkett had not as yet thought fit to bring to trial "even for their own justification" any of the whites implicated. "Such events being allowed to pass away without further comment than the inquiry originally entered into by this department has tended to inspire the settlers with the idea that these whole-sale slaughters are permitted," Sievwright wrote. "I would earnestly recommend that a check may be given in this district to such an opinion."[28]

The outburst against the legal authorities had been prompted in part by Croke's refusal to agree to charges being laid against the Whyte brothers for the mas-sacre they'd committed. But Sievwright was annoyed that he was still awaiting the advice he'd sought months earlier on what to do about his supposedly "incomplete" depositions relating to the Winter brothers, whom he believed should also be charged with murder. As well, he'd just received a letter from Croke in relation to the recent killing of five Tjapwurong people by the Wedge brothers and their men. Croke had promised to seek the Attorney-General's

Monthly List of Persons who have taken out Depasturing Licences in the District of Portland Bay from the 4th to the 31st October 1840 inclusive

Names	Residences	Station	Date of Licence	No. of	Date of Licence	Amount	Remarks
						£ s.	
O'Brien Henry	Geelong	Geelong		245	19 Aug 1840	5 -	
do	do	do		246	do	10 -	
Bird Alexander	The Hopkins	The Hopkins	23	257	do	10 -	
do	do	do		252	do	10 -	
Conolly John Port	Wardo River	Wardo River		349	do	5 -	
do	do	do		350	do	10 -	
Davidson, Davidson, Thom. Creek Running into Port Fairy	Brisbane	Brisbane	1	325	do	do	10 -	
Fenwick Nicholas	Geelong	Reserve of the town of Geelong	1	317	do	10 -	
McCrae Duncan	Portland Bay	Merino Plains	1	314	do	10 -	
do	do	do		345	do	20 -		in a district
Peace Robert Gardiner	Geelong	Warruna	1	326	do	10 -	
McCallan R. M.	Geelong	Geelong		337	do	10 -	
Patrick Robert Ann	Bryant's Creek	Bryant's Creek		342	do	5 -	
do	do	do		341	do	10 -	
Robertson Bro. Geo. E	Wardo River	Wardo River		360	do	5 -	
do	do	do		361	do	10 -	
Ritchie John	Port Fairy	Port Fairy		347	do	5 -	
do	do	do		346	do	10 -	
Noble David	do	do	7	323	do	10 -	
Fuller The Fiery	Portland Bay	Geelong		338	do	5 -	
do	do	do		339	do	10 -	
White Brothers	do	do		355	do	10 -	
do	do	do		356	do	10 -	

Total £ 210 -

Reproduced courtesy of State Records New South Wales

Instead of accepting Sievwright's recommendation to lay charges against the Whyte brothers over their admitted massacre, the colonial authorities would soon be issuing them with two new 10 pound squatting licences, one back-dated to cover the date when the massacre occurred. In the same month, Police Magistrate Nicholas Fenwick received a depasturing licence for the "reserve of the town of Geelong".

opinion on the killings, but he would not be recommending that any charges be laid against the whites involved. It appeared, he asserted, that the Wedges had only acted in self-defence, or at least defence of their property. "Taking possession of sheep amounting to 1290 is no trifling offence, and not only taking possession of them but also killing many of them," Croke wrote. "On this branch of the case, my opinion is that the perpetrators of the outrage ought to be punished, if only they can be caught and identified."[29]

Croke's letter had angered Sievwright, who did not believe that any amount of sheep stealing justified the killing of blacks. In fact, his attack on the legal officials may have been even stronger had he awaited another letter from Croke, which arrived a few days after his report had been sent to Robinson, then on to La Trobe. This letter related to the clash involving Peter Aylward, Robert Tulloh, and R. W. Knowles the previous June, in which Aylward had admitted several Tjapwurong people had been killed and "a great many wounded". Sievwright had been ready to take the three settlers into custody and commit them for trial for murder, but had been advised by Fenwick to first seek Croke's opinion. Again, the Crown Prosecutor told Sievwright he'd forward the depositions to Plunkett without a recommendation that charges be laid. According to Croke's reading of the depositions, the blacks involved in the clash had not acted defensively when the settlers had arrived at their camp, but had initiated hostilities. The white men had testified that the Aborigines had "placed themselves in battle array" and had accompanied a challenge to fight with the throwing of a spear. The rounds of gunfire to which they were then subjected were therefore justified. "I do not think under the circumstances the evidence in this case raises such a strong presumption of the guilt of Mr Aylward and party, as would warrant you to commit them," Croke wrote.[30]

The Attorney-General did not agree with Croke. "I think it is evident that more than one homicide has been committed by Mr Aylward and his party," Plunkett told Croke. But Aylward appeared to be the only one who'd admitted seeing a dead body, and as Sievwright had taken his statement on oath, it could not be used in evidence against him. The fact that a homicide had occurred would have to come from a white witness who could testify in court. Plunkett added that it would be "highly unconstitutional" for him to direct magistrates such as Sievwright in the discharge of their duties. He enclosed another copy of the letter he'd sent the previous May, in which he'd told Sievwright his depositions in the case of the Winter brothers were "incomplete". This was the letter on which Sievwright had sought clarification. The Crown Prosecutor, however, had not passed on Sievwright's request for more detailed instructions. And once again, an attempt by the Assistant Protector to bring white settlers to trial for murder would be allowed by Croke to lapse.[31]

About the same time, another massacre of Bunganditj people would occur in the far west of the Port Phillip District. Ironically, it would be first reported to La Trobe by Peter Aylward's partner, Augustine Barton. A total of either 15 or 17 Aborigines, mainly women and children, were fed damper laced with arsenic at a station operated by the Henty brothers near the junction of the Wannon and Glenelg Rivers. Barton said the blacks had reported that a hutkeeper at the station had divided the damper among the Aborigines who were visiting the station. Soon afterwards, the blacks were "seized with violent pains in the stomach accompanied by retching" before they died. The white men had found a new way of ridding themselves of their unwanted black neighbours -- a way which would prove both highly effective, and virtually untraceable.[32]

CHAPTER 8
Hallucinations

INVARIABLY, there is a gap between theory and practice in a government decision on a means to deal with what has been deemed a problem. The size of the gap -- the extent to which the politicians' stated intent is achieved -- depends on their willingness to allocate adequate funding...and to a large degree on the goodwill, competence and commitment of those responsible for implementing the decision. A poorly-funded government project launched as little more than a policy outline, with details to be worked out later by bureaucrats pre-occupied with other matters, is likely to achieve little. If the project is subject to widespread public opposition as well, and the lobbying of the representatives of those it's meant to benefit is ineffectual, its chances of success are even further diminished. Many whites -- among them colonial officials such as Foster Fyans -- hoped that Port Phillip's Protectorate was such a project. They regarded the experiment as an expensive hindrance to settlement by "the greatest people upon the face of the earth"[1], and they looked forward to the day when it would be abandoned. As far as the do-gooders back in London were concerned, it would still appear that an attempt had been made to address concerns about the Aborigines. Unfortunately, it just hadn't worked. After all, there was no group of influential heretics with the gall to question the morality of the British invasion itself.

Notwithstanding their primary role of ensuring a smooth white takeover of the land, Gipps and La Trobe never wanted to be indentified with the anti-Protectorate sentiment. Mindful of the considerable support in Britain for the objectives of the department, they were eager to be seen to be giving it a fair trial. But in many ways their actions were fatal to the cause. Complex and delicate cultural issues that had to be taken into account for the Protectorate to have a chance of achieving its stated aims were ignored by Gipps and La Trobe. And their parsimony and petulance would deprive the officers of the department of the means fundamental to the discharge of their supposed duties. The biggest mistake by Gipps and La Trobe, however, was the decision to leave the workings of the Protectorate entirely up to Robinson, in whose abilities far too much unaccountable faith was placed.

The British government had acknowledged that it would not make sense for details of the department's operations to be dictated by men in London who had no first-hand knowledge of the unique local circumstances in New South Wales. Robinson and his assistants had been told that Gipps would give them full instructions on their arrival in Sydney.[2] The Governor shirked the responsibility, quickly passing it on to the Chief Protector. In doing so, he declared: "Mr Robinson received his present appointment because he is supposed to have acquired experience in these matters superior to that which is possessed by any other individual in the Colony. I am willing to give him the widest discretionary power, to judge his labours only by their results."[3]

To the constant detriment of the endeavours of Sievwright and his colleagues, this would result in implementation of the Protectorate being from the outset inefficient and inconsistent. At the same time, fear that his expertise might come into question, coupled with a desire not to offend Gipps or La Trobe, crippled Robinson's willingness to make prompt and resolute decisions on matters crying out for urgent action. Much of the voluminous correspondence produced from Robinson's office was vague or contradictory, and the Chief Protector failed to win the respect of his assistants. When they were sent into the field, they had not received the instructions they'd been promised on how they should carry out the eight duties outlined before their departure for the colony: the longest amounting in the convoluted verbiage of the day to less than 80 words.[4] While ignoring their numerous subsequent pleas for more guidance, and for the material support they'd been promised, Robinson was ever willing to blame any perceived failings of the Protectorate on their incompetence.

In a report in January 1840, giving his first detailed views on the department, La Trobe regretted he could provide no evidence of the Protectors having made any "reasonable or decided" progress. It was apparent that they'd made "but little advance" in acquiring a knowledge of the habits, character and language of the tribes with which they'd been in most frequent contact. Without this information, it was impossible to have a reasonable hope of the Protectorate being ultimately successful in its efforts "for the protection and moral and physical improvement of the Aborigines". And the Superintendent believed that after having lived with the blacks for a few months, the Protectors should have been able to induce them to start abandoning a practice thousands of years old -- the migratory search for food according to seasonal availability. Robinson and his assistants had not achieved even "some slight power of controlling their movements", he lamented.

The Protectors' duties, La Trobe acknowledged, were "exceedingly difficult of attainment", and if firmly and conscientiously discharged they could stir up "men's prejudices and passions". Nevertheless, they were armed with the advocacy of a good cause, were supported by the authority of both the British and colonial governments, and had "the full terror of the law on their side" through their magisterial powers. This should have made them sufficiently strong to set opposition at defiance, and command a degree of respect among the white population. Their failure to have won at least the goodwill and co-operation of the "better class" of white settlers had greatly added to their difficulties. As well, La Trobe was still in doubt whether Robinson had "any very clear and sober conception of the extent and character of his own peculiar plans" for the Protectorate. Worse still, he believed Sievwright and his colleagues were equally mystified. "I regret to state that it is but too evident that the Assistant Protectors have not understood his plans nor entered into their spirit, and that but little harmony of operation or common bond of union can thus far be detected," he wrote.

The Superintendent said Robinson did not dispute that little progress had so far been made by the Protectorate, and had given two reasons. The first related to his pay. "Mr Robinson states that his personal pay and allowances, far from giving him that power of action which would be desirable, are such as to render him of but little utility to the cause: and are, in fact, such as to place him below his assistants in point of both private emolument and official power."[5] It was an exaggerated claim, already rejected months earlier by Gipps, and La Trobe did not feel it was justifiable.[6] Robinson's second excuse for lack of progress was "the incapacity and unsuitable character" of the men chosen to help him. La Trobe agreed that the Assistant Protectors were generally "gentlemen not calculated by previous habits and attainments" to be suitable. But before their arrival in the colony, they could not have had "the smallest conception" of the true nature of the task they'd agreed to undertake. Only Robinson had the necessary knowledge, La Trobe believed, and he should have visited them in the field to impart "that instruction and encouragement which they could expect from none but himself". Instead, he'd chosen to sit in his office in Melbourne for seven months. Robinson's "state of inaction" was reprehensible, and was retarding the operations of the Protectorate more than any other cause. "It must be termed inaction," La Trobe wrote, "however well and usefully employed Mr Robinson may consider himself to have been employed in studying the languages and political relations of the tribes...or in culling anecdotes or noting down traits of character amongst the large band of natives allowed to remain congregated for so long in the immediate vicinity of the town, to their own undeniable ruin."

Furthermore, Robinson was avoiding the responsibility of discretionary spending of the special fund the Governor had made available for the use of the Port Phillip Aborigines. La Trobe stated he would recommend expanding the fund, if he was convinced it would further the aims of the Protectorate -- and he believed Gipps would endorse the recommendation, despite having emphasised the need to limit the size of handouts to the Aborigines.[7] However, Robinson's behaviour precluded him from being able to make such a suggestion. "Until order and system are introduced into the Department, it cannot be otherwise, but that the Government will frequently be called upon to interpose obstacles to the speedy execution of the wishes of the Protectors, and to assume the appearance of checking the work, instead of promoting it," he concluded.[8]

A month later, the obstacles proved too great for one of the Assistant Protectors. In a lengthy resignation letter, James Dredge argued his prescribed duties, with the means furnished by the government, were "of such a character to defy the possibility of performance". For example, he'd been given only one bullock and a cart and told to proceed almost 140 kilometres into the bush. It was well known that one bullock could not draw the cart there had it been empty, let alone loaded with all his equipment and supplies, so he'd been forced to buy another three bullocks with his own funds. He'd also been expected to move about his vast district gathering statistical information on its numerous Aboriginal tribes, yet at the same time take charge of the government stores at his camp, and provide a monthly return showing how they'd been used. If any of the stores became spoiled or were stolen he would be held responsible, although no store was provided for their security. To the public, Dredge noted, it would appear that his salary and allowances were extravagant. But after two years on the government payroll only "a miserable balance" remained. There'd been heavy job-related expenses such as freightage to get to Melbourne, the cost of the extra bullocks, food and clothing for the two prisoners assigned to him, and repairs to his tents and cart.

Reproduced courtesy of the La Trobe Australian Manuscripts Collection, State Library of Victoria
An Assistant Protector addresses some Aborigines, as sketched by William Thomas

Most disappointing of all to Dredge, however, was that the office of Assistant Protector was not what had been represented to him by Sir George Arthur in London, who'd drawn up the Protectors' duty statements. He'd been led to believe that he would be acting basically as a missionary "promoting the extension of Christianity amongst heathen tribes". But his duties were entirely of a *civil* character, and not religious. He'd also believed that one of the reasons for his selection had been his family, which "might form the nucleus of civilization amongst the natives". Arthur had given him to understand that the colonial government would "render the situation respectable, and provide for the Protectors and their families a suitable residence, and all other facilities for the accomplishment of the great objects of their undertaking". But on reaching Sydney from London the Protectors had encountered "a chilling reception", and had to "endure an amount of obloquy which could not well have been exceeded had we been expatriated for notorious offences". On their arrival in Port Phillip not only was no residence provided, but the government had refused to recognise that his wife and four children existed, beyond giving a small allowance to feed them. The office of Assistant Protector was far from being "respectable". No degradation, short of banishment, could exceed it. He could no longer receive money from the resources of the colony, Dredge concluded, when he could see no way of discharging his responsibilities "with credit to myself, the satisfaction of the public, and the benefit of the suffering Aborigines".[9]

La Trobe received a copy of Dredge's resignation letter with regret, believing him to be the "best fitted" of the Assistant Protectors for the duties required, and the only one who from the start had shown "a disregard for his private convenience and interest in attempting to carry the intentions of the Government into effect". The Superintendent asked him to come to Melbourne, and tried to talk him out of resigning, but to no avail. All Dredge would agree to do was to return to his district until Gipps had accepted the resignation, and arrangements were made to replace him.[10] In his comments on the resignation letter, the Governor declared he knew nothing of the circumstances which had led to Dredge's appointment, or whether his large family was considered an advantage. But the then Secretary of State for the Colonies, Lord Glenelg, had expressly informed him that no promise or expectation was held out to the Assistant Protectors "of any emolument whatever" above their salary of 250 pounds a year. Furthermore, Glenelg had stated that Robinson's assistants were "to attend to the Aborigines, if practicable, in their movements from one place to another" until they could be "induced to assume more settled habits of life". If Dredge had come to the colony expecting to act only as a missionary, with a house provided at a fixed location, and all his expenses paid, he'd "very greatly misunderstood" the terms of his employment.[11]

It was also wrong, Gipps asserted, for Dredge to claim that for the conveyance of himself and family into the bush he'd been provided with only one bullock and a cart. He'd also been given an ample daily allowance of 10 shillings and sixpence "for travelling and other incidental expenses", raising his pay to about 440 pounds a year. "Mr Dredge says he was dissatisfied from the beginning," Colonial Secretary Thomson wrote to La Trobe. "The Governor believes he was, and so also were the other Protectors; and this is one of the reasons perhaps, why His Excellency, from the beginning, has had so little reason to be satisfied with them or their exertions. From the beginning he observed in them all, and even in their Chief, a disposition to complain a great deal, and to write a great deal, but to bestir themselves, in their proper avocations, very little..."[12]

Gipps' comments provoked an angry response from Dredge, in which he questioned whether the Governor could seriously imagine that Glenelg had appointed men with families "with a view to reducing them to the vagrant habits of the Aborigines". He also questioned whether Gipps really believed he could have so misunderstood the terms of his agreement with the government to not, with the greatest reason, expect a house to be provided, and all expenses paid, above his annual salary. "Does he think that I could possibly entertain, even a suspicion," he wrote, "that the Colonial Government would require me out of such a paltry sum to defray expenses incurred in the performance of (a Protector's) work? I have yet to learn that either usage, or common honesty, requires a servant to expend his stipend for his employer's benefit instead of his own."

Dredge rejected Gipps' denial that he'd only been given one bullock and a cart to carry himself and family into the bush, pointing out that the daily allowance of 10 shillings and sixpence hadn't been for "travelling and other incidental expenses". According to the Governor's own instructions, the allowance specifically comprised one shilling and sixpence for each Protector to feed himself, three shillings to feed his wife and children, three shillings and sixpence to feed and clothe his two convict servants, and two shillings and sixpence for forage. No allowance had been made for the Protectors to pay for the extra bullocks needed to pull their carts. If Gipps had really meant the allowance to be spent on "travelling and other expenses", Dredge stated, then he'd been deceived by the Governor's instructions. He added that he'd not complained of the size of the allowance, though it hadn't covered the actual expenses.

Gipps' remark that he and his colleagues had shown a lack of a disposition "to bestir themselves, in their proper avocations" also riled Dredge. He had no misgivings about his own efforts to carry out his duties, and wouldn't shrink "from the most searching enquiry" into them. "That I should have cost the public so large a sum, and have rendered such small service in return, was one of the reasons which induced me to tender my resignation," he remarked. "I submit, how-

ever, that the inefficiency of my services is to be attributed rather to the inadequacy of the means placed at my disposal, and the absence from the beginning
of that countenance which I had the right to expect..."[13] So ended Dredge's
employment as an Aboriginal Protector. A short time later, he and his family had
moved back to Melbourne, where he opened a shop selling glass and china ware
"of taste and elegance".[14]

The disillusionment which led to Dredge's resignation was of course shared by
the other Protectors. They, too, had been seriously misled by Arthur on what to
expect in the colony, and on how the Protectorate would operate. And they'd
also been forced to spend substantial amounts of their own money to buy bullocks, to pay for stationery and medicines, and to otherwise establish themselves...only to find that having done so, adequate funding wasn't forthcoming
to allow them to carry out their supposed duties. A large part of the problem was
Robinson's stinginess with the annual fund of 300 pounds which Gipps had allocated for the "contingent expenses" of the Protectors. It was more than a year
after the fund was authorised when Dredge submitted his resignation, having
never heard of it.[15] While the Chief Protector kept the fund secret from his
assistants, and largely unavailable to them, they missed many opportunities to
establish friendly relations with tribes with which they had only occasional contact. The chance that Gipps might increase the size of the fund was also lost.

Each of the Assistant Protectors had been told that in his dealings with the
Aborigines, he should be "endeavouring to conciliate their respect and confidence and (making) them feel that he is their friend".[16] But after 18 months in
his district, during which he'd ridden thousands of kilometres through it,
Sievwright's progresss towards this goal had been dismal. On his most recent
trip to the west, lasting three weeks, groups of Aborigines had fled from him on
several occasions.[17] Most of the Aborigines theoretically under his care still
knew nothing of the purported reason for his presence, or of the odium he was
receiving from his fellow whites as a result of his efforts to achieve it.
Sievwright had been making urgent written appeals for supplies at the rate of
one a month since his arrival in the district. But these appeals, reiterated verbally to both Robinson and La Trobe, were falling on deaf ears. In October 1839
-- almost five months after setting up camp in Geelong -- he'd received his first
batch of food and gifts for the Aborigines under his care: 25 rugs, 77 kilograms
of rice, 36 kilograms of sugar, 180 rows of beads, 14 tomahawks, 12 hanks of
twine, and 24 mirrors.[18] Since then, he'd been able to win the confidence of the
Barrabools to a certain extent by providing "partial relief" to some of them with
the limited supplies he'd been given. A few elderly and sick Colijons who'd
made their way to his camp had also received a little food. But further to the
west, the Jarcoort, Elangamite and other Kirrae people had only been given

Day of Month.	Names and Tribe.	Male.	Female.	General Remarks.
STATEMENT of ABORIGINES fallen in with by Assistant Protector				
15	*Largest*	5	..	*Fled across the River Hopkins*
19	*Unknown*	3		*near Mount Rouse fled in much alarm*
25	*Unknown inhabiting between the grass reads & River Wannon*	3	1	*Employed at station of Mr Barton on River Grange language that understood*
24	*Unknown inhabiting on River Wannon & Glenelg*	2	4	*one domesticated the Winters station River Wannon language not understood*
30	*Unknown met near Mount Napier*	11		*fled in alarm*

Extract from "Statement of Aborigines fallen in with by Assistant Protector Sievwright in September 1840". On three occasions, Sievwright recorded Aborigines had fled as he approached. One group near Mt Rouse "fled in much alarm". Another near Mt Napier also "fled in alarm". Sievwright recorded finding one man "domesticated" on the Winter brothers' station on the River Wannon. On two occasions, he couldn't understand the language of Aborigines he met, including some who were employed on the station of Augustine Barton on the "River Grange". Soon after Sievwright's visit, Barton would report the killing of up to 17 Aborigines with poisoned damper in the same area.

"trifling donations" which with difficulty he could spare from his own supplies while passing through their territory. He'd had no supplies at all to help win the goodwill of the tribes even further from Geelong, and induce them to remain with him for any time. They were therefore virtually "unknown" to him. There was a "very hostile state of affairs" in their territory, and he recommended that "the Herald who shall approach them as peacemaker be possessed of every adventitious aid to ensure his safety, as well as his success".

Though he'd spent less than half his time in Geelong, he'd been with the Barrabool blacks more than any other tribe, and it was only their language with which he felt any degree of familiarity. He reported that it was "nearly devoid of any labial articulation, being chiefly composed of lingual and gutteral aspirations which require an extreme nicety of ear to understand". He knew of no European language "to which their pronunciation has the least analogy". There was no Barrabool equivalent to the English "f", "s" or "v", and it appeared that "perfect communication in it could not be held by writing". In this respect, it was similar to the Maltese language "which although copious and expressive for oral communication, is not a written language and cannot be expressed by the European alphabet". Sievwright gave some examples of Barrabool words, spelt "as nearly as possible" in the English alphabet: Na-ni (enough); Ma-lo (by and bye); Coop-mo-ang-eet (there, take it); and Kno-bu-nut (to drink). Certain syllables, he noted, were pronounced in staccato fashion. Barrabool numerals did not exceed five, or rather three, as four was expressed by twice two, and five by two and one, thus: Cai-mote (one); Bal-ait (two); Kal-caar-een (three); Bal-ait po Bal-ait (four); and Bal-ait po Bal-ait Cai-mote (five). "To express any quantity beyond this they hold up one or both hands, as many times as will make up the number required," he recorded.

In the same report, Sievwright provided the first tentative information he'd gained on the customs and beliefs of the Barrabool people. He was certain that they had no religion. However, they had "a superstitious belief in the existence of an Evil spirit whom they fear and propitiate by what may be termed incantation, in which spell they seem to have great faith." Each year, as spring approached, the tribe would assemble and retire to a part of the Bush where they were free from intrusion to perform "some secret ceremonies", which he imagined were connected with their superstition. "Twice I have been refused admittance amongst them at this time, and on one occasion having been conducted to them by a woman who had been left sick at my tents, I was desired to return and not remain with them," he wrote.

"As to the subject of cannibalism which has been attributed to them, I have in no instance met with it, nor do they speak of it but with so much disgust as we ourselves regard it," Sievwright continued. "In order to amuse, I have heard the women and young men repeat such fables, as such anecdotes are generally sought for, and received with much avidity by the white population. Their old people they do not inter, but consume by fire, and they also preserve by a process of steaming or baking, and smoke drying, portions of the bodies of their enemies, which they are anxious to retain and preserve as long as possible as trophies of victory, or rather revenge, and their greatest pride and desire seems to be to procure the Fat of their enemies with which they grease and keep in repair their spears and other weapons..." The Protector added he could enter into a more detailed account of Barrabool ceremonies, customs and habits, but he was not yet confident enough with the language to be sure that he would be giving correct information, instead of mere opinion. "I must defer entering further on these subjects until a matured intercourse, and more intimate acquaintance with the natives, shall qualify me to do so," he concluded.[19]

In an exchange of caustic letters over the following month, marking an acceleration in their deteriorating relations, Robinson castigated Sievwright for not providing more detailed information. Until now he'd refrained from insisting that Sievwright conduct a complete census of the Aboriginal population of his district, as instructed before moving to Geelong, because he'd not wanted to "intermeddle". But Sievwright had now had enough time to acquire the necessary language skills to comply. The absence of the required information was preventing him from recommending "in a definite form" suitable sites for Aboriginal reserves. Confusingly, Robinson stated that these reserves should be set up "for the exclusive benefit and advantage of each tribe". Yet at the same time, he argued Sievwright had been wrong in expressing the view many months earlier "that the tribes could not be united for the purposes of civilisation". Political alliances were common among the Aborigines, and this view was an example of the "hallucinations" he'd anticipated Sievwright would have.

Robinson rejected Sievwright's explanation that a lack of supplies to win the confidence of the Aborigines, and thus induce them to remain with him for some time, had left him unable to conduct the census. Every application for supplies "submitted in accordance with the Forms and Rules" of the department had been granted, he claimed. The Chief Protector also dismissed Sievwright's complaint that he'd not been given enough guidance or instructions. It wasn't his intention to "multiply directions" until the census had been completed. Finally, Robinson remarked it wasn't a sign of neglect that he'd so far not granted Sievwright's requests to visit his district, even though he'd visited the ones for which his three fellow assistants were responsible. "There are reasons why (the visit to) your district should be postponed, principally on account of its magnitude," he wrote.[20]

In replies to the Chief Protector's letters, Sievwright declared it was the first time he'd heard that he'd been left to conduct the census in his "own way" because Robinson hadn't wanted to "intermeddle". His troubles, he retorted, were largely due to his supervisor's policy of non-interference. He'd long ago been promised "ample and definite" instructions, and as a subordinate he had a right to expect them. Robinson's communications relating to the census amounted only to "orders to obtain information without any means or assistance being granted to enable me to do so". They couldn't be regarded as "instructions" because they taught him nothing from Robinson's experience, to help him avoid the "hallucinations" he'd been expected to have. Furthermore, in seeking proper instructions he'd made no reference to his language difficulties. It was therefore "preposterous" for Robinson to have suggested that he was waiting to be taught the languages of his district. On the question of supplies, Sievwright recalled that the Chief Protector had finally told his assistants the previous April of the discretionary power granted by Gipps to distribute food and clothing "to those tribes with whom an intercourse was to be established for the first time". He gave the dates of six written requests he'd made since then for information on how to apply for these supplies, while "having stated the necessity for their immediate issue". So far, the requests had been ignored.[21]

Unaware of the debilitating effect on the operations of the Protectorate of such squabbling, the *Port Phillip Patriot* published yet another article on the department, blaming Gipps for its "utter uselessness" in checking inter-racial violence. "It seems to be a characteristic feature of the Sydney Government to expose its officers to every species of annoyance and degradation, and no class more so than the Protectors," it remarked. "With duties as arduous (if properly performed) and equally as disagreeable as those of other Government servants; endeavouring to prove the efficacy of a plan as yet in its incipient state; they are divested of the means and shorn of the power of testing its merits." While the white settlers viewed the Protectorate with alarm, the Aborigines had been led to believe it would provide them with both security and "food and raiment in abundance". But the Aborigines were beginning to realise that their expectations weren't likely to be fulfilled and they were consequently running riot.

Such was the predicament in which the Governor left the Protectorate, the article continued, "and such are the steps by which he seeks to conciliate the evil passions and jealous dispositions of the sable lords of this soil; but he may depend on it, that if he does not cause more effective means to be taken to check the hostile incursions of these children of nature, the settlers will unite, en masse, for their own defence, and the consequences can hardly be foretold." The *Patriot* shared La Trobe's view that the main task of the Protectors should be to establish "secure and friendly relations with the aborigines" rather than try to "civilise" them. "It is ridiculous, we fear," the article concluded, "to attempt to domesticate these unfortunate beings, or to bring them to sit down quietly in any establishment that may be found in the interior for that purpose; their nature is too erratic, and disposition both too indolent and wild ever to accomplish a "consummation so devoutly to be wished for". This is a question which must yet form matter of grave consideration by the government."[22]

CHAPTER 9
A mass escape

WORD reached New South Wales in September, 1840, that the British government had finally stopped banishing convicts to the colony. The news took no-one by surprise, Governor Bourke having warned three years earlier of notice he'd received from London that the days of assigning convicts as labourers to the colonists were numbered.[1] The warning was issued as the government came under sustained pressure from a range of interest groups to radically change its imperial policy. Notable among these groups were promoters of "systematic colonisation" led by an English writer, Edward Gibbon Wakefield, who'd developed the theory while in prison for kidnapping a child heiress. Wakefield and his supporters advocated colonisation by men of capital and carefully chosen free emigrants to work for them as labourers. A select committee of the House of Commons concluded in 1838 that the 50-year-old practice of transportation of convicts wasn't efficient either as a means of punishment or reform. The government adopted the committee's recommendations to end transportation to New South Wales and the settled parts of Van Diemen's Land -- and to stop assignment of convict labour altogether. It also accepted the committee's suggestion that the minimum price of "waste" land in the colonies should be substantially increased. This was in line with Wakefield's theory that the price of land should be set high enough to be beyond the reach of the majority of emigrants, thus ensuring that they would have to remain labourers for some years. Proceeds from land sales were to continue to be used to promote emigration.[2]

Convicts and former convicts had provided the main source of labour in the Australian colonies for decades, and the abolition of transportation and assignment would aggravate a chronic labour shortage in New South Wales. But at the same time, the move to end the colonies' reputation as "the dunghill of England" removed one of the main impediments to the emigration of "respectable" families.[3] Many thousands of people were willing to migrate to escape from dismal economic and social conditions in Britain and Ireland, and two systems had been developed to induce them to make the much longer and more expensive voyage to New South Wales rather than North America. Both involved subsidising the cost of their passage with land sale funds. Under the first system, naval surgeons who'd been superintendents on convict ships were sent back by the colonial government to select emigrants and escort them to the colony. The second system involved payment of bounties, initially to individual colonists whose agents recruited emigrants on their behalf, and later to shipowners who brought emigrants back. However, there was widespread dissatisfaction in the colony with the schemes. They couldn't provide enough immigrants, and many of those arriving didn't have the occupational skills most needed. Partly because of fear of the Aborigines, others were unwilling to leave the towns to work in the bush, where the demand for labourers was most acute.[4]

   The way in which immigration was handled by the colonial government caused much resentment in Port Phillip, and fuelled growing agitation for separation from New South Wales. The Port Phillip settlers pointed to the much higher wages being paid in their district as evidence of a more severe labour shortage than elsewhere in the colony. They argued that the number of immigrants being brought to Melbourne should be in proportion to Port Phillip's contribution to the Land Fund. But as they saw it, the Sydney authorities were using a large portion of the money they'd paid for land to encourage free labourers to replace convicts in areas of the colony where white settlement had occurred earlier, and in which assignment had been more extensively practised.[5]

   Various proposals were put forward in Sydney and Melbourne on what else

Reproduced courtesy of the National Library of Australia
"Bushman's Hut" by S. T. Gill. Some squatters in New South Wales used Aboriginal labour.

could be done to relieve the dearth of labour. One popular idea was the mass importation of cheap "coolie" labour from India -- even though this had previously been opposed in London, Calcutta and Sydney. Glenelg had told Gipps that Indian labourers would probably permanently become "a distinct class of persons separated by origin and habits from the rest of the labouring Population, subject to restrictions not generally imposed, and regarded as of an inferior and servile description". Gipps had agreed that any substantial immigration from India would be fraught with "evils of the highest magnitude".[6] Nevertheless, the *Sydney Herald* reported that the few coolies who'd been imported so far had "proved themselves to be excellent shepherds, and slow but hardworking and sober, temperate people". It suggested that coolies were essential for the continued prosperity of the colony. "Our mechanics and imported emigrants are getting mad with the high wages they demand for their services," it argued, " and the settlers must endeavour to obtain at moderate rates some accessible source and fountain of labour, unless we give up the struggle and ruin the colony."[7] Encouraged by the Sydney paper's Port Phillip namesake, a group of settlers had already chartered a ship to sail from Melbourne to Calcutta to bring back 300 coolies on an experimental basis. But questions were raised about the accuracy of reports that the Colonial Office had lifted a ban on the export of coolies to Australia, and when Gipps made it known he wouldn't make any application to the Governor of India on the group's behalf, the voyage was abandoned.[8]

On a sweltering Saturday in December 1840, a large group of Port Phillip settlers -- most of them squatters -- packed the rooms of the Melbourne Auction Company to form an Immigration Society. Chaired by La Trobe, the meeting rejected a proposal that it should merely be a branch of a similar society recently formed in Sydney. Instead, it was decided to form a separate association to encourage to Port Phillip "healthy and able emigrants from Great Britain under the Bounty System, as also from other European and Oriental countries, when circumstances may permit". An unwieldy management committee of 42 members was elected, with La Trobe as its patron, to draw up plans for putting the society's objectives into effect. The committee members included the merchant Arthur Kemmis, who'd been treasurer to the short-lived Coolie Committee, and a number of Western District squatters -- among them Alexander Thomson, John Thomson, and Hugh Murray.[9]

As the meeting was underway in Melbourne on how to consolidate white occupation of Port Phillip, the Chief Protector of Aborigines sent a letter to his Western District assistant instructing him to prepare to come to the town for what would be its first Supreme Court session. Robinson told Sievwright that the alleged murderers of John Thomson's shepherd were expected to stand trial. "I am unable to inform you at what date precisely, but it is possible that it may

be before the close of this month," Robinson advised. "I have to request, therefore, that you take prompt measures to ensure the attendance of Witnesses...and
adopt any other arrangement that you may deem necessary." The Chief
Protector added that this would include attempting to obtain an interpreter for
the trial of the two Elangamite brothers charged with the murder of Thomas
Hayes.[10]

But Sievwright believed his duty was to help defend Kowcanmarning and
Wawarparneen against a false allegation -- not to make sure that prosecution witnesses appeared in court. The only people capable of helping the defence by
providing alibis were black, and therefore not allowed to be witnesses, even if
the impossible task of finding a competent interpreter had been achievable.
Nevertheless, Sievwright was eager to peruse the statements Fyans had used the
previous July to commit the brothers for trial for murder...and their tribesman,
Burguidningnang, for theft. He wrote back to Robinson, repeating a 16-week-
old request for copies of Fyans' depositions. Receiving no reply, he rode to
Melbourne to discover that Robinson hadn't been given copies. Fyans had
handed the depositions to Police Magistrate Fenwick, who had sent them to
Crown Prosecutor Croke. They had then been sent to the Attorney-General in
Sydney, because Croke expected that the trial of the Elangamite men would have
to take place before the Supreme Court there. A decision had since been made
to appoint a resident Supreme Court judge to Port Phillip, but he'd not yet
arrived, and the depositions were still in Sydney.[11]

Kowcanmarning and Wawarparneen had been charged with a capital offence,
so could only be tried before the Supreme Court. Burguidningnang, however,
could and should have faced his theft charge before the Court of Quarter
Sessions in Melbourne the previous October, when the three Elangamite men
had been transferred from the Geelong jail to the one in Melbourne.[12] Instead,
Burguidningnang had languished in chains for another three months, merely
because the documents on which he'd been committed for trial had been wrongly sent to Sydney and not returned. Robinson had done nothing about his case
because of a mistaken belief that he, too, had been charged with murder.
Realising what had happened, Sievwright insisted that Burguidningnang be
brought before the Court of Quarter Sessions the following week, when it was
due to hold its latest sittings -- either to be tried for the crime he'd allegedly committed, or to be discharged. Hearing that Sievwright was also making a fuss
about the way in which Burguidningnang and the brothers had been captured,
Crown Prosecutor Croke agreed. Croke had recently sent off a letter to the
Secretary of State for the Colonies in London, asking to be appointed Port
Phillip's first Attorney-General, or a judge. He didn't want his application to be
adversely affected by Sievwright raising questions about the legality of

Burguidningnang's incarceration.[13]

Croke and his superiors were also eager to put on trial nine of the Aborigines who'd been in jail since being captured the previous October by Major Lettsom. Their eagerness to bring the whole Lettsom fiasco to an end had since been intensified by another tragedy. One other Aborigine who'd been on the major's prime suspect list had been captured, although he wasn't destined to stand trial with the rest. Jaggerroger, called Harlequin by the whites, was wanted for an attack on a sheep station earlier in the year, during which he'd been shot.[14] Caught north-east of Melbourne, he'd been brought in relay to Melbourne by a number of Mounted Police, a total of about 360 kilometres. Occasionally, he'd ridden behind one of the police. But most of the way he was dragged alongside their horses on a short dog chain, one end padlocked around his neck, the other tied to a stirrup. The chain was also used to secure him at night, when handcuffs were placed around his ankles as well as his wrists. After Harlequin complained of feeling ill, a sergeant had given orders to speed up his transfer to Melbourne, and the last 130 kilometres of the journey had been covered in two hot days. Harlequin had collapsed in the watch-house cell into which he was placed, exhausted and feverish, and his face swollen from the tightness of the chain. The following day, his condition had worsened, and Assistant Colonial Surgeon Cussen had ordered him to be removed to the town's hospital. He'd remained there for less than two days. After a bout of severe diarrhoea, brought on by a purgative prescribed by Cussen, Harlequin had died.[15]

So it was that on January 6, 1841, Burguidningnang and nine other bewildered blacks in handcuffs were ushered and into the crowded Melbourne court building to face the next stage of the white man's "equal and indiscriminate" justice. For the occasion, their leg irons had been removed, and they'd each been dressed in a new suit of cotton prison slops ordered by Gipps.[16] In the court to provide moral support for the defendants were the Chief Protector, and Assistant Protectors Sievwright and Thomas. But the atmosphere was decidedly hostile. All of the colonists who came to witness the proceedings, and those chosen as jurists, were well aware of a strong feeling throughout the colony that it was high time a group of Aborigines received harsh punishment. Word would hopefully then soon spread that even if there wasn't immediate retribution for raids on the property of white men, it would come eventually.

It was also obvious that conviction, at least of the nine Aborigines captured by Lettsom, was of vital importance to deflect criticism of the orders of Gipps and La Trobe, and of the subsequent actions of the lesser functionaries in the law enforcement branches of their administration. Prosecutor Croke told the bench of magistrates chaired by Edward Brewster that he was presenting three indictments. The first charged one of the defendants, Tarrokenunnin, with aggravated robbery, as an alleged organiser of the robbery of some food from Peter Snodgrass' station, north-east of Melbourne, the previous March. The other eight taken prisoner by Lettsom -- named as Nandermile, Logermakoom, Cowinyowlit, Morrermalloke, Peebeep, Lambiderruc, Pinegingoon, and Wilegurn -- were also charged with aggravated robbery, as accessories. The third indictment charged all defendants generally with common robbery.[17]

Snodgrass' former shepherds, McCarrick and Deighton, gave evidence that on the day of the robbery a group of black men had approached their hut. They claimed the group had been led not by Tarrokenunnin, but by Winberri, the man shot dead when Lettsom had taken his prisoners. In broken English, the Aborigines had asked for food, saying they had a right to some because the white men's sheep had scared off their kangaroos. As they'd done on many previous occasions, McCarrick and Deighton at first refused to hand over any food. But when the blacks had produced firearms, they'd allowed them to take quantities of flour, damper and mutton from the hut, most of which was immediately divided among the party and consumed. The witnesses were then cross-examined by Redmond Barry, an able and eloquent Irish barrister whom Robinson had engaged as counsel for the defence. Under Barry's questioning, the shepherds admitted several facts which might have been seen to mitigate the actions of the defendants. For instance, McCarrick and Deighton had made death threats against blacks in the neighbourhood, and when the group had approached their hut on the day in question they'd actually been busy making ball cartridges for their guns in anticipation of a clash. As well, they'd shot dead many of the blacks' dogs: one they'd killed the day before the robbery for disturbing their sheep. They admitted, too, that if the law had permitted one of the defendants to give evidence, and he told the court that on that day a black woman had been in their hut, he might be telling the truth. Thomas, who'd been sworn in as an interpreter, attempted to expand on this point. But Brewster upheld Croke's objection that it was irrelevant.[18]

Barry then made a lengthy appeal for the peculiar nature of the case to be considered. Such was the defendants' understanding of British law, and of what was transpiring in the court, that even as he spoke in their defence, they probably thought he was speaking against them, he noted. While the actions of the defendants couldn't be justified, they could be explained, and even condoned. According to the white man's law, they'd committed a crime. But according to their own "laws of uncivilised nature" they'd merely taken what was their right to have, to satisfy their hunger. He urged the court to look on the defendants as members of a race whose land had been appropriated by Europeans, and who were now subjected to starvation and countless acts of cruelty and oppression. Arrangements should have been made to ensure that the Aborigines could provide for themselves at least as well as before the Europeans arrived, and that their rights as adopted British subjects were maintained. Until this was done, it was unfair to make them rigidly accountable to British law. In the current case, mitigating circumstances such as the shooting of the defendants' dogs, and interference with their women, had been deemed inadmissible as evidence. But, Barry argued, the court and jury could consider these as a reason for deviating from the strict application of the letter of the law. Instead the spirit and design of the law should be applied, based on equity and justice to suffering fellow human beings who'd been provoked into committing petty larceny.[19]

The defence counsel's spirited arguments cut no ice with Brewster. In his summing up of the case, he made no mention of the disadvantages the defendants faced in not understanding British legal principles, and in not being allowed to speak in their own defence, even if they'd understood the language in which they were being tried. Nor did the chairman of the court mention any of the facts outlined by Barry which might partially excuse their behaviour. Brewster told the jury that all the defendants, with the exception of Burguidningnang, had been identified by McCarrick and Deighton, and the evidence had proved their guilt on the charge of robbery at Snodgrass' station. The jury, comprising both squatters and Melbourne residents, didn't take long to agree. Burguidningnang was immediately discharged, and the court room was cleared for a few minutes while Brewster consulted the bench of magistrates on sentencing for the others. Then, as Burguidningnang stood outside the court stunned, his shackles removed for the first time in five months, his nine fellow defendants were led back in to receive their sentence: 10 years' transportation.[20]

One observer, the Reverend Joseph Rennard Orton, recorded in his journal that night that the trial had been "an abominable mockery". Orton, a Wesleyan Methodist missionary who'd helped establish the Aboriginal mission near Geelong, had observed many trials. However, he wrote, he couldn't remember having seen a prosecutor "more bent upon a conviction". Croke had seemed "determined to bring the whole of British jurisprudence upon the untutored heads of these unhappy creatures whose common law right has been...grievously transgressed". Brewster's behaviour he also condemned. The court chairman had summed up the case "according to the most ex parte notes" he'd ever heard taken, before giving his "gratuitous" and "unconstitutional" opinion that the nine blacks must be found guilty.[21] According to the *Port Phillip Patriot*, the sentence against the Goulburn blacks was "monstrously severe", but the *Gazette* and the *Herald* would carry no such condemnation. "Whether their punishment will have any effect in checking the aggressions of their kindred, a future period will determine," was the only remark on the sentence by the *Herald*.[22]

Early one afternoon a few days later, as Burguidningnang recuperated in

Proceedings of Asst Protector Sievwright Western District from 1st December 1840 to 28th February 1841 inclusive.

Kilambeet 1st March 1841.

Till the latter end of December I was employed with the Wodowro tribe in the Geelong District endeavouring to acquire the language & when being ordered to Melbourne to attend the opening of the Supreme Court I repaired thither on the 29th where I remained until an Aboriginal Native 'Burguidningnang' was brought up & dismissed from the Bar after an imprisonment of five months, he being one of the three natives, apprehended by the Crown Commissioner of this District and a party of Settlers in the latter end of July last. — His individual while harmlessly employed with his family & others of his tribe in the imagined security of the Forest, distant from the dwellings of White Men, was surrounded by twenty two persons seventeen of whom were Settlers & the remainder Police, and this under the sanction & presence of the above Government Officer & after a severe struggle was appre=hended & dragged a distance of one hundred & fifty Miles to Jail, where he remained heavily ironed for five Months, without knowing why he was thus treated, nor were even the

means

Reproduced courtesy of the Dixson Library, State Library of New South Wales
"Proceedings of Asst Protector Sievwright, Western District, from 1st December 1840 to 28th February 1841 inclusive." *In this report, Sievwright would condemn the treatment of the young Elangamite man, Burguidningnang, who was arrested by a posse of 17 squatters and five police led by Foster Fyans, and who was eventually released without conviction after being "heavily ironed" for five months. At the time of his arrest, Sievwright says, Burguidningnang had been "harmlessly employed with his family and others of his tribe in the imagined security of the forest, distant from the dwellings of white men".*

Robinson's home to gather strength for the trek home to his family, the two other Elangamite men arrested with him, Wawarparneen and Kowcanmarning, suddenly found themselves with a little space to stretch out in the Melbourne jail, when 23 other inmates were taken from the building. They comprised the nine Goulburn men and 14 whites -- all but one of them men -- convicted of offences ranging from assault and being Prisoners of the Crown at large, to horse and cattle stealing. Two faced transportation for 15 years, and one for seven years, to Norfolk Island, the most feared of all penal establishments where Flogger Fyans had earned his nickname while Superintendent. The others faced prison terms of up to three years in irons, or forced labour in an iron gang. The jailer handed over the prisoners to a police constable and four soldiers to be taken to a cutter on the Yarra River, which was to ferry them to a larger vessel in the bay, bound for Sydney. The escorts had prepared themselves for the assignment with a morning drinking session: constable John Robinson was showing signs of drunkenness; private John Robson was so drunk he could barely be trusted with carrying some luggage. A large crowd which had gathered to watch the prisoners being trudged down to the river was entertained by some of the whites taunting the blacks with signs that they were being taken to be hanged.

A decision was made to place the white prisoners below the deck of the *Victoria*. The trembling blacks were left on the deck, and for the short voyage the handcuffs and shackles which had joined them two together were removed, though their leg irons -- and a cross bar which connected them -- were left on. A short time later, near the mouth of the Yarra, where it narrowed and the sails of the ships on the bay came into view, the cutter tacked close to the southern bank. Simultaneously, the blacks made a break for freedom, jumping overboard and frantically splashing their way towards the thick tea-tree on the bank. The soldiers, the constable, and the skipper of the cutter opened fire with muskets and pistols. Three of the blacks were hit: two sank, although the third managed to struggle on a little further. As the guns were reloaded, a passing dinghy was commandeered to quickly reach the bank and seize the wounded man, Tarrokenunnin. He was thrown into a dinghy, and two of the soldiers furiously paddled off to raise the alarm in the town. But by the time a search party reached the scene, the other six Aborigines had disappeared. Some would later be reported to have managed to escape after removing their leg irons with the help of blacks camped on the edge of the town.[23]

For 11 days after the trial of the Goulburn blacks and Burguidningnang, Sievwright remained in Melbourne. He'd vowed not to leave the town this time without some supplies, and managed to have a marked effect on Robinson's previous reluctance to allocate funds for his use. To Sievwright's surprise, the Chief Protector not only issued some food for distribution to the Western District

Aborigines, but also authorised him to obtain hoes, shovels, axes and other means to enable him to start farming operations at the site at Keilambete which he'd recommended for a reserve. As well, Robinson told Sievwright he could buy some extra bullocks to use for ploughing, and hire both a free immigrant with farming experience as an overseer and a constable to help maintain order. Sievwright pointed out to Robinson again that the formation of a reserve at Keilambete would involve disturbing John Thomson, who on La Trobe's recommendation had just joined the prestigious list of settlers and officials who could act as magistrates.[24] Sievwright requested that the Chief Protector visit the site to confirm his choice, before he set up operations. Robinson, however, was waiting for an opportunity to make an extensive tour of Sievwright's district. It wasn't likely, he remarked, that a brief visit would allow him to be as well qualified to judge the selection of a site as Sievwright, who'd "made the selection the object of careful enquiry". His recommendation that Keilambete was the best site, Robinson added, had already been forwarded for government approval. Formation of the reserve -- and the start of agricultural operations -- should go ahead as soon as possible.[25] At last, it seemed to Sievwright, he was being given the means to help at least some of the Aborigines of his district to help themselves cope with the white takeover of their land.

Chapter 10
Possessors of the soil

IN a series of auctions that started in June 1837, the New South Wales government limited the amount of land made available for purchase in the Port Phillip District to relatively small areas in and around the towns of Melbourne, Geelong and Portland. By October 1840, only about 65,000 hectares had been sold, for a total of about 313,000 pounds.[1] The policy of not releasing large amounts of land for sale suited the squatters who, away from the towns, could still lease vast unsurveyed areas for 10 pound annual fees. Most of their capital remained available for maintaining and expanding their flocks and herds, instead of being tied up in real estate. But new instructions from London on the sale of "Crown land", based on the recommendations of a newly-formed Board of Colonial Land and Emigration Commissioners, were to cause panic among the squatters.

Regulations issued by Governor Gipps in line with the instructions decreed that land sales by auction in Port Phillip would in future be confined to the towns in which auctions had already taken place. All other land sales would be at a fixed price of one pound per acre (0.4 hectares) for "country land" and 100 pounds per acre in any new towns. From time to time, the public would be notified in what size lots land was to be available for purchase. Selection of land at the fixed price would start on 1 March 1841. The aim of the Commissioners was to encourage potential British migrants to invest in land in Australia by allowing them to know exactly how much they could buy before migrating. The price of rural land was fixed at one pound per acre in Port Phillip so it had no comparative advantage over land being offered for sale for the same fixed price in the province of South Australia, being established on Wakefieldian principles across the border, just beyond Sievwright's area of operations.[2]

Insofar as they indicated the willingness, if not the intention, of the British government to declare Port Phillip a separate colony from New South Wales, the new regulations were welcomed in Melbourne. A well-attended public meeting in the town on the second last day of 1840 expressed the hope that they would be a preparatory step to granting Port Phillip its own government and legislature.[3] Gipps certainly believed this was the intention in London, and he supported such a move.[4] But the new regulations placed him in the classic administrator's dilemma of being forced to implement a policy with which he didn't agree. He'd told the British government many months earlier he was strongly against fixed price land sales instead of auctions anywhere in New South Wales, believing they would place new immigrants at the mercy of land speculators who would buy up all good land. A fixed price policy might be appropriate for a new settlement like South Australia, where there were few "great Capitalists", especially if only small portions of land of fairly uniform quality could be released for purchase. However, he'd argued, a fixed price policy wasn't appropriate for an older colony like New South Wales, where occupation had already been authorised in large areas of land of extremely varied quality, and where men of very large capital were already engaged in speculation. "I feel perfectly satisfied that such a measure would lead to what I think I can only properly designate as a scramble," he'd exclaimed. "I cannot indeed imagine anything that would throw this Government and the whole Colony into more complete confusion..."[5]

The Port Phillip squatters, too, were worried that the new regulations would encourage land speculation, damaging to their interests. In a petition to La Trobe, a large group of squatters requested the right of pre-emption, should the land they were occupying come up for sale -- or at least the right of compensation for any improvements they'd made to the land, such as housing, stockyards, and cultivated paddocks. The system of sale by auction, they pointed out, had been "sufficiently unfavourable" to squatters. They'd been forced to pay prices that reflected not only the value of the land, but also the value of their own improvements. Under the new regulations, their situation was infinitely worse. They could buy "orders" from the Land Office in Melbourne, and specify the land they wanted to buy the day it became open for sale. But as the new regulations stood, anyone with orders of prior date who claimed the same land on the same day would have first option to buy. This would encourage speculators with no intention of occupation, but "simply to sell over again to the former occupant or some other party, at an exorbitant profit". Without any certainty of possession, settlers "would erect nothing but the most superficial habitations, and cultivation would scarce be attempted". The right of pre-emption or compensation for improvements would, however, have a markedly different effect. Each man secure in the possession of his station would feel that it was his home, and would strive to surround it as far as possible with "the comforts of civilized life". Good cottages would be built and cultivation would proceed...and the appearance of the countryside and the habits of the settlers would become closer to those of the land they'd left behind.[6]

Alarm among the squatters over the new regulations was heightened when it was realised that Port Phillip land orders had been on sale in London for months. Henry Dendy, an English brewer, was the first to arrive in Melbourne with an

Sir George Gipps, painting based on a portrait by Eden Upton Eddis, 1836.

order giving him the right to buy more than 2000 hectares of land -- eight times the size of the blocks previously sold at auction. Supplementary instructions not yet having arrived from London, La Trobe and Gipps were surprised to learn that Dendy's order authorised him to buy either already surveyed land when it came up for selection on 1 March, or to request a special survey of any other land he fancied. The only conditions were that he buy the land in one block, and con-form to any local regulations, such as those defining the limits of the towns.[7]

While he awaited the latest instructions, and the outcome of further protests to London over the fixed price policy, Gipps approved a distance of eight kilome-tres in any direction from the town centres as their limits. At the same time, he told La Trobe he was opposed to granting the Port Phillip squatters' request for the right of pre-emption. The squatters at best must be regarded as "mere Tenants at Will" -- meaning the government could at any time terminate their occupancy. "If we ever allow them to be considered more, we shall make them too strong for us: I expect even now that it is the point in our management of Crown lands on which we are most open to attack by the Advocates of the (South) Australian system," he wrote. "They will ask how we can expect persons to buy Land, if we allow them all the advantages of ownership over thousands of Acres, for 10 pounds a year?"[8]

Throughout the debate over Port Phillip's new land regulations, and squatters' rights or lack of them, little mention was made about any Aboriginal rights to land. In fact, the existence of thousands of Aborigines, and their strong attach-ment to particular territory, had no bearing whatsoever on the formulation of land policy in the colony. The authorities simply assumed that as white settle-ment expanded the Aborigines would, with some coercion, move further away. Gipps had authorised the establishment of one reserve for each of the four Assistant Aboriginal Protectors, initially covering slightly more than 20,000 hectares -- 10 times the size of the blocks being sold to individuals such as Dendy. If the reserves proved successful, the Governor might be prepared to sanction more. The question remained, however, just how much support the Protectors would receive in trying to give the reserves a fair trial -- both from their superiors and from the public, notably the squatters.

As Sievwright joyfully went on his unexpected spending spree in Melbourne, obtaining the supplies he'd been authorised to buy for the Keilambete reserve, he followed with intense interest efforts by his colleague, Edward Parker, to set up a reserve in the district to the north of his own. Parker had occupied the site chosen for a reserve almost two months earlier, but the "Port Phillip Herald" was still conducting a vigorous campaign against his right to have done so. The site on the Loddon River where Parker had set up camp, about 140 kilometres north-west of Melbourne, fell within the area being used by squatting partners James

Monckton Darlot, Donald Campbell Simson, and William Hampden Dutton --
co-proprietor of the *Herald*. The day after he arrived there in November 1840
with 11 blacks, most of them children, Parker had sent a letter to the partners
advising them that, with La Trobe's authority, he'd taken possession of a stretch
of the river flats about three kilometres below their head station. He requested
that the squatters immediately move their cattle from it, so cultivation could proceed. Parker, like Sievwright, had told Robinson the previous July of his recommended site for a reserve. There'd been no objection from the Chief
Protector, so he assumed that his choice had been accepted, and that once the site
was ready to be occupied, either Robinson or La Trobe would tell Crown Lands
Commissioner Frederic Powlett to advise the squatters that it had been appropriated. He told the squatters to expect such notification soon.[9]

In a tirade against Parker and the government that began just over a fortnight
later, the *Herald* declared that there'd not been "a subject of more vital importance" in the history of the colony. Parker's "summary and arbitrary" actions in
occupying the site, it alleged, had resulted in massive financial loss to Darlot
(mentioning only *his* name). It was well known to every settler, and couldn't
have been a secret to Parker, that cattle wouldn't remain in the vicinity of blacks.
His unannounced arrival "with his whole tribe at his heels" had caused Darlot's
cattle to scatter: 650 head of cattle, worth 4,875 pounds, had gone missing. The
financial disaster for Darlot was bad enough. But worse still was the fact that
Parker's actions might set an "iniquitous precedent"", allowing the legalised
claims of the squatters to be destroyed, and "to substitute in their stead the
caprice of the Protectorate".

Government regulations under which Darlot held his squatting licence stated
that he could only lose it before its expiry the following June if he was convicted of any of a range of offences, such as illegally selling liquor or not reporting
the correct number of stock he was keeping. But Darlot hadn't been charged
with any offence, let alone convicted. Nowhere in the regulations was there a
provision for the government to cancel his licence without notice, as Parker was
seeking to do. If the government had such power, the only purpose of the
licences they were buying would be to prescribe the limits of squatters' runs.
And if this was the case, the licences would be no protection against the
vengeance of a vindictive government officer. "Let the aborigines be protected,
and their every necessary want supplied to the utmost extent that humanity may
dictate or justice demand," the *Herald* declared, " but never at the sacrifice of
the pledged rights of the settlers".[10]

The campaign against Parker reached its peak just as Sievwright was about to
return to Geelong from Melbourne with his supplies for Keilambete. In an article headed "The Protectors versus The Colonists", the *Herald* reported: "We

have heard of other inroads having been already planned and on the eve of being executed; perhaps while we write, ruin is marking the devastating march of the Protectorate, destroying the brightest hopes of the settlers, and bringing disgrace upon British Law." The article included the text of Parker's letter to Darlot and Dutton asking them to move their cattle from the river flats. If, as the letter stated, he'd been authorised by La Trobe to occupy the site, the Superintendent had "wantonly exceeded" his authority, and should be made to pay in full the loss Darlot had sustained, it affirmed. If, however, Parker had lied, a mere denial was not now enough: an outraged public must be given an assurance that such illegal proceedings would not occur again. According to the *Herald*, Darlot had received the letter only the week before, though it was dated seven weeks earlier. Parker was either guilty of "the most culpable carelessness" in transmitting the letter, or had antedated it "to at least palliate his offence by endeavouring to make it appear that he had given notice of his destructive intents".[11]

The allegations prompted an incensed Parker to take the highly unusual step of writing to the *Herald* in his defence, rejecting its accusations. The letter, he stated, had been delivered without delay to the squatters' head station, addressed to Darlot, Dutton, or their overseer. A few days later, he'd asked the overseer verbally to move the cattle from the river flats, pointing out at the time that the measure may only be temporary: he may not be staying at the site because the soil was "of a doubtful character". He denied, too, the claim that the Aborigines had disturbed the squatters' cattle: even after the tribe with him had assembled in considerable numbers, the cattle had still fed almost daily within sight of the camp. True, a stockman had complained to him that he'd lost 200 head of cattle, and had asked that the blacks be restricted to entering and leaving the camp by only one route. This he'd rejected, as "neither just nor necessary". He had, however, asked the blacks to keep away from the cattle, which they'd "generally" agreed to do.

Parker also implied that the campaign by the *Herald* had been motivated by personal rather than public interest. Why, he asked, had the paper's co-proprietor not been mentioned as one of the squatters involved? To conclude, Parker noted he'd abstained from discussing the rights possessed by holders of squatting licences because this was a matter outside his line of duty. "I have higher claims to urge," he wrote. "I assert the paramount rights of the original possessors of the soil. And I cannot but remark that it is a painful indication of the inhuman state of feeling prevalent towards the aborigines in this colony, that as soon as they are concentrated and employed in raising the means of subsistence, private interests clamorously urge their expulsion from every spot calculated to yield a profitable return to their labour and it is sought to drive them back to the arid desert or the barren 'scrub'."[12]

In yet another bitter attack, the *Herald* claimed the somewhat awkward letter must have been sanctioned by the Chief Protector, and La Trobe. There wasn't one sentence, it alleged, put forward to refute, justify or lessen the severity of Parker's actions. Nor had any attempt been made to deny the principal point at issue: that Darlot's legally-held station had been seized illegally and without notice. Only the extent of Darlot's loss had been questioned. The *Herald* left it up to the public to judge who was more likely to be correct: a *stockman* who had put the loss at 200 head of cattle, or *its* source, the *overseer*, who had reported 650 missing. As well, Parker had stated his Aborigines had "generally" followed his request to avoid going near the cattle. He must be "well aware that one single instance of disobedience of orders was quite sufficient to do the whole injury". On the question why no mention had been made of its co-proprietor in articles on the affair, the *Herald* lamely explained that Darlot had received Parker's notice of his intention to set up camp. Dutton had been in Sydney at the time, and it "did not want to confuse the public by the introduction of other names". Finally, the *Herald* declared that on behalf of the white settlers, it indignantly denied Parker's assertion that there was "an inhuman state of feeling prevalent towards the Aborigines". There wasn't a settler in the Port Phillip District who wouldn't heartily rejoice at seeing the Aborigines really and well protected, and who wouldn't do their utmost to contribute to this end. "But," it snapped, "let us never measure our love for the blacks by our hatred of the whites -- justice to both is not incompatible with the duties of the Protectorate."[13]

Even before he wrote to the *Herald* defending his actions, Parker had written to Robinson recommending that he move to a site further up the Loddon, which he'd decided was more suitable for cultivation.[14] The proposal prompted complaints to La Trobe from two squatters who feared the "great injustice" of eviction from the proposed new location. He assured them that care would be taken to minimise any inconvenience or losses they might suffer. But the "moral and physical improvement" of the Aborigines was of paramount importance: it was certain that Aboriginal interests would take precedence over those of any squatters.[15] Gipps endorsed La Trobe's stand. "The Protectors cannot of their own authority remove persons who hold licences to depasture stock on Crown Lands," he told the Superintendent, "but if any portion whatsoever of Crown Lands be required for a public purpose, there can be no doubt that the person in occupation of it must give it up. As little doubt can there be that the protection of and civilisation of the aborigines is a public purpose -- and one too of the very highest consideration."[16]

Crown Lands Commissioner Powlett, meanwhile, who'd visited the area on La Trobe's instructions, had reported that he considered "the trespass and injury complained (of) by Messrs Dutton and Darlot to have been much overrated". Their overseer had informed him that only 30 or 40 head of cattle, from a herd of 1300 to 1400, had gone missing. The only mistake Parker had made was assuming that either Robinson or La Trobe would inform Powlett of his intention to set up camp on their station. Powlett concluded by saying that he'd apparently reached agreement with Parker that a site called Jim Crow Hill, further up the Loddon, appeared to be the most suitable site for the proposed reserve. This would require a fifth squatter having to relocate some of his sheep. Within six weeks, the Governor had approved the new site.[17]

"Sievwright drew a rough map in a patch of dirt..."

From what he knew of Parker's experience, through the press and Robinson, it was with a curious mixture of excitement and apprehension that Sievwright had meanwhile returned to Geelong to announce to his family and the Barrabool people his imminent departure for Keilambete. Reaching agreement with Christina on what the family should do was easy. The Aborigines around Keilambete and beyond had had much less contact with whites than those near Geelong, and it was obvious that the possible dangers of living with them would be greater. Until he'd established a residence, and was confident that the whole family could live at Keilambete in safety, Christina would remain in Geelong with 18-year-old Frances, their 10-year-old twins, Frederica and Melita, and their two youngest children, Georgina and Falkland. Only their two eldest boys,

14-year-old Marcus and 11-year-old Charles, who expressed a strong desire to accompany their father, would go with him. Trying to convince the Barrabool tribe to make the move was far more difficult.

Calling the elders and those who knew some English together, Sievwright drew a rough map in a patch of dirt, indicating how far west he was going to set up his new camp. As best he could with the limited ability to converse, he assured them that if the tribe accompanied him to Keilambete, it would at last be able to obtain food and clothing in return for labour. It took a while for the elders to understand the full import of what he was proposing. When they did, they were dismayed. Many of the Barrabool men had been into Kirrae territory, but only by invitation for great meetings of the tribes, on war expeditions, or as special envoys. To be invited there by a white man was unprecedented, baffling, and frightening. When it became clear that Sievwright couldn't be dissuaded from moving, the elders convened an urgent meeting to decide what the tribe should do.[18]

Since Sievwright had begun living with the Barrabool people14 months earlier, he'd at least provided some protection from his fellow whites, and he'd occasionally been able to meet the basic needs of some members of the tribe. The elders realised that the future of the tribe in its own territory would be even bleaker without his presence, but they feared that moving outside it into enemy territory could result in rapid annihilation. A few months earlier, when Sievwright had asked some Barrabool men to accompany him to Keilambete to investigate the murder of John Thomson's shepherd, a small group had escorted him to the edge of their territory, but had then turned back.[19] None of the Barrabool people had been near Keilambete for some time and for all they knew, Kirrae territory could by now be worse affected than their own by the white invasion. After two days of intense discussions, the elders approached Sievwright's tent in a group with their decision: before they'd give any further consideration to the previously inconceivable idea of quitting the land of their ancestors, they would need an up-to-date report on the situation around the spot where he wanted to take them. To obtain the report, they would send five of the tribe's best fighting men. He readily agreed to their demands that he must take responsibility for the warriors' safety during the day, and allow them to sleep in his tent at night.[20] The stage was almost set for Sievwright to take on the greatest challenge of his life.

CHAPTER 11
Move to Keilambete

FROM the early days of white settlement of the Port Phillip District, vigorous efforts were made by the authorities to prevent Aborigines from obtaining or retaining firearms. Undermining these efforts were white men willing to trade guns and ammunition for animal skins and lyre bird feathers. Others saw advantages in fuelling inter-tribal strife by selective donation of small quantities of white weapons. Nevertheless, there was never any large-scale use of guns by the Aborigines, and long after white settlement began, there hadn't been a single case of a white man having been shot dead by a black. The relatively few whites killed in reprisal attacks for the many blacks killed by white men's firearms had all been killed with the contents of traditional armouries.

Robinson told Sievwright and his colleagues in July 1839 that most Aborigines couldn't be trusted with guns because they had only a vague concept of morality, and were prone to be "initiated into most baneful practices" by white farm labourers. Unless something was done, he argued, it was only a matter of time before they started using guns against white men who refused requests for food and clothing. As well, the Chief Protector believed, "numerous" blacks had already been shot dead by enemies among their own race, often at the instigation of "nefariously disposed" whites. Except for a few individuals under the immediate control of an authorised white man, the Aborigines must therefore be prevented from having firearms. Court chairman Brewster and Crown Prosecutor Carrington had advised that this was "not only perfectly legal but highly proper". Robinson warned his assistants that disarming those who already had guns would require caution and prudence. Whenever possible, the police should be asked to retrieve the weapons so any resultant ill-feeling was directed at them, rather than the Protectorate.[1]

In the Western District, Sievwright could expect no such assistance from the police under Flogger Fyans' command. When Fyans and Lonsdale had been the respective Geelong and Melbourne Police Magistrates more than a year earlier, they'd decided unofficially to use their constables to seize guns from the Aborigines. But the retrieval of white weapons from the blacks was another example of the duties which Fyans felt after Sievwright's arrival was no longer his responsibility.[2] Within a fortnight of receiving Robinson's views on firearms, for instance, Sievwright was forced to attempt alone the "delicate task" of recovering muskets believed to be carried by a group of 13 blacks who'd reportedly been hired by some white men to kill some troublesome Colijon tribesmen. The group, also "abundantly armed with spears", denied having any guns.[3] When Assistant Protector Parker reported that the same blacks were on their way back to Melbourne, having successfully carried out their mission, Robinson wrote to Gipps suggesting that "nothing short of a legislative enactment" would be enough to prevent the Aborigines from obtaining firearms.[4]

The Governor decided to refer Robinson's suggestion to La Trobe, who was then about to become Port Phillip's Superintendent.[5] Meanwhile, however, Gipps issued a decree threatening to not renew the licence of any squatter who gave arms or ammunition to the blacks, or whose servants may be found to have done so, "for any purpose whatever". He echoed Robinson's sentiments that guns couldn't be entrusted to "people as yet but in a very few instances restrained by civilization, or any moral or religious instruction". As well, the dangerous practice of giving guns to Aborigines "must often lead to the perpetration of crime, not only among their own tribes, but also among the white population". Gipps also directed that the Crown Lands Commissioners should endeavour "by quiet and persuasive means" to retrieve white weapons from the

Reproduced courtesy of the Mitchell Library, State Library of New South Wales
"Settler and Aborigine", by S. T. Gill.

Aborigines -- and to report the names of any squatters on whose runs they may have obtained them.[6]

Soon after his arrival, La Trobe wrote the first of many communications on the subject. His immediate concern was that some of the large number of blacks camped near Melbourne had firearms, at least two "undisguisedly so". One was a young man named Derrimut who'd been among the group Sievwright had unsuccessfully tried to disarm more than three months earlier. But La Trobe did not initially agree with Robinson that the police should be used to retrieve the weapons. "I am quite persuaded," he told the Chief Protector, "that a firm and prudent exertion of your authority, personally exercised, will be sufficient to do this in an amicable manner, without any assistance from constables or other attendants, whose very presence would imply the meditated employment of force." La Trobe added that Robinson by now should have arranged for the blacks to leave the vicinity of the town. On reading La Trobe's letter, Gipps commented that if necessary, all the Protectors' allowances and rations should be suspended until they'd ensured that the move took place.[7]

Less than a month later, the number of Aborigines camped on the south bank of the Yarra near Melbourne had tripled, to almost 300. While constantly trying to make them move, Assistant Protector Thomas also attempted to encourage them "in a friendly manner" to give up their firearms. But instead, they hid them from him. Thomas had spent most of his time dealing with blacks frequenting Melbourne, who'd had more opportunities to acquire guns than other members of their race. He therefore had a distorted view of the extent to which firearms were being used by the Port Phillip Aborigines, believing it to be widespread. "It is no easy task to persuade the savage to give up his gun," he reported. "It has become the tool for his subsistence. I am persuaded that he would as soon part with his lubra or child as his gun, nor do I consider it prudent to attempt it." When the Aborigines finally decided to disperse, some to shift to the reserve he was trying to establish about 60 kilometres south of Melbourne, they took their guns with them. La Trobe, angry that the move had taken so long, rebuked Thomas and refused to authorise him to take any supplies to induce the blacks to remain at the reserve. It was a petulant and short-sighted decision that soon resulted in the reserve being abandoned, and Thomas being forced to return to Melbourne to try to persuade another large group of blacks to leave the town.[8]

Alarmed that the number of guns being acquired by the blacks was "greatly on the increase", and having lost hope of the Protectors being willing or able to stop this "evil", La Trobe ordered the Melbourne police to retrieve the weapons whenever they could do so without force. The first weapons seized under this order were the muskets given to five Barrabool men recently chosen by Sievwright to be his Native Police, who'd wandered up to the town from

Geelong while he was away in the far west of his district. La Trobe was then astounded to learn that Thomas had been encouraging the blacks camped near the town to hand over their guns to him for safe keeping at night, to be returned each morning. The Superintendent told Gipps that when questioned on this "singular policy", Thomas had replied that he didn't feel at liberty to betray the trust placed in him by confiscating the weapons. While normally careful not to interfere with the procedures which the Protectors deemed proper to follow, La Trobe stated, he'd immediately written out an order "which relieved Mr Thomas from all responsibility" and sent a constable who'd recovered a number of firearms from under the bed in Thomas' tent.

Subsequently, La Trobe reported, he'd managed with "great difficulty" to enforce an order for the immediate dispersal of the almost 500 blacks who'd assembled on the outskirts of Melbourne: 203 of the local tribe, 111 Goulburn blacks, 95 of the Barrabool tribe, and 87 from an area north-west of the town. Despite the moves to disarm them, the blacks still had many guns when they left. The Goulburn blacks -- and reportedly the Barrabool Aborigines -- had since caused "great annoyance" to the white settlers. The time had come, he declared, for tough action to prevent the Aborigines from obtaining any further firearms. The Governor's decree threatening to refuse to renew squatting licences if the Aborigines were given guns in the bush wasn't enough. As La Trobe pointed out, the squatters and their men weren't the blacks' main source of guns: while a few guns in the right black hands could help reduce Aboriginal numbers, they would only be endangering their own lives by allowing too many of their superior weapons to be acquired. The main source of firearms was in Melbourne, and the periodical visits of the blacks to the town must be stopped, regardless of the consequences. As well, a law to prohibit the supply of firearms to the blacks should be urgently introduced. "Its provisions can scarcely be made too peremptory and too severe," La Trobe advised, "and it should award heavy penalties against anyone who under any pretext should either give, lend or sell arms or ammunition to the Aborigines, whether in town or country."

In conclusion, La Trobe decided to sow further doubts in Gipps' mind about the wisdom of the advice he might receive from Robinson or his assistants on the best way to deal with the Aborigines. He didn't want Gipps to suspect, he stressed, that his view of the colonial government's political, social and religious duties towards the Aborigines was based on principles less sound than those of the Protectorate. Nor did he want the Governor to believe that his efforts to discharge these duties might be less sincere. However, he had to admit that his views and those of the Protectors on how to attain the end to which they were all striving were "widely different". Instead of weakly yielding to and following the "movements and fancies" of the Aborigines, he suggested, they should be wisely controlled by a "just and firm degree of authority".[9]

Without waiting for endorsement from Gipps, La Trobe went ahead with his ban on the Aborigines entering Melbourne. He also decided to apply his ban on black access to Geelong -- the move which was to end the loose employment and trading arrangements the Barrabool tribe had established in that settlement, and provoke bitter condemnation from Sievwright. After the bans went into effect, Gipps advised La Trobe that Attorney-General Plunkett had been requested to prepare the suggested legislation on firearms to submit to the Legislative Council as soon as possible. The Act would eventually be proclaimed in the Government Gazette in Sydney in August 1840, almost exactly a year after Gipps had issued his decree on the subject. As La Trobe had suggested, the Act went much further than the decree. Notwithstanding the supposed "equal and indiscriminate" application of the law to both races, it declared that no Aborigines, or half-castes living with them, could have firearms of any description or ammunition in their possession without the written authorisation of a magistrate. Any white person, other than convicts, could seize guns or ammunition held by a black without permission "provided that no personal violence be used...further than may absolutely be necessary". Anyone convicted of supplying guns to an unauthorised black would be fined the hefty sum of between 10 and 25 pounds for each offence.[10]

Proclamation of the Act in Sydney coincided with the start of the return to Melbourne of another sizeable group of Aborigines, despite the ban on their entry. La Trobe despaired that the "utmost exertion" of the police to stop the influx was proving "quite insufficient". Once in the town, the blacks were being supported in their defiance of the authorities by a number of white residents -- particularly the vendors of arms and ammunition, in whose shops they were seen not only by day but even after dark. Again, the Superintendent insisted that it was up to Robinson and his assistants to ensure the departure of the Aborigines who'd already arrived, and to prevent the arrival of any more.[11] When copies of the Act reached Melbourne from Sydney a few days later, La Trobe decided to stretch the law to the limit. He sent a circular to Robinson, and the Melbourne and Geelong Police Magistrates, drawing their attention to it. Though the Act didn't say so, he'd decided that the clause allowing blacks to possess firearms with a magistrate's permission didn't apply in the Port Phillip District. This clause, La Trobe stated, had been introduced to take into account the situation in parts of the colony where the blacks had been living for years among the whites. But in Port Phillip's present state, the only safe course would be to grant no exemptions "under any pretext".[12] Major Lettsom had just arrived in Melbourne, and within two weeks dozens of guns held by the blacks camped near the town had been forcibly recovered with his help, despite Robinson's objections.[13]

After the Barrabool Aborigines were banned from Geelong and were forced to fall back on ever-dwindling traditional food sources to save themselves from starvation, Sievwright regularly joined the men on hunting expeditions. On many of these occasions, his rifle proved effective in ensuring the hunting parties' success. While he could of course have done all the shooting himself, he taught certain blacks he regarded as trustworthy how to use the weapon. This practice, he found, delighted the tribe, and became an important way of "obtaining that ascendancy amongst them" which was so crucial to his overall mission.[14] Sievwright was therefore dismayed to learn that La Trobe had deemed that there should be no exemptions in the Port Phillip District from the firearms law. He could continue to allow some of the Barrabool men to use his gun while they were hunting in areas remote from squatters' runs, with little chance of being spotted. But he realised that although the risk might only be minimal, the consequences of detection -- for both himself and the Protectorate -- could be severe.

Some weeks after the introduction of the law, Sievwright decided to seek La Trobe's permission to grant exemptions. In a brief note to the Superintendent, he explained the advantages of having been able to share his rifle with the Barrabool hunters, pointing out that the permission he sought would apply merely to the use of his own gun, and only when he was a member of the hunting party. Sievwright had recently received a letter from his brother, John, saying he'd taken up the idea of coming to Australia, and would be aboard a barque called the *William Hughes* that was daily expected to arrive in Melbourne from London. When he went to the town to await John's arrival, Sievwright took his note to La Trobe, in the hope of being able to deliver it personally. In a chance meeting later that day, he was able to do so. La Trobe appreciated the arguments he put forward, but having stated unequivocally that there would be no exemptions to the firearms law, he wasn't willing to lay himself open to charges of inconsistent decision-making by giving the Protector written permission to grant them. Sievwright's request for such authority, however, he "acceded to verbally".[15]

The verbal permission was an important psychological fillip for Sievwright, making him feel that he may have finally made some headway in improving his poor relations with La Trobe, and it was with renewed confidence that he returned to Geelong with his brother to at last make the move to Keilambete. But before the move took place, he was to come under yet another attack from the press -- ironically, this time for the way in which he'd made previous trips through his district. According to the *Geelong Advertiser*, recently launched as the town's first newspaper by John Fawkner, Sievwright was "fast acquiring an unenviable notoriety". The *Advertiser* stated its criticism didn't concern his dealings with the Aborigines, for he had "a licence *ex officio* to commit any absurdity or iniquity in that department". However, it commented that besides protecting "the black bushrangers", Sievwright rode about the countryside like Harun Al-Rashid, the tyrannical Caliph of Mesopotamia featured in *The Thousand and One Nights*. With him he took two large dogs that were in the habit of "worrying and scattering the settlers' flocks, even in open day".

The paper referred to sworn statements that had been made at the Geelong Police Office, complaining that on a recent occasion when Sievwright had been riding near the town, one of his dogs had terrified a flock of young ewes "heavy with their first lambs". This had occurred on land bought by the Derwent Company, the affairs of which were under the management of Fyans' friend and neighbour, David Fisher. Despite the sheep being on purchased land, Sievwright had demanded to know what right they had to be grazing so near the road. The "bold Protector" had then haughtily and wantonly ignored the warning of one of

"He explained the advantages of having been able to share his rifle with the Barrabool hunters..."

Fisher's shepherds and created similar havoc with his dogs among a flock of wethers just ahead. The damage caused to the flocks was considerable, but couldn't be fully ascertained until it was known how many of the traumatised ewes would either die or slip their lambs. For the sake of the Derwent Company and the public, the *Advertiser* declared, Fisher should make every effort to have Sievwright charged with some offence. "Whether the action be civil or criminal, we hope it will be vigorously prosecuted, for the official rank of the offender as Protector and Justice of the Peace is a considerable aggravation," it asserted. "The Protectors seem to think that it is their duty to trample upon the white usurpers of the soil; at least that is the only way they show their regard for the interests of its original possessors."[16]

Instead of "rushing the settlers' flocks", the *Advertiser* added, Sievwright should pay some attention to the case of Mumbowran, a young Barrabool man who'd been chained for 17 days in solitary confinement in the Geelong watch-house, without any formal charge having been laid against him. "The pitiful cries of this poor wretch often disturb the neighbourhood," it claimed. Although it was difficult to establish the truth, no official inquiry having been made, the paper believed Mumbowran had been arrested for the murder of a Colijon who'd attempted to kill a white shepherd near Lake Colac. The Barrabool blacks, who considered themselves civilised and the Colijon tribe "barbarians", had decided to take the law into their own hands and punish the Colijon who'd attacked the shepherd by spearing him to death. Mumbowran had later boasted that he'd thrown the last spear. The paper alleged that Sievwright had then "gammoned" him into carrying a parcel to the watch-house, where he'd been arrested. Such *"white perfidy"* was "rarely equalled in the annals of *black treachery*". Should this account be substantiated, the *Advertiser* remarked, it had no hesitation in saying that the conduct of the Barrabools had been not only blameless, but praiseworthy. "Though ignorant of European law, they outraged none of its maxims; if they did not go through its forms, they at least acted according to its spirit," it observed. "They are now punished for *protecting the whites* -- a crime they will take care not to be guilty of again."[17]

The *Advertiser* had recently scoffed at the professed attempt to grant the same legal rights to the Aborigines as to the white population of the colony. "The grand error committed by our legislators, and the source of all discontent of our settlers," it had declared, "lies in the *a priori* hypothesis adopted by the Home Government that, as the aborigines are human beings, and within the dominions of Her Majesty, therefore the same laws which are applicable to other British subjects must also be suitable for them..." It was not surprising that the "liberal affectation" of the British government should lead it to commit such an error, but it was absurd for the colonial authorities to perpetuate it. The paper "would be as little surprised to see Caesar and Pompey meet again on the plains of Pharsalia, in the shape of two poodle dogs, as to see any of our newly-titled British subjects assume the character as well as the name". Mumbowran and the rest of his race needed to be put on special settlements where the whites could "civilise them by compulsion", the *Advertiser* argued. "The present system of *protection* merely ensures to them their unrestrained indulgence in their vicious propensities," it argued. "They are protected when they ought to be punished, and neglected when they ought to be instructed. Some change in the system must be made, and it will require to be a sweeping one."[18]

Mumbowran had in fact been arrested on one of several warrants issued by Fenwick after Robinson decided to show the blacks "that murders even among themselves, could not be permitted with impunity".[19] Sievwright had merely been acting on instructions from Robinson when he formally requested the warrants at the Geelong Police Office. Mumbowran had been wanted for the murder of a Goulburn black known as Tommy at Melbourne. Poleorong, alias Billy Lonsdale, and Wingolabel, alias Captain Turnbull, were also suspected of involvement in the murder of Tommy or another black at Melbourne. But the warrants for their arrest were for the recent murder of a Jarcoort at the Wesleyan mission station south-west of Geelong. To Sievwright's disappointment, a fourth man named Winerderd was also being sought for involvement in the murder. Winerderd had been one of the five Barrabool men Sievwright had chosen a little over a year earlier to act as his Native Police.[20]

Three of the murder suspects -- Mumbowran, Poleorong and Wingolabel -- had been among the group of blacks hired 19 months earlier by some whites to kill some Colijon blacks, and whom Sievwright had unsuccessfully tried to disarm.[21] So at a time when he was about to try to promote peaceful relations between the Barrabool people and the tribes to the west, Sievwright was not unhappy that at least one of the group was in detention. The move to Keilambete would take him through Colijon territory, and he wanted that tribe to regard the reserve he was about to form as a sanctuary as well. If the Barrabool blacks were to accompany him there, his chances of success could only be jeopardised by the presence of men such as Mumbowran against whom unsettled scores remained. When Sievwright finally set off on the dusty track out of Geelong for Keilambete, Mumbowran remained in jail. It was a strange procession, Sievwright and his brother leading the way. Behind them rode the newly-appointed overseer, Alexander Davidson, and constable, Joseph Godwin. Next came a team of eight bullocks, being driven by one of Sievwright's servants, sitting on a cart that also carried the Protector's two sons, the wives of the overseer and the constable, and supplies. The five heavily-armed Barrabool warriors selected for the mission walked alongside. Sievwright's other servant stayed behind, to look after Christina and the girls.

Less than a week later, Sievwright had set up camp at Keilambete, despite vehement protests from John Thomson, and -- much to the squatter's horror -- had begun gathering the first inhabitants of the new reserve. He dispatched messengers to encourage Aborigines in the area to bring in other members of their tribes, so he could attempt to explain his plans. He also went on recruiting missions himself. One in particular would have profound memories. In the forest about 30 kilometres south-east of Keilambete, he came across a group of

Elangamite people -- among them Burguidningnang. Sievwright later recalled: "Upon recognising me, he evinced the most lively symptoms of joy and gratitude, having closely embraced me in silence, with his head leaning on my shoulder, for upwards of a minute; he then suddenly turned to those who were with him, and most vehemently and loudly proclaimed who I was and what I had done for him, upon which the old men of the party came up to me and severally placed their right hand upon my left shoulder..." The Elangamite blacks then beckoned Sievwright to their huts nearby, and treated him as an honoured guest. In quick succession, he was offered water, witchetty grubs, possum and fish. He

"He came across a group of Elangamite people -- among them, Burguidningnang..."

accepted some of the latter, and "having superintended the cooking of it", he remained with them for some time. On leaving, he received a necklace of kangaroo teeth, and a promise that the group would arrive in two days at Keilambete with other members of the tribe.

The Elangamite people were true to their word, and on their arrival Sievwright gave them blankets and tomahawks to present to the Barrabool ambassadors -- resulting in "a most friendly and confidential intercourse". That evening, Burguidningnang solemnly approached the Protector's tent, followed by the elders of his tribe, bearing in his arms his two-year-old daughter. Sievwright was dumbfounded when he realised that Burguidningnang wished him to take the infant and give her to his 11-year-old son, Charles. Across the cultural chasm, it was an extraordinary gesture of good faith, possibly unparalleled in the history of the colony, and Sievwright could not reject it outright. "Having taken the child, I endeavoured to have explained to him that such was not the custom with white people, but that the child should remain with my children, and be clothed and fed like one of them, upon which they retired seemingly much satisfied...", he recorded. A short time later, a strong dome-shaped hut made of bark and mud had been erected next to Sievwright's tent, where Burguidningnang left his wife and daughter while he went on expeditions to encourage more Aborigines to join the reserve.

Under the guidance of overseer Davidson, preparations for farming activities started immediately. The blacks' complete lack of agricultural experience did not hamper the initial task allotted to them: clearing and fencing the area John Thomson had been using as a fold for his sheep at night. For most, it was the first chance to use the white man's tools, and there was lively competition among the young men to try out the axes, saws and hoes. Davidson would pay each of the blacks who contributed a few hours' labour with a small circular piece of tin. In the evenings, as the stumps of the felled trees smouldered away, the labourers would gather at his tent to exchange the coins for quantities of

Reproduced courtesy of the National Library of Australia
"Corrobori", by S. T. Gill.

flour, rice, sugar, tea, mutton, or tobacco. Then around the campfires, those who had worked would share their novel rewards with their families. On some nights, a large blazing fire would be lit, and the members of the various tribes would gather for a corroboree. Mostly men, but some boys, would dance to a song sung by a leader near the fire, as a group of women beat time on their possum skin rugs, rolled up tight.

After only two weeks at Keilambete, Sievwright was quietly confident of achieving his vision of a haven for the blacks of his district, where they could live together in harmony and safety. They'd already shown they could embrace the totally new concept of payment for labour -- and as long as they continued as they'd started, it appeared they could be taught to satisfy some of their food needs by growing their own crops. As well, there was still an abundant supply of traditional food in the forest and the lakes between Keilambete and the coast. The suitability of the area for hunting and fishing could be seen in the physical characteristics of the Kirrae people, in whose territory the new reserve lay. Unlike the "shrivelled and emaciated" tribes closer to Geelong, Sievwright reported, the Kirrae blacks were "in a state of not merely copulency, but of decided obesity". The Barrabool representatives had certainly been delighted with the site, and had returned to their tribe to urge them to move to the reserve, describing the country around Keilambete as "covered with kangaroo instead of sheep, and undisturbed by the white men, like their own country long ago".[22]

CHAPTER 12
Bureaucratic panic

K
EEPING abreast of a massive amount of paperwork was a time-con-
suming and tedious task for the New South Wales colonial administrators. Letters and reports relating to the Aboriginal Protectorate added
considerably to their workload. The long-winded correspondence of the head of
the department, in hand-writing appallingly difficult to decipher, was at first
treated facetiously by those to whom he reported. The Colonial Secretary
remarked that the Chief Protector may soon have to be forbidden "the use of pen
and ink", while La Trobe told the Governor he was coming under "a terrible file
fire" from Robinson.[1] But gradually, the large quantity of correspondence was
in itself responsible for a degree of resentment towards the Protectorate -- and
tended to dissuade the authorities from paying due attention to the tragic events
its officers were reporting, or to the means they were proposing to deal with
them.

Usually, the periodic reports of the Assistant Protectors were passed on by
Robinson, and then by La Trobe, with superficial comment...and on reaching
Sydney they were merely filed away with what was largely regarded as all the
other nuisance material generated by the department. Often, the reports would
not be read by Gipps.[2] When Sievwright submitted his report for the months of
June to October 1840, Robinson's covering note was confined to carping about
the fact that it covered a five-month period instead of the specified six. The
Chief Protector made no comment whatsoever about the report's damnatory contents.[3] However, La Trobe quickly realised that some of its stinging criticism
was directed at him, and he had much more to say about it.

In an initial covering letter to Gipps, the Superintendent attempted to dismiss
the report as a good example of the irregular and "meagre character" of the information which the Chief Protector was receiving from his assistants. Sievwright's
report was "mainly occupied with expositions of his own views, complaints of
the arbitrary line of conduct pursued by the authorities in seeking to prevent visits by the natives to the townships, unsupported statements of the misconduct of
the Government Officers in his district, or allusions to the neglect of the
Government in delaying the adoption of measures which he considers necessary
for the tranquillization of his district..." These measures, La Trobe argued, could
only be taken when Sievwright himself had provided the local information

required by Robinson, and when he'd exhibited "proof of some experience in the discharge of his Magisterial and other official duties".[4]

Before sending on the report a week later, La Trobe realised he should comment on Sievwright's allegations about the tardiness of the colony's legal authorities. In a second covering letter, he told Gipps he was quite ready to join the Protectors in lamenting that there'd not been a single instance of a settler being brought to trial as a result of the frequent clashes with Aborigines. But, he alleged, it was not clear that the legal authorities were to blame to the extent that Sievwright had alleged. La Trobe claimed that Sievwright had been given clear instructions by Attorney-General Plunkett and Crown Prosecutor Croke in Melbourne on the correct way to act in cases in which he believed unjustified

From "The Chronicles of Early Melbourne"
Charles Joseph La Trobe

homicide had occurred. He was unable to explain why Sievwright -- and his fellow Assistant Protectors -- had persisted in attempting to launch prosecutions on the basis of depositions that had not been legally recorded.

The Superintendent went further: "No decided step has been taken by him in any of the lamentable cases of collision between the settlers and the aboriginal natives of his District although it appears to me that if his opinion of the character of the Homicides in question were really that which he conveyed, it was clearly and imperatively his duty to do so." La Trobe made no mention that Sievwright had in fact appealed for more detailed instructions on how he should record depositions. Nor did he outline what "decided step" he believed Sievwright could have taken in any of the cases in which he'd recommended that murder charges be laid, but in which Croke had ruled that no further action was warranted. "The Chief Protector is fully aware," La Trobe concluded, "of the disposition of the Government to give him every assistance in its power, and that no obstacle would be allowed to intersperse itself in the way of the direct course of justice."[5]

Gipps had recently told La Trobe he could not prescribe what measures to take to repress "the unceasing acts of aggression" by the Port Phillip blacks and the equally lamentable acts of reprisal which they were provoking. However, he directed La Trobe to make it known in the district that if no other way of restoring peace could be found, the Government was willing to restrict squatting licences to stations which Crown Lands Commissioners Fyans and Powlett could protect with the small number of police under their command. Squatting would be made illegal in areas where clashes with Aborigines were likely to occur.[6] In threatening this drastic move, Gipps was responding to a series of documents from La Trobe relating to the abysmal state of inter-racial relations in Port Phillip. The Governor was keen to be seen to be doing all he could to minimise the violence -- especially as he was still fearful that officers of the Protectorate may address grievances about his administration direct to London. Sievwright's report containing the allegations against La Trobe, Fyans and the legal authorities would only increase this fear. In his first official reaction after skimming through it, Gipps only instructed that La Trobe be told he agreed that the Assistant Protectors' reports were of poor standard. As the Protectors were immediately under the Superintendent's orders, it was up to him to ensure that the reports improved.[7]

But in a private letter to La Trobe later that day, Gipps outlined his real feelings -- suggesting that the Superintendent try to prevent Sievwright and his colleagues from making comments in their reports that could embarrass the colonial government. "I fear you have a great deal of trouble before you with the Protectors," the Governor wrote, pointing out that most of the documents relating to the Aborigines he'd received recently from Melbourne had been sent to the Attorney-General for advice because they related to judicial matters rather than to any measures of the executive government. "I think you should not allow them to trouble you with such matters -- they do not properly belong to you," the Governor wrote, "and if I were in your place I should make the Protectors confine themselves in their reports to the Government to matters on which they have been desired to report. At the same time, it is necessary to do this with great caution, as they are evidently trying to get up a case for England."[8]

Just over a month later, Gipps would sit down to wade through the paperwork he'd received relating to the Protectorate, deciding what to send on to the Colonial Office in London himself. It was only then that he noticed to his horror, for the first time, the allegation Sievwright had made about the way in which Fyans had made an "indiscriminate attack" in capturing the three Elangamite men, renewing "a spirit of antipathy and hostility" towards the Western District Aborigines.[9] The Governor instructed Colonial Secretary Thomson to write to La Trobe immediately, demanding an explanation. "A charge of this sort against a public officer ought not to have been made in so informal a manner, but being made, it should have been inquired into," the letter instructed, "and even now no time must be lost in making strict inquiry into it..." Gipps added that he'd initially overlooked Sievwright's allegation because of the "extremely irregular and unsatisfactory" manner in which Robinson forwarded information to the government. Papers sent by the Chief Protector through La Trobe should be brief and lucid, clearly identifying points requiring attention. Instead, Robinson seemed to be passing on copies of the entire correspondence of his department "without note or comment". Mixed up in this "unintelligible mass of unimportant and unnecessary matter" were the uncalled for opinions and observations of the Assistant Protectors, which were tediously repetitious, and "frequently disrespectful to the Government".[10]

The same day, Gipps wrote another private letter to La Trobe about a disturbing report he'd just received from the Reverend Joseph Docker, a Church of England clergyman who'd set up a sheep station near that of Doctor George Mackay, where Major Lettsom had initially been sent. Docker told Gipps he had more than 6000 sheep under the sole charge of Aboriginal shepherds, who were faithful and honest workers. However, it was his painful duty to report that the doctor and the Mounted Police in the area had almost destroyed his hopes of showing from his experiment that blacks could be used as shepherds on an extensive scale. Parties of police, sometimes led by Mackay, were constantly scouring the area. "As soon as the natives get a glimpse of them they flee to the hills for safety, and thus are my sheep scattered and left in the bush without shepherds," Docker complained. On one occasion, two blacks had been wounded when shots were fired as a group of five escaped from Mackay's custody. The following day, police had arrived at his station and fired shots at a black against whom no charges had been laid. More recently, a policeman had come to his hut, accompanied by two drunken employees of Mackay, and seized an "intelligent and well-behaved" young Aboriginal man named Moleleminner, known to the whites as Joe. After "much unnecessary rough usage", Joe had been dragged -- handcuffed and neck-tied -- to a nearby station then on to Melbourne, after a stockman swore on oath that he was among the party that had attacked Mackay's station earlier in the year.

"There exists unfortunately, among most of the settlers around me, a most inveterate and deadly hatred of the Aborigines, which I cannot account for," Docker wrote. "For my own part, I dread the visits of the police more than I should those of the wildest savages in the bush."[11] Gipps could not afford to dismiss Docker's report: if it happened to reach official ears in London, immediately after news of the disastrous Lettsom affair, his government's handling of Aboriginal matters would certainly look even more questionable. Besides, the Governor had also only recently heard about Harlequin, the black who'd died in Melbourne after the Mounted Police had dragged him from the same area by a dog chain around his neck.[12] Gipps told La Trobe that Robinson should investigate Docker's claims.[13]

Ironically, that same day in Melbourne La Trobe would write to Gipps, inform-

Reproduced courtesy of the Mitchell Library, State Library of New South Wales
"Mounted police and blacks" by Colonel G. C. Mundy.

ing him of the latest development in the Lettsom affair: the escape on the Yarra of the black prisoners who'd been sentenced to transportation.[14] When he received the Governor's letters more than a week later, La Trobe still did not know how many of the blacks had been shot dead while trying to escape, or how many had got away.[15] Preferring to try to settle this matter first, he held off ordering the immediate inquiry he was supposed to launch into Sievwright's complaint about Fyans' behaviour. However, La Trobe instructed Robinson to leave as soon as possible to investigate Docker's allegations.[16] The Chief Protector would take with him Joe, the Aboriginal man whose arrest Docker had decried. With La Trobe's authority, Robinson would also gain the release from the Melbourne jail of two other blacks arrested at the same time two months earlier: Joe's brother, Coyamber -- called Larry by the whites -- and Tanrougen, also known as Simon. Robinson told the Superintendent that all three had been arrested at Mackay's instigation, but there was no evidence against any of them. For the journey back to their country, he added, he'd given Joe, Larry and Simon each a suit of slops, a blanket, and food rations.[17]

While he awaited Robinson's return, La Trobe again turned his attention to Harlequin's death, hoping to quickly resolve the incomplete inquiry into it. But to add to the Superintendent's woes, he was being stymied in this case by the outright refusal of Police Magistrate Simpson to co-operate. Simpson pointed out that Robinson had already inquired into and reported on the circumstances of the death. In calling on him to make a separate investigation, Simpson argued, La Trobe was in effect asking him to cancel the proceedings of a fellow magistrate of equal authority, and one whose duties were "admitted more particularly to enjoin the execution of such authority". This he would not do. "However complimentary the nomination may be to myself individually the duties are so invidious that I trust after this explanation of my feelings, they will not be pressed upon me," he told La Trobe. If the Protectors were not regarded as competent enough to carry out such investigations, they should be conducted by other magistrates in the first instance, and not be subject to "the stigma of a revision".[18]

Simpson's attitude left La Trobe in a quandary. The Police Magistrate had taken a similar stand on a previous occasion when called upon to inquire into the death of Narrokemulluc, the Lettsom detainee shot dead while trying to escape from the government store. Then, too, he'd refused to carry out a request to investigate on the ground that the death had already been inquired into by Robinson and Parker. On this occasion, La Trobe had been quite willing to let the matter quickly lapse -- when he heard that the Attorney-General had advised that the key issue in question was whether Narrokemulluc had been escaping from *legal custody* at the time he was shot. Plunkett had told Simpson that the depositions taken by Robinson and Parker did not say by whose authority, or why, the Aborigines had been detained in the store. "It is quite clear that unless the imprisonment was legal, the Homicide cannot be justifiable," Plunkett stated.[19] The Attorney-General did not realise it had been La Trobe who'd ordered the detention of the blacks -- quite *illegally* -- in line with Gipps' instructions to Lettsom to ignore the law and seize hostages.[20] In Harlequin's case, La Trobe was much less inclined to allow Simpson to decline to investigate, but he was unsure what steps to take to force his compliance.

As the Superintendent pondered over what to do next about Harlequin's death, he would receive some welcome news about the black prisoners who'd escaped on the Yarra. Crown Lands Commissioner Powlett told La Trobe he'd been informed by Assistant Protector Thomas that six of the blacks -- one of them "severely wounded" -- had been seen not far from Melbourne. "I have since heard that two natives with Irons on were seen near the Goulburn River, and have every reason to believe that the eight natives who escaped are all at large," Powlett wrote.[21] La Trobe did not ask Thomas to verify the report, or order any other investigation into it, lest it should prove false. Nor did he want to aggravate the situation any further by encouraging Powlett to act on warrants that had been issued by Simpson for the recapture of the escapers. In a confidential message, he told Powlett: "However little it may appear justifiable in me in ordinary cases to interfere with the course of law, I consider it my imperative duty in this instance to request...that if the warrants in question cannot be executed without the employment of force and probable bloodshed, that you will unhesitatingly avoid attempting their recapture."[22] Gipps, also preferring to let the matter rest, would later endorse his stand.[23]

Hopeful that the Lettsom affair was all but over, La Trobe sought Crown Prosecutor Croke's advice on what he should do about Harlequin's death. Croke told the Superintendent that statements by the Mounted Police commander, Lieutenant F. B. Russell, appeared to be "extenuations" of the treatment Harlequin had received from the policemen who'd brought him to Melbourne. But the Prosecutor was quite satisfied that there was evidence that the "disease" from which Harlequin had been deemed to have died had been "superinduced" by the manner in which he'd been dragged to the town on the choking dog chain. His police escorts were therefore "as guilty of his death as if they had shot him without justifiable cause".[24] It was certainly not what La Trobe wanted to hear, and in reporting to Gipps that Simpson was refusing to investigate the death, he would make no mention of Croke's opinion.[25]

Soon afterwards, Robinson would confirm the accuracy of Docker's claim that there appeared to have been no just cause for the police having taken Joe into custody. Benjamin Reid, the drunken stock-keeper who'd given evidence against Joe, was believed to have killed many blacks in a number of clashes. He'd been present when the blacks had attacked Mackay's station, and there was reason to suppose that he was a cause for the attack, if not the main one. Robinson recommended that Reid, a convict whose ticket-of-leave had been suspended after turning up drunk when called as a witness in a recent court case in Melbourne, should be removed from the area. The Chief Protector also brought back to Melbourne the revelation that another Aborigine, known as Micky, had been arrested on George Mackay's orders at the same time as Larry and Simon. The doctor's brother, John, told Robinson that he'd shot Micky dead as the prisoners made "a desperate attempt" to escape, helped by a large number of their tribesmen. This raised the officially-known death toll among the tribes north-east of Melbourne from Lettsom's operation, and the subsequent actions of the police and the Mackay brothers, to four. In the same three-month period, at least six other blacks from the same tribes had been shot and wounded, if not killed, while trying to escape from custody. Robinson recommended that another Assistant Protector be appointed to the area.[26]

It was only after Robinson's return from Docker's that La Trobe passed on a letter he'd written three weeks earlier saying that Gipps wanted an explanation of Sievwright's charge against Fyans.[27] Notwithstanding the fact that he'd known for four months the circumstances to which his assistant had alluded in making the charge, Robinson wrote to Sievwright demanding the explanation.[28] On the same day, the Chief Protector sent a second letter to Sievwright, requesting details of the site where he'd set up camp at Keilambete -- including which squatters were affected.[29] This letter was in response to a complaint to La Trobe from John Thomson, who'd ridden to Melbourne to show the Superintendent a note he'd received from Sievwright asking him to move his property from the site. La Trobe had angrily demanded that Robinson give Thomson a letter to deliver to his assistant, "calling his attention to the informality and impropriety of his proceedings". He believed that Robinson was not yet ready to propose a site for an Aboriginal reserve in the Western District. Even if a selection had been made, the choice would have to be approved by Gipps. It would then be Fyans' responsibility to remove any squatters occupying the wanted land. Finally, La Trobe advised that Sievwright should have been "particularly guarded" in his dealings with Thomson because of their "previous differences" -- a reference to the confrontation that had occurred when the squatter had refused to make a statement to Sievwright about the murder of his shepherd, on the ground that he'd already made one to Fyans.[30]

Still unaware of the stir in Melbourne over his actions, Sievwright had just written his first report at Keilambete, expressing satisfaction with his choice of the site and its prospects as a haven for the blacks under his care. About 230

Aborigines, representing several tribes, had already come to the site...and the challenge now was to teach them to live like Europeans. Sievwright admitted that it would be a mammoth task. The Kirrae people, in whose territory Keilambete lay, could be "classed in the lowest scale of human beings", he wrote. "The women and children are wholly unclothed; they seem to have no idea of decency or even that inherent propriety which would lead (one would imagine) even the most savage beings to avoid the presence of each other, when from necessity they are called upon to do so. Their habits and practices will not admit of being described. Their food is generally devoured in the most revolting manner, cooking of any description seldom performed, the reeking entrails and warm blood of the newly slain kangaroo being consumed and quaffed by them until repletion puts a stop to the disgusting banquet."[31]

Eighteen months earlier, after having been with the Barrabool blacks in Geelong for only a few weeks, Sievwright had reported that he saw little chance of the "stubborn and stiff-necked" older generation of Aborigines changing their ways.[32] After a short time at Keilambete, he still believed that teaching the younger generation a new lifestyle was the only hope of "civilising" the Aborigines. He reported that the Kirrae adults were already confident enough to leave their numerous children with him whenever they left the camp. Regretting that he had neither the time nor the expertise himself, he called for the early appointment of a missionary or teacher to the reserve to take advantage of the "ample field" this left open for the children's education and religious instruction. There was no pursuit of more importance, and he would do his best to facilitate it by maintaining peace in the camp through constant surveillance

Reproduced courtesy of the La Trobe Picture Collection, State Library of Victoria
"Lake Colongulac, a view in the Western District", by John Gully, engraver. Lake Colongulac was close to the centre of the territory of the Kirrae people, not far from Lake Keilambete.

and discipline over the adults.[33]

Only the previous day in Sydney, Gipps had tacitly accepted a recommendation from La Trobe to reject a proposal from Assistant Protector Parker for the immediate appointment of a missionary to his reserve. It would have given him "exceedingly great pleasure", La Trobe had told Gipps, to endorse the idea of appointing missionaries and teachers to the Protectorate. But first, Parker and his colleagues would have to show that their reserves were really established -- and that the adult blacks of their districts were willing to at least leave their children at the homesteads while they wandered.[34] Although this was what Sievwright was now claiming to have achieved, La Trobe would even not learn of it until Robinson finally passed on his assistant's report many months later.[35]

Meanwhile, the five Barrabool envoys had returned from Keilambete to Geelong, where their tribe was becoming increasingly restive over the continued detention of Mumbowran. The *Geelong Advertiser* was still championing his cause, alleging that six weeks after his detention, still no formal charge had been laid against him. "This is a case of cool cruel atrocity on the part of his detainers," it declared. "They are guilty of cowardice, for they would not dare do the same to a white man. That they are guilty of inhumanity must be acknowledged by the greatest enemy to the blacks, for anyone who would use a dog in the same way would be a dog himself. We have noticed this subject so often, that we would be wanting in our duty if we did not deepen our imprecations upon these violators of the law, justice, and humanity. Where are the Protectors, the accusers, the Crown Prosecutor, the Superintendent, and the Magistrates? Are they all implicated in this disgraceful affair?" The *Advertiser* hoped that a judicial inquiry into the case would lead to a "severe reprimand" for those who'd deprived Mumbowran of his liberty. "When the Aborigine's trial does come on, it is twenty to one that no case will be made out against him," it concluded.[36]

Oblivious to the efforts of the *Advertiser* to secure Mumbowran's release, the Barrabool elders decided that the time had come for the tribe to free him. On several occasions, the Geelong police forced back groups of warriors who attempted to storm the stone watch-house in which the murder suspect was being held. Then word reached Police Magistrate Fenwick that the Barrabool blacks were planning to gather in the town "in considerable numbers", and had threatened to murder all its 450 or so white inhabitants if Mumbowran was not released. Fenwick decided to act quickly to defuse the situation. Heavily ironed, Mumbowran was taken from the watch-house by a party of soldiers with fixed bayonets and constables armed with carbines. Amid the angry yells of a crowd of Barrabool people, he was marched to the nearby beach, then taken by rowboat to a cutter called the *Governor La Trobe* which was about to set sail on a night voyage to Melbourne. Sending Mumbowran across Port Phillip Bay had achieved the desired result, Fenwick proudly wrote to La Trobe the following morning: hardly a black could be seen in Geelong.[37]

Even before Fenwick's letter reached La Trobe, however, Mumbowran had escaped. As the cutter had sailed down the Yarra River in the dark close to Melbourne, the prisoner had feigned illness and convinced his escorts to free one of his hands from the handcuffs around his wrists so he could clamber onto the deck. Suddenly, he'd managed to free his other wrist and slipped overboard into the river and disappeared. The rowboat was instantly manned and a search was made, but no trace of him found. The white authorities did not know for sure whether he'd managed to reach the river bank, or sank under the weight of his chains.[38] A fortnight later, the *Advertiser* reported a sighting of Mumbowran back in the Geelong area, free from his fetters. Having campaigned for weeks for his release, the paper remarked it was far from sorry to hear of his escape. But the effect that Mumbowran's treatment would have on "the widening breach" between whites and blacks was cause for concern. "The latter have lost all respect for the former; they have been taught to laugh at the idea of punishment; and find that there is not so much difference between them as was formerly supposed," it lamented. "They will imitate the worst traits of their oppressors, and accelerate their own final extinction." An incident had already occurred a few days earlier, when about 150 Barrabool blacks had used "threatening language and gestures" towards two policemen sent to a station near Geelong to apprehend a runaway seaman.

The *Advertiser* reiterated its call for a complete overhaul of the Protectorate, whose Western District agent it considered to be an inferior human being to Mumbowran -- for reasons it could not explain without prying "into private character". The paper asserted it did not question what it saw as the object envisaged for the Protectorate: making the Aborigines fit for "a higher range of duties", and inducing in them a different set of wants "in order to make their interests less opposite to those of their more civilised conquerors". But, as the *Sydney Gazette* had recently pointed out, the Protectorate had become a disgraceful "piece of downright jobbery" that only benefitted the "greedy sinecurists" it employed to grow fat on the public purse. The *Advertiser* suggested that the Governor of the province of South Australia, George Gawler, had set an example well worth following the previous year "by shooting a few blacks in a summary manner, to strike terror into the remainder". While such a practice may appear revolting, ultimately it would be found to be more merciful than the "blank cartridge system" of the New South Wales government, which was not helping either race.[39]

A letter from Gipps was already on its way to the Colonial Secretary in London in which the Governor declared that he was losing hope in the Protectorate. The deployment of the Protectors had not reduced the number of inter-racial clashes, which had in fact increased in the Port Phillip District in recent months. "By many of the settlers it is said that the presence of the Protectors is the occasion of outrage, inasmuch as their appointment has tended to embolden the blacks, and to render the stockmen and servants of the settlers less resolute than they used to be in defence of their masters' property," Gipps wrote. The Governor was more inclined to believe that the increased frequency of clashes was due to the rapidity with which white pastoralists had been moving into the District, which until recently had been "the undisputed heritage of the savage". However, his hopes of any advantage being derived from the Protectorate were "every day diminishing".

In his more confined theatre of operations in Van Diemen's Land, Gipps went on, he believed Robinson had shown considerable merits. But as Port Phillip's Chief Protector he was "afflicted with such a love of writing that much of his time must be spent that way, which would be far better devoted to active employment". His assistants were, he believed, even more inactive. The formation of the fixed station he'd approved for each Protector would give their duties "a still more missionary character" -- and while confined to these stations, the Protectors would not be able to check the atrocities that occurred whenever land was occupied for the first time by white stockowners. Nevertheless, under proper management the stations would be places of refuge for the blacks. They would also be places for the education of Aboriginal children -- which was perhaps the only measure on which a reasonable hope could now be founded "for effecting any improvement" in the colony's Aborigines. Gipps would also make a strange passing reference to Sievwright. The Governor had not yet been informed that Sievwright had just been told to move to Keilambete. However, Sievwright's most recent report to the government had been in Gipps' office for two months. In this report, the Assistant Protector had reiterated a five-month-old complaint that the government had yet to decide on where he should move to form his reserve. Without elaborating, Gipps told the Colonial Secretary that La Trobe had complained in strong terms of the difficulty in getting Sievwright to move from Geelong.[40]

CHAPTER 13
"A hideous pandemonium"

THE use of exotic gifts to win favour among strangers of another culture was a common practice during the age of exploration of the Earth's surface. Often, the motive was commercial: the donors would hope that the gifts would serve as product samples, leading to lucrative trading arrangements. In other cases, gifts were meant to be examples of a weird but obviously superior culture. Coupled with promises of more to come, they could establish sufficient goodwill to guarantee safe passage through otherwise hostile territory. By 1841, it was a ploy well developed by Port Phillip's Chief Protector of Aborigines. While preparing for his first trip into the Western District of his domain since his arrival more than two years earlier, Robinson took great care to procure what he believed would be an impressive range of gifts. In doing so, he would dig deep into the fund allocated for the "contingent expenses" of his department, access to which he'd only very sparingly allowed his assistants.

Among the items Robinson bought in Melbourne for the trip were a quantity of squibs, Catherine wheels and other fireworks, four kaleidoscopes, and 204 rows of coloured beads. There were also 110 metres of ribbon, to make pendants of 372 medals -- some struck to mark Queen Victoria's marriage to her German-born first cousin the previous year, the rest to mark her coronation in 1837. Other gifts would be of varying practical use to their intended recipients: 100 blankets, 60 cotton shawls, 50 print dresses, 204 cotton handkerchiefs, 50 tomahawks, 200 pocket knives, 576 tobacco pipes, 300 fish hooks, 12 fishing lines, six hanks of twine, and quantities of cotton and needles.[1] With La Trobe's permission, he intended supplementing these gifts with food purchased whenever practical along the way.[2]

The day in March 1841 on which Robinson finally set out on his journey, Sievwright sat down at Keilambete almost 200 kilometres away to write a reply to the letter he'd just received from the Chief Protector demanding an explanation why the site had been chosen for his district's reserve. Again, he pointed out that it had been first recommended to him by the Jarcoort Kirrae people -- and that his own experience had since confirmed the wisdom of the selection. The site was in the middle of the district, and near the edge of an extensive and thickly-timbered forest that comprised its "principal hunting ground". The Jarcoort blacks had originally asked him to live with them on the fresh water lake, Terang, about three kilometres away. However, he'd decided to set up his homestead on the salt lake because his overseer had advised that a marsh next to it -- once properly drained -- was the best spot in the area for cultivation. As well, the limits of the reserve with Keilambete at its centre would only require John Thomson to give up *part* of the land he'd been using for grazing. If the reserve was centred at Terang, Thomson and four other squatters would have to be disturbed.[3]

The Chief Protector would receive Sievwright's letter on his arrival in Geelong two days later. That same morning, Thomson would meet him in the town and

Reproduced courtesy of the La Trobe Picture Collection, State Library of Victoria
A group of Aboriginal women and children in bushland. When Robinson left Melbourne in March 1841
for his tour of the Western District, 100 blankets would be among the items he took to give away.

hand him a note from Fyans stating that the Crown Lands Commissioner presumed Sievwright had been authorised to occupy the squatter's run. When Thomson added that he was about to ride to Melbourne to make another complaint to La Trobe, Robinson not only explicitly denied having authorised Sievwright's actions, but also suggested that the squatter pursue the matter further with Fyans. Overjoyed, Thomson lost no time in asking the Commissioner to take the necessary proceedings under the Squatting Act to evict Sievwright from his run. Fyans, however, would tell Robinson he felt "a delicacy in interfering with a gentleman in the Public Service". Urging the Chief Protector to make Sievwright move, he pointed out that if Sievwright was allowed to take over the run, it would be to Thomson's ruin. Besides, Fyans advised, it was also unnecessary in "a country abounding in all the requisites" for which Sievwright could wish.[4]

When Robinson arrived in Geelong, the Barrabool tribe had quit the neighbourhood -- having just witnessed Mumbowran being taken away. Except for one black youth on horseback who was living with a squatter near the town, Robinson had not yet seen any Aborigines since leaving Melbourne. Eager to get on with his journey and meet some, he soon headed off with replenished food, forage and other supplies. The first day after leaving Geelong, he was disappointed to find that the Wesleyan mission to the south-west was also temporarily without any Aboriginal residents. The next day, he passed the low range of hills on the east side of Lake Colac used privately by Fyans as a cattle run, before arriving at the station of Hugh Murray. Camped there, he found about 40 Colijon people who "appeared quite at home" and who were "highly amused" by a fireworks display he put on for their benefit. Visiting the Colijon tribe was one of the few remaining Jarcoort warriors. Eurodap, aged about 23, had survived being hit seven times by buckshot or slugs fired from British guns. Nevertheless, he had continued to associated with some whites, who'd named him Tom Brown, and who'd taught him some English. He understood that Robinson intended visiting his country, and agreed to accompany him there. The Chief Protector would also pick up another escort: waiting for him at Murray's to volunteer for the task was John Thomson.[5]

The party would pass within a short distance of Keilambete two days later -- and Thomson would go there for the night -- but Robinson was in no hurry to visit his assistant. First, he would go to Boloke -- a salt lake more than 50 kilometres to the north which abounded in eels, and home territory of the Bolagher section of the Kirrae people. Lake Boloke was a favoured spot for settlers in the area to collect slabs of thick salt from its banks, used for curing meat. While loading about half a tonne of salt onto his cart for this purpose, Robinson would hear that a nearby station on the Hopkins River, managed by Henry Gibb, had been robbed by some Kirrae blacks of guns and other items for the second time in 10 days. According to the report, passed on by the Manifold brothers, a shepherd was feared to have been killed. Robinson, still accompanied by Thomson, went to investigate. The Chief Protector found that the robberies had taken place, but not the reported murder. However, he was told that a hutkeeper employed by Gibb had been struck on the head while setting some fishing lines in the river. Although the man had been severely beaten, his life was in no danger. "I am inclined to think that the attacks on Gibb were occasioned by revenge for the outrages committed on the natives by this individual, as reported upon by Sievwright," Robinson wrote in his journal. He would also later record that

Gibb and two of Fyans' police had responded by attacking a group of Elangamite people who'd had nothing to do with the robberies. Burmudgerlong, described by Robinson as the Elangamite chief, had received gunshot wounds to his head and body. Other members of the group had also been wounded.[6]

From Gibb's station, Robinson proceeded over several rainy and windy days towards Keilambete. On the way, he would stop for a meal at the station of Niel Black, who handed him a note from Sievwright giving directions to his camp. Sievwright's convict servant, who was at Black's to purchase supplies from the squatter, added that he was willing to come to meet Robinson if required. The Chief Protector was offended. "This whole proceedings of Sievwright was most strange and quite out of character of a subordinate," he wrote. "It was his place to have come to me and tendered his services." As he arrived at Keilambete that night, Robinson would run into Thomson, who'd ridden on ahead of him. Over refreshments in the squatter's slab hut, they discussed his claim that 28 of his sheep had gone missing, believed stolen by the blacks. Thomson also made yet another complaint about Sievwright's behaviour before the Chief Protector walked over to the nearby camp to finally make his first visit to his assistant in the field, and to meet the 136 blacks there: 42 men, 33 women, and 61 children. "I shook hands with them and, if I was to judge their inward feeling by their outward acts, I believe they were highly gratified to see me," he recorded. Robinson was particularly touched by the welcome he received from Burguidningnang, who showed "great glee" to see him and extolled him "in the greatest manner".[7]

The pleasure Robinson derived from the blacks' reception was soon tempered, however, by his tense relations with Sievwright. The strains were immediately exacerbated when Robinson told his assistant he doubted if Keilambete would be sanctioned as a reserve. The constant complaints he'd received from Thomson over the previous two weeks were not given as the reason. Rather, he told Sievwright, he believed that the site was too close to the Wesleyan mission station -- which was already catering for the needs of the Colijon and Jarcoort people. Sievwright rejected the claim, saying his operations were independent of those of the missionaries. Certainly, it had been the Jarcoort Aborigines who'd recommended the site. But they were only one section of the Kirrae tribe. And Keilambete was obviously acceptable to more than just the Jarcoort blacks. Even the combined strength of the Jarcoort and Colijon people was less than the number of Aborigines who'd already registered at the site -- and he believed the Barrabool tribe was due to arrive any day. Sievwright told Robinson he was ready to fight any suggestion that the Protectorate capitulate to Thomson's demand that he shift. He would also not quietly submit to La Trobe's censure over his actions. Sievwright read Robinson the draft of a letter he was about to formally write to him, further defending himself against La Trobe's claim of "informality and impropriety" in the way in which he'd moved to Keilambete.[8]

Three months earlier, Sievwright pointed out, he and Robinson had held several conversations in Melbourne about the selection of a site for his reserve. Robinson had then provided the means and authority for him to go to Keilambete, erect the necessary buildings, and commence agricultural operations without delay. He'd also been instructed to convey provisions to the site which would be used as payment for the blacks' labour. In line with another instruction from the Chief Protector, he'd provided details as soon as possible of the exact location chosen for the homestead in consultation with the overseer. As a matter of courtesy, Thomson had been given early notice of what he was likely to hear formally from Fyans about the need to give up some of the land he'd been using. The squatter had also been requested to move about two tonnes of flour being stored in a shady spot a few hundred metres from his hut because a large number of blacks were coming to the site who'd had little interaction with the whites, and over whom Sievwright could not expect to have control for some time.

In light of the fact that he'd been acting according to Robinson's orders, he could not understand why -- on the basis of Thomson's ex-parte statement -- La Trobe had censured his actions, which were solely connected with a public and urgent duty. It had also been unfair for the Superintendent to have suggested that his actions may have been biased by his previous dispute with Thomson over the taking of statements in relation to Thomas Hayes' murder. He could prove that he'd recommended Keilambete directly to La Trobe in February 1840, months before the squatter's arrival. His later recommendation to Robinson had been made before he'd ever met Thomson -- and two months before their confrontation. Finally, Sievwright yet again expressed satisfaction with the selection of Keilambete. The area of his district in which it was located was "closely occupied" by white settlers, and to his knowledge there was no other suitable location which would require only one squatter to move. About 250 blacks had so far come to the site, some of whom had been daily employed in clearing the land and ploughing in preparation for crop planting. In the hope that another planting season would not be lost, he would endeavour to continue this work unless he received an order to the contrary.[9]

The order would come the following day, after Thomson complained to Robinson that the blacks had again raided his flocks, stealing 12 sheep. The Chief Protector told Sievwright to suspend agricultural work, and to confine his operations to the erection of a store and temporary huts. It was to be a memorable day for Sievwright in other ways as well. After a fireworks display by Robinson, the blacks at the camp decided to hold a corroboree. However, before it could get underway, a general fight broke out over members of another tribe allegedly interfering with the Elangamite women. Robinson and Sievwright managed to separate the combatants, but not before the elderly Elangamite, Burmudgerlong, and others were wounded with blows from clubs and other heavy wooden weapons. An angry Burmudgerlong urged the whites to shoot the Elangamite opponents. Instead, Sievwright confiscated his spears and on Robinson's instructions took him away to give him tea and damper while he calmed down. Later, the Chief Protector ordered that all the blacks be given a feast of mutton, potatoes and tea. It was not enough for some, however. That night, a group attempted to steal some more of Thomson's sheep. They fled when the squatter's overseer caught them in the act, and opened fire.[10]

The following morning, Sievwright, Burmudgerlong and a Jarcoort elder arrived at Robinson's tent with four blacks who'd admitted being involved in the attempted robbery. Robinson strongly reprehended them before ordering them to leave the camp. It was an unsatisfactory means of punishment, he recorded, but they seemed relieved to submit to it. If they had not been banished, he believed, their fellow Aborigines would have inflicted their own punishment, which would have served no good purpose. Thomson was happy enough with Robinson's decision, inviting him to roast chicken dinner. As they dined, confusion reigned among the blacks in the camp over the suspension of agricultural work -- and the subsequent absence of food payments. Sievwright wrote to Robinson, outlining what he believed would be the consequences. It would be a bad precedent to set, he argued, to continue issuing food without exacting any labour from his charges. But if they were deprived of food at the camp, they would obviously have to go elsewhere to obtain it. "Since they are here in such a body and others are hourly expected, the nearest settlers are likely in this case to suffer from their visits," he wrote. The government would also miss the opportunity to make substantial savings by the Aborigines being taught to grow some of their own food.

Until now, Sievwright added, he'd believed that the government had sanctioned Keilambete as the site for his reserve. His recommendation of the site had been before the government for many months. "I am consequently induced to believe that had any objection to its permanent occupancy been contemplated, that a notice to this effect would have been issued previous to my being directed to come here," he pointedly remarked. Furthermore, the Protectorate had gained some "moral influence" over the blacks of the district by informing them that a certain area had been allotted for their exclusive use. If he was now forced to move, and this influence forfeited, the chances of success of any future civilisation efforts would be highly questionable.[11] What Sievwright did not know was that La Trobe had been awaiting a report from Robinson on the suitability of

Keilambete ever since the Assistant Protector had recommended it six months earlier. La Trobe was not prepared to seek final approval of the site as a reserve from Gipps until Robinson had used his "experience and judgement" to endorse the recommendation.[12]   And after a week at the site, Robinson was not convinced Sievwright had made a good selection.   In fact, after dining with Thomson again, Robinson decided to write to La Trobe stating that he could not decide on the matter until he'd further explored the district.[13]

The discovery the following morning of the spot nearby where a dozen of Thomson's sheep had been disembowelled would lead to a caustic exchange between Sievwright and Robinson. The Chief Protector believed his assistant had heard that the robbery of the sheep was about to take place the previous week -- and knew who'd committed it. "Sievwright, with his usual finesse when spoken to, said he should leave it to me and requested me to tell him what to do," Robinson recorded. "I said I was not going to do his work and if he thought so he was mistaken. He knew well nothing could be done excepting apprehending them for their conduct. Had he, when the circumstances were first reported to him, made an investigation it might have been avoided." Sievwright, Robinson wrote, treated the matter with levity. Some other heated words were swapped, then a silence of ten minutes, before Sievwright stated he regarded Robinson as a "dangerous man" against whom he would be on guard. "I desired him, if he was not disposed to assist, not to disturb me," Robinson continued. "He walked off and said if I wanted him I might send for him."[14]

On one earlier occasion, Robinson had recorded in his journal that Sievwright was "officious and interfering". Yet another outburst had followed Sievwright's explanation that he could not lead the blacks in worship on Sundays until he had a prayer book and a structure of some kind to serve as a chapel. "With such a man it is not possible to affect any good," the Chief Protector had written. "He is evasive and orders are, by him, kept in abeyance and he has not the ability to execute them." But the clash that followed the discovery of the sheep remains turned the rift between them into a chasm. "It is time I was away from this man, for it is now impossible that I can regard him as faithful or assistant...," Robinson wrote. If he was to remain at Keilambete any longer, the blacks would be sure to become aware of their differences, and take advantage of the situation -- as he believed they'd done with Sievwright's differences with Thomson. One black had explained: "Plenty good Mr Sievwright, no growl, black fellow steal sheep and turnips and parsnips."[15]

Before Robinson was ready to leave Keilambete, the blacks would make another raid on Thomson's sheep. Around sunset on a wet and windy evening, a group of about 20 men approached the sheep-fold and hoisted several of the animals over the hurdles that enclosed it. The robbers fled when one of Thomson's shep-

herds opened fire on them. Sievwright sent his overseer and constable to investigate while he quickly went around the camp to see if all the blacks were in their
huts. Some blacks were missing from four huts, he found, but when he checked
again a few minutes later they'd returned -- claiming merely to have been at the
other end of the camp. Reporting to Robinson on the incident, Sievwright
wrote: "Although you have already declined allowing me the benefit of your
assistance and advice relative to the measures that ought to be adopted towards
the natives for the purpose of checking the reported attacks, I deem it my duty
again to apply for those orders on the subject which you may think fit to give."[16]

The Chief Protector blamed his assistant for the raids. "Sievwright did wrong
to bring the natives here until the question of the reserve was settled," he recorded. "Moreover, had it been settled it was wrong for him to collect the natives
until he had a season in advance, so as to ensure a constant supply of flour, potatoes etc. He ought to have placed his overseer in charge, to have carried on the
improvements, and gone himself among the natives, itinerating with the tribes.
He would then have gained useful information and saved me the necessity of
doing it for him. And the natives would, moreover, have regarded him with
more confidence." Thomson's employees had also informed Robinson that
Sievwright was declining to act on complaints about the blacks' behaviour while
his superior was present. When Thomson's overseer had reported the theft of all
his turnips, Sievwright had laughed in his face. And when a bullock driver
employed by the squatter had told Sievwright that the blacks in the camp had
insolently pointed their spears at him, the Assistant Protector had replied "with
a haughty air and a contemptuous look" that the matter should be raised with
Robinson because he knew so much about the Aborigines.[17]

It was no longer possible, Robinson decided, for Sievwright to remain at
Keilambete. A curt note to his assistant read: "I feel it my duty in consequence
of the repeated attacks made by the Aboriginal Natives upon the property of Mr
John Thomson to request that your encampment be removed (for the present) to
a locality removed from Mr Thomson's station and until the pleasure of the
Governor be known in reference to the reserve." It was an oddly-worded
instruction, given that Robinson had only just written to La Trobe saying he was
not convinced that the site was the best available -- and could not yet recommend it for the Governor's approval. Verbally, Robinson added that Sievwright
should move to Terang, the fresh water lake nearby, and with great reluctance he
agreed to comply.[18]

Robinson, Sievwright, his brother John, and one of two Jarcoort men the Chief
Protector had taken on as guides -- known to the whites as Charley -- then set
off for an inspection of Burguidningnang's home territory to the south-east. On
the way, they came across an unoccupied Elangamite camp, where they found

several native baskets -- the contents of which were of great interest to Robinson. They included sharpened kangaroo bones used as needles, pieces of iron hoop and broken glass, lumps of clay and lava, sticks for stripping bark, and even some European clothing. In one basket there was also a walnut-sized piece of what Robinson thought was either the fat or bone of an enemy warrior, designed to be worn as an amulet. It was wrapped in possum skin, tied with sinews, and suspended on a cord of possum fur. Charley wanted to take it away, so Robinson left in its place a new cotton handkerchief. He also left a handkerchief for a lead pencil found in another basket, believing it would be of more use to himself than the Aborigine who had somehow acquired it.[19]

It would be another two days before Sievwright moved his camp to Terang, prompting a complaint from Thomson's neighbour, Neil Black, that he would no longer be able to use the lake to water his cattle. Threatening to send a letter of objection direct to London, Black requested a written assurance that Sievwright would be at Terang no longer than three months. The Chief Protector rejected the request, but told the squatter that if Keilambete did not become a permanent Aboriginal reserve, neither would Terang.[20] Unaware that the camp had been moved, Thomson would meet La Trobe in Melbourne the following day to complain again about Sievwright's actions at Keilambete. After his previous complaint, he'd believed Robinson would force his assistant to shift. But, he told La Trobe, Sievwright had continued to fell all the trees close to his hut, plough the ground in front of his door, and collect blacks at the station without any supplies for their support. As a result, he was sustaining "serious loss in sheep and other minor pilferings every day". Robinson had declared his inability to make Sievwright move, referring him again to Fyans as "the proper officer" to assist him. Fyans, the squatter complained, was still declining to act without instructions from La Trobe.[21]

The Superintendent acted quickly, handing Thomson a letter to deliver to Sievwright condemning his behaviour. La Trobe reiterated in the letter that he was fully prepared to ensure that the interests of the Aborigines did not succumb to the comparitively petty interests of the squatters. "I cannot nevertheless consider the step you have taken, otherwise than improper and unadvised," he wrote. The difficulties involved in the selection of reserves for the other Assistant Protectors, La Trobe told Sievwright, had made him realise that "the utmost caution and circumspection" would be needed in choosing one for him. Robinson had been distinctly and repeatedly told that without "a decided assurance of the eligibility of the situation" from the Chief Protector, no location would be recommended to Gipps. So far, all he'd received from Robinson was the letter saying it would be premature for him to make a judgement about Keilambete -- and a copy of the note he'd sent to Thomson stating that

Sievwright had not been authorised to take over the squatter's run.

"Whatever degree of encouragement you may have received from the Head of your Department to presume that your choice of a locality had been officially brought under my notice and sanctioned by His Excellency, and that you were at liberty to go at once and without ceremony and displace the occupier of the land," La Trobe wrote, "I cannot bring my mind to sanction a proceeding which entails the infliction of an act of positive injustice upon a settler -- a proceeding which in my opinion is as uncalled for as it is against established rule." Not realising that Robinson had already issued the same order, La Trobe instructed that Sievwright should suspend his operations, and move his camp from the immediate vicinity of Thomson's homestead. "I should exceedingly regret if the step were productive of inconvenience to you, loss to the Government, or of any real injury to the interests of the Natives, but for any such consequence, I hold that the Department is alone accountable," he concluded.[22] In an accompanying letter, La Trobe told Thomson that his criticism of Sievwright did not preclude Keilambete being required by the government. If Robinson endorsed his assistant's selection, the squatter would still be required to move. La Trobe also outlined the developments to Gipps, who would agree "entirely" with the steps the Superintendent had taken.[23]

Unrest soon became prevalent in the Terang camp, following the suspension of agricultural operations and the subsequent loss of food payments. And more Aborigines were arriving on the basis of what had become a false promise borne by the messengers that a haven had been established for them where they would not go hungry. The result, Sievwright would later recall, was that "the evil passions and uncontrollable ferocity of the savage became apparent", and the picturesque shores of Terang were converted "into a hideous pandemonium".[24] The day before La Trobe wrote his letter of condemnation, intense fighting broke out in the camp involving the use of spears, clubs and boomerangs. According to Robinson, the fight was started by a black Thomson had taken on as a servant. Again, the old Elangamite, Burmudgerlong, was among those wounded -- as was Burguidningnang. In further fighting a few hours later, a woman and a child were severely beaten. But the most serious clash in the camp so far would occur early the next Sunday morning, after Robinson had resumed his journey to the west with what he regarded as a "burlesque" farewell from his assistant.[25]

Around 2 a.m., Sievwright was awoken by shouting from some Bolagher huts erected close to his tent. Jumping up from his mattress, he looked out to see the fully-armed Bolagher men rushing towards the Jarcoort section of the camp about 50 metres away. Fierce hand-to-hand fighting immediately broke out between what seemed like more than 100 warriors. As he hurriedly lit a lamp, some Jarcoort people burst into Sievwright's tent pleading for protection. They were quickly followed by some Bolagher women who earnestly beckoned him to one of their huts. There he found a 13-year-old girl, Worangaer, unconscious and blood pouring from two deep spear wounds in one side of her face. As he frantically tried to stop the bleeding, hundreds of spears, boomerangs and other weapons were being exchanged outside in the dark.

The fighting continued for about an hour before dying down, and the Bolagher men returned to their part of the camp to see if the mysterious contents of Sievwright's medicine chest contained sufficient magical powers to save Worangaer. When it became apparent that his efforts were in vain, the Bolagher men prepared to renew the combat. Just before dawn, they again attacked. Kinship obligations required the Elangamite men and a small party of Warrnambool Kirrae men in the camp to join the Jarcoort men in the battle, which would leave few of the fighters without fractures or spear wounds. Although outnumbered, the Bolagher men fought hard, and after about two hours, managed to force their opponents to flee to a spot several kilometres away where their women and children had already fled. The Bolagher fighters gave chase, and selected a 17-year-old Jarcoort girl named Mootenewharnong for their revenge. She was felled by about 20 spears. Satisfied, the Bolagher men returned to the camp as the wailing Jarcoort people made a fire to burn her body to ashes.

Back at the camp, the Bolagher blacks gathered around Worangaer's hut, waiting silently and solemnly for her death. When this occurred, they expressed "the

Reproduced courtesy of the Mitchell Library, State Library of New South Wales
"Native Fight" by S. T. Gill.

most violent and extravagant grief", throwing themselves on the ground, weeping and screaming loudly. With sharp stones, they lacerated their bodies, and inflicted wounds on their heads with their clubs. About an hour later, Worangaer's father and brother lifted her body and carried it off a few hundred metres into the bush. The rest of the Bolagher people came behind in single file, surrounded the body again, and lit a fire. Sievwright, who'd also followed, was asked "rather sternly, and by impatient signs" to return to his tent. However, he indicated that he'd like to stay, and sat down on a log laying close by. Worangaer's father walked up to him and pointed his finger to his mouth, and then to the body. As the Bolagher blacks intensely watched his reaction, Sievwright signified his intention to remain, and with as much indifference as he could feign, stretched out on the log to watch what followed.

With a sharp flint, an old man made a small incision on one of Worangaer's tiny breasts -- prompting "the same scenes of violent grief" that had already taken place in the camp. After a short pause, the incisor continued the operation, and in a few minutes had disembowled the body. Then, to Sievwright's fascinated horror and disgust, he witnessed "the most fearful scene of ferocious cannibalism". As the old man began to portion out the entire contents of Worangaer's viscera, there was "a general scamble" by some of the women for her liver. It was snatched in pieces and eagerly devoured. Next, the women avidly tore up and ate Worangaer's kidneys and heart, as the old man cupped his hands and quaffed the blood and serum that had collected in her chest cavity. The flesh was then cut from Worangaer's ribs and back, and her arms and legs were twisted and wrenched from her shoulder and hip joints. Teeth were used to sever difficult tendons. The arms and legs were bent and stuffed in baskets, while a portion of the flesh was put on the fire to cook.

Suddenly, it seemed to Sievwright, the Bolagher people remembered his presence. Something was said to one of the women, who went to her basket and extracted one of Worangaer's legs, cut off the foot, and offered it to him. Sievwright thought it prudent to accept it, wrapping it carefully in his handkerchief. He then pointed towards his tent, and when the blacks nodded assent, gladly walked off. Soon afterwards, the funeral party disbanded. Impressed that Sievwright had apparently agreed to participate in their ritual feast, the Bolagher people tried to involve the other whites in the camp as well -- including Sievwright's two young sons -- but they declined offers of some half-picked bones and other parts of Worangaer's body. At the end of the day, Sievwright rode off to secretly bury Worangaer's foot, passing on the way the tree hollow where her severed head had been placed between some stones heated in the fire, and was undergoing a process of baking.

Reporting the series of events to Robinson and La Trobe, Sievwright stated that on the testimony of about 100 Aborigines, a Jarcoort man named Warawil had been identified as the one who'd murdered Worangaer. It was imperative that something be done to eradicate such "wretched and most savage actions". If necessary, a special law should be introduced to overcome the legal inability of the Aborigines to give evidence in the white men's courts. There was no point, he argued, in apprehending Warawil for the murder, only to discharge him without trial because there was no white witness. The effect would be "to create with the Aboriginal community a hostile feeling, and unsatisfactory opinion of our administration of justice, without any beneficial result accruing to them, or to us, by so partial and an imperfect interference in their polity".[26]

CHAPTER 14
Divine visitations

AS early as June 1837, when the white population of the Port Phillip District had reached more than 500, Attorney-General Plunkett told Governor Bourke it was time to appoint a resident Supreme Court judge in Melbourne. The distance between the settlements, Plunkett argued, made it obvious that the Supreme Court sitting only in Sydney could not administer justice to the inhabitants of Port Phillip "with any degree of convenience or necessary despatch". The Melbourne magistrates, led by William Lonsdale, were not empowered to deal with cases of felony, or even most misdemeanours. The result was that Port Phillip was "almost without the pale of the law". So great was the hardship of having to travel to Sydney for trials that many crimes were going unreported. And while individuals felt they could not seek redress for private wrongs through the legal system, Port Phillip's peace and tranquillity was under threat.[1]

More than three years later, Melbourne still did not have a resident Supreme Court judge. A Court of General Quarter Sessions and a Court of Requests had been set up in the town to hear some criminal and civil matters. But the most serious cases were still reserved for the Supreme Court in Sydney, so the problem outlined by Plunkett had only been partly addressed. For instance, the *Port Phillip Patriot* lamented, delays in getting civil matters heard before the Court in Sydney meant that the "swindling geniuses" who occasionally appeared in Melbourne were able to "decamp with the kernel, leaving their unfortunate creditors nothing but the shell". Only one of the New South Wales Supreme Court judges -- irascible Irishman John Walpole Willis -- backed the campaign for a resident judge in Melbourne. He would later recall that in expressing support for the proposal to Gipps: "I remembered that the policy of the ancient English Constitution, as established by the great Alfred, was to bring justice to every man's door, by constituting local courts where injuries could be redressed in an easy and expeditious manner by the suffrages of members of the same community."[2]

In March 1839, Willis had told Gipps he felt "almost incapable" of discharging his judicial duties. He had frequent pain in one side, believed to be caused by "derangement of the liver", which was "greatly augmented" whenever he had to sit in court for long. The judge had suggested he be retired, but Gipps did not believe he'd served in New South Wales long enough for the colony to have to pay any portion of his retiring allowance...and Willis had been forced to continue serving on the bench.[3] After the New South Wales Legislative Council finally authorised the appointment of a Melbourne judge in October 1840, Willis was selected. Gipps was glad to have somewhere to send Willis for a number of reasons -- notably the fact that for some time, he'd been in open conflict with the Chief Justice, Sir James Dowling, who'd argued strongly against the creation of the Melbourne post. Gipps would report to London that during one altercation between the judges in their robing room, Willis had made "indecorous" remarks in front of witnesses which Dowling had found offensive. At other times, Willis had apparently sought rather than tried to avoid opportunities to make observations from the bench which showed the little respect he had for Dowling. On one occasion, he'd referred to the Chief Justice having convicts assigned to him as servants, comparing this to the possession of slaves. On another occasion, in an address to a jury, Willis had accused Dowling of an inappropriate lack of "dignity of demeanour" by making frequent attempts at humour by "punning" during trials.[4]

Gipps told Lord John Russell he believed that Willis' behaviour did not warrant a reprimand, or even a call for an apology from him. Instead, he'd attempted a reconciliation between the judges and thought he'd achieved this over dinner at the Governor's residence. Since then, though, other matters had arisen which proved this was far from the case. The poor relations between Willis and Dowling would have been reason enough for Gipps to be thankful of the opportunity to send Willis to Melbourne. But the judge's character gave the Governor an extra incentive. Willis was not only contrary and argumentative, but also a stickler for correct procedure. His previous judicial appointments in Upper Canada and British Guiana had been marked by controversy. In the former, he'd been removed from office by the Governor after taking a stubborn stand on a procedural issue -- but was reinstated after an appeal to the Privy Council in London. Gipps' attitude to the administration of justice was pragmatic, extending to a willingness to issue instructions to his subordinates to act illegally when he deemed it expedient. If any of the Supreme Court judges would challenge his actions, it would be Willis. It was therefore better for the Governor for Willis to be busy with matters in Melbourne.[5]

Willis officially opened Melbourne's Supreme Court in April 1841, almost four years after Plunkett had argued it was urgently needed. The judge warned that those convicted before him could not expect lenient treatment. They would find, Willis told the court, that he did not suffer from "a spurious humanity" or "weak tenderness" manifesting itself in undeserved sympathy for the guilty. Crime could only be prevented by instilling a terror of punishment in would-be offenders. In the first two sessions of the court, 14 criminal cases would be brought before it -- all involving men who were formerly convicts in Van Diemen's Land. Two cases were dismissed, but all but one of the rest resulted in convictions. A man named Alexander Wilson was sentenced to death for uttering a cheque for 20 pounds -- although Willis decided to recommend to Gipps that the sentence be commuted to transportation for life. Two men, each convicted of stealing a horse, were transported for 15 years. A young man found guilty of embezzling his employers was transported for 14 years; four thieves for seven years. Another man was jailed for two years with hard labour for "assault with intent to commit an unnatural offence on the person of a youth". The only case result-

Reproduced courtesy of the La Trobe Picture Collection, State Library of Victoria
"The Opening of the Supreme Court" by W. F. E. Liardet.

ing in an acquittal involved a charge of "assault with intent" on a seven-year-old girl. Willis stressed the accused man, Henry Watson, escaped what would have been a certain conviction and death sentence only because the girl had been deemed too young to be aware "of the nature and responsibility of an oath" to give evidence.[6]

After he'd dealt with the 14 cases, Willis was informed by Croke that despite fears of an outbreak of disease in the overcrowded Melbourne jail, no other criminal cases were ready for trial. In some cases, Croke complained, he'd not received the depositions from the police needed to prepare his prosecution. In other cases, no depositions had been sent to him by the magistrates who'd committed prisoners for trial. Another case involved a man named John Payne, who'd been in custody awaiting trial for manslaughter for more than a year, for stabbing dead a fellow employee of the Henty brothers near Portland. The committing magistrate had been Charles Sievwright, who happened to have been in the area at the time investigating clashes involving the Bunganditj. Payne had been sent to Sydney, but then back to Melbourne to stand trial when the new court opened. The case could not proceed, Croke told Willis, because it had been impossible to get witnesses to attend in time for the present sittings from where they resided, more than 200 kilometres beyond Geelong. The judge described Payne's case as "decidedly the most cruel, arising from error or accident" that had ever come to his notice. Calling Payne before the bar, Willis told him that if Croke could not arrange for the witnesses to attend the next sitting of the court in just over a fortnight, he'd be set free.

Next, Croke referred to the two elderly Elangamite men who'd been in custody for almost nine months, pending trial for the murder of John Thomson's shepherd. The Crown Prosecutor told Willis that the brothers had also been expected to stand trial in Sydney. The depositions on which Foster Fyans had committed them had been sent to Attorney-General Roger Therry there, and had not been returned. Consequently, he had no power to prosecute. Told that the blacks were very ill, Willis asked for them to be brought before him. Wawarparneen was supported into the court; Kowcanmarning was too weak to be removed from the town's tiny hospital. Appalled at the prisoners' "wretched" state, the judge reminded the court of instructions from London relating to the treatment of Aborigines. From a legal point of view, the Prosecutor could produce no evidence against them. Furthermore, the prisoners should have been given the opportunity to cross-examine their accusers through an interpreter -- a matter which Croke had raised with Sievwright, Fyans and Fenwick, in a gross underestimation of the linguistic difficulties. Declaring that he would always see justice done to those brought before him, regardless of skin colour, Willis added that he was discharging Kowcanmarning and Wawarparneen and ordering them to the hospital's care.[7]

The judge's act of compassion came too late for the emaciated Elangamite brothers. They were doomed to end their days far from the country in which they'd spent their lives, and where their wives, children and grand-children would wait in vain for their return. Kowcanmarning lingered on for only another four days before dying. So great was Wawarparneen's grief and despair, it killed him. Not only had he lost his brother, but also the only person with whom he'd been able to converse for months -- and for an unknown period ahead, if he'd stayed alive. There was no-one with whom he could share his mourning, or discuss what enemy might have used the evil magic that caused Kowcanmarning's deterioration and death. Nor was there any hope of helping to convey his brother to the spirit world through performance of the appropriate tribal ceremony. It took only hours for Wawarparneen to also die. And so went much ancient Kirrae knowledge and wisdom, more of which the two elders had been planning to pass on to the rising generation when they'd felt the end of their days approaching.

It was decided that formal inquests should be held into both deaths. Kowcanmarning's was held first, before a jury in a room at the Lamb Inn in Collins Street. Evidence was given that from the time of his incarceration in Melbourne, the Aborigine had apparently been convinced from the sign language of the white prisoners that he was going to be hanged. Assistant Colonial Surgeon Cussen gave evidence that an examination of the body had revealed no sign of disease. It was Cussen's opinion that Kowcanmarning's death was the result of "the confinement he had undergone, combined with a broken spirit". The jury returned a verdict that death was due to "the visitation of God": natural causes. Later that day, an inquest was held at the rear of the jail into Wawarparneen's death. The jury was told that he'd died "under precisely similar circumstances" after hearing of the death of his brother. "The sympathetic affection even in the bosom of this savage appeared too finely strung to bear up against the loss," observed the *Port Phillip Herald*. In the view of Assistant Protector William Thomas, the deaths of the two Elangamite men were remarkable evidence that the Aborigines were "tenacious of freedom", while Judge Willis believed Wawarparneen had died "from an excess of sympathy rarely instanced in the human race". The jury settled for the conclusion that Kowcanmarning, too, had had a divine visitation.[8]

Later that day, Police Magistrate Simpson would meet his predecessor, William Lonsdale, at the Melbourne Police Office to conduct an inquiry into the death in the town's hospital back in December 1840 of another Aborigine -- Harlequin. Simpson had hitherto adhered to the principle that he was not legally authorised to inquire into the case, fellow magistrate George Robinson having already done so. Attorney-General Plunkett had accused Simpson of allowing "an absurd etiquette" to stand in the way of carrying out his duties. If he were not about to take leave in Ireland, Plunkett declared, he would recommend that criminal charges be laid against the Police Magistrate for obstructing the ends of justice. Gipps endorsed Plunkett's view, but Simpson remained defiant. He told La Trobe it was "distressing in the extreme to be exposed to such unheard of threats". Assuring the Superintendent he was not being "led by any captious feelings", Simpson stated he was maintaining his stand until Plunkett withdrew his insulting and intimidatory remarks. After La Trobe expressed regret at Plunkett's note, and appealed again to Simpson's "sense of public duty", the Police Magistrate finally agreed to conduct the inquiry -- as his last duty before resigning in protest.[9]

The inquiry by Simpson and Lonsdale would result in manslaughter charges against two of the mounted troopers who'd dragged Harlequin to Melbourne on a dog chain. Michael Goodwin and Thomas Connock had been responsible for bringing the Aborigine the last 130 kilometres to the town, in two days. Evidence was given in their Supreme Court trial that when arrested, Harlequin had been in good physical condition. When he was delivered at the jail in Melbourne, the temporary watch-house keeper could not fit a finger between Harlequin's neck and the chain around it. The black's face was swollen, he was having great difficulty breathing, and was developing a fever. Assistant Colonial Surgeon Cussen told the court he'd visited Harlequin several times before he died two days later. Although he'd never seen anyone with similar symptoms die so quickly, he hadn't thought an inquest was necessary, and had only inspected the body "generally". Willis told the jury that the evidence showed the prisoners had only been obeying orders and had committed no "culpable excesses" in conveying Harlequin to Melbourne -- treating him kindly and giving him provisions whenever they'd stopped. The jury did not entirely agree with Willis. But nor did its members think that Goodwin and Connock should be punished for their actions. After a brief discussion of the judge's remarks without retiring, the foreman expressed the jury's deep regret that a life had been lost through "wanton neglect". Nevertheless, the verdict was not guilty.[10]

In the same sittings of the court, both Sievwright and Assistant Protector Parker were to provoke rebukes from Willis over the way in which they'd recorded and used depositions. The criticism of Sievwright came in the case of John Payne, the shepherd of the Henty brothers charged with manslaughter. Before sentencing Payne after his conviction to only an extra 24 hours in prison, Willis said Sievwright should never have taken the "most irregular and illegal" step of asking him under oath whether he killed his fellow shepherd. Similarly, Parker was censured by Willis for having taken statements on oath from five assigned servants in relation to the death of an Aborigine named Nahargabeen -- otherwise known as Abraham or Jemmy. Nahargabeen had been shot dead at the station formerly operated by James Darlot, Donald Simson and William Dutton, whose partnership had since broken up. William Jenkins, John Rennington, Edward Collin, Robert Morrison and William Martin were all charged with shooting with intent to do grievous bodily harm. Willis again had to make the point that statements on oath by the accused could not be used as evidence against them. Then when the only *prosecution* witness gave evidence that *he* had fired the first shot in self-defence when Nahargabeen and about 150 other blacks had attacked him and the defendants with spears, the case was quickly dropped.[11]

The *Port Phillip Herald* seized the opportunity to condemn Sievwright and Parker's "unwarrantable disregard of the laws of the land". Such "disreputable practices" should arouse the indignation of a free -- and British -- people with a sense of the wrongs they'd suffered and with the awful dangers to which they were being exposed by the tyrannical Protectorate and its ignorant officials. "The whole system of the Protectorate is rotten at the core, reform cannot be introduced; its constituent elements are subversive of every principle of equity, or justice, and being thus *radically* bad, must be wholly extirpated from the province. The Protectors, as a body, instead of a blessing, have proved a curse to the community at large, and as such we will not lose sight of them until they are removed from place and power," the *Herald* vowed.[12]

The following day, Willis would provide one final farcical episode in the ignominious chain of events that had started with Gipps' decision to send Major Lettsom to the Port Phillip District. Opening another Supreme Court session, Willis announced that because of a technicality he'd discovered, all convictions at the Quarter Session trials in Melbourne 20 weeks earlier had been illegal. Gipps, he told the Court, had agreed that the convictions should be annulled. Those convicted at the trials included Tarrokenunnin -- the only Lettsom detainee still in detention. He'd been in prison in Melbourne since being captured after escaping because La Trobe had been awaiting Gipps' instructions on where he would serve his sentence of 10 years' transportation. Suddenly declared a free man with Willis' shock announcement, Tarrokenunnin was released into the care of Assistant Protector Parker.[13]

There were some whites in Port Phillip who welcomed Tarrokenunnin's release. According to the *Port Phillip Patriot*, the sentence he and the other eight Goulburn blacks had received had been unjustifiably severe, inasmuch as it referred to crimes they were suspected of having committed, rather than to those of which they'd been convicted. Now that the convictions had been declared illegal, it was fearful to contemplate who was responsible for the wanton waste of human life that had occurred when the nine Aborigines were fired on as they jumped overboard from the cutter taking them down the Yarra. As well, the *Patriot* added, it had now been ascertained beyond doubt that the blacks had made their escape bid at the instigation of the white prisoners also on board, who'd hoped to take advantage of the confusion by escaping themselves.[14] However, the number of whites sympathetic to the Aborigines would soon drop dramatically, as news spread of the murders of three more white men -- this time in the far west of Sievwright's district.

The first murder to be reported to the authorities was that of Thomas Williams, a shepherd employed by a former wine merchant turned squatter named Matthew Gibson on the Glenelg River, in Bunganditj territory. Williams' murder was reportedly related to an incident involving a group of Bunganditj people who'd been prevented from stealing young potatoes from a garden at

Gibson's tent residence. Although they'd previously been on good terms, the incident had turned nasty, and Gibson's wife had produced a pistol to stop a black called Yarra from hitting another white woman at the station with a rake. That same day, Williams was murdered. The shepherd's dog brought some of Gibson's sheep back to the station long after dark, and several hundred more were found alive the next day before Williams' body was located, stripped naked. Then about 110 valuable ewes just about to lamb were found dead at an abandoned Bunganditj camp. The first two blacks to die in reprisal attacks by whites in the area included Yarra. They were only the first of many. One of Gibson's fellow squatters, John G. Robertson, would later describe the total number as "fearful".[15]

Even before Williams' murder became widely known, the grisly details of the murder of another squatter in the area, Edmund Morton, and a man he employed, William Lawrence, would set off a much bigger wave of fear of the Aborigines and thirst for revenge among the whites of the district. Morton for some time had been associating with a Bunganditj woman called Lewequeen, whose husband -- known as Long Yarra -- was the sole survivor of the massacre by the Whyte brothers a little over a year earlier. According to John Robertson, Morton's behaviour was "very unpardonable" and "at times deranged" -- implying that this had been the motive for his murder. In mid-May 1841, Morton and Lawrence -- nick-named Larry -- took Long Yarra and another black with them on a bullock-cart to strip bark about 10 kilometres from their head station. The white men were attacked that night as they slept.[16]

In a letter published in the Melbourne newspapers, sheep station superintendent Thomas Grant described what he found when he arrived at the scene a few days later: "A little on the right of the track, I observed what I considered at first was a white log with a large Eagle Hawk pecking upon it. Upon my nearer approach, the bird rose slow and heavily from the mangled remains of poor Mr Morton. He was stripped quite naked and lying on his face, the greater part of which was actually cut away. His head was one mass of frightful wounds, and (there were) many bruises on different parts of his arms and body, which was torn by birds of prey. About fifty yards nearer the dray lay the remains or skeleton of Larry, from whose bones the flesh had been completely cut off. The skin was cut a little above the wrists and ankles with a sharp knife or instrument; from all other parts the flesh was cut and nothing left but bare bones. God only knows whether they did not this before life was extinct, as the struggle with him had been long and dreadful. His arms were extended, and were speared through the wrists to the ground."[17] In a statement before Fyans, Grant added that he'd covered the remains of the two men with sheets of bark, but when he returned to the scene to bury them the following day, Lawrence's "nearly scalped" head had gone missing.[18]

The murders of Williams, Morton and Lawrence had already been reported to James Blair, a young Irishman with a limp who for six months had been the first Police Magistrate at the haphazard collection of mostly wooden buildings that comprised the township of Portland. The reports coincided with visits to the area by both La Trobe and Chief Protector Robinson, who was camped just outside the settlement. In fact, it was La Trobe who first told Robinson about the murders of Morton and Lawrence -- advising him to drop a plan to take a group of blacks into the township. They would have been the first Aborigines to enter Portland for several years, but the timing could not have been worse. Not only had the three murders just been reported, but there were rumours that other whites had been murdered by blacks in the area as well. There was a real danger of an immediate outbreak of violence if any Aborigines dared to enter the settlement.[19]

Referring to inter-racial clashes that had already taken place in the area, La Trobe had months earlier told Blair that he must use every means in his power to discourage "the spirit of reprisal which evinces itself among many of the (white) settlers, however cloaked beneath the natural desire to recover their property".[20] But Blair had responded by saying he was finding it "quite impossible" with the limited force at his disposal to produce anything like order in the district. "The labouring population appear to comprise the very dregs of society, who have been so long accustomed to act as they please that they cannot brook the slightest control," Blair had told La Trobe. He'd suggested that a small party of Mounted Police be permanently stationed in Portland, to be used to quell disturbances in the area. He'd also asked for a strengthened constabulary under his command to gain and maintain law and order in Portland itself. Most of the settlement's 250 or so residents, Blair complained, were men who'd absconded from indentured employment in the whaling industry started there by the Henty family. These men had lived lawless lives for years, and a much stronger force was needed to subdue and then control them, especially because Portland's remoteness precluded the possibility of procuring help from Melbourne in an emergency.[21]

La Trobe passed on Blair's request for reinforcements to Gipps, but the Governor quickly rejected the idea of any further increase in Port Phillip's police establishment. If he felt the need, La Trobe would have to redeploy the 10 Mounted Police based in Geelong under Fyans' command.[22] Less than two months after receiving this reply, La Trobe would inform Gipps of another appeal for reinforcements from Blair following the escape of three prisoners from the Portland lock-up. The Superintendent feared that as a new whaling season approached, the police force at Blair's disposal would be found to be

"altogether inadequate for the preservation of order or the repression of violence". He suggested that Portland be sent a corporal and 13 privates from
among a party of soldiers that was daily expected to arrive in Melbourne from
Sydney.[23] Gipps would eventually endorse the suggestion, some time after the
whaling season had started -- as had the reprisals over the killings by the
Bunganditj.[24]

Soon after returning to Melbourne from Portland, La Trobe would receive two
letters from Blair relating to Robinson's visit to the area. In the first, the Police
Magistrate remarked it appeared that Robinson's main purpose in setting up
camp near the township was "to establish a communication between the
Government authorities and the natives" by introducing some to him. Blair told
La Trobe that to Robinson's annoyance, he'd declined any such introduction
because of the murders recently committed by the blacks. "It would afford them
a pretext for congregating about the township and so lead to disturbances, or perhaps murders, which with the weak force at my disposal I could not possibly
prevent," he wrote. Blair added that Robinson had justly designated the tribes
in the area the wildest he'd met. He could therefore not understand why the presents which the Chief Protector had handed out to them had included a large
quantity of knives.[25] In the second letter, Blair added there'd been reports of
three or four more whites in the area having been killed. "I suggested to Mr
Robinson that he might confer a lasting benefit on the District by using his influence to have the murderers given up, but he gave me to understand that such
measures formed no part either of his duty or system," he wrote.[26]

Robinson had recorded in his journal his disgust at Blair's attitude towards the
Aborigines. The Police Magistrate had told him that he believed the government
should send troops to the area, to be used to round up the Bunganditj people and
demand the surrender of those involved in the recent killings. If they did not
surrender, Blair had declared he would "shoot the whole tribe". Such a measure
was not without its supporters. The *Port Phillip Gazette*, for instance, had commented it could not conscientiously condemn Morton or Lawrence's relatives if
they were to exterminate the tribe in retaliation. At a time when tensions were
already high, Robinson believed Blair was instigating further ill-feeling towards
the blacks. When Edward Henty had stated he had no doubt that the white settlers in the area were "dropping" the blacks, Blair had remarked in Robinson's
presence that he hoped so. "I thought of all men he is the most improper for his
present post," the Chief Protector wrote. "It is not the duty of any government
officers to neglect the one portion of Her Majesty's subjects for the sake of the
other. This is not justice." Robinson also recorded that judging by the reception
he'd received, the hatred that men such as Blair and Henty had for the Aborigines
-- whom they regarded as "hardly human" -- extended to those who'd been

appointed to be their Protectors.[27]

La Trobe had also just received a letter from Sievwright, in which he vigorously defended himself against the Superintendent's criticism of his actions in having started formation of his district's Aboriginal reserve at Keilambete. Notwithstanding what Robinson may have said, Sievwright stressed that he'd acted "with the distinct concurrence and authority of the Chief Protector". Robinson had instructed him to choose the actual site of the reserve. When he'd then suddenly been given the equipment and the men to start operations, he assumed his almost year-old recommendation of Keilambete had been endorsed. Furthermore, even during Robinson's recent visit to the site, he'd been assured that the recommendation had been forwarded to the government. Finally, Sievwright told La Trobe he was forwarding a copy of the letter outlining his defence to Robinson. He finished off: "I would respectfully add that when the discrepancies which now exist are explained by the Chief Protector, I trust your Honour will exonerate me from having acted 'improperly' or 'inadvisedly' -- as my proceedings have been actuated by a lively desire to carry out the duties entrusted to me, with that promptitude and diligence which the pressing claims of the Aborigines demand."[28]

In a quarterly report sent direct to La Trobe five days later, Sievwright highlighted the devastating effects of Robinson's order suspending agricultural operations at Keilambete and making him move to Lake Terang. During the five weeks before Robinson's arrival, the young and able-bodied among the 250 or so Aborigines who'd gathered at Keilambete had been actively employed in helping to form a homestead on the reserve. They'd cleared about 2.5 hectares of land, formed wells, and started a garden. When the work was suddenly stopped on Robinson's order -- and consequently the supplies on which the blacks had been depending were no longer available -- they'd become "highly insubordinate and in several instances extremely hostile". Since the move to Terang, there'd been the killings of the Bolagher girl, Worangaer, and the Jarcoort girl, Mootenewharnong. As well, a Bolagher man aged about 40 had died as a result of a spear wound received in one of a series of subsequent "alarming fights". Sievwright lamented he was now only authorised to hand out food to the sick, aged and children. In accordance with custom, this was shared with everyone in the camp. The number of blacks registered with him had now grown to 348, and there was not enough food to go around. If he'd been able to continue operations at Keilambete, the building needed for safe custody of the stores and equipment under his control would long ago have been built. The lack of such a building had proved such a massive problem that he was now unable to leave Terang to carry out his duties elsewhere in his district.

On three occasions while he was away from the camp for only a few hours, the blacks had taken the opportunity by threats to obtain from his sons the food that had been prepared for their own use. "On another occasion, the spears of two contending tribes, which I had placed in my tent for the better security of all parties, were in my absence forcibly taken away; on which occasion the overseer, constable and their wives were so alarmed, they declared they would not remain an hour amongst them were I to absent myself (unless firearms were furnished to them for their protection); their indecision and alarm being at once perceived by the natives, they do not fail to avail themselves of it," he added. "This alarm, however, has not been without cause, for at one time the party could not have

"Collecting such a body of savages was at the outset fraught at least with uncertainty..."

sustained more serious threats and decided indications of hostility, without actually coming to extremities -- and it is a matter of thankfulness and surprise a collision between them and the Crown prisoners attached to the service has hitherto been avoided." Even when he'd been at the camp, Sievwright reported, two of the blacks had used the threat of violence in unsuccessful attempts to make him hand over food. One had threatened him at spear point; the other with a firebrand. "As it is, nothing can for a moment be lost sight of that is not purloined, even to the abstraction of our own food while being cooked," he wrote.

"The experiment of collecting such a body of savages was at the outset fraught at least with uncertainty when supported by all that was required for success," the Assistant Protector declared. But the position of the whites involved had now certainly become dangerous. Sievwright noted that the Aborigines of the area had been encouraged to gather at Keilambete, under the assurance that their daily wants would be provided in a safe haven. But then he and his staff had been compelled to break faith with them. They'd had to explain as best they could that most supplies had been stopped, and the camp at Keilambete broken up, not because the Aborigines had failed in any way. Rather, they'd had to try to explain "that it was deemed proper that their interests and pressing wants, together with the efforts that were being made for their benefit and amelioration, should still be postponed, and the ultimate success of the object of the establishment hazarded, because the operations of the department had been commenced in the neighbourhood of a settler who had not received due notice". Furthermore, John Thomson had not been notified that a portion of the Crown land on which he was squatting was needed "for the purposes of a national undertaking" because the necessary communication on the subject had not been sent to the government by the Chief Protector -- even though he'd had 11 months to do so. "Under such circumstances, the claims of the settler were declared predominant to those of the Aborigines," Sievwright bitterly complained.[29]

CHAPTER 15
Pay backs

BY mid-1841 -- with transportation of British convicts already stopped, and assignment of convicts to private employment about to end -- the New South Wales pastoralists again started expressing deep concern over a shortage of cheap labour. Nowhere near enough people, they argued, were taking advantage of the systems devised to promote emigration from Britain. According to a petition to Gipps circulated in Sydney, the flocks which provided the colony's principal export to Britain were being subjected to "the most alarming deterioration and loss" because of a shortage of shepherds. At the same time, those British labourers who had arrived were demanding wages quite disproportionate to the value of wool "and to the general profits of agricultural and pastoral pursuits".[1] There were suggestions that more impoverished peasants could probably be induced to come from Ireland, but there was a strong belief in some quarters of the predominantly Protestant colony that a disproportionately high number of Roman Catholics had already arrived from there.[2]

There was even a proposal that the labour shortage could be at least partly addressed by bringing in some "proverbially sober and industrious Flemings" from Belgium as tenant farmers.[3] The pastoralists, however, wanted a much larger source of cheap and compliant labour. China had been mooted as one possible such source. Britain had since ruined this idea by launching a war there, in response to the Chinese government's impudence in trying to stop a lucrative trade British merchants had established based on large numbers of Chinese people becoming addicted to Indian opium. The pastoralists came to the overwhelming conclusion that despite the official opposition they'd previously encountered, they must revive their call for the mass importation of cheap "Hill Coolies" from India. The Sydney petition to Gipps argued that immigration of Indian coolies would be "the readiest and most effectual means" of averting a crisis that was jeopardising the prosperity of the colony.[4]

There could be no question, the *Sydney Herald* argued, that the best sort of labour for New South Wales was that supplied by British emigration. But this was providing only a quarter of the labour needed, and almost every intelligent colonist was now asking why coolies could not be imported to meet the demand. When the proposal had been raised back in 1837, the *Herald* recalled, the "hateful monster" of slavery had not long been abolished throughout the British

Empire. Such was the mood in Britain that the continued use of indentured Indian labour on sugar plantations in Mauritius and the West Indies was being denounced as slavery in disguise -- and when the proposal to send coolies to Australia was raised in the British Parliament, orders were sent to the colonial government in Calcutta to make sure it did not occur. Although doubtless motivated by "an amiable philanthropy", it had been "altogether gratuitous, impertinent and not less unkind to the Coolies" to compare the situation in the slave colonies to that in New South Wales -- where slavery had never existed. Besides, any doubts about the way in which coolies may be treated in Australia could easily be removed by enacting legislative safeguards.

The *Herald* envisaged two objections within the colony to the importation of coolies. "First, they are *foreigners*, bearing a different complexion, and speaking a different language from our own; and if incorporated in great proportions with our population by permanent settlement and by intermarriage, they would deteriorate our species, effeminating our British veins by an infusion of Asiatic blood," it commented. "But the inference thus educed is a begging of the whole question. *Would* they intermarry? The instinctive repugnance between the two races would be against such an alliance, and would prevent its taking place to any considerable extent. *Would* they permanently settle? We think not, both because their unconquerable attachment to their native soil, and to the social system peculiar to their own country, would unfit them for sitting down in the Colony as a home for life; and because it would be provided by law, as it was in the Mauritius, that at the end of the term of their engagement, a free passage back to India should be at their command. The prevailing idea under which they should emigrate should be, that they were leaving their native shores only for a season, and to return to them with a little fund for the evening of their days."

The second point that could be raised against the coolies, the *Herald* remarked, was that they were *pagans*. "But as their paganism would not impair their capabilities as shepherds and farm servants, what is the objection to it?" the paper asked. "Our recent opposition to a redundant immigration of Roman Catholics was grounded upon the sole consideration, that the Romish Church is essentially and unchangeably adverse to public freedom. But we have yet to learn that the coolies have any hierarchy at all, or that it ever entered their heads to claim the whole world as a spiritual appanage of their Hills. We have no fears of a Coolie priesthood undermining our Protestant institutions, nor of a Coolie Pontiff commanding us to do homage to his toe. We never heard of Coolie anathemas thundering over a heretic world, or of Coolie rescripts absolving subjects from their allegiance to unbelieving sovereigns. The Coolie superstition, however much it is to be deplored by Christians is, compared with the restless ambition of the Tiara, a quiescent and harmless dream. There would be no hope of them paganising us, but would there be no hope of our *Christianising* them?"5

In Port Phillip, too, there was renewed interest in the importation of coolie labour from India. If the proposal was again blocked by the British authorities, the *Port Phillip Patriot* suggested, the colonists of New South Wales should take advantage of the apparently far laxer attitude of the Paris government to such matters, and send ships to pick up labourers from the French-held port of Pondicherry, in south-east India. "The French Government has none of the mawkish sensibility which prevents the British Government from allowing the Coolies to leave the country, where they are frequently in a state of starvation, to come to a land of plenty, lest the pseudo-philanthropists of the mother country should again rave of slavery," the *Patriot* observed. It had consequently long been France's policy to encourage rather than check emigration from the parts of India it held. According to the *Patriot*, Gipps had often expressed support for the proposed introduction of Indian labourers. However, Gipps would that same week write to the latest Secretary of State for the Colonies, Lord John Russell, reiterating his opposition to the idea because of the "ultimate evils" he believed it would entail.6

A sub-committee of the New South Wales Legislative Council had just been formed to consider the subject of immigration. Headed by the first Anglican

Reproduced courtesy of the Mitchell Library, State Library of New South Wales
"Native encampment near the Murray, S.A. (South Australia)". The Governor of South Australia, George Grey proposed a plan to encourage Aborigines to adapt "to European habits and mode of life".

Bishop of Australia, William Grant Broughton, the committee was asked to look at the extent to which Aborigines may be used as farm labourers. "In a country where labour is so much in demand, it must appear strange to all who have their eyes directed on us that we should neglect the nearest source from which it is to be obtained," Gipps had told the Council. "I mean the real children of the soil, the aboriginal inhabitants of the country. Though by nature wild, and with difficulty induced to submit to the restraints which are imposed on ordinary labourers, abundant proof exists that they may be made to do so. I have seen some establishments myself, and am informed of others in which they have been, and still are, profitably employed." The issue was not to be taken lightly, Gipps stressed. Russell had just informed him that 15 per cent of the revenue of Crown land sales must be applied "to the civilisation and improvement of the Aborigines". Thankfully for Gipps, Russell had given him flexibility to decide how this 15 per cent target should actually be achieved -- and the Governor immediately announced that half the cost of maintaining Border Police should be included in it. The justification for this: "A police and Government Officers might have been necessary if the wilds had been entirely unpeopled, but not so numerous nor of so expensive a character."[7]

As the immigration committee sent out questionnaires to various parties around the country -- including Port Phillip's Aboriginal Protectors -- Gipps also put into circulation a report he'd received from Russell on how best to "civilise" the black Australians. The author was George Grey, a former British army captain who'd come to public attention by leading two exploratory missions in the west of the continent, and who'd recently taken up the post of Governor of the colony of South Australia. Half of Grey's report was devoted to what he regarded as the reason for the failure of all previous civilisation efforts in Australia: allowing the Aborigines to continue to practice their own "barbarous laws and customs" in matters not involving whites. In Grey's view, the Aborigines had been led to believe that certain actions, including murder, were only criminal when they were exercised towards white people -- and could be committed with impunity among themselves. Instead, the blacks should have been gradually taught that British laws had replaced their own -- even in matters only involving each other. The greatest obstacle in applying British law to them was their inability to give evidence in British courts. But Grey suggested that to help make them amenable to the white man's laws, their evidence could be accepted in cases involving themselves when borne out by strong circumstantial evidence. The report made only passing reference to the fundamental problem of language, even if this suggestion was to be adopted.

The other half of Grey's report related to how the Aborigines could be led to "civilisation" by teaching them to work for their colonisers. He suggested that white settlers be rewarded by receiving land either as a grant or at a discounted price for helping to "reclaim" Aborigines by employing them for at least six months. Under Grey's plan, inducements would also be held out to the black labourers. Those who could produce a certificate from a Protector saying they'd been employed by the same white settler for at least three years should also be entitled to land grants -- if possible in the territory of their birth. As well, they should receive a portion of the funds raised by government land sales to start their own farming operations by buying, for example, goats or poultry. Grey suggested that in areas where there were few whites, it would be "imprudent to induce many natives to congregate at any one point". But in areas with large white populations -- and where police or military forces were stationed -- they should be encouraged to "assemble in great numbers". These blacks, the captain asserted, could be used in opening new roads, or in repairing old ones. This mode of employment would be "singularly suited" to the habits of the Aborigines because it would keep them moving from place to place.[8]

Grey's plan was similar in some respects to the one that had been promoted in London by John Helder Wedge, the former Port Phillip Association surveyor whose nephews were still squatting in the far west of Sievwright's district. Wedge had argued that the Aborigines could hardly be expected to remain indifferent to being deprived of the land which had provided their means of subsistence. It was in the whites' interests to try to avoid the otherwise inevitable violence "by supplying them with food and raiment, to minister to their wants, to teach them domestic and useful habits, and to instil in their minds religious precepts". A certain quantity of land, Wedge suggested, should be granted to the colonists "for each individual native that was reclaimed and domesticated" for at least three years. As well, he proposed that stations should be established where huts should be built for the blacks' use. At these stations, they should be given daily rations of flour, potatoes, tea and sugar -- and occasionally blankets and tomahawks. As much as possible, they should be encouraged to trade "some commodity of their own produce" for these handouts. "The native women make a very neat and useful basket," he noted, "which would afford them constant employment, and for which a market might be found in the colonies, and they might even be sent to England." The adult male Aborigines might be encouraged to perform some "light employment" which should "bear the appearance of amusement", such as fishing.[9]

Gipps and La Trobe didn't much care for detailed proposals on how to deal with the Aborigines being made to the Colonial Office. There was always the danger that a new Secretary of State for the Colonies may decide in London that they were worthwhile -- and go beyond the usual practice of making only vague policy decisions. In Wedge's case, Russell merely asked for a report from La Trobe on the suggestion that the scheme could be tried on an experimental basis in Port Phillip.[10]   The Superintendent passed on the matter to the Chief Protector of Aborigines, and it was then forgotten until Gipps received another letter from Russell -- written more than a year later -- again asking for the report.[11] Informing La Trobe of the renewed request, Gipps described Wedge as a "troublesome and self-sufficient gentleman". The Governor promised to try to fob Russell off by telling him that Wedge had made "nothing but the most commonplace suggestions and observations that might have been made by anyone, whether acquainted or not with the Port Phillip District". He'd add that "in all essential particulars" the colonial administration had already gone far beyond what Wedge was suggesting.[12] In fact, when he wrote to London about the matter, Gipps would confine himself to this last remark -- without offering any explanation what he meant by it.[13]

An even more confounding letter was already on its way to London from Gipps aimed at dampening Russell's belief that George Grey's "civilisation" plan appeared to be "fit for adoption generally" in New South Wales.[14] In reference to Grey's suggestion that British law should apply to both races, the Governor wildly asserted that this was already the policy in the colony "in every respect". Gipps then acknowledged that there were differences in enforcing penalties, both by the colony's judges and by its executive government -- although this was "invariably in favour of the savage". He acknowledged, too, the inability of the blacks to give evidence in trials, but pointed out that the attempt by the colony's Legislative Council to partially overcome this had been blocked by the British government. Gipps went on to claim that the inability to give evidence worked in the Aborigines' favour as often as against them. Indeed, he reported, complaints had been long and loud among the settlers that the penalties of the law were rigorously enforced against whites who committed violence against the blacks -- while Aborigines were "almost invariably acquitted". At the same time, he admitted, there was some reason to believe that the difficulty in bringing the blacks to justice had engendered a disposition "in the minds of the less principled portion of the white population to take the law into their own hands". This had been the case when, nearly three years earlier, at least 28 Aborigines had been "barbarously murdered" in northern New South Wales, for which seven white men had been hanged. The Governor failed to remind Russell that no action had been taken against the squatters responsible for an even bigger massacre in the Port Phillip District -- the Whyte brothers -- despite Sievwright's insistence that they should face trial for murder.

The most important part of Grey's report, Gipps told Russell, was the one relating to the employment of the Aborigines. He was firmly convinced that, next to "the diffusion of Christian instruction", the enjoyments which the use of money

commanded would be the most effectual of all means of civilisation. Gipps
asserted that on various occasions he'd tried to persuade the colonists to look to
the blacks for a supply of labour. He'd also seriously considered a system of
rewards to people employing them as labourers for wages. However, he'd so far
been deterred from attempting it "by the fear of the abuses to which such a practice might lead, and the certain difficulties that would attend on the distribution
of the rewards". Gipps also pointed out that his opinions on the employment of
Aborigines were at variance with those of many people who considered it essential to keep them as far as possible out of contact with white men. It must be
admitted, he stated, that contact with whites would frequently expose the blacks
"to temptations which they may not be strong enough to withstand -- the men to
the use of ardent spirits, the women to be seduced from their husbands or natural protectors". But he believed that it would be by contact with whites," and by
being placed as nearly as possible on a par with them", that the civilisation of
the blacks was most likely to be advanced. Laws already existed providing for
penalties against whites who helped blacks obtain spirits or firearms, Gipps
concluded, and perhaps one would be devised to give "further protection" to
Aboriginal women.[15]

*A report by Sievwright on deaths of Aborigines in the Western District, from April to August, 1841. As
well as "where death took place", Sievwright has recorded the name, sex, tribe, marital status, and "supposed age" of the deceased. The names on the list are: Worongongaer, the 13-year old Bolagher female
killed at Lake Terang "by the Targurt (Jarcoort) Tribe"; Mootenewharnong, the 17-year-old Targurt
killed the same day in revenge by the Bolagher people; Canawarn, aged 50, "chief" of the Canawarn
tribe, who died at Lake Canawarn "from inflammation of bowels"; Camethon, a 40-year-old Bolagher
man who died at Boloke "from a spear wound in foot"; Yaradil, the young Targurt "killed when travelling with the Chief Protector" on the River Wannon (called Eurodap by Robinson); Jangite, a 50-year-
old Mainmait female who died at Terang from "inflammation of bowels"; Tatardeen, aged 40, a
Bolagher who died at Terang from pleurisy; Worongarite, a 40-year-old Targurt "chief's wife" who died
at Purrumbeet; and Werdong, aged 20, a Targurt woman who died at Leura from a spear wound. Thus,
assuming Camethon's wound was not accidental, five of the nine died at the hands of other Aborigines.*

One man who certainly believed such a law was warranted was the superintendent of the Buntingdale Wesleyan mission station south-west of Geelong, Benjamin Hurst. In a letter to La Trobe, Hurst dissented "in toto" from Grey's proposal to encourage blacks to work for white settlers -- partly because of "the awful and alarming extent to which the females are prostituted". The missionary told La Trobe he had ample evidence that his countrymen were "deeply and disgracefully" involved in this "abominable practice". Venereal disease was already "almost universal" among the blacks -- and was causing the early death of many. "I am driven to the conclusion that an attempt to civilise this people by attaching them to the stations of settlers would not only fail, but would be inflicting one of the greatest possible evils upon a people who are already sinking under the hand of oppression," Hurst wrote. "We have heretofore abstained from alluding to the share of guilt which attaches to individuals who would deem it an insult to be classed with shepherds and hutkeepers; but now that the welfare of the people for whose benefit we left our native land is so deeply in question, I think it is time to speak out. I have, therefore, no hesitancy in informing Your Honour that there is every reason (excepting only absolute proof) to believe that the prostitution of the native women is not confined to the lower order of Europeans. From these circumstances, it appears to me that should Captain Grey's plan be adopted, one of the most effectual measures would be taken to annihilate the wandering tribes of Australia, especially when I call to mind the fact that the half-caste children are destroyed almost as soon as they are born."

Hurst's letter had actually been written in response to a request from La Trobe for details of the killing of a black at the Buntingdale station. Relating this incident, the missionary reported that a party of about 200 blacks of a tribe or tribes he did not identify had arrived at the station for the avowed purpose of committing a murder in revenge for the death of an old man who had died of disease in the camp several months earlier. Their appearance and behaviour caused "the utmost alarm" among the Jarcoort Kirrae and Colijon people who'd been living at the station for some time, and several of them fled during the night. The following day, Hurst and his colleagues had tried every means they could devise to conciliate, but to no avail. About an hour after sunset, a number of the visitors clandestinely surrounded the breakwind of a Jarcoort man and drove several spears through his body. A few hours later, the rest of the Jarcoort blacks left the camp. The next day, the hostile party had left, apparently satisfied with its mission, taking with them a Colijon woman given up by her husband. Immediately afterwards, the other Colijon Aborigines announced that they were also all leaving, with the exception of six boys who'd previously been left in the missionaries' care by their parents or guardians.

"This is the second time during this year, that our people have been scattered by the same cause," Hurst wrote. "In both instances, they assigned as the reason for their leaving us, that we are unable to protect them from the aggressions of their enemies when they come upon them in large numbers, and that they are safer when wandering in the bush, where they cannot be so easily found." The victim in the previous incident had also been a Jarcoort. Two years earlier, the Jarcoort section of the Kirrae tribe had had numerous members. But nearly all of the Jarcoort fighting men had been "butchered in cold blood by Europeans". Hurst believed the Jarcoort people were now being victimised by other tribes because their numbers were now too small to dare to seek revenge. The missionary added that he believed reserves of land should be set aside for each tribe. However, the Jarcoort Kirrae blacks and the Colijon tribe -- being now both small groups -- might be prevailed upon to live on the same reserve, as they'd done at Buntingdale.[16]

Certainly, the massacre by Frederick Taylor and his accomplices near Mt Elephant had seriously depleted the number of Jarcoort warriors available for self-defence. They felt even more vulnerable after the second murder of a Jarcoort at the Wesleyan station, and their elders decided that the tribe should again seek refuge with Sievwright. Terang, after all, had originally been recommended by them to the Assistant Protector, and some Jarcoort people were still living in relative safety there. In fact, three young women who'd recently given birth at or near Terang had all been Jarcoorts. But an unsettled score remained against Warawel -- the Jarcoort man who'd murdered the Bolagher girl, Worangaer, at Terang a few weeks earlier. The Jarcoort girl, Mootinewharnong, had lost her life in immediate revenge, but a Bolagher man had since died of a spear wound received in the fighting that had taken place after Warawel's attack. He'd been a relative of Worangaer, so Warawel still had to submit himself to the united wrath of the family. If he survived the ordeal, he would have expiated his offence. After leaving Buntingdale, the Jarcoort people crossed into the territory of their Colijon allies, and sent a "wergher" to negotiate with the Bolagher people at Terang on the conditions for their return.[17]

Werghers were messengers chosen for their linguistic and diplomatic skills, sent for instance to issue an invitation to a meeting to settle a dispute. The nature of a particular mission was indicated by the colour and pattern of the stripes of clay painted on the face and body of the wergher. The actual message was often carried on a piece of wood, engraved with notches and other markings. A code of behaviour relating to werghers which transcended tribal boundaries was strictly observed. Their duty was sacred, and their personal safety was assured while in foreign territory, regardless of the nature of the tidings they brought.[18] Sievwright recorded what happened when a wergher arrived at his destination:

"They at once proceed to the Hut of the Chief, or in his absence to that of one of the Elders of the Tribe, with whom they are to communicate. Room is made for them, and food and water brought to them. They remain silent and preserve the most impertunable gravity of demeanour, nor is a question asked of them until they have finished their meal and choose of themselves to begin the conversation. I have known an hour to elapse ere a word has been uttered. Before I knew the nature of their office, or the dignity and importance attached to it, I have endeavoured by every method to induce these werghers at once to speak, and reply to my questions, but without success. Nothing would overcome their silence and gravity, and I have been astonished to find the active, lighthearted and merry companion, who had left me a few weeks before, return as I imagined an austere, sullen and apparently evil-disposed savage, until all was explained when he in the course of the evening came to my tent, disburdened of his mission, and relieved from its ceremonies, not less willing to relate what he had to tell, than anxious to learn every particular connected with what had occurred in his absence."[19]

The meeting at which Warawel would undergo his ordeal was arranged by werghers painted with red stripes who travelled between the Bolagher people camped at Terang and the Jarcoort blacks who'd moved into Colijon territory in June 1841. Warawel would arrive at Terang late in the month accompanied by 53 other blacks. Sievwright would later record that most were Colijon. Most of the rest he would register as Woordy Yalloc -- the section of the Barrabool tribe who frequented the country north of Colijon territory. On their arrival at the camp, Sievwright reported, the Colijon and Woordy Yalloc chiefs deposited their spears at a distance, then walked over and sat down in silence in front of the Bolagher huts. One of the Bolagher elders immediately went and picked up the spears, carried them to the hut of the Bolagher chief, and placed them among his weapons. This was an invitation for the visitors to stand and enter the hut. A short time later, the visiting chiefs went through a similar ritual before entering Sievwright's tent to tell him they would be staying at Terang for "one moon". Most of their people had gone to visit the rest of the Barrabool tribe, with whom they intended returning when he sent a messenger to fetch them. Meanwhile, Warawel would be offering battle to Worangaer's relatives.

Warawel and two fellow Jarcoort men accompanied the chiefs on their visit to Sievwright's tent, but they did not leave their weapons outside, remaining fully-armed. Their faces and bodies were painted with red clay, in various designs, and their hair was gathered into a knot. Around their waists and ankles they wore bands of green leaves, as was often the practice during corroborees. Warawel, Sievwright would recall, had the air of "a haughty and courageous warrior" -- refusing to even acknowledge questions put to him. The two Jarcoort

June 1841.

Statement of Aborigines fallen in with in Western District by Assist. Prot. Sievwright

Day of Month	Names	Male	Female	Remarks	Day of Month	Names	Male	Female	Remarks

"Statement of Aborigines fallen in with in Western District by Assistant Protector Sievwright". Listed are 53 members of the "Woordy Yalloc" and "Colijohn" tribes, who accompanied the Jarcoort man, Warawel, to Terang when he was to undergo his ordeal for killing the Bolagher girl, Worangaer. For a full list of the 53 names, see table opposite page.

warriors with him were apparently meant to be body-guards, but Warawel seemed to consider that his safety depended on his own constant vigilance. His eyes never rested for a moment on the same object, and the slightest movement he watched "with intense distrust". Warawel's nervous behaviour would continue for four days, while the various tribes represented at Terang held corroborees -- and more of Worangaer's relatives arrived at the camp. Finally, Sievwright was informed that the battle would take place the following morning at dawn. Then late that evening, a group of terrified Bolagher blacks went to Sievwright's tent, saying they'd discovered that Colijon friends of Warawel had a musket which they intended using to support him. It was with "much difficulty" that the Protector persuaded them he would ensure this did not occur.

Soon after dawn, the pre-battle ceremony began. Warawel and the other two Jarcoort men were painted and decorated as before -- with the addition of a quantity of feathers and the down of large birds attached to their hair and beards. Gesticulating and screaming, they ran backwards and forwards in front of their huts, holding a shield in one hand and spears and other weapons in the other. Behind them, the Jarcoort and Colijon men were preparing to fight, as were the Bolagher men on the other side of a stretch of flat ground. After a few minutes, Warawel and his two comrades slowly advanced towards the Bolagher fighters by a zig-zag route, stamping their feet violently, and stretching their limbs in various directions. Then they performed pirouettes, first on one leg, then on the other, before finishing the challenge by dropping on one knee, supporting themselves on their shields, while holding their weapons aloft at arms length.

Three Bolagher men immediately responded by approaching the open ground in a similar manner. As they did so, two Bolagher women, with wreaths of leaves tied around their waists and ankles, also came forward. They moved between the two groups of fighters, continually shaking small branches they were holding, dancing, stamping their feet, and singing. At one time, it seemed to Sievwright, their songs were meant to encourage their own party, while at another they were meant to scorn the enemy. Warawel threw a spear towards the Bolagher men, but it was easily avoided, and thrown back, again missing its target. The three Bolagher men continued their approach until they, too, dropped on one knee. All the men of the various tribes then followed suit, until more than

---

fifty heavily-armed and apparently ferocious men a side had formed what appeared to Sievwright to be "an assembly of the most infuriated and intrepid beings that could possibly be witnessed".

The stature of the warriors, Sievwright would recall, seemed to have been increased by the manner in which they were painted and ornamented. At the same time, their attitude conveyed a strong impression that their courage would not be easily subdued, or their fortitude shaken. A general engagement seemed inevitable. But suddenly, a pistol shot rang out from the Colijon huts, and Sievwright was astonished by the reaction. Instead of the men launching into the disciplined fight for which they'd so elaborately prepared, the battle ground

"Soon after dawn, the pre-battle ceremony began..."

was in an instant deserted "like a well-rehearsed scene in a Pantomine". The warriors had been prepared to subject themselves to possible dreadful injuries from the crude weapons of their opponents, but the pistol shot sent many flying for shelter into the forest. Others rushed into Sievwright's tent for protection. Some of the Bolagher people approached Sievwright, accusing the Colijon blacks of unacceptable treachery, and demanding that they be immediately ordered from the camp. After unsuccessfully trying to obtain the firearm, Sievwright with much regret complied with the Bolagher demand. The Colijon people left straight away to return to their territory.[20]

A few days later, Fyans' Border Police would add to the turmoil among the Aborigines in the district when they dispersed a gathering of Barrabool blacks

at Geelong, and drove them from away from the town. It was a "salutary" measure, the *Geelong Advertiser* declared, which had become necessary for seasonal
reasons. "During the summer, nothing could exceed the honesty and general
good conduct of the blacks," it acknowledged. "But as the winter set in, and
their necessities increased, they have been less scrupulous, and several thefts
have taken place, particularly of intoxicating liquors. The whole tribe has several times managed to get drunk, and they were fast becoming more and more
degraded. A few more seasons of such conduct would soon bring them down to
the level of the Sydney blacks, and lead to their final destruction."[21]

In the same edition, the *Advertiser* would refer to the "very troublesome"
behaviour of the blacks around the series of hills to the north of Mt Rouse grand-
ly called the Grampians by the whites, though they were hardly of the scale of
the mountain chain of that name across Scotland. One station just east of the
Grampians, operated by brothers George and Harry Thomson, had recently been
raided twice. Armed parties were sent in pursuit, the *Advertiser* reported, but
even though the flocks were only in the blacks' possession for short periods, a
total of about 150 "of the finest wethers" had been lost. No mention was made
of any violence having been committed by the whites -- before, during, or after
the robberies.[22] George Robinson, who would pass through the area soon after
the incidents, found it easy to see why the Thomson brothers had been attracted
to the area. It included "extensive, open downs, green and covered with a close
and luxuriant herbiage".[23] But the Chief Protector would also be stunned by the
evidence he found of why the area was so important to the Tjapwurong people.

CHAPTER 16
Explanations

ONE notion widely accepted by British colonisers was that the Aborigines of the Port Phillip District were accustomed to a nomadic lifestyle. According to this belief, as the European settlement gradually expanded, displaced blacks were not being greatly inconvenienced because they could simply move to other areas. In the western part of the district, the number of semi-permanent Aboriginal dwellings that were occupied on a regular or seasonal basis -- some partly made of stone -- could have shaken this misconception. But before their existence could become widely known, many had been destroyed by whites who did not want recognition of attachment by particular Aborigines to specific territory. In other cases, the number of semi-permanent dwellings simply dwindled along with the number of their users. At the same time, suggestions that the Aborigines may have had considerable technological skills would be treated with mirth by most whites. Yet in the Western District where whites had so far ventured in relatively small numbers, there was ample evidence that this was the case.

There was also widespread ignorance among the white population of the fact that a great cultural diversity existed among the Aborigines. Just among the tribes whose territory fell within the Port Phillip District there was, for instance, a wide variety of languages, religious beliefs and ceremonies, ornamentation, and weaponry. The language barrier of course made it extremely difficult for any interested whites to gain information about the Aborigines beyond what they could personally observe. Without the ability to verbally confirm suspicions, it was easy to draw wrong conclusions. As well, an ever-present element of mutual mistrust, if not fear, was not conducive to the two races reaching a basis for peaceful co-existence -- if ever the question of land-sharing could be resolved. Unique among the whites in being able to at least try to bridge the gulf were those paid to live and move and among the blacks -- George Robinson and his assistants, and a handful of missionaries. Most of the other whites who came into regular contact with the Aborigines would rather they had not done so, except when the men were needed for cheap labour, or the women for sex.

Despite his misgivings about the Protectorate, La Trobe realised he and Gipps were under pressure from London to at least be seen to be giving it a fair trial, especially after the violence both by and against the Aborigines in the last half of 1840. When he ordered Robinson to make his trip into the Western District, La Trobe declared it was primarily a peace mission. According to the Superintendent's instructions, the Chief Protector was supposed to use the trip "to attempt to open a friendly communication" with the tribes to the west of Lakes Corangamite and Colac. He also made particular reference to the tribes in the vicinity of the Grampians, north of Mt Rouse. La Trobe promised to take whatever steps he could to repress any further clashes between the Aborigines and the white settlers of the district. But first, Robinson would need to gather the detailed information which he'd been unable to obtain from Sievwright on the causes, character and results of the clashes which had already occurred. As usual, the Superintendent had expressed excessive confidence in Robinson's

Reproduced courtesy of the La Trobe Picture Collection, State Library of Victoria
"View of Mount William in Western Victoria" (in the Grampians) by Eugene von Guerard.

abilities. "Your acknowledged experience in the proper line of conduct which it is recommendable to pursue in effecting the objects proposed by your journey, relieves me from the necessity of offering you any suggestions," he'd remarked.[1]
  In response, Robinson had pointed out that the area he'd be visiting was extensive, and that he could not tell how easily he'd be able to carry out his mission.[2] He gave La Trobe no indication how long the journey may take -- and once it was underway he was in no hurry to complete it. Robinson did not confine himself to an investigation into the state of inter-racial relations. Rather, he took the opportunity to mount a self-promotion exercise among the Western District Aborigines. In addition to the considerable supplies he took from Melbourne,

La Trobe had authorised him to acquire any further gifts he wanted "to conciliate the goodwill of the tribes" with which he came into contact.[3] The Chief
Protector's purchases along the way would include more than 200 extra rugs and
blankets, and dozens of tin pannicans and clay pipes. As well, he would buy
sacks of flour and potatoes, and quantities of mutton, sugar, tea and tobacco. On
numerous occasions, he would dole out his largesse to groups of blacks -- most
of whom had received nothing from his ill-supplied assistant responsible for
their welfare.[4]

Backed by La Trobe's inordinate faith, Robinson tackled his mission with an
undoubted belief that he had an exceptional ability to relate to the Aborigines
and gain their confidence. Unfortunately, his jealous and destructive relationship with Sievwright only reinforced this belief. He set off on the journey convinced that his abilities would enable him to overcome the massive language difficulties which had been hampering Sievwright's operations. His strategy was
to induce blacks from different tribes to accompany him into the territory of others, to act as interpreters. Robinson would later boast that the strategy had
worked perfectly well, enabling him to open a friendly communication with all
of the tribes of the Western District -- most of them personally, the rest by word-
of-mouth. But his report to La Trobe of his journey would include the names of
more than 60 supposed "tribes" or sections of tribes.[5] It would not give the
Superintendent a clear picture of which Robinson believed were the major ones,
and what territory they occupied. La Trobe would have been even more confused if Robinson had included the names of all the alleged tribal groups he'd
mentioned in his journal. Near part of the border between Bunganditj and
Gunditjmara territory, for instance, he'd recorded the names of nine so-called
local tribes.[6]

Robinson would tell La Trobe he'd conducted a census of the Western District
tribes, and gathered details of their habits, manners, customs, languages, and

Reproduced courtesy of the La Trobe Manuscripts Collection, State Library of Victoria
Examples of Western District Aboriginal huts, as sketched by Assistant Protector William Thomas

"every other useful information that time would permit". Robinson also claimed to have obtained information about inter-tribal relations, but his report would give few details of them. There was even less information about the causes and results of inter-racial clashes, despite La Trobe's explicit instructions to obtain it. The reason of course was largely because the Chief Protector had faced the same language difficulties as Sievwright. Robinson acknowledged in his report that it was impossible for Protectors or missionaries involved with the Western District Aborigines to be "perfectly cognisant" of all their activities in such a large area. But he declined to mention to La Trobe the difficulties he'd faced with the language barrier.[7] The Chief Protector made no attempt to hide the fact in his private journal. He would realise that there were wide differences in the languages of the district, and he certainly experienced problems in verifying information. "The difficulty and uncertainty of persons getting correct information from the natives is apparent from the mistakes of all who have attempted it," he recorded in the journal. "I am compelled to use, with all my experience, much caution, and it is only by confronting several natives and repeating it often that I can consider it correct. And notwithstanding this, I am liable to err -- but how much more those who have not the same advantages."[8]

Robinson's main interpreter for more than half of the journey would be the young Jarcoort named Eurodap who'd been among the very first group of Western District Aborigines he'd encountered. Two months into the journey, he realised that Eurodap's skills as an interpreter were far from perfect, but he'd found no better. Then, a little over a month later, Eurodap was dead -- speared by a fellow black called Pongnorer while in the territory of the Bunganditj, far from his own. Robinson would mention the killing in his report -- and that one of Eurodap's grieving tribesmen, Inergerook, had vowed to return with other Jarcoort warriors to destroy Pongnorer and his people. But it evidently did not occur to Robinson that the incident showed his modus operandi was perilous for the participants. Although saddened by the incident, it did not cause him to review his policy of taking Aborigines into the territory of other tribes, without any knowledge of existing or potential strife.[9]

Language difficulties of course did not stand in the way of Robinson making observations about aspects of the lives of the Western District Aborigines, and there was much he found fascinating. He was, for instance, impressed with some of their housing. In Kirrae territory, he found several camps of mostly dome-shaped huts. He recorded that they were usually made with a framework of sticks, closely packed together, then covered with bark and turf, the grass side downwards. In one camp, he found a camp of nine such huts. Each hut, with an open doorway at one end, was large enough for seven or eight people. Almost a month later, about 100 kilometres to the north-west, he would find a village of 13 similar huts. One of them, about three metres in diameter, was "sufficiently strong for a man on horseback to ride over".[10]

But probably the feature of the lifestyle of the district's Aborigines which impressed Robinson most was the elaborate systems they'd devised for catching eels and other fish. In Kirrae and Gunditjmara territory, he found weirs up to about 90 metres wide built across creeks and rivers. The weirs were made initially by driving thick forked sticks vertically into the river bed. Other sticks were then closely interlaced across the river, using the vertical ones as supports. A few small gaps were left in the wall of the weirs, which each held a long tapering "arrabine" made of plaited matting material, in which the eels would be caught as the water rushed through. Even more impressive to Robinson, though, were the eel-trapping systems he found in Tjapwurong territory, near where the robberies had recently occurred on the run operated by George and Harry Thomson.

These involved the digging of networks of trenches "at great cost of labour" by using a stick chisel sharpened at one end, the soil displaced being used to form embankments. In one spot, Robinson estimated that there were trenches dug over an area of about six hectares, with their total length amounting to several kilometres. The system would be in full operation after heavy rains, when the whole of the water of a creek was made to pass through it before reaching a marsh. Here and there along the way, small gaps were made in the trench walls where water was allowed to escape through eel traps. Around the trench network, many large mounds had been made, similar to those common at Aboriginal campsites in other parts of the Western District. There were ovens dug into each of the mounds for baking the catch. One mound covered almost 20 metres by 30 metres of ground, and over years of use had built up to about two metres high.[11]

Some of the Aborigines whom Robinson met had had little or no contact with Europeans, and he was occasionally amused by what happened during his meetings. One day, he would record an incident in which a group of blacks were given a muslin dress. It was "much admired", especially by one man who would put it on himself instead of his wife -- back to front! On another occasion, Robinson's horse was "an object of great attraction", especially to one man who was highly surprised to see the Chief Protector take off the saddle. "Had it been part of the horse, his wonder could not have been greater," Robinson wrote in his journal. "He probably thought it belonged to the beast". On other occasions, groups of Aborigines were surprised to see Robinson putting on gloves, and writing with his pen and ink.[12]

However, by the time Robinson made his journey, most of the blacks of the Western District had at least had some interaction with the whites -- and numerous times he was disturbed by the physical and psychological effects. He would witness many examples of what he regarded as the evil influence shepherds and other white labourers were having among the black population. One obvious manifestation of the problem was the extent of venereal disease among the Aborigines which Sievwright and Benjamin Hurst had already reported. Robinson would also see many examples of what he believed was moral degradation. One evening, he would record having heard two young Aboriginal girls repeating "obscene, scurrilous and blasphemous language", apparently with no understanding of what they were saying. "Some of the words were: well done fuckumoll, go it fuckmoll, good-night fuckmoll," Robinson recorded. "Fuckmoll and fuckomoll were often repeated." These girls were among the many Aboriginal females he believed were encouraged to stay at certain stations by nefarious white men "for improper purposes".[13]

At other stations, the Chief Protector found that the squatters were not particularly fond of employing emigrant labourers because they tended to be frightened of Aborigines. "They prefer the emancipated convict," he wrote. "That is, in other words, the conscience of the latter are seared, and they will meet their wishes in destroying blacks." Overall -- whether emigrant, convict, or former convict -- Robinson found the class of white labourer to be a great impediment to good race relations. The Chief Protector would report to La Trobe that most of the white servants were "depraved", and all were armed. "And in the estimation of some of these characters, with whom I conversed, I found that the life of a native was considered to be of no more value than that of a wild dog," Robinson wrote. On one station, he described the whites as "the most profligate wretches" he'd met. On another station, a squatter would tell Robinson his men were "a great set of scoundrels" who were impossible to manage. Then a few weeks later, he would be shocked by the heartless manner in which Charles Winter and his men reacted to the murder of Eurodap. So dismayed was he by their reaction that he "could almost become a misanthrope".[14]

The following day, Robinson would hear details from the young squatter, Robert Tulloh, of an event which had occurred while he and others were searching in Tjapwurong territory for sheep stolen from Peter Aylward's station a year earlier. A Tjapwurong boy aged about six had been captured in a river, then taken to a fire, where he'd been tortured by burning by one of Tulloh's men named George Robson. When the child had thrown a stick at Robson, the "natural ruffian" had kicked him to death. Tulloh claimed he'd cocked his pistol and pointed it at Robson, but had then been too frozen with horror by what he'd seen to pull the trigger. It was another example of what the Chief Protector would see and hear on his Western District trip that would lead him to record: "There are persons who have no more of humanity about them than their shape."[15]

Reproduced courtesy of the Public Record Office of Victoria

"Return of Work done by the Aboriginal Natives of the Mainmait, Elangamite, Bolagher and Targurt (Jarcoort) tribes, Western District, during the month of July 1841." With most work at Lake Terang suspended on Robinson's orders, Sievwright was able to provide employment for only 11 blacks, 10 of whom worked every day of the month except Sundays "fencing and stripping bark". A separate return in the PRO shows the daily payment was one pound (454 grams) of rice and one ounce (28 grams) of sugar. During the month Minmuck also received four ounces of tobacco.

Nevertheless, as Sievwright had reported, Robinson would find that ill-feeling towards the blacks in the district was not universal. In fact, the Chief Protector would find that those squatters who'd made the effort to have good relations with the local Aborigines were generally pleased with the results. Several white settlers would tell Robinson that they'd had no trouble at all with the blacks. Aboriginal labour was being used by many squatters, even by some with a history of violent relations, such as the Whyte and Winter brothers. The range of duties assigned to the blacks included bullock dray driving, ploughing, felling and grubbing trees, and stock-keeping. One squatter told Robinson he'd been saving money by using black instead of white shearers. At a station operated for the previous three years in Barrabool territory by two sons of a Scottish baronet, Thomas and James Dennistoun Baillie, the blacks had been constant visitors and labourers. One of the brothers told Robinson that the Barrabools had been given free access to the homestead, and in the entire time nothing had been stolen.[16]

The most extensive employer of black labour, though, had been the Western District's Assistant Aboriginal Protector. And he would have much to say about it in his reply to the questionnaire about black employment sent out by the Legislative Council's immigration committee while Robinson was on his tour of the district. Sievwright told the committee that he'd known of the Aborigines performing a service for which no European could be found -- namely the unloading of vessels onto the beach at Geelong, and then carrying the cargo to the stores, in the heat of summer. He'd also known Aborigines to be employed from sunrise to sunset for days washing sheep, and to be employed for months at a time as efficient shepherds. "Their average services as such, were esteemed by the settlers, much superior as to carefulness and assiduity of conduct than those reckless characters which have hitherto chiefly composed the servants of the district," Sievwright reported. As labourers, Sievwright found, the prevailing feature in the Aborigines was "indolence, or that love of ease which all nations indulge in when there is no immediate call for activity". He told the committee: "A few hours' daily excursion in the Bush is quite sufficient (where their country is not overrun with the white population) to supply their wants, and knowing this they are quite improvident of the morrow." Sievwright believed he'd found the solution to overcoming this attitude. "Creating amongst them fictitious wants, by the introduction of our luxuries, such as Tea, Sugar, Tobacco, Flour etc., has succeeded with most of them in enducing them to work," he reported.

Nevertheless, Sievwright had not been in a position for some time to pay for work performed. Since his activities were suspended, pending the outcome of Robinson's tour, he'd been restricted to handing out small amounts of food to the sick, aged and children at Terang. This food, along with what could be obtained

RETURN

Shewing the total quantities of Provisions and other Articles issued during the month of *August* 184*1*, from *1st* to *31st* inclusively, for the *Western* District.

TO WHOM ISSUED.	PROVISIONS, &c.									ARTICLES OF CLOTHING AND OTHER NECESSARIES.									
	Flour, lbs.	Meat, lbs.	Tea, lbs.	Sugar, lbs.	Rice, lbs.	Salt, lbs.	Soap, lbs.	Tobacco, lbs.	Blankets, No	Rugs, No	Police Jackets, No	Jackets, No	Trowsers, No	Shirts, No	Frocks, No	Chemises, No	Caps, No	Shoes, No	Pannicans, No	Knives, No	Tomahawks, No
To Aborigines, sick, aged, and young children	1108½	288	10.7	744.9	34.5	12	8	0	9	4	4	4	4	4	4	4	11	11	11	11
To Aborigines, for work performed																				
To Native Police																				
To Native Women and Girls																				
To Native Men and Boys																				
+ Europeans	139½	93	2.14	14.8	11	2.14	117	4	4	4	4	4	4	4	4	4	4	4		
Total	1328	381	13.6	59.1	34.5	14.14	9.7	0	9	4	4	4	4	4	4		4	4	4	
Quantity remaining on hand	3723½	490	22¾	63½	7	9½	36¼	100	26	0	0	0	0	0	0	0	0	0	0	0

I hereby certify that no Provisions or any other Article belonging to the Government, under my charge, have been issued to any person except to those entitled and duly authorised to receive the same.

N.B. The articles marked with an asterisk are given as rewards for merit, good conduct, or work performed.

To   The Chief Protector.

+ *Ratios for 1 Constable + 2 drawn prisoners attached to establishment.*

[signature]
ASSISTANT PROTECTOR.

Reproduced courtesy of the Public Record Office of Victoria

During August 1841, Sievwright was able to issue a total of just 1188 pounds (539 kg) of flour; 288 pounds (130 kg) of meat; 345 pounds (157 kg) of rice; 44 pounds (20 kg) of sugar; and small quantities of tea, salt and soap to "sick, aged and young" Aborigines.

from hunting, was still being shared among all the 270 or so Aborigines camped with him, meaning that none were getting enough. Sievwright believed that with so many blacks collected in one spot, and a scarcity of food, it was surprising that he was able to maintain discipline of any kind in the camp. "When idleness and inactivity are allowed to prevail, the worst propensities of the individual, be he savage or civilised, are sure to predominate," he reported. "Hence, daily contentions among themselves, petty thefts in the camp, hourly complaints of want of food, have been followed by depredations of the most serious description upon the flocks of the adjacent settlers..." The settlers had stated that they'd recently suffered more from Aboriginal theft than at any previous time. "I would therefore again urgently and respectfully entreat that the intentions of the government, with the orders for my future proceedings, be communicated with the least possible delay, in order that no further odium may be incurred in the district from the protracted operations of this branch of the department."[17]

The Protectorate's bad reputation in the Western District was certainly becoming even worse, as reports increased of sheep thefts by the Aborigines. In one raid on the station of John Bromfield, near Geelong, 125 sheep were said to have been stolen. A search party was organised, the *Geelong Advertiser* reported, but by the time the sheep's tracks were traced to a deserted Aboriginal camp, all the animals had been eaten. In the middle of the camp, there was "a good log yard" where the sheep had been held. The author of the report, apparently a squatter, said he could state that more than 300 blacks had participated in the feast -- 200 of whom had left Sievwright's camp at Terang a week earlier. "As we are debarred from the pleasure of teaching them right from wrong ourselves, to whom are we to look for protection?" he asked. "For what do we pay the assessment on our stock? Is it not to afford us some security against ravages of this nature?" In a commentary on the report, the *Advertiser* lamented the squatters were showing a remarkable degree of apathy over such "scenes of rapine", which were the inevitable result of the policy of concentrating large numbers of Aborigines in one spot. "Let the matter be taken up vigorously by the local press, backed by the settlers, and the subject will ultimately be forced upon the notice of our rulers, and the influential part of the British public, through a thousand channels," the *Advertiser* suggested. "We are not without advocates at home, and a hint dropped in the colonies may be picked up in England, and made use of in the promotion of colonial reform and the substitution of some sounder system of policy than the present, which is alike injurious to the interests of the settlers and of the Aborigines."[18]

One of the squatters to complain about the gathering of blacks at Terang was former trading vessel captain, James Webster, based only about 20 kilometres from Sievwright's camp at the hill the Kirrae people called Bo'ok -- known to

the whites as Mt Shadwell. Webster told La Trobe that the "dreadful depredations" of the Aborigines had reached such a pitch that if something was not done
to stop them, he had every reason to believe there would be "the most serious
consequences" for both races. "Their attacks, I may say, are almost nightly,"
Webster wrote. "And sometimes even in open day the shepherds are rushed."
The squatter claimed that every white settler in the neighbourhood had suffered
losses. He'd personally lost more than 200 sheep in the past three months. On
one occasion, the blacks had attacked one of his shepherds and stolen about 400
sheep. Most had been located by a search party "secured in a regular bush yard",
but 44 of his best ewes, just about to lamb, had been slaughtered.

"I may remark that last year, and up to the time that the Protector of Aborigines
settled in the neighbourhood, I never lost a sheep -- scarcely even saw a native
-- and never on any occasion came into collision with them," Webster added. "I
have repeatedly reported their aggressions to the Assistant Protector, taken the
nooses that have been found round the sheeps' necks that have escaped from
them, shown him the spears that have been thrown, but it appears that he can do
nothing to put a stop to these enormities and acknowledged the natives were

Reproduced courtesy of the Public Record Office of Victoria
*Between 1 March and 31 August 1841, Sievwright recorded the births of six Aboriginal children in the
Terang-Kilembeet (Keilambete)-Mt Leura area . The births are listed by date, mother's name, sex, tribe,
where born, and age of mother. The 20-year-old mother of the first of five Targurts (Jarcoorts) born in
the period was Baridgerneen. Her boy was born at Keilambete. The other four Targurt births were:
Ninegobeen (girl at Terang); Borborneuck (boy at Leura); Cararderneen (girl at Terang); and
Walanagourk (girl at Terang). The sixth birth was to a 17-year-old Colijon mother, Cocodelingong, who
had a girl at Leura on an unspecified date in July.*

utterly beyond his control." Webster obviously understood Sievwright's diffi-culties. "If tribes are encouraged to come from all quarters and not fed, it is nat-urally to be expected that they will rob and plunder especially if not punished," he wrote. The squatter had no doubt that the blacks who were committing thefts were well known to the others, and could be identified and punished -- or at least ordered away from Sievwright's camp. The stationing of a couple of Mounted Police in the area would do "incalculable good, by showing that their depreda-tions have attracted the attention of Government". The police would also be a means of preventing the bloodshed which he believed would occur if the blacks' repeated and daring attacks continued. Webster suggested that the police should be placed under the command of either himself or John Thomson -- the two hon-orary magistrates in the area.[19]

Immediately on receiving Webster's letter, La Trobe wrote to Foster Fyans, requesting a report on the situation around Mt Shadwell, at the same time autho-rising him to take whatever steps he might deem necessary to prevent clashes.[20] The following day, La Trobe would inform Robinson that he'd decided to sus-pend Sievwright's salary, over his criticism of Fyans' actions in the area after the murder of John Thomson's shepherd more than a year earlier. The reason: La Trobe had not received the statement demanded from Sievwright months earli-er, in which he was supposed to explain his claim that the Crown Lands Commissioner had made an "indiscriminate attack" on some blacks while attempting to apprehend the murderers of Thomas Hayes. After taking his own depositions in the case, Sievwright had been in great haste to ensure that they reached the legal authorities, lest those taken by Fyans were believed to be the only ones relating to the matter. But in his haste, Sievwright had committed a basic bureaucratic mistake: he did not go through the laborious but necessary process of writing out copies of all his depositions to keep for his own records. Thus, when called on to explain his charge against Fyans, his first urgent step had been to write to Robinson, in the hope that copies had been kept in the Chief Protector's office. Sievwright had then been forced to await Robinson's return from the Western District before receiving a reply to his appeal. At the same time as telling his Assistant he could not help, Robinson took the opportunity to point out to La Trobe that Sievwright had still not provided the explanation demanded -- prompting the decision to suspend his salary.[21]

Gipps had approved the salary suspension in Sydney before Sievwright heard of it at Terang, and had time to send back the explanation demanded from him. Because Robinson had told him the depositions could not be found, the expla-nation was, he admitted, partly based on memory. In reply to Gipps' remark that he should not have made his charge against Fyans "in so informal a manner", Sievwright pointed out that he'd made it in his next periodical report to the government after hearing of the manner in which the Crown Lands Commissioner had captured the alleged murderers of Thomas Hayes and committed them for trial. He imagined that he could no longer, with propriety, completely withhold his knowledge about the affair, although he wanted to reserve a special communication on the subject until Burguidningnang and his two Elangamite tribesmen had been brought before a proper tribunal. He was confident that when this occurred, their innocence would be established. There would then be an additional reason for laying details before the government of what he considered to be Fyans' "dangerous and reprehensible conduct" in the way in which he'd led 17 armed settlers to assist in capturing the prisoners.

The Assistant Protector pointed out that in dismissing the charges against the three Elangamite men, Judge Willis had declared that there was no evidence against them. At the same time, the judge had called upon the Aboriginal Protectors to see justice done to them, as the Justice of the Peace who'd committed them for trial had failed in his duty to allow them an opportunity to cross-examine the witnesses giving evidence against them -- one of the complaints Prosecutor Croke had made about depositions received from Fyans. It was also his painful duty, Sievwright went on, to provide details of the consequences of Fyans' actions in accepting the aid of armed settlers in their capture. "While travelling through the district at this time, I found the settlers in a state of violent excitement against the natives," the Assistant Protector wrote. At Henry Gibb's station, for example, where he used to see the blacks "domesticated and employed in shepherding and otherwise working", he found the attitude of the people totally changed. "Where kindness and conciliatory measures had before invariably been adopted, I now found a spirit of hostility existing," he commented.

In a statement given to him by Gibb, Sievwright had learned of "a second attack made upon the natives by the settlers, under the authority of the Crown Commissioner". This was a reference to Fyans having authorised the Mounted Police corporal, William Brack, to join Gibb, his brother, and three of their shepherds in an unsuccessful attempt to capture a Jarcoort youth who'd thrown a spear at the squatter. The operation led by Fyans, along with the one involving Brack, had also inspired a third incident, in which Gibb had called on a group of fellow squatters to form another posse to capture the youth. The Assistant Protector reported that until this time, Gibb had been prepared to overlook what he believed were frequent thefts of sheep by the Aborigines because he found them useful, especially as shepherds. But Gibb had "imbibed" the sentiments shown by Fyans in leading his posse until it had made the "indiscriminate capture" of the three Elangamite men -- not hesitating to pursue a similar line of conduct after Fyans had left the area.

There were other examples, Sievwright asserted, of the ill effects of Fyans' actions in using squatters to perform what should, if deemed necessary, be police duties. For instance, the Commissioner's posse had also included Claude Farie and Niel Black -- both large proprietors in the district. The manner in which Farie and Black conducted their stations had proved how much the conduct of the servants could be influenced by their masters. There'd been no complaints of oppression or injustice towards the Aborigines by the people they employed. "Nor were the females of the different tribes encouraged or were permitted to approach their several stations," Sievwright wrote. "Yet strange as it may appear, under the sanction of such a leader, these Gentlemen were found foremost in the ranks of his auxiliaries. On charging these Gentlemen with the incongruity of that conduct with their former sentiments, they replied that they as settlers were bound to make common cause with the others, and while acting under the sanction of a Magistrate and officer of the Government, did not imagine they were all to blame."

Having elucidated on his remarks about the "indiscriminate attack" led by Fyans, and the "spirit of antipathy and hostility" towards the Aborigines it had engendered, Sievwright added that he now wanted to remind the government of the results of Fyans' commitments of the three Elangamite men for trial. Burguidningnang, he recalled, had been discharged after being imprisoned for five months on a charge of theft. After a confinement in irons for nine months on the murder charge, Wawarparneen and Kowcanmarning had also been discharged, although they'd both died just a few days later. "Having thus had the honour to furnish the particulars of their capture, confinement, and death of these unfortunate men, whose free spirits were broken and whose hardy frames sunk ere tardy justice could deliver them from their protracted sufferings," Sievwright wrote, "I would again respectfully refer to my original report upon this subject, in the hope that the Aborigines may be secured from such extreme measures as they have in this instance been exposed to, and especially from the risk of being again brought into collision with the settlers of the district."[22]

Knowing that Sievwright had a wife and seven children to feed and clothe besides himself, Robinson might have been expected to try to speed up the restoration of his assistant's wages. But not even a notification from La Trobe that he considered Sievwright's pay suspended for the previous *three months* would make Robinson hurry. He would take another nine days concocting a covering letter that would play down the fact that it had been his own prolonged absence from Melbourne which had delayed Sievwright's ability to provide the explanation demanded from him. Robinson pronounced it was Sievwright's own fault that he'd not kept copies of all his depositions, which would have allowed him to have provided the explanation when it was sought. Then, instead of backing his assistant's remarks about what had happened to the three Elangamite blacks, the Chief Protector decided to berate him. Robinson told La Trobe that Sievwright could not be used as an interpreter in the trial of the two murder suspects because he did not know a single syllable of their language. Nor was he able to find an interpreter. Robinson finished with the extraordinary claim that he now knew for certain there were whites to be found "who understood the dialect, and who might have been obtained by a little exertion". When La Trobe passed on Sievwright's explanation to Fyans for comment, the Assistant Protector's salary remained suspended.[23]

CHAPTER 17
A squatter on trial

RESENTMENT about being governed from Sydney was well-developed in the Port Phillip District by August 1841, when Governor Gipps informed La Trobe he was planning to make his first visit. Gipps of course was well aware of the degree of support for separation of Port Phillip from New South Wales. A petitition calling for separation, adopted at a public meeting in Melbourne more than a year earlier, had been signed by many prominent Port Phillip residents before being sent to the British Parliament. The petition had argued that Port Phillip, or Australia Felix, was a "free province" subsidising a penal colony through the sale of its land. The district should be entirely separated from New South Wales, with a "free representative government" of its own. A permanent committee was in place in Melbourne to promote the proposal, and a Parliamentary solicitor had been appointed in London to lobby politicians on the committee's behalf.[1]

News that Gipps was about to visit coincided with the public release of a letter from the London agent, John Richardson, giving the initial reaction in London to the separation petition. Richardson informed the committee that the Secretary of State for the Colonies, Lord John Russell, had acknowledged receiving the document, without revealing his attitude to it. Nevertheless, Richardson had been informed that Russell would be inclined to favour the Port Phillip District having a government separate to that of New South Wales, if not its own legislature as well. But with the possibility of an imminent dissolution of the British Parliament, this was as far as the separation cause could at present be advanced, the solicitor advised.

This was relatively positive news for the proponents of separation. But the joy it could have provoked was tempered by the recent alarming revelation that the Land and Emigration Commissioners who advised Russell had recommended that the western half of the Port Phillip District be attached to the colony of South Australia. A public meeting in Melbourne called to discuss the Commissioners' proposal passed a series of resolutions decrying the plan. With no small degree of exaggeration, they claimed that there was a stretch of more than 300 kilometres "of barren and uninhabitable desert" between Portland and the habitable portion of South Australia. The only transport link between the two parts of the new colony would be by sea. In contrast, there was "a continuous tract of available territory" already covered by the flocks and herds of the colonists between Portland and Melbourne, comprising a most valuable part of Port Phillip. One speaker pointed out that South Australia, founded on Wakefieldian principles, was supposed to be self-supporting, but was 210,000 pounds in debt. This would mean that 210,000 acres of land would have to be sold at one pound per acre just to pay off the debt, without any of the revenue being available to promote emigration.

The closing resolution asked the separation committee to prepare another petition to the British Parliament outlining the sentiments of the meeting, to be forwarded to London as soon as possible. Like the previous petitition, this would be sent with the knowledge that several members of the Parliament had a direct financial stake in Port Phillip's prosperity. They included at least one member of the House of Lords -- Archibald Kennedy, the first Marquess of Ailsa, who was in partnership with other Scottish aristocrats in one of the biggest pastoral companies in the district. At least one member of the House of Commons was also an absentee squatter in the district. Sir John Owen, who held the Welsh seat of Pembroke, had a station being managed on his behalf in the territory of the Bunganditj, which extended across the border into the supposedly "uninhabitable" part of South Australia.[2]

The forthcoming visit of the Governor left the separationists in a dilemma. They'd argued long and vigorously for an end to his administation of their affairs. But the proposal to annex the western part of Port Phillip to South Australia was a far more disturbing scenario than continued rule from Sydney. It had now become more imperative to seek Gipps' support in opposing the Commissioners' proposal, rather than trying to convince him of the need for Port Phillip to have autonomy. As the sycophants started drafting their welcoming speeches, the Governor told La Trobe he was certainly hoping for a less hostile reception in Melbourne than he might have received a few months earlier. Accounts he'd received from people who'd just come from Melbourne indicated that "a less angry feeling" was beginning to prevail there towards his government. Gipps would be "rejoiced" if this was so. For the sake of popularity, he would not indulge in extravagant spending similar to Colonel George Gawler, the Governor of South Australia who had led that colony into bankruptcy. But, Gipps asserted, he was certainly not indifferent to the prosperity of Port Phillip, or to the "good opinion of its inhabitants".[3]

When he first told La Trobe he was thinking of visiting, Gipps expressed a desire to visit Geelong, which under the annexation proposal could become part of South Australia.[4] It had been four-and-a-half years since Gipps' predecessor, Richard Bourke, had visited the settlement, long before it could be called a town. So when La Trobe let it be known that another vice-regal visit was imminent, the white residents of the Geelong area were keen to welcome him. The *Geelong Advertiser* acknowledged that in the past, it had been fanning the flame of discord against Gipps' administration, by painting what it regarded as mis-deeds "in vivid colours". While it did not now abjure from its opinions, the paper stated, it was appropriate to receive the Governor in person with "a degree of propriety". Gipps' visit could produce considerable benefit to the district. Notably, the *Advertiser* suggested, the Governor could declare Geelong to be a free warehousing port. This would remove the need for trading vessels to gain customs clearance across Port Phillip Bay in Melbourne, on their way to or from Geelong.[5]

At a public meeting in Geelong, a special committee was formed to draw up a "congratulatory message" to present to Gipps on his arrival in Geelong. Members of the committee included the chairman of the meeting, Alexander Thomson, his friend David Fisher, and other squatters -- William Roadknight, Hugh Murray, and G. F. Read. They decided to also invite "any other gentleman who may wish to attend the presentation".[6] As it transpired, much of the organ-isation for the Governor's visit would fall to Foster Fyans. It was his responsi-bility, for instance, to ensure that the Governor's party had access to enough horses to make a short tour of the area. The Crown Lands Commissioner also agreed to provide lunch for the party, the only meal it would be having in the town.

Arriving in Melbourne on a Saturday, Gipps would be on his way to Geelong early the following Tuesday aboard the gaily decorated steamer, the *Aphrasia*, which for the previous few months had been operating a twice-weekly service from Melbourne. Five hours later, the Governor -- accompanied by La Trobe -- was disembarking at the Geelong jetty, to the cheers of a large crowd of whites who'd gathered on the cliffs overlooking the harbour. A trumpeter in Fyans' Border Police played the British National Anthem, reportedly the first time that the tune had been heard at an official occasion in the settlement. On the wharf to welcome the visitors were Fyans, Police Magistrate Fenwick, other petty offi-cials, and Alexander Thomson's committee -- swollen by a number of other toad-ies who'd accepted the invitation to join.

Arrangements had been made for the Governor to immediately make a whirl-wind tour of the area, conducted by Fyans. During the tour, Gipps and La Trobe would pass the hut where Christina Sievwright and five of her seven children were starting to starve because of the suspension of her husband's salary over his allegation against Fyans. But they did not stop to speak to her, a short time later being at the Geelong Court House where Gipps was to be officially welcomed as Queen Victoria's representative. The address would rival the one he'd received in Melbourne for obsequiousness. "The long-expected visit of your

Excellency to this remote portion of the colony revives the hope that our wants of every kind, when brought respectfully before your Excellency, will meet with that consideration which our numbers and respectability as well as the wealth and importance of the district require," the signatories stated. "We further beg to express our earnest and heartfelt wishes for your Excellency's personal and domestic happiness and prosperity, and our fervent prayer to the Author of all good is that you, sir, and Lady Gipps, may be blessed and cheered through the anxious cares of your high and exalted stations."

In reply, Gipps declared he'd been "highly delighted" by what he'd seen, and promised to do all in his power for the benefit of the district. He regretted that the state of the treasury prevented him from agreeing to every claim made upon

From "The Chronicles of Early Melbourne"
Foster Fyans' residence in Geelong

it. Nevertheless, he could see that Geelong required a new court-house, and he would issue immediate directions for one to be built. Gipps and La Trobe then joined "a large number of the resident gentry" for a sumptuous lunch at Fyans' residence "served in quite a princely style" by the Crown Land Commissioner's servants. Throughout the meal, the Governor would hear first-hand of the attitude of the white settlers to issues such as the desire for Geelong to have direct trade with South Australia, without being part of it.[7]

After the meal, Gipps and La Trobe would make another short tour of Geelong before returning to the jetty to board the *Aphrasia*. After a few more grovelling remarks, some more cheers from the re-assembled crowd, and a salute from the funnel of the steamer, the visitors were on their way back to Melbourne. It had been a pleasant day, with fine weather, and the Superintendent was pleased with the way in which the Governor had been introduced to the representatives of the white community in the western half of his fiefdom. La Trobe was therefore horrified by a conversation with one of the other passengers aboard the steamer -- Benjamin Hurst, one of the Buntingdale missionaries. Hurst related various claims about the mistreatment of Aborigines by the whites. There was not much in the missionary's remarks which had not been stated before by Hurst or Sievwright, but La Trobe feared that the Governor's visit could be marred by them. He quickly brought the conversation to an end with a promise to investigate if full details were provided. Hurst declined for the time being, saying he was relating information provided by one of his colleagues, whose informant he could not recall. La Trobe did not mention Hurst's remarks to Gipps.[8]

Hurst had been on his way to Launceston, in Van Diemen's Land, for an anniversary meeting of the Wesleyan Missionary Society, now with operations in France, Spain, Germany, the West Indies, Africa, Ceylon, India, the South Sea Islands, and Australia. He would address the meeting the day Gipps arrived back in Sydney. Speaking in support of a resolution proclaiming the "truth and transcendant excellency" of the Wesleyans' religion in helping to provide for the moral wants of the human race, Hurst "startled" his audience by repeating the allegations he'd made to La Trobe aboard the *Aphrasia* about the actions of white men in Port Phillip's Western District towards the Aborigines. "He said it was usual for some to go out in parties on the Sabbath with guns, for the ostensible purpose of kangarooing, but in reality to hunt and kill these miserable beings," the *Launceston Advertiser* reported. "The bones and the bodies of the slaughtered blacks had been found -- but because the evidence of the native was not admissable in a court, the white murderers had escaped with impunity, and were still pursuing their career of crime and blood."[9]

After word reached Melbourne of Hurst's address in Launceston, La Trobe demanded that he provide details of his allegations. Hurst called on La Trobe with his colleague, John Skevington, who told the Superintendent that his informant had been the young Scottish squatter, Robert Tulloh. La Trobe replied that verbal reports were not good enough, and he ordered that they give him a written statement that could form the basis of an investigation. Before this could be provided, however, a meeting would be held to mark the anniversary of the establishment of the Wesleyan Missionary Society in Melbourne. Hurst would also address this meeting, and was unrepentant. He reiterated the allegations, while again emphasising that they related to the behaviour of the men the squatters employed, rather than the squatters themselves. This time, though, he pointed out that the claims had originally come from the mouth of a "respectable" squatter.[10]

Before Hurst's latest outburst became known, the white community of the Port Phillip District was rocked by another sensational development: for the first time in the history of the district, a white man had been charged over the shooting of an Aborigine. And it was not a shepherd or stockman who was facing trial. On the basis of depositions taken by Sievwright, Crown Prosecutor Croke was allowing the indictment of Sandford George Bolden, a wealthy English "gentleman" squatter. Bolden was one of a number of brothers who were believed responsible for bringing the first pure-bred Shorthorn cattle to the district. Their herds, and the stations on which they grazed, were among the biggest. The prosecution of Sandford Bolden related to an incident near one of

From "The Chronicles of Early Melbourne"
Irish barrister Redmond Barry, who later became a judge, had been appointed standing counsel for any Aboriginal defendants. But he would appear on behalf of the first squatter charged over a black's death.

their stations in Gunditjmara territory, about 30 kilometres west of Terang. At least one black, a man named Tatkier, had been shot while on his way to Sievwright's camp -- the very day that Hurst had related Tulloh's claims to La Trobe aboard the *Aphrasia*.[11]

The swiftness with which Bolden's trial was brought on reflected his standing. Unlike the Aboriginal murder suspects caught by Fyans, for instance, there would be no nine-month wait in jail for a court appearance. Rather, Sievwright would allow Bolden bail, and the trial would take place within weeks. Croke would tell the opening of the trial that Bolden was charged with feloniously shooting at Tatkier, with intent to kill, with a pistol loaded with ball, shot or other "destructive materials". The shooting incident occurred while Bolden had been riding with his brother, Lemuel, and two stockmen -- Peter Carney and William Kearnan. The group had come across three blacks crossing the run -- Tatkier, his wife Terang-gerang-coe, and a boy, Bong-il-bong. Croke told the court that Bolden had rashly come to the conclusion that the Aborigines had intended committing some mischief and ordered them to leave his run. "Not paying due respect to this order, they were ordered to be beaten off with whips," the Prosecutor submitted. Tatkier had run off, pursued by Bolden on horseback. Finding the pursuit "hot and dangerous", the Aborigine had whirled in circles around the squatter's horse, and tried to defend himself with one of his weapons, at which point Bolden shot him in the abdomen. Tatkier had jumped into a waterhole, and Bolden had galloped off to get more ammunition, telling Carney and Kearnan to secure the wounded black if he tried to escape. When the squatter returned, he had again shot at Tatkier, who then fell into the water.

Carney deposed that before being shot at the first time by Bolden, Tatkier had twice swiped at the squatter with a kind of club, the edges of which were so sharply carved that they could cut a horse's head off. Bolden had been about three metres away when he fired with a small double-barrelled pistol, but he could not say whether Tatkier was pretending to be wounded when he ran off, clutching his abdomen. He'd seen no blood. By the time Bolden had returned Tatkier had come out of the waterhole and his fellow stockman had been struggling with him. The second shot fired by Bolden had been with a short-barrelled pistol, at a distance of about 15 metres. Again, he could not say whether the shot hit the black, because he, Kearnan and Bolden had immediately ridden away.

Cross-examined by the Irish barrister, Redmond Barry, appearing for Bolden, Carney stated he'd not seen the squatter load his pistols, and could not swear that there was anything in them but gunpowder. The stockman added that the woman with Tatkier had been carrying an axe and a net full of bullock fat. Croke interrupted, saying this was irrelevant, prompting an extraordinary outburst from Judge Willis. If the government was prepared to declare itself the owner of the land, those licensed to lease parts of it had a right to use all lawful means to recover any property a would-be thief was attempting to carry away. They also had a clear right to drive off anyone who may come onto the land "for the purpose of aggression or not". This applied to both races. "The blacks have no right to trespass unless there is a special clause in the licence from the government," Willis asserted.

When cross-examination continued, Carney revealed that the whites were certainly driving the blacks from their runs. "It is a common course to frighten the natives by snapping or presenting a pistol at them", he admitted. William Kearnan told the court that he'd been the first to encounter the three blacks crossing Bolden's run on the day of the shooting incident. When he'd told them to move on, they'd defiantly replied that Mr Sievwright would "widgel widgel" him, meaning hang him. However, Kearnan denied that he'd made any attempt to drive them off. He corroborated Carney's evidence about the circumstances of the shots being fired. Like Carney, he also stated it was common to intimidate the blacks with firearms. He'd also seen smoke coming from Bolden's double-barrelled pistol after the first shot, but could not say whether the weapon had contained anything but gunpowder. And he also could not state whether Tatkier had been hit by any projectile from the second shot, fired after he'd received several blows from a heavy wooden club while struggling with the black near the edge of the waterhole. Kearnan added a claim that he'd seen Tatkier as a member of every Aboriginal party involved in recent incidents of cattle and calf killing at Bolden's station, including one time just eight days before the day of the shooting.

Next to give evidence was Sievwright, who told the court that Bong-il-bong, aged about 10, had told him at Terang that both Tatkier and Terang-gerang-coe, had been shot dead. The Protector told the court Bolden had at first denied that any shooting had occurred when he arrived at the squatter's station two days later to investigate. But when he'd made it clear to Bolden that he knew there'd been a clash, the squatter had then asked whether the bodies had been found. When Sievwright had replied that he believed so, Bolden had suddenly admitted the incident, claiming to have been too busy with some cattle sales to report it. As the squatter had been "in a state of extreme agitation", he'd decided to return the following day to resume the investigation when a calmer statement could be made. Although he'd told Bolden that he believed the bodies had been found, he'd made no such remark to Carney and Kearnan before taking their depositions in the case.

The Assistant Protector had gone to the waterhole into which Tatkier had dropped with several of his tribesmen, and his white constable, to search for the body. But the search had had to be abandoned because of the arrival of a white boy on horseback who the blacks with him had threatened to kill in revenge. Sievwright stated he'd not made any other search at the waterhole, but had twice made searches for Tatkier in his territory since the day of the shooting, without success. The Protector told the court that Tatkier had been personally known to him. It was possible, he admitted, that Tatkier was still alive, but he believed it was "highly improbable". According to his inquiries, Bong-il-bong had been wrong in claiming that the woman had also been killed. Although he'd not seen her since the incident, he believed she was alive. He had not mentioned this to Bolden or his stockmen.

At the time, Bong-il-bong had reported to Sievwright that he'd fled and hidden up a high tree after the whites started "beating them severely a considerable time with their whips" to drive him and the two adult blacks from the run. When the whites had left, he'd found Tatkier's body "shot through the body and head", and Terang-gerang-coe also dead, "much wounded about the head". Kiernan had told Sievwright that Carney's horse had accidentally trampled her. He'd later seen her laying against a tree, not moving, although he did not believe she'd been dead. Lemuel Bolden had told the Assistant Protector that Terang-gerang-coe had got up and fled into the bush after frightening his horse by swiping at him with a stick.

Whatever happened, the blacks camped with Sievwright at Terang at the time had believed Bong-il-bong's version of events, and they'd wanted revenge. "The grief and rage which this intelligence occasioned among the natives who were with me cannot well be described," Sievwright had told Robinson. "The men of two of the tribes immediately armed themselves, declaring they would go and kill the white people, and called upon me in a manner most peremptory and energetic, to accompany them. I succeeded after a time in allaying this ferment, by saying I would immediately go and procure the bodies (for the possession of which they seemed most anxious) and inquire into the circumstances attending the deaths -- if two, only, of the principal men of their tribe would accompany me, to which proposal they apparently assented." Six warriors had ended up joining him for the unsuccessful search for the bodies.

When the matter came to court, Willis would criticise Sievwright for having told Bolden he believed the bodies had been found before taking the squatter's statement. This made the statement's legality highly questionable. The judge also declared he was "excessively shocked" that Sievwright had failed to inform Bolden of Tatkier's wife having since been seen alive, although it was never established in either the squatter's statement or in evidence how he might have believed he'd also contributed to her death. The judge declared he would be ashamed to wear his gown if *he* had acted the same way as Sievwright. Furthermore, the Assistant Protector's information about the alleged finding of the bodies had been based on what he'd been told by a "wholly savage" Aboriginal boy aged only about 10.

"Why, the testimony of the most respectable Christian child would be, at that age, scarcely believed in a Court of Justice," Willis observed. Yet he was prepared to allow the case against Bolden to proceed, as he was eager to have the matter investigated as fully as possible. This was because he'd recently been publicly subjected to the "despicable" accusation of allowing his private feelings to interfere with his administration of public justice. The defendant was the younger brother of the Reverend John Satterthwaite Bolden, a Church of England clergyman who was "a near and respected neighbour" of the judge in an area known as Heidelberg, just outside Melbourne. He did not wish the public to think that this might influence the way in which he dealt with the case.

In his final address to the jury in Bolden's defence, Redmond Barry argued that the prosecution had failed to produce any evidence to show that the squatter's pistols had been loaded with anything other than gunpowder. Nor had it been shown that Tatkier had been the person whom Bolden had allegedly fired at. While these points in themselves were fatal to the prosecution case, he would go further and state that Bolden had been justified in firing his pistols. On the first occasion, he'd done so in defence of his own life. The second time, he'd fired to defend the life of one of his servants from "an infuriated cannibal". The small size of the pistols used, and the hasty manner in which they were fired, made it "very doubtful" that the shots could have taken effect, even if the weapons had been loaded with "ball, shot or other destructive materials".

Notwithstanding his earlier claim to administer impartial justice, it was then Willis' turn to denigrate the prosecution case. Had Bolden been indicted for shooting at an Aborigine whose name was unknown, there was a possibility that there could have been a case to answer. But the judge argued that the Crown Prosecutor had failed to prove that the black shot at by Bolden had been named Tatkier, as stated in the indictment. On this ground alone, he told the jury, the prosecution case had completely failed. He therefore wanted to know why the time of the court should be so abused as to be wasted by investigating such an unsupported case. Croke objected, expressing the view that there was sufficient evidence to show that Bolden had shot at an Aborigine, earning another rebuke from Willis.

The judge concluded by reiterating his view that there was no evidence against Bolden in terms of the indictment. Nor had the prosecutor proved "one iota" of malice in the actions of the squatter, and the jury must acquit him. Again Croke objected, arguing that animosity by Bolden had been shown. Furthermore, the Crown Prosecutor defiantly rejected the judge's claim that he'd wasted the court's time. On the basis of the same depositions, he would file a thousand indictments. In fact, he was prepared to file another one in the Bolden case the following day, this time taking up Willis' suggestion not to name the black at whom the shots had been fired. If he dared do so, the judge threatened, he would be recommending that Croke be declared unfit to continue as Crown Prosecutor, but Croke showed no immediate sign of backing down. After this heated exchange, the jury retired for a few minutes to consider its verdict. It accepted the judge's instruction, finding the prisoner not guilty. One jury member, John Manton, asked to express on behalf of his 11 fellow jurymen that Bolden left the court "without the slightest imputation upon his character". However, the foreman, David Charteris McArthur, revealed this was not the unanimous opinion of the jury.[12]

Those elated with the verdict and quick to crowd around Bolden included several fellow squatters, some of whom had come to Melbourne for the trial, and the judge. To the amazement of this crowd of supporters, Bolden would also be approached by Sievwright. In line with his training as a gentleman and officer, willing to accept defeat graciously when necessary, the Protector offered to shake the squatter's hand in congratulations. "This is just about as *cool* a piece of impudence as any we remember on record," the *Port Phillip Herald* commented. "Mr Sievwright must be dismissed from a situation he is wholly unworthy and incompetent to fill, and a petition must be set on foot, praying His Excellency to lose no time in doing this bare act of justice to the inhabitants of Mr Sievwright's district," the *Herald* suggested. "It will, we feel assured, be signed by every respectable settler in the place."[13]

A few days later, the *Herald* was more vicious. "We have had frequent occasions to point out the total worthlessness of the Protectorate as a Department, and our comments have been free and pointed whenever the delinquencies of any of its officers required exposure," it remarked. But never in the wide range of the Protectorate's "abuses" had anything occurred either in its nature, operations or consequences, which had the least resemblance to the "disgracefully trumped up" case against Bolden. Sievwright had admitted telling Bolden that he believed that the body of the black at whom he'd shot had been found. Thinking he'd been responsible for Tatkier's death, albeit in his own defence, the squatter had then given the statement which had formed the basis for his committal. The "merest novice" in legal matters would know that threats or inducements must never be used to extract confessions. But, the *Herald* argued, by making the remark about the body, Sievwright had violated this principle. Furthermore, he'd done so as a government officer who was supposed to mediate between blacks and whites, and as a magistrate who had the power "of inflicting the utmost injury upon his fellow men".

"From several quarters we have received the strongest possible comments upon

Mr Sievwright's uniform demeanour as a private individual, as an Assistant Protector, and as a Magistrate," the *Herald* went on. "With his private character we, in our official capacity, have nothing to do, and as such we care nothing for the reports respecting the manner in which he regulates or is regulated by his household. We only say and reiterate that his public conduct in the present instance is a disgrace to the colony at large and the magistracy in particular. It is criminal in its nature, and alarming in its consequences." Bolden was "a respectable young man, against whose spotless fame the voice of slander had never breathed an insinuation". But the squatter had been forced to suffer from the thought that his friends in the colony and back in England would be much distressed to learn that he'd been put on trial.

The *Herald* again called for Sievwright's dismissal for his "unprincipled" and "fiendish" conduct. "As long as Memory retains her seat within the breast, and honour and virtue are respected by the wise and good, so long will the late conduct of Mr Sievwright be kept before the mind, and its polluted nature be viewed with a feeling of the utmost abhorrence," the paper declared. "If the Colonists have the least regard for their own safety; if they respect truth and honour, and the credit and welfare of the province, they will bestir themselves like men sensible of their rights and their power to defend them, to rid the country of such an officer." The Governor had just visited Port Phillip and promised to ascertain and address its grievances. A petition calling for Sievwright's dismissal as a Protector and a magistrate should be the first test of the sincerity of the Gipps' pledge.[14]

The *Herald* did not confine itself to criticism of Sievwright's actions. If Crown Prosecutor Croke's had shown more common sense, and prevented the case from going ahead, the books of the Supreme Court could have been "still unsullied with such a disgraceful entry". "There was not a tittle of evidence to give the least colour of justification to such a cruel and unheard of procedure, and we defy Mr Croke to produce a precedent, from the legal records of any country on the face of the earth, to exculpate himself from that ignorance of his duty which has now been indelibly affixed to his character," the *Herald* remarked. A separate petition could also be organised calling for his replacement, it suggested.[15] It was an alarming development for Croke, who was awaiting the outcome of an application to the Secretary of State for the Colonies, Lord John Russell, to be appointed Port Phillip's first Attorney-General, or a judge. When La Trobe was informed of the initially secret application, he'd told Russell that after having had Croke as his legal adviser for two years, he could not offer an "unhesitating" opinion about his abilities. Gipps, too, had already told Russell that he could not recommend Croke "for any appointment in the Colony of greater importance than that which he now holds".[16]

It was not until after Bolden's trial that the Port Phillip press gave details of the speeches Benjamin Hurst had made in Launceston and Melbourne, with their inflammatory allegations about the Portland Bay squatters. The reports would include copies of a letter to Hurst signed by 10 squatters -- among them Sandford and Lemuel Bolden. They were sorry, the letter stated, that the missionary had thought proper to stigmatise the settlers of the Portland Bay District as cruel and cold-blooded murderers. "We, sir, take leave to state that the information by which you seem to have been guided is false and calumnious as far as relates to those with whom we...have any acquaintance; and we would call upon you to justify yourself, for having made such statements, by attempting to prove at least some of your heavy charges," the Boldens and their friends challenged.[17]

The *Herald* lost no time in condemning Hurst. "We may now mention that almost every individual holding any appointment whatever connected with the Aborigines seems determined to do the utmost in his power to vilify and belie the respectable inhabitants of the Province," the *Herald* opined. The Portland Bay squatters had shown "great and exemplary" forbearance, in the face of innumerable Aboriginal attacks. It was both false and cowardly for Hurst to have so maligned them. "He may be a clergyman in name, but the individual who could be guilty of such language upon no other authority than mere hearsay, even granting that he possessed so much and which is all he claims -- such a person, we say, is neither a man in principle nor a Christian in practice," the article went on.

"Here we have an individual assuming to himself great credit for his disinterested conduct in volunteering his services to civilise his more benighted brethren, by which he would wish it to appear that he sacrificed every domestic comfort and submitted to every hardship," it continued. "Here we have a person wearing the insignia of an honorable profession, and in his intercourse with his fellow men using all the bland expressions of an earthly saint. Here we have a person paid by the government and the people for rendering signal service to the country, and the cause of humanity and religion, in the Christianising of savage tribes -- but who, in direct opposition to all that his situation and *profession* would lead us to infer, basely maligns the people by whom he is supported, and seems to wish that his love of God may be tested by the hate of his brother!"[18]

The *Geelong Advertiser* also assailed Hurst. "It is painful to discover that men whom the world have been accustomed to look upon with respect, are not underdeserving of reprehension," it lamented. Yet Hurst must be guilty of one of two charges -- either uttering unfounded slander, or gross neglect of his duties as a missionary. "This individual -- we will not disgrace his calling by treating him as a minister of the gospel -- has, according to his own statement, been

[handwritten manuscript reproduced — Precis of Quarterly Reports of Asst Protector Sievwright, dated Western District, 1st December 1841 and 1st March 1842]

"Precis of Quarterly Reports of Asst Protector Sievwright dated Western District, 1st December 1841 and 1st March 1842." Sievwright reported that 443 blacks had registered at his Lake Terang camp, but they were suffering food shortages. He warned that attacks on the flocks and herds of the settlers of the district had assumed "an alarming character", and that "decided measures" -- notably food supplies -- were needed "in order to check the impending evil".

surrounded by scenes of wholesale murder and bloodshed during the last two years. He has looked on carelessly, with a smile upon his countenance, and done nothing to stem the torrent of iniquity." Instead, he'd kept quiet until he went to *exhibit* himself at a meeting in another colony, and then endeavoured to produce a "startling effect" by alleging that his friends in Port Phillip were "a band of murderers".[19]

While the tirade against Sievwright and Hurst continued, La Trobe would write to Gipps, informing him of the result of his investigation into the claim about Fyans' behaviour made by Sievwright, whose salary remained suspended. The Superintendent reminded the Governor that Sievwright had alleged that Fyans had made "an indiscriminate attack" on some Aborigines while searching for the murderers of John Thomson's shepherd almost 17 months earlier. According to the investigation, La Trobe concluded, it did not appear that more violence had been used than was "absolutely necessary" during the apprehension of the two murder suspects by the party led by Fyans, and no blood had been shed. La Trobe ignored Sievwright's explanation that his use of the word "indiscriminate" related to the fact that the three blacks apprehended -- the two murder suspects and Burguidningnang -- had been members of the first group of blacks encountered by Fyans' posse. La Trobe also did not believe that the way in which the three Elangamite men had been dragged to Geelong in chains, being urged on with stock whips, was of any consequence.

"Whatever informalities there might have been in the form and manner of the committal of these men, I cannot conceive that Mr Sievwright has borne out his charge against the Crown Commissioner," La Trobe told Gipps. "From all the evidence produced, it appears that nothing occurred of the character of an indiscriminate attack, and Captain Fyans' explanation shows that however he deemed himself authorised under the peculiar circumstances of the case, to accept the assistance of the neighbouring settlers in endeavouring to apprehend the murders, he did his utmost to guard against the possible occurrence of such a result. Mr Sievwright seems to have forgotten what, living at that time within sight of Captain Fyans' barracks he might have recollected, that though the Crown Commissioner had been furnished with six men as a Border Police force, the men had not yet received their accoutrements from Sydney, and were therefore not available for the service. With reference to Mr Sievwright's statement that by this indiscriminate attack a spirit of antipathy and hostility to the Aborigines had been renewed, which had been in a great measure overcome in the District, I must observe that as far as I can ascertain, or have evidence to guide me, the Assistant Protector is not borne out in making the first assertion, or justified in drawing the closing inference."

The Superintendent added that the enclosed correspondence, which included a reply from Fyans to Sievwright's allegations, showed that the Protector had been in Geelong when news of the murder of John Thomson's shepherd reached the authorities. Sievwright had allowed Fyans to proceed to investigate and attempt to catch the Aborigines responsible "without any intervention or offer of assistance". His own investigation had not started until after the arrests had been made. "It also appears to me that Mr Sievwright's investigation had less reference to the murder of the white man by the natives than to the conduct of the Crown Commissioner in attempting to apprehend the murderers," La Trobe wrote. Without any reference to Fyans, as the magistrate who had preceded him, Sievwright had taken a second set of depositions from the same parties. When Thomson, a brother magistrate, had declined to make a second deposition on oath, Sievwright had threatened to commit him to jail. "Upon a review of these facts, I cannot consider Mr Sievwright's conduct in the matter, however zealous in appearance, either just towards the Crown Commissioner, or free from censure," La Trobe concluded.[20]

Gipps would reject La Trobe's suggestion to censure Sievwright when he received the Superintendent's report in Sydney a few days later. The Governor would inform La Trobe that although he shared his sentiments on the matter, he'd decided that no further action against Sievwright was necessary.[21] Only the day before, one of Sandford Bolden's brothers had called on Gipps to request Sievwright's dismissal from the magistracy. The Governor had replied that he'd read a newspaper report of Bolden's trial, and it was "by no means clear" to him from this that the Assistant Protector had done anything wrong. Besides, the best way of testing allegations of wrongdoing by a magistrate was through Supreme Court action against him.[22]

It would not be until early in 1842 that Sievwright would learn of the reinstatement of his salary. In the meantime, he'd returned to Terang after Bolden's trial. On his way back to Terang, he'd spent a few days in Geelong -- the first time in 10 months that the whole family had been together. In these few days, Sievwright and Christina made the tough decision that despite the dangers, it was time for her and the younger children to rejoin him. Still not knowing when the suspension of his salary might end, the Sievwrights and their seven children set off one morning in December 1841 for Terang -- in what would prove a masterstroke in his relations with the Aborigines. "The arrival of my children amongst the natives was hailed by them with the most vehement demonstration of extravagant joy," Sievwright would later recall. "It was long after nightfall when we reached the lake, and on passing through the encampment, the shouts of the men, and the screaming of the females, demonstrated that this act of confidence was thoroughly appreciated by them."[23]

The Western District Aboriginal Protector had taken his bravest step yet towards achieving the purported aims of his appointment. Ironically, at the same time, the situation of the Aborigines under his protection had become more precarious as a result of the other bold step he'd recently taken -- initiating the prosecution of Sandford Bolden. Even La Trobe in Melbourne was alarmed by Judge Willis' declaration during Bolden's trial that the squatters had the right to drive off anyone trespassing on their runs. Until now, La Trobe told Gipps, it had been "generally understood" that the Aborigines' "natural right of occupation" had been extinguished on land sold by the British government. However, the same was not true of unsold land covered by a depasturing licence. Apart from the presumed illegality of attempting complete expulsion of the Aborigines from such land, it had been regarded that "there was a manifest inhumanity in pursuing such a course". Such was the extent of squatting that: "In many parts of the country it would in fact drive certain tribes from every portion of the wide district to which their wanderings were ordinarily limited before any provision could be made for their support and benefit."

But publication of the judge's remark, La Trobe warned, had had a profound effect -- especially in "parts of the country most exposed to depredations". It had removed "a degree of wholesome restraint" which with difficulty had been established towards the Aborigines. The squatters now felt they had the backing of the law when they ordered the blacks off their runs. If such an order was not obeyed, the law gave the right to use force. "I question whether even in the midst of civilisation that power is often exercised without leading to something which renders a resort to violent means justifiable, and when it is to be exercised among armed and ignorant savages it is easy to foresee what must almost in every case be the result," La Trobe wrote. He suggested that the colonial government take urgent action: when squatting licences came up for renewal in a few months, legislation should be in place allowing insertion of a clause stating that it was *not* legal to forcibly expel Aborigines from leased land.[24]

CHAPTER 18
Claptrap and deceit

D ESPITE an economic slump in South Australia in 1841, along with a severe austerity drive by its new Governor, George Grey, demand for stock to expand the flocks and herds in the grazing land of the colony was high. Good profits were to be made by white men willing to make the hazardous overland journey with sheep and cattle from New South Wales. The most favoured route for the overlanders took them just outside the Port Phillip District, on the north side of the Murray River, through country in which there was no white settlement. And the actions of the overland parties soon made revengeful Aborigines the biggest hazard of the journey -- especially near the junction of the borders of South Australia, the Port Phillip District, and the rest of New South Wales.

In August 1841, Grey reported to London that the blacks of this area had recently become more hostile than ever before. In the three most recent attacks on overland parties, several Europeans had been killed or wounded. The Governor observed it was impossible to restrain the enterprise of profit-driven individuals who were "virtually making war upon their own account" by voluntarily proceeding into the territories of inimical tribes. But men were being hired for overland missions without realising that there would almost certainly be serious clashes with Aborigines along the way. At the same time, the Aborigines were being subjected to "much ill-usage" by members of overland parties who were trying to protect themselves through "terror and awe".

It would be impossible, Grey acknowledged, for the British government to offer protection with troops or police stationed along the many hundreds of kilometres which the overland parties travelled. However, he'd devised a plan under which each overland party would be escorted into safe territory by a force of about eight to 10 Mounted Police. This force, and the rest of the party, would be placed under the command of an officer appointed by the government, whose duties would include trying to establish friendly relations with the blacks. The cost of the scheme would fall upon the proprietor of the stock being moved, as the one whose actions were placing both his employees and the Aborigines in danger.

The Governor told the Colonial Office he'd already put his plan into effect. Approval had been given for a sub-inspector, a sergeant, and 10 recently retrenched constables to accompany 12 volunteers to join up with an overland party of 26 white men on their way to South Australia from New South Wales with 7,000 sheep and other stock. The party sent from Adelaide was to be under the orders of South Australia's Protector of Aborigines, Matthew Moorehouse, except in the event of an Aboriginal attack, when the sub-inspector would take command. An Aborigine had also been sent to act as an interpreter. A representative of the owner of the stock had agreed to cover the cost of sending the party -- including arms provided by the government -- for nine weeks. The idea was for the party from Adelaide to rendezvous with the overlanders near the Rufus River, just across the border in New South Wales. Grey added that if a similar system was adopted in that colony, he believed it would stop a repetition of the "frightful scenes" which had recently taken place.[1]

By permission of the National Library of Australia
"Overlanders" by S. T. Gill.

Gipps had already received a letter from Grey suggesting that he issue an official notice informing the public of New South Wales of what had occurred to the overland parties on their way to South Australia, and suggesting that any future parties should be well-armed. Gipps immediately dismissed the proposal. "Such a notice would I fear be construed into a Licence to shoot Blacks, and our Squatters are not at all in want of a Permission from Govt. to do this," he told La Trobe in a private message.[2] Besides, Gipps believed the public was well aware of what had happened to overland parties through "the ordinary channels of communication" such as newspaper reports: there was no need for him to issue a special notice outlining the dangers.[3]

Reports of the result of implementation of Grey's police escort plan would emerge soon before Gipps' visit to Melbourne. For the stock proprietor and his men, it was a resounding success, but for the Aborigines it was a disaster. As it turned out, the party coming from New South Wales had reached the Rufus River area just ahead of the party from Adelaide. Some of the 26 overlanders would later testify to an official inquiry that about 300 blacks had menacingly blocked the track on which they were travelling. They had not waited for the blacks to actually attack before they simultaneously opened fire. The shooting would last almost three-quarters of an hour. The leader of the overland party, William Robinson, told the inquiry: "When a shot was fired, they instantly dropped down, making such a noise that we could scarce hear the report of the gun. They were all around us wherever we looked, making the most horrid noises, jumping about and shaking their spears." Matthew Moorehouse, the Aboriginal Protector, deposed that when he arrived at the scene, he counted 21 bodies. The blacks retreated, but were then attacked the following day by the police party sent from Adelaide. This time, there were about 30 blacks killed, and "a good many" wounded.

Ironically, the bench of magistrates which conducted the inquiry into the Rufus River affair was chaired by the man who had led the first group of white men through the area on an exploratory mission back in 1830. Indian-born former

Reproduced courtesy of the Mitchell Library, State Library of New South Wales
"Conflicts on the Rufus, S.A. (Murray)" by W. A. Cawthorne.

soldier and now assistant Crown Lands Commissioner Charles Sturt had in fact been responsible for "discovering" and naming the Rufus, in honour of the red-headed George McLeay, son of the then Colonial Secretary of New South Wales, Alexander McLeay, and second-in-command of the expedition. At the time, they had been travelling in a whaleboat down the Murray, also given its European name by Sturt, in honour of the then Secretary of State for the Colonies in London, Sir George Murray.

The expedition led by Sturt had had several meetings with apparently hostile groups of Aborigines. On one occasion he'd even had his gun cocked and pointed at a black man, ready to fire, before "the almost miraculous intervention of Providence" -- in the form of the sudden arrival at the scene of a previously befriended black, who'd been able to cool passions. That was as close as Sturt's group had come to a clash with the the Aborigines. Once a degree of mutual suspicion was overcome, he'd found the blacks of the area to be "a brave and confiding people" who were "by no means wanting in natural affection". The bench of magistrates Sturt chaired in 1841 also included his English friend and fellow explorer, Edward John Eyre. Both Sturt and Eyre had brought stock overland from New South Wales. During his first overland journey in 1838, Eyre had also found the Aborigines to be "tractable and friendly". But Sturt, Eyre, and the other magistrates realised that the behaviour of members of more recent overland parties had resulted in much change in inter-racial relations since those relatively calm initial contacts.

The bench would find that the actions of the police party which had accompanied Moorehouse to the scene had been unavoidable. Indeed, much praise was due to him and the police "for the great forbearance evinced by the force when placed under circumstances of the most trying nature". Robinson's party was also exonerated. The magistrates found that it "did not act with unnecessary severity against the natives when obliged to fire upon them, such firing appearing to have been in defence of their lives and property". The bench recommended that some soldiers, or armed police, be stationed in the Rufus River area to try to prevent further clashes between overland parties and the blacks. Sturt summed up by stating that the affair had received "anxious and deliberate attention" -- and expressing the hope that the inquiry and its findings would have "a good effect" both in South Australia and in England.[4]

The mention of England was a candid admission of the importance to the South Australian colony of the opinions formed about it back in London. Obviously, a favourable picture of a colony coping with the Aboriginal "problem" would be better for attracting potential investors -- and for enhancing the career prospects of the colony's administrators. Across the border in New South Wales, George Gipps and Charles La Trobe faced the same problem. And it was with this problem in mind that La Trobe chose the person to conduct the inquiry into the allegations by Benjamin Hurst late in 1841. The task should have gone to the British government official most directly concerned with the welfare of the blacks in the Portland Bay district: Charles Sievwright. But the Superintendent would instead choose the Portland Police Magistrate, James Blair, whose hatred of the blacks the Chief Protector had noted during his recent tour of the district. And in requesting a report from Blair on the Hurst allegations, La Trobe would make it clear that he was not expecting the claims to be substantiated.

The difficulties in ascertaining the exact character and number of inter-racial clashes were at one time "exceedingly great", La Trobe commented. But he believed these difficulties should have been eliminated. Not only had Blair been appointed as Police Magistrate, but Crown Lands Commissioner Fyans had made frequent visits into the district with parties of Mounted Police. If atrocities such as those alluded to by Hurst really occurred, the ability to conceal them had been made "yet more doubtful" by the more recent appointment of Englishman Acheson French as Police Magistrate near the Wedge brothers' station at The Grange. As well, the "principal settlers" in the remote part of the district towards the Glenelg and Wannon Rivers were the Henty brothers. The Hentys were also magistrates, and were "necessarily cognisant of what happens in that neighbourhood". This should be, La Trobe believed, "an additional guarantee" to the government that the events on which the allegations were based could not be "of recent occurrence".[5]

Blair would find no shortage of white men willing to discredit Robert Tulloh, the squatter on whose statements Hurst's allegations were largely based. Anger against Tulloh over the remarks attributed to him was exacerbated by the fact that he was known to have been visiting a certain young woman in Geelong. Like himself, she was Scottish and educated on the Continent. In a community in which unmarried young women were rare, and attractive ones even rarer, any suitors were sure to attract some attention, and some envy. But Tulloh had attracted amazement: he'd been courting Fanny Sievwright, the eldest daughter of the detested Assistant Protector of Aborigines. Tulloh was from the Scottish highlands, where his father was laird of a small castle. The family was well-connected, but had fallen on hard times, and he'd come to Australia hoping to improve his fortunes. One of his brothers had told George Robinson that Tulloh -- once betrothed in Scotland -- had no intention of marrying Fanny, because "two poor people coming together would not do". According to the brother, "paying his addresses" to Fanny was as far as Tulloh wished to go. Whatever his intentions, the fact that Tulloh was prepared to keep company with the Assistant Protector's daughter was considered treachery by many of his fellow squatters. His brother was among those who disapproved. Fanny and her mother, he told Robinson, "drank like the devil".[6]

Realising his future as a squatter was in grave jeopardy, Tulloh went to Portland to make a statement as soon as he heard Blair's inquiry was underway -- and he was quick to deny almost everything he'd reportedly stated at Buntingdale. Under oath before Blair, he explicitly denied having made the remark about white men going on Sunday expeditions to shoot Aborigines. Nor had he ever heard of such a practice, although it was possible that white men had retaliated against black aggressors while out shooting on Sundays. He'd told the Buntingdale missionary that the blacks were now less troublesome than in the past, but he'd not offered any explanation why. "I told him that the settlers in general had done everything they could to conciliate the Aborigines," Tulloh swore. "They had endeavoured to domesticate them, and finding that fail, had endeavoured to terrify them without doing them injury, but without effect."

The 23-year-old squatter claimed he'd never seen a dead Aborigine. On two of the six occasions when he'd been a member of a party assembled to recover stolen sheep, shots had been fired, but no lives had been lost. The only Aboriginal remains he'd seen had been some bones in a black camp, found while searching for sheep stolen from his neighbour, Peter Aylward. Despite this claimed lack of evidence, Tulloh added: "I am aware that the Aboriginal natives are cannibals, and I have every reason to believe that a number of each tribe are annually sacrificed, in conformity with their religious rites or customs."

Six months earlier, Tulloh had clearly stated to Robinson that one of his men, George Robson, had kicked to death a Tjapwurong boy taken prisoner while searching for Aylward's sheep. This he had again related at Buntingdale. But when it came to making a statement on oath to Blair, Tulloh suddenly recanted. Sure enough, Robson had kicked the boy, causing him to fall backwards. But he'd then been so disgusted, he'd walked away and had never asked what became of the child. Recalled by Blair two days later to elaborate, Tulloh stated Robson may have only used his foot to push the boy. "The child uttered a sound at the time, which I considered to be a cooee for the natives in the scrub," the squatter swore. "I do not believe the child was killed. I mentioned the circumstances to two or three persons. They might have inferred from the way I told it, that the child had been killed." In his first statement to Blair, Tulloh swore that the boy had tried to bite him before he handed him over to Robson. In the second statement, he claimed the boy had bitten him several times. In a footnote to the statement, Blair would tell La Trobe that from the evidence he'd been able to collect, he did not believe the case even warranted Robson being charged with common assault.[7]

Blair, whose fear of the Aborigines made him reluctant to leave Portland, would confine his inquiry to depositions from squatters who happened to be visiting the town, plus a few other white men who lived there -- such as the Winter brothers' brother-in-law, squatter Cecil Pybus Cooke. To a large degree, the statements would reflect the Police Magistrate's own feelings about the Aborigines. The reference to the Aborigines being cannibals which Blair extracted from Tulloh would be a common theme. The wording of some statements on the matter would be almost identical to Tulloh's, including the reference to the blacks supposedly making annual sacrifices in line with "religious rites or customs".

According to Thomas Norris, a squatter in Bunganditj territory: "I do not consider the diminution of their numbers is to be attributed to the attacks of the white people, but altogether to their conformity to those rites or customs, and to disease." Norris was one of the squatters keen to add details of the claims about cannibalism. "A case occurred about a fortnight ago when a child of about three months old was killed and eaten by its own tribe," he alleged. Stephen Henty was also quick to jump on the bandwagon. "Some of their cases of killing and eating each other, which have been reported to me, are of a most revolting nature," he stated. "In one case, a mother assisted to kill, roast, and eat her own child." John Henty would add his tuppence worth, claiming that the Aborigines ate "fleshy parts of the body" before entombing the bodies of tribe members who died from accidents. "A white man once shot himself accidentally at my station, and the blacks asked me for his body, to eat it," Henty concluded, without saying whether he complied with the request.

The overall aim of the depositions was obviously to portray the squatters as a fine set of Britons, somehow living in harmony alongside the wild and cannibalistic Aborigines. The squatters were unanimous in rejecting the allegation about Sunday shooting expeditions against the blacks, adding that such a practice could not occur without their knowledge. Several were also eager to portray Tulloh as an extremely unreliable information source. According to station superintendent David Edgar, Tulloh even boasted about his own clashes with the Aborigines whenever he could find anyone willing to listen: "Before I knew him I heard of his exploits, as narrated by himself, in which he stated he expended a pound of powder per day on the blacks. I never heard him give the same version twice to the same story. It is ridiculous for anyone who knows the truth, to hear him tell a story. He has a constitutional taste for making mis-statements. He is proverbial all over the country for telling untruths; so much so, that an extraordinary story is always called a Tulloh." Thomas McCulloch swore that he'd never heard a report by Tulloh confirmed by anyone, while a Grampians squatter, Edward Barnett, declared that Tulloh was "addicted to gross exaggeration". The Portland clerk of petty sessions, James Allison, stated that he'd been laughed at for believing one of Tulloh's tales. "I have since heard a number of these extravagant stories which he has told," Allison said, "and that in fact he is quite proverbial for it."

While accusing Tulloh of gross exaggeration, the squatters were quite prepared to allow their own statements to be riddled with misleading omission, half-truths, and outright lying. John and Stephen Henty, for instance, referred to the deaths of three Bunganditj on one of the stations they operated with their brother, Francis, back in March 1840. The Hentys, in whose qualities La Trobe had so much faith, both stated that the deaths had been inquired into. But neither mentioned that their attempt at concealment had delayed the inquiry by Sievwright, and given three shepherds he wanted to interview time to abscond. Nor did the Hentys mention that even as they made their statements to Blair, one of their men, Thomas Connell -- after whom they'd named one of their runs -- was under investigation by Sievwright for killing a group of Aborigines by feeding them poisoned damper.

Thomas McCulloch mentioned the clash that had occurred after the theft of some sheep from his station in mid 1840. However, he again failed to mention that two blacks had been shot dead -- specifically denying that any lives had been lost. Robert Savage admitted that at least one black had been killed in a clash while looking for stolen sheep back in early 1840. He claimed he'd not heard of an inter-racial clash in his area since which had resulted in a black death. Edward Barnett deposed that shots had been fired while pursuing black sheep thieves a few months earlier. But he claimed that he'd not asked whether any of the shots had hit their targets, and therefore did not know whether there had been casualties![8]

A few months before Blair's inquiry, Robinson had recorded in his journal: "The settlers at the Bay (Portland) spoke of the settlers up the country dropping the natives as coolly as if they were speaking of dropping cows. Indeed, the doctrine is being promulgated that they are not human, or hardly so, and thereby inculcating the principle that killing them is no murder." One inland squatter, Arthur Pilleau, had told Robinson that the settlers were encouraging their men to shoot the blacks "because thereby they would the sooner get rid of them". Pilleau himself seemed inclined to the doctrine. "He said, and others have said -- and said it to me -- that there would never be peace until they were extirpated," wrote the Chief Protector. As well, Pilleau had stated that for every white man killed, 20 blacks were shot. The squatter had admitted that just before Robinson's arrival in the area, "a number" of blacks had been killed in reprisal for the murder of Matthew Gibson's shepherd, Thomas Williams. "He said they did not kill them when there were many together, lest they should be known, but singly."[9] A little over six months later, Pilleau would downgrade his story to only one black prisoner having been killed after Williams' murder -- and claim that he'd not heard of any other blacks being killed in the previous 12 months.[10] Even the death of this prisoner would be denied by Thomas McCulloch, who swore that the black had managed to escape by swimming across the Glenelg River after he fired shots at him.[11]

Despite the very limited nature of his inquiry, Blair was enthused by his findings. In a covering letter to La Trobe he declared that there was not a single authenticated instance of an Aborigine having been killed by a white man in the Portland Bay district within the previous 18 months, although several white men had been "murdered and eaten" by the blacks in the same period. At the same time, acts of aggression by the Aborigines were reported to have been more frequent over the past few weeks than in any other period in the past year. Yet the incident reported by Edward Barnett, in which shots had been fired at Aborigines who'd stolen sheep, appeared to have been the only case of an inter-racial "collision" during the previous 15 to 18 months.

A reference by Hurst to 43 out of 44 blacks being shot dead on one occasion referred to the Whyte brothers' affair, which had taken place about two years earlier. A further inference by the missionary that the hostile acts of white men had already made many Aboriginal tribes extinct was "perfectly indefensible". It appeared from the evidence of George Winter that the number of blacks in the district had not been diminishing. Winter had sworn that there were generally from 70 to 80 blacks on his station, and at times 150. And Winter's evidence was important, Blair stressed, because he'd done "as much or perhaps more than any other individual to conciliate and domesticate the Aborigines".

To further undermine Tulloh's credibility, Blair also told La Trobe that the Scottish squatter had stated on oath that his horse had been speared under him by the blacks. But David Edgar had now sworn that he'd witnessed Tulloh accidentally wounding his own horse with a sheep-shear blade, lashed to a pole, with which he'd been pursuing some blacks. In conclusion, Blair stated that the Portland Bay settlers were the most respectable body of settlers whom he'd met in six years of living in New South Wales. "The penal character of the colony has necessarily introduced into the early settlements many persons with whom it would not be desirable to associate," the Police Magistrate wrote. "But the settlers of this district are, I may say without exception, gentlemen of education. Most of them have arrived from home within the last two years, and who cannot, therefore, be supposed to have so soon forgotten the principles in which they were educated as to render their society dreadful. In a young community like Portland Bay, every little irregularity attracts observation; and it is much to be regretted that the only individual who has shown himself unmindful of the respect due to the society should thus think it necessary to stigmatise its reputation."[12]

Even if the squatters had been as virtuous as Blair claimed, however, he'd ignored the fact that it was the employees of the squatters which had been the accused in the remarks made by Hurst -- not the squatters themselves. And it was preposterous to suggest that the behaviour of the shepherds and stockmen could always be governed by the supposed high principles of their masters! During his tour of the district, Robinson had heard many complaints from squatters -- including Tulloh -- of the difficulties of controlling their men. The saying was common among the settlers "that the men, and not we, are the masters", the Chief Protector had told La Trobe. "If therefore, the settlers could not control their men in matters where they were personally concerned, it was scarcely to be supposed they could do so in matters regarding the natives, and on that account many of the respectable settlers assured me they kept the natives from their run, and prohibited their servants from holding any intercourse with them," Robinson had written.[13]

In some areas at least, the squatters found their discipline problem was worse when alcohol was freely available. "When I first came the lower order were a debauched, drunken, good for nothing set," Thomas Norris stated to Blair. When he'd had to take his men to Portland, it had been impossible to say within a week when he might induce them out again. Norris claimed that in the previous year or so, there'd been "a great change for the better among the labouring classes". Stephen Henty, who resided in Portland, would make similar remarks. "The lower orders were formerly a most turbulent and unruly race, and the place was the most lawless I ever met," he stated. "They are now much more orderly, and the offence of drunkenness is wonderfully abated."[14] Yet in one remote part of the Western district, a group of squatters had just successfully lobbied for a new store to be banned from selling or stocking alcohol. In a petition to La Trobe, the squatters stated that the store had become "an intolerable nuisance" instead of a convenience, even though they were far from a town. "Since its establishment, our servants have been able to procure spirits, directly or indirectly, whereby our Flocks and stations have been neglected, nay even abandoned, and outrages committed, which have hitherto been unheard of in our district," the petition complained.[15]

It was not uncommon for squatters like Stephen Henty to be absent from their stations for extended periods. Fyans had reported one station he'd visited near Mt William, on the edge of the Western District, which had been left entirely in the hands of a large number of convict servants. Englishman William Kirk, who held the squatting licence, had returned to Sydney, from where he'd made an overland journey of almost three months the previous year with "a fine lot of 6000 sheep".[16] Kirk's overseer had also been absent for some time, and Fyans "could find no person to answer for the establishment". La Trobe had later told

Gipps: "I quite agree with Captain Fyans in the view he has taken of the evil that must result from such a state of things."[17] Just a week before La Trobe wrote these words, Robinson had been at Kirk's station, nearing the end of his tour of the district. And he'd seen and heard plenty to make him even more apprehensive than La Trobe about the situation.

Though it was two months after Fyans' visit, the squatter and his overseer were still absent. Aborigines in the area gave the Chief Protector the names of two blacks recently shot dead by one of Kirk's shepherds, seven of whom were assigned convicts. Two convict servants had recently absconded from the station, while another two still there were former convicts. During Robinson's visit, a former employee of Kirk's who'd been dismissed was among a group of white men who arrived and "behaved in a disgraceful manner to the natives, endeavouring to incite them to a breach of the peace, making use of the most infamous and provocative language". Robinson believed there was a danger of violence breaking out, which would result in a massacre of the blacks because of the number of whites present with a large quantity of weapons. When he asked the visitors to desist, trying to assert his authority as Chief Protector, Kirk's former employee had "put himself in a fighting attitude and swore he would knock my bloody head off". Black men at Kirk's told Robinson that this man and one of the other visitors had in the past fired at them, and taken away their women. The use of the black women was obviously a common practice. "The white shepherds at the station appeared to devote more of their time to the native women than to their sheep," Robinson recorded. "I have not seen such shepherding all the time I have been out."[18]

Despite their official responsibilities and experience, La Trobe would feel no need to seek any comment from either Sievwright or Robinson before sending on Blair's report to Gipps. Nor would he ask for comment from Fyans, as the Crown Lands Commissioner for the Portland Bay district. He would not even consult Police Magistrate Acheson French, whose base at The Grange was closer than Portland to the stations of most of the settlers whose sworn statements were submitted with Blair's report. La Trobe was obviously very conscious of the fact that his comments on the report may be needed to help Gipps respond to any queries from London about the remarks attributed to Tulloh or Hurst. He was also mindful of Gipps' warning to him a year earlier to be careful in his correspondence on Aboriginal matters because the Protectors were "evidently trying to get up a case for England".[19] La Trobe decided that the best way of assisting the Governor was to use George Robinson's favourite ploy -- shameless deceit.

"That frequent and fatal collisions took place in 1839 and at the commencement of 1840, between settlers in the Portland Bay district and the natives, however difficult of legal proof, is too notorious to be denied," La Trobe wrote. "They must always be deplored by every friend of humanity." The Superintendent stated it was clear that whatever basis existed for the statements made by Hurst was to be found in this period. The various measures taken by Blair for the better government of the district, since the start of 1840, had been "attended in a great measure with the desired results". Atrocities such as those mentioned by Hurst, if they were ever practised, would never be tolerated by the present class of settlers. "I dare not yet hope that in such a wide expanse of country, thickly occupied by sheep and cattle runs, and so much exposed to incursions of wild natives, further collisions may not occasionally occur," La Trobe added. "But it appears to me that the chances of concealment are now exceedingly diminished."[20]

The picture painted by Blair of a district which had long been relatively tranquil was palpably false, and both La Trobe and Gipps knew so. La Trobe's letter to the Governor failed to remind him of a series of communications from Blair complaining of his difficulties in producing order in his district with the limited force at his disposal for law enforcement. In December 1840, for instance, Blair had complained that he was finding the task "quite impossible".[21] Six months later, Blair had told La Trobe there were "almost daily" reports of whites being murdered by Aborigines in the district. Then, not long before being asked to report on Hurst's allegations, Blair had complained to La Trobe about the "disturbed" state of the region because of the presence of runaway convicts and "other bad characters".

So concerned had La Trobe been about what he was hearing from Blair and others that he'd decided to send the new officer-in-charge of the Mounted Police in the Port Phillip District, Lieutenant A. W. Riley, on an extensive tour of the Western District. Riley had visited various stations between Melbourne and the Grampians, then south to Portland. He reported that the number of runaway convicts said to be at large and causing disturbances was greatly exaggerated. Most of the runaways, he believed, had left the colony and had crossed into South Australia. However, Riley added: "The country appeared to be in a rather disturbed state, owing to the frequent outrages committed by the Blacks, and the great want of protection to the Settlers in the district." Blair still only had three foot constables, and it was ludicrous for La Trobe to be suggesting that in such a short time, he'd been able to restore order in the district and reduce the incidence of inter-racial clashes to "occasional".[22]

La Trobe had also received the recent complaint of the "dreadful depredations" of the Aborigines from James Webster, in the centre of the district, with the warning that serious clashes were imminent in his area.[23] And the Superintendent himself had recently acknowledged the likelihood of considerably more inter-racial violence. It was precisely for this reason that he'd called for the appointment of a Police Magistrate at The Grange, admitting to Gipps that he believed only "a certain proportion" of the frequent inter-racial clashes in that area had "reached the ears of Government". The blacks of this area were "exceedingly numerous" and were "of far bolder and more warlike disposition" than others in the Port Phillip District. Acheson French had not been appointed to the post for another two months, with the assistance of only one foot constable.[24]

The Superintendent would also send the Governor a copy of a scathing letter he'd sent to Hurst, informing him of the result of Blair's inquiry. The British government could not blame Hurst, La Trobe acknowledged, for taking up the matter of Tulloh's claims zealously and fearlessly. Such would have been his duty if he'd been a simple inhabitant of the district, instead of a missionary whose time and powers were especially devoted to the benefit of the Aboriginal inhabitants. "But in whatever degree the result of the investigation now instituted be satisfactory or unsatisfactory to the government and the friends of humanity," the Superintendent wrote, "I do not conceal my opinion that the circumstances under which you judged it your duty to publish those statements to the world lay you open to reprehension."

In common justice to the district, and the local government, matters which were "exceedingly improbable, to say the least of it" should have remained publicly unstated until they had been "tolerably proved". Nevertheless, before Tulloh's "claptrap" had even been investigated, Hurst had publicised it in Launceston "with the hope that it might be believed and produce a sensation". Hurst may have been acting as a conscientious man in aid of a holy cause, but La Trobe believed the means he'd used would not receive divine sanction.[25] In a separate letter written later the same day, La Trobe would tell Gipps that he believed Tulloh did not deserve the privilege of being a squatter on Crown Land. As soon as the Governor read Blair's report, he directed that Tulloh's depasturing licence should not be renewed.[26]

Meanwhile, Hurst had responded to the demand by the Bolden brothers and their friends for him to provide proof of at least some of the claims by Tulloh which he'd repeated in Launceston and then in Melbourne. And he was unrepentant. Hurst asked the *Port Phillip Gazette* to publish the response, pointing out that he would not at the same time be commenting on the attacks on him by the other Melbourne papers, such as the *Herald*. This was because he shared a view expressed by the Sydney-based Scottish Presbyterian clergyman and political activist, John Dunmore Lang. "It is the men who have the least character to lose who are loudest in defence of the commodity when assailed by others," he quoted Lang as having remarked.

Hurst began his response by saying that when he'd met some squatters in Melbourne at the time of Sandford Bolden's trial, he thought he'd given a "full and sufficient explanation" -- particularly in relation to the claim about expeditions to shoot blacks on Sundays. He had nothing more to offer than what he'd said then: a "respectable" white settler had volunteered the information "that great numbers of the natives had been shot in the district in which he resides, some in cold blood and on the Sabbath, by persons who had gone out for the ostensible purpose of kangarooing". Yet again Hurst emphasised that the white men reported to have "murdered the unoffending blacks" were *employees* of the squatters, not the squatters themselves.

Was he not justified, Hurst asked, in believing the statements of a gentleman whom he believed was equally as respectable as the squatters who'd since complained. "If the settlers themselves make statements similar to the above, can they justly complain if others repeat them?" he wrote. "If you say nothing ought to be published on hearsay authority, I reply that then the whole race of Aborigines might be destroyed, and no-one would have any right to complain." Hurst believed that the squatters knew that "a great many" blacks had been shot in the Portland Bay district. Certainly, he thought this to be so, and could if necessary produce the names of "a host of individuals" who'd been missing ever since they were reported to have been shot. Perhaps, Hurst proposed, the squatters could provide an estimate of the number of Aborigines who'd been shot dead in areas west of Lake Colac. He suggested that it might be around 200. He did not necessarily mean *murdered*, but perhaps -- to use the words of the *Gazette* -- legally shot either "in defence of life and property" or in retaliation. And perhaps the squatters could say how many bodies had been "put out of the way, that vexatious and harrowing inquiries might be avoided".[27]

Only four of the squatters who'd criticised Hurst, not including the Boldens, responded to his letter. Without explanation, they claimed that he'd contradicted what he'd stated at the Launceston and Melbourne meetings. The squatters were not, they added, representatives of the whole district, as Hurst had suggested, and could answer only for themselves and those with whom they associated. "We are astonished, sir, that you presume to ask us how many hundreds have been shot, how many bodies have been made away with, and at what rate day by day the Aborigines are disappearing from the soil," the squatters protested. "We are surprised, sir, that you think proper to put these questions tauntingly, as if you triumphed in the knowledge that we could answer them. We tell you, sir, that we know nothing of such proceedings, and if you do, it is a crime in you to have concealed your information until now."[28]

In his communications with Gipps and Hurst on the storm over the missionary's remarks, La Trobe highlighted Blair's finding that there had not been a single authenticated case of an Aborigine having been killed by a white man in the previous 18 months. The word *authenticated* was cleverly chosen. Despite La Trobe's claim that it was now harder for killings of Aborigines to escape the notice of the authorities, there was evidence to suggest otherwise. As the squatter, Arthur Pilleau, had told Robinson, blacks were being killed singly, rather than in large groups. Often the tribesmen of the victims would make concealment even easier by taking away the bodies and disposing of them soon after the killings. And some whites were becoming adept at new forms of surreptitious murder -- notably by feeding unsuspecting groups of Aborigines damper laced with arsenic, as had occurred on one of the Henty stations near The Grange.

Even as Blair was taking his statements in Portland, inter-racial clashes were occurring, some not far from the town, in which Aborigines were being killed. One clash which occurred the day George Winter made his statement, only about 50 kilometres north-east of Portland, left at least one black dead.[29] In his report to La Trobe on the Tulloh affair, Blair claimed that the whites were showing extreme forbearance despite an increase in the number of black aggressions in recent weeks. He soon had to admit he'd understated the situation. Only a fortnight after sending in his report, Blair would write another letter to La Trobe, informing him of a number of recent attacks by the blacks. "There appears, I am sorry to say, to be a general move among the Aborigines," he wrote.[30]

CHAPTER 19
The black cap

S INCE the Puritan-dominated British government had banned Christmas celebrations in the 17th Century, religious festivals had never been particularly popular in Scotland, and the most important time of the year for celebration was New Year, known as Hogmonay. Details of the customs practised would vary in different parts of Scotland. But the most important Hogmonay ritual, "first footing", would be universal. The first person to visit the family home in the New Year, preferably just after midnight, should be a dark-haired man. He should bring with him a piece of coal, a piece of bread, and perhaps some salt or a little money. This would auger well for the family's chances of having enough warmth, food and wealth during the year.

New Year's Eve in Edinburgh in 1841 was quieter than in previous years. But a good enough crowd of mainly young people gathered on the High Street and bridges of the Old Town to give a noisy welcome to the arrival of the New Year -- as Charles and Christina Sievwright had done on numerous occasions when they'd lived in Edinburgh.[1] In later years, as they started travelling around England with Charles' regiments, then to the Mediterranean, and eventually to Australia, the Sievwrights would maintain the Hogmonay tradition with their children. Only just reunited for the first time in months, on New Year's Eve in 1841 it was obvious that the family was going to need whatever good fortune the "first footing" may bring during 1842. Thus, it was with even more fervent faith than usual in the power of ancient and unknown forces that the ceremony was performed at the Lake Terang camp.

Chosen to be the first visitor through the door of the slab hut that had been used as a store, but which was now temporarily the family home was the overseer, Alexander Davidson, a fellow Scot. In accordance with the Hogmonay tradition, as he stepped through the door with a piece of coal, a piece of damper, and some salt, he was given a drink of whisky which had been set aside for the occasion. In return, Sievwright then "first footed" at the tent of Davidson and his wife. In the bush setting, far from any sizable group of fellow whites, it was the strangest Hogmonay the family had ever experienced. So, too, was it for Davidson and the few other whites present -- and for those blacks who gathered in amazement to watch the ceremonies!

The desire for good fortune Sievwright was hoping that Hogmonay would bring in 1842 was prompted in the first instance because as far as he knew, his salary still remained suspended because of the allegations he'd made about Foster Fyans. He'd not yet received notification that Gipps had decided that payment of his salary could now be resumed. What Sievwright did know by then, however, was that he was supposed to be going to Mt Rouse, about 70 kilometres north-west of Terang, where Patrick Codd had been murdered on the station of the squatter, John Cox, back in May 1840. It was there that he was supposed to be setting up a new reserve for the Western District Aborigines, although much had been going on behind the scenes to try to thwart the plan.

At the end of his recent tour of the district, Robinson had recommended four sites as future reserves. One was Sievwright's initial choice, Lake Keilambete. Another was at the junction of the Wannon and Glenelg Rivers, near The Grange where Police Magistrate Acheson French was based. A third reserve, he'd said, should be at a hill known to the blacks as Burrumbeep, about 100 kilometres north-west of Geelong, on the edge of the Western District. The fourth reserve should be at Mt Rouse, and it was this one which Robinson wanted set up first. "It must be presumed that the Chief Protector has made his selection with prudence and care," La Trobe told Gipps. In anticipation of the Governor's approval, the Superintendent had already put in motion the steps necessary to clear the Mt Rouse site. Gipps would quickly endorse the decision, at the same time approving the other sites selected by Robinson for future reserves.[2]

According to the author and one time Western District squatter, Thomas Alexander Browne, such was the suitability of the country around Mt Rouse for grazing that it "made the mouth of a cattle-man to water". In parts, the lava country around the extinct volcano was marshy, but the rest of the lightly-timbered area more than made up for this slight imperfection. "Once cattle were turned out there, they never seemed to have any inclination to roam, being instinctively aware, doubtless, that they could never hope to find such shelter, such pasture, such luxurious lodging anywhere else," Browne wrote. It was with heavy heart that Fyans received a letter from La Trobe giving him the task of notifying John Cox that his station was wanted for government purposes. "As Commissioner of Crown Lands, I was compelled to order one of my best friends in life off," Fyans would later recall. "He remonstrated with me on the hardship. However, he could not blame me; I had to act according to my instructions from Government. A protracted correspondence followed, and a time limit given to him of six weeks, when he was to vacate at an enormous loss of property."[3]

So it was that Sievwright, who had not been consulted on the proposal, was about to be ordered to abandon the camp at Lake Terang, and move to Mt Rouse. But towards the end of 1841, before the move could take place, La Trobe would receive a memorial from Fyans signed by 15 white settlers or their representatives, strongly objecting to the plan to make Mt Rouse an Aboriginal reserve. The signatories suggested that the government "would exhibit greater benevolence" if it selected locations for black reserves which were "not in the occupation of a licenced stockholder". They argued that certain un-named spots where the Aborigines had congregated were more suitable than Mt Rouse. The fact that the Aborigines had chosen these spots, the petition said, was proof of the capacity of the surrounding country to support them.[4]

Asked by La Trobe to comment, Robinson rejected this opinion as "the height of absurdity". In a rambling reply penned on Christmas Eve, he stated the blacks had been forced to gather in hilly and forested areas by necessity -- and their attacks on the whites' flocks proved the inadequacy of the natural food resources now available to them. These attacks would continue, the Chief Protector feared, until the Aborigines' food needs were satisfied "either by means of their own industry, or by the bounty of Government". Robinson was adamant that Mt Rouse was the best site in the Western District for a reserve where the Aborigines could be taught to grow their own food. It was in the middle of an area with a high black population, and it was isolated. And Robinson did not share Thomas Browne's enthusiasm about the area's suitability for grazing. Swamps and volcanic rocks meant that much of the surrounding country was "unavailable to settlers". As well, the movements of the blacks for a considerable distance around could be monitored by observing the smoke of their fires from the summit of Mt Rouse.

In an accompanying private note to La Trobe, Robinson claimed that most of the signatories to the petition objecting to a Mt Rouse reserve were young men with little experience in the colony. They were "but indifferent judges" as to what was, or what was not, best suited for the Aborigines. All but two of their stations were at least 30 kilometres from Mt Rouse. And finally, the Chief Protector pointed out that the "most extensive stockholders" in the area had not signed the document. La Trobe reiterated to Gipps that he had no reason to doubt Robinson's argument that his choice of Mt Rouse had been "a wise one in every respect". Besides, whatever merit there may be in the squatters' case against the selection had "come under notice at far too late an hour to have any weight". The formation of the Mt Rouse station, he recommended, should be allowed to go ahead without hesitation, a decision which Gipps would endorse.[5]

On the same day that he approved Robinson's selection of Mt Rouse, La Trobe would write a separate letter to Gipps expressing further serious doubts about the Chief Protector's department. The letter was prompted by reports from the Assistant Protectors which had just been passed on by Robinson. One report from Sievwright related events which, by the time they were read by La Trobe, had occurred more than a year earlier. Robinson had not been prepared to forward the report before he'd gone on his lengthy tour of the Western District. This was because Sievwright had used the report to outline his reasons for choosing Keilambete as the location for the Western District reserve. More importantly, Sievwright also mentioned that he'd proceeded to Keilambete on Robinson's orders *to start forming the reserve* without delay. The Chief Protector had received the report just after a note had arrived from La Trobe demanding that he question Sievwright over the apparent "informality and impropriety" of taking over Keilambete from John Thomson without due authority.[6]

It could well have been argued that it was preferable for Robinson to defer a decision on a Western District reserve until after he'd made his personal tour of the district. But he'd made a decision to order formation of the Keilambete reserve before the trip, and when he received La Trobe's note he could have at least admitted that perhaps he'd been a little hasty. He chose instead both to suppress his Assistant's report, and to allow him to bear the obloquy from the Superintendent alone. And when Robinson had been confronted on the matter by John Thomson, he'd even gone so far as to deny having issued the orders which Sievright specifically mentioned in the report. It was ironic that a few months after Sievwright had been forced to move to Terang, Keilambete should be one of the four sites recommended by Robinson and approved by Gipps for a future reserve.

The batch of reports from Robinson's assistants which included the suppressed one from Seivwright upset La Trobe. "I cannot forward these documents to His Excellency without expressing my opinion that after nearly three years' trial, there is but little appearance of order and general system observable in the conduct of your Department, and that as at present constituted, I cannot hope for their establishment," he told Robinson. La Trobe was concerned that the reports were arriving with "very great irregularity" and contained an "exceedingly small amount of really useful information". Furthermore, some remarks loosely scattered through them were "disparaging" to the government. He would tell Gipps he was unsure how to react to these remarks. "The Department of Protection of Aborigines in this District is so peculiar and so anomalous that common rules are scarcely applicable in dealing with it," he wrote. "I can only assure His Excellency that I am ready to assist any investigation on any point that it would be satisfactory for him to have elucidated, and as far as the local Government is deemed culpable by the Protectors, to invite any investigation His Excellency may think proper to institute."[7]

One recent incident had certainly caused untold damage to both Robinson's reputation, and the credibility of his department -- at the same time heightening white antogonism towards the Aborigines. In a penal colony in which brutality was common, the lives of common working men were not highly valued among the white community. But the murder of two whalers at Cape Paterson, about 110 kilometres south-east of Melbourne, caused a sensation. It was not the victims who were regarded as important, neither of whom was ever even fully identified. Rather, it was the fact that the murders had allegedly been committed by a group of blacks who'd been under the constant care of the Chief Protector for 13 years, and who'd been brought by him to Port Phillip from Van Diemen's Land.

A total of five blacks would stand trial for the murder. They would include Robert Timmy Jimmy Smallboy and Jack Napoleon Tarraparrura, known to the whites simply as Bob and Jack. Because the defendants could not give evidence, the court had to rely on what they'd allegedly said to Crown Lands Commissioner Frederick Powlett and Border Police corporal William Johnston when they were captured. Powlett and Johnston would give evidence that Bob and Jack had admitted shooting the two whalers, named only as William Cook and Yankee. One of the three women charged, named as Leilah Rooke Truganini, had stated that she'd watched the murders. She'd reported that Cook had not died immediately from his gunshot wounds, and had been finished off by the blacks beating his head with sticks. No motive was established for the murders, and no evidence produced of any involvement by the other two women charged -- named as Fanny Waterfordea, and Maria Matilda Natopolina.

Realising that his own reputation as a "civiliser" was also on trial, Robinson did his best to convince the jury that despite the evidence against them, Bob and Jack were "not wanting in humanity". The defendants had both been members of his first official mission into the Van Diemen's Land bush to try to arrange friendly relations with the remnant tribes of that colony, and on subsequent journeys. The Chief Protector told the court that Jack had recently accompanied him on his tour of the Western District of Port Phillip, and his conduct had been "exemplary". Bob had also been used for similar purposes on a trip to Adelaide by way of the Murray River by George Langhorne, an Anglican catechist who had operated as a government-appointed missionary among the Aborigines of Port Phillip between 1837 and 1839. Robinson said Langhorne had told him he and other members of his party owed their lives to Bob's actions when they'd been attacked by some Murray blacks. The Chief Protector added that on one occasion back in Van Diemen's Land when he'd been in danger of being killed by hostile Aborigines, Truganini had saved him by helping him to escape across a river.

Redmond Barry, as counsel for the defendants, endeavoured to introduce some mitigating circumstances in their favour. "It must be remembered," he argued, "that these men and their fellow countrymen once roamed over the green hills

Reproduced courtesy of the Geelong Art Gallery
"The barter" by Eugene von Guerard, depicts either the Barwon or Moorabool River in Geelong. Before his move to Terang, Sievwright's camp was near the junction of these two rivers, just outside the township.

and wide plains of their native soil, the lords of all around, subject to no will but their own, no master but their own passions." What now had they come to? Barry submitted he did not wish to trace the course of the destruction of the Van Diemen's Land Aborigines, which had ended up with the remnants of that once numerous people being transported to a foreign and, to them, a distant shore. It was impossible from a relatively short association with Robinson for them to have forgotten what had occurred, and it was not surprising that feelings of revenge should "burst forth with redoubled fury on the first opportunity".

Willis was unimpressed. In a summary of the case for the jury that lasted almost three hours, he pointed out that Robinson had claimed back in 1836 that all five defendants, along with the other blacks he'd taken to Flinders Island in Bass Strait, were "civilised". It was legitimate for Barry to have pointed out that the defendants had been brought to the foreign land of Port Phillip by Robinson, Willis asserted. But the jury should also bear in mind the words of the Attorney-General in a recent and somewhat similar case elsewhere in New South Wales. The foremost legal authority in the colony had stated that members of a jury had a duty to themselves and to their fellow colonists, to protect not only their property, but more especially their lives -- and if they deemed the prisoners to be guilty, to use their verdict to try to prevent the recurrence of similar acts of aggression. After retiring for a short time, the jury returned to inform Willis that it had found the women prisoners not guilty. Bob and Jack they found guilty, with a recommendation for mercy because of their previous good character "and the peculiar circumstances of the case".

Bob and Jack would be returned to the court the following day for sentencing. In accordance with the ritual he was obliged to follow, Willis placed a black cap upon his head, before telling the defendants, as though they might understand what he was saying: "Painful as it is at all times to pronounce the sentence of the law upon a fellow creature, yet that pain is greatly increased when the delinquent has not the consoling hope of his crime being pardoned hereafter, by means of true repentance and the mercy and forgiveness of Almighty God. The light of Christianity, the only rational piety, if ever distinguishable in your minds, can but have glimmered for a moment, instead of continuing to illuminate by its calm splendour, your journey through a world of misery, and directing you to the Haven of Eternal Rest. All men, even in an uncivilised state, are said to entertain, however imperfectly and however clouded with vain imaginations, some expectation of a future state. May the latest spark, if it exist in your minds, kindle, by God's blessing, that holy flame of piety and repentance, that may make you wake unto salvation before that period shall arrive when that world must close upon you forever, for I can hold out no hope of pardon."

"The punishment that awaits you is not that of vengeance, but of terror, that others by the example you will afford, may be deterred from similar transgression," Willis added. "The civilisation and instruction imparted to you, under the kind protection of Mr Robinson, who has behaved like a father to you, and who has brought you to these shores, has not, I lament to say, been attended with the salutary consequences that might reasonably have been expected. You are not like the wild Aborigines who inhabit the native forests of this district. You are not, as was said by the people in England, ignorant savages about to be made amenable to a code of laws of which you are absolutely ignorant, and the spirit and principles whereof are foreign to your modes of thought and action. You, for years, have associated with and become familiar with the manners, customs, and ordinary laws of the British people, sufficiently so at least to know that the circumstances of which you have been convicted, could not have been committed by you with impunity. What I have said will be better explained to you by those under whose care you will be until the period of your execution."[8]

Willis told Bob and Jack that they would be hanged in a public place, on a date to be set by the Governor. "The convicts were then removed, seemingly much affected, the perspiration pouring off one of them in large drops," reported the *Port Phillip Herald*. In a commentary on the case, the *Herald* claimed that during their years with Robinson the convicted blacks had learned English, could read and write, and were "perfectly conversant with the customs of the settlers". As well, they were "not insensible of moral and religious obligations, and knew well their legal responsibility for the crime which they committed". It was therefore astonishing that the jury had recommended mercy for the murderers. "The oft-repeated and in certain circles the so popular argument of pseudo philanthropists, that the soil is the property of the blacks, and therefore the laws of nature force them to resist invasion on the part of the whites, cannot be advanced as an excuse for the bloody deed of which these wretches have been so clearly convicted," the *Herald* declared.

Bob and Jack were not from the Port Phillip district, and could not claim that the murders they'd committed were in any way connected with intrusion upon the land which they originally possessed, the paper continued. They'd brutally murdered two innocent white men, and must be hanged for the crime. "If they are not to suffer the consequence which the British laws award to such culprits, then from such announcement their more savage brethren will naturally imbibe encouragement in their career of blood and plunder, and the whites will reasonably infer that whilst the blacks have their protectors, *they* have no security against their incursions and crimes," the *Herald* argued. "When, in addition to this, the colonists call to their recollection that in Sydney white men suffered the extreme penalty of the law, and we justly admit, for taking summary vengeance against the natives, and that they if guilty of a similar offence are liable to a similar punishment, the public will instantly perceive that whilst the laws protect the blacks, the white man's blood must go unavenged."[9]

Forwarding his trial notes to La Trobe, Willis made it clear he did not agree with the jury's recommendation for clemency. "The case strikes me as one of great atrocity," the judge advised. "There were also charges of arson and robbery against the Prisoners, which their conviction for murder rendered it unnecessary to try. It now therefore rests with His Excellency the Governor to decide whether these wretched men, or either of them, shall be speedily executed; or reprieved until their case be submitted to Her Majesty."[10] Passing on the judge's notes and comments, La Trobe told Gipps he could not offer any words in Bob and Jack's favour. The Governor wasted no time in deciding not to exercise his prerogative of mercy, and a date for the execution was set -- one week after the letter informing La Trobe of the decision reached Melbourne.[11]

Before receiving confirmation from Sydney that Bob and Jack should be hanged, La Trobe would initiate further inquiries into the reported murder with poisoned damper of a group of Bunganditj people on a station operated by the Henty brothers on the Wannon River, back in October 1840.[12] When he'd visited the area a few months after the incident, the Chief Protector told La Trobe, the Henty brothers had claimed that the alleged poisoner, overseer Thomas Connell, was expected back from a trip to Van Diemen's Land any day. But the Hentys assured him that Connell knew nothing of the affair. Robinson had tried to trace two Bunganditj who had reportedly survived by vomiting up the poisoned damper. But at the time, the Aborigines in the area had been dispersed by the wave of the revenge killings which followed the murders by the Bunganditj of Edmund Morton and William Lawrence, and he'd been unable to find the survivors. He told La Trobe he'd later been "astonished" to learn that Sievwright had not obeyed his order to investigate the matter. "I have since reiterated my request and have ordered this officer to proceed forthwith to investigate the case, and have distinctly informed him that in the event of any further neglect, that his conduct would be represented," Robinson wrote.[13]

When he'd first been asked to inquire into the case by Robinson, Sievwright had been too afraid to leave Terang because the camp had been in so much turmoil. At that time, the blacks had been "highly insubordinate" and had been attempting to obtain the government provisions in the camp "by threats and violence". There being no building for the safe custody of the stores, he'd wanted to be present to at least try to prevent any raids on them.[14] Robinson told La Trobe he'd rejected this explanation, saying the overseer and constable could have managed to protect the stores in his assistant's absence.[15] In any event, on being ordered again by Robinson to go to investigate the poisoning, Sievwright did not have the same fears. This time, he was ready to even leave his family at

Terang with more than 200 blacks, believing they were safe because of the "natural confidence" that had been established by bringing them to live there.[16]

According to the information given to La Trobe by Augustine Barton, 15 to 17 Bunganditj had died a horrible death after eating the poisoned damper on the Henty station.[17] Robinson had recorded the names of seven victims.[18] When he got to the scene of the massacre, Sievwright would separately record eight names, obtained through a young boy called Bulajoe who stated his father was among them. Four names were common to both Robinson's and Sievwright's lists. Thus, the names of at least 11 victims became known to the Protectorate, though it is doubtful if the two lists were ever compared. Sievwright would report that the four women, three men and one child on his list had all died on the evening on which they'd been given the poisoned damper, or the next day, "in much pain, accompanied by retching". Bulajoe showed the Assistant Protector where the bodies of two of the victims, including his father, had been burned -- and the spots where others had wandered to die. The young black and another Bunganditj would also take Sievwright to the *Merino Downs* station of the Henty brothers where the damper had been handed out.[19]

Stephen Henty would claim to have first heard of the poisoning while visiting the nearby station of the Wedge brothers. Instead of heading straight back to his own station, the squatter stated, he'd gone to Portland. From there, he'd written to Thomas Connell asking about the matter. Henty would provide what he said was a copy of Connell's reply -- in which the overseer denied his involvement, and called for the report to be "properly investigated". The squatter asserted that he'd not complied with Connell's request for a full investigation because he knew that "a gentleman" -- presumably Augustine Barton -- was about to report the matter in Melbourne, and he'd expected an immediate inquiry to result from this. But Henty told Sievwright he'd made his own inquiries, and he was "perfectly satisfied" that Connell was innocent. If the overseer had been guilty, he could have declined a new employment contract and stayed in Van Diemen's Land when he was sent there to hire more staff. Besides, the squatter argued, Connell was a Wesleyan "of the most quiet and orderly nature", and could not commit such a "revolting crime".[20]

At the station where the poisoning reportedly occurred, Sievwright would run into a wall of professed ignorance of the matter. However, in a sworn statement to Sievwright denying involvement, Connell would raise very serious questions about Stephen Henty's account of events -- and doubts about his own innocence. Connell would claim that on first hearing reports of the poisoning, he'd written to Henty asking for an investigation, with the aim of clearing his name. But he did not know whether Henty had made any inquiries. In fact, he claimed, he had not even discussed the matter with the squatter in the 15 months or so which had

since elapsed.   Connell further alleged that on hearing that Robinson was
approaching the area a few months after the reported poisoning, he'd been eager
to see him, to answer any questions he may have about it.   Unfortunately,
Edward Henty had ordered him to go to Van Diemen's Land to procure more servants -- just as the Chief Protector had arrived in the vicinity.

"I positively assert and declare that no such circumstance regarding the poisoning of natives took place to my knowledge amongst the people under my
charge," Connell swore. "Such an event could not have taken place at this station without my having been acquainted with it. It might have happened on an
outstation, but there has been no cause for such conduct as the natives have
never annoyed us nor done any harm since I have been here except on one occasion when the men said a ewe was killed by them." One of Stephen Henty's
shepherds, John Daley, would also deny knowing anything about the poisoning
-- and would claim that there had been no sheep stolen at all from the station in
the two years he'd been employed there. This included the period of 1840, just
ahead of the poisoning incident, when a wave of Aboriginal attacks on sheep stations had swept across the Western District. And there certainly had been sheep
thefts on neighbouring stations.[21]

From the testimony of Bulajoe and other Bunganditj blacks, Sievwright was
convinced that the poisoning had occurred. But once again, only Aboriginal evidence was available, and it could not be used to launch any prosecution. "We
can only hope that sooner or later circumstances may transpire which will bring
to punishment the perpetrators of this diabolical act," Sievwright lamented.[22]
The Assistant Protector's frustration over his inability to launch a prosecution
over the poisoning would be tempered by one event during his investigation,
which had lasted almost two weeks. He'd met about 150 Bunganditj blacks at
the station of the Winter brothers, whom ironically he'd wanted to commit for
trial for murder back in 1840 -- but whose prosecution had been blocked by the
Attorney-General in Sydney. And with his move to Mt Rouse imminent, it
appeared that the Bunganditj people at the Winters could form a key part of his
future plans for protection of the Western District Aborigines.

George Winter said he'd heard the Assistant Protector was in the area, and had
assembled the blacks to meet him. Sievwright had been keen to seize the opportunity to invite the Bunganditj blacks to join him at Mt Rouse, even though it
was well outside their territory. He'd had to wait until the following morning for
the reply: the Bunganditj elders indicated that they'd be willing to accept the
invitation, provided he first returned with their counterparts from the tribes
already there to establish goodwill by paying "the accustomed preliminary
visit". This he assured them he would arrange, and he left in no doubt that as
soon as the necessary ceremony had been performed, the Bunganditj people

would make the move. He was looking forward to being joined by them. "Mr Winter has generally the greater part of this tribe upon his station and reports most favourably of their conduct," he recorded.[23]

The day Sievwright returned to Terang, Bob and Jack would be hanged. It was the first public execution in Melbourne, and the ghouls were excited. The crude gallows was erected on a grassy patch on the edge of the town, and a crowd of several thousand gathered to watch. More than half, according to the *Port Phillip Herald*, were women and children. As well, about 20 Aborigines would watch the proceedings from the top branches of nearby gum trees. The Irish journalist, Edmund Finn, later recorded that the black spectators had behaved with decorum -- unlike some of the whites "who shouted and yelled and vented their gratification in explosions of uproarious merriment, as if they were participating in the greatest sport". As the Church of England chaplain, Adam Compton Thomson, spent 20 minutes reading prayers at the foot of the gallows,

Reproduced courtesy of the La Trobe Picture Collection, State Library of Victoria
"The first execution" by W. F. E. Liardet depicts Bob and Jack being taken from prison.

there were calls from the impatient crowd to "cut it short". Eventually, the two prisoners were led up the rickety ladder onto the scaffold, their arms pinioned, and white hoods and then nooses were placed over their heads by the hangman.

Chosen as executioner from a sizeable field of volunteers was an Englishman, John Davies, a former farm labourer transported to New South Wales to serve a life sentence for sheep stealing. Davies, who'd been forced to leave behind his wife and two daughters in England, had been brutalised by almost 10 years as a Crown prisoner. He thus had no hesitation in jumping at the offer of a payment of 10 pounds (later reduced by Gipps to five) and a "ticket-of-leave" for carrying out the task. When the Reverend Thomson uttered the words: "In the midst of life we are in death", Davies signalled for fellow prisoner John Styleman below to pull the cord that was supposed to release the drop. But the system did not work properly, the drop falling only half-way. For a few seconds, Bob and Jack "twisted and writhed convulsively in a manner that horrified even the most hardened" until a bystander had the presence of mind to kick away the piece of wood obstructing the drop, allowing it to fall the full way. The executioner "grinned horribly a ghastly smile" in response to cries that he'd botched the job. Davies was later quoted as saying that Jack, whose end was almost instantaneous, had "hung beautiful" because the noose around his neck had been better adjusted. Bob, however, was not so fortunate, his chest "labouring and heaving violently for some time after his fall".

"May their fate have a beneficial effect upon the Aborigines of the province," declared the *Port Phillip Herald*. It was vaguely possible, the *Herald* said, that the hangings would provoke summary vengeance upon the whites from blacks "goaded on by the dark and untutored passions of nature". But it would have been absolutely certain that many more Aborigines would have suffered if the hangings had not taken place. The white population would have quickly and correctly concluded that the colonial government was not willing to give the death penalty to blacks for crimes which deserved them. The incensed whites would have immediately declared "open warfare", and hundreds of Aborigines would have died. This in turn would have caused the character of Port Phillip to sink "in the estimation of all civilised nations" -- and immigration would have ceased. "The authorities with their utmost power would be unable to stay the evil, and the nature of the result would be only equalled by the cruelty of the means by which it was effected."[24]

CHAPTER 20
To Mt Rouse

OR several million years, volcanoes spewed lava across a large part of the south-east of the Australian continent. The volcanoes were mostly relatively small, with cone-shaped craters, although the eruptions from them were spectacular, and the extensive lava flows resulted in major topographical changes. By the time the first white settlers arrived there had not been an active volcano for about 7000 years. To the whites, hills such as Mt Elephant and Mt Rouse would be merely silent reminders of the region's violent volcanic past. But these hills would have particular significance to the Aborigines, whose ancestors had been living in the region long before the volcanic activity stopped. In some cases, the hills would serve as markers of tribal boundaries. In other cases, they would form the basis of Aboriginal folklore.

One story of the Gunditjmara people told how a great tidal wave had swept across the coast, to put out the fires in the volcano called Benwerrin, in the south-west of their territory. The tidal wave had killed many humans and animals, and had caused widespread destruction. Only the ancestors of the Gunditjmara camped on the summit of a hill called Yayon, about 20 kilometres inland, had survived. The Gunditjmara believed that if the lake-filled volcano known as Berrin in neighbouring Bunganditj territory ever began to erupt, and the earth began to shake, another giant tidal wave would come.[1] The Bunganditj had their own legend about Berrin, called Mt Gambier by the whites. The first Aboriginal man in the region, Craitbul, had once lived happily inside Berrin's crater with his wife and two sons. But one day, the water deeper inside the crater had risen up and put out the fire in their earth oven. With three more new ovens, the same thing happened. Finally, the family -- whose feats would include creation of kangaroos -- would settle in a cave near the top of the outside of the crater.[2]

Probably the biggest lava flow in the Western District occurred from a volcano which 19,000 years later the blacks would call Puutch beem, meaning "high head", but which the whites would call Mt Eels or Mt Eccles. Over a period of perhaps a few weeks or months, a huge flow of lava would pour southwards from the volcano for more than 50 kilometres, out onto the then dry continental shelf. Part of the flow would later be covered by the sea, not far from what the whites would call Portland. Lava would also spread westwards over the surrounding plains, forming what would become known as the Stony Rises or The Rocks. The area would be a popular location for the Gunditjmara people, who fished in its lakes, swamps and streams, with the volcanic stones being used to make both fish traps and circular houses. The area was also important for hunting. In the spring, it was "one immense preserve of every kind of wild fowl and wild animal that the country owned".[3] Then after the white occupation, The Rocks would reveal themselves as advantageous to the Gunditjmara in another way.

The country to east of The Rocks was not the best for grazing purposes in a district that was so rich in suitable land. Yet by early 1842, most of it had been claimed by white settlers who, like their counterparts elsewhere in the district, soon resented the presence of the local Aborigines. And, when it became apparent to the Gunditjmara that the arrival of the whites was to their distinct disadvantage, a guerilla campaign was launched. The Rocks were centrally located in Gunditjmara territory, and the extreme danger of riding horses through them made them ideal as staging points for raids on the white settlers' flocks and herds, and then as refuges from any pursuers. One squatter would recall of the jagged rocky area: "As a natural covert for savages, it could not be surpassed."[4]

Among the stations to suffer worst from Gunditjmara attacks staged from the rises was one which immediately adjoined them, operated on the Eumeralla River by three partners -- John Hosking, John Terry Hughes, and James Arthur Carr Hunter. Hosking and Hughes were the wealthy principals of a leading mercantile firm in Sydney, and were large land-owners in Port Phillip as well as absentee squatters.[5] Hunter, a Scottish youth not yet 18 years old, held the squatting licence on behalf of the partners, and was supposed to live at the station, although he was given the assistance of an overseer, James Guthrie, and three other men. It was a large run, geared mainly for beef and dairy production.[6]

Gunditjmara raids on the run started in December 1841, not long after its establishment. But the first serious clash would occur in the first week of 1842. Overseer Guthrie reported that he'd returned from looking for a horse believed to have been stolen to find the huts and the nearby dairy apparently abandoned by his three subordinates. A black named Jackey had come out of one hut, followed by another black armed with a wooden leanguil. Guthrie would depose a few days later that he believed he was about to be struck with the weapon, so he shot the Aborigine holding it dead. Seeing more blacks inside the hut, he leapt on his horse and galloped off to a neighbouring station. When he returned the following day with assistance, he found that the huts had been ransacked, but there was no sign of the stockmen he'd expected to find dead.[7]

Police Magistrate Acheson French, before whom Guthrie made his statement, decided to swear in the overseer and five other white men as special constables in an effort to catch the black thieves. They included the squatters William Forlonge, Thomas Norris, and David Edgar. On the basis of information from Guthrie and Hunter's housekeeper, Jemima Purnell, about the most recent and other events, French would also issue warrants for the arrest of Jackey and several other Gunditjmara men who'd been given European appellations. Among them were Mercury, Jupiter, Billy and Bumbletoe. There was also Cocknose, so named for "the highly unclassical shape of the facial appendage".[8] And a warrant was issued for the man known to the whites as The Doctor, reputed to be responsible for extracting the prized kidney fat of members of rival tribes killed in battle.

By permission of the National Library of Australia
"Natives attacking shepherds' hut" by Samuel Calvert.

French and his special constables would visit Hunter's station, finding it still abandoned, the stockmen and the housekeeper having fled to Melbourne. They would also ride into the bush to inspect what was believed to be a temporary shelter, or mia mia, recently used by The Doctor. French reported that they found no traces of the horse alleged to have been taken there and eaten. Informing La Trobe of the matter, the Police Magistrate pointed out that in part he'd been induced to issue the arrest warrants because of complaints from the squatters "that the government is very ready to take notice of any injury committed by the whites on the blacks, but not so in the contrary case". When such remarks were made, the squatters would cite murders such as those of Patrick Codd and Edmund Morton.[9]

Young James Hunter was not impressed with the rigorous life of squatting in the Australian bush, much preferring to spend his time in the towns. He'd been absent from his station for some time when the incident involving Guthrie occurred, making a leisurely trip to Melbourne. Hunter had only got as far as Geelong when the overseer caught up with him to tell him what had happened. He would immediately seek help from Foster Fyans, who decided to send two of his Border Police -- a corporal named Bird, and private John Carty -- to the station, where the three stockmen had agreed to return after initially fleeing to Melbourne. Carty believed he was fortunate to be chosen: only a month before, he'd appeared before the Geelong court, charged with being a Crown prisoner "lurking about the town without a pass". Being "of previously bad character", he'd been sentenced to 12 months' labour in irons. He was also supposed to have been dismissed from his attachment to the Border Police, so he was grateful when Fyans decided to reinstate him for the dangerous assignment at Hunter's.[10]

According to the version of events as later reported by Fyans, two days after the arrival of the troopers at Hunter's, two blacks had appeared. They'd been armed with eight spears tipped with volcanic glass. The troopers had watched in hiding from a hut as the blacks entered one opposite. When one of the three stockmen had told the corporal he recognised the two Aborigines as instigators of recent acts of "injury and destruction", the police moved to arrest them. A scuffle took place, as four of the white men grabbed the blacks and shackled them together, while the fifth white man stood watch in case some more Gunditjmara should arrive. But the handcuffs were too big for the wiry wrists of one of the blacks, and he managed to pull his hand free, grabbed an axe, and struck Carty on the head. As Corporal Bird drew his sword to defend his comrade, he received a blow to the head with a garden spade which the other black had picked up. Then Bird saw Carty being dragged by the hair towards the door of the hut, and the axe in the air poised for another blow. Bird swiped with his sword, cutting the black holding the axe across the cheek and through the jaw. The other black he also managed to wound with the sword before they fled, leaving him regretting that he did not have a better firearm he could have quickly used.

Carty had been so badly wounded, Fyans would report, that it had been impossible to move him from Hunter's station. As well, as Carty lay terrified in the hut, two days after the clash the blacks had staged a night raid on the station, stealing one of the finest Border Police horses. "There can be little doubt that this noble animal has shared the fate of numerous others, particularly in this District, where the Natives appear to me daily to grow worse and more vicious," Fyans wrote. It was a matter of considerable regret that the "vile murderers and savages" responsible for wounding Carty and stealing the horse had not been captured. There was only one consolation: at least the two who'd been in the hut had been "marked well with good sabre cuts" so they would now be easily recognised.

The Crown Lands Commissioner was convinced that "great credit" was due to Bird for his actions. But, he told La Trobe, instructions were needed from the Governor on how the Border Police should act when dealing with the Aborigines in the future. Fyans had not yet been informed of the result of the belated inquiry into Sievwright's criticism of the way in which he'd acted when capturing suspects for the murder of Thomas Hayes, back in 1840. Since explaining his actions, he pointed out to La Trobe, he'd been in "anxious expectation" of a ruling from Gipps on whether Sievwright's charge against him was justified. Fyans added that he believed he was in a unique position, as a magistrate "between Missionaries, Gentlemen, Natives and Protectors". Without directions from Gipps, it was impossible for him to know how he should act. "I shall feel glad to be guided by His Excellency's orders, and submissively take this opportunity to offer my opinion that it is high time to protect the Europeans in this District, who have suffered so much, and for years, and without redress," he concluded.[11]

A week later, the *Geelong Advertiser* would report the arrival back in the town of Bird and Carty. Although both troopers had received severe head wounds, neither was in a critical condition. After relating what had occurred, as outlined by Fyans, the *Advertiser* told its readers: "Mr Hunter, whose run has been the scene of these transactions, is one of the kindest and most indulgent of our settlers towards the blacks. He repeatedly supplied them with food and clothing, and thought that he could trust them in return, but mark the result! The moment his back was turned, they commenced a series of gross outrages, and have stripped his establishment of every kind of property they could carry off." It would be impossible, the paper suggested, to try to pursue the guilty blacks into the Stony Rises, where they'd fled with the Border Police horse. But further attempts would no doubt be made to capture them when they again came out of the rocks, and the white community should act resolutely. "After such occurrences, it will be absolutely necessary, for the safety of the settlers, that a striking example should be made among the blacks in that quarter; else they will be emboldened by impunity to commit still more serious outrages."[12]

What the *Advertiser* didn't realise was that the Gunditjmara people had already decided to launch more attacks against the white invaders of their territory, and the clash with Fyans' troopers at Hunters had strengthened their resolve. Furthermore, members of the tribe had started going beyond stealing the white men's animals for food, staging some attacks that were purely sabotage. Near the hill known to the whites as Mt Eckersley, north of Portland, Gunditjmara guerillas burned down a large field of oats planted by the Henty family. "The men saw the blacks in the act of firing the oats, and took immediate steps to check the flames, but unfortunately without effect," recorded Police Magistrate Blair. The Gunditjmara would also be blamed for setting fire to a large field of wheat on a farm near Port Fairy established by Scottish whaling station manager, Captain Colin Campbell, who'd been one of the first cultivators of Gunditjmara territory. Campbell would later tell Robinson he believed his wheat had been set alight by sparks from a nearby bushfire, but the accusation against the blacks would by then have been well circulated among the whites.[13]

Within a few days of the attack on the Henty brothers' oats, the Gunditjmara would take a step the tribe had not previously taken in its guerilla campaign -- the killing of a white man. By a strange coincidence, he would have the same surname as the corporal involved in the clash at Hunter's. The victim would be Thomas Bird, hutkeeper to John Ritchie, in a coastal area between the mouth of the Eumeralla River and Port Fairy. Ritchie's two shepherds, John Salvage and John Wilson, would later relate how on the day of the murder, they'd returned to the hut in the evening to find it had been robbed. Then they would find Bird's body nearby, still warm. He'd been laying on his back, his arms extended, with several spear wounds in his chest, one through his forehead, one through the nose, and another through an eye. Bird's musket was gone, along with a quantity of balls, shot, and a canister of gunpowder.

Salvage and Wilson reported that stolen from the hut were two skin rugs, a pea-jacket and trousers, and quantities of sugar, tea and flour. Oddly, also missing were two wooden beds and a mattress. They claimed there had not been any previous violence at the station involving the Aborigines. But the blacks had been "very troublesome", making three earlier attempts to rob the hut which they'd just emptied, and one raid on a hut on another outstation. The shepherds said that after discovering Bird's body, they'd both left their sheep in a yard and ridden off to the head station, believing it was too dangerous for only one of them to remain behind. The following day, both Bird's body and the sheep had been brought back to the home station, and all of Ritchie's outstations had now been deserted.[14]

Three days after Bird's murder, Gunditjmara warriors would also attack a station on a creek in their territory, next to the Bolden brothers' run. The squatting licence was held by an Englishman, Robert Whitehead, who operated a drapery business in Melbourne. Robinson had seen trouble brewing months earlier at

Whitehead's station, managed by a fellow Englishman, R. W. Sutton. The Chief Protector had been disturbed to find an Aboriginal skull hanging in the shepherds' hut, which Sutton claimed to have been that of an old woman who had died in her mia mia on the creek. But Sutton had also admitted an incident in which both he and a shepherd had opened fire on some blacks after two lambs were stolen. The overseer didn't think any of the blacks had been hit, although he made it clear they may not be so lucky on any subsequent occasion.

"This young man could not conceal his bad feeling towards the natives, and said the squatters must protect their property of all hazards," Robinson wrote in his journal. The Chief Protector also recorded that Sutton was one of a number of white settlers who'd told him they didn't fear acting contrary to the law, because in the isolation of the bush "nobody would know about it". In the attack on an outstation of Whitehead's early in 1842, a large party of Gunditjmara would drive off 85 sheep, leaving behind a shepherd, John Prentice, with three spear wounds "and a severe blow to the stomach". One of the spear wounds would be serious enough to confine him to bed for many weeks.[15]

"It was another extraordinary procession which he led on the 70 kilometre trek..."

Before reports of the latest Gunditjmara attacks would become widely known, Sievwright would leave Terang, in Kirrae territory, on the journey to take up his new base at Mt Rouse, on the border between Gunditjmara and Tjapwurong country. It was another extraordinary procession which he led on the 70 kilometre trek, over three days. There were 17 whites travelling either on horseback, or on a cart pulled by six bullocks -- Charles and Christina Sievwright, their seven children, overseer Alexander Davidson and constable Alexander Donaldson and their respective wives -- Anne and Betty. There were also the four convict servants assigned to Sievwright -- John White, James Evans, William Kay, and Peter Littleher. Sievwright had told his brother, John, who'd been with him for a year, that a farming venture they'd planned together could not proceed, so John set off back to Geelong to try to find employment. A total of 210 Aborigines also left Terang for Mt Rouse -- 69 men, 65 women, and 76 children -- the biggest group of which were Jarcoort Kirraes. Again, it was unprecedented for a white man to be leading such a large group into the territory of another tribe, and it was fraught with the danger of an outbreak of either inter-tribal or inter-racial violence. But Sievwright found the behaviour of his charges to be exemplary.

"On the road we passed the several stations of the settlers, and encamped both nights in the immediate vicinity of their flocks and herds, without the slightest attempt having been made by the natives at an irregularity or depredation," the Assistant Protector proudly reported. "Nor was the line of march at any time broken, or even progress impeded, by any straggling or disorder, and on each day's halt their first care was to provide, most abundantly, for the comfort of my family by erecting screens of branches to protect them from the weather and in furnishing firewood, water etc. and I could not but look upon their diligent, provident and orderly conduct at this period without referring to the scenes of inebriation and moral disorganisation I had frequently witnessed under similar circumstances amongst our best disciplined troops -- the contrast being much in favour of the uncivilised community by which I was surrounded."

On arrival at Mt Rouse, Sievwright's family took up residence in the stone hut formerly used by John Cox's overseer, James Brock. Relations with Christina still being strained, he moved into an adjoining hut, formerly used by Cox. Then, the day after the party's arrival, Sievwright started his long-awaited agricultural operation. The blacks were soon involved in daily work, preparing ground allocated for wheat paddocks, a vegetable garden, and a kitchen-hut. A large area had to be cleared of its volcanic stones, and brush fences made to enclose the paddocks. Sievwright would soon be telling Robinson there was a need for more bullocks to allow ploughing to go ahead. The six bullocks already assigned to him were constantly engaged pulling the cart on trips to collect supplies, including those needed to pay his black labourers. On most trips, the cart would go to and from a store at Port Fairy to collect flour, meat, sugar, and tea. But it also had to be sent to Lake Boloke to collect salt.

Besides the extra bullocks, Sievwright asked that the Chief Protector take urgent steps to supply him with teachers for the "imperative" task of the education and religious instruction of the large number of children already at the camp. Sievwright promised to give high priority to the construction of a school building. The sooner a system of education started, the sooner progress could be made in restraining the younger children "from the habits and pursuits of their parents", while eradicating the undesirable traits which the older children had already acquired. "This I imagine may be now rapidly achieved, as the confidence of those natives who are now with me, has been gained, and their respect conciliated," the Assistant Protector reported. "They know me as their friend, and trust me as such." From the outset, Sievwright had dissented from Robinson's idea of forcing different tribes to live together in the one spot. His early experience at Mt Rouse, however, indicated the Chief Protector's plan may work after all. Several tribes were now "living amiably together" which 12 months earlier had no dealings with each other. Most of the blacks who had accompanied him to Mt Rouse had never seen that part of the district, and the fact that the men of the tribes had brought their women and children was "indicative of their confidence and of their intention to remain".

"Restraining the younger children 'from the habits and pursuits of their parents'..."

As well, Sievwright reported, the conduct of the Jarcoort and other blacks who had been with him for the previous year or so augered well for the prospects for the Mt Rouse reserve. Significant "progress in civilisation" had been shown by these Aborigines, and this was having a positive effect among the others who'd joined him more recently. "Instead of the outrageous ferocity which charac- terised their general demeanour and conduct, the adults are now under a disci- pline, to which they unhesitatingly submit, and the younger branches are at all times anxious to do what they imagine will be acceptable," he wrote. "They now conduct themselves peaceably and circumspectly at their meals, and all observe the general rules laid down for their guidance. They willingly employ them- selves at the task allotted to them, and their time is spent with cheerfulness and contentment."

Almost all of the Aborigines with him, Sievwright added, had had little or no contact with the white population. The children especially had been free from "any contaminating example", except from the Crown prisoners assigned to him as servants. It would be most desirable, Sievwright advised, if these prisoners were replaced by free servants of good character.[16] Despite the minimal contact between the blacks at the Mt Rouse reserve and the whites, it had been enough to introduce venereal disease among them. And it would not be long before Sievwright would report that one of his prisoners, James Evans, had been involved in "improper connection with native women" at the reserve, contract- ing syphilis as a result. Sievwright immediately sent Evans to Geelong, urging the authorities to punish him after medical treatment. La Trobe would agree that Evans "doubtless" deserved punishment, but would initially make a ludicrous request for "proof" from Sievwright of how the prisoner had caught the disease! It would not be until Evans boldly applied for a ticket-of-leave some weeks later that La Trobe would punish him by rejecting it. Gipps would uphold the deci- sion, and Evans would continue as a labourer assigned to public works in Geelong, while the syphilis slowly killed him.[17]

CHAPTER 21
"The impending evil"

IT would take 36 years after the arrival of the first white settlers in New South Wales before a special party would set off on an overland journey to explore the southern part of the colony. The expedition leaders were Australian-born Hamilton Hume and Englishman William Hovell, a former merchant ship captain. After a 10-week journey in 1824 over hundreds of kilometres, Hume and Hovell would reach the shores of Port Phillip Bay, near Geelong, mistakenly believing it to be Westernport Bay, further to the east. They and their six convict servants had been the first white men to cross the territory of several Aboriginal tribes, yet it was not until the party was about to start its return that it had its first meeting with some blacks. Hovell would attribute the low number of encounters with the Aborigines to a simple cause. "They did not appear to be astonished at the sight of the horses and bullocks, but they were very much afraid of them, much more so than they were of us, and dreadfully alarmed if they saw the bullocks look towards them, notwithstanding they were at a great distance from them," he recorded after the first meeting. "This fear we encouraged, as we considered it the greatest security against any attack. I have no doubt but this is the principal cause of our not seeing any of the natives during the whole of our journey before."[1]

A popular story among the Gunditjmara people, always told with "great glee", related how members of the tribe saw their first bullock, possibly a runaway from the Henty brothers. The incident occurred at a waterhole known as Wuurong Yaering, on Spring Creek, about 30 kilometres north-east of Port Fairy. A group of Gunditjmara people fishing at the waterhole had suddenly been surprised by the bullock, wearing a sheet of tin on its head designed to act as blinkers. At the time, the blacks had apparently already seen white men, or at least knew something of them. But never before had they seen such a large animal, and they fled. They were even more terrified that night when the bullock wandered into their camp, bellowing. At daylight, the bullock was still there, and the consensus was reached that it must be a muuruup, a bad male spirit, or perhaps some form of white man that had not been seen before. Its horns, the Aborigines surmised, were tomahawks that had been driven into its head. After the beast walked off, a council of war was held, and it was decided that all those present should follow it. Finding it a few kilometres away grazing in an open part of the forest, the bravest warrior approached the animal, asking it whether it was a white man, and whether it was prepared to hand over the tom-ahawks! The bullock responded by pawing the ground, bellowing, then charging at the blacks, causing them all to flee. The story would be told time and again at gatherings of the tribe.[2]

Ironically, Wuurong Yaering, where the bullock story originated, would later become part of a 19,400 hectare cattle station. The white men who took out the squatting licence for the station were both former doctors, Englishman William Dallas Bernard and James Kilgour, a Scot. Bernard and Kilgour would invest a large sum establishing their operation, paying the relatively high price of more than seven pounds a head for their initial 600 cattle. As well, they would hire an overseer from the Scottish highlands to help ensure the success of their venture. However, the doctors had no previous experience with cattle farming and the overseer was not up to the task. The station was soon in a shambles. The cattle had a variety of old brands, and had not been re-branded -- a major problem when they were allowed to wander "all over the country" by the stockmen Bernard and Kilgour employed.

During his 1841 tour, George Robinson would visit the station and meet Kilgour. The Chief Protector recorded that the stockmen were "a great lot of blackguards" and "inhuman scoundrels". Three of them were former convicts. They, in Robinson's view, were "a thousand times worse than the actual convicts". He was shocked at the cruel way in which Kilgour's men treated the animals under their care. "I told the Doctor and his overseer that I had had 16 years' experience with men in the colonies and that the men he had were as bad as any I had met with," Robinson recorded. "I hoped he would keep the blacks from coming in contact with such characters. For my own part, I would rather live among the worst blacks than with such men." Robinson regarded Kilgour as "foolish". He was, like all new arrivals, "a declared enemy" of the Aborigines. "And yet they have never injured him except by their being on his run, which he says is of itself an injury as the cattle run away when they see blacks," he wrote.

The land covered by Bernard and Kilgour's station, which the doctors called Tarrone, was of prime importance to the local Gunditjmara people. As well as having an abundance of kangaroos and other game, the relatively light tree cover included wattles which provided gum for use as food as well as cement. There were also she-oaks, the hardy wood of which was good for making weapons. And there were "Australian honeysuckles" -- banksia trees -- used for making a sweet drink by soaking the flower cones in water, and mixing in a little gum. As well, Tarrone took in part of a river known to the whites as the Moyne. Before the doctors' arrival, the spot had been a favourite haunt of the Gunditjmara tribe -- especially in spring time, when hundreds of eels could be caught as they tried

By permission of the National Library of Australia

"*View of Moroit (Koroit) or Tower Hill, extinct volcano between Lady Bay and Port Fairy in Australia Felix*". *Squatters with runs in this area included Dallas Bernard and James Kilgour, and the Bolden brothers. In this picture, a Gunditjmara family with a conical hut is depicted, bottom left.*

to make their annual pilgrimage downstream to the sea to breed.

During his Western District tour, Robinson had found an elaborate fishing weir at Tarrone. The weir was about 60 metres long, stretching across the river and turned back at each end. It was about 1.5 metres high, and had holes for eel pots at the ends, and at two or three places in the middle. Ducks were also plentiful in the waterholes along the river, and one of the few Gunditjmara who guided him through the area showed him several places where the tribe had had huts. But by the time the Chief Protector made his tour, the area had well and truly been taken over by Bernard and Kilgour. And although Robinson did not realise, his request for the doctors to keep their men away from the blacks need not have been made: the Chief Protector's guides were the first Aborigines who'd had the courage to visit for some time.[3]

Bernard would soon tire of the squatting life, deciding to leave the colony to pursue a long-standing interest in China, where he would end up off the coast on an iron paddle steamer of the East India Company, involved in the first Opium War. But before he left, Bernard would write a lengthy letter to Fyans complaining about the recent upsurge in Aboriginal violence and the devastating effects it was having. The letter stated that since accompanying Robinson onto the station, Gunditjmara people had visited numerous times. They had "continually disturbed" the cattle, and were believed to have killed many of them. On several occasions, groups of up to 40 of the blacks had gathered near the squatters' huts in a menacing manner. Bernard claimed they had been "made to retire", but without guns being fired, and "without their having been in any degree injured".

Despite this lack of violence against them, the doctor complained, the Gunditjmara people had not responded in kind. In the first week of 1842, a stockman had been attacked just near the huts by a large party of blacks, who threw about 10 spears. The attackers had ignored warning shots fired over their heads by the stockman, and had fled only when two other armed white men arrived at the scene. About three weeks later, a far more serious incident had occurred. A party of seven or eight Gunditjmara men had arrived at the stockyard at milking time, early in the morning. They had attacked the overseer, who received spear wounds on both sides of his body. One spear had penetrated about 10 centimetres into the Scotsman. A spear had also been thrown at the man employed to run the dairy at the station, but it had missed. The overseer had managed to strike two of the blacks with a large stake, causing them to drop their weapons, before they fled when men with guns heard the commotion and rushed from the huts.

In the next few days, Bernard told Fyans, the blacks had stolen three valuable horses from close to the huts, and had attempted to get into the paddock where the three remaining horses had to be kept. Then another serious incident had occurred only a week after the spearing of the overseer. A stockman had been watching a mob of cows within a few hundred metres of the huts when he was suddenly grabbed from behind by a group of Gunditjmara men that included one wounded by a blow from the overseer's stake. After seizing his musket, the Aborigines had tormented the white man by patting him on the back, and declaring with a grin: "White fellows no good; must kill 'em". The man was struck with a leanguil by one of his captors. Then another tried to shoot him, but could not work out how to discharge the gun. When the man managed to break free and run towards the huts, Bernard reported, he'd saved his life by dropping his whip, which the blacks stopped to pick it up rather than pursue him. The next day, a party had been sent out to search for two horses which had been with the man. Part of their flesh was found roasting on a fire at a deserted Gunditjmara camp nearby, where bones were scattered about. The blacks had heard the whites coming and had fled in such a hurry they'd left behind all their spears and other weapons.

Since this incident, a mob of cattle had been driven off by the Gunditjmara tribe, Bernard complained. Although many had been recovered, some were believed to have been killed. "The natives have evidently planned fresh attacks during the last week, prowling about the place at dawn of morning," he wrote. "On another occasion they threw spears from a distance at Dr Kilgour himself. Under these circumstances, the whole property of the station is going to ruin. Five horses out of six being killed, the cattle cannot be watched; the calves are lost about the run, the dairy ruined, and no man's life is safe. These outrages have been committed on a station on which I have myself seen, within the last few days, hundreds of kangaroo, ducks, pigeons, and other birds, besides great quantity of fish, thereby removing every possible excuse of insufficiency of food for the blacks." Nor had the blacks ever been maltreated on the station, Bernard claimed. It was common, he added, for them to say: "You touch black fellow, Mr Sievwright hang you." It was the same defiant remark attributed to the Gunditjmara people involved in the shooting incident over which Sandford Bolden had faced trial.

The squatters in the area, Bernard observed, feared with good reason that their dangers and difficulties would be aggravated by the arrival of Sievwright with his blacks at Mt Rouse. This was "not only from the violent bearing of the blacks towards the whites, but also from the hostile encounters between the several black tribes themselves". The doctor would list examples of the other "many other outrages" which had recently occurred. These included the murder of John Ritchie's hut-keeper, Thomas Bird, the serious wounding of Robert Whitehead's shepherd, and various robberies. He also listed the burning of

Colin Campbell's field of wheat, which Campbell himself did not blame on the blacks. Bernard requested that Fyans raise the issue urgently with La Trobe, on behalf of all the squatters in the Port Fairy district. No time should be lost, he suggested, in sending every available assistance, whether police or military, to protect the whites' lives and property -- "and to prevent a state of open war between the two races, which must otherwise inevitably arise".[4]

Bernard's partner had told Robinson he realised that the numerous dingoes in the neighbourhood had probably been responsible for killing of some calves at the station for which the Aborigines were being blamed. But Bernard's letter would make no mention of this. Nor did the squatter mention the possibility, as Robinson believed, that the blacks could also have been unfairly accused of being responsible for all of the horses that had gone missing. The letter of complaint against the blacks, in which the Englishman highlighted the loss of his horses, came just two months after one of his former stockmen had been transported to Norfolk Island for life after pleading guilty in the Supreme Court in Melbourne to horse theft. Robinson would later tell La Trobe that the stockman, Irishman Patrick Kelly, was one of what he regarded as the "depraved set of servants" employed by Bernard and Kilgour. He was "noted" for horse stealing.[5]

The *Geelong Advertiser* would certainly have no reservations about the accuracy of Bernard's claims against the Aborigines. Reporting the incidents complained of by the squatter just five days after his letter was written, the *Advertiser* would even embellish them. Backing his call for the colonial government to quickly provide protection for the white settlers of the district, the paper expressed fear that no effectual stop would be put to the "ravages" that were occurring "until the settlers be stirred up by their repeated wrongs to make a fearful example among the barbarians". According to the *Advertiser*, the blacks had killed Bernard and Kilgour's five horses, worth a total of 300 pounds, "by thrusting spears down their throats", then devoured the carcases on the spot. This was "the most characteristic instance of their combined dishonesty, brutality, and savage grossness" the paper had yet heard about the Aborigines. "The barbarians have got tired of fat wethers and fat bullocks, and nothing now will gratify the refined appetites of the gourmandising thieves but horse-flesh!" it declared. And the "pseudo-philanthropists of England" would argue that the interests of the Aborigines and the settlers were identical! This ought to be so, but it assuredly was not so at present.[6]

Flogger Fyans had recently told La Trobe he believed the Aborigines had suffered "a very trifling disadvantage and injury", despite the rapid occupation of their country by Britons. He'd made the extraordinary claim in a letter crafted for consumption in London, after La Trobe requested information about the Aborigines for the Secretary of State for the Colonies. "Though their hostile aggressions have been great, the settlers have borne all, and only in a few instances have they protected themselves and property with the loss of life on the part of the native," Fyans wrote. "Under every circumstance, I conceive that much praise is due to the character of the Europeans in this country. They have displayed great forbearances, and evinced an inclination to benefit the Aborigines on every occasion. I also remark that the most trifling act on the part of the European is noticed, and if possible turned to their disgrace, when murder, outrages, and destruction of property pass un-noticed on the part of the native. Situated as the settler is, he dreads to protect his property, and tacitly submits."[7]

Just a few weeks later, while forwarding Bernard's letter, Fyans would suggest to La Trobe that the days of tacit submission should be declared over. It was time, he asserted, for the government to use military force against the blacks. He asked for the immediate deployment of "a strong party of soldiers" to help the white settlers fight Aboriginal attackers. "Under every circumstance, it is necessary that strong measures are immediately taken with these savages, to prevent a continuance of murder and destruction of property," Fyans wrote. The soldiers should be quartered "on the different establishments about Mt Rouse". Fyans told La Trobe that the same tribe was responsible for the attacks on Kilgour and Bernard's station and others in the Port Fairy area. This tribe had also been responsible for wounding his policeman, John Carty, and stealing a police horse. When he moved against the culprits, he would rather not be putting more horses at risk. From the nature of the country around Port Fairy, he pointed out, infantry would be more useful to him than Mounted Police.[8]

To emphasise the urgency of his request for military action, Fyans would end his letter by informing La Trobe that the blacks had murdered another white man. The latest victim, he advised, was a hut-keeper of Thomas Woolley, in what the whites called the Victoria Valley, in the southern part of the Grampians. Fyans reported the murder as fact, although the man had only gone missing, and no body had been found. Woolley's station was in the territory of the Tjapwurong people, adjoining that of the Gunditjmara. So if confirmed, it would show that the new wave of resistance against the invaders was not confined to one tribe. Certainly, inter-race relations in the Victoria Valley were dismal. It had been after a visit to Woolley's station six months earlier that Robinson had recorded his remark of there being people "with no more humanity about them than their shape". And while he was in the area, he would hear of one of Woolley's employees, perhaps the missing man, being among a party of whites who had rushed a Tjapwurong camp and seized all the spears. Although Robinson believed the weapons had been returned on demand, such incidents had obviously only aggravated tensions.[9]

With either astoundingly naive optimism, or another bout of culpable self-delusion, La Trobe had just written a letter declaring his belief that the situation in the most disturbed part of his realm had become more peaceful. The Superintendent was replying to the report from the Portland Police Magistrate, James Blair, on the allegations made by Robert Tulloh. He told Blair he agreed with his opinion on "the general improved state of the Western district during the last year or 18 months". This was the period in which Blair had claimed there had not been an "authenticated" case of a black being killed "by the hands of a white man" -- and which La Trobe had stressed when castigating Benjamin Hurst for his "reprehensible" conduct in spreading Tulloh's allegations.

The Superintendent also enclosed for Blair's information, and then delivery, the reply he'd written to 19 white men who'd signed a petition objecting to Hurst's actions. La Trobe told the signatories he'd assured Gipps that even if atrocities such as those referred to by Tulloh and then Hurst had ever been practised, they would not be tolerated "by the present class of settlers". The character of the squatters now inhabiting the district, the "better class of servants employed", and "a really improved state of feeling with reference to the Aboriginal inhabitants", was a far stronger guarantee against acts of cruelty or lawless retaliation than any mere extension of police arrangements, he added. This would be of little advantage, if not altogether futile.[10]

To his embarrassment, within the next few days La Trobe would receive the report from Blair telling him of the apparent "general move among the Aborigines", and he would hear of the murder of Thomas Bird. Then he would receive Fyans' letter mentioning the murder of another shepherd, and calling for the use of the military against the blacks. The Superintendent quickly realised he'd lost touch with what was happening on the frontier, and moved to appear as though he hadn't. In a reply to Fyans, he stated he'd taken it for granted, on receiving previous information about "the aggressions of the natives" in the Port Fairy area, that Fyans would have immediately sent "a strong detachment" of police. "This must be done immediately," he declared. "The duty of affording, as far as practicable, protection to the settlers, under the circumstances detailed, is of paramount importance."

On Fyans' proposal for the deployment of infantry at the stations of the squatters around Mt Rouse, La Trobe was ambivalent. "It is my duty to state that past experience leads me to differ from you in opinion as to the real benefit to be derived from such a course, and has shown me that there are strong objections to it," he told the Commissioner. Nevertheless, he he was willing to give Fyans the use of a military detachment, then stationed at Portland, if this would help to preserve order in the district. The soldiers could be deployed wherever Fyans may recommend. La Trobe enclosed a copy of a letter he was sending to the

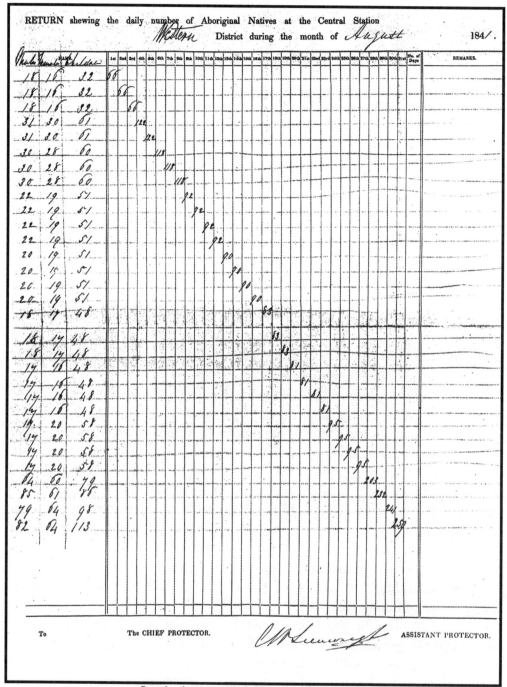

"*Return shewing the daily number of Aboriginal Natives at the Central Station, Western District, during the month of August 1841.*" *At the start of the month, at the Lake Terang camp there were 66 Aborigines: 18 adult males, 16 adult females and 32 children. The numbers fluctuated, but quickly climbed in the last days of August, reaching a total of 259 at the end of the month: 82 adult males, 64 adult females, and 113 children. Still the work-for-food scheme remained suspended on Robinson's orders.*

commanding officer of the detachment, requesting him to make available "a steady non-commissioned officer and such party of men as may be considered sufficient" if Fyans requested them. The soldiers should be ordered that the sole object of their mission would be "to afford the settlers protection in case of attack". These orders must be unambiguous, and not departed from.[11]

At the same time, La Trobe would write to George Robinson, instructing him to leave immediately for the area around Port Fairy and Mt Rouse to inquire into "the real character" of the recent Aboriginal attacks. "I wish particularly to learn from you in how far Mr Sievwright possesses the power of control over the natives by whom he is accompanied; in how far these are concerned in the outrages complained of; and what is the line of conduct adopted by Mr Sievwright in reference to them," La Trobe wrote. The letter, written just two days after Sievwright had arrived at Mt Rouse, was received with delight by the Chief Protector, who saw it as giving him the opportunity he'd long awaited to rid himself of his assistant. Robinson had already stuck a dagger in Sievwright's back, less than a month earlier, and now La Trobe was giving him the chance to drive it deeper. The initial stab by the Chief Protector came in comments on Sievwright's report for September to November 1841. Robinson wrote the comments while still smarting over the damage to his reputation from the series of events that had culminated in the execution of Bob and Jack only the day before. He'd been in no mood to give any credit to anyone else claiming to know how to deal with the Aborigines.

The report by Sievwright, he told La Trobe, was "vague and unsatisfactory". It also did not comply with his instructions to provide a daily journal of proceedings, and did not provide a single useful fact. "The present paper is quite in character with the other documents from this Assistant," Robinson complained. "It is obtruding his opinions uncalled for and unasked, a line of conduct which His Excellency the Governor so strongly deprecates, and I am sure that he is totally incompetent and unable to give a decided opinion on the present subject, namely the issue of rations indiscriminately to all the Aboriginal natives of his district." The report, Robinson claimed, was also inconsistent. To prove this claim, he quoted Sievwright's remark that the young and able-bodied should at all times be required to perform "a task suited to their capabilities" in return for their food. "Mr Sievwright was at perfect liberty and was authorised to supply food to the natives on these terms in return for the work done -- the sick, the aged, orphans, mothers of families and chiefs being provided for," the Chief Protector claimed.[12]

It was grossly deceptive for Robinson to make such a statement. First, Sievwright had never been told he could issue rations to "mothers of families" or "chiefs". But secondly, and more importantly, Robinson was ignoring the fact that the amount of work which his assistant had been able to ask his charges to perform was extremely limited because his agricultural operations had for months been largely suspended. Sievwright had reported that on average during September, he'd had 209 Aborigines with him each day at Terang. Robinson -- and La Trobe -- would make no comment on his calculation that the daily allowance he'd been able to give to them amounted to only about 135 grams of flour. They would also ignore his frank admission that it was the blacks with him who were making attacks on the flocks and herds of the neighbouring squatters because they were hungry. As well, when the report was forwarded to Sydney, neither Robinson nor La Trobe would comment on Sievwright's reminder that he'd again been making monthly appeals for the ability to issue more supplies -- or on his warning that "decided measures ought at once to be taken to check the impending evil".[13]

CHAPTER 22
In the balance

AS the colonisation of the Port Phillip District proceeded, the fate of its original inhabitants would continue to be one issue of concern pursued by the Aborigines Protection Society, based in The Strand in London. The day Sievwright and his charges arrived at Mt Rouse, the *Port Phillip Gazette* would publish an open letter from the Society, addressed to the clergy, magistrates and other colonists of Port Phillip. The letter stated bluntly that from information reaching London, it was feared that the blacks of Port Phillip were "rapidly extirpating". "The Aborigines Protection Society is friendly to colonisation, and includes in the number of its committee and supporters some who are largely interested in colonial prosperity," the letter pointed out. "But it is impossible as men, patriots, philanthropists or Christians to behold, without anxiety, the ruin of the people we shall be accessory in supplanting, unless our modes of colonisation be directed with greater humanity and wisdom than in times past."

"In Port Phillip, the land which once constituted the support of tribes of natives, now scarcely knows them, it is understood," the letter went on. "And if this not be the case yet, that it soon must, is a conclusion which obviously results from the mode of colonisation pursued there -- from a system which entirely over-looks the moral and substantial claim of the natives." Not realising that reserves had already been set aside, the Society called on the Port Phillip colonists to demand their establishment. At the same time, the colonists should "impress sentiments of humanity and consideration for the natives" upon their shepherds and servants. The Society had also not yet heard of the storm created in Melbourne by the Wesleyan missionary, Benjamin Hurst. The colonists, it suggested, should be supporting the efforts of those trying to convert the Aborigines to Christianity. "It is in their power to sustain the noble exertions of Christian missionaries by illustrating, in their intercourse with the natives, those principles which the missionaries are engaged in inculcating -- more especially by keeping ardent spirits and liquors from the natives, and by stamping with their strongest censure, and with virtuous severity, everything approaching to the character of licentious intercourse with their women."[1]

Word had not yet reached London of the recent commotion over the public remarks by Hurst about the treatment of the Port Phillip blacks. The most serious allegation by the Wesleyan missionary had been that white men had adopted the practice of going out on Sundays professedly to shoot kangaroos, but in reality to shoot Aborigines in cold blood. In admonishing Hurst for spreading this allegation, La Trobe had claimed that Police Magistrate Blair's inquiry had shown it was "untrue as regards the past and the present time". A few days later, replying to the petition from 19 squatters who'd objected to Hurst's actions, he'd been a little more circumspect, acknowledging that atrocities may have occurred in the past. But he was confident that none would now be tolerated by the better class of squatters, or the men they employed. It would not be long before an incident would occur that would make La Trobe eat his words.[2]

A group of eight Kirrae blacks -- two men, their wives, two other women, and two children -- would leave Sievwright's camp at Mt Rouse, planning to return to their country for a time. Two days later, they'd travelled about 20 kilometres to the south-east, where Thomas Osbrey and Sydney Smith operated a station as joint agents for a wealthy Dublin-based Irishman, Charles Fitzgerald. The eight blacks set up camp in a clump of tea-tree in a gully known as One-one-derang, about a kilometre from Osbrey and Smith's head station on what had become known as Muston's Creek. Late at night, the group was suddenly awoken by eight white men who rode up, dismounted, then opened fire with guns. Three of the women and one of the children were shot dead. Wooigouing had one gunshot wound through her chest, and her right thigh broken by another shot. The child, a boy aged about three, was also shot through the chest. So was Niatgoucher, a widow who'd been several months pregnant. The scorching on her side would later show how close the killer had been when he'd opened fire. Coneyer, another widow, was shot through the abdomen, her left arm broken by another bullet. The fourth woman, Wonigoniber, was severely wounded, with a gunshot wound in the back and another through her right hand.

Pwebingannai, who'd been married to Wooingouing, and Calangamite, the husband of Wonigoniber, managed to avoid the shots, one of them grabbing Coneyer's child, Unibicquiang, as they fled. Taking turns at carrying Unibicquiang on their shoulders, the two men started running back towards Mt Rouse. Trying as much as possible to avoid open areas on the way lest the horsemen returned to complete their slaughter, the distraught and exhausted blacks would take until almost midday to reach Sievwright's camp. There was much excitement among the Kirrae and the other blacks at the news of what had happened. Worried that members of his family could be selected for revenge, Sievwright nevertheless decided to set off for the scene in his box cart at daybreak the following morning. Grief-stricken Pwebingannai, painted white in mourning for the death of his wife, would agree to go as his guide. When they reached the scene of the massacre, they found Wonigoniber still alive, but weak. The Assistant Protector gave her water and made her as comfortable as he could before driving his cart up to Osbrey and Smith's hut and demanding that they accompany him back to the site. There he made both the squatters sign a document giving detailed descriptions of the wounds on the bodies of the three dead women, and dead child, as well as Wonigoniber's.

After cutting off one of his dead wife's arms to take with him back to Mt Rouse, Pwebingannai would -- on Sievwright's orders -- burn her body and the other three. As he did so, Sievwright would return to the squatters' hut, and call all the white men together. They included the station manager, Richard Guiness Hill, a nephew of the Dublin brewer, Sir Richard Guiness, the hut-keeper, Joseph Betts, and labourer, George Arabin. The killing of three women and a child, Sievwright declared, could not go unpunished, and if necessary he was ready to provide a reward of 50 pounds for information that would lead to a conviction. Despite this inducement, all of the white men present denied knowing anything about the murders. All of them were lying. All of them knew that Hill, Betts, and Arabin had been members of the party which had attacked the blacks. Other members had included three visitors to the station on the day -- squatter Charles

"When they reached the scene of the massacre, they found Wonigoniber still alive..."

Smith, Melbourne draper and squatter Robert Whitehead, and Arthur D. Boursiquot, a cousin of Hill who practised as an accountant in Melbourne. Sievwright would return to Mt Rouse with Pwebingannai, now a widower, and Wonigoniber, close to death, in his cart. And the whites at Osbrey and Smith's renewed their warnings to each other that anyone giving information to the authorities would be shot.[3]

That same day, while Sievwright battled with his scant medical supplies to save Wonigoniber's life, her relatives milled anxiously around him, Gipps in Sydney would write a letter to La Trobe that would have profound consequences for all the Aborigines of the Western District -- and their Protector. It related to the comments Robinson had made on one of Sievwright's recent reports. He had accused his assistant of being "totally incompetent and unable to give a decided opinion on the present subject, namely the issue of rations indiscriminately to all the Aboriginal natives of his district." Somehow, Gipps interpreted this comment on *what Robinson regarded as a proposal* by Sievwright to be a comment on what Sievwright was *actually doing*. "To bring together large parties of natives from distant parts and to issue to them indiscriminately rations from the government is quite at variance with the orders under which Mr Sievwright is acting," the Governor declared.

But Gipps would not stop there. Robinson, he knew, would never have the effrontery to question the actions of the New South Wales government. Sievwright was showing no such obsequious pliability, and the Governor was alarmed that word of the Assistant Protector's criticism of his administration may reach London. As well, Gipps had received information which raised doubts about Sievwright's character and behaviour, most recently from one of the Bolden brothers, eager to besmirch him after the squatter's trial. Gipps instructed the Colonial Secretary to send a letter to La Trobe suggesting it was time to get rid of Sievwright, who appeared to pay no attention to the instructions of either the Chief Protector or the government. "The repeated reports of the inefficiency of Mr Sievwright made to His Excellency officially, added to extremely injurious reports affecting his moral character, which have reached the Governor through channels which though not official, are such as to have little doubt of their correctness, force him to request Your Honour to report whether the continuance of Mr Sievwright in the public service can be creditable to government, or calculated to advance the cause, for the furtherance of which he was sent to Port Phillip," the letter stated.[4]

When La Trobe received the letter, the Chief Protector had just left on the trip to the Western District on which he'd ordered him. He'd already told Robinson to provide a report on Sievwright's degree of control over the Aborigines with him, and on how the Assistant Protector was dealing with the "outrages" being committed by them. There was therefore no need to send a message to Robinson informing him of the Governor's letter. He could await the Chief Protector's report first. Robinson would take a week to reach Mt Rouse, arriving on a rainy 15 March 1842 -- just over a month since the establishment of the reserve. The number of Aborigines present had risen to 263, about a quarter of what Robinson estimated to be the population of the area, with the arrival that day of a group of Bolagher people. There were 91 men, 71 women and 101 Aboriginal children at the camp. For the previous two weeks, some of the Jarcoort Kirrae blacks who'd come from Terang had been engaged in helping to dig a channel to drain a marshy area constantly supplied by a spring at the foot of Mt Rouse. The drainage plan was starting to work, Sievwright told the Chief Protector, and would "amply repay the labour expended upon it" by opening up a larger part of the best soil in the neighbourhood for cultivation. His black labourers had also been involved in felling and rooting up trees, and in continuing to erect brush fences to enclose the proposed wheat paddocks, and vegetable garden.

Over the next two days, Robinson would help his assistant to lay out the site of a future black "township". He directed Sievwright to vacate the huts he and his family had taken over from John Cox, and to build new huts on a slight rise at the northern base of Mt Rouse. Robinson would also endeavour to provide some entertainment for the blacks at the camp, for example by showing them how he could use sunlight shining through a magnifying glass to burn marks on a sheet of paper. The demonstration wasn't appreciated. "The marks excited fear and the wild blacks said there would be plenty of sickness," the Chief Protector recorded. Then Robinson decided that he and Sievwright should both ride off to investigate the recent "outrages" involving the Gunditjmara, as outlined in William Bernard's letter to Fyans. Accompanied by one of Sievwright's servants, they would first set off for John Cox's new station, about 40 kilometres to the south-west, where two weeks earlier a whaler-shepherd whom the squatter employed had been speared in the chest and abdomen during a raid on a flock of sheep. The man was not seriously wounded, and was recovering. Cox's overseer, James Brock, told the Protectors that a few days earlier, a small number of Aboriginal men, women and children had come to the station. When the shepherd had stated he thought he recognised the man who'd speared him, an unsuccessful attempt was made to capture him. Shots were fired, Brock admitted, but he made no mention of casualties.

Next, Robinson and Sievwright rode to James Hunter's nearby station to investigate the raids there, and the clash with Fyan's Border Police. After Sievwright had taken statements from Hunter's employees, he and Robinson set off into the stony rises nearby to try to make contact with the blacks alleged to have been involved. As guides, they took one of Hunter's stockmen, and a black who had accompanied them from Mt Rouse, named Bartburnborrite, or Charley. They were led across a large dry swamp to the rises, where they had to dismount and carefully lead their horses through the rocks towards where they could see a camp-fire. As they approached, a few Aboriginal women fled from the camp, comprising some huts made of mud, others of stone. Along with a spear, and some baskets, also found in the camp was evidence of one of the recent thefts from Hunter's -- the backbone and hooves of a horse.

Spotting the fire of another camp in the rises, Sievwright proceeded there, but it too had been abandoned by the time they reached it. After waiting some hours for the return of the blacks, a few women eventually approached, wondering what had happened to the food they'd left baking. Through the imperfect conversation Bartburnborrite was able to have with them, not really understanding their language, Sievwright managed to convince the women of their peaceful intentions. The women eventually went off and returned with some more members of their tribe, the total numbering 33. Again a difficult conversation was held, at the end of which Sievwright believed the group had agreed to meet the following day at Hunter's, and then visit the Mt Rouse reserve. On their way back to Hunter's in the evening to camp for the night, Sievwright and Robinson would see a large fishing weir, and numerous snares "of a very large scale" built in open areas by the blacks for catching kangaroos and birds. It had been a fascinating day for both of the Protectors, and one on which they'd had the opportunity for unprecedented co-operation. But Robinson had been irked by the fact that Sievwright had acted independently by going to the second camp and setting up a communication with the blacks. Such was the Chief Protector's wrath that on their return to Hunter's station, he did not speak to his assistant.[5]

Just after dawn the following morning, about 30 Aborigines arrived at the station from the rocks. Mostly men, but with some women and children, they included Jupiter, Jackey, Billy, The Doctor, and Bumbletoe -- five of the blacks for whom Acheson French had issued arrest warrants. There were 15 white men at Hunter's, other than the Protectors, and they urged the new overseer at the station, Richard Manifold, to demand that the warrants be acted on. Some of the men, former convicts who now made a living splitting logs ready for sawing, had been among those who'd made statements to French, on which the warrants were partly based. Manifold approached Robinson and Sievwright, but they rejected an offer to help seize the blacks. "I came not to apprehend nor to persecute, much less to act treacherously to these people whose confidence I am called upon to gain," was Robinson's explanation.

To the astonishment of the white men, the Protectors requisitioned 11 kilograms of flour and half a kilogram of tobacco from Hunter's store, which they distributed to the Gunditjmara people. Robinson then ordered Sievwright and

Bartburnborrite to quickly lead the blacks away from Hunter's station, towards Mt Rouse. Sievwright would accompany the group for about 13 kilometres, occasionally driving the old men of the party in his spring cart. Then he would leave them with Bartburnborrite for the rest of the journey, and when he turned to rejoin Robinson he believed they were on their way to the reserve, with Hunter's flour and tobacco as samples of what they could earn if they became labourers there. Sievwright reported to Robinson that they'd made the right decision. One of the blacks had told him that the splitters at Hunter's had interfered with Gunditjmara women. This is what had provoked the clash at John Cox's which the splitters had reported to Acheson French.[6]

Next, the Protectors proceeded together along the rough track to Port Fairy, more than 50 kilometres away, through country that was mostly either densely forested or swampy, and which had not been taken up by squatters. For part of the way, Robinson tied his horse to the back of Sievwright's gig and travelled in it, until one of the wheels caught on a tree and he was thrown out. However, he managed to catch hold of the shaft, and saved himself from a heavy fall. A little later, Sievwright and his servant were thrown from the cart, but they too escaped injury. It was almost dusk by the time they reached Colin Campbell's farm, where they received a rare warm welcome. Campbell had told Robinson on his previous visit to the area almost a year earlier that the Gunditjmara blacks who lived in the area had stolen at least four tonnes of potatoes, and about 100 sheep. But he was now "on better terms with them than ever" and his potatoes were seldom touched. Black labour was also useful to him, especially during the whaling season, and on several occasions he believed the Gunditjmara had protected his property from other tribes.[7]

The previous year, at a large swamp not far from Campbell's, Robinson had witnessed one Gunditjmara gathering which he estimated to number between 300 and 400. It was the biggest group of blacks he'd see during his tour of the Western District. When he and Sievwright visited the swamp, they would come across about 60 blacks. Through a young boy who knew some English, and who acted as an interpreter, Sievwright would invite them to join him at Mt Rouse. But they would reject the invitation, "being afraid of the other tribes they would meet there". It was, the Assistant Protector believed, a minor setback, and probably just as well for the time being. "I imagine this objection will be easily overcome when it shall be expedient to congregate more than are at present at the reserve," he recorded.[8]

It would have been regarded by their fellow whites as partial behaviour for Sievwright and Robinson to have passed through the area without visiting the station of John Ritchie, where Thomas Bird had been killed, as well as Robert Whitehead's, where his speared shepherd was still in bed recovering. On a hot day towards the end of March 1842, the Protectors would also go to the station of English partners, Henry Loughnan and Lewis Innes Lynch, on the Merri River, near Whitehead's. There a serious robbery had recently occurred. A party of Gunditjmara had driven off 353 sheep, firing a shot at Loughnan. The employees at the station, who included a Barrabool man, had managed to catch up with the thieves and recover the sheep, but they were then seized again by the blacks and taken away after a clash when the whites ran out of ammunition for their guns.[9]

At one other squatters' station -- that of brothers John and William Allan, near where the Hopkins River met the sea -- the Protectors would hear positive reports about the blacks. The Allan brothers had introduced tobacco smoking among the Gunditjmara who lived in the area, and ever since had managed to remain on good terms by providing regular figs of tobacco. So good had relations been that a shepherd formerly employed by the Allans had briefly gone to live with the blacks. But soon before the arrival of the Protectors, one of the brothers had asked the tribe to send him away, and he'd since left the district. Robinson was pleased this had occurred. He had intended arranging for the white man to be "removed" from the tribe because he believed "such a connection would lead to mischievous results".[10]

It was not the first such case. One young white servant had twice recently appeared in the Police Office at Geelong for absconding from his master and living with either the Colijon or the Kirrae people, "apparently determined to renounce a civilised life altogether". On the first occasion, he'd been sentenced to several days' solitary confinement with bread and water rations. On the second occasion, he'd been jailed for three months, prompting the *Geelong Advertiser* to call for the establishment of an institution for the "reformation" of such people. "Means of punishment we have in abundance, but it is very questionable how far the conduct of this youth can be considered *criminal*, springing as it does from misdirected education, rather than from any vicious propensity," the paper remarked.[11]

About two months before the youth's first appearance in the Police Office, a case even more disturbing to the white authorities had been reported in the Western District. A white man named Edwards, believed to be a runaway convict who'd earlier been reported killed during a raid on the Wedge brothers' station further north, had been seen leading a group of Gunditjmara on a station operated by Stephen Henty, north of Portland. The informant was an employee of Henty, who'd stated the blacks with Edwards had been "extremely troublesome". Much of his and his fellow employees' time was now spent defending the property of their master. Portland Police Magistrate James Blair told La Trobe that without Mounted Police, he could do nothing to try to capture

Edwards. All he could do was to tell Henty to try to apprehend him, if necessary under the "Rogues and Vagabonds Act".[12]

Edwards did not stay around long enough to be arrested. In any event, the Gunditjmara hardly needed a white man to lead them in their resistance to the invasion by his fellow whites. It was at the same station of Stephen Henty that they set fire to the field of oats, months after the report about Edwards being with them. Then Gunditjmara guerillas would attack the station again, driving Henty's men from it, even as Sievwright and Robinson were travelling through another part of their territory. "In the present instance, they displayed the same disposition to mischief," James Blair reported, "beating down a building with large stones, breaking a plough, and destroying as much property as they could." Blair told La Trobe that the blacks could not be allowed to keep "undisturbed possession" of the station, as it was one of the resting places for bullock teams travelling to and from Portland, the main road passing close by. He'd requested the officer-in-charge of the military detachment at Portland to send a party of soldiers to the station "to preserve order" until the expected arrival in the next few days of Foster Fyans.[13]

Before he would receive Blair's letter about the Henty station, La Trobe would be visited by James Kilgour, who would present a memorial from squatters and other white men in the Port Fairy area. It complained of the "great and increasing want of security to life and property" because of "the absence of any protection" against the blacks. "Their numbers, their ferocity, and their cunning, render them peculiarly formidable," the whites protested, "and the outrages of which they are daily and nightly guilty, and which they accomplish generally with impunity and success, may, we fear, lead to a still more distressing state of things, unless some measures, prompt and effectual, be immediately taken to prevent matters coming to that unhappy crisis." When life and property were in constant danger, the petitioners remarked, there could be no prosperity. "No immunity is to be purchased; such treatment only accelerates the fate it was meant to avert," they claimed.

"We would represent to your Honour that this district is eminently well qualified for the support of stock, as well as for the purposes of agriculture, and that a large population would be attracted here by these advantages, if the knowledge of this dreadful drawback did not oppose it," the petition continued. "Your Honour will doubtless learn with regret that some of our number intend leaving the district wholly and entirely, on account of the natives." And the signatories believed Sievwright was at least partly to blame for their woes. "Their usually large number is swelled by the addition of those resident with the Protector, and we are bound to say that these latter are in nowise better disposed towards the settlers than are the former, and their knowledge of our habits makes them still more dangerous as neighbours."

Kilgour's petition then outlined what it alleged were the recent "outrages" committed by the blacks in the Port Fairy area. The list included the killing of four white men and the wounding of eight others. As well, it claimed that the Aborigines had stolen about 3000 sheep, 10 horses, seven head of cattle, 16 cows, more than 100 calves, and 10 tonnes of potatoes. Most of the attacks and thefts, the petition stated, had occurred within the previous two months. In fact, one of the murders listed was that of Thomas Hayes, 20 months earlier. One of the other reported killings on the list was that of the hutkeeper of Thomas Woolley who'd gone missing, but whose fate was unknown. The other two murders had been confirmed and *had* occurred recently. One was that of Thomas Bird. The other murder, which had only just become known, had been that of a shepherd employed by squatting partners, Peter Hutcheson and James Kidd, on the Hopkins River. He had reportedly been found with a spear through his heart, although little else would ever become publicly known about his death. Several of the thefts which were said to have been committed recently were also those which had been reported back in 1840, and others were exaggerated. For example, the 10 tonnes of potatoes, allegedly stolen from Colin Campbell, was a much higher figure than Campbell had given to Robinson for a theft that had occurred long ago.[14]

It would not be for some time that La Trobe would learn that Kilgour had not only exaggerated, but had faked signatures to his petition, and he would initially assume its details were accurate. In his reply to the document, the Superintendent expressed sympathy that the whites of the Port Fairy area were suffering great losses, and were in "constant expectation of attack" from the blacks. "From my own knowledge of the circumstances under which many of you betake yourselves to the life of a settler, and my belief (which I hope never may be shaken) that in the case of the majority, these losses have been unprovoked by any proceeding on your part, beyond that of placing yourselves and your property in manifest peril, I consider that your position presents a strong claim upon the immediate attention of the government," he wrote. "But situated as you are, it is far easier to deplore your losses than to prevent them. The evils you complain of are those which have everywhere accompanied the occupation of a new country inhabited by savage tribes."

It was greatly to be deplored, La Trobe went on, that the presence of Sievwright "and other means of prevention" had not done more to repress "aggression and retaliation" by the blacks, and had failed to establish a good understanding between the races. The colonial government would continue to try to achieve these objectives without delay. At the same time, the settlers could make a just claim for sympathy and pity for the loss of European property or lives. But this claim could only be made if the Aboriginal attacks were unprovoked and unre-venged. One act of "savage retaliation or cruelty" on the part of the whites would make abhorrence the dominant feeling in the minds of most men. "And, I regret to state that I have before me a statement presented in a form which I dare not discredit, showing that such acts are perpetrated among you," La Trobe told the petitioners.

The Superintendent was referring to a report from Sievwright on the recent murders of the three Aboriginal women and the child at the Muston's Creek sta-tion operated by Thomas Osbrey and Sydney Smith, both of whom were appar-ent signatories to the petition. The Assistant Protector's report was the first La Trobe had heard of the murders, and he reacted with abhorrence. "Will not the commission of such crimes call down the wrath of God, and do more to check the prosperity of your district, and to ruin your prospects, than all the difficul-ties and losses under which you labour?" he asked the Port Fairy settlers. "I call upon you as your first duty to yourselves, and to your adopted country, to come forward in aid of the authorities, to clear up the obscurity with which this deed is as yet involved; and purging yourselves, and your servants, from all knowl-edge of and participation in such a crime, never to repose until the murderers are declared, and your district is relieved from the stain of harbouring them within its boundaries."[15]

At about the same time, La Trobe would receive a letter from the Grampians squatter, Horatio Wills, complaining of "the present alarming state" of that area. Wills claimed that for about a year, from the conciliatory measures adopted by himself and his fellow squatters, the local blacks had been "pacific". For some time, his station had been "a general rendezvous" for the local blacks. But in the past two months, there had been attacks on his property and employees. These attacks he blamed on "predatory tribes" which had come from a distance. "The cattle herd of my immediate neighbour, from 1200 head, are now supposed not to exceed 600 on the run or its vicinity," Wills told La Trobe. "They have been driven through the country, and within the last seven days he has had two of his best horses killed in endeavouring to collect them. This is too serious a loss to be submitted to with patience. The blacks of my neighbourhood assure me that the 'wild blacks' have destroyed a considerable number, and have frequently urged me to go out with them to drive their enemies away from the cattle of my neighbour."

On his visit to Wills' station eight months earlier, Robinson had received plen-ty of evidence from the local blacks -- not intruders -- of killings in which Wills and his men had been involved. It was these killings which the Chief Protector believed had prompted the murder of one of Wills' shepherds, John Collicoat. Presumably, Wills apparently did not want to add to his list of victims without having at least warned the authorities that it was imminent. "Situated as this neighbourhood is, at a remote distance from magisterial authority, we are subjected to loss of life and property, without redress, unless we infringe the laws," the squatter wrote. "We submit in many instances to loss of property without repining, but when life is at stake, unless some effectual means of lawful resistance be applied, we shall be compelled, in self-defence, to measures that may involve us in unpleasant consequences."

A few evenings before writing, Wills told La Trobe, an Aboriginal woman had alerted the whites at his station that a certain black man who'd been at the nearby camp the previous night had threatened to murder one of the shepherds. The squatter decided to try to take the would-be murderer into custody. Along with one of his men, and a black guide, Wills stated he'd sneaked up to the camp at night. "A feeble light was emitted by the dying fires, and I could distinguish nothing but a mass of blacks, with a great quantity of weapons around them," he wrote. "One glance at the numerous warlike implements convinced me that they were strangers." But Wills obviously thought they would speak the same language as the locals. He claimed that he'd stood on a log, "and desired them, in their own language, to remain quiet". The squatter gave no indication of whether they'd understood his imperfect Tjapwurong dialect, before one of them had sprung at him. According to Wills' account, the white man he'd taken with him opened fire, causing the black to fall back, wounded. Hearing the rustling of spears, the squatter then fired over the Aborigines' heads, and they retreated. Wills gave no other instance of violence against the blacks in his area. But he told La Trobe that force would be needed "to suppress the incursions of distant tribes". He suggested that an unpaid magistrate be nominated in the area, and given "special constables", to exercise this force when necessary.[16]

A report from a squatter like Wills should have been checked for reliability before being further circulated in the colonial bureaucracy. But once again, La Trobe would conduct no such check before sending it to Gipps. With Wills' letter, La Trobe would send Gipps a copy of Kilgour's fraudulent petition, and the reply he'd made to it. He told the Governor he believed the document's claims were accurate. For example, he accepted the claim that four white men had been killed in the previous two months in the Western District. At most, the figure was three, although still only two had been confirmed. Crucially, La Trobe would also believe the petition's claim that Sievwright had been partly responsible for the disturbed state of the Western District.

"Without pretending to determine the various causes that may have conspired to render the preventive measures adopted by the government by the appointment of a Protector for the Western District, of little or no avail, I cannot but consider it a complete failure," La Trobe told Gipps. "Further, it would appear as though the existing danger had been seriously aggravated by the course pursued by the Assistant Protector, in collecting from far and near a large number of natives, whom circumstances neither enabled him to employ nor feed, and over whom he could exercise neither physical nor moral control. A catalogue of robberies and aggressions in the adjacent stations, by parties so brought together, both in the vicinity of Mr Sievwright's temporary station at Keilambete, and now in the vicinity of Mt Rouse, would convince his Excellency of this. On the other hand, I fear that the demeanour of the Protector towards the settler has been in too many instances that of defiance rather than that of conciliation, and very much calculated to give the latter the impression that their interests were neither considered nor protected, thus fostering a spirit in the European residents which it is the most anxious desire of the government to remove."

Plans to use the military detachment at Portland to help to protect the Western District settlers from the Aborigines had meanwhile fallen through, with its pending withdrawal because of the role of its commanding officer in a disturbance in the township. La Trobe reminded Gipps that he'd ordered Fyans to the area where the blacks were most troublesome with the whole of the Border Police under his command, numbering 12 men. The Lands Commissioner had been told not to withdraw the troopers "until the disorders were repressed". In addition to two Mounted Police sent to The Grange to help Police Magistrate French, three were now being sent to Portland to be under the orders of Police Magistrate Blair. No further police were available. As well, La Trobe told Gipps he was still awaiting the outcome of a visit to the area by the Chief Protector, who'd been given a particular brief to ascertain the line of conduct pursued by his assistant in relation to the attacks by the blacks. Sievwright's future, and that of the Western District Aborigines, was in the balance.[17]

CHAPTER 23
An arrest at Mt Rouse

UNDER an Act passed by the British Parliament in 1823, New South Wales was given a limited form of constitutional government. The autocratic powers of the colony's Governor were curbed slightly with the introduction of an appointed Legislative Council, and the Supreme Court was given full independence from the Governor. The Legislative Council had the power to pass laws that applied specifically to the New South Wales. Legislation, however, could only be initiated by the Governor, after the Chief Justice had certified that it was not contrary to English law. When the 1823 Act expired in 1827, it was replaced by another one with similar provisions. But even after this came into effect, there was still confusion in the colony over whether the Supreme Court had jurisdiction over one type of case. Forty years after the arrival of the first white settlers, even the judges of the Supreme Court could not decide whether they should become involved in crimes committed *among* the Aborigines. Rather than make a decision, on several occasions they allowed cases to lapse.

It was not until 1836 that the Court was finally forced to make a ruling, in a case in which an Aborigine named Jack Congo Murral was arraigned for the murder of a fellow black named Jabinguy. A defence lawyer appointed by the Court argued that it had no jurisdiction. Neither the accused nor the victim was a subject of the King of Great Britain, in whose name their country had been occupied. Nor had this occupation changed the "usages and customs of their own" which the Aborigines had been practising from time immemorial. If Jabinguy's relatives believed Jack Congo Murral had committed murder, they would be inflicting possibly fatal punishment on him by spearing. The Chief Justice, Sir Francis Forbes, and the then puisne judges, James Dowling and William Burton, rejected the defence argument, and ruled that the court *did* have jurisdiction. Jack Congo Murral would stand trial, although he would be acquitted.

The judges' ruling on jurisdiction was reinforced in a case in 1838, in which a black named Long Jack stood trial for the murder of his wife, Mary, north of Sydney. The court was told that Mary died after being beaten on the head with a waddy by a very drunk Long Jack. In summing up the case for the jury, Judge Burton declared that "wherever the British standard floats, the inhabitants are within the pale of British law, and whatever savage customs may have been in existence must cease". A guilty verdict was reached, and Long Jack was sentenced to death. Nevertheless, because of the impossibility of determining what the motive for the murder may have been, the judge sent a recommendation to Gipps for a pardon on the condition that the sentence be commuted to transportation for life.[1]

Towards the end of 1841, confusion would again arise on the jurisdiction question, in a case which came before Judge John Willis in Melbourne. It involved a Barrabool named Bonjon, who was accused of murdering a Colijon named Yammening in July of that year. According to statements taken by Foster Fyans, Bonjon had accused Yammening of having taken his woman before shooting him in the back of the head with a carbine on the Barwon River station of Andrew Brown, not far from Geelong. Bonjon, who was seen with the woman the following day, was well known to Fyans. For some time, the young black had been used as a horse tracker in the Border Police, being paid with food and clothes. Fyans had found him to be "intelligent in his own way", and although his English was limited, his services had been "very useful".[2]

The Lands Commissioner had been one of the magistrates who committed Bonjon for trial for murder, not realising that the case would take up hours of Supreme Court time, and end up in London for a final decision on jurisdiction. The question would be raised at the opening of Bonjon's trial by the Irish barrister, Redmond Barry, who was assigned as defence counsel. Bonjon, he declared, could not even plead because he was not a Christian, and did not understand "the nature and obligation of an oath sufficiently to verify the plea according to law". After Judge Willis told the court he believed that jurisdiction was doubtful, the jury would unanimously agree "that the prisoner was not competent to put in a plea as to the jurisdiction of the court". The jury would also decide that Bonjon was capable of knowing whether he killed Yammening. But he was not capable, it deemed, of deciding whether he was guilty of the crime with which he was charged because murder was not always a crime with the Aborigines. Willis commended the jury on its decisions before discharging it, saying a new one could be sworn in if necessary after the unresolved question of jurisdiction was decided.

Barry and Crown Prosecutor Croke were called on to present their arguments. Barry's centred on *how* Britain was seen to have acquired New South Wales. If it had been *conquered*, the defence counsel asserted, there could be no question that British law applied to the Aborigines. But this certainly had not been the case. The original settlers had not been opposed by the blacks, so the colony could not be said to have been conquered. Nor could it be said that the territory had been *ceded* to Britain. Rather, New South Wales had been *occupied*,

without any treaty or agreement having been entered into by the British authorities with the Aborigines. They remained an independent people, and could not
possibly be made subject to British laws in matters involving only themselves.
As well, evidence could be produced if necessary to show that the blacks had
their own form of laws, based on a feeling of revenge which was "imprinted universally in the breast of the savage". Such being the case, wrongs would never
go unpunished. Croke counter-argued by outlining various examples of similar
cases in Sydney in which Aborigines had been tried and punished, the judges
maintaining "that wherever the British colonised, there the British laws became
supreme, and the natives must be amenable to them". Also, as the murder for
which Bonjon had been charged had occurred on lands "possessed and claimed
in ownership by the British government". It was therefore right that offences
committed on such land should be tried by the authorities acting on behalf of the
British Crown.

Such was the seriousness of the jurisdiction question to Willis, he would spend
three hours delivering his decision. According to the commission under which
Britain governed New South Wales, the judge pointed out, the sovereignty of the
Crown was asserted over the whole of the territory within the limits it defined,
including a large portion of the north island of New Zealand. "There does not
appear to be any specific recognition in this commission of the claims of the
Aborigines, either as sovereigns or proprietors of the soil, although it is in the
recollection of many living men that every part of this territory was the undisputed property of the Aborigines," he stated. The question was whether the
commission had legally destroyed the blacks' "existence as self-governing communities", and effectively made them British subjects. Or had it merely reduced
the Aborigines "to a state of dependent allies, still retaining their own laws and
usages", subject to certain conditions?

Under the law of nations, as acknowledged by the British government, Willis
continued, there were examples of "rude" people within British colonies being
recognised as self-governing, dependent allies. In the United States, which had
been colonised in the same way as New South Wales, the Indians had been
regarded as such. In 1738 in Jamaica, the British Crown had sanctioned a treaty
that allowed former slaves known as Maroons to keep some of their own laws.
And on the island of St Vincent in the Caribbean, ceded to Britain by France, a
treaty had been entered into with the Charib people in 1773 which stated that
British laws did not apply to "their intercourse and customs with each other".
More convincing proof could not be found, Willis declared, to refute Croke's
argument that all people in a British colony were subject to British law. In India,
too, the judge added, the Christian British government had tolerated the Hindu
practices of widows burning themselves on their husbands' funeral pyres, and

devotees throwing themselves under huge wheeled vehicles during Juggernaut processions.

There was no legislation, Willis went on, which expressly stated that the Aborigines of New South Wales were subject to British law. The 1828 Act which had started the process of constitutional government had declared that the laws of England would be applied in the administration of justice in the colony as far as circumstances would permit. "But this, I think is very different from declaring that the Aborigines shall, as among themselves, be amenable to British law," the judge asserted. "The only acts of legislation with regard to the Aborigines that I remember are the local ordinances to prevent their being supplied with spirits, and to prevent them bearing firearms, but it has never been attempted to deprive them of their weapons. These laws are perfectly consistent, I think, with the character of the Aborigines as dependent allies, and necessary for the protection and due regulation of intercourse between the Aborigines and colonists." Willis therefore concluded there was strong doubt about the propriety of exercising jurisdiction in the Bonjon case, and suggested an adjournment.

As it turned out, Croke would decide not to proceed with the prosecution, and Bonjon would be freed. But then Willis would become aware of Gipps' view that the Aborigines *were* subject to British law, even in matters not involving white men. He immediately sent full details of the case to the Governor, with a request that it be brought before not only the colony's legal authorities, but also the British government. In seeking the opinion of the Chief Justice of New South Wales, James Dowling, Gipps made the point that in numerous official documents, the Aborigines had been referred to as subjects of Queen Victoria, and as such were amenable to the same laws as any of her other subjects. As well, even if they were regarded as having been conquered, the Aborigines had never had "any code of laws intelligible to a civilised people". Dowling was quick to assure Gipps that the issue had been decided "after a solemn argument" by the colony's Supreme Court back in 1836. There was no need, Dowling advised, for the Governor to introduce a special bill to the Legislative Council declaring that British laws applied to the Aborigines. Pleased with this opinion, Gipps nevertheless was still obliged to refer the matter to London. And until he received a reply from the Secretary of State for the Colonies, Lord Stanley, the matter was not really resolved.[3]

By a strange coincidence, the very day that Gipps would write to Stanley on the matter, Sievwright would write to Robinson seeking guidance on it. The question of what to do about murders of one black by another had first been raised by Sievwright in April 1841, after the killings that took place at the Lake Terang camp of the Bolagher girl, Worangaer, and then the Jarcoort girl, Mootenewharnong. The Assistant Protector had told Robinson that it was imperative to eradicate the system of revenge killing, such as had just occurred. "I would respectfully entreat that the attention of the government be called to this subject, in order that measures may be adopted, or a law enacted, calculated to meet such cases," he'd advised. Sievwright added that he could identify Worangaer's killer, the Jarcoort named Warawel. He could also produce the testimony of 100 witnesses to use against him if he committed Warawel for trial for murder. But of course this testimony would have no legal standing in a British court. Warawel would be discharged, and the whole affair would only serve to create hostility in the Aboriginal community, and a poor opinion of the way white men administered justice "without any beneficial result accruing to them, or to us, by so partial and imperfect interference in their polity".[4]

Any interest in the issue Sievwright was raising would be swamped by fascination with the details he provided of how the Bolagher people disposed of Worangaer's body. To Robinson, it was a "diabolic transaction". Gipps would describe it as perhaps "one of the most ferocious acts of cannibalism on record".[5] But Sievwright would be confronted with several more cases of one black being killed by another while still camped at Terang. On one occasion, early in January 1842, a woman named Elingapooterneen was speared through the heart while asleep by a man named Onebeeturon. The sole cause of the murder appeared to be that Elingapooterneen had refused to carry water from the lake for Onebeeturon, Sievwright reported. He believed that both the victim and killer were Elangamite. However, the other tribes present had also been involved in the fighting which immediately broke out in the camp after the killing. Onebeeturon had been "severely wounded", and had been carried away by his friends towards Lake Colac. The Assistant Protector reminded Robinson of the letter he'd written the previous April, and which had so far been ignored. Unless measures were taken to suppress the "barbarous" crimes being committed by the blacks on each other, they must imagine that they were tolerated by the whites, he stated.[6]

This time, Robinson would eventually pass on Sievwright's request for action, asking for instructions from La Trobe. The Superintendent would refer the matter to Crown Prosecutor Croke, who would devote most of his petulant reply to ridiculing of the Assistant Protector. In his "usual general state", Croke opined, Sievwright had given "a pathetic narrative" of what he'd called strife and contention resulting from the current practice of non-interference. Surely, the Prosecutor snarled, if the acts complained of amounted only to strife and contention, it was Sievwright's "bounden duty" to put them down, without calling for help. If, however, the Assistant Protector was referring to cold-blooded murder committed by one Aborigine against another, it was a different matter. Notwithstanding the opinion recently rejected by Judge Willis in the Bonjon case, he'd be willing to launch a prosecution over the murder of Elingapooterneen. But Sievwright had been long enough as a magistrate to know at least that he would have to offer more than inadmissable Aboriginal evidence. "Mr Sievwright should also know that no power short of the Legislative Council (with the sanction of the Privy Council at home) can remedy the evil he alludes to," Croke concluded. Had he requested a copy of the April letter to which Sievwright had referred, Croke would have realised that the Assistant Protector well understood this, but he did not bother to do so.[7]

By the time La Trobe referred Croke's letter to Gipps, the first murder among the blacks gathered at Mt Rouse had occurred -- almost a year after Sievwright had first requested instructions on the subject.[8] Unaware of this killing, or the fact that Gipps was seeking guidance from London, La Trobe was keen to enter the debate. "My own opinion is that unless we assume power to interfere to prevent or at least punish murders of the natives among themselves, we shall never teach them to respect European life," he wrote. The amount and character of the punishment to be awarded was a separate question. But it appeared to La Trobe that the blacks should be made aware of the "sense of the enormity of taking away life" felt by the whites, regardless of the circumstances. And when the Aborigines stood trial for murdering their own race, a defence should not be able to be made based on "very doubtful interpretation of their manners and customs or intentions".[9]

Just two days later, Sievwright would again be doing his best to convince the blacks at Mt Rouse, some of whom had now been living with him for more than 12 months, to adopt European religious values -- holding his first big outdoor Sunday service at the newly-formed reserve. Once again, he chose one of his favourite doxologies, the simple tune and lines of which were starting to catch on, to be the main part of the service. A total of 264 blacks attended, and some at least joined the Protector and his family in singing: "Praise God, from whom all blessings flow; Praise Him, all creatures here below; Praise Him above, ye heavenly host; Praise Father, Son and Holy Ghost." Later that day, there was thunder and lightning, traditionally blamed by the blacks on hostile tribes that lived further west. But some of those at Mt Rouse must have wondered whether there was some connection with the ceremony they'd performed with their Protector before they all sat down together near their bush "church" for their special Sunday meal of damper.

It was 20 years to the day that Charles and Christina Sievwright had been in a proper church in Stirling in Scotland, taking their marriage vows before the elderly Episcopal Bishop of Brechin, George Gleig. The bishop had been dressed as usual in short cassock, with knee-breeches and buckles, and silk stockings; Charles in his Rifle Brigade uniform, and Christina in her bridal finery, made for the occasion in Edinburgh. What a different scene it was now, in the isolation of the Australian bush on the other side of the world, surrounded by a large group of dark-skinned and mostly naked men, women and children with whom they could hardly converse! On their "tin anniversary", the only items of the metal which Charles could find to give to his wife hardly seemed appropriate as gifts to mark the occasion -- pannicans, eating utensils, and the small "coins" used to pay his black labourers!

Continuous rain the day after the Sievwrights' anniversary would confine the

"Holding his first big outdoor Sunday service at the newly-formed reserve..."

blacks to their huts, and no work would be performed. Then early the next day, two white men from the nearby station of Scotsman Alexander Cameron would arrive to complain that a flock of sheep had been stolen by some blacks. The Protector was horrified to find that during the night, the sheep had been brought close to the reserve, and many of them had been killed. With the assistance of his overseer and constable, Sievwright recovered 160 sheep, mainly rams, and returned them to their owner. But 228 sheep had been reported lost. "The proprietor of part of these sheep states that much blame was to be attributed to the shepherd who had this flock in charge, he having been in the habit of leaving them unprotected," Sievwright would report.

Nevertheless, he could see that the theft would soon be cited by opponents of the Protectorate as evidence of its futility. It was crucial that he moved quickly to show that he would not be tolerating such behaviour. Sievwright called together the elders of the tribes at Mt Rouse, and using Jarcoorts as interpreters he explained "in as forcible manner as possible" that he intended apprehending the thieves. "Their present improved position, with constant supplies for the comfort of themselves and families, which were assured to them by the government, so long as they should conduct themselves according to the rules laid down for their guidance, together with the security which was now assured to all who should deserve it, was brought under their notice," he told Robinson. As well, Sievwright told the elders that he held them responsible for good order in the camp. He now required them to identify the thieves, so they could receive punishment. If they did not do so, the innocent members of their tribes would suffer along with the guilty.

After much discussion among themselves and "a great deal of recrimination" the Protector believed that the elders understood what he was saying, and had agreed to hand over the culprits. When this did not occur, he immediately carried out his threat of mass punishment. Rations were suspended, and the blacks were not permitted to earn any by working. The suspension of rations would last more than two rainy days. Sievwright would then be told that two men who'd lived in the camp a short time had been responsible for the theft of Cameron's sheep. Both of them had since left. After the blacks promised that no further thefts would occur, and pleaded with Sievwright to be allowed to resume work, he relented. The blacks were once again involved in helping with ploughing a five hectare paddock, grubbing, and fencing -- some of the working women leaving their babies in woven reed baskets suspended from the lower branches of nearby trees which were being retained for shelter.

A few days later, Sievwright would witness a marriage: the bride a young member of the tribe he called the Moborcondeet, apparently meaning a section of the Gunditjmara, the groom a Bolagher. As the assembled tribes watched in silence, the ceremony began with the young Bolagher men approaching the huts of the Moborcondeet in a group. Two of them carried a large quantity of flour and other provisions, which the tribe had managed to collect despite the suspension of supplies by the Protector. These provisions were placed in front of the hut of the bride's father, and after a few minutes, two of the Moborcondeet elders removed them. The Bolagher men then went a short distance away and arranged themselves around several fires which the Moborcondeet women had in the meantime prepared. Still silent, they maintained an "apparently ceremonious demeanour".

The bride, with white streaks painted over and under her eyes and red lines on her cheeks, was led out near the fires by an old woman of her tribe, and started dancing before the crowd, which gathered around her in a circle. With short rests, she would dance for almost half an hour, occasionally being joined by other Moborcondeets. The older women of the tribe would switch her on the legs with branches, which seemingly "excited her to further exertion". From time to time, her mother would lead her by the hand to the edge of the circle, and loudly proclaim what Sievwright later ascertained were statements relating to the achievements of the family. These were met with silent nods of the head "and other gestures of complacency".

"The Bolaghers retired as they had approached in a body, and the young woman was again switched and rubbed with leaves by a youth of her tribe while uttering some words in a loud and quick voice," Sievwright recorded. "She was shortly afterwards conducted to the hut of the chief of her tribe which was well stored with provisions which were distributed amongst the party -- he occasionally placing with his own hands portions of the food in the mouths of his visitors." That was the end of the ceremony. But the Moborcondeet people had been offended by the behaviour of the Jarcoort Kirrae blacks. After work the following day, fighting broke out in the camp, and many of the men involved received severe wounds. The cause of the fighting, Sievwright told Robinson, was that the Jarcoort people had "neglected to furnish the accustomed presents on the preceding night". When the fighting stopped, about 60 of the Jarcoort blacks left the camp, although they would return in about a week.[10]

Flogger Fyans, meanwhile, had been flabbergasted to learn what had occurred a little over three weeks earlier when Sievwright and Robinson had been at James Hunter's station and the Aborigines had come out of The Rocks. He'd just taken depositions from Hunter's employees, who had again deserted the station because of "constant depredations" by the Gunditjmara people. Fyans told La Trobe he'd by-passed Croke by sending the depositions direct to Judge Willis, seeking his opinion on the propriety of the recent actions of Sievwright and Robinson at Hunter's. Among the group the Protectors had gathered at the station -- and fed from the squatter's store -- had been five of the Gunditjmara blacks with arrest warrants against them issued by French. But it appeared that the Protectors had "declined their service as magistrates" to apprehend them, though they were "guilty of the most heinous outrages". And it was not because of the difficulty of capturing the five, the Crown Lands Commissioner pointed out. There'd been 14 or 15 other white men present who'd all been "ready and willing to act".[11]

The Commissioner certainly had no reservations about trying to enforce the warrants, and the 14 troopers he led on his mission were also eager. He would later record that they'd been "in hopes of taking satisfaction" in revenge for a number of incidents, including what had occurred at Hunter's station three months earlier to Private Carty, still suffering in Geelong from his head wounds.

Also in the party, armed with a sword, was Bonjon, the Barrabool Fyans had recently committed for trial for murder of a Colijon. And for a time there was another black in the party. The Commissioner believed that on the promise of a sack of flour, he'd found a Gunditjmara willing to point out Mercury, Charley and the others they were seeking. But after two days of searching, one of them involving nine hours of riding, the guide slipped away at night.

The following day, Fyans left the rest of the party and set off into The Rocks near Hunter's station with Bonjon, and a young Border Police trooper named Potter. There they met a black who identified himself as Charley, and who fitted the description of the wanted man. When Fyans moved to seize him, he responded by throwing two of the three heavy spears tipped with volcanic glass which he'd been carrying, without effect. Potter opened fire at the Aborigine, but he too missed. Still mounted, Fyans then charged at Charley, making vigorous swipes with his sabre, but which according to the Commissioner all hit the black's shield. Twice the black tumbled over the rocks when he was knocked down by Fyans' horse, but he still managed to strike at it with a leanguil. Then Charley drove the pointed handle of the leanguil through the nose of the horse, being instantly covered in the blood that spurted out. The horse quickly weakened and started the falter, and Fyans was obliged to dismount and force his handkerchief into the wound to stop the bleeding. As Bonjon came to Fyans' aid, Charley ran off.[12]

Within a week, Fyans would have two more encounters with some of the Gunditjmara warriors he sought. The first would occur after the party reached Hunter's abandoned station. Hiding among some nearby trees, the whites waited until a scout reported that about 30 Gunditjmara men had arrived and entered the squatter's hut. Two men were ordered to seize the spears and leanguils which the blacks had left about 100 metres from the hut, while the rest of the troopers joined Fyans in approaching the building. "The riot and confusion within on our appearance was terrific," he would later record. "The two doors were well secured, the only entrances to the habitation. We thought it impossible for any to escape, but (with) these wild savages, bounding through the hut from room to room, roaring piteously, giving the loud war coohey for assistance, the hut appeared almost to move with its contents!"

Suddenly, two of the blacks escaped through the chimney, then about a dozen heads appeared through the thatch roof, as others worked their way to freedom, jumping from the roof over the troopers' horses. They made for their spears, only to find them tied in bundles, under the guard of a policeman. "Some still remained inside, guilty of great crimes, and (it was) highly necessary that they should be made prisoners," Fyans wrote. "But the difficulty was how to lay hands on them. Fearing the consequences, I dreaded ordering the men in, for life must be lost, and by doing so we might lose three natives we so anxiously wished to apprehend -- Cocknose, Bumbletoe and Jupiter." In any event, Jupiter soon made his appearance through the roof, and along with another black with a warrant against him, Jackey, jumped to the ground and started running off as their tribesmen had done.

Jupiter being recognised by a trooper who'd been stationed at the hut, the party rode off in pursuit of him and Jackey. The two blacks managed to get as far as a spot in a forest several kilometres away before being overtaken and seized after a scuffle. Jupiter was well secured by handcuffs, but after being held down by a number of men for some time, Jackey managed to break free and make another run for freedom. For several more kilometres he managed to evade capture, running into the thickest parts of the forest where it was most difficult for his pursuers to ride, and to keep sight of him. But he finally "fell from wounds" and was secured. "He died in less than half an hour after he was taken," Fyans would report to La Trobe, with no hint of regret. "I beg to state that the two natives were of bad character, cannibals, and were destroying the horses throughout the country," the Commissioner declared. He would offer no details about what wounds Jackey had received, and the Superintendent would never ask.[13]

Just two days later, Fyans would report the apprehension of two more of the blacks with warrants against them -- Cocknose and The Doctor. They had put up "considerable resistance", he remarked, and "a serious scuffle" had taken place in which The Doctor had received a gunshot wound from which he had since died. A black boy had also been wounded. Again, Fyans had no regrets. Cocknose and The Doctor had been charged with attempting to take life and steal property at Hunter's station, and during their apprehension, the Border Police had suffered extensive damage to their clothing and weapons. "I beg leave to bring to Your Honour's notice that the tribe on Mr Hunter's station are of the wildest and most savage nature, that great destruction of property has taken place, and I have great hopes that the examples made will be the means of bringing them to good order," he told La Trobe.[14]

Next on Fyans' hit list was an Aborigine known to the whites as Roger, whose clan claimed the territory around Mt Rouse. La Trobe had ordered the Commissioner to investigate a report that Roger had been one of the blacks involved in the murder of the Wedge brothers' former employee at Mt Rouse back in 1840, Patrick Codd. The apparent breakthrough in the case had come from Codd's brother, Clement, who happened to work as an assistant in the Melbourne drapery store of the Western District squatter Robert Whitehead -- one of the whites who'd just carried out the Muston's Creek murders. Codd had told La Trobe that Roger could now be at Sievwright's reserve, north-west of

Muston's Creek. Furthermore, he could be identified by James Brock, who'd been wounded in the same attack in which Codd's brother had died, and who still lived nearby on John Cox's new station. If evidence could be obtained to back Codd's claims, La Trobe told Fyans, Roger should be arrested.[15]

Almost two years had passed since Patrick Codd's murder, but Fyans could well remember it, having arrived at the scene just a few days after it had occurred. James Brock had not been game enough to go out of his hut to bury the body, which had been "dreadfully decomposed" and "almost torn to pieces by wild dogs". After burying Codd together, Fyans and Brock had turned their attention to Patrick Rooney, the shepherd whose jaw had been broken in two places in the attack. Together, they'd removed pieces of broken bone and teeth, then applied strong plasters and a bandage. They'd also shaved the old shepherd's head to treat other wounds. After two days of "simple nourishment", Rooney had shown a wonderful improvement. Fyans would later recall that the shepherd would live for almost another three years, apparently without pain. During this time, he could "barely articulate a word". Yet according to Fyans, he would often point to his jaw and achieve the remarkable feat of saying "Roger". But this was a claim recorded long after the operation Fyans would lead to Mt Rouse from Hunter's station to arrest Roger, just three days after the capture of Cocknose and the killing of The Doctor.

After two days' riding, Fyans decided to camp for the night only about 10 kilometres from the Mt Rouse reserve so he and his party of about 12 troopers could arrive there by surprise early the following morning, in the hope of apprehending the "vile savage" for whom he already had an arrest warrant written out. It had been less than a month since word had reached Sievwright's camp about the murder of the three Kirrae women and a child at Muston's Creek by Clement Codd's employer and his accomplices. Wonigoniber, shot in the back and through a hand, was still clinging to life after having been brought back to the camp, her groans of pain serving as a reminder to all of the more than 200 blacks present of the incident. News of the deadly operations of Fyans and his troopers over the previous few days may also have already reached the camp before they rode in to wake everyone just before sunrise, although it had not yet reached Sievwright's ears. The camp was immediately "in a state of great excitement". The Aboriginal men quickly took up their weapons, and sent their women and children off to a distance.

At first, Fyans refused to tell Sievwright why he was demanding that Roger be indentified and handed over. But then, to the Protector's surprise, James Brock arrived at the camp and revealed that the black was wanted for Patrick Codd's murder. Sievwright's immediate reaction was to pretend that Roger was not in the camp, at the same time strenuously asserting his innocence, pointing out that

at the time of the murder, Brock had denied Roger's involvement. Fyans, however, was determined to act on what he said was La Trobe's order to arrest Roger,
whom he was convinced *was* in the camp. Pointing out that Jackey and The
Doctor had just been killed for resisting arrest, he warned that he was willing to
use force if necessary. The Protector could either hand Roger over, or the troopers would be ordered to find him by searching the huts. Fyans' stand left
Sievwright with a bitter dilemma. Roger was well-known to him, having struck
up a friendship and spent many hours with his brother, John, back at the
Keilambete and Terang camps. He did not believe the black was guilty of
Codd's murder, and he was loathe to help in his apprehension, especially by
Fyans. Yet if he continued to shelter him, there would obviously be a bloody
confrontation which would scatter his charges, perhaps permanently. With
much reluctance, he agreed that Roger had to be surrendered, for the sake of the
future of the reserve, the prospects of which were just starting to look so promising.

What made matters even worse for Sievwright was that his credibility as a
friend and Protector of the Aborigines would soon be destroyed if he was seen
to be co-operating with Fyans in Roger's arrest. He felt he had no choice but to
stoop to the very ungentlemanly acts of betrayal and subterfuge, to avoid his co-
operation being known. Sievwright told Fyans that if he left the camp, he would
send Roger with overseer Davidson and his cart to the nearby station of English
brothers, Charles and Frederick Burchett, purportedly to buy supplies of mutton.
The black, Sievwright reluctantly suggested, could be seized at a distance from
the camp, and he would not be seen to have played any part in it. To this, the
Commissioner agreed, and a few hours later, the cart carrying Roger and
Davidson was on its way towards the Burchetts' with Fyans and his troopers
waiting in hiding in a designated area of forest.

Just after it passed, four of the troopers would overtake the cart "at full gallop",
force it to stop, and seize Roger. However, the powerful black, his naked body
greased with animal fat, was not easy to hold. He managed to slip from their
grasp and start running for his life, heading back towards Mt Rouse. In the
melee, the four police horses had broken loose, so Roger had a good start,
although it was not long before some other troopers were in pursuit. Roger as
much as possible led them across stony ground, where he knew it was difficult
to ride. Fyans would later report that as a result, his party would "suffer in horse
flesh considerably", with every horse involved in the chase receiving serious leg
injuries on the jagged rocks. But the rocks would take their toll even on Roger's
tough bare feet and legs, and after about 20 minutes he would collapse, being
easily seized by four other troopers who dismounted.

The result of the chase would even provoke a rare display of compassion in

Flogger Fyans. "Bad as the character of Roger was, a murderer and leader of every riot which took place in the country, still we could not but look with pity on him, laying on the ground almost unable to move, his legs streaming with blood, and feet so lacerated he could not stand," the Commissioner would recall. Shackled with two pairs of handcuffs, Roger had to be carried a few hundred metres out of the stones, to be placed on a pack horse. Reporting the capture of Roger to La Trobe, Fyans suggested that Gipps should reward the efforts of his men. "I beg leave to again recommend the men of the Border Police for His Excellency's favourable consideration," he wrote. "They have undergone considerable fatigue, and willingly do their duty. They are good soldiers and deserving men." The help of James Brock, too, had been crucial to the successful capture of the "vile assassin", and he deserved thanks from the white community. "I have also to thank Assistant Protector Sievwright for sending Roger for the *mutton*," Fyans sarcastically added.[16]

As Roger was being taken back to Fyans' camp on Hunter's run, Sievwright would write to Robinson, explaining at length why he believed the prisoner was innocent. After Patrick Codd's murder, he stressed, Brock had stated that he was certain he could identify the blacks involved. Roger's name having been mentioned as a suspect, he'd brought him before the overseer. Brock had not only denied the black's involvement, but had added that he would have recognised him by now because he'd seen him about John Cox's station for almost the previous fortnight. About eight days after this conversation, Brock had come to Sievwright and told him he'd started to think that Roger *was* one of the party. The Protector stated he'd "wholly disregarded" this testimony then "as I believed that he had argued himself into his present position". Furthermore, Sievwright remarked, Roger's tribe had positively stated that for some months before and after Codd's murder, he'd been near Lake Boloke, "unable to move from a loathsome disease" -- presumably venereal. As well, they'd pointed out two individuals who they advised had been of the party which killed Codd, but who Brock had not been able to recognise. Finally, Sievwright added a request that Robinson bring the circumstances of the arrest of Roger under La Trobe's notice.

Except in cases of crimes committed when the Aborigines were under his direct charge, he suggested, no further attempts should be made to make arrests of blacks at Mt Rouse without giving him to chance to negotiate a peaceful surrender of any with warrants against them. Arrests at the camp by parties of police would soon destroy the confidence the blacks had in him. "They have been collected together under an assurance of protection, as long as they shall adhere to the rules laid down for their guidance," he wrote. If these rules were broken, he would have no hesitation in handing over the offenders to face trial. This he'd suggested just a fortnight earlier, for instance, in the case of those who'd stolen Alexander Cameron's sheep. But he'd just been called upon to deliver over to justice an individual charged with a crime of which he had every reason to believe him innocent. Roger had been absolved "from the unanimous testimony of his people". As well, the offence for which Roger had been charged had occurred almost two years earlier, and before Sievwright had had any dealings with the tribes of the area. "I feel myself placed by such a post facto interference, in a position as practically untenable as it will, I am afraid, ultimately be unprofitable," he declared.[17]

Roger, Cocknose and Jupiter would remain at Fyans' camp for a few days while he decided the best way of getting them to Melbourne for trial. The risk of an escape attempt, or possibly even a rescue bid, would be too great to take them overland, he concluded. There was no ship due to leave soon from Port Fairy or Portland for Melbourne. So instead, Fyans directed that the prisoners be loaded aboard a schooner which was about to sail for Launceston, across Bass Strait in Van Diemen's Land, with a cargo of sheep and cattle. Two constables sent as escorts arranged a transfer in Launceston to a brig sailing to Melbourne. For three Aboriginal men who had never been aboard a boat it was a terrifying experience being shackled in the cargo holds of the two vessels, as they sailed a total of about 1000 kilometres over 17 days, 11 of them in the rough seas of the Strait. After the second leg of the journey, the trio would end up in the Melbourne jail, still in chains. Not long afterwards, they would be joined by another Gunditjmara captured near Hunter's station by Fyans -- Bumbletoe.[18]

Soon before the black prisoners arrived in Melbourne, the town's white community had learned of the recent raid on Alexander Cameron's sheep by Aborigines from the Mt Rouse reserve. In a letter to the "Patriot", Cameron had complained his district had been in "a most wretched state" since the arrival of the Protector and his charges. Two of his shepherds had been attacked "by Mr Sievwright's tame tribe". The 228 sheep he'd lost, mostly valuable rams, had been slaughtered within metres of the hut which was the Protector's residence. "He says that finding the mutton in the possession of the blacks is not a sufficient proof in justifying a commital or conviction," Cameron wrote. "Now if those thieves are under British protection, why should they not be under British prosecution, when my property, which they had forcibly taken, was found in their possession?"[19]

No publicity was given to any of the steps taken by Sievwright to try to prevent such thefts recurring, as outlined in his recent report to Robinson. The Chief Protector was still sitting on the report. And when he finally passed it on to La Trobe, more than six weeks after it was written, Robinson would make no comment whatsoever on Sievwright's suggestions about the best way of dealing with Aborigines accused of crimes against the whites. In putting forward these proposals, the Assistant Protector had made specific reference to the theft of Cameron's sheep. It would have improved the attitude of the white community towards Sievwright, and the Protectorate itself, if it had been known that he was willing to hand over Aborigines with warrants against them -- even in cases like that of Roger, whom he believed to be innocent. But once again, the Chief Protector was prepared to allow his assistant to bear the increasing wrath of his fellow whites alone.[20]

Another murder had also since occurred among the Aborigines at the Mt Rouse camp -- as a result of Roger's arrest. After Roger had been taken away by Fyans, Sievwright reported, his family had been "under much excitement and great grief". A brother of Roger named Kalkinwherdon had killed an Aboriginal boy named Wawallowbron "while in a paroxysm of lamentation". It seemed that the boy had been speared dead merely because he happened to be the first person who came in the enraged black's way. "I sent for Kalkinwherdon and questioned him on the subject," Sievwright wrote. "He acknowledged having killed the boy, because the white men had taken away his brother. The deed was not witnessed by an European although the body was immediately seen by the overseer, on the outcry being raised in the camp." Once again, Sievwright asked for instructions on how he should deal with such cases.[21]

Not long after Fyans used the Barrabool, Bonjon, to help capture Roger, a party

"Aborigine defending himself against an attack by spears" by W. A. Cawthorne.

of blacks from Mt Rouse was said to have staged a deadly raid on the Barrabool blacks. News of it would come in the form of a letter to the *Geelong Advertiser* from the squatter, John Bromfield -- named by the Jarcoort people back in 1839 as one of the whites involved in the massacre near Mt Elephant. According to Bromfield, the Barrabool camp near his station had been left "deluged with blood", the raiding party having killed three men and two young women. One of the women had still been alive when he'd arrived at the scene the following morning. With two spear wounds in her abdomen, and her intestines falling out, it would have been "a charity" to have immediately shot her. Instead, she'd been left to die later that day. Bromfield claimed that some of the victims had been "partly eaten" by what he termed "their Christian brethren" from Mt Rouse. "These are civilised Aborigines who have been well instructed by our Assistant Protectors, and certainly have profitted no little by the time and expense that have been lavished upon them," he quipped.[22]

CHAPTER 24
"A fair moral name"

DESPITE the vast distance from Britain, and differences in climate, the fashion houses of Europe would still be influential among many of the early British settlers in New South Wales. All the colonial newspapers featured advertisements from stores claiming recent shipments of clothing that would be stylish in London. "The largest and most fashionable assortment of Bonnets in Melbourne," boasted one store, that also stocked "Splendid Mousselin de Laine Dresses, of the latest designs", as well as gentlemen's opera ties, silk parasols with printed borders, and French Cambric handkerchiefs. Another store offered Victoria and Tartan Earlston Gingham dresses "composed of the finest fabric, most chaste and tasteful patterns, warranted fast colours, which have been so much admired and universally worn by the fashionable circles of society in the Mother Country and on the Continent".[1]

In early 1842, George Robinson decided that the often naked Aborigines of Port Phillip should at least start a transition to British clothing. The Protectorate had given high priority to putting in place the means of food production. But the Chief Protector believed that unless the blacks were clothed as well as fed, they "could not be civilised". He wanted every Aborigine under the care of his assistants to have an annual gift of one blanket and one handkerchief. For the men, he would also request permission to hand out one serge shirt, one check shirt and two pairs of strong linen or cotton trousers. For the women, he wanted enough material, plus needles and thread, to make each of them a dress. The number of blacks he estimated that could be recipients of the handouts was at least 2590 - 1000 of them in the Western District. The bold requisition made on the basis of these figures, however, would be immediately rejected by Gipps as "very extravagant". The Governor had been told that the estimated cost of the supplies was more than 856 pounds, and he ruled that the order must be "very greatly reduced". Furthermore, Gipps directed that the Chief Protector be told that the requisition had resulted in diminished confidence "in his prudence and discretion, or in his regard to a proper economy in the expenditure of the public money".[2]

When La Trobe passed on the Governor's comments, Robinson was quick to defend himself. "Notwithstanding the reiterated applications and complaints from the Assistant Protectors, and the repeated importunities from the

Aborigines, for blankets and clothing, scarcely any issues were made during the year 1841, such was the rigid system of economy observed by me in reference to those articles," Robinson told the Superintendent. "The condition, however, of the natives towards the close of the year was in consequence deplorable, and numerous cases of extreme wretchedness in this respect were met with, and so marked did this appear, that animadversions were made in the public prints, and charges of injustice and oppression brought against the department." Robinson would make no mention of the fund allocated for the contingent expenses of the Protectorate, or the considerable expenses incurred during his tour of the Western District for half of 1841. Nor would he offer any explanation why he'd so long ignored the pleas of his assistants and the Aborigines themselves.[3]

While sending a copy of the Chief Protector's letter to Gipps, La Trobe would take the opportunity to present a scathing summary of how he viewed the first three years of the operations of the Protectorate. He was not disposed, he remarked, to assert that absolutely no good had been achieved by Robinson and his assistants. But the inherent difficulties of their anomalous duties had been

Reproduced courtesy of the Mitchell Library, State Library of New South Wales
"Blackfellows' camp", as depicted in the "Illustrated Melbourne Post". In early 1842, George Robinson would ask for every Aborigine under the care of the Protectorate to be given an annual allocation of one blanket and some European clothing. Governor Gipps would reject the idea as "very extravagant".

complicated by the way in which Robinson had structured the department, and whatever achievements it had produced "might have been secured by far more simple and unpretending machinery". La Trobe reminded Gipps that a year after the formation of the Protectorate, he'd reported on its "total inefficiency". He would be "exceedingly happy" to now present a different opinion. But two years further on, there was "the same want of harmony, the same absence of system in details, and of co-operation in pursuance of the object in view, and the same spirit of internal distrust and dissatisfaction".

"It follows that no result, commensurate with the importance assumed by the department, with the magnitude of the object aimed at, or even with the expense incurred, can be looked for," La Trobe lamented. "In little more than three years, a sum exceeding 16,000 pounds has passed into the hands of the department, and this outlay has neither contented the individuals composing it, nor been of any essential benefit to the Aboriginal natives." The amount of correspondence between the Protectors and the government was "exceedingly heavy". Yet it was impossible after the most careful sifting to glean from it "any quantity of really valuable and trustworthy information, capable of being employed in taking those important steps for the better government of the natives, in their various relations to one another, or to the Europeans, which are so imperatively called for".

To date, the Superintendent observed, the government still had not even been given correct information on the numbers, position, and character of the various tribes in the Port Phillip District, or on its borders. Few men in ordinary life, he acknowledged, could be found capable of performing with judgement and success the varied duties imposed upon the Assistant Protectors. This conviction would perhaps relieve him of the disagreeable duty of making a close examination to determine to what extent the Protectorate's "want of success" was due to the personal failings of the individuals of which it was comprised. Without having to do that, La Trobe suggested, it was time for "a complete change of system".[4]

As La Trobe's report was being sent to Sydney, the Port Phillip press gave an indication of the way in which the British government had decided to treat Aborigines suspected of stealing food or other items from the whites. The news came in the form of an extract from a letter to Gipps from the Secretary of State for the Colonies, Lord John Russell, commenting on reports on "aggressions by the natives on the flocks and herds of the settlers" in the Port Phillip District. The Assistant Protectors should be required to "deliver up for trial any one or more of their number who might be identified by a settler complaining of an attack or loss of property," Russell advised. In the same letter, the Secretary of State commented on the operation in Port Phillip back in October 1840 by Major

Samuel Lettsom. Russell advised he "could not commend the mode in which he executed his duties". Yet at the same time, Russell stated any Aboriginal Protector who refused to hand over crime suspects would render all the blacks under his care liable to similar action to that taken by Lettsom.

The fatal results of Lettsom's illegal operation had been sheepishly reported through the bureaucracy to the authorities in Sydney, and then London. At every step along the way, there had been an expectation of it being condemned. But, 17 months after the operation, the whites of Port Phillip had now learned that the British government had endorsed it. Gipps could still make pronouncements that the black and white people of New South Wales enjoyed "equal and indiscriminate justice". But the reality was that, with the sanction of London, special parties could be organised to indiscriminately round up large groups of Aborigines and hold them hostage as Lettsom had done. The only rider which Russell added was that Lettsom-type operations "should not be undertaken without some hope of convicting the parties guilty of outrage or theft". The *Geelong Advertiser* welcomed Russell's remarks. "The principles upon which the Home Government have founded their instructions appear to be of the most enlightened kind, and will ultimately do more good to the Aborigines than the mawkish philanthropy of the present protectorate system," it commented.[5]

Soon after Russell's remarks were published in Geelong and Melbourne, Fyans would set off on the mission that would result in the deaths of at least two Gunditjmara men, and the arrests of Roger, Cocknose, Jupiter and Bumbletoe. Fyans was pleased with the outcome of the expedition, and saw no need to make large-scale arrests like Lettsom had done. But the squatters of the area were not satisfied with Fyans' efforts. In a letter to La Trobe written two days after Roger was arrested, 12 of the squatters complained that until now the only time Fyans' Border Police had been seen in the area was when the Commissioner made his annual rounds. The troopers, they suggested, should be removed from his control in Geelong. Instead, they should be broken up into smaller units and stationed under the control of magistrates throughout the Western District -- the appointment of one or more of which was needed in the Port Fairy area.

But the main purpose of the letter from the 12 squatters would be to object to some of the remarks La Trobe had recently made when replying to the memorial organised by James Kilgour. The group -- which included Kilgour, Niel Black, James Webster and Armyne Bolden -- was particularly concerned about what the Superintendent had said in relation to the murders of the Kirrae women and child at Muston's Creek. "We cannot comprehend upon what principle of reason or justice any stain can rest upon the inhabitants generally of a district on account of the crime of a few cold blooded and heartless miscreants perpetrated in their neighbourhood," the letter protested. But this was implied by La Trobe having called upon the signatories to the memorial to purge themselves and their servants of all participation in or knowledge of the murders of the three women and a child.

Then the squatters dropped a bombshell, virtually accusing Sievwright of having "doctored" his report about the affair to make it more emotive. La Trobe could not possibly view the crime with greater abhorrence than they would, were they as confident as he appeared to be of the truth of what had been reported to him about it. "But we have strong reason to believe that the information transmitted to your Honour may not be altogether correct," the letter asserted. Several of the squatters had heard servants on Smith and Osbrey's station say that Aboriginal men as well as women had been shot. The blacks themselves had also stated this, they claimed, "thus leading to the belief that an affray had taken place" on the day in question. "And we have had proof in too many instances of late, that the natives do not often resign their plunder without a fight for it, which may have been the cause in this instance also, and led to the melancholy event referred to".[6]

It was the first time La Trobe had had reason to doubt the accuracy of Sievwright's report on the murders, and he told the squatters their claims would be investigated. But the fact remained, he replied, that the killing of a child and three women, one of them pregnant, was "a most detestable crime". It might fairly be supposed that the murderers at Muston's Creek had been residents of that part of the district. It was the common duty of the government and the "respectable settlers" to detect them. Under the circumstances, the "ultimate concealment" of those responsible would scarcely be possible if "a general spirit of zealous inquiry" had been aroused among the white settlers. And if the murderers did remain undetected, it was certain that this was a case in which the actions of a few *would* leave a stain on the whole community.[7]

The Superintendent had already shown a determination to ensure that the Muston's Creek murders did not go unpunished. La Trobe had immediately endorsed Sievwright's initial offer of a reward of 50 pounds for "any free person or persons" giving information leading a conviction. If the informant was a convict, he'd pledged, an application would be made to Queen Victoria for a conditional pardon. Informing Fyans and Police Magistrates Blair and French of the reward, La Trobe had also told them they could ensure the co-operation of the squatting community by saying, if necessary, that they had the authority to remove every station within 50 kilometres of the spot where the murders were committed. It was a sensational proposal, and La Trobe did not initially mention it when he informed Gipps of the murders three days later.[8]

On the day of Roger's arrest, Sievwright had gone back to the scene of the Muston's Creek killings to find out whether publication of the reward had helped

Fifty Pounds Reward, or a Conditional Pardon.

Superintendent's Office,
Melbourne, 21th March, 1842.

WHEREAS it has come to the knowledge of the Government, that on the night of 23rd of February last, a party of six or more Europeans surprised a number of aboriginal natives, sleeping in a tea-tree scrub, in the immediate vicinity of the station of Messrs. Smith and Osbry, in the Portland Bay District, and then and there barbarously murdered three aboriginal females, and one male child, by gun or pistol shots, besides wounding a fourth female. It is hereby notified in His Excellency the Governor's name, that with the view of bringing the perpetrators of this great crime to justice, a reward of fifty pounds will be paid to any free person, or persons, who may give such information as shall lead to the conviction of any of the guilty parties ; and if such information be given by a prisoner of the Crown, application will be made to Her Majesty for an allowance to him of a conditional pardon: Whereas also, it has become known that in divers instances of recent date, certain European settlers, or their servants, have been murdered in different parts of this district by native blacks, and amongst others, whose names are yet unknown, Alexander Moffat Allan, on the river Loddon, on the 13th of March last, Thomas Bird at the station of Mr. Ritchie, near Port Fairy, on the 6th of February; notice is hereby given, that the above reward of £50 will be paid, in either of the cases cited, to any free person or persons who may give such information as shall lead to the conviction of any of the guilty parties ; and if such information be given by a prisoner of the crown, application will be made to her Majesty for an allowance to him of a conditional pardon.

In his Excellency's name,.
(Signed)   C. J. LA TROBE.

Superintendent La Trobe would endorse Sievwright's initial reward of 50 pounds for any "free" person who provided information leading to the arrest of the Muston's Creek murderers. If the informant was a convict, application would be made for a free pardon. As this official notice shows, La Trobe felt it prudent to offer the same reward over recent murders of white men by blacks. But when Governor Gipps heard details of the Muston's Creek murders, he decided to double the reward to 100 pounds for a free person. Instead of a conditional pardon, a convict would be eligible for a full pardon -- with a free passage back to England.

to jog any memories. Again, however, he would hear a chorus of denials. He would report that in his view, Thomas Osbrey and others were lying. Even if all of the murderers had been visitors, it was "next to impossible" that none of the white men at the home station knew anything of the affair. The firing of a gunshot was "the usual signal of alarm throughout the country". So many shots could therefore not have been fired so close to the station without having excited at least the attention, if not the alarm, of the white men there at the time. "On questioning Mr Osbrey as to whether he had endeavoured to learn any circumstance that might lead to the discovery of the guilty parties, he replied 'He was just come from a country (Ireland) where there was a great deal of crime and that there, the people did not meddle with what did not concern them, so he did not think it his business to make inquiries on the subject'."

Not having been informed of the controversial proposal which La Trobe had already made about the squatters within a 50 kilometre radius, Sievwright recommended that at the very least, the licence in Osbrey's name should be cancelled. Smith, acting as overseer, and station manager, Richard Hill -- who he believed were on the verge of applying in their own right for licences -- should have their applications rejected. "By such an example, a check may be given to that system of co-operation amongst a portion of the settlers, who would rather abet a crime, even of this magnitude, against the Aborigines, by every concealment in their power, than lend their aid to bring the guilty parties to justice."[9] That same day in Sydney, Gipps would decide that the 50 pounds reward being offered for information about the murders was inadequate. At at around the same time, the Bolden brothers, for example, were offering 50 pounds for information leading to the conviction of anyone responsible for stealing a missing white Durham bull.[10] Gipps decided to double the reward to 100 pounds for a free person. Instead of a conditional pardon, a convict would be eligible for a full pardon -- with a free passage back to England.[11]

This more tempting incentive was certainly not enough to make Osbrey and Smith talk. The day after it was advertised in the Melbourne press, they would visit La Trobe in Melbourne to personally deny any knowledge of the murders.[12] As yet unknown to the Superintendent, the number of murder victims had just risen to four women and a child. Pwebingannai, the distraught husband of Wonigoniber, the woman wounded at Muston's Creek, and other members of his tribe, had told Sievwright they wanted to take her away from Mt Rouse. Her condition from the gunshot wounds in her back and right hand had gradually deteriorated over the two months that she'd been at the reserve. The Assistant Protector had applied for a doctor to be sent to treat her, but none had arrived. There was nothing more he could do for her, so he did not try to stop Pwebingannai carrying his wife away from the camp, to a spot about three kilometres away. There she had died two days later.[13]

Soon after Wonigoniber's death, two more white men would be murdered by Aborigines in the Western District -- Scottish squatter Donald McKenzie, and his hutkeeper, Frederick Edinge. The killings occurred on McKenzie's station in Bunganditj territory, about 70 kilometres west of Mt Rouse. A shepherd employed by McKenzie, Joseph Lillycross Wheatley, would later depose that he believed one of the murderers had been a black named Koort Kirrup, who had been living with his wife and children on the station. He was "perfectly domesticated", understood everything that was said to him in English, and could speak enough words to make himself understood. "Mr McKenzie placed unbounded confidence in him, as he frequently described the great assistance he should render in case any blacks should attack the station," Wheatley stated. Koort Kirrup had done as much work as a white station hand would have done, including erecting a sheepyard. In return, McKenzie had given him rations for his family.

It had been obvious to Wheatley on the still, clear and frosty morning of the murders that something was amiss, and when he went out to watch the sheep he'd taken with him McKenzie's double-barrelled gun as well as his own pistol. Koort Kirrup, who had been behaving strangely in recent days, had not as usual come up to McKenzie's hut for some breakfast for his family. And only the day before, one of Koort Kirrup's sons -- known as Tom -- had told him that there were "plenty of blackfellows about". Not long after being left in charge of the sheep, Wheatley heard a gunshot, then McKenzie's voice shout "murder" from the direction of the hut occupied by Frederick Edinge. He ran across and called out McKenzie's and Edinge's names, but received no reply. Koort Kirrup was beating something dark on the ground with a waddy, and as he tried to get into the hut he noticed several blacks were already inside. Others were closing in on him, so he ran up some elevated ground behind the hut to ready himself for defence. A spear was thrown, sticking in a tree close to him.

Koort Kirrup, the right arm of a shirt he was wearing covered in blood, had then called out "come on you bloody wretch" to Wheatley before throwing two spears in his direction. Another black had then thrown a spear at him from a distance of about nine metres, which also missed him. Wheatley opened fire with the pistol. He saw the black fall with a wound to the left side, although "there was some life still in the body". Koort Kirrup ran down towards an open area alongside a creek, to which some Aborigines were trying to drive the sheep. Wheatley fired five more shots from his pistol as the blacks went to surround him, but was unsure whether he hit his targets. Having only the two charges left in McKenzie's gun, the shepherd fled into the bush on the other side of the creek. He managed to elude his pursuers for a while. But then Wheatley's dog, which knew Koort Kirrup well, guided him and at least two other blacks to him. The blacks overtook Wheatley, and confronted him on the edge of a forested area. However, the white man quickly turned back, and by a circuitous route managed to reach the nearby inn of Daniel O'Neill.

The publican agreed to take his bullock dray back to McKenzie's station with the "greatly frightened and excited" Wheatley. With them went two men who worked for O'Neill, and two employees of one of the Henty brothers who'd been drinking at the inn. Edinge's body they found first. He was laying on his back, his little dog faithfully sitting on his chest. Edinge had been "severely beaten about the head, apparently with some blunt instrument", and he had a spear wound in one side. As well, he appeared to have been shot in the back. Then McKenzie's body was found. His head had been "battered to pieces" and he'd been speared in the chest. The spear had apparently been thrust at him, rather than thrown: lacerations on one of his hands indicated that he'd tried to ward it off. Other wounds on the squatter's body gave a clue to the possible motive for the murders. McKenzie had been "dreadfully beaten about the private parts, which were frightfully swollen and almost shapeless". Horrified by their discovery, the white men covered the bodies with some branches before Wheatley took off to report the murders to Police Magistrate Blair in Portland, about 50 kilometres away.

Police Magistrate French, whose base at The Grange was roughly the same distance away from McKenzie's station as Portland, would hear of the murders at about the same time, and unlike Blair immediately set off to to the scene. French would help to bury the bodies and conduct an inquest, amounting to a statement from O'Neill. Informing La Trobe of what had occurred, French said about 700 of McKenzie's sheep had also been driven off, about 600 of which had since been recovered. The rest had been found with their legs broken. French told La Trobe he'd organised a posse of his two Mounted Police and some "volunteer settlers" to search for the blacks involved whom Wheatley believed he could identify. However, no blacks had been apprehended. French added that the murder of McKenzie was particularly tragic because from what he could learn, the squatter had "behaved with the greatest kindness to the natives, frequently feeding them with flour and meat". La Trobe would tell Gipps it appeared that the murderers had been among those who'd been both fed and employed at McKenzie's station.[14]

In its report of the murders of McKenzie and Edinge, the *Port Phillip Gazette* would allude to the outcry over the recent murders of the Aboriginal women and child at Muston's Creek. If "whole districts of civilised inhabitants" could suffer the odium of actual or presumed aggressions against the blacks, it argued, those who were paid to watch over and direct them should be called on to explain how murders such as those at McKenzie's station were occurring. "Shall they not be required to prove, that notwithstanding diligent observation, they were in perfect ignorance of the movements of their proteges?" the *Gazette* asked. "And if they do prove this, do they not then, themselves, show that the Protectorate system is what the public voice has long pronounced it -- delusive, useless, worthless? The application of the law of highly civilised England to fierce revengeful savages, in conjunction with the Protectorate, is like making the same law to govern the wolves and the lambs, with the additional absurdity of employing a shepherd for the wolves, and leaving the lambs to take care of themselves."[15]

"Most of his black labourers...were applying themselves cheerfully to their agricultural duties..."

Only a week later, Sievwright would be reporting that he was satisfied with the progress he was making with the almost 300 blacks who were living with him at the Mt Rouse reserve, despite the fact that there was "much sickness prevailing". Because of the total lack of medical aid and clothing, this sickness -- including several cases of "severe rheumatic fever and pleuritis" -- was likely to increase. Articles of clothing promised by Robinson almost three months earlier had not yet arrived. But there were some positive signs. "During the last three months, the natives have shown that they fully appreciate the benefits that are daily accruing to them at this establishment," he stated. Most of his black labourers had become "regular in their habits of industry", and were applying themselves cheerfully to their agricultural duties without daily orders having to be reiterated. "Some act as stock-keepers and have charge of the bullocks and cows upon the station," he wrote. "Others have charge of the horses, and are employed at regular duties about the station. Others have been taught to plough and drive the team and are much pleased with the responsibility attached to such employments."

"So soon as they have breakfasted, the men and children proceed to the field to work, while the women generally go off in a body to procure roots, oppossums, etc," Sievwright added. "All generally return to the station about 3 p.m. then retire to their huts, happy and contented, and the evenings are passed by the children in play." Sometimes, the women had not gone off searching for food during the day and had joined the men and children in the learning and then practising agricultural work. As the men had dragged a harrow over the ploughed land, the women and children had helped break up the sods by pulverising them with sticks. This, he noted, had been "better than cross-ploughing". Wheat had been sown in two parts of a large field, and progress had been made in establishing a vegetable garden.

Except for the recent theft of 228 sheep from Donald Cameron's nearby station, Sievwright declared, he had "every reason to be satisfied" with the conduct of the blacks since the Mt Rouse reserve had been established. The white settlers in the immediate vicinity of the reserve had expressed to him "satisfaction and surprise" at the security they had recently enjoyed, having expected "quite another result". This was quite an achievement, the Protector remarked, when it was considered that the blacks with him were "of the wildest and most savage description". Most of them had had no communication with the whites, "having but lately been deprived of their country by those settlers who have so rapidly overrun this part of the district". It was an acknowledged fact that the Aborigines had been displaced to the extent that there was "not a pool of water for the purpose of a station of which they are not bereft".

The claims being made by the Assistant Protector were in direct contradiction to the assertion made about his effect on inter-racial relations in the memorial recently presented to La Trobe by James Kilgour. That memorial, Sievwright advised, purported to be a correct account of "the recent misdeeds" of the blacks. Instead, it contained an exaggerated report of all of the losses experienced by the white settlers over a period of two years. This time period the document had failed to mention. "It would not, I presume, under such circumstances tend to excite the impression which the memorialists would wish to establish," he wrote. When the Chief Protector had inquired into the accounts of some of the events mentioned in the memorial, Sievwright noted, he'd found the facts to be "of a totally different complexion". The Assistant Protector concluded optimistically: "If a comparison is to be drawn between the condition of the natives of a portion of the country which for the first time has been encroached upon by the white population, and those other parts of the colony which have been for years occupied and settled, it should be borne in mind that the first collisions between the savage and the settlers are, to both parties, the most fatal -- and that now, the tranquillity of this portion of the district may be rapidly established, since an asylum has been instituted to provide for the wants of the Aborigines."[16]

When he'd received Kilgour's memorial, La Trobe had told Gipps it appeared that Sievwright's behaviour had "seriously aggravated" the disturbed state of the Western District, without checking the accuracy of the document. He'd since received the report he'd ordered from Robinson on the recent actions of his assistant. The Chief Protector would be surprisingly restrained in his direct comments on Sievwright, going nowhere near as far in denigrating him as La Trobe had done. He would confine himself to the comparitively mild remark that Sievwright "appeared unacquainted" with most of the "outrages" attributed to the blacks of his district. However, Robinson would by implication suggest that Sievwright be replaced. The Aborigines of his area were not under the control they should be, he advised. To help gain the desired control over these and other blacks, the Chief Protector suggested the appointment of "men of good character" as "travelling overseers". Such men, he believed, could be hired for 50 pounds a year, with rations. This would be one fifth of the cost of each of the four Assistant Protectors, "some" of whom, he alleged, were averse to this kind of duty, and had "not yet travelled".

With typical ambivalence, while making this vague proposal for "travelling overseers", the Chief Protector lauded the prospects for the Mt Rouse reserve. If properly conducted, he stated, it "would be found of great advantage and utility to the Aboriginal natives and the white inhabitants". More blacks could be encouraged to join the 300 already there, and religious instruction and educational classes could be started among the 100 or so children. "A religious missionary, a medical attendant, and a schoolmaster are required," he told La Trobe. As well, Robinson suggested, the convict servants at the reserve should be replaced. "I am apprehensive they will do harm," Robinson wrote. "Ex-convicts are equally objectionable, and none but men of good character should be employed on such establishments." These had been key recommendations from Sievwright, ignored by Robinson at the time they'd been made. After many weeks of unnecessary delay, they'd at last gone one stage further in the bureaucracy. But that was as far as they would go. When La Trobe sent on the Chief Protector's report to Gipps more than two weeks later, there would be no mention of the recommendations in the covering note.[17]

That same day, La Trobe would receive a reply from Robinson to his request for comment on the suggestion from Gipps that Sievwright should be sacked. The Chief Protector needed no encouragement, and was uncharacteristically

concise. "In reply I do myself the honour to state that under all the circumstances and judging from past proceedings that in my opinion it would be desirable the services of this officer be dispensed with," Robinson joyfully wrote.[18]
To add fuel to the fire, La Trobe would tell Gipps that all of the other Assistant
Protectors had managed to achieve "at least that degree of respect which will be
accorded to a fair moral name and an evident desire to effect good, however limited the success". The same could not be said for Sievwright. "Mr Sievwright
has unfortunately for himself not been in a position to claim even these
advances," La Trobe wrote. "Neither can he claim the approbation of the government as to the general tenor of his proceedings, and I can but agree with the
Chief Protector that his further services should be dispensed with."[19]

Nine days later, Gipps would send a batch of documents relating to the
Aborigines to the Secretary of State for the Colonies in London, Lord Stanley.
In one covering letter, the Governor stated he was obliged to draw Stanley's
attention to La Trobe's complaints about the "inefficiency" of the Aboriginal
Protectors. "I am painfully convinced that the Protectors have as yet effected no
good that can be put in comparison with the irritation which they have created,
though at the same time I feel very reluctant to put a stop to their proceedings,
so long as the remotest hope can be entertained of a better result from their
labours," Gipps wrote. Later that day, the Governor decided he'd better send on
a copy of La Trobe's letter recommending "a complete change of system" for the
Protectorate. In a separate note to Stanley, Gipps remarked he'd "entertained
doubts as to the necessity or propriety" of forwarding La Trobe's letter. But he
now thought he ought not withhold it any longer.

"With the exception of the Chief Protector, Mr Robinson, it would be difficult,
I think, to find men less equal to the arduous duty of acting as Protectors of the
Aborigines, than those who were selected for this purpose in England in the year
1838," Gipps wrote. "And the Chief Protector, though efficient as far as his own
mode of holding intercourse with the blacks is concerned, is quite unequal to the
control of what is becoming a large and expensive department." Robinson,
Gipps added, was "already advanced in years, and far beyond the prime of life"
-- though at 54, he was only three years older than the Governor. "The course
pursued by the Protectors has been, as far as I am able to form a judgement of
it, one from the beginning, of feeble action, and puling complaint," Gipps continued. "With power in their hands to command the respect of the settlers, they
have failed to make themselves respected; and I greatly fear that their measures
have tended rather to increase than allay the irritation which has long existed
between the two races.[20]

Back in Melbourne, La Trobe had told Robinson he'd recommended that
Sievwright be sacked as soon as possible. In a considerable understatement of

the Assistant Protector's perilous position, La Trobe remarked it was "but just" that Sievwright be informed "that the question of his services being discontinued has been mooted".[21] The Chief Protector was in no hurry for justice to be done. He waited another three weeks before addressing a brief note to Sievwright. "I am directed to acquaint you that the subject of your appointment will be brought under the consideration of government, and the question of how far it is desirable to continue the same has been mooted," the note bluntly stated.[22]

Ironically, as the note from Robinson was on its way to Mt Rouse, Sievwright's optimistic report about the prospects for the reserve he'd established was on its way to Melbourne. And it was not the only bad news in the mail for Sievwright. Also on its way to Mt Rouse was notification that Melbourne flour and general store merchants, William Porter and George White, had acted on a threat to sue him in the Supreme Court for an unpaid debt for goods supplied while his salary had been stopped, and which he'd still not paid. The Court had ruled in the merchants' favour, awarding them damages of 53 pounds, plus costs of 10 pounds. The total was more than a quarter of Sievwright's annual salary. Another Melbourne merchant, John Wyberg Shaw, had also filed a summons against the Assistant Protector at the Prothonotary's Office, although Porter and White's was the first case to be tried.[23]

The note from Robinson informing him that his suspension was being considered would not reach Sievwright until two weeks after it had been written. Shocked, he immediately sent a reply. "As I am in utter ignorance of any circumstance that can have possibly led even to the expediency of such a measure being adopted by the government, I have to beg that you will do me the honour to inform me from what it has arisen, and at the same time to procure me permission from His Honour the Superintendent, to proceed to Melbourne in order that I may be enabled promptly to meet this case," he wrote. Sievwright sent a copy of the letter direct to La Trobe.[24]

The campaign to dispense with Sievwright's services had already gathered momentum by the time his letter reached Melbourne. Even before the Assistant Protector had written the letter, Gipps had authorised his suspension "until the pleasure of the Secretary of State shall be known". Informing La Trobe of the decision, the Governor requested to be provided with a statement on "the reports injurious to Mr Sievwright's moral character which have been current at Port Phillip". La Trobe should also state the grounds, if any, which made him believe that these reports were well-founded.[25] The Superintendent in turn would seek reports on the matter from former Melbourne Police Magistrate William Lonsdale, and Foster Fyans. In particular, he would ask Lonsdale and Fyans for "succinct" statements on what they knew about the circumstances relating to

Christina and Fanny Sievwright having run away from Geelong to Melbourne, back in 1839. La Trobe knew that the runaways had spent several days at Lonsdale's house, and that Fyans had been involved in an unsuccessful reconciliation attempt at the time.[26]

A statement would also be sought from Robinson on the rumours about Sievwright's moral character. At the same time, La Trobe told the Chief Protector to send Sievwright a letter informing him that he'd now been suspended, and requesting him to prepare to give up control of the Mt Rouse reserve to the person appointed to replace him. "You are aware that it is not so much from a consideration of the perverseness and incapacity which have been displayed by Mr Sievwright in the department, that His Excellency has been induced to take this step, as from that of the charges which have existed and still exist against Mr Sievwright's moral character, and it is but just that Mr Sievwright should know this, and have an opportunity to urge anything that he may think proper to do in defence," La Trobe concluded. Again, however, Robinson was not interested in justice for his assistant. He would write the letter suggested, about two weeks later, but not send it.[27]

Another inquiry had meanwhile been launched into a matter in which Sievwright was inextricably involved -- the Muston's Creek murders. La Trobe had been informed of the death at Mt Rouse of the wounded woman, raising the number of murder victims to five. He'd also read a report from Sievwright on the progress of his investigations into the case, including fresh depositions he'd taken on another visit to Smith and Osbrey's station. But La Trobe was not satisfied. Almost four months had passed, and still no-one had been arrested. He appointed Crown Lands Commissioners Fyans and Powlett, and an aristocratic Irish squatter and magistrate, Charles James Griffith, to carry out what he expected to be a "rigorous" inquiry into the murders. The inquiry panel was ordered to investigate the claim that Sievwright had "doctored" his report on the case by omitting mention that there'd been an "affray" and that men as well as women had been shot. La Trobe pointed out he could not see any reason to doubt the accuracy of what Sievwright had reported. It appeared that the murder victims had not been members of "a marauding party returning with their plunder". But the source of the claim about Sievwright's report could have primary information about the affair.

Fyans, Powlett and Griffith were sent copies of every document relating to the case in La Trobe's possession. In his confidential instructions, he told them he expected the inquiry to result in several other documents. One would list the names, character and occupation of every white inhabitant of the stations "within a certain limit of the place" at the time of the murders. Any parties known to have visited at about that date should also be noted. If any had left the district, it should be ascertained when they did so, and where they'd gone. La Trobe added that he also wanted notes prepared "of all credible Aboriginal evidence bearing on the subject, however inadmissable in court of law". If nothing else, the inquiry would at least produce ample evidence to show that all possible means had been tried to find a clue that could have ultimately led to the apprehension of the murderers.

For reasons which he did not feel the need to outline, the Superintendent feared that the panel of inquiry would not receive "hearty co-operation" from the settlers of the area. But if it was correct that eight horsemen had been involved, there must be many white men who must have either direct knowledge of the identity of the culprits, or at least suspicions who they were. The 100 pounds reward had not been effective in inducing any one of them to come forward. This was perhaps because granting of the reward was dependent on a conviction being gained. The panel might be able to find men willing to provide useful information with the inducement of a few pounds quietly slipped to them, rather than in the form of a reward. He was authorising them to spend up to 50 pounds for this purpose, at their discretion.[28]

Three days later, La Trobe would write to Fyans saying he'd been informed that the Commissioner had just returned from his extensive tour to the west of his district. It may be difficult, he acknowledged, for Fyans to immediately undertake another long trip, and if he wished he could excuse himself from participation in the Muston's Creek inquiry -- a suggestion which would be readily accepted. In a separate letter, written the same day, La Trobe would request details from Fyans of the operation that had resulted in the deaths of Jackey and The Doctor. As the Commissioner concocted his reply, the prisoners he and his Border Police had taken alive -- Roger, Cocknose, Jupiter and Bumbletoe -- would start their second month in the crowded Melbourne jail, in complete ignorance of what their fate could be.[29]

In the same time advertisement offering a reward for information about the Muston's Creek murderers, La Trobe had offered a reward for information about two white men murdered by Aborigines. One was John Ritchie's hutkeeper, Thomas Bird, who'd been killed the same month only about 60 kilometres southwest of the site of the Muston's Creek massacre. The same terms were offered: 50 pounds reward for a free person, or an application for a conditional pardon for a Crown prisoner. The only proviso in each case was that the information given would have to lead to convictions.[30] Soon after the arrest of Roger, Jupiter and Cocknose, Police Magistrate Blair would report that he had in custody an Aborigine who he believed had been one of Thomas Bird's murderers. The arrest of the Gunditjmara man had been recommended by none other than George Robinson.

After his visit to the district earlier that year, the Chief Protector had told La Trobe that most of the recent stock losses suffered by James Kilgour and other white settlers in the Port Fairy area could be attributed to a band of Gunditjmara warriors led by Puntkum, also known as Mr Murray. He'd also been the one who'd fired a gun at Henry Loughnan during one recent robbery. No black should be apprehended, the Chief Protector commented, unless a conviction could be obtained. But in Puntkum's case, be believed there were enough sworn statements from white witnesses to convict him and he had "advised his apprehension".[31] Robinson had omitted two key facts about Puntkum in his report. First, he failed to tell La Trobe that Puntkum had been one of the blacks who'd accompanied him on part of his lengthy Western District tour in 1841.[32] But the Chief Protector also failed to mention he'd been told by an Aboriginal informant that Puntkum was one of Bird's murderers.[33]

Blair would soon learn of this more serious allegation against Puntkum -- and lost no time in informing La Trobe of it, after he'd been arrested near Portland by District Constable Thomas Finn. The only problem was that no evidence could be gained against Puntkum except "that of his own people". Their evidence of course was inadmissable. The only hope was that Puntkum could be committed for trial on a lesser charge of involvement in one of the attacks on James Hunter's stations. The prisoner was being held in the Portland lock-up, Blair told La Trobe, pending possible identification by a boy who worked for Hunter.[34] Blair would soon be issuing an arrest warrant for another suspected black murderer -- Koort Kirrup, the Bunganditj man accused of killing Donald McKenzie and Frederick Edinge. But the process of getting him to court would prove even more frustrating.[35]

CHAPTER 25
Roger's trial

THE hills which the white men would later call the Grampians, to the north of Mt Rouse, played a major role in Aboriginal tradition. The Grampians belonged to three tribes -- the Bunganditj, the Tjapwurong and the Jaadwa. In rock shelters in parts of the hills, Aboriginal artists had left their mark, with a wide variety of paintings. In the Bunganditj part of the hills alone, there were thousands of motifs painted in red and yellow ochre and white pipe clay on the walls of rock shelters. Many of the motifs were simple bars or strokes. But some were of human figures in various forms and animals such as fish, kangaroos and birds. Others depicted human hands, or emu and kangaroo tracks. In the eastern range of the Grampians, in Tjapwurong territory, there was a painting of particular significance in a cave in a huge granite boulder. It was of Bunjil, believed by initiated Aboriginal males throughout the region to be their supreme creator -- with ongoing powers which included the making of medicine men.[1]

According to one Aboriginal legend, all fire which could be safely used originated in the Grampians. At one time, the fire belonged exclusively to the crows which inhabited the hills. They realised the great value of the fire, and prevented all other animals from getting any of it. But one day, when the crows were amusing themselves by throwing firesticks about, a wren called Yuuloin Keear swooped down, picked one up, and flew away. Then a hawk called Tarrakukk took the firestick from the wren, and set fires burning across the Western District. From that time, there had always been fires from which lights could be safely taken. The Western District Aborigines would never take a firestick from a fire suspected of having been started by lightning, which was one form in which the evil spirit Muurup visited the earth.[2]

As the tribe with the territory furthest to the west, the Bunganditj were believed by the Aborigines to the east to have a particular link with Muurup, because it was always from Bunganditj territory that thunderstorms with lightning came.[3] The concept of other tribes with malevolent intent was an integral part of Aboriginal culture. Natural deaths were usually attributed to the ill-will and evil spells of an enemy in another tribe -- and when this occurred, retribution had to be sought, just as much as when death had occurred as the result of a violent encounter. Avenging of death by the male friends and relatives of the deceased was regarded as a sacred and necessary duty, and one death could start a series of payback killings.[4]

While the Bunganditj people may have control of the weather, and the ability to direct lightning strikes, members of the southerly section of the Tjapwurong blacks at Mt Rouse were also renowned for having particular spiritual and supernatural powers. Before he was shot dead by a white man, members of various tribes would travel great distances to seek access to the famous healing powers of the Tjapwurong elder, Tuurap Warneen. At corroborees and great meetings, he would have his face painted red, with white streaks under his eyes, and a head-band of the quill feather of a turkey bustard, or the crest of a white cockatoo. His widow was a celebrated sorceress, known as White Lady, who would maintain her reputation with no small degree of quackery and tall stories. For example, she would acquire a coil of fur formerly owned by a European woman, and tell her people it was the tail of a lunar kangaroo she'd brought back from a trip to the moon.[5]

A depiction of Aboriginal rock art in the Grampians

After the arrival of white men, the inter-tribal suspicion which often led to violence was made acute by large-scale displacement, and further fuelled by the introduction of new diseases among the Western District tribes such as influenza and syphilis. Sievwright would do his utmost to minimise the extent of disease among his charges. But the very limited medical supplies which Robinson was prepared to provide were soon expended. Sievwright was forced to use his own funds to buy more supplies for emergency use.[6] At the same time, he would apply the limited medical knowledge he'd gained in the army whenever the Aborigines would allow him. He'd shown a special interest in the ill health of the blacks since his arrival in the colony, it being the subject of one of his first communications to the government while still in Sydney.[7] In Melbourne, he'd lobbied hard for action on the dismal medical situation of the blacks, as he saw them dying around him. The final moments of one ill black he described thus: "He squeezed his lubra's hand, pulled the blankets over his head, and died like a lamb."[8]

More than three years later, Sievwright was still making urgent appeals for medical aid for the Aborigines. In a letter to Robinson in July 1842, Sievwright cited three communications earlier that year relating to the ill health of the blacks at Mt Rouse, all of which had been ignored. The 1842 winter was aggravating the suffering. "From the extreme severity of the season, and the total absence of blankets or clothing of any description, rheumatic fever has now made its appearance amongst the natives, from which they are suffering severely," Sievwright reported. Five had died from the fever in the previous nine days. "My hut is daily crowded with others whose distress I in vain endeavour to relieve," he complained. The deaths, he sadly added, had prompted the Jarcoort blacks to leave the camp the previous day. The Jarcoort people, with many of their warriors already dead, had been living under his protection for most of the previous 16 months. But they were afraid of being left open to retaliation if they were blamed for the deaths by the other tribes present at the camp. This "superstitious belief", Sievwright reported, was "general amongst them".[9]

This latest appeal for medical aid from Sievwright would arrive in Melbourne not long before he became aware of the growing case for his dismissal. Ironically, Robinson had finally taken up his pleas for medical assistance, and had gained approval for the appointment of a medical officer for the Mt Rouse reserve. The officer had already been chosen: unsuccessful squatter John Watton, who happened to be father-in-law of Police Magistrate Acheson French at The Grange. La Trobe had approved Robinson's plan for Watton to take "temporary charge" of the Mt Rouse reserve during Sievwright's suspension. Subject to the Governor's endorsement, Watton was due to take over running the reserve from Sievwright in just a few weeks.[10]

First to reply to La Trobe's request for information about reports detrimental to Sievwright's moral character was the former Melbourne Police Magistrate William Lonsdale, to whom Christina had appealed for help after she and Fanny had run away from Geelong back to Melbourne in 1839. Lonsdale would relate how Christina had made serious complaints to him and the then Crown Prosecutor, Horatio Carrington, about her husband's behaviour when they'd met at her request at a Melbourne hotel. "Her principal cause of complaint appeared to be that Mr Sievwright, who lived in a tent apart from his family, was indulging in everything he wished, whilst herself and family were in want of many necessaries of life both in food and clothing," Lonsdale told La Trobe.

"This I readily believed from the manner in which I had observed they lived, when they were in the neighbourhood of Melbourne," he wrote. "She stated she never had the command of money to purchase articles necessary for her children, and that to assist her on her way to Melbourne one of her convict servants had lent her a small sum. She then entered into an account of their past life by which it appeared Mr Sievwright had abandoned her for about two years in the Mediterranean, where he had been quartered with his regiment, and that after being without receiving intelligence of him for some time, she learnt he was living a very disreputable life in London, and that through the interference of their friends, she had again joined him a short time before they came out to this country."

"Thinking their position at the inn a very unprotected one, as well as one which would be inconveniently expensive, I invited them to my house till their complaint should be enquired into," Lonsdale went on. "I then wrote to Mr Sievwright, begging him to come to Melbourne forthwith, as I thought his wife's statement was such as to throw great discredit on him, and that arrangements should be made to prevent a recurrence of such exposures. He excused himself from coming, stating he had a child sick, and had no-one with whom to leave it and the others in charge. This I afterwards found was not a correct statement. Mrs and Miss Sievwright remained several days at my residence, during which

From "The Chronicles of Early Melbourne"
Captain William Lonsdale's cottage in Melbourne

time many things were related of him which were disreputable and abominable; among others, that he had made advances to Miss Sievwright on board the ship they came from England in, of so plain a nature that it could not be misunderstood but he meditated her seduction."

"Whether these accusations were true, I could not of course tell, but my impression from various circumstances was, that enough had been said to prove him to be anything but a moral man; and the strongest reason for my coming to such a conclusion was his own conduct at the time these accusations were made, and his evident desire to avoid meeting his wife before me to discuss her complaints. The neglect of his family was also evident to all who saw them, whilst his own comforts appeared to be well attended to. Some time after Mrs and Miss Sievwright left Melbourne and returned to Geelong, he called upon me, but I gave him to understand I could not again admit him into my house from what had transpired, but at the same time that my opinion was very much against Mr Sievwright's character. I must at the same time say I saw enough of the wife and daughter to cause me to regret having invited them to my house, and to convince me that considerable laxity of morals existed with them as well as with Mr Sievwright."[11]

Next, La Trobe would receive a report from Sievwright's arch enemy, Flogger Fyans. He also reported that Sievwright had tried to use the excuse of having to look after his other six children as the reason why he could not go to Melbourne to see his runaway wife and daughter. Then when he'd offered to mind the children, Sievwright had stated that if Christina and Fanny could find their own way to Melbourne, they could find their own way back. About a fortnight later, the English solicitor, William Meek, had arrived at Fyans' cottage, saying he was attempting to conciliate in the Sievwright family "as a disinterested and honourable man". The Crown Lands Commissioner told La Trobe that he'd been reluctantly drawn into this attempt the following day, at the request of the Sievwrights.

"On entering a very dirty and miserable tent, I was introduced to Mrs and Miss Sievwright," he wrote. "I then requested to know what I was required for. Mr Sievwright said to hear the complaints of an old married woman. Mrs Sievwright proceeded, and was interrupted by Mr Sievwright directing his daughter to withdraw. The girl not immediately complying, he in a loud and most commanding voice directed her to immediately withdraw, and comply with his commands. She very quickly did so. Mr Sievwright then opened a small box, and taking from it some letters and bills...now, gentlemen, he said, this woman brings me before you, but if you allow me to read over some of her bills of extravagance, you can then judge of me and her complaints, or if she leaves me a sufficiency to support my family."

As Sievwright proceeded giving details of a bill amounting to almost 50 pounds, Fyans stated, his wife had "appeared not a little astonished at the items given of her extravagance", and accused him of needing glasses. She'd taken the bill from him, and started reading it. The first item was a box of cheroots. Christina had laughed, saying she did not smoke cheroots. The next item was several dozen jars of pickles. Here Christina had declared that such things were only consumed in Sievwright's tent, into which his family was not admitted. She and the children were each given a small daily allowance of mutton and flour with a little salt, without any vegetables. Another item on the bill was some boxes of claret. This Christina had also claimed had been entirely for her husband's consumption: the only glass of wine she'd had since arriving in New South Wales had been when she'd stayed at Lonsdale's house.

The only item on the bill which could be related to Christina's spending, Fyans reported, was two pairs of children's stockings, costing only two shillings. "She then handed the bill to Mr Meek, and so fully satisfied us that no extravagance attached to her or family that we acquitted her of the imputation," Fyans declared. "She then explained her extreme poverty for many years, that from her industry and charity she managed to bring up the family, that she had no allowance, that she had been deserted for many years when her fortune was squandered away in London gaming houses and other places, and with improper females, that his conduct was always of the same nature, and constantly attaching blame and extravagance to her. She then remarked to us, you may perceive that we are poorly clad, even to a shoe we barely have, holding up her foot. She had no stockings on, and her great toe sticking through an old boot. We could see no appearance of extravagance in dress, and cannot for a moment hesitate to declare the utmost value of the dresses did not exceed five shillings."

From what he and Meek had seen and heard, Fyans continued, they believed that it would be "a fruitless task to attempt to bring them in a state ever to live together". He'd suggested a separation, and a yearly allowance to Christina. Sievwright was willing to separate, but declined giving any allowance, saying only that he would pay her fare back home. To this, Christina had agreed, with the condition that Fanny would go with her. When Sievwright refused the demand, Fyans quoted Christina as having stated: "My child shall never be out of my sight with you. Not for the world would I leave her under your care, you vile creature. You well know your conduct, and the indecent liberties which you have taken with my poor child." At this point, Fyans told La Trobe, he left the tent, "never wishing to meet or see such people again".[12] Meek would verify the accuracy of the Commissioner's account of the meeting. "I can further bear testimony to the miserable manner in which the wife and daughter of Mr Assistant Protector Sievwright were then living (so much so indeed that the meanest labourer must have felt astonished and disgraced to have seen his wife in such a state of poverty and wretchedness) whilst he himself was revelling in comforts and luxuries," Meek added.[13]

More was hardly needed to rip Sievwright's reputation to shreds, but Fyans had kept a damning copy of an 1839 letter written by Christina. Soon after the incident in the Sievwright family tent, Christina had complained to Fyans that her domestic affairs had not been "at all ameliorated". Since Meek's departure, she'd attempted to submit quietly to all of Sievwright's "degrading and coercive treatment" of herself and their children. But she was finding that "in every trivial circumstance" his conduct was "more tyrannical and unlawful". The daily provisions were locked up from her, while he and one of the servants weighed up and distributed what he deemed necessary. He'd frequently refused to give her tea and sugar for the evening meal or breakfast, prompting her to steal supplies by removing slabs from the hut containing stores of the "treasures".

This had been known only to her and Fanny, but one day she'd defiantly called him to show what she'd been doing. He'd responded by calling the Barrabool men and the white convict servants together and proclaiming to the crowd that she was both mad "and a bad person" whom he would call a constable to take away. "This to you, my dear sir, may appear ludicrous," Christina told Fyans. "But need I assure you, to me it is quite unsupportable. He has refused it again this morning, and we are now without breakfast. My children are still without shoes, and I am without money. Pray assist me by your valuable advice, either as a friend or professionally. My conduct can be proud to be unexceptionable. I say this, as it is necessary to assure you (a stranger to my character) of it in this my untoward position."[14]

Next to respond to the Superintendent's request for information was the Chief Protector. He told La Trobe that reports detrimental to Sievwright's character had first been brought to his attention by his fellow Assistant Protectors, soon after he'd arrived in Melbourne. "Mr Dredge informed me that an improper and he believed a criminal intercourse had taken place between Mr Sievwright and Mrs Parker on their passage from Sydney to Port Phillip which had continued until my arrival in the harbour," Robinson wrote. "His treatment of his wife and daughter was said to be cruel and oppressive. His language to them was often of a disgusting description. They had frequently to leave their home on account of his cruelty. The family at times were in want of food. It was moreover said he had attempted the seduction of his own daughter. The proceeding is the common talk of the district, which is not surprising since the same was testified to and made public by his own family." The unhappy manner in which Sievwright lived with his wife was apparent, Robinson asserted. For a long time, the family occupied at Geelong "a miserable hut without windows or chimney", and now at Mt Rouse they were living in a solitary hut in the middle of an open area more than two kilometres from the black settlement, where Sievwright was living in John Cox's former hut.

Aborigines were the source of some of the detrimental reports about Sievwright, Robinson claimed. "The natives (who are acute observers) over whom Assistant Protector Sievwright was placed, noticed the impropriety of his conduct, and reported the same to the settlers," Robinson wrote. "Mr Parker informed me recently, that the natives had mentioned to Mrs Parker at the Loddon that an improper intercourse had existed between Mr Sievwright and his daughter. It is unnecessary to offer comment upon the proceeding, or to go into detail. Suffice to say, such is the common report of the district, and knowing as I do, that 'example' with the natives teaches before 'precept', I am of opinion that the unhappy manner in which he lives, is alone sufficient, independent of any other circumstance (or indeed want of capacity, or perverseness he may have evinced since his connection with the department) to disqualify him for the office of an Assistant Protector."[15]

There was more dirt that could have been thrown at "the most unpopular man that ever breathed". But the Chief Protector had managed to cover the key points in the scuttlebutt that had been pedalled by Sievwright's many detractors, doing his best to lend it credibility. If La Trobe had bothered to investigate, he would have found that much was at least second-hand hearsay or exaggeration. For example, the barque on which the Assistant Protectors had travelled to Melbourne had been crowded with the first batch of government immigrants to be sent to Port Phillip. As well as the 103 immigrants, including 30 women and 44 children, there was also a detachment of 34 soldiers aboard, jammed into the steerage "like herrings in a barrel". Two army officers and the Protectors and their families travelled in the cabins. The atmosphere aboard the boat was convivial. "We were altogether a jolly lot...an agreeable companiable set of passengers," one of them would later record. But with much of the voyage through stormy weather, the Protectors and their wives had their time cut out preventing their 22 children from falling overboard. Seven of the children were Charles and Christina's, so the circumstances were hardly ripe for him to be having an illicit affair with Mary Parker![16]

Certainly, after they arrived in Melbourne, Sievwright had spent some nights drinking with both of the Parkers at the military officers' mess, much to James Dredge's disgust. Dredge would record that Edward Parker's "abominable" conduct, drinking brandy and water before and after preaching, gave his profession the lie. What made it even worse was that he was a fellow Wesleyan, and Dredge had even been moved to complain to the Buntingdale missionaries about him.[17] About two months later, Parker had accused Sievwright of having attempted to seduce his wife. Sievwright had denied the claim, but it was of course enough to end their friendship. And there had been witnesses to their "sad altercation", providing more raw material for the rumour-mongers to craft and pass on.[18]

But the fact that Christina Sievwright had made sordid accusations against her husband was undeniable. And Robinson would provide La Trobe with further damning documentary evidence to prove it. He produced a letter written to him by Christina back in March 1839, complaining of her husband's behaviour. Her complaints had not been prompted by the "temporary annoyances" of having to live in a tent at that time on the edge of Melbourne, Christina wrote. Rather, she wanted Robinson to understand that Sievwright's conduct for some years had been "guided by a cold selfishness", which had been more fully developed since they'd left England, where they'd been surrounded by friends. "His behaviour is at present outrageous and ungentlemanlike," Christina declared. "These may appear harsh expressions, but they are mildly descriptive of his conduct." She pleaded with Robinson to "make any arrangements" which might render it unnecessary for her to accompany Sievwright into the bush. "I should then be enabled quietly to continue the education of my little ones," she wrote.[19]

At the time, Robinson had not been willing to act on Christina's letter. "Of course, I cannot interfere," he'd told his own wife, Maria.[20] But he'd kept the letter, and 40 months later he was eager to send it on to La Trobe, even though he knew there'd been a reconciliation. The Chief Protector would also enclose a more recently-written letter which in his view also amounted to a complaint about Sievwright's conduct -- this one written by Sievwright's brother, John. He'd written to Robinson from Geelong, where he'd moved after having lived at Keilambete and then Terang for about a year. As John explained in the letter, when the Western District reserve had been relocated to Mt Rouse, plans he'd had with his brother for a joint farming venture fell apart. The Assistant Protector was going to Mt Rouse with a wife and seven children, as well as more than 200 blacks, and could hardly spare the time to do any farming beyond that involving the reserve. He'd told John he would have to find a squatting partner, and should proceed to Geelong to start looking. John told Robinson that he'd arrived in Geelong "in very bad spirits", knowing no-one, although he'd had one stroke of good fortune, from an unlikely source.

"On my introducing myself to Captain Fyans, I was received with very great kindness, indeed I shall never forget, I may say, the affectionate manner in which he was pleased to express himself towards me," John wrote. Fyans had immediately allowed him to take over the site where his brother and his family had initially lived with the Barrabool blacks, and where Christina had continued to live with their younger children until they'd been reunited for the journey to Mt

Rouse. John had taken out a squatting licence for the site, and he was writing in case Robinson knew of a "quiet industrious person" who might be interested in becoming a partner. "It is certainly a most beautiful place for the purposes of agriculture etc. and a considerable sum might be made yearly by the supply of all kinds of vegetables and milk, to the inhabitants of Geelong, rearing stock etc. etc.," he wrote. In contrast to the description which Robinson had just given as evidence of his brother's neglect of his family, John Sievwright stated the residence at the site was "a very good large hut". As well, there was a stockyard, a paddock, and a good water supply. Finally, John suggested that Robinson might feel inclined to make use of his year of experience with the Aborigines by employing him in some other way.[21]

In July 1842, a week after Robinson sent on this letter to La Trobe, John Sievwright *would* be called upon to use some of the expertise he'd acquired from living with the blacks. The Assistant Protector's brother would be summonsed to Melbourne to be an interpreter at the opening of Supreme Court proceedings against Roger. John Sievwright had written to Robinson expressing disbelief that Roger, or Tagara as he knew him, could have murdered Patrick Codd at Mt Rouse. "I have been acquainted with Tagara for the last 12 months, and I have been more intimate with him than any other native at the Aboriginal establishment," he wrote. "He was very much attached to me, and we were constantly together, and ever found him faithful and trustworthy. He is a great favourite with all the people from Terang to Mt Rouse, and is known to them by the name of 'The Russian'. When I was at Mt Rouse in January last, I was told in Mr Brock's hut the native who killed Mr Codd was a tall man with grey hair. This does not answer the description of Tagara."

Perhaps, John Sievwright suggested, Robinson could refer to the list of Aborigines residing at Keilambete and Terang at the time of the murder. But he was confused about dates: the Keilambete camp had not been established until nine months after the murder. There was no list which might provide an alibi for Roger. Sievwright added that Tagara had a brother called Color with a strong physical resemblance, suggesting that Brock may have seen *him* at the murder scene. Color had only joined the Terang camp the previous November, having before then remained in his own country around Mt Rouse. "In conclusion, if you think any of the above points will be of service to my poor friend Tagara, pray make use of them for his benefit," he pleaded. "I feel very much interested about his fate, and I sincerely trust he will find a friend and Protector in yourself, and the jury, who are bound if they have a doubt, to give it in favour of the unfortunate prisoner."[22]

As standing counsel for the Aborigines, Redmond Barry would state at the opening of Roger's trial that he'd only just become aware of "a material witness" who was some distance from Melbourne, and who he may be able to use to establish an alibi. This matter, however, was put aside while the court considered whether Roger understood the proceedings sufficiently to be able to plead. Through John Sievwright as interpreter, Roger said he was aware of the murder, but had been more than 50 kilometres away at Lake Boloke at the time, catching eels, and helping some white people with wood cutting and other work. He added that he was like a Barrabool black, always fond of the white men, and would never harm any of them. Judge Willis took this as a plea of not guilty.

The judge then directed the court to decide whether Roger was "of sufficient mental capacity" to enable him to stand trial. In an address to the jury, Barry suggested he was not. "The capacity of this prisoner reduces him to the very level of a deaf and dumb man," he argued. "He has never been actuated by other feelings than those dictated by nature, and being restrained by no known law, he might have considered that by killing a man under certain circumstances he was doing that which was right." As well, Barry said, Roger's inability to understand English meant that he would understand neither the nature of the proceedings, nor the details of the evidence. John Sievwright agreed, adding that he was not familiar enough with Roger's language to explain what was happening to him. Sievwright was able to ascertain, however, that Roger knew two of the witnesses for the prosecution, and they were "no good" and had "no right" to appear against him. At this point, one of the witnesses to the trial, English lawyer Robert Deane, shouted out: "That is not the way of trying the man." Ordered by Willis to keep quiet, Deane stormed out of the court-room.

After this interruption, the Wesleyan missionary, Benjamin Hurst, told the court he did not believe Roger understood the nature of a jury. He estimated that he'd need six months to explain to him, for example, his right to challenge jurors. Nor did Hurst think Roger understood the nature of an oath. Asked by Barry whether the Aborigines had any notion of a supreme being, Hurst replied that they had "an idea of an evil spirit" who they believed lived on the moon. The Aborigines also had a practice of punishing criminals by throwing spears at them. But he didn't know whether they had a "civil judicature". Next, George Robinson was examined. The Chief Protector told the court he'd visited Roger in the Melbourne prison, and attempted to explain the nature of the proceedings against him. Not only had he failed, but he knew of no-one who was competent enough in Roger's language to be able to do any better.

In an address to the court, Willis showed that 54 years after the start of white settlement of New South Wales, some colonial officials were still making the same arrogant assumption that there was only one Aboriginal language. The Aboriginal Protectors, the judge stated, should learn *the* language of the blacks as soon as possible, so they would be able to converse with them "freely and familiarly". In the current case, he wanted Roger "to receive all the instruction" it was in the power of the court to give. This was the prisoner's right, as one of "the original possessors of the soil" from which the wealth of the colony had been derived, and as a subject of Queen Victoria. But, Willis declared, he also wanted to state most emphatically that the Aborigines would be held "responsible to the law of England" for any violence against the colonists. It was important that the Aborigines be made to realise that such violence would meet with severe penalties. At the same time, he declared, violence against the blacks by the whites would be similarly punished.

The jury in the current case, Willis directed, must decide whether Roger -- with proper advice and caution -- was able to make a defence. Deliberations would take several sessions. At one stage, the jury would return for guidance, the foreman pointing out concern among the jurymen that if Roger was declared incapable of standing trial, it could affect all cases involving the Aborigines. In the West Indies, Willis replied, he'd tried hundreds of negroes. With a solitary exception, all had been able to understand the proceedings against them "to a reasonable extent". This, he stressed, was all that was required. It was not necessary that Roger should be "intimately acquainted" with court proceedings. After deliberating for another half an hour, the jury would decide that the accused was "of a sufficient mental capacity to enable him to take his trial". John Sievwright had to face the horrible thought that he may have inadvertently contributed to the decision. If he had not offered his services as an interpreter, in a bid to save Roger from trial, the jury may have decided that he was not capable of making a plea, or a defence -- and he may have been discharged. It was a thought that would grow stronger during and beyond the trial.[23]

Three days later, Roger would again appear in court, with John Sievwright and Benjamin Hurst as two of four purported interpreters. James Brock, would swear that Roger had been leading the party of about 18 blacks at John Cox's station the day of the murder. He was positive that Roger was among the ones who'd killed Patrick Codd with a leanguil. Brock testified there was no doubt about identification. Roger was taller than the rest, and he'd seen him on other occasions. The other white man at the station at the time of the murder, Patrick Rooney, also told the court that Roger had been leading the party of blacks, although he had not seen him strike Codd -- and in a conversation with him about the incident, the prisoner had denied having done so.

In Roger's defence, Redmond Barry argued that no direct testimony had been adduced that the prisoner had been the one who inflicted the mortal blow on Codd. In this respect, the indictment against Roger was unsupported. No post mortem examination of Codd's body had been made, and the court had not been given any description of the wound he'd suffered. When considering these facts, members of the jury should also bear in mind that they were not only carrying out the laws of their country. They also had a duty "to do justice to an untutored savage". In an address to the jury, Willis would state that Charles Sievwright should have been in the court, instead of having his brother and Hurst acting on his behalf in Roger's defence. Nevertheless, he was grateful for the assistance of John Sievwright and Hurst. "If there had not been interpreters, the prisoner would have been acquitted of the charge, and perhaps a very dangerous person again let loose amongst society," Willis concluded. After retiring for only about 10 minutes, the jury returned to a court-room in which "the most breathless silence prevailed" to announce its verdict: guilty.

Before sentencing, Roger reiterated that he'd been at Lake Boloke at the time of the murder. With John Sievwright interpreting, he said he'd been helping to wash sheep for the squatter, James Webster. Roger gave the names of six men who could verify his statement. One was a brother called by the whites "Milk and Water". The other five were white men, named Carey, Jack, Sandy, Muggie, and Charley. When some blacks had come to the spot and told him of the murder, he'd asked why they'd done it. But Willis did not believe the statement. Donning his black cap, the judge went through the charade of addressing Roger, in the same way that he'd done seven months earlier when sentencing Bob and Jack. The prisoner, he declared, had been judged by "an intelligent jury" to be of sufficient mental capacity to understand the nature of the trial -- and he'd been given the best professional assistance available.

"You are not an ignorant savage, nor perhaps more unacquainted with the forms of courts of justice than many of the immigrants arriving on these shores," he told Roger. It was a constant defence of white people to say they'd never been in a court of law before. "The period which has elapsed since you murdered Mr Codd (now about two years) shows that sooner or later guilt will meet with punishment -- that enormity like yours will be manifested by that Power to whom nothing in the whole system of a thought or action can be hid, and who in His good time will drag forth the murderer from amidst his hidden deeds of darkness and disaster, to receive that punishment which the very voice of nature calls for to be inflicted on the slayer of the innocent. You would not, had you killed a man of your own description, long have escaped with life. Neither will the laws by which you have been tried for killing a white man, suffer you for any length of time, to remain alive. The sentence of the court is that you be taken hence to the place from which you came, and thence to some place as His Excellency the Governor may appoint, and there be hanged by the neck until you are dead, and may God, of whom unfortunately you are ignorant, have mercy on your soul."[24]

Despite having written a lengthy letter to Robinson asserting Roger's innocence, Charles Sievwright was not summonsed to Melbourne for the trial, and it was over before he learned of it being held. If he'd been able to come to Melbourne to give evidence, he could have pointed out that Codd had boasted of the number of blacks he'd killed, and that his murder had been a revenge killing. The Assistant Protector could have told the court that Roger's tribe supported his claim to have been at Lake Boloke at the time of the murder. He could also have outlined why he believed Brock had "argued himself into his present position" of regarding Roger as one of the blacks who had killed Codd.[25] And Sievwright could have drawn the jury's attention to contradictions in Brock's evidence which might have helped Roger's case. Brock, for instance, had told the court that Roger's older brother was "chief of the Mt Rouse tribe", although Roger was a member of the "Colac tribe" -- an obvious impossibility.[26]

The Assistant Protector could have travelled to Melbourne for the case on his own volition, and requested to be summonsed as a witness for the defence. But he had no idea when the trial was going to be held. And he'd received no reply to his request for permission to go to Melbourne after receiving notification that his employment was in the balance. He and the other Assistant Protectors had been warned long ago that unauthorised visits to the town would result in the suspension of their allowances. They were not supposed to come within 30 kilometres of the town without La Trobe's express permission.[27] Sievwright could hardly afford to further jeopardise what was obviously the very precarious state he was in by making an unauthorised visit. He was on the brink of bankruptcy following the recent Supreme Court judgement against him, and could not afford to lose his job.

More than a month before Roger's trial, Robinson had passed on to La Trobe the letter in which Sievwright had expressed his belief that Roger was innocent.[28] So the blame for not ensuring that Sievwright was summonsed did not lie entirely with the Chief Protector. La Trobe, at least, would feel some compunction that he'd allowed the moves to isolate Sievwright to take precedence over the utmost being done for Roger to present a case in his defence. In a private note after the trial, La Trobe would tell Gipps that "in spite of judge and jury" he had some doubt about Roger's guilt. As well, he remarked, he'd received other information while visiting the Portland Bay district which made him believe that Codd's murder was far from being unprovoked. "If my information was really to be relied on, Mr Codd's conduct towards the natives had been criminal in the highest possible degree, and I fear that by his death the sly murder of many of that race was avenged," La Trobe added.

Although provocation, however just, could not palliate murder among white people, the Superintendent argued, "it may be allowed some weight in considering the case of a rude savage". And the more he saw "of the actual state of things" in the Port Phillip District in regard to the relations of blacks and whites towards each other, the more cautious he felt "in stigmatising the excesses committed by the former as unprovoked".[29] The note was written to accompany a formal letter from La Trobe to Gipps expressing the view that he'd be "gratified" if Roger was granted clemency, despite Willis having stated that he could see no mitigating circumstances.[30] The judge had further said that it would have "a better effect" if the hanging took place at Mt Rouse, where the murder had taken place.[31] La Trobe could see no benefit in this idea, particularly because the Western District reserve had been established there. "I think it exceedingly doubtful whether, from what we know of their temper, it would be productive of the good effect intended upon the natives in that part of the country," he wrote. "It would possibly not only disgust them with the spot which has been chosen for their future location, but might arouse feelings which it is of the greatest importance to avoid exciting."[32]

"The natives partake of a plentiful breakfast..."

The Mt Rouse reserve had just been visited by Charles Griffith and Frederick Powlett, who were investigating the Muston's Creek murders. Griffith would later record that there were 300 to 400 blacks at the camp, and he left with a lasting impression of how the Assistant Protector tried to provide for their "immense" appetites: "In the morning they were put into a pen, and run out, one by one, as sheep are when they are counted, when each received a mess of a kind of burgoo, or porridge, which he carried away in a hollow piece of bark. In the middle of the day they were all drawn up in a row, squatted on their heels, and a wheelbarrow, full of pieces of beef, was wheeled round, the overseer giving a piece to each in turn. It was amusing to observe the anxiety with which they eyed every piece as it was delivered; each of them, as they received their allowance, squeezing it in his hands, to ascertain whether it contained any bone or no; when it had much of this, or little fat, they freely gave vent to their feelings of rage and disappointment. They all appeared sulky, and had completely the appearance of sturdy beggars receiving a dole."[33]

Another observer who visited the Mt Rouse reserve about the same time would be somewhat more positive. He would report that the reserve had the pleasing appearance of "a regular village". There was "a neat collection" of about 60 Aboriginal huts, erected along streets from which the blacks had removed all trees and other obstructions. "The discipline of the community is extremely regular," he remarked. "Exactly at the hour of six o'clock, a bell is rung at the quarters of the Assistant Protector, and its last tones witness the assemblage of every person upon the station. Prayers are then offered up for the protection of a beneficent Providence throughout the remainder of the day, and after these are concluded the natives partake of a plentiful breakfast provided by one of their number. This meal over, they betake themselves, under the direction of white overseers, to the further pursuit of their labours in felling trees, tilling ground, and other methods of beautifying the village."

"When night closes in, Divine praise is again celebrated, and protection implored through the watches of the night," the *Portland Mercury* quoted the observer as saying. "The little community then retire contentedly to rest, to await the coming of another day, in which they may again pursue their round of harmless and commendable occupations."[34] The rival *Guardian* would challenge the accuracy of the report. The only huts that could comprise a "neat collection" at the Mt Rouse reserve, it commented, were five expropriated from John Cox when his run was taken over -- unless a few scattered bark mia-mias, such as were to be found "almost everywhere in the bush", were to be counted.[35] The *Mercury* responded by saying that its informant stood by his report about the huts, and the discipline being applied at the reserve. "He also states, however, that the remainder of his assertions are at best a fanciful picture of what an Aboriginal home station might be, if the unfortunate race for whose benefit it is designed were capable of sufficient improvement, and the men appointed their Protectors possessed the required degree of competence for the difficult task they have undertaken."[36]

CHAPTER 26
Intensified resistance

OR almost half of the 1700s, Britain was ruled by two men born and educated in the Hanover region of Germany -- King George I, who never even learned the English language, and his son George II. During the reign of George II, many thousands of Britons would be sent abroad to fight in various conflicts, often prosecuted more to preserve the King's German interests rather than Britain's. Notable among the conflicts that occurred during this period was what would become known as the Seven Years' War, fought on three continents. In one battle in the war, in 1759 at Minden in Hanover, six British infantry regiments would win everlasting glory. Against overwhelming odds, and with heavy losses, the British foot soldiers would rout the opposing French forces, much of it cavalry.

On their way to the battle, the British troops had passed through rose gardens, and it would become a tradition of all the Minden regiments to mark the anniversary of the battle on August the 1st by wearing roses in their caps, in memory of the 10,000 or so men on both sides who died. The Minden regiments included the 25th Foot, the first regiment that Charles Sievwright would join 56 years later. The Royal Fusiliers, in which Sievwright ended his army career, would also eventually inherit the rose tradition from one of its components -- the 20th Foot, another regiment at Minden. It was a tradition which Sievwright observed throughout his military career, and which he tried to maintain even after he left the army.

In 1842, on the eve of the 83rd anniversary of the Battle of Minden, Sievwright went for a long walk around Mt Rouse searching for a wildflower resembling a rose. In the end, he had to settle for an early spring flower that lacked a resemblance, but which would serve the symbolic purpose. The next day, he would pin the flower to his cap, before climbing to the top of Mt Rouse, to sit on a rock gazing wistfully southwards, where almost 60 kilometres away he could just catch a glimpse of the sea. It was a time of quiet reflection on the past, rather than the uncertain future, but it would not be long before Sievwright was brought back to the harsh reality of the present when a black from the camp below disturbed his solitude with the news that a horseman had arrived with some mail.

It would include the letter which Sievwright had been fearing for some time.

Written by Robinson, it informed the Assistant Protector that Gipps had authorised his suspension because of charges against his moral character. Astounded
not so much by the letter, but by the ground for his suspension, Sievwright
immediately ordered one of his servants to saddle his horse, and he set off for
Melbourne to seek an audience with La Trobe. Two days' travelling later, he'd
reached Mt Shadwell. There, Sievwright was informed by James Brock that La
Trobe had left Melbourne for Portland, and could be planning to visit the Mt
Rouse camp, so he rode back. In a letter to La Trobe explaining his return,
Sievwright emphasised that he was fully prepared to rebut any charges against
either his private or public character. This he "fearlessly and conscientiously"
asserted he would be able to do, and asked the Superintendent to meanwhile
withhold judgement. Sievwright would wait in vain for a week for a reply
before setting off again to Melbourne, this time with Christina.[1]

On his arrival in Melbourne, Sievwright would discover that his suspension had
been public knowledge well before he learned of it himself. The letter informing him of the decision had been written by Robinson a month before he
received it. La Trobe had instructed the Chief Protector that it was "but just" for
his assistant to be told why he was being stood down, and be given an opportunity to defend himself.[2] But Robinson had not had the decency to comply with
this instruction until after the Melbourne press got wind of the story. The *Patriot*
told its readers that Sievwright's imminent suspension was "generally known".
His successor had not yet been named, but it was to be hoped he would "show
himself more desirous of conciliating the settlers, and securing their co-operation" than Sievwright had done.[3] A few days later, and before Robinson's letter
reached Mt Rouse, the *Gazette* would report that Sievwright had been suspended until he could satisfactorily meet an inquiry directed to be held into "certain
practices" which had elicited La Trobe's "disapprobation". The Assistant
Protector having been appointed in London, it pointed out, he could be suspended but not dismissed until the case had been referred to the Secretary of
State for the Colonies.[4]

After Sievwright arrived in Melbourne with his wife, Robinson would provide
a copy of another letter from La Trobe. It was both proper and just, the letter
instructed, that Sievwright should be made aware of the "distinct character" of
the charges against his moral character which had caused Gipps to suspend him.
Sievwright, the Superintendent wrote, was "fully acquainted" with his personal
opinion on the subject, expressed "without disguise" during their meeting in
Melbourne more than two years earlier. He'd made it clear to Sievwright that
whether they were true or false, the graver charges against him, and the manner
in which they'd been advanced, "were such as to render it impossible for him to
retain his appointment with any expectation of really benefiting the cause that

he was deputed to serve".

"From this I never wavered, and have had since ample reason to know that it was correct," La Trobe stated, without offering an explanation why it had taken so long for him to act. He added that he had confidence in the sources through which the existence of the more serious claims against Sievwright had become known to him. He'd informed Gipps that even if they were false, the claims had been "from the outset fatal to him and his recent career". If there was any basis to half of what Sievwright's own family had stated about his behaviour in Europe, both while in the army and after he left it, his appointment "could only have been sanctioned in complete misconception of his real character". In conclusion, La Trobe promised to forward for Gipps' consideration "any explanation or other remarks" which Sievwright may consider in his interests to put forward.[5]

Although he still did not know the details of what had been said about him, for the first time Sievwright was aware of the extent of the damage Christina had done to his reputation when she'd run away from Geelong three years earlier. Obviously realising that her future was also at stake, she agreed to seek an immediate personal meeting with La Trobe to try to repair the damage. The request being rejected, Christina would write the Superintendent a note. "I have only taken the liberty to see your Honour, to request that I may not be brought forward as one or any of the causes of Mr Sievwright's present disagreeable position," she wrote. "That which occurred three years ago was dictated by a woman's feeling. I am afraid that judgement had little to do with it. I have been told that letters of mine addressed to Mr Lonsdale are to be produced. Surely this is impossible. I shall only add that Mr Sievwright's character in the army was unimpeached, and his duty as Protector I think has been faithfully performed. By so doing, he has foregone the goodwill of many of the gentlemen of the district of Portland."[6]

The same day, Sievwright would also write to La Trobe, sending him copies of correspondence that had taken place back in 1836 and 1837 when his friends in London were trying to find him a job after he'd been forced to sell his commission in the army to pay off his debts. The letters, he remarked, were among many he'd received from the same individuals, whose friendship he'd had the "distinction" to enjoy for the previous 15 years. Sievwright mentioned three of the letter-writers in particular -- Major-General Sir Frederick Ponsonby, the former Governor of Malta, the Viscount Falkland, the present Governor of Nova Scotia, and General Lord Frederick Fitzclarence, his former commanding officer, and son of King William IV. All three must be known to La Trobe, he believed, perhaps personally.

The letters showed an obvious affection for Sievwright by Ponsonby, Falkland

and Fitzclarence -- and extensive efforts by them to help him find a job. Ponsonby's elder brother, Lord Duncannon -- a former Home Secretary - had also joined the campaign. Those approached by Sievwright's supporters included the Home Secretary, Lord John Russell, the Foreign Secretary, Lord Palmerston, and the Irish Secretary, Viscount Morpeth. Palmerston's response was that with such patrons, he certainly felt goodwill towards Sievwright -- but lacked the opportunities to do anything for him. Other senior officials approached complained of the same problem. The Master-General of the Ordnance, Sir Richard Hussey Vivian, with responsibility for military supplies, had to decline a suggestion that Sievwright be given a civilian job at some barracks, saying he was "overwhelmed" with applications for employment. So, too, was the Lord-Lieutenant of Ireland, the Earl of Mulgrave. In the end, it had been Duncannon who had made the successful move. At Sievwright's request, he would approach the Colonial Secretary, Lord Glenelg, just at the time that the Assistant Aboriginal Protectors were being chosen for New South Wales.

The correspondence showed that Sievwright's friends, especially Falkland, had been prepared to sustain the campaign to find him a new position for as long as necessary. Even at a time when he'd been "knee deep" in House of Lords business, Falkland had vigorously pursued every avenue he could. Suspended from the job that had eventually been found for him, Sievwright could only turn to the words his friends had used in a bid to convince La Trobe that he'd been held in high regard by people of influence in London. "I would respectfully beg to state that I have been induced to lay these credentials of former associates and friends before your Honour in justice to myself, in order that my career and character previous to my arrival in this colony might not be withheld from your knowledge, as it will now become my duty to bring every act of my public and domestic life, since my arrival here, for examination before any tribunal which your Honour may choose to appoint."[7]

Although he'd later claim not to have read them, the letters would prompt La Trobe to agree to a brief meeting, which Sievwright would leave with the understanding that he'd not been dismissed -- only suspended. The suspension would be lifted, he believed, if he managed to refute the charges against him -- and the case for his dismissal had certainly been much weakened by Christina having virtually recanted on her 1839 remarks. But then Sievwright received a notice from Robinson informing him that he was considered to have vacated his office by having made an unauthorised visit to Melbourne! The new medical officer at Mt Rouse, John Watton, whose appointment happened to become effective that day, would now replace him. The Chief Protector directed Sievwright to return to the Western District reserve and hand over whatever government property he had in his charge. In another letter to La Trobe outlining this development, Sievwright requested to be given a written copy of the charges outstanding against him. If they were not yet ready, he was prepared to return to Mt Rouse -- although, he pointed out, this would deny him the "most desirable" opportunity of seeking legal advice on his situation from a Melbourne lawyer.[8]

Four days later, Robinson would send Sievwright a letter from La Trobe which would include details of the charges against his moral character. The Superintendent would include a reference to the most serious claim which Lonsdale alleged Christina had made about him -- having contemplated the seduction of his own daughter. "In reply to the fearful and unnatural crimes that have been imputed to me, I have but one remark to offer, which is that, with the assistance of God, on whose support I rely in this trial with which He has though fit that I should be visited, I shall be able to rebut and disprove those foul calumnies that have been attached to my name, and of which I now for the first time have learned the extent, with that horror which such accusations must inspire," Sievwright wrote back to Robinson.

Working through the document from La Trobe, Sievwright recalled how, more than two years earlier, he'd offered to appear before a tribunal to answer the rumours then in circulation, and which were making the Superintendent want to shun him. "His Honour replied, that he did not see how he could then interfere in the matter and it was the duty of the Chief Protector to have done so, at the time the accusations against me were first made," Sievwright wrote. La Trobe had advised that he resign because if there was an investigation it would drag the names of his wife and daughter "before the four quarters of the world". The resignation suggestion he'd found "most extraordinary", and he'd repeated his request for an inquiry, again requesting that he not be prejudged. Nevertheless, he'd been willing to resign if he had to, rather than bringing Fanny's name more before the public than it appeared it had been already. But that had been the end of the matter until he'd received the letter at Mt Rouse at the start of the current month, informing him of his suspension -- more than14 months later.

One charge against Sievwright listed by La Trobe was "gross immorality in carrying on an improper if not criminal intercourse with the wife of one of his colleagues". Although no names were given, this was a charge provided by Robinson, based on information he'd been given by Dredge. In reply, Sievwright stated that the first time he'd spent any time with the wives and families of his fellow Assistant Protectors was when they all left Sydney together to travel to Melbourne. "For the short time we were together during the passage from Sydney to this place, we were under the accumulated miseries of an extremely crowded vessel, and very tempestuous weather," he wrote. "Tis true that on the third or fourth day of the voyage, I was jocularly asked by one of my colleagues if my lady was generally of a jealous disposition, as he had just been informed by her that she thought that his wife and her husband were too intimate -- to which he had replied that whatever she might attribute to her husband, that he knew his wife sufficiently to have no uneasiness on the subject."

Still without giving names, Sievwright added that after their arrival in Melbourne, Parker and his wife, Mary, had set up their tents close by in the encampment used by the Assistant Protectors before they'd headed off for their respective districts. Parker being "more companionable in every respect, as an associate and friend" than either Dredge or Thomas, they'd spent much time together -- both during the day, and in each other's tents in the evenings. This, he'd since learned, had "much offended" the pious Dredges, who he did not at any time feel inclined to visit. It was the Dredges who he believed had invented "the foul charge" about himself and Mary Parker, and then induced Christina to believe it. "The character of the lady referred to, and her husband, are, I imagine, sufficiently known to render such a report highly absurd, did not the sudden and highly improbable nature of the charge render the whole truly ridiculous," Sievwright remarked.

Next, Sievwright tried to deal with the claims of his "unfeeling and harsh conduct", originally made by Christina. This charge, he declared, was also false. "On sitting down in our tents in the bush, three miles from Geelong, more than usual privations were at first to be endured," Sievwright wrote. But the family had shared the inconvenience. He'd never partaken of comforts or indulgences which were denied to his family. Still unaware just how scathing Christina had been in her 1839 letters, Sievwright said she and their children would deny the claims that they'd been neglected. His family could also prove the falseness of the charge of his illtreatment of them while still in Europe, where he was alleged to have led a "dissolute" life.

Not realising that William Lonsdale and William Meek had both just provided negative reports about him, Sievwright challenged Robinson to seek written statements from them on the way he'd treated his family -- as well as from Meek's fellow solicitor, Horatio Carrington. It was Lonsdale's letter which provided the basis of what Sievwright would describe as "the most revolting and fearful" charge against him: having allegedly contemplated incest with Fanny. This charge too, he declared, was utterly false. He told Robinson that back in 1839, Meek and Carrington had made him aware of a rumour concerning himself and Fanny -- and that the rumour could be sourced to Christina. He'd immediately dealt with the matter, both Fanny and her mother making statements in which they'd given an "indignant disavowal" of any knowledge of it. Meek and Carrington had accepted their denials, and he'd believed the issue had been "set at rest".

La Trobe's letter next listed claims that there was evidence of continuing disunity in Sievwright's family, and that it had suffered "indecent neglect" near Geelong until relatively recently. These claims he also declared were false, and in his defence he offered to produce the bills of various traders for supplies furnished for the family's use. It was true that on one occasion, he'd been absent from most of his family for 10 months. On another occasion his absence had lasted five months, and on another three months. But it had been a necessary part of the job to itinerate across his district, and to try to win the confidence of the blacks by living among them in a tent, before the Mt Rouse reserve was established. "If I am charged with neglecting my family while thus engaged, upon those arduous duties upon which I was ordered, I can only answer that my family inform me, that upon no occasion did they ever make a complaint to anyone on that subject, which position they as well as I know was unavoidable, as I at all times considered my public duties paramount to my own comfort, and the wishes of my family that I could reside occasionally with them when doing so, must have been to the detriment of my vocation," Sievwright wrote.

"I would remark that a general reference to every settler in my district who may have known me for three years past can be obtained, as to their knowledge of my character, conduct, conversation, and general demeanour," the Assistant Protector bravely added. As well, Sievwright suggested that an opinion on his character could be sought from the commander-in-chief of the armed forces in New South Wales, Sir Maurice O'Connell. A member of both the Executive and Legislative Councils in Sydney, O'Connell had served with Sievwright in the Mediterranean. Sievwright would also enclose for Robinson's information copies of the correspondence he'd received from Ponsonby, Falkland, Fitzclarence and the other nobles while looking for a job. Someone who had the friendship of such men, he argued, was "not likely to be the miscreant depicted in the charges now brought against him".

Such was what Sievwright described as "a short outline" of his response to the charges outlined in La Trobe's letter. He requested that this be given to La Trobe, along with a "most urgent request" for a commission of inquiry. "You are aware that in similar cases to mine, this is the course usually adopted, and I firmly trust that the government will authorise this course, as being that alone, by which the truth or falsity of the charges brought against me can be fully and clearly ascertained," he argued. "The severest scrutiny into my past and present conduct, my moral and domestic character, and the discharge of my official duties, I am ready, willing and most anxious to submit to -- and every facility will be given by myself and my family towards arriving at the truth of these subjects." In justice to himself, his family, and the government itself, his request for a commission must be granted.[9]

While Sievwright awaited the result of his request, the Chief Protector would decide to blacken his suspended assistant's name a little more. In an unsolicited letter to La Trobe, Robinson would add another allegation against him -- assaulting Christina. This claim, he alleged, had been made when she'd called at his temporary office soon after his arrival in Melbourne in 1839, to complain of Sievwright's "ill usage" for a number of years. "She said his conduct had been but nothing in comparison to what it had been since his arrival in the colony," Robinson told La Trobe. "He withheld from her and her children the common necessaries, made use of approbrious epithets, and what was worse, struck her with his fist. In consequence, she begged to be prevented going into the bush with her husband." This, he claimed, had been before she'd put her complaints

"Some of the Aborigines...had begun the most intense and sustained resistance..."

about Sievwright in writing, in the note now in La Trobe's hands.[10]

With the case against Sievwright still gathering strength in Melbourne, he and Christina would return to Mt Rouse to rejoin their children. They would discover that in their absence, some of the Aborigines for whom he was responsible had begun the most intense and sustained resistance that would ever be launched against the whites in the Western District. Notably, the renewed attacks were mainly occurring in the territory of the Bunganditj and the Gunditjmara people -- the two tribes over which Sievwright's influence had so far been limited. In Gunditjmara territory, some of the upsurge in attacks on white men and their property could be attributed to the return of two of the other blacks sent to Melbourne at the same time as Roger to stand trial -- Jupiter and Cocknose -- who'd been released along with Bumbletoe. Prosecutor Croke had ordered them to be released because of inconsistencies in statements made against them.

For example, James Hunter's housekeeper, Jemima Purnell, had made one statement in which she'd said her husband, John, had given some Aborigines who visited the station "a little flour". This statement had been made before Acheson French, soon after the incident. Six months later, in a second statement before Foster Fyans and another magistrate, the amount of food involved had increased to "half a sack" of flour, and some beef and damper. A former employee of Hunter called McCurdy had meanwhile told Fyans that John Purnell had given the blacks a full sack of flour. McCurdy had also alleged that Jupiter had thrown two spears at him. In one of two statements before Fyans, he'd given this as his reason for abandoning Hunter's station. But he'd apparently neither voluntarily stated nor been asked whether he'd been close enough for the spears to hit him. If he'd not been within range when the spears were thrown, Croke noted, not even a charge of "constructive" or intended assault could be sustained.

As well as the contradictory statements and other irregularities, Croke told La Trobe, the charges of assault and robbery brought against Jupiter and Cocknose had been couched in such vague terms as "threats and motions of resistance", "endeavoured" and "supposes". And Jemima Purnell had not stated that her husband had been forced to give the blacks the food, which would have made it a case of robbery. There were no words used "significant of a positive charge" in any of the depositions. Indeed, the best the Crown Prosecutor could hope to do with the depositions was to make out a case of intended assault against Jupiter, rather than actual assault. This, he'd decided, was not of sufficient weight to justify the expense of a trial, which would have included the costs of bringing witnesses to Melbourne from more than 300 kilometres away. Thus, though their apprehension had cost the lives of two of their tribesmen, they would be released without trial almost three months later.[11]

Acheson French was horrified to learn in particular of Jupiter's release. Less than a month later, he reported to La Trobe that almost every day there was fresh news of an Aboriginal attack. In the previous two weeks, sheep had been taken from at least six separate stations -- and on each occasion, attempts had been made to kill the shepherds. Even the life of a shepherd employed by the Police Magistrate had been threatened. French would enclose a statement from Samuel MacGregor, superintendent on the station of James Hunter, to give La Trobe an idea of what was happening. "I am sorry at the same time to say that I think the natives will be more emboldened in their depredations on account of the escape of the native Jupiter with impunity from his confinement," French lamented.[12]

James Hunter's station was one of the hardest hit in the renewed Gunditjmara attacks after the release of Cocknose and Jupiter. In early and mid-August 1842, raids were staged on three separate days. In the first raid, Cocknose and Jupiter led a party of about 12 black men which drove off a large flock after causing the two shepherds in charge of it to flee by throwing spears at them. When the shepherds rushed back to the home station and reported what had happened to overseer MacGregor, several of the whites armed themselves with guns and set off in pursuit. They caught up with the blacks with the sheep about eight kilometres away. The Gunditjmara men tried to fight off the whites with spears, but after a "severe skirmish" eventually gave up and fled. MacGregor would later claim that on this occasion, none of the blacks had even been wounded by the whites' gunfire.

Three days later, Jupiter and Cocknose were among a much larger group of Gunditjmara men -- estimated to number between 150 and 300 -- which struck again, trying to drive off a flock of sheep. "They carried green boughs before them for the purpose of concealing themselves, and were close upon us before we were aware," shepherd Robert Cochrane would depose. When spears and boomerangs were thrown, and death threats made, Cochrane and a fellow shepherd started to retreat, firing as they did so. Hearing the gunshots, Samuel MacGregor rode over and found the blacks had split into two groups -- one to drive off the sheep, and one to pursue the shepherds, whose ammunition was expended just as he joined them. Cochrane and MacGregor would claim that on this occasion, the blacks had fled when he shouted, as if for assistance. Again, to his knowledge there had been no black hit by gunfire, and again there had been no loss of sheep.

The Gunditjmara warriors would wait another eight days before making a third attempt to capture Hunter's sheep. According to shepherd William Brice, about 300 blacks suddenly arrived early in the afternoon and drove off more than 1000 sheep, as they threw spears and waddies at him and another shepherd. "Seeing it useless to contend with such a number, we retreated towards the station," Brice later told Sievwright. The Gunditjmara men followed them for several hundred metres, and the shepherds "occasionally fired upon them when they came close". MacGregor's uncle, Samuel Gorrie, who acted as overseer, and who would earn a reputation of being "stalwart and iron-nerved" in the face of Aboriginal attack, set off in search of the sheep. He was assisted only by "a Sydney native boy" who lived at the station. There was no difficulty in tracing the route taken by the thieves. Besides the tracks of the hooves, the way was littered with sheep -- some dead, others with their legs broken. The Scotsman and the boy caught up with the Gunditjmara men at sundown at a camp in the rocks more than 10 kilometres away, where he saw a feast of roast mutton being prepared.

Gorrie returned to Hunter's station for reinforcements before attempting to recover the sheep. He would be joined on the moonlit mission back to the Gunditjmara camp by MacGregor, who'd since returned from a trip to Port Fairy, three shepherds and the black boy. When MacGregor shouted at the blacks, a spear was thrown at him. The whites opened fire, and the blacks retreated. In the semi-dark, the whites managed to round up about 100 sheep which were still alive and drive them out of the rocks, to watch them until morning. No-one slept. "During the night, the natives continued yelling at a very little distance," Gorrie later recalled. At daybreak, a larger number of sheep were recovered. The dead bodies of two black men and a boy, shot the night before, were also found, but left where they fell. Some Gunditjmara people appeared as the whites started driving the sheep back to the station, but they did not come very close, and no further spears were thrown or shots fired.

Just how many black lives were lost as a result of the theft would never be known to the white authorities. In a letter to Acheson French soon after the incident, MacGregor stated the shepherds had fired "about 40 rounds" while retreating from the scene of the robbery. He admitted that more shots were fired later in the rocks, although he'd lie about the three bodies which had been found. "We had recourse to use a quantity of powder and lead in the retaking of the sheep, though I cannot say that any took effect," MacGregor wrote. A month later, MacGregor, Gorrie and one of the shepherds would all admit that at least three blacks had been killed. And the death toll may have been higher.

Informing La Trobe that he'd issued warrants for the re-arrest of Jupiter and Cocknose for the raids on Hunter's, French reported: "I regret to state that the people at the station were obliged to fire on and to kill some of the natives, not only for the recovery of the sheep, but in defence of their lives, as in more instances than one, I believe the blacks closed with their antagonists and fought hand to hand, so determined were they to keep possession of their booty." Later, a fellow squatter would describe Gorrie as the "envied possessor of a rifle of great length of barrel and the deadliest performance" which he used to exact revenge on the blacks. On just one occasion, the squatter recorded, Gorrie had shot dead two men as they fled.

The August 1842 raids had a devastating effect on Hunter's squatting operation. The third raid resulted in an immediate loss of more than half of the 1000 sheep driven off, most of them "maiden ewes". About another 40 would die over the next few weeks from injuries they received while being driven to the Gunditjmara hideout in the rocks. The raids also caused a staffing crisis at the station. Hunter told La Trobe he'd had 25 men and women employed there, besides MacGregor and Gorrie. "But I am sorry to say the number is considerably reduced now, in consequence of the men running away and forfeiting their wages, rather than exposing their lives to the attacks of the blacks," he wrote. There was a need, Hunter told La Trobe, for "some immediate steps for the protection of the settlers" from the continued black attacks. "Otherwise, they must lead to our irretrievable ruin," he warned.[13]

James Hunter was by no means the only squatter complaining of the behaviour of the Western District Aborigines. Even before Hunter sent his letter to La Trobe, the first edition of *The Portland Mercury* had published a detailed list of recent attacks on almost 20 sheep and cattle stations -- a few by the Gunditjmara blacks, but most of them by the Bunganditj men. The *Mercury* claimed that in the previous four months, 3500 sheep had been killed by the blacks, 500 of them Hunter's. At the same time, four white men had been murdered, and another two seriously wounded. One squatter with large flocks in the area was quoted as saying that "the country might as well be in a state of civil war, as few but the boldest of the settlers will move from their home stations".

"Many of the principal sufferers from the depredations of the blacks are now running from two to three thousand sheep in a flock, and these are tended by as large a number of shepherds as they can afford to hire," the *Mercury* commented. "As it is impossible that such large flocks can be properly fed, the consequences will soon evince themselves in the ill-condition of the animals, the prevalence amongst them of scab, and the consequent deterioration, both in quality and quantity, of their wools." The need was urgent, the paper argued, for the New South Wales government to provide protection for the settlers. If this was not forthcoming, it feared that a cry of vengeance would shortly ring throughout the length and breadth of the land, the "disastrous sating" of which would long be remembered "with horror and awe".

One of the four murders mentioned by the *Mercury* was that of a shepherd named Freeman, who'd worked for Thomas Ricketts, a squatter on the Glenelg River, about 130 kilometres north of Portland. Ricketts, the report claimed, had shown the local Bunganditj people "innumerable acts of considerate kindness". However, the blacks had recently driven off a flock of sheep, taking Freeman as well. A party of white men which set off in search of Freeman had found his boots, with the strings broken as if they'd been forcibly taken from his feet. Next to the boots lay the unfortunate shepherd's faithful dog, covered with wounds, "which had evidently been received in a spirited defence of his master", the *Mercury* reported.

"On the following day, they came upon the camp of the natives, who saluted them with a shower of spears, and then took to flight, all escaping save one woman who was not sufficiently swift to elude the pursuit," the article continued. "The only trace of Freeman at the camp was his gun, which the party found with the breech taken out, but the woman they had taken prisoner informed them that the tribe had killed Freeman, chopped him into pieces, which they had eaten as they proceeded with their march with the sheep." Ricketts' station had since been again attacked, the *Mercury* added, and one of his shepherds speared, although he'd managed to recover most of the sheep driven off on both occasions.[14]

At about the same time as Freeman's murder was reported, a group of Bunganditj men also struck at the adjoining station, operated on behalf of the Welsh Member of the British House of Commons, Sir John Owen. A shepherd, John Hickey, was reported missing, along with the 1300 sheep over which he'd been left in charge. The English station superintendent, Francis Desailly, later deposed that he'd set off with a party of whites, following the tracks of the sheep for more than 70 kilometres, into the Grampians. On the way, they picked up various pieces of clothing which had been worn by Hickey. Deep in the Grampians, they came across a Bunganditj camp, where most of the sheep had been driven. The blacks had shown "a disposition to fight", the head of the pursuing party almost being hit by a tomahawk thrown at him, Desailly stated. The whites had been forced to open fire, and although he did not see any of them fall dead, he supposed that one or two of the 30 or so men among the blacks must have been hit as they fled.

In the camp, more pieces of Hickey's clothing were found, along with his still loaded gun, and several tomahawks, axes, gimlets, a butcher's knife, quart pots and pannicans, and some human bones in a bag. The sheep were in such a "wretched state" it would take five days to drive them back to the station. When he got there, Desailly would learn that it had again been attacked. This time, a party of Bunganditj blacks had driven off the bullocks, and his brother George had taken some men and gone off in pursuit. As he anxiously awaited their return, Desailly went looking for his missing shepherd. Hickey's decomposing body he found in an open plain nearby, covered with spear wounds, and with a large gash in the back of his head. The squatter believed it had been caused by a tomahawk, although Police Magistrate Blair would speculate that it may have been caused by a boomerang. After Hickey's burial, the second search party would return with the bullocks, which Blair reported had been driven by the attackers more than 160 kilometres, in the opposite direction to the sheep.[15]

Yet to hear of Hickey's murder, La Trobe had already expressed fear that the state of the Western District was "beyond all remedy under present circumstances". There were no funds available to hire any more Mounted Police to help Police Magistrates French and Blair at The Grange and Portland to restore order.[16] However, French had suggested that the Mounted Police under his command could be augmented by some members of a newly-established Native

Police force. Comprising young men of tribes in the east of the Port Phillip District, under the command of an English-born former army captain, Henry Edward Pulteney Dana, the Native Police had been formed for training as Mounted Police auxiliaries. French believed they could be of "great benefit" in both tracking stock stolen by the blacks, and in "hunting out the perpetrators from their own dens".[17]

Desperate enough to take up French's suggestion as an experiment, La Trobe was nevertheless apprehensive about what effect the deployment of Native Police may have on the volatile situation in the Western District. The Superintendent told Dana that on an initial mission, which would require "great caution", he should take 10 of the "most trustworthy" of the members of the new force to The Grange. In particular, La Trobe was interested in finding out how the "tolerably close discipline" to which the Native Police had "cheerfully sub-mitted" in the past few months at a camp near Melbourne would be preserved "in a perfectly new position at a distance from their own district, and in a coun-try occupied by native tribes to which they are strangers".

At first, La Trobe instructed, Dana should not take the Native Police to Mt Rouse, and he should avoid them making contact with white employees at the squatters' stations. When they got to The Grange, French would be responsible "for their proper and legitimate employment", and strict conditions would apply for their use to recover stolen property or as trackers. Such duties could only be performed by the Native Police either with French as a member of the party, or under such specific and written directions to Dana "as may ensure that what may be done is under the direction of a magistrate, and according to law". As well, La Trobe was prepared to accede to Dana's request to take with him 100 rounds of ammunition, but it must remain in his personal charge, and he must give a regular account of how it was used.[18]

Dana's black police -- one sergeant and 24 constables -- were each given a uni-form comprising a green jacket, with possum skin facings, black or green trousers, with a red stripe on each leg, and a green cap, with a red stripe around it. They were also each issued with a short carbine with bayonet, although they were not supposed to load the weapon without permission. "The relation between the Australian Aborigines and a civilised people, as regards their untu-tored simplicity, is as children to adults; and the relation of a body of these men, when organised as a police force, and those who are to command, should be as the private soldier to the officer," Dana told La Trobe. "Taking into considera-tion, then, that these people are as children, they should be treated with lenity and proper indulgence."

At the same time, Dana believed there was a need for the occasional use of "a wholesome rigour of punishment" against the black police to deal with "certain refractory principles or features in their character which would be opposed to discipline and command". For minor offences, he suggested solitary confinement, with restricted meals of "inferior quality" food. However, corporal punishment would be needed "in cases of flagrant neglect, disobedience, and insolence". Anything approaching violence towards himself, or the white superintendent or sergeant, should be punished with both the lash and imprisonment. "By such means, discipline, order, implicit obedience and respect to officers would at all times be enforced," Dana wrote. "Such opinions may not agree with your Honour's, but with lenity and a little severity they may have a good effect in the end."[19]

Nine of the black constables -- only four of them mounted because of a lack of horses -- would accompany Dana on the 1842 mission to try to reduce guerilla activity around The Grange. All were single men, aged between 18 and 30.[20] From the whites' point of view, their lack of alliances with the Western District tribes would prove a major benefit. In fact, the new recruits would soon demonstrate that being fellow Aborigines did not act as a constraint when the Native Police were called upon to engage in a series of largely secretive operations against the Western District blacks. Rather, they would show themselves to be eager participants. Their effectiveness would be beyond Acheson French's highest hopes, playing a major role in what would be the start of the end of Aboriginal resistance in the District.

CHAPTER 27
A declaration of war

B Y 1842, the range of public entertainment available in Melbourne had developed well beyond bar room singing and brawls. There were, for instance, occasional horse race meetings and cricket matches. Other events held that year included the first two shows of the Pastoral and Agricultural Society of Australia Felix. A rickety structure called the Theatre Royal also opened in 1842, putting on regular performances for those who could afford the admission fee. But the colonial government would be responsible for the form of entertainment which would prove to be by far the most popular of the year, drawing the biggest crowds -- the town's first hangings. Thousands of Melbourne's white residents would turn out in January for the public execution of the convicted black murderers from Van Diemen's Land, Bob and Jack. Then in June, thousands more would treat as "a great gala celebration" the hanging of three fellow whites convicted of bushranging.[1]

The ghouls who had so enjoyed the first five hangings were thrilled to learn late in August that there was to be another one. La Trobe would receive notification that Gipps would not be exercising his prerogative of mercy to save the Western District Aborigine, Roger, from going to the gallows for Patrick Codd's murder. At a meeting of the Executive Council in Sydney, Gipps had tabled both Judge Willis' opinion that there were no mitigating circumstances, and La Trobe's letter asking for clemency to be considered. The Governor had even tabled La Trobe's private note to him, in which he'd frankly stated he doubted Roger's guilt, and suggested that Codd's conduct towards the blacks had been "criminal in the highest possible degree". But the Chief Justice, James Dowling, told the meeting he was convinced from Willis' notes that the evidence against Roger had been sufficient to support a conviction, and that the sentence was "according to law". It had been enough to convince the Council that Roger should be hanged, though it was left up to La Trobe to decide whether to take up Willis' suggestion that the execution take place at Mt Rouse.[2]

When La Trobe informed Willis that clemency had been denied, the judge decided that he would personally inform the condemned man of it. Roger, the *Port Phillip Herald* reported, did not show "the slightest symptoms of alarm or consciousness" at Willis' news. He'd shared the same cell with about 26 other prisoners since his conviction, and they'd seen him occasionally shedding tears, although they'd not been able to ascertain why. "He still denies that he committed the murder, and says that it was done by other wild black fellows," the *Herald* reported. At the same time, he seemed to be regarding his approaching fate with apparent indifference. All attempts "to impress him with a sense of religion or the immortality of his soul" had hitherto proved quite ineffectual, his only remark being that he would "rise up a white man". The *Herald* suggested that in the 10 days Roger had to live, he should be separated from the other prisoners, and an effort made "to bring him to a sense of his perilous position".[3]

The day the *Herald* made this suggestion, Roger would be visited in prison by George Robinson. He would give the Chief Protector the names of two other blacks whom he claimed were the murderers of Patrick Codd. As well, he alleged, the main witness for the prosecution in his trial, James Brock, had killed two Aboriginal men and one woman.[4] But it was too late for Robinson to do anything with this information, even if he'd felt inclined to try. There was no avenue left for an appeal against Roger's scheduled execution. Early in the morning on the appointed day, Robinson was back at the prison, hearing Roger again assert his innocence. He would reiterate, too, that the man he'd allegedly murdered had taken liberties with Aboriginal women, and had killed several blacks. The Chief Protector watched as Roger ate a little of his breakfast of mutton chops, bread and tea, before calmly allowing his fetters to be removed on a chopping block, and be replaced with handcuffs. A white calico cap was with difficulty stretched over his head, before a horse-drawn cart pulled up to take him to the gallows, with an escort of Mounted Police and soldiers.

After the handcuffs were removed, and Roger's arms were pinioned instead, he was directed to climb up a ladder to the scaffold. Before he reached the top of the ladder, however, the ceremony was suddenly stopped, and Roger ended up sitting on a step, "looking about him like a wild beast at bay". The crowd of at least 1000 whites, most of them men, grew restless, as rumours spread that the promised spectacle would not be provided -- that the government had merely wanted to give Roger a scare, and would now hand him over to the Protectorate. But then the reason for the delay became apparent, with the hurried arrival on the scene of an embarrassed Sheriff, without whose presence the Aborigine could not legally be "launched into eternity".[5]

For the benefit of readers unable to be eye-witnesses, the *Patriot* would provide a vivid account of the final moments of Roger's life. "The arrangements having been completed, the wretched man ascended the fatal platform. The rope was adjusted, and the bolt having been withdrawn, he appeared for about a second to have lost all power of motion, when suddenly his body exhibited the most dreadful convulsions. His whole muscular system was in agitation, and his efforts to free himself from the cords lasted upwards of four minutes. When his struggles had ceased, his legs were drawn up to his neck, showing the violent nature of the dreadful struggle for life in which he had been engaged. The body was then cut down and buried." Thus ended one more life which, given the opportunity, Sievwright could have saved.[6]

Having been opposed to the hanging in the first place, La Trobe's big regret once it was over was that it had taken place on a Monday morning. Because of a law forbidding labour on the Christian sabbath, the scaffold had had to be erected on the previous Saturday. This had meant that the structure on which Roger would die had remained "during the whole of Sunday under the charge of the police, as an object of curiosity to the lower part of the populace of the town". This, the Superintendent believed, was undesirable. If the "melancholy necessity" of a further hanging in Melbourne again arose, he requested that the Executive Council set the execution date towards the end of the week. The scaffold could then be erected just the day before the hanging.[7]

There would never be any way of telling whether, as Willis had suggested, Roger's hanging would have had a deterrent effect on Aboriginal attacks in the Western District if it had taken place at Mt Rouse. But having the execution in Melbourne certainly had no such effect. Within days of the execution, Portland's second newspaper, the *Guardian* would be joining the *Mercury* in making an urgent call for protection for the white squatters and their men. "The aggressions upon the settlers by the Aborigines are now coming upon them so thick and fast, and attended with waste of property to an immense amount, and loss of life to a fearful degree, that to be supine when such tragical events are going forward among our fellow countrymen, would betray an indifferency that wants a name, and so highly culpable as to deserve the highest censure that could be inflicted," the *Guardian* thundered. "And the man that would not sympathise with them, and do all in his power to remedy the grievous evils that they are now continually subject to, would be undeserving the name of man, and ought to forfeit all claim to the privileges of civilised life."

The *Guardian* scoffed at the view expressed by Sievwright and others that many acts of Aboriginal robbery and murder could be traced to white men having interfered with black women. At the same time, it ridiculed the idea that the blacks may have customs governing sexual relations among themselves. "The delicate sensibilities imbibed in civilised life, in reference to conjugal fidelity, surrounded and supported by the awful mandates of Heaven, and the careful guard of human laws, can find no place in the breasts of savage tribes, with whom intercourse between the sexes is all but absolutely promiscuous -- who have no power higher than their own passions to consult, and no law to bind them but the want of cunning to elude, or the deficiency of physical strength to overcome," it declared. "And as the one sex is in a state of complete subjection to the other, and the female used for no other purpose than to minister to the wants and gratification of the male, when opportunities serve, that allows of the latter being better served according to the impulses of his appetite, by the prostitution of the former, than by her continence. Her wretched person is offered as the price of the procurement of such service, to afford him, it may be, a morsel of bread or a grain of sugar."

It could not be denied, the *Guardian* acknowledged, that there may have been acts of cruelty committed by the whites of the Portland district against the blacks. But it had never heard or seen any detailed statement of such acts. "On the contrary, we are far more inclined to believe that the settlers in this district, as a whole, have unintentionally erred by an excess of kindness, believing that the natives were to be reconciled, and the continuance of their favour purchased by an occasional present, an article of dress, or a supply of food," the article fantasized. "They for a while acted upon these conciliatory measures, but when the accustomed supplies were withheld, or found inconvenient to bestow, and came not with that frequency which Aboriginal wants required, the favour and conciliation of the natives at the same time ceased. First pilfering, then open robbery followed -- and, if resistance by either the settler or his servants was offered, either instant murder or meditated revenge, was the consequence to be looked for."

"The present state of the Aboriginal population, in the vicinity of the Glenelg and some other parts of the district, is that of open and undisguised hostility against the settler," the *Guardian* continued. "They now, we believe, rarely appear at the stations but in great numbers, for predatory purposes; and their approach if at all perceived is to the settler an infallible signal of attack. Or the lonely shepherd, at a distance from the homestead, in an unwary moment is surrounded, and if the nature of the situation favours a simultaneous mode of attack, a hundred spears are pointed at him, when his death is inevitable if he attempts to use the arms he bears, and he either falls at once a prey to savage ferocity, or driven away with the sheep he tended, to be dealt with as circumstances or a sudden and ungovernable impulse of the lawless horde might dictate. This, however, is a matter little short of absolute certainty that, if killed, the flesh of his body quickly becomes entombed in the bowels of his murderers, and its bones, scattered about the plains, are left to bleach in the open air."

There could be no reasonable objection made, the *Guardian* added, to the setting up of reserves such as the one still under Sievwright's control at Mt Rouse, as places of safety and retreat for the blacks. But the settlers were at the same time offered no protection by the government. And if a black was charged with an offence against the person or property of a white man, he had the advantage of a "double trial". In the first instance, the Supreme Court would decide whether he had sufficient understanding of the proceedings to be able to stand trial. If it was decided he was not, he could be acquitted and there was no need to even proceed to the second stage, regardless of the strength of the case against him. And the blacks facing trial in Melbourne were being offered as their standing counsel the services of Redmond Barry -- a barrister "of the highest professional attainments".

"Is it fair and consistent with even-handed justice, that the government should throw so many special guards and protective rights around the Aborigine, to secure him from European injustice, and leave the settler exposed to all the violence of cannibal hordes, when they may choose to make their attacks upon him?" the *Guardian* inquired. "And yet, we ask, what has been hitherto done, suited to the peculiar circumstances of the Australian settler, to protect him from the incursions of the natives, any more than as though a savage had never shown a murderous propensity, or an Aboriginal of the country had never been seen?" Some settlers in the Portland area believed that the government would not provide the protection they urgently required. "We have nevertheless so much confidence in the vigour of British rule, that we feel persuaded it can never suffer, with impunity, a British subject to be a meal for a cannibal stomach, or the blood of the industrious labourer of Great Britain to gorge the Australian savage," the commentary concluded.[8]

Unbeknown to the *Guardian*, the Port Phillip Superintendent had already virtually decided to declare war on the Western District Aboriginal resistance leaders. The decision was prompted by a letter he received the day Roger was hanged, in which the Portland Police Magistrate, James Blair, had complained of further Aboriginal attacks in the district and of "fruitless attempts made to repress them". La Trobe was sick of receiving such reports. He'd immediately written to Fyans, ordering him to take "the most decided measures" to quell the disorder. "I have to request that you will consider this paramount to everything other at the present time," he told the Crown Lands Commissioner. All available police in the Western District were to be deployed in the operation -- the 12 Border Police usually under Fyans' command, plus the seven Mounted Police in the district, and the 10 Native Police recently sent there. Both James Blair and Acheson French were ordered to allow Fyans to take command of the Mounted and Native Police at Portland and The Grange "until he may be able to dispense with their services".

It was a major extension of orders issued just three days earlier, in which La Trobe had merely told Fyans to use "every means" in his power to afford protection to James Hunter and other squatters, and to capture as soon as possible the blacks responsible for the recent attacks on Hunter's station. La Trobe had also just ordered French to report on the attacks on Hunter's. The

Superintendent had stated he assumed that French had made "every exertion" to apprehend "the authors of these outrages" -- including Jupiter and Cocknose, if sufficient evidence against them could be obtained. Only a day later, an urgent letter would arrive from French, telling La Trobe that the situation in the far west of the district was worsening by the day. The blacks had even attempted to drive off the Police Magistrate's own flock of sheep, and to spear a shepherd employed by him. "I am obliged to keep my horses tethered close to home to be ready at a moment's warning to render assistance either to my own men or to those of my neighbours," he wrote.[9]

Fyans didn't like young Hunter, whom he regarded as a "street-walking villain" who spent too much time in Melbourne instead of looking after his station.[10] However, the Commissioner was eager for the opportunity to lead what would be the biggest official party assembled for an operation against the blacks in the Port Phillip District since the one led by Major Lettsom against the Goulburn Aborigines back in 1840. Fyans was angry over the release of Cocknose, Jupiter and Bumbletoe, and believed it was time to teach the blacks a lesson. And he knew of course of the recent suspension of the only man who'd been willing to officially challenge his previous actions -- the Western District's Aboriginal Protector. The mission on which he was being ordered could be conducted without any official monitoring or questioning from Sievwright.

At the same time as being told to use "the most decided measures" against Aboriginal troublemakers, however, Fyans was reminded that murder was not officially sanctioned. He would receive notification from La Trobe that the government had decided to extend the terms of the reward being offered over the murders of four Kirrae women and a child at Smith and Osbrey's station at Muston's Creek. It had been more than six months since Sievwright reported the murders, and no progress had been made in efforts to identify the culprits. La Trobe told Fyans, French and Blair that Gipps had decided that the reward for information leading to a conviction would remain at 100 pounds for a free person or a free pardon for a convict, with a free passage back to England. But the terms had now been extended to make the reward available to "any of the parties who were not principals in the first degree or did not actually fire the shots causing death" -- if they were willing to give evidence against the other whites involved. Copies of the new terms were also sent to commandant Dana, of the Native Police, and to John Watton, the newly-appointed medical officer at Mt Rouse -- but not to Sievwright.[11]

The new terms of the reward had been recommended by Frederick Powlett and Charles Griffith, sent by La Trobe to inquire into the accuracy of the information from Sievwright on the murders. Their inquiry, La Trobe told Gipps, had confirmed the "general accuracy" of the first report of the Muston's Creek murders made by Sievwright. The killers must have been from stations "at no very great distance from the scene", but Powlett and Griffith had also not been able to gain even a faint clue as to who they may have been. La Trobe added that Sievwright may have been partly to blame for the perpetrators still being free. "I cannot but express a regret and surprise that the first measures adopted by the Assistant Protector upon his being informed of the murder were not more decidely taken and better directed, and especially that so obvious and certain a method as that of carefully tracking their steps in returning was not seemingly even thought of." There was no mention of the fact that Sievwright at the time was desperately trying to keep alive a critically wounded woman with severe gunshot wounds -- and that he had to quickly get her back to Mt Rouse where he at least had some scanty medical supplies.

Despite Powlett and Griffith's lack of success, the Superintendent had remained optimistic that the murderers would sooner or later be discovered. "Under the supposition that the individual and united efforts of the settlers and residents of the district were directed to attain this end, I cannot conceive of the possibility of their escaping detection and I would still fain hope that however late such may be still secured," La Trobe told Gipps. Should this not occur, he agreed with the Governor that it might be necessary to refuse to renew squatting

By permission of the National Library of Australia
"Native Police" by S. T. Gill.

licences in an area around the scene of the murder. However, he'd suggested that they wait two to three months to see what happened.[12]

While the Muston's Creek murders remained unsolved, the affair inevitably stained the general reputation of the squatters of the district. The longer they were forced to suffer this ignominy, the more they hated Sievwright for having brought it to the government's attention -- and the more they looked forward to being rid of him. But even as the hatred against the Assistant Protector intensified, he and his family did not give up hope that he might be reinstated. And realising that they had at least in part been responsible for his downfall, Christina and Fanny would make a last-ditch attempt to save him before he had to hand over control of the Mt Rouse station to John Watton.

In one letter to La Trobe, Christina declared that she was prepared "to subscribe upon oath", should it be deemed necessary, to the "correctness and truth" of the lengthy statement her husband had made a month earlier in response to the charges against him. There'd been a great exaggeration, Christina protested, of the events which had led to the first charge, in which Sievwright's name had been linked to Mary Parker. "I do believe that the intimacy was not improper, and as to criminality, that imputation never even occurred to my mind," she wrote. Christina also rejected the accusation that her husband had been neglecting his family, challenging La Trobe to inspect the family's accounts. "Since 1839, I have both from choice and necessity resided with the younger part of our family near Geelong, as Mr Sievwright has been from that period until February last the present year, without a permanent residence, and has been with our boys itinerating with the natives and living in tents," Christina added.

"How shall I give your Honour my opinion upon the last and foulest accusation?" Christina continued, referring to her alleged statement back in 1839 that she believed Sievwright had contemplated Fanny's seduction. "Such a charge was never even hinted at by me, and never was made either by me or by my daughter to Captain Fyans or any other person, and I must state, twenty years' knowledge of Mr Sievwright's principles, practices, and tastes, entitle me to asseverate that he is wholly incapable of the unnatural debasement which I believe even in the most abandoned and profligate society never existed," she concluded.[13]

Fanny would also declare her willingness to swear on oath the accuracy of her father's denial of the charges against him. "But how shall I write of those strange and imcomprehensible charges, where my name is coupled with that of my father, in a style, the import of which I do not altogether understand," Fanny added. "It seems to me impossible that the conduct attributed by this accusation has been penned by one who is a parent, or that any stranger could so gratuitously blight my position in the world by so publicly promulgating such foul calumnies against one wholly unknown to him. I can only solemnly assert to your Honour that this charge is untrue, as it is to me inconceivable. I feel so utterly overwhelmed by those cruel reports that my inclination leads me to beg a contradiction from your Honour, which may be as widely disseminated, as the original document of 12th August must have been -- nay, I deem this request my right, tho' it is a poor indemnification for my present sufferings."[14]

It was a severe embarrassment for La Trobe. Sievwright had already emphatically denied each of the charges against him. And they had now been repudiated by Christina. Fanny, too, had denied the most serious charge. Documentary evidence of the allegation concerning Fanny was confined to reports of what Christina had *allegedly* said back in 1839. Thus, the only *recent* statement against Sievwright was that from Robinson, expressing the view that he was unsuitable to be an Aboriginal Protector. The only other verifiable grounds for his suspension boiled down to the letters sent by Christina to Lonsdale and Robinson, complaining in 1839 of Sievwright's behaviour. La Trobe had soon known at least the general content of those letters. But the Superintendent had declined Sievwright's request to investigate the claims against him then, choosing to take no action at all. The grounds for his suspension more than three years later, especially with Christina and Fanny's denials, were looking increasingly flimsy.

The letters from Christina and Fanny had not even reached Melbourne from Mt Rouse before John Watton arrived at the reserve to take over from Sievwright. It was 23 September 1842 -- almost four years since he'd arrived in Australia to take up the appointment. The Assistant Protector had continued his official duties up to the last minute -- one of the last ones being the taking of statements about the recent attacks on Hunter's station by the Gunditjmara guerillas.[15] The handover to Watton would involve a stocktake of supplies he was leaving behind, some of them personal, for which he intended seeking reimbursement from Robinson. Though he resented the circumstances, Watton was affable enough, and Sievwright had a vested interest in having the reserve continue because he was hoping for the lifting of his suspension. So he took pains to give whatever assistance he could to Watton, including an outline of the system he'd developed for labour and payment for it.

That spring evening, Sievwright sadly looked around the Mt Rouse reserve, wondering whether he would have any further role in trying to bring "the beacon of civilisation" into the lives of the Australian Aborigines. At the same time, 240 kilometres to the east, some of the sharpest British minds in the colony were grappling with the topic of whether uncivilised man was benefited by his contacts with civilised man. The Melbourne Debating Society had convened to discuss the question for the third consecutive Friday. One Aborigine who'd been living at Mt Rouse before being taken into white custody featured in the first session. It was the week that Roger had been hanged, and two of the speakers -- including the editor of the *Gazette*, George Arden -- would highlight his case as an example of an uncivilised man who had hardly benefited from the arrival of the British in his land. Roger, they argued, had been "judicially murdered".[16]

Other speakers in two subsequent sessions would give details of how they also perceived various Aboriginal or native people to have suffered as a result of contact with "civilised" people such as the British. The debate was finally brought to a vote on the issue by show of hands at the end of the third session, the day Sievwright gave up control of Mt Rouse to Watton. Surprisingly, despite the remarks by a number of speakers lauding the benefits of colonisation for the colonised, only one hand voted in the affirmative. The almost unanimous view was that contacts with civilised people could *not* be regarded as beneficial to uncivilised people -- the destructive effects just being an inevitable part of human evolution.[17] A week later, the Debating Society would meet again, this time to discuss the probable origin, and destination, of the Aborigines of Australia. No vote was taken on the first part of the topic. But the consensus on the second part was that "the probable destination" of the native Australians was "extermination".[18]

CHAPTER 28
Mr Cold Morning

AHEAD of the series of attacks launched by the Aborigines of Port Phillip's Western District during and beyond the winter of 1842, one of the squatters affected by them would put forward a radical scheme for the "better treatment" of the blacks. The proposal came from John Hunter Patterson, whose other pet projects would include helping to found a Presbyterian Scots Church and a hospital in Melbourne, where he lived. Patterson had two stations run on his behalf at the time in the Western District -- one a sheep run near The Grange, formerly operated by the Wedge brothers, the other a cattle run near Mt Napier, about 20 kilometres west of Mt Rouse.[1] He argued that rural parts of Port Phillip would never be fully or speedily developed until something was done "to restrain the predatory habits of the Aborigines". At the same time, the white settlers had to be given a reasonable guarantee of safety for themselves and their property.

In a pamphlet printed in Melbourne, Patterson noted it had been established beyond dispute that white occupation had caused a scarcity of those plants and animals which formerly constituted the Aborigines' staple articles of subsistence. "If the occupation of the country by our flocks and herds has had the effect of depriving its natural possessors of their customary supplies of food, we are bound, on every principle of justice, either to provide them with an equivalent, or patiently to submit to their irregular excursions, whatever be the individual annoyance, or positive detriment arising out of them," the pamphlet argued. "It is from a want of attention to this fundamental principle, we conceive, that the measures resorted to by the government have proved so notoriously ineffectual. For without entering into unnecessary details, it is admitted, even by those who are disposed to give the greatest credit to the measures adopted by the local authorities, that those stock-holders who are immediately under the eye of the District Protectors have invariably suffered the greatest amount of injury from the depredations of the blacks."

The Port Phillip Aborigines, Patterson believed, should be fed "gratuitously" with meat and flour at depots established in the territory of each tribe. Food distribution should be handled through a redirected Protectorate, with "Sub-Protectors" assigned to each tribe. The Sub-Protectors would ensure that each member of the tribe received "an adequate supply of wholesome food".

PROPOSED PLAN

FOR THE

𝕭𝕰𝕿𝕿𝕰𝕽 𝕿𝕽𝕰𝕬𝕿𝕸𝕰𝕹𝕿

OF THE

ABORIGINES OF AUSTRALIA FELIX,

BY

John Hunter Patterson,

OF

MELBOURNE PORT PHILLIP.

JUNE 7, 1842.

ALTHOUGH much has been done by the Government and enterprise of individuals to advance the interests of this Colony, it is a matter of general complaint, that no efficient means have been adopted to restrain the predatory habits of the Aborigines. At the same time it is universally admitted, that unless these are restrained, and the Colonists furnished with a reasonable guarantee, for the security of their persons and property, the resources of the country can neither be fully nor speedily developed.

It now appears to be established beyond the reach of dispute, that the extensive occupation of the Territory has produced a scarcity of those plants and animals, which constituted the staple articles of their subsistence,—and this view is confirmed by the fact, that the depredations of the Aborigines have been hitherto committed with the sole purpose of obtaining *food* or *clothing*.

In these circumstances it is sufficiently obvious, that before any system can be devised for ameliorating their condition, an adequate provision must be made, for supplying them with the first necessaries of life, for it is idle to talk of reforming, or even of restraining, by punishment or otherwise, *a starving population*. Nor is this a mere matter of expediency. If the occupation of the country by our flocks and herds has had the effect of depriving its natural possessors of their customary supplies of food, we are bound, on every principle of justice, either to provide them with an equivalent, or patiently to submit to their irregular excursions, whatever be the individual annoyance, or positive detriment arising out of them.

It is from a want of attention to this fundamental principle, we conceive, that the measures resorted to by the Government have proved so notoriously ineffectual. For without entering into unnecessary details, it is admitted, even by those who are disposed to give the greatest credit to the measures adopted by the local authorities, that those Stock-holders who are more immediately under the eye of the District Protectors have invariably suffered the greatest amount of injury from the depredations of the Blacks.

In respectfully submitting the following details to the consideration of the Government, I would be understood then to take it for granted, as an essential pre-requisite to any radical or permanent improvement, that the Native population be, in the first instance, *fed*, and *fed gratuitously*, let the cost and sacrifice be what they may,—this in my opinion would be best effected;—

When he put forward his radical plan "for the better treatment" of the Aborigines, John Hunter Patterson had sheep and cattle stations in the Western District. The plan, suggesting that each tribe be fed "gratuitously" with meat and flour at special depots, was distributed throughout the colony and among ruling circles in Britain, but was not seriously considered. Patterson would later be pushed to the brink of bankruptcy by Aboriginal attacks on one of his stations.

Encouragements such as quantities of tea, sugar, tobacco and soap would be offered to those who cultivated the soil or who engaged in some other "useful employment". And there would be annual gift of one pair of blankets and two suits of clothing for every Aborigine. Patterson felt that this system would gradually wean at least the younger blacks "from their roving and unsettled habits". It should never be forgotten, he remarked, "that indolence, or neutrality on the part of the Aborigines, is infinitely preferable to active and open hostility".

One key flaw in Patterson's proposal was that it was based on the assumption that there were a much smaller number of tribes, and members of them, than those actually still in existence. He would give an estimated costing of the scheme, amounting to more than 14,500 pounds a year for 1000 blacks. This was almost double the direct amount the existing Protectorate system had cost to run the previous year.[2] But Patterson's costing provided only for a Chief Protector and just three "Sub-Protectors", each with one medical officer and four overseers. The number of tribes in Port Phillip was of course much higher than three, and according to Robinson's estimate, there were more than 2500 blacks.

Some of the funds needed for his scheme, Patterson suggested, could come from the money saved from a reduced need for Mounted and Border Police. The rest -- and this would be his most controversial proposal of all -- could come from a form of taxation on all the colonists, payable in either cash or food. "From the calculations I have made, I am almost satisfied that the tax, if levied in this way, would not greatly exceed in amount, the outlay at present imperatively necessary on the part of stockholders, for the protection of their flocks -- especially when coupled with the losses to which they are subjected from actual depredations," Patterson stated.[3]

At least two of Port Phillip's Aboriginal Protectors would disagree with Patterson's assertion that it had been the squatters closest to the Protectorate reserves had "invariably suffered the greatest amount of injury from the depredations of the blacks". Just days before the publication of Patterson's pamphlet, Charles Sievwright had boasted that the squatters near Mt Rouse had expressed to him "satisfaction and surprise" at the security they had recently enjoyed.[4] And in a letter to Robinson, Edward Parker declared "an unqualified contradiction" to Patterson's claim, at least as far as his reserve was concerned. He was apprehensive that Patterson's pamphlet could produce "an erroneous and unfavourable opinion" about the beneficial effects his reserve was producing "upon the Aboriginal character". No doubt this "misrepresentation" had been unintentional, Parker added, requesting that his remarks be brought to the attention of the government. Robinson would comply with the request, in a letter to La Trobe, without giving the faintest hint of his own opinion on Patterson's pamphlet.[5]

Patterson would seek support in Britain for his proposals, sending copies of the pamphlet to the Secretary of State for the Colonies, Lord Stanley, and other members of the British parliament. Stanley would agree to pass on copies to the Duke of Wellington, the Duchess of Northumberland, and others. Without commenting on Patterson's proposals, however, the Secretary of State told Gipps that he would not in future allow the squatter to use his office as "the medium of his correspondence".[6] The pamphlet was also widely distributed in New South Wales. In Melbourne, the *Herald* would publish the entire text, recommending it for the attention of its readers. But there would be little serious public discussion of Patterson's plan before details started becoming known in Melbourne of the new series of attacks by the blacks in the west of the Port Phillip District -- including the murders of two more white shepherds. One of Patterson's stations would be among those which suffered "repeated" attacks and heavy losses, and would help to push him to the brink of bankruptcy. Even he would later agree that the "aggressions" of the blacks justified La Trobe's order for the operation against them led by Foster Fyans.[7]

Just before Fyans set out on his mission, another example would occur of what the Crown Lands Commissioner and others considered to be the apparent futility of taking black prisoners. Yet another Western District Aboriginal leader, sent to Melbourne for trial, was released from prison, able to rejoin the resistance, without even being tried. Partpoarermin, known to the whites as Cold Morning, had been charged with highway robbery and assault by Police Magistrate Blair at Portland. The charges related to an incident four months earlier near Mt Eckersley, on the track that went north of Portland to The Grange. A group of Gunditjmara men had attacked two bullock drays carrying supplies up the track north of the town, bound for the stations of Thomas Tulloh and James Riley, about 80 kilometres away.

One of the dray drivers, Joseph "Tiger" Ellis, would later depose that led by a man known as Jacky Jacky, the blacks had thrown "a whole shower of spears" at the other un-named driver employed by Tulloh, who responded by firing a double-barrelled gun. One of the spears went through the man's hat, but he was not wounded. While this was going on, Ellis stated, Cold Morning had called out to him: "Bloody rogue, you Tiger, plenty spear for you!" Then, as one team of frightened bullock teams took off with one dray up the track, one of the blacks grabbed a whip from the other dray, and drove the second team off the track, into the bush, calling the bullocks -- by name. The two white men ran after the first dray, and managed to catch up with it not far away. Ellis remained guarding it while the other driver went for help at the nearby station of Scottish squatter, David Edgar.

The stolen dray was found not far from the track, one wheel stuck on a tree

stump. The bullocks had been unyoked, and the load on the dray had been plundered. The prize most sought by the raiders had been the 10 full sacks of flour
the dray had been carrying. The flour sacks had been too heavy to carry off, so
most of the sacks of wheat and barley had been emptied near the dray, and then
re-used to divide the flour into smaller quantities. A search of the area found
much of the missing flour "concealed in hollows of trees and covered with
bones". At the end of the search, one-third of the flour was still missing, along
with a small quantity of the wheat. A tarpaulin that belonged to one of the Henty
brothers, and a jacket belonging to Ellis "in which were 14 bank notes", were
also gone. But the eight bullocks were all found nearby, two of them "chained
up to a tree, as a bullock driver would fasten them". In recently-vacated
Aboriginal camps in the area, the searchers discovered quantities of half-baked
damper, but no blacks were to be seen.[8]

Three days after the robbery, Cold Morning would be captured at a part of the
beach near Portland known to the whites as the Convincing Ground. It was
reportedly so named years earlier, even before white settlement of Melbourne,
by whalers employed by the Hentys, who had used their guns to convince a
group of Aborigines that the whales brought to the shore belonged to the white
men. Edward Henty would tell Robinson that a whale had broken its moorings
and washed up on the shore. When the whalers went to retrieve it, they were
attacked by a party of Gunditjmara people, who for centuries had feasted on
beached whales. The whites had retreated to arm themselves, and were again
attacked when they returned to the spot, Henty stated. "And the whalers then let
fly, to use his expression, right and left upon the natives," Robinson recorded.
"He said the natives did not go away but got behind trees and threw spears and
stones. They, however, did not much molest them after that."[9] Another white
man would tell Robinson that the violent "convincing" that had taken place at
the spot was related to the whalers' desire for Aboriginal women.[10]

One of the Henty's stockmen, John Robson, had recognised Cold Morning
when he'd appeared at the Convincing Ground with a large number of
Gunditjmara people. With the help of some whalers, Robson had seized him and
another Aboriginal man, also suspected to have been involved in the dray robbery. Despite "a violent resistance", the whites managed to get the two blacks
to Portland, where they were placed in prison, pending identification by one of
the dray drivers. "Cold Morning has a fresh gunshot wound on the arm, probably inflicted by Mr Tulloh's man, and a cut on his head, apparently from a sabre
which he says he received from a white man -- most likely in some skirmish with
the Border Police," Police Magistrate Blair had told La Trobe.[11] Certainly, the
Border Police sent to James Hunter's station had reported wounding two
Gunditjmara men in a clash four months earlier. At least one of them had

received sabre cuts to the head.[12]   Robson deserved a reward for his efforts, Blair suggested.   "The difficulty experienced by the police in apprehending Aboriginal natives charged with any crime is so very great, owing to their immediately escaping to a different part of the country from that in which it has been committed, seems to render it desirable that some encouragement be held out to private individuals whom chance may afford an opportunity of apprehending them," he told La Trobe.[13]   The Superintendent had passed on the proposal to Gipps, but the Governor had rejected it, saying he did not believe a reward was justified in such a case.[14]

When he'd committed Cold Morning for trial for highway robbery and assault back in May, Blair's interpreter had been a Portland shoemaker named Richard Claxton -- better known as Black Dick.   Through him, Cold Morning had allegedly declined to ask any questions about his committal, stating only in his defence that other Aborigines had been involved in the robbery.[15]   Blair would later confess that his interpreter's linguistic abilities were very limited.   Black Dick seemed to have "much difficulty" in making Cold Morning understand anything which he said to him.   "In fact the man appeared almost as fully to understand what was said to him in English as what was explained to him by the interpreter," Blair would admit.[16]

For weeks, Cold Morning would be in the Melbourne prison with four other Western District Aborigines -- Roger, Jupiter, Cocknose and Bumbletoe -- the latter three being fellow Gunditjmara men.   Crown Prosecutor Croke would decide to put Cold Morning on trial in the same July sessions of the Supreme Court as Roger.   Just nine days before those sessions were due to start, Croke decided to ask George Robinson for the two defendants' Aboriginal names. Ludicrously, he wanted interpreters as well![17]   Robinson would refer Croke's letter to Sievwright, but the Assistant Protector would reply that he could not act as an interpreter in either case.   He'd only been in communication with Roger's tribe since moving to Mt Rouse less than six months earlier, and was not yet familiar enough with his language.   Cold Morning he did not know, and no-one had even informed him of the circumstances of his arrest.[18]   Nor would the Assistant Protector ever be officially informed.   Prosecutor Croke would not even bother to wait for Sievwright's reply before continuing legal action against the two blacks.

Even before Sievwright's letter reached Melbourne, a Supreme Court jury had decided that Roger understood enough of the proceedings to stand trial, largely because of faith in the abilities as an interpreter of the Assistant Protector's brother, John.   Two days later, a jury comprising most of the same men would rule that Cold Morning was not ready for trial because of the absence of an interpreter. While Roger went on to be convicted and sent to the gallows, Cold Morning had remained remanded in custody, supposedly undergoing instructions in court proceedings, in accordance with an order from Judge Willis. More than a month later, Croke would write to La Trobe suggesting that Robinson be instructed to comply with the judge's order.[19]

Although La Trobe agreed with Croke's suggestion, Robinson of course was no more able to interpret than Sievwright. Cold Morning would languish for another fortnight before Croke would decide there was no point in detaining him any longer. He would finally be released, after almost four months in detention, for Robinson to make arrangements for his return to Portland by boat. There was a schooner leaving for Portland in just a few days, and Robinson would have liked to have had Cold Morning on it. But although Cold Morning was technically free, La Trobe was not keen to send another Western District resistance leader back to his territory before Fyans had completed his imminent mission. He decided to delay Cold Morning's return by seeking an explanation from Croke on why he was being released. And he was in no hurry to ask for the explanation, waiting more than two weeks before he did so.[20]

As commandant at Norfolk Island, and then as Geelong's Police Magistrate, Flogger Fyans had shown a propensity for swift and severe punishment. His first major operation against the Western District blacks in 1842 had resulted in two dead suspects, and four prisoners. Of those prisoners, Roger had been hanged. But after hearing of the exploits of two of the others -- Jupiter and Cocknose -- after their release, he was not keen to capture any more prisoners to send to Melbourne for interminable arguments about amenability for trial. And when he arrived in Gunditjmara territory, just as Sievwright was handing over control of the Mt Rouse reserve to Watton, there would be plenty of fresh reports of Aboriginal attacks in the area to strengthen his resolve to deliver a deterrent blow.[21]

A month after being ordered on his mission, Fyans was again at James Hunter's station, this time leading a party of 16 police. But partly because of the rainy weather, and partly because of the terrain, he'd so far had no success. "I regret to inform you that, after a long journey at a bad season, we are unable to do any service in this part of the country," he told La Trobe. "We find the horses almost useless, and are obliged to lead them for miles." Fyans had led one expedition into The Rocks from Hunter's, at times wading through marshes, but without having found any blacks. He now wanted to go to the Winter brothers' station, on the Glenelg, about 70 kilometres to the north-west, where at least one Bunganditj man had recently been shot dead as a large flock of sheep was being driven off. Fyans had decided to leave Dana and the Native Police behind, close to Mt Eels. "A hut can easily be thrown up to accommodate them, and I really believe that is the only means of our ever being able to take Jupiter and Cocknose again, or to restore peace to this place," he wrote."[22]

Although Fyans would spend a further 10 weeks on his mission, few details would ever be revealed of what measures he took to try to quell the unrest. He would end up telling La Trobe that he'd travelled more than 3200 kilometres, investigating claims against the blacks. He'd confirmed the losses of well over 3000 sheep and lambs in recent raids at nine stations. But at the end of his mission, Fyans didn't believe the future was necessarily bleak. Gunditjmara blacks around Port Fairy had started to behave "extremely well", and he believed the Bunganditj people further west would become quieter. "I do not consider them to be in a worse state than the different tribes were in other parts of the district some years ago," Fyans wrote. The Commissioner even conceded that the Western District Aborigines were being blamed -- and punished -- for offences they hadn't committed. "The newspaper accounts exaggerate all their crimes, and I am of opinion that many of the settlers act in accordance with them, and in returning their lists of losses far exceed their bounds," he stated.[23]

Contrary to Fyans' initial plan, Dana and his Native Police wouldn't stay in The Rocks near Hunter's trying to seize Jupiter and Cocknose. Some would accom-

"Attack on store dray" by S. T. Gill

pany Fyans for other parts of the mission, although only four horses were available for them, so most had to be left at The Grange with Acheson French. Those who could be mounted would be involved in one operation, for instance, on the Glenelg River, in Bunganditj territory. This would result in the capture of four blacks suspected of involvement in at least one of the recent murders of white men. It would be the only report of the capture of prisoners during the Fyans-led operation, and their fate would remain a mystery. Bumbletoe, who was delivered back to Portland while the operation was underway, would also disappear.[24]

The commanding officer of the Native Police told La Trobe he wanted to express "in the highest terms" his satisfaction with the conduct of his men during their Western District mission, which had covered almost 2000 kilometres. Neither he nor French had had cause to be dissatisfied with their behaviour, and those without horses had shown themselves to be "ready and willing to march to any part of the country ordered to". Two young troopers, named Buckup and Yuptun, deserved special mention. They had "gallantly" saved him from drowning while attempting to cross the flooded Wannon River. Dana would provide few details of the actual operations in which the Native Police had been involved. However, he gave a strong hint that his men had at least threatened to use their carbines or bayonets against their fellow Aborigines -- a threat they would carry out a few months later, if not then. "I anticipate that the trip to Portland Bay will be attended with some good results, for the fear with which the wild blacks regard the men and their knowing that now they can be followed to any place they go to will have a good effect in preventing them from thinking that they can commit depredations with immunity," Dana wrote.

Yet another mysterious matter would be how the Native Police had been used to try to force large numbers of Aborigines to move to the Mt Rouse reserve. Soon before Sievwright's suspension became effective, there were between 300 and 400 blacks living at Mt Rouse. But soon after John Watton took over, many had left. Dana would tell La Trobe that his police had driven between 200 and 300 Aborigines to Mt Rouse from Lake Boloke and the River Hopkins. The circumstances had been "very trying", but the Native Police had shown themselves to be "faithful and true" during the operation. Either the Aborigines delivered to Mt Rouse by the Native Police didn't stay there long, or else Dana was greatly exaggerating the numbers. Soon after the operation took place, French would inform La Trobe that Watton had been to the Hopkins and had brought back about 60 blacks -- making the total number at Mt Rouse between 180 and 200.[25]

There was no indication from Dana whether the blacks driven to Mt Rouse were ones who'd been living at the reserve before it started to break up after Sievwright's suspension. He would also offer no information on how the "very trying" operation had been carried out. However, La Trobe would later learn that at least one young Aborigine "forcibly carried away" by the Native Police from the Hopkins River area had been missing for months.   Lachlan MacKinnon, a Scottish squatter in Kirrae territory, north of Terang, told La Trobe that an Aboriginal boy who'd been living at his station had been abducted by Dana and his men. "His parents evince a degree of distress for the loss of their child, for which few would give them credit, and have frequently requested me to ascertain his fate," MacKinnon would write, belatedly asking La Trobe to investigate.[26]

Just after La Trobe learned that the Fyans-led mission was being wound up, with the return of the Native Police to their headquarters near Melbourne, Cold Morning would arrive back in Portland -- an event reported with a mixture of scorn and cynicism by the Port Phillip press. Not knowing Cold Morning's language, the Melbourne *Herald* suggested that if his suspension was lifted, it would take Sievwright at least six or seven years to make the black acquire the knowledge of court proceedings which judge Willis had expected him to obtain in prison. In an article headed "Mr Cold Morning", the *Portland Guardian* would also mock the judge's ludicrous suggestion: "We have to announce the safe arrival in the district, as cabin passenger per *Alpha*, of the distinguished person above named. Mr Croke, though feeling seriously the want of a clerk, does not deem the progress that the sable gentleman made while under Protectorate instruction in Melbourne, sufficient to tempt that legal gentleman to retain the services of the sable scholar. Cold Morning after landing, quietly walked through the town, and with his wardrobe on his shoulder, proceeded to join his tribe, but not before he had amused many of the townspeople with a graphic description of the proceedings of the Supreme Court in his own case, and represented His Honour the Judge as having 'big one *flour*' on his head."[27]

The *Guardian* would not be making jokes about Cold Morning for long. Only a week later, it was reporting another attack involving him near Portland. Cold Morning, it alleged, had led a group of about 20 Gunditjmara men in an attack on a "Sydney native" called Bradbury, who worked for James Hunter, as he passed by with a white employee of the Survey Department named Cooke. Cold Morning had thrown the first of three spears at Bradbury, all of which missed. Cooke, who'd been unarmed, had urged Bradbury to open fire with his pistol. In the confusion, as he hastily drew the weapon from his belt, it went off, "the contents passing through his hand". But the gunshot had been enough to make Cold Morning and his companions flee. After Bradbury had returned to Portland to have his shattered hand dressed, and to make a detailed statement to the Police Magistrate, three troopers had been sent to the scene.

Through this incident and others, the *Guardian* observed, Cold Morning had evinced an "unrelenting disposition to continue in the commission of crime". This was no doubt strengthened by his recent discharge from custody. "With regard to absence of capacity to comprehend the nature of proceedings instituted against him, we feel inclined to differ from the learned gentlemen in Melbourne, who have so humanely provided him with clothing, and given him a free passage to the scene of his depredations," the paper remarked. Cold Morning had given "shrewd and cunningly evasive replies" while being examined by Blair, with Black Dick as interpreter, before being committed for trial in Melbourne. On his return to Portland, he'd given a "well delineated account" of the Supreme Court proceedings, including a description of the reading of the indictment, the peculiar dress of the judge, and the evidence of witnesses. This account had been delivered, the *Guardian* claimed, "with a degree of perspicuity seldom equalled by those parties to whom we look for a higher degree of 'mental capacity' than the Melbourne philanthropists are disposed to attribute to our sable friend, Mr Cold Morning".[28]

A little over a fortnight later, the *Guardian* would report that Cold Morning had revisited Portland. With his tribe assembled nearby, he'd entered the settlement with the apparent purpose of "reconnoitring the movements of the bullock drivers -- in order to ascertain the practicability of making an attack upon them when a safe distance from the town". Cold Morning was reported to have made a similar visit before the robbery for which he'd been sent to Melbourne for trial, and the residents of Portland were apprehensive about his reappearance in the town. "The reception met with by his sable highness on this occasion was quite unbecoming a person of his importance, and we trust that he may resent it with proper spirit, and absent himself from the town entirely", the *Guardian* quipped. "We understand the Police Magistrate dispatched two of the Mounted Police in pursuit of the tribe, in order to further their removal from the township -- a close acquaintance with these gentlemen being deemed to be undesirable."[29]

The fears of the *Guardian* were well-founded. Within a week, a large group of Aborigines would attack a bullock dray as it passed through the same area of forest where the earlier raid had occurred, not far from Portland. Ironically, this time the dray attacked was carrying supplies ordered by the Police Magistrate at The Grange. After the two white drivers jumped from the dray and fled for help, the bullocks were forced off the road into the forest with their load. Later that day, Chief Constable Thomas Finn and two Mounted Police from Portland would trace the tracks of the dray to a waterhole, about three kilometres into the forest. The dray had been backed in after the bullocks had been unyoked, and was completely under water. Nearby, the police managed to find all of the bullocks, several of them speared, as well as some of the goods which had been on the dray.

An unidentified Aborigine would then guide the police to a nearby black camp. As the white men approached, all the blacks except one woman fled into a thicket of tea-tree. Without explaining how, Blair would later report that the police had spent "some hours of exertion" in an unsuccessful bid to drive the blacks out of the trees. The woman caught in the camp, he reported, had told the Aborigine guiding the police that two tribes had combined for the attack on Acheson French's dray. The attackers had included several "tame blacks", including one employed by the Whyte brothers. He was a very good bullock driver, and had been responsible for taking the dray into the forest, as well as unyoking the animals. It could well have been a youth called Calpert, alias Harry, whom George Robinson had seen helping with a dray of the Whyte brothers the year before. Robinson at the time had recorded that Calpert was from the Glenelg River, which would have made him a Bunganditj Aborigine, a large number of whom had been slaughtered by the Whytes. It is possible, then, that there were both Bunganditj and Gunditjmara men involved in the attack on French's dray.

Chief Constable Finn, Blair told La Trobe, had set fire to everything possible in the blacks' camp, including all the spears and other weapons they'd left behind when they'd fled. He'd also destroyed quantities of flour, tea, and sugar robbed from the dray which he'd had no way of bringing back to Portland. French would later report that more than 27 pounds worth of government goods had been lost in the raid -- including three bags of flour, two bags of sugar, about nine kilograms of tobacco, three jackets, three pairs of trousers, six shirts, six palm hats, three pairs of boots, one vest, one new tarpaulin, two bows with yokes, and two chains. As well, French had lost "a good deal" of his own property, for which he sought government compensation.

The Police Magistrate suggested that two Mounted Police needed to be permanently stationed in the area where the attacks on the drays had occurred to dissuade future attacks. There was a stretch of about 45 kilometres of forest between stations along the track heading north from Portland. This afforded "great advantages" to the blacks in plundering drays which had been loaded in Portland and were heading to the interior. French was afraid that this was the commencement of a system which if not immediately suppressed would "reach an alarming height", as the blacks found that they could acquire "provisions more to their taste" with greater ease and less risk of being discovered than in raids on the settlers' flocks and herds. "Having ascertained the names of some of the parties connected in the robbery," he added, "I have issued warrants against them, amongst whom is the notorious Cold Morning, and I shall set about every means towards their apprehension."[30]

In Melbourne, meanwhile, La Trobe had been unimpressed with letters he'd received from the Western District Aborigines' suspended Protector, and his wife and eldest daughter. The Superintendent had told Gipps that Sievwright, Christina and Fanny had given "the most unqualified denial" of the truth of the charges against the Protector's moral character -- and they were willing "to substantiate that denial upon oath". But after comparing letters he'd just received from Christina and Fanny with those written by Christina to Robinson and Fyans in 1839, he'd been confirmed in the view "that the employment of Mr Sievwright and his family in the public service has been from first to last, a discredit to it".[31] Gipps, however, had decided he did not need any further confirmation from La Trobe that he'd made the right decision in suspending Sievwright. Belated notification to Stanley of the decision was already on a ship on its way to London.

"I regret to say that my reasons for suspending Mr Sievwright are not founded solely on his general inefficiency as an officer, but on certain reports injurious to his moral character, which have long prevailed at Port Phillip, and the truth of which he has taken no steps to disprove," Gipps had written. "In respect of these rumours, I transmit to Your Lordship a copy of a confidential paper, which I have received from Mr La Trobe." In this document, the Superintendent had summarised the various aspersions against Sievwright's moral character made in the reports by Robinson, Lonsdale and Fyans -- as well as those made in the letters written by Christina. La Trobe had given no reason why he'd not acted on the allegations, even though he believed they'd been hampering Sievwright's crucial operations. "It may be easily comprehended that they should give rise to much scandal from the very outset, and have thrown serious obstacles in Mr Sievwright's way," La Trobe had remarked. "Their existence has cast an air of ridicule over the presumed efforts of Mr Sievwright to discharge his duty as an Assistant Protector and a Magistrate -- deputed, in conjunction with his family, to pave the way by Christian precept and Christian example for the regeneration of a most degraded race."

The respect of his superior or his colleagues had never been gained by Sievwright, La Trobe remarked, and his unpopularity among the settlers had been strengthened by the knowledge of the charges against him. The Superintendent was even willing to give credence to the suggestion that the rumours about Sievwright could have been known to the Aborigines, and could have been at least partly responsible for his alleged lack of authority over them. "If my information is correct," he wrote, "there are those among them who are fully acquainted with the character of the charges against him, and shrewd enough to draw their conclusions from them." La Trobe failed to mention that this was third-hand information from Robinson which had passed through a highly dubious translation process! La Trobe hastened to add that he could scarcely said to be acquainted with Sievwright, having shunned him since hearing of the rumours about him soon after his arrival in Melbourne.[32]

In his letter to Stanley enclosing La Trobe's report, Gipps promised to transmit "any remonstrance which may be made by Mr Sievwright against his removal from office".[33] The first protest from Sievwright, calling for an inquiry into the charges against him, had in fact already been made in Melbourne three weeks earlier. Even before he finally sent Sievwright's letter on to Gipps, La Trobe would inform Robinson, Fyans and Lonsdale to prepare themselves for an inquiry. The suspended Protector's "indignant denial" of every charge against him, La Trobe warned them, extended even to their statements of the circumstances under which the allegations had been made. The Superintendent would provide extracts of the relevant parts of Sievwright's letter, to help them gather any further information or evidence against him. Whether an inquiry would be necessary "to vindicate the propriety" of Sievwright's suspension was a decision which would have to be made by Gipps.[34]

So while Sievwright awaited the inquiry he felt sure would be held, without his knowledge the case against him continued to build. Notification of his suspension was on its way to the Colonial Office in London, without his letter of denial. His main accusers had been given details of his likely defence, and told to strengthen their case. And the Aborigines for whose protection he'd been responsible for more than three years were also about to enter an uncertain phase. While Sievwright was suspended, John Watton would not be taking over all of his duties. He'd been appointed as a medical officer at the Mt Rouse reserve, not as a protector for the Western District. Without saying how he thought it could be achieved, La Trobe wanted Watton to only perform those duties of an Assistant Protector which were "imperatively necessary" to enable Robinson to exercise a control over the reserve from 240 kilometres away in Melbourne, and to keep the government aware of what was happening there. Any matters requiring the services of a magistrate could be performed by the man who had issued most of the arrest warrants for the Aboriginal resistance leaders in the area -- Watton's son-in-law, Acheson French.[35]

CHAPTER 29
Holding ranks

THE ability of Governor Gipps to maintain authority over the white men of New South Wales was always tenuous, especially as the number of free settlers in the colony increased. There was the example of the American Revolution to show what could occur if the behaviour of representatives of distant rulers in London became to be regarded as oppressive. Gipps and Superintendent La Trobe had relatively small military forces available to suppress any uprising they might provoke among the well-armed settlers of New South Wales. In particular, it was important for Gipps and La Trobe not to antagonise too much the squatters who with the approval of the colonial government had taken over a large portion of the colony. It was far more territory than the military would be able to control if the Governor's authority was ever challenged in an open revolt.

One cause of serious unrest among the squatters, beyond the belief that they were being overtaxed by Gipps, was the insecurity of tenure which squatting licences gave over the land on which they were investing their capital. It was a sensitivity which the Governor could not ignore. Yet avoiding acts which might incur the displeasure of the New South Wales squatters was not Gipps' top priority. It was far more important to him to keep a good reputation back in England than to be popular among the squatters. And there was one factor which he feared had the potential to damage that reputation more than any other -- the perception that his administration had not done enough to prevent the Aborigines of the colony from being maltreated by the squatters and their men. The British parliament had decreed that Aboriginal protection should be a primary concern of the colonial government. So seriously did Gipps feel a need to demonstrate a commitment to this decision that he was at times willing to risk the wrath of the squatters by the manner in which he showed it.

In July 1842, Gipps suddenly felt more vulnerable to criticism from London over the issue than ever before. He'd just had to report to the Colonial Office the circumstances, as far as he knew them, of the recent murders of four innocent Aboriginal women and a child at Muston's Creek in the Western District of Port Phillip, and the lack of progress towards finding the culprits. To make matters worse, he'd just suspended the Aboriginal Protector who'd been responsible for looking after the murder victims and the rest of their tribe -- and who'd been the one who'd brought the slaughter to official attention. Gipps had not yet been told that the report on the killings commissioned by La Trobe from Charles Griffith and Frederick Powlett had upheld the accuracy of Sievwright's initial claim that the murders appeared to have been wanton. But Gipps knew that he would have been quickly informed if any evidence had been uncovered to support the allegation of exaggeration by the suspended Protector. Furthermore, it was obvious that Sievwright was not going to disappear quietly.

The whole affair made Gipps extremely nervous. He felt certain that the publicity which would be given in England to the Muston's Creek murders would reflect "most prejudicially" upon the character not only of the district in which they had been committed, but on the whole colony. The Governor would feel so much at risk of damaging criticism from London that he would make an extraordinary threat. If acted upon, it could easily have provoked insurrection among the New South Wales squatters. Asserting the supremacy of his duty to try to ensure the protection of the Aborigines, the Governor declared he was willing to take extreme steps to bring the perpetrators of the Muston's Creek murders to trial. Unless progress was made in apprehending suspects, he was willing to consider cancelling all the squatting licences in the part of the colony where the murders had occurred -- and then declaring "the whole district" an Aboriginal reserve. "He shall not shrink from the performance of such a duty, if justice and humanity seem to require it at his hands," La Trobe was told.[1]

It was a substantial advance on the action which La Trobe himself had suggested over the massacre almost four months earlier. Taking away a few squatting licences would be one thing. Declaring the whole area to be an Aboriginal reserve, unavailable for squatting, would be quite another. When the Governor's potentially explosive proposals reached Melbourne, La Trobe felt obliged to broadly endorse them -- and to pass them on to Niel Black and the small group of other Western District squatters who'd complained that their reputations were being unfairly tainted over the colonial government's reaction to the murders. However, the Superintendent was quick to try to minimise the squatters' anger by giving the narrowest possible definition of what the Governor might have meant by "the district" which could be declared an Aboriginal reserve. Gipps might have meant just the area around Muston's Creek. Or he could have meant the Western District, or even the whole of Port Phillip. La Trobe went for the easiest option. Certainly, he said, the squatters whose licences were closest to the scene of the massacre should face licence cancellation if no further information on the killings came to light. But he suggested to Gipps that they wait another two to three months before deciding whether any such severe action was necessary.[2]

Even before the expiry of La Trobe's suggested deadline, the issue of the colonial government's ability to withhold squatting licences because of mistreatment of Aborigines would again arise -- this time as a result of an event much closer to Sydney. In August 1842, a petition would be brought before the Legislative Council from about 90 squatters in the Bathurst area, about 200 kilometres west of Sydney. They were outraged by the cancellation of the squatting licence of one of their number, William Lee, on the ground that at least 12 Aborigines had been shot dead in a confrontation with his men while he was absent. In making this decision, the squatters believed, the authorities had gone way too far. The petition was presented by a conservative Sydney-born landowner who helped to represent the pastoralists on the Legislative Council, James Macarthur.

The incident which had provoked the cancellation of William Lee's licence had occurred during a drought almost a year earlier, when Lee's employees had been forced to move his stock further down the Bogan River in search of water. According to Macarthur, Lee's overseer and the men under his control had been accompanied by a group of Aborigines with whom they'd thought they were on good terms. But the blacks had suddenly "without the least cause or provocation" attacked the whites, killing three of them. The rest of Lee's men had fled, to return later with Mounted Police from the town of Bathurst. There'd been another clash, in which the blacks had been shot dead, who included three of the murderers. Two of the other killers had been committed for trial, but because of the usual language difficulties, they'd since been discharged.

Macarthur emphasised that the incident had not involved William Lee, whose general conduct and character was "exemplary in the extreme". A former shepherd, he'd gradually improved himself to the position of being a squatter through hard work. In so doing, he'd earned himself the appellation of "Honest William Lee" throughout the whole Bathurst district. It was unfair, Macarthur argued, for such men to be penalised for incidents in which they did not participate. He agreed with a call by the Bathurst squatters for an amendment to the Squatting Act, under which reports of "delinquencies" or "unfavourable" behaviour by squatters would not be left entirely to Crown Lands Commissioners to rule on. Rather, they would have to be examined by panels of three, five or more "disinterested gentlemen". These panels would make recommendations to the Governor. Macarthur conceded there was no doubt that the Aborigines of New South Wales considered the whites to be "guilty of a gross outrage in taking possession of their country". But he believed the British people had been acting "in accordance with the Divine command to occupy and cultivate the earth". As long as the British settlers treated the blacks with "humanity and Christian mercy", they could not be guilty of any injustice.

Having allowed Macarthur to speak at length on the subject, Gipps gave a forceful response. He told the Council he believed that the squatters had taken up the case to test their strength against his government. But the squatting interest was already becoming too powerful, and he was determined to take "the most firm and determined stand" against it. Two of his duties were stronger and more imperative than any others. One was "protecting the domain of the Crown in trust for the whole Empire, and not for any particular class of individuals". Still more sacred was his duty to "protect the rights of the Aborigines" -- and it was in line with this duty in particular that he had acted in cancelling Lee's licence. He was being accused of having dealt unjustly with an unoffending individual. But Lee, as the licence-holder who employed the men involved in the clashes with the Aborigines, had to take responsibility for them.

The Council, Gipps continued, had not been told the full facts of the case. The Bathurst squatters had made much of sheep and cattle losses which Lee had suffered, without one word of regret about the loss of human lives which had occurred because he'd broken government regulations. Lee's men -- led by an assigned convict -- had in fact taken his stock a distance of about 115 kilometres, into an area from which they knew squatters had been banned for more than a year. The local Crown Lands Commissioner, Francis Allmann, had designated the area to be entirely for the use of the Aborigines, for whom there was barely enough water. Gipps believed that seeing these scant water supplies being consumed by Lee's cattle, the blacks had attacked with that "instinct of self-preservation" which was common to all men. If it was considered noble in the Swiss or the Tyrolese to fight for their beloved mountains, it was without question equally praiseworthy for the Australian Aborigines to fight for the protection of their water-holes. No European had ever drawn a sword in a purer cause.

If it was true that the blacks involved had accompanied Lee's men on their journey to the murder scene, the Governor added, they must have been well acquainted with the power of the whites' superior weapons. They would therefore not have turned on them "without a considerable degree of provocation". Furthermore, according to the circumstances as outlined by Macarthur, the Mounted Police who returned with Lee's men had been "very temperate" in their efforts to apprehend the murderers of the white men. But, Gipps told the Council, the evidence of a corporal showed that the blacks had been "shot and sabred indiscriminately" after the police galloped among them. This had caused the loss of the lives of at least 12 Aborigines, the Governor noted, who he had been entrusted by the British government to protect. It was evident that the whole distressing affair had resulted from the "mismanagement" of employees for whom Lee was morally and legally responsible. It was therefore fair that Lee should have had his licence cancelled.[3]

The squatters and their supporters were even more incensed after Gipps' remarks. The case had shown, the *Sydney Morning Herald* said, that checks needed to be made on the Governor's "far too formidable" power to withhold a squatting licence. Gipps was in effect the lord paramount of an ancient feudal dynasty -- with the licensed graziers of New South Wales little better than slaves. "Twenty thousand human beings, hundreds of thousands of horned cattle, and millions of sheep, are subsisting on a soil from which he can at any moment, without the intervention of Judge or Jury, expel them as trespassers," it bleated. This was "radically and glaringly wrong", the *Herald* declared. It backed the Bathurst squatters' call for special tribunals to consider calls for the cancellation or refusal to renew squatting licences -- based on the testimony of sworn witnesses.

Gipps was attempting to justify his power on the ground that the relationship between the British Crown and the licensed graziers was the same as that between landlord and tenant. But this was not so, the *Herald* argued. A landlord had exclusive rights to certain soil, and in considering its use he was not bound to consider anyone's interest but his own. On the contrary, the Crown was not a proprietor of land in New South Wales, but a *trustee*, on behalf of the society of which the graziers were members. Licences to use the land were given for the mutual benefit of the state and the licence-holders. As trustee, the state was obliged to ensure that this was the case. But before the land of New South Wales could be made advantageous to the British Empire, it had to be made profitable to the white colonists. And for this to occur, the state was entirely dependent on the private industry of individuals. "Private industry is, in short, the only instrument with which the state can work; and it is obviously her interest to see that nothing be done that would blunt its edge, to take every precaution for keeping it in good repair, and for facilitating the whole of its beneficial operations."[4]

The idea of withholding squatting licences as a means of punishment for what the colonial authorities regarded as unacceptable behaviour was not new. In the Port Phillip District, it would be used several times during 1842, even before the resolution of either the Muston's Creek or the William Lee affairs. One Western District squatter who would receive the sanction was Robert Tulloh, who had first earned himself the ridicule of his fellow squatters for dating Fanny Sievwright, and then their ire for accusing their employees of murdering blacks. After the whitewash inquiry by James Blair into the accusations, Gipps would endorse a recommendation from La Trobe that Tulloh be refused renewal of his licence as punishment for having exaggerated.[5] Tulloh would plead for a review of the decision, saying it would reduce him to "a wretched and miserable man". Pointing out that he was only 23 years old, he told La Trobe he'd never been accused of a dishonourable action. He was of good family, his father being not only laird of a small Scottish castle, but also related to the Duchess of Gordon and Sir William Gordon-Cumming of Altyre Castle.

If he had a chance to lay his case before a jury of his countrymen, Tulloh protested, he was sure he could prove himself "honourably not guilty" of any misdemeanour. "What have I done to receive such a sentence?" the squatter asked La Trobe. "Your Honour, you are a father. Place your son in my present situation, banished without a hearing. Fancy the disgrace it will throw on my friends." Tulloh also pointed out that he did not own all the sheep he controlled. Most of them belonged to Augustine Barton, the squatter who'd been the princi-

"Natives chasing game" by Eugene von Guerard. While still able to rely entirely on traditional food sources, Aborigines did not run the risk of being given arsenic-laced food by white men.

pal informant in the Henty poisoning case investigated by Sievwright. If La Trobe would not reconsider the decision to refuse him a new squatting licence, then he asked to be at least given time to dispose of the sheep. Tulloh's appeal had limited effect. La Trobe would give him four months to settle his affairs, but that was as far as he would go. A week later, Gipps in Sydney would write to London, informing the Secretary of State for the Colonies, Lord Stanley, that a further squatting licence would not be given to Tulloh because he'd made "exaggerations of the grossest nature" about the way his fellow whites had been treating the Western District Aborigines.[6]

Two months later, Flogger Fyans would decide to apply the same sanction against a second Western District squatter. Ironically, the squatter involved would be one of those who'd given evidence to help to bring about Tulloh's downfall -- though the decision to act against him would be for an entirely different reason. Fyans would inform La Trobe that Thomas Norris had taken the wife of one William Morgan from Portland to live with him at his station in Bunganditj territory, about 130 kms north of the town. In discussions with Police Magistrate Blair, Fyans had learned to his disgust that Norris had collaborators in absconding with Morgan's wife. "I need not bring to your notice that an occurrence of this nature is most injurious to so young a place," Fyans told La Trobe. The Commissioner had lost no time in telling Norris what he thought of his "disgraceful proceedings" -- and that on the basis of Morgan's complaint of wife-stealing, he would not be renewing the squatter's licence when it came up for renewal a few weeks later.[7]

Blair had already brought La Trobe's attention to the matter the previous month, prompting the Superintendent to suggest to Gipps that Norris' licence be cancelled. But the very day that Fyans would take his action against Norris, Gipps in Sydney would rule that a squatting licence could not be withheld on the ground of mere "impropriety of conduct or immorality", unless it had something to do with holding of the licence. It was a very narrow reading of the Squatting Act, which gave wide powers for licence cancellation for behaviour considered to "endanger the peace and good order of any district". La Trobe would inform Blair and Fyans of the decision, at the same time saying he agreed with Fyans' views on the subject, and would ask the Governor to reconsider. In doing so, La Trobe would point out that Fyans believed Norris' behaviour would have an adverse effect on the morality of the Western District. Still worried that the legality of Fyans' move against Norris could be challenged, Gipps would reluctantly decide to reverse his decision and endorse it.[8]

Then, just as the William Lee affair was being debated in the Legislative Council in Sydney, Gipps would be dismayed to receive a letter from La Trobe informing him that a third Western District squatter -- James Kilgour -- was

going to be blocked from renewing his licence. The decision related to the petition the Scottish squatter had organised, complaining of alleged Aboriginal
depredations. Sievwright, whom the petition accused of aggravating inter-racial
strife in the Western District, had disputed the accuracy of its claims. In a letter
written just three days later, La Trobe drew Fyans' attention to discrepancies
between details in the petition, and those in depositions recorded by George
Robinson after it was sent in. But that was not all. In more than one instance,
La Trobe had been told that Kilgour may have fraudulently added signatures to
the document. La Trobe requested a report from Fyans on whether this was the
case, and whether the petition exaggerated the state of affairs.[9] When there was
no response to a demand for an explanation, Fyans decided that Kilgour was no
longer fit to hold a squatting licence -- a decision endorsed by La Trobe.[10]

The Governor was appalled at the timing of this development, but was as usual
loyal to his subordinate. He told La Trobe that his letter informing him of it did
not "absolutely require an answer" from him. He would therefore simply write
the word "read" on it, which according to official practice indicated tacit
approval. "I think the course of proceeding which you have adopted is right, and
you need not be afraid of my leaving you in the lurch; but if you have read the
late proceedings in Council in respect to the case of Mr Lee of Bathurst, you can
scarcely fail to see, that there is a growing disposition on the part of the squatters to try their strength against the Govt. and that therefore in all we do we must
take care to proceed on sure grounds," Gipps wrote. "Nothing at present would
better suit their purpose, than to be able to get up a plausible case of hardship
inflicted on a squatter by the Govt. I do not mean to turn you from the course
which you have (and in my opinion very properly) adopted; but simply to put
you on your guard, not to give to Dr Kilgour and his neighbours, any advantage
over you."[11]

News that the Kilgour's licence would not be renewed reached his station,
about 40 kilometres south of Mt Rouse, around the time that Sievwright's suspension became effective. With no Aboriginal Protector active in the district for
the first time in more than three years, some of the anger over the government's
decision would be taken out on Kilgour's station against the Gunditjmara
Aborigines. According to John Watton's belated inquiries some weeks later, a
"considerable number" of the blacks would be given what they believed to be
flour by a man named John Lyons. But when they ate the damper they made
from it, they were "immediately seized with burning pains in the throat, excru-
ciating pains in the stomach, vomiting, sinking of the abdomen, and intense
thirst" -- symptoms of arsenic poisoning. The following morning, at least three
men, three women and three children were dead. When Watton arrived at the
scene, he found another woman still seriously ill, whom he took to Mt Rouse for

treatment.

Also implicated in the affair were Kilgour's then overseer, a Scottish highlander named Robertson, and two Irishmen, named Paddy and Jack. Watton discovered that a few months before the incident, Robertson had received from Port Fairy almost one kilogram of arsenic. About a quarter of a kilogram of it was missing. It was believed that the white men implicated, who had all since left Kilgour's employment, could be located in Melbourne. But with characteristic resolve not to become involved in any prosecution, the Chief Protector would casually tell La Trobe more than two months later that although Robertson was willing to give information if required, there was no evidence against him. There was not even any evidence of any Gunditjmaras having been murdered, the bodies of the victims having been burned by their relatives. And no trace of Paddy and Jack been found.[12]

The Gunditjmara people's suspended Protector, meanwhile, was well into the first phase of what would be a long battle for justice. Sievwright had been astonished to learn that his calls for a full and urgent inquiry into the allegations against him were not being addressed. La Trobe had initially told him that the subject had been referred to Gipps for a decision. Raising the matter for a third time, four months after his first request for an inquiry, La Trobe would try to fob Sievwright off by saying that no reply had yet been received from Sydney. Then, during a meeting in Melbourne another month later, the Superintendent had told Sievwright he was not expecting a reply from the Governor on anything to do with his suspension until word had been received from the Secretary of State in London. It was time, Sievwright realised, to start carefully documenting what was happening to him.

"I take the liberty of expressing my complaint of the treatment I have received, and of protesting against the proceedings of the government, as harsh and arbitrary, and in their effects to me and my family, overwhelming and ruinous," he wrote to La Trobe after returning to his Melbourne hotel after their meeting. "Ere the meanest subject in the British dominions, or the lowest soldier in Her Majesty's service, can be punished for imputed misconduct or crime it is, I presume, necessary that he should be brought to trial, his accusers produced, and the opportunity afforded him of rebutting the charges and of vindicating his character. What then must be the feelings of an officer who, for the last 25 years of his life, has had the honour to serve Her Majesty, with a name hitherto unimpeached, on finding himself suspended from his appointment on the mere report of anonymous slanderers -- *rumours* taken against him as *charges*, and conviction following without trial, and dismissed not only unheard, but with contemptuous silence in regard to my request for a Court of Inquiry."

"If these clandestine rumours, thus adopted as charges, were so heinous as to require my immediate dismissal in this summary manner, how, I would take the liberty of asking, is it that the government has permitted an officer against whom they have been in possession of every charge now brought forward against him for several years past, to disgrace their service without inquiry? Especially after I had invited, nay pressed an inquiry, more than three years ago when your Honour first referred to these reports, and your Honour declined to interfere. I have for several months past indulged in the hope held out to me not only by your Honour's correspondence, but personal communication, that my urgent request for an inquiry would be granted; and the ignorance in which I have been kept of the intention of the Government, not only to refuse my application, but to treat it with silence, has prevented me at once from hastening to England, to meet in *due time*, the charges that have been as I am informed, carried home, without any communication of that fact to me.

"I have therefore, Sir, still to demand in the most emphatic terms, justice at your hands. More than five months have been permitted to elapse, since I earnestly solicited, that which I now demand as my right -- a Court of Inquiry, whereby alone the truth or falsehood of the rumours that have reached your Honour can be tested, and the opportunity afforded me of exposing the machinations of those whose names have hitherto been withheld, and in whom your Honour has occasion to feel confidence, as the sources through which your knowledge of the existence of the graver charges, and the manner in which they were brought forward, has been drawn. In conclusion, I beg to intimate my intention of taking the earliest opportunity of transmitting to her Majesty's Secretary of State a knowledge of my present unprecedented position, together with the whole of the correspondence to this date of the Colonial Government on this subject, reserving to myself the privilege of directly addressing His Excellency the Governor upon the subject, as a last resource for obtaining in this country, that justice and impartiality for which His Excellency's administration has hitherto been so conspicuous."[13]

Less than a week later, Sievwright would be writing to La Trobe again, this time over how he was supposed to support his family during his suspension. Since returning to Geelong from their talks in Melbourne, the Assistant Protector had received a note from La Trobe saying he was not entitled to any special salary until his fate was known. Sievwright protested to La Trobe that it was "the common and acknowledged practice" in all British colonies for suspended officials to be paid half salary -- the balance to be paid in the future if and when they were cleared of any wrongdoing. Unless the practice was followed in his case, he and his family would be "left in sudden and utter destitution". This, Sievwright explained, was partly due to the fact that Robinson was withholding his salary and allowances for the two months up to the time of his suspension.[14]

Asked for an explanation, Robinson confirmed that he'd decided to withhold payment of more than 60 pounds due to Sievwright because there were competing claims for the money. Almost a month after Sievwright's suspension took effect, the Mt Rouse overseer, Alexander Davidson, had told him that he was still owed two months' wages, amounting to more than 16 pounds. Robinson told La Trobe he'd then received a letter from the constable at the reserve, Alexander Donaldson. He'd claimed that Sievwright owed him more than nine pounds in wages. Robinson had also investigated claims that Sievwright had been making unauthorised issues to his family from the government stores at Mt Rouse *after* his suspension began. A conservative estimate of the value of the government wheat, flour, meat, tea, sugar, rice and soap consumed by the Sievwrights over two months amounted to 49 pounds.

The wages owed to Davidson and Donaldson, Robinson told La Trobe, had been paid into Sievwright's bank account. These wages and the unauthorised issues together amounted to more than what the government owed Sievwright. In fact, according to the Chief Protector's calculations, his suspended assistant was in debt to the government to the tune of more than 13 pounds. To complicate the matter, Robinson would include copies of the letters from Alexander Davidson and Alexander Donaldson. Davidson's letter alleged that as well as his wages, Sievwright owed him another 20 pounds for supplies he'd given to the Aboriginal reserve -- a water cask, a bullock yoke, and quantities of butter. Donaldson's letter also mentioned that his wife had a private claim for 29 pounds in unpaid wages for her services as a maid to the Assistant Protector's family. Yet Robinson would also include a more recent letter, in which his assistant had told him he'd settled the claims from Davidson and Donaldson, with the exception of the claim for the butter supplies -- for which he denied liability. And Robinson would make no reference to Sievwright having explicitly denied making any unauthorised supplies to anyone at Mt Rouse.[15]

Without seeking Sievwright's response to Robinson's claims, La Trobe would refer them to Gipps, who would deal the suspended Protector another cruel blow. During his suspension, the Governor said, Sievwright could receive no pay unless it was ordered by the Secretary of State for the Colonies, Lord Stanley. It was a matter on which Stanley had not even been asked to rule in the letter informing him of Sievwright's suspension, which was still aboard a ship on its way to London! Gipps added that Sievwright, if he wished, was at liberty to go to England to defend himself "should he think it proper so to do".[16] A week later, Gipps would dismiss Sievwright's claim for salary outstanding. Such salary would normally be paid, the Colonial Secretary wrote to La Trobe. But according to Gipps' interpretation of the correspondence, the Chief Protector had failed to certify that Sievwright had "performed his duty". The Governor could only presume that Robinson had acted justly in deciding that the salary owing should be withheld.[17]

Amid his struggle to gain reinstatement through an inquiry, Sievwright was flabbergasted by Robinson's new claims against him over unsettled accounts, and the willingness of La Trobe and Gipps to accept them without investigation. His rejoinder that he held receipts showing he'd paid the wages due to Davidson and Donaldson was ignored. And the allegation of having misappropriated at least 49 pounds worth of government stores for the use of his family was completely unjust. When he'd left Mt Rouse to go to Melbourne to try to defend himself, Sievwright had left behind at the reserve goods of his own worth much more than that. It was these goods which had been issued to his family -- not the government's. But beyond the overall denial that anyone had received unauthorised handouts, Sievwright could not yet take the matter any further. No-one had even told him the extent to which Robinson had alleged he'd thieved government property.

With the allegation of misappropriation still unresolved, La Trobe told Sievwright he should move from Mt Rouse. Now without an income for seven months, the suspended Protector would decide to move his family back to Geelong, where his eldest children at least might have a chance of picking up some casual work. Fanny was now 19, Marcus 16, and Charles 14. The twins, Frederica and Melita, were about to turn 13, Georgina was nine, and Falkland was eight. To transport the family and their belongings over a distance of about 190 kilometres, a bullock dray was needed. Sievwright rode to the squatters around Mt Rouse, but could find no-one willing to loan him the use of a dray. Some were willing to hire one to him, but he could not afford the fees they wanted.

In desperation, he wrote to La Trobe, requesting permission to borrow one of the drays used to bring supplies to the Aboriginal reserve from Port Fairy. Marcus would ride to Melbourne to personally deliver the letter, only to be told by La Trobe that it was quite out of his power to accede to the request.[18] Sievwright was thus forced to hire a dray by dipping into scant and rapidly dwindling funds which he'd hoped to save for food. It was with heavy heart that the Assistant Protector loaded the dray, then went around shaking the hands of the Aborigines in the Mt Rouse camp, wondering if he'd be returning to live with them. And he cursed his inability to even attempt to explain to them why he'd suddenly stopped conducting the affairs of the camp a few months earlier, and was now going away.

The same frustrating language difficulty would present itself as Sievwright met other groups of Aborigines known to him as he passed through Kirrae, Colijon and Barrabool territory on the way back to resume residence in the family's old hut near the rapids on the Barwon River just outside Geelong. It was almost four years since they'd started living at the spot in tents, their first home in the bush after leaving Melbourne. Again, they would be joined by some of the Barrabools -- including Mumbowran, the young man who had escaped from custody by jumping overboard in the Yarra two years earlier. While Fanny amused herself by compiling a list of tribe members, and some Barrabool words and expressions, her "kolorneen" (sad) "peet-ya-rik" (father) could only hope that "burra-burra" (by and by) he'd be able to lift the family out of the quagmire into which it had plunged.[19]

CHAPTER 30
To rags

A LTHOUGH the British Empire in 1843 was well short of its eventual
zenith, those charged with its management still had an enormous responsibility. Decisions made in London would affect the lives of millions of
people across the world. However, there was only so much that could be done
from London. Great faith had to be placed in the administrative competence of
those in charge of each British colony or "possession" -- unless clear patterns
emerged that this faith was ill-deserved. Correspondence between London and
Sydney showed that through successive Secretaries of State for the Colonies,
confidence was maintained in the abilities of George Gipps and his underlings
to administer New South Wales. And when the Secretary of State was an auto-
crat like Lord Stanley, the chances were slim indeed that lengthy consideration
would be given to a recommendation from Gipps about the need for disciplinary
action against a single servant of the Empire.

Even before Stanley learned of Sievwright's suspension, he'd made harsh
judgements about him, based on reports of his behaviour from Robinson and La
Trobe. These reports, tainted by malice and deception, had been among a mass
of material relating to the Aborigines recently sent on to London by Gipps.
Included was the letter from La Trobe in which he'd declared the efforts of the
Protectorate in the Western District to be a complete failure -- largely because of
Sievwright. It was this letter in which the Superintendent had accused the
Assistant Protector of having "seriously aggravated" the existing danger by
gathering a large number of blacks over whom he had neither physical nor moral
control. The settlers in the vicinity first of Keilambete, and then at Mt Rouse,
had been the victims of robberies and aggression. Further, La Trobe had accused
Sievwright of having a demeanour of "defiance" towards the settlers, rather than
conciliation.[1]

Stanley would accept La Trobe's description of Sievwright's actions without
verification, and was quick to condemn the Assistant Protector. "The practice of
collecting large bodies of natives in one spot, and in the immediate vicinity of
the settlers, without any previous provision for their subsistence or employment,
was a proceeding of singular indiscretion," the Secretary of State concluded.
"That these people would commit depredations rather than suffer want, and that
thus ill blood and probably collisions would be caused between them and the

settlers, must, I should have thought, have occurred to any man of common observation, and no-one could have better reason than Mr Sievwright to know his utter inability to control them." Stanley told Gipps that in such circumstances, he was not surprised at the Governor's opinion that the measures of the Protectors had tended "rather to increase than allay the irritation which has long existed between the two races".[2]

When a letter arrived from Gipps three months later, informing Stanley of Sievwright's suspension, the reply was curt. "I have to convey to you my approval of Mr Sievwright's removal from office, and of the appointment of Mr Watton to the vacancy," was the Secretary of State's hasty decision. Stanley's only concern: that Gipps had waited several months before writing to inform him of the suspension. "I notice this delay in order that it may be avoided on future occasions," he commented.[3] Stanley saw no need to investigate any of the claims against Sievwright. He did not even question the fact that Gipps or La Trobe had been in possession of the most serious claims against the Assistant Protector for almost four crucial years on the New South Wales frontier, without having done anything about them. And Stanley obviously believed Gipps' fallacious assertion that Sievwright had done nothing to try to disprove the aspersions against him.

It would be some weeks before Stanley would receive a copy of the lengthy letter which Sievwright had written after hearing of his suspension, denying or dismissing the allegations against him one-by-one. Gipps had received the letter just after sending notification of the Assistant Protector's suspension to Stanley. The Governor would decide that it constituted an adequate "defence" and there was no need to comply with Sievwright's demand for an inquiry at which his accusers could be revealed, and the reliability of their claims examined. But the Governor did not dispatch the so-called defence letter urgently, so it could be considered alongside the statements against Sievwright. By the time it got to London, Stanley's letter approving of Sievwright's dismissal was already on a ship well on its way back to Australia. Not only had Sievwright's call for an inquiry been ignored, his "defence" had not even been considered.

To compound the injustice, Gipps had done his best to undermine Sievwright's credibility before belatedly sending on his "defence" letter. With the letter, the Governor would send a range of statements which La Trobe had provided -- including some from Robinson, Fyans and Lonsdale, refuting or at least calling in to question many of the statements Sievwright had made. No opportunity whatsoever had been offered to the accused man for denial, counter-accusation, or explanation. Gipps would also send to Stanley the statements which La Trobe had received from Christina and Fanny Sievwright, denying impropriety by the Assistant Protector. But the Governor would try to undermine even these.

Despite the different styles of expression, Gipps would state that in his view, they bore "internal evidence of having been written under Mr Sievwright's dictation". And Robinson, Fyans and Lonsdale were "persons of unquestioned credit". When Christina and Fanny's letters were contrasted with theirs, they added little to Sievwright's defence, Gipps told Stanley.[4]

In any event, the Secretary of State was not about to change his mind about the Sievwright case. Having made his decision, Stanley was determined to stick to it. He would be unmoved by Sievwright's "defence". On the scale of things, it was a minor matter to Stanley for one official in one colony to be claiming to have been unfairly treated in being suspended. Besides, he did not want the matter to be too closely scrutinised. "I should wish, if possible, to avoid pursuing this affair further, as it is not of a character fit for public investigation", Stanley would tell Gipps. It would, of course, be exactly what the Governor had hoped to hear from the Secretary of State. The Governor, too, did not want the matter to be prolonged by an inquiry, lest his own actions -- or those of his administration -- should come into question.[5]

Back in Australia, Sievwright was still expecting an inquiry into his suspension. It would still be months before he would hear that he had been sacked, without an inquiry. As he waited for that news, he and his family's circumstances became increasingly tragic, as they slipped further into poverty. A small alleviation in the family's plight would come as the result of a letter to La Trobe from Geelong, signed by a man calling himself Frederic Nesbitt. It is possible that, ironically, the letter had in fact been written by the man regarded as the best actor of tragedy plays in the Australian colonies. Francis Nesbitt McCrone, an Englishman, had just spent his first year in the colony performing in Sydney, playing Othello, Shylock, Richard III, William Tell, and others.

Francis Nesbitt, as he called himself on stage, had been on a brief visit to Melbourne at the time the letter was written to La Trobe about the Sievwrights, trying to expand his fame by convincing the management of the Royal Victoria Theatre to hire him for a few performances for a substantial fee. Unsuccessful in his efforts because his fee was regarded as too high, the "great tragedician of the Sydney boards" could have made a side-trip to Geelong before he moved on, and could have gone exploring up to the Barwon River rapids. In any event, whether he was the actor or someone else, the writer had been moved "by feelings of the deepest commiseration" to see the "heart-rendering position of a talented virtuous family" resulting from Sievwright's suspension. The youngest six children were "without shoes and otherwise slightly clothed", Nesbitt told the Superintendent. He implored La Trobe to assist the Sievwrights, either directly or indirectly, to stop them from starvation until they could obtain assistance from their friends back in Britain.

"Mr Sievwright's situation precluded him from making friends among the white population," Nesbitt wrote. "Therefore, they are now suffering the penalty of having done their duty to the Aborigines." He'd heard examples of Christina and Fanny's musical and linguistic abilities, and he was impressed. They were, he observed, "highly accomplished in vocal and instrumental music, Italian and French languages etc. etc.". They'd been unsuccessful in trying to find work in Geelong, but perhaps La Trobe could help find them employment as tutors in Melbourne. "As to Mr Sievwright's conduct, that will I doubt not be ultimately proven to have been correct in the graver charges," Nesbitt added. But this at present was irrelevant. Common sympathy necessitated urgent assistance for the family. "I as a stranger to you beg and pray you may not allow one day to pass without, as a Christian, inquiring in what manner you can assist them," he told La Trobe. "I beg to state their case is I think unprecedented."[6]

Strangely unaware whether Nesbitt's description was accurate, La Trobe would send his letter to Police Magistrate Nicholas Fenwick in Geelong asking him to investigate, while taking care "not to excite attention". Fenwick would report that after having made "every inquiry at the Public Houses and elsewhere" in the settlement, he'd found no-one who knew of Nesbitt. But the letter had not exaggerated. "As to the actual state of Mr Sievwright's family, as described in Mr Nesbitt's letter, I have every reason to think that the picture is not overdrawn, and that they really are in the greatest state of destitution," Fenwick reported. "Nobody here it appears will give them anything on credit now that Mr Sievwright has been suspended, and how they manage to get their daily bread, nobody can tell, and their children are in rags."[7] Reporting Nesbitt's letter and Fenwick's report to Gipps, La Trobe said he was not aware whether it was in the Governor's power to render the family any assistance.[8]

Having been made aware of the destitution of Sievwright's family, Gipps could not totally ignore it. Besides, the Governor possibly felt a twinge of guilt over the matter -- realising of course that he'd notified his superior in London of Sievwright's suspension without having given the Assistant Protector a chance to defend himself. Gipps would send La Trobe 10 pounds of his own money, which was to be given to the Sievwrights "without saying from whence it comes". At the same time, Gipps told La Trobe he was considering whether anything could be given to the family "out of the public funds". Less than a fortnight later, the Governor would decide that this was not possible.[9]

Without telling Sievwright, La Trobe would arrange for Fenwick to give the 10 pounds from Gipps to Christina in instalments of 10 shillings a week. The *weekly* sum was less than half of what the family income had been on an average *daily* basis, but with Sievwright's salary and allowances stopped, it was better than nothing. It was enough to buy a loaf of bread a day. Fearing that her husband could allow personal pride to interfere with the arrangement, a desperate Christina did not inform him of it. She would receive the first instalment through Fenwick soon after Sievwright was required to cross Port Phillip Bay on the *Aphrasia* to Melbourne to give information leading up to another sensational trial in which he would be a prominent figure. This one would be the most sensational of all. The Western District Aborigines were claimed to have often taunted the whites with threats along the lines of: "You touch black fellow, Mr Sievwright hang you."[10] Finally, it appeared that such a threat may have some basis. For the first time in the Port Phillip District, white men were facing the possibility of being hanged for murdering Aborigines.

One of the whites present at the time of the slaughter of the black women and child at Muston's Creek had finally decided that the lure of the reward for information was too great to resist. Christopher McGuinness, a bush carpenter, had confessed to Robinson that he knew who was involved. The Chief Protector had passed on the information, and three men had now been arrested. In statements at the Police Office in Melbourne, McGuinness gave evidence against station manager Richard Guiness Hill, hutkeeper Joseph Betts, and labourer John Beswicke -- two of whom had denied involvement in statements sworn before Sievwright. According to McGuinness, the three had been among a party of six white men who'd ridden off from the station together on the day of the murders. Betts, who'd claimed he was planning to shoot kangaroos, had a brace of pistols in his belt, plus a gun loaded with ball.

Wanting a kangaroo skin, McGuinness swore he'd followed the party to a small gully with tea-tree scrub not far from the head station. Two shots were fired by Joseph Betts, and he saw two unarmed blacks run out of the trees. Then he heard four more shots, but he could not see who'd fired them. He'd returned to the station huts without investigating. Soon afterwards, the party had returned and gone into the hut used by the squatters, Thomas Osbrey and Sydney Smith. The white men had been carrying boomerangs, leanguils and shields. That night, Betts had stated that some black women and a child had been shot dead. He'd been too frightened to immediately inspect the scene, McGuinness said, in case there were other Aborigines around. But the following day he'd passed the spot where the shooting occurred. He'd seen three blacks who were "apparently dead", although he'd not gone close enough to examine them.[11]

Acting on the information from McGuinness, Fyans had apprehended Osbrey, who confessed that he'd been falsely claiming to know nothing of the affair. The squatter confirmed much of what McGuinness had deposed. Osbrey gave the names of three others involved: fellow squatters Charles Smith and Robert Whitehead, and Richard Hill's cousin, Arthur D. Boursiquot. These three, along with Hill and Betts, had ridden off with all the available firearms after Betts reported that "a mob of blacks" was close by. "I saw or heard nothing further until they returned in about an hour," Osbrey stated. "They brought with them some of the arms which belonged to the natives. They talked together of what they had done. On remonstrating with them on the impropriety and danger of what they had committed, they made light of it, but threatened one and all to shoot any person who dared to give any information against them, which I considered a threat to myself, and the same language was frequently repeated to me; and I was on one occasion asked by Charles Smith, would I swear that Whitehead was not in my hut on the day the blacks were shot, which I refused to do." The threats against him, Osbrey explained, meant that if he'd revealed what he knew when Sievwright had arrived to investigate the murders, he would have had to have abandoned his station, as he'd now been forced to do.[12]

Despite the statement by Osbrey, only Hill, Beswicke and Betts would be charged over the murders. The start of their trial would be delayed by moves to rid New South Wales of another troublesome employee of the British government whose behaviour was bringing it into ill-repute: Judge Willis. As a result of his erratic and intemperate behaviour, Willis had made himself extremely unpopular with many residents of Melbourne, and had provoked memorials for him to be amoved. Crown Prosecutor Croke would be among "nearly all the Officers of any consideration" in the Port Phillip District who signed one memorial. Many people would also sign a counter-petition expressing *support* for the Willis. But Gipps would conclude that the overwhelming weight of opinion was against the judge. Willis, the Governor would later tell Stanley, was not capable of "the calm and dispassionate administration of justice". Melbourne, he declared, had been "kept in a state of continued excitement" by Willis' proceedings, and "the extraordinary nature of the harangues" he'd been in the habit of delivering from the bench.[13]

One such public "harangue" from the judge had directly concerned the Muston's Creek murders, and the colonial administration's efforts to detect and put on trial those responsible. Gipps told Stanley that Willis had openly accused the government "of partiality in pursuing to Justice the perpetrators of crimes committed on the Aborigines, and allowing those committed by them to pass with impunity". This, the Governor feared, could only be explained by a desire by the judge to gain popularity in the Port Phillip District "by encouraging the vilest and most inhuman passions of the dispersed occupiers of Crown Lands". Some of the Aboriginal Protectors were among those who had called for Willis' amoval, the Governor pointed out.[14] Robinson had told La Trobe that because of Willis' comments over the Muston's Creek case, he could no longer have confidence in the judge's administration of justice, at least as far as the Port Phillip Aborigines were concerned.[15]

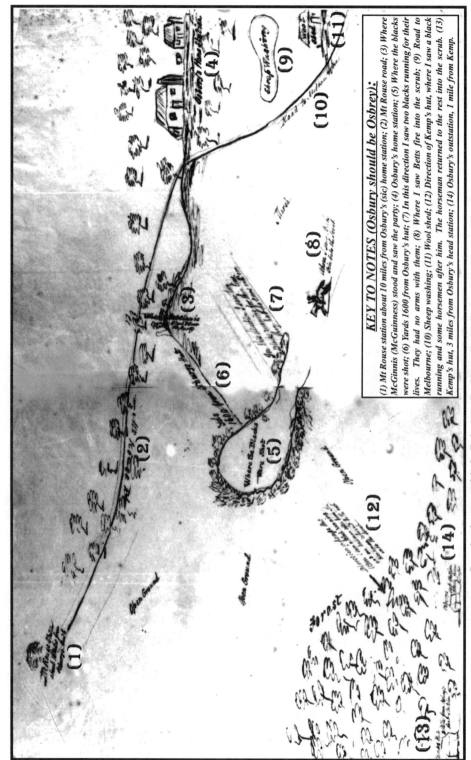

KEY TO NOTES (Osbury should be Osbrey):-

(1) Mt Rouse station about 10 miles from Osbury's (sic) home station; (2) Mt Rouse road; (3) Where McGinnis (McGuinness) stood and saw the party; (4) Osbury's home station; (5) Where the blacks were shot; (6) Yards 1600 from Osbury's hut; (7) In this direction I saw two blacks running for their lives. They had no arms with them; (8) Where I saw Betts fire into the scrub; (9) Road to Melbourne; (10) Sheep washing; (11) Wool shed; (12) Direction of Kemp's hut, where I saw a black running and some horsemen after him. The horseman returned to the rest into the scrub. (13) Kemp's hut, 3 miles from Osbury's head station; (14) Osbury's outstation, 1 mile from Kemp.

Reproduced courtesy of the La Trobe Australian Manuscripts Collection, State Library of Victoria

A sketch of the Muston's Creek murder site, by Assistant Protector William Thomas, prepared after confessions by Christopher McGuinness

   The Muston's Creek trial would eventually go ahead during the first session for Port Phillip's new Resident Supreme Court judge, Irishman William Jeffcott, appointed to replace Willis. The first witness for the prosecution would be Charles Sievwright, who would feel a strange mixture of sadness and pride. Until the mail arrived from London with word that he'd been dismissed, Sievwright was still an Assistant Protector of Aborigines -- and it was as such that he would give evidence. More than four years had passed since his first unsuccessful attempt to have a murder trial in Melbourne over the killing of Western District Aborigines. Here at last he was giving evidence in such a trial. He would undergo rigorous cross-examination on the wounds on the decomposing body of one of the women killed, Coneyer. One defence counsel, beaknosed Scottish barrister Archibald Cunninghame, would make him admit that he could not swear for certain that the wound to Coneyer's abdomen had not been inflicted by an unbarbed spear, rather than a gunshot. Then Colonial Surgeon Patrick Cussen would further weaken the prosecution case when he told the court that from Sievwright's evidence, it would be almost impossible for him to conclude that Coneyer's wounds had been inflicted by a gun.

   In his statements at the Melbourne Police Office, McGuinness had admitted seeing Betts fire at something at the murder scene. In his evidence before the court, however, he went further: he believed Betts had shot an Aboriginal woman. That is, he'd seen a black fall when Betts fired, and judging from the shriek, it had been a woman. Osbrey, as another Crown witness, would tell the court that only Hill and Betts were among the armed men who set out from the station on the day of the murders. Beswicke, who worked for Robert Whitehead, hadn't even been at the station on the day. Another of Osbrey's former labourers, George Arabin, would contradict this part of his master's testimony -- agreeing with McGuinness that the three prisoners, and three others, were among the party which had ridden off, purportedly to shoot kangaroos. But Betts was the only one he knew had been armed, because he'd loaned a loaded gun to him. He'd heard shots fired, before the party returned to the station with some Aboriginal weapons. The gun he'd lent to Betts was no longer loaded. When Sievwright had visited the station to inquire into the affair, he'd kept his silence because he'd been afraid of Hill. With this statement from Arabin, the case for the prosecution closed at 11 o'clock at night.

   When the court re-opened the following morning, the defence would produce witnesses who depicted McGuinness, a former convict, as a constantly drunk and disorderly man whose statements under oath couldn't be believed. Archibald Cunninghame would also produce two witnesses who swore that Beswicke had been at Whitehead's station at the time of the murders. One witness to provide an alibi was James Brock, whose brother worked in Whitehead's

drapery store in Melbourne, and on whose evidence Roger had gone to the gallows. In Beswicke's case, the jury was left with the choice of believing Osbrey
and the two alibi-providers that he was not at the scene -- or McGuinness and
Arabin. They would choose the former. Having chosen to believe the evidence
presented on Beswicke's behalf, the jury obviously had to have doubts about
what McGuinness and Arabin had sworn in relation to the other two defendants
as well. Further suspicion was raised about the accuracy of their testimony
when discrepancies were pointed out between their statements at the Police
Office, and their evidence in court. Suggestions were also made that
McGuinness had tried to increase the chances of receiving the reward being
offered for a conviction by meeting Arabin before and even during the trial to
try to corroborate their evidence.

As Judge Jeffcott commenced his summing up of the case to the jury, the foreman rose and said it had already agreed on a verdict: not guilty. Jeffcott would
later tell La Trobe he believed that Hill, Betts and the other parties named by
Osbrey as having been at his station on the day of the murder had been involved
in the "atrocious affair". But the "gross contradictions" in McGuinness' evidence, his attempts to make the case one of direct proof instead of circumstantial, along with his bad character, had thrown such discredit on the case as to
make the jury "fully justified" in rejecting a guilty verdict. The judge made no
suggestion that the case could be re-opened, and no comment on why, for
instance, Osbrey should not have at least been charged with being an accessory
after the fact, instead of being made a Crown witness. Nor was any comment
made on why charges had not been pursued against the other men who'd been
implicated by Osbrey -- squatters Charles Smith and Robert Whitehead, and
Richard Hill's cousin, Arthur Boursiquot. At Robinson's suggestion, Arabin and
McGuinness would later receive 50 pounds between them from the colonial
government to help them join the culprits in leaving the Port Phillip District.[16]

Thus, what could have been a triumph for Sievwright before he learned he'd
been dismissed as an Aboriginal Protector turned out to be a disaster. Like
Jeffcott, he was convinced of the guilt of at least Hill and Betts, but he was hardly in a position to be pursuing the case. He was embroiled in an increasingly bitter battle for survival for himself and his family. Robinson had recently upped
the ante by accusing Sievwright of even greater misappropriation of government
stores at Mt Rouse than previously believed. Initially, the Chief Protector had
estimated that Sievwright had taken at least 49 pounds worth of government
goods at Mt Rouse for unauthorised use by his family. Using information provided by John Watton, Robinson had now calculated the figure at more than 132
pounds worth of goods during 1842. "From all the information I have received,
there is strong reason to suppose that like misappropriations of provisions have

been made anterior to 1842...especially at Lake Terang," Robinson told La Trobe, without offering any evidence to back the aspersion.

Furthermore, Robinson complained, Sievwright had ignored repeated requests to hand over books relating to his administration of government stores at Mt Rouse. La Trobe could have granted Sievwright's request for an inquiry into his dismissal, with terms of reference that covered the alleged theft of government property. Instead, he chose to get the Crown Solicitor, Henry Field Gurner, to write to the Assistant Protector demanding that he give the books to Robinson -- with the obvious inferred threat of legal action if he refused. Amazingly, Gurner would write the letter requested by La Trobe, but not post it. It would only be presented when Sievwright called at the Crown Solicitor's office several weeks later, having heard of the letter from Robinson. Within hours, the Mt Rouse accounts were in the hands of a Melbourne accountant, Archibald McLachlan. After a process lasting more than a month, during which McLachlan would have to consult Sievwright for certain explanations of the figures, they would be forwarded to the Chief Protector.[17]

According to McLachlan's calculations, 32 pounds worth of Sievwright's personal property had been used for official purposes. Some had been in the form of rations given by his overseer to the Aborigines, and some to pay some sawyers who'd cut some timber for the station. There were also receipts from John Watton for taking over personal supplies of timber, wheat, tea and sugar, with a total value of 26 pounds. Thus, Sievwright was *owed* 58 pounds by the government, in addition to two months' pay and allowances still being withheld. Confident that his accounts would show no wrong-doing, Sievwright wrote to La Trobe telling him they'd now been provided to Robinson. His family, Sievwright pointed out, was in "extreme" need of the money owed to him. It had now been almost a year since the family had been deprived "of all means of subsistence", and he hoped La Trobe wouldn't allow their suffering to be unnecessarily prolonged.[18]

Receiving no reply, Sievwright would write to La Trobe again two weeks later, enclosing a copy of his earlier letter. The fact that he was now without the means of procuring food for his children should be "sufficient apology" for repeating his request for immediate payment of the money due to him.[19] This time, La Trobe would send a reply, accusing Sievwright of having impeded the settlement of the Mt Rouse accounts up to the period when he was suspended. In handing over charge of the Mt Rouse station to John Watton, La Trobe alleged, Sievwright had failed to give an account of the manner in which the large quantity of stores under his charge had been used. He'd also taken away the overseer's account book containing details of the receipt and spending of the stores. Under the circumstances, the Superintendent remarked, the claim he was now making against the government was "extraordinary".

The outburst from La Trobe would prompt a lengthy and spirited defence from Sievwright, with copies of 11 enclosures to back his claim that the accusations were quite unwarranted. Throughout his time as an Assistant Protector, Sievwright pointed out, he'd kept accounts on the prescribed printed forms provided by Robinson. These accounts, remitted in duplicate every month to the Chief Protector, had outlined the daily and cumulative monthly use of the stores under his control. As well, they'd stated the amount of stores on hand on the last day of every month. They'd been provided up to the last day of August 1842 -- the last full month in which he'd been in control at Mt Rouse. "My monthly accounts have invariably been passed, not only without any required explanation, but have been referred to by the Chief Protector in terms of courtesy and approbation," Sievwright told La Trobe. It was true that the store book kept by overseer Davidson hadn't been handed over to Robinson. But this was because it was the only document in Sievwright's possession which had details of the *private* as well as public stores which had been at the station. This book had been needed for his accountant to calculate what he was owed by the government.

It was mysterious, Sievwright added, that Robinson had claimed to have made "repeated applications" for him to hand over the accounts and other documents relating to Mt Rouse finances. The enclosures he was now sending to La Trobe included copies of all letters received from the Chief Protector in relation to the matter. La Trobe could see that no such "repeated applications" had been made. It wasn't likely, Sievwright pointed out, that he would refuse to help any measure which could result in settlement of his claims against the government, and thus relieve his suffering family. A "still more paramount consideration" was to remove the "vile allegations" against him about the accounts, which had been "so pertinaciously adhered to" by Robinson despite Sievwright's denials, and then readily propogated by La Trobe. "In conclusion, I would most respectfully state that whatever may be the impression your Honour may have received from those, or any other statements made to you concerning me, I can but reiterate the prayer (that has hitherto been unheeded by your Honour and the Government) for investigation, and the 'severest scrutiny' on any part of my conduct as a private individual, or as a public servant, which your Honour may now think fit to institute," Sievwright concluded.[20]

A month later, Sievwright would again be writing to La Trobe defending himself over the Mt Rouse accounts. Yet another allegation had been made by Robinson, after he'd perused the overseer's store book. The Chief Protector had accused Sievwright of having used government stores to pay his two Crown prisoners for almost two years. During this period, Robinson claimed, he'd been receiving a cash allowance to pay them. The sum he now calculated his assistant owed the government was 123 pounds.[21] Sievwright was outraged by the allegation. "I cannot but feel that the conduct and proceedings of the Chief Protector are now...malevolent and personal," he told La Trobe. He called again for the speedy appointment of a board of inquiry which he believed the Superintendent had indicated he was prepared to set up to investigate this allegation and others. He was confident that he would be vindicated, and that the justness of his claims against the government would be upheld.[22]

To La Trobe's relief, the word from London for which he'd been stalling would finally arrive before he had to make a decision on Sievwright's renewed request for an inquiry. The Superintendent would receive a copy of the letter from Stanley to Gipps, approving of Sievwright's dismissal, and saying the case was not fit for public investigation.[23] Informed of the contents of Stanley's letter, Sievwright was incredulous. He would have been even more so, had he known Stanley had made his judgement before the arrival of his so-called defence letter. Wrongly assuming that this letter had been taken into account, Sievwright asked whether a 60 word response really purported to be the final word from the Secretary of State on his case. Did it mean that Stanley was denying him the inquiry which he'd been earnestly seeking, deciding to entirely rely on his so-called letter of defence to make his judgement? And what of his claim for half-salary during the period of his suspension? Would that now be paid? It suited La Trobe, of course, for the matter to be officially declared over -- and he decided it was worth an unpublicised ride down to Geelong to try to persuade the former Protector to quietly accept his fate. But yet another misfortune had just been added to the series which had struck Sievwright, and he was in no mood to capitulate.

Within weeks of the end of the Muston's Creek trial, Sievwright had found himself again in court on a matter relating to his duties as an Aboriginal Protector. This time, the case in the Court of Requests in Geelong arose from an administrative bungle by Robinson back in 1841. Just before the Chief Protector had set off on his tour of the Western District early that year, he'd told Sievwright he'd arranged for a consignment of flour to be sent from Melbourne to Geelong. On Robinson's instructions, Sievwright's dray driver had gone all the way from Keilambete to the merchant in Geelong to whom the flour had supposedly been delivered, Frederick Champion, only to be told it was not there. Champion had refused to accept the flour, and it had been taken to the store of another Geelong merchant, Charles Ruffle, where it had been stored for months before it had finally been delivered to Terang on Sievwright's dray. Ruffle was now claiming payment for storage of the flour, and cartage of it from Champion's store to his own. Sievwright had referred Ruffle to Robinson, but the merchant wasn't willing to wait any longer for the slow bureaucratic wheels to turn. He wanted his

From "The Chronicles of Early Melbourne"

Scenes of Melbourne in 1844, the year in which two boards of inquiry would investigate Sievwright's outstanding financial claims against the New South Wales government. The scene above shows Batman's Hill, from the south-east bank of the Yarra River. The scene below shows "Melbourne from the falls". Although Sievwright was suspended in 1842, La Trobe and Gipps had resisted his repeated calls for an investigation into his financial claims throughout 1843. At the end of 1844, Sievwright would still be demanding a more wide-ranging inquiry into the real reasons for his suspension.

payment immediately, and had now won a judgement against Sievwright -- as the apparent agent in Geelong of the Protectorate, even though he'd been suspended.

The judgement against him, Sievwright told La Trobe, would leave his family even more impoverished, at a time when the government had left it with no support whatsoever. Then to his severe embarrassment, the strength of his argument would be weakened when he learned from the Superintendent about the small payments Christina had been surreptitiously receiving through Fenwick for the previous 24 weeks.[24] He'd been denying reports of continuing disharmony in his family, saying he and his wife had been reconciled. At the same time, he'd been saying his family was destitute, and that he'd been forced to sell their few possessions to buy food. On his return home after the meeting with La Trobe, Sievwright would angrily demand that Christina write to the Superintendent explaining why she'd not mentioned the payments to him. When the payments unexpectedly began, she would tell La Trobe, she'd been so desperate that she was considering making a public appeal for help. With her children asking for bread, she could not afford to risk the payments being stopped by Sievwright's pride, so she'd decided it was best just not to tell him.[25]

Just two days later, Sievwright himself would write to La Trobe, giving more details of the consequences of the recent judgement against him in the Court of Requests. The bailiff had been to his residence and had seized some of the family's last remaining personal property -- to the value of ten times the amount for which Robinson had so far refused to admit liability, plus court costs. "I have been compelled to bring these circumstances under the notice of your Honour, to show, to what my family has been reduced, by another unjust and arbitrary act of the Chief Protector towards us," Sievwright wrote. "A portion of the suffering of my family have been made known to your Honour, but the startling facts which I cannot longer withhold, that I and my children have not now for ten days tasted either flour or meat, which wretchedness might have been avoided, had my property (thus sacrificed) been left to me for their support, will be sufficient to obtain for us, that consideration and redress which simple justice demands."[26]

At last, La Trobe would give in, appointing a three-man board of inquiry to look into the unsettled accounts between Sievwright and the government. One member would be Fenwick. There would also be former Royal Navy lieutenant and fellow magistrate, Edward Brown Addis, and former Melbourne merchant, Alfred John Eyre, now Clerk to the Bench at Geelong. Fenwick, Addis and Eyre would be asked to investigate not only the actual state of the accounts, but also the reasons why they remained unsettled, well over a year after Sievwright's suspension.[27] The implication was that the matter should have been settled long ago, but still the board didn't move quickly enough for Sievwright. Before it would report to La Trobe, he would send the Superintendent another poignant letter.

This time, he requested that Gipps be informed of "the state of suffering and destitution" to which he and his family had been reduced by the measures adopted against him by the government. "When it pleased His Excellency suddenly, and at once, to suspend me from my office of Assistant Protector, I was left without the means of supplying the daily wants of my family," Sievwright wrote. But for "the trifling personal property" he had at hand to use for the family's support, they would have starved. But this property was now exhausted. Optimistically, Sievwright would repeat his request for half-salary during the period of his suspension, again claiming this was the customary practice in British colonies. Such a salary was particularly necessary in a place like Port Phillip, with the family deprived for so long of a source of income. Nor had there been any financial help from family or friends in Britain.

"However expedient the extraordinary measures adopted towards me may have appeared to the Government, it cannot, I feel assured, be the wish of His Excellency to reduce to beggary and unmerited disgrace, the family of an old officer, who until now has held an honourable, and I may be permitted to add, a distinguished position in society," Sievwright wrote. "It is now essential that I proceed to England to restore to my family what they have been deprived of, and to endeavour to leave them, at least, the inheritance of a good name. To be enabled to do so, and in the meantime, that I may not be compelled to leave them to the charitable consideration of private friendship, nor be subjected in my own person to the indignity of being obliged to accept even of menial employment on board, so that I secure a passage to England, I deem it my duty to my family, myself and to His Excellency to thus make a valedictory appeal to the Government previously to being compelled to resort to those painful, though imperative measures, which are as foreign to my consent as under the circumstances they might become derogatory to His Excellency's administration."[28] The veiled threat to bring Gipps' administration into disrepute did not faze the Governor. "He cannot but feel compassion for the distress into which he is well aware that the family of Mr Sievwright has fallen, but His Excellency regrets that he is not at liberty to allow his official acts to be influenced by such considerations," was his response.[29]

A few days later, Fenwick, Addis and Eyre would begin their inquiry. The board would conclude that Sievwright had himself to blame, in part, for the delay in settling the Mt Rouse accounts. This was because of his "highly inconsiderate" decision to take away the store book when he'd moved back to Geelong. The board would also criticise Sievwright's "highly irregular system" of having allowed his private stores at Mt Rouse to be mixed with those of the government. According to Alexander Davidson, there had been no distinction between the property of the government, and that of the Assistant Protector, when supplies had been issued at the station to the blacks and whites. But the fault was not all Sievwright's. The board was also critical of the "very imperfect manner" in which Davidson had kept the accounts in the store book. This had made it a matter of considerable difficulty, if not altogether impossible, to clearly determine the state of the accounts.

Despite this difficulty, the board told La Trobe it had concluded that one of Davidson's entries in the store book was quite wrong. This related to the delivery of more than 700 kilos of flour, 160 kilos of sugar and 36 kilos of tea to Terang in January 1842 -- just before the whole camp made its amazing move to Mt Rouse. The overseer had entered these in the book as "government stores", but the board believed they had in fact been Sievwright's. At the time, the Protector had made no recent requisition for stores to Robinson, and he'd been able to prove to the board that he'd made a recent purchase of similar quantities of stores to those delivered at Terang. "Consequently, the supplies charged to Mr Sievwright as having been issued to his family in 1842 appear to have been his own private property," the report concluded. On the question of the goods to the value of 58 pounds which Sievwright claimed to have loaned to the government, the board had been unable to reach a conclusion. But Robinson had stated that Sievwright's monthly accounts had been correct. "We may mention also that nothing has come under our notice which would warrant us in attributing to Mr Sievwright any charge of misappropriation of Government Stores," it added.[30]

It was enough to convince La Trobe that Sievwright should at last be paid the 61 pounds in salary and allowances due to him 18 months earlier. But the claim for the further 58 pounds would have to wait. After Robinson admitted he, too, was unable to form an opinion whether the claim should be allowed, La Trobe told Sievwright the matter would have to be referred to Gipps for a decision.[31] The Governor's reply was brief. He approved of Sievwright being paid his outstanding salary and allowances. But he wouldn't entertain the claim for 58 pounds. "His Excellency regrets he can see nothing in the report of the Board which would justify his paying it," La Trobe was told.[32]

Not knowing what Gipps had already decided, Sievwright a few days later would seek a written statement from La Trobe clearing him of the imputation of having made an unjust claim. Robinson had told him that such a statement would have to come from the Superintendent. Perhaps from the evidence it considered, the board had been unable to make a decision on the claim, Sievwright suggested. But the board should have taken its investigations back *before* Davidson had been appointed and taken control of the stores. Details should have been obtained of the amounts of goods supplied for the Western District operations of the Protectorate by the government in the whole period prior to his suspension. From his monthly returns, a calculation could have been made of what had been issued to the Aborigines, and how much remained. This would have revealed the surplus which he was now claiming as his own property, and for which he'd not been paid.[33]

It would take months more of haranguing before La Trobe would reluctantly agree to call on Addis and Eyre to have another look at Sievwright's claim.[34] Convening in Geelong, they would again examine documents provided by the former Assistant Protector. But again, they would criticise the way in which he'd allowed his private stores to be mixed with those of the government -- and the way in which these stores had then been issued. Addis and Eyre told La Trobe they still couldn't come to a conclusion about the validity of the claim. The Chief Protector remained the only one who might be able to shed some light on the matter by comparing Sievwright's figures with those of the supplies received and *officially* issued at Keilambete, Terang and Mt Rouse.[35]

At the board's suggestion, Sievwright would send all his documentary evidence to Robinson. But in a letter to La Trobe, the Chief Protector would only add to the board's criticism of the way in which his former assistant had kept his stores. However much he may be "disposed to assist" Sievwright, it was "altogether impossible" to gain a clear picture of the validity or otherwise of his claim. Robinson would also take issue with remarks by Sievwright that the Western District's Aboriginal reserve had been "left by the Chief Protector to sustain itself as it best could", and that he'd been forced "to advance his private stores for the necessities of the station". Sievwright himself had admitted, Robinson stated, that during 1841, he'd been supplied with 6760 kilos of flour and 2850 kilos of meat. During 1842, the Chief Protector claimed, the figures had jumped to 15,000 kilos of flour, and 15,436 kilos of meat. There were big discrepancies between these amounts and those contained in other documents in his office.[36] But even if they were correct, Robinson did not include a daily calculation of how far the amounts mentioned would have gone. During 1841: only 18.5 kilos of flour and 7.8 kilos of meat per day -- very small amounts considering the large number of Aborigines living with Sievwright at the time. Even in 1842, daily average allocations to 200 Aborigines could only have amounted to about 200 grams of flour, and 200 grams of meat. And usually, there were more than 200 Aborigines at Mt Rouse.

The letter from Robinson, with the report from Addis and Eyre, was all La Trobe needed to decide that Sievwright's claim could not be admitted. He would write to the former Assistant Protector telling him of the decision, then informed Gipps. As expected, the Governor would not overrule the Superintendent. He would agree that Sievwright's claim should be disallowed. "His Excellency concurs with Your Honour in considering Mr Sievwright's claims now finally disposed of," the Colonial Secretary told La Trobe.[37] It was an excessively optimistic remark. Even before these words were written in Sydney, Sievwright had launched a renewed and increasingly bitter quest for justice in Melbourne.

CHAPTER 31
Fightback

D ESPITE a high level of illiteracy, a notice in a New South Wales newspaper was one of the most effective means of an individual conveying
information to fellow colonists. Most notices of course were just advertisements for goods or services. Others sought support for various causes, or
informed the public of new government regulations. But some were of a distinctly personal nature. Early in 1841, for instance, an Englishman named John
Winstanley was so enraged by his wife Matilda running off with another man
that he was moved to inform the public of the fact in the *Geelong Advertiser*.
Winstanley, whose clock-making business in Geelong would later include the
sale of wedding rings, claimed that Matilda had left the marital home "without
the slightest provocation". She'd since been seen in the company of one Henry
Perks. Winstanley warned the public against "harbouring or giving credit" to
her, adding that he would not be responsible for any debt she incurred.
Furthermore, a warrant had been issued for Matilda's arrest, presumably for
adultery, and he was willing to offer a reward of five pounds for anyone who
could apprehend and lodge her in prison. It was half the reward being offered
at the same time in Geelong for recovery of a missing dark bay mare.[1]

An alternative means of gaining publicity among the whites in New South
Wales, particularly attractive to those who could not afford to advertise, was
through letters to the editors of the papers. Often these letters were mere commentary or expressions of opinion, published as contributions by anonymous
correspondents such as *An Old Tar*, *A Settler in the Grange District*, *A Solicitor*,
Nauticus and *Hibernicus*. But sometimes the letters contained news of great
public interest. For instance, it was through a letter from the squatter, Thomas
Grant, to the *Patriot* in Melbourne that the Port Phillip colonists first heard of
the murder by the Bunganditj Aborigines of Edmund Morton and William
Lawrence a few months after Matilda Winstanley ran off with her lover.

By early 1845, two-and-a-half years after his suspension, Charles Sievwright
would decide to try to use the local press to embarrass the colonial government
into giving him the inquiry he was still seeking to clear his name. He would
approach the fellow Scot who'd taken over as editor and proprietor of the
Geelong Advertiser, James Harrison, and plead for assistance. Sievwright told
Harrison he was prepared to provide copies of his official correspondence with

Robinson and La Trobe from 1839, and through them expose the shabby way in which he'd been treated. After reading through the documents, Harrison decided to take the extraordinary step of publishing what could be the longest letter to an editor of a newspaper in Australian history. The letter would incorporate about 40 copies of correspondence relating to the Aboriginal Protectorate and Sievwright's dismissal, as well as extracts from six of the former Assistant Protector's official reports, all linked with comments from him. It would take up four broadsheet pages of the *Advertiser* over two days, much of it in tiny type-face, and would require production of a special supplement on the first day.

Not surprisingly, the financial nightmare which had dominated Sievwright's life since his suspension featured heavily in the material published. The former Protector's still outstanding claim for 58 pounds, which Gipps had tried to declare a dead issue seven weeks earlier, was still well and truly alive. In statements and letters published in the *Advertiser*, Sievwright was able to describe in detail the case he'd presented to the boards of inquiry and the colonial government to try to recoup the money. Any other evidence relating to the matter was held by the Chief Protector, and to his knowledge, nothing had been produced to show his claim was unjustified. In one published letter, sent to La Trobe after the inconclusive second inquiry, Sievwright had stated that if an allegation was being made that his accounts were incorrect, Robinson should be made to specify in what way. At the same time, he would again express extreme lack of confidence in his former superior's ability or willingness to treat him fairly.

"I regret that it becomes imperative upon me here to state to your Honour that the Chief Protector is my openly declared enemy," Sievwright had written. "And in knowing him to be so, I did not object to his being associated with the late board, or to any reference that could be made by them to him alone, knowing the correctness of my position, and feeling satisfied that from your Honour I would receive ample justice, and thus be shielded from the effects of personal animosity." Instead, though, he'd become the victim of "intangible aspersions and unmerited obloquy" and an ambiguous accusation about the accuracy of his accounts. It was also his duty to state that during a recent meeting in Geelong, Robinson had told him that on one occasion he'd been unjustly made to personally cover the cost of an expense relating to the Western District which the government had disallowed. And the Chief Protector had added that for all he knew, he could be made to pay for Sievwright's claim for the 58 pounds. "This of itself will prove the incompetency of the Chief Protector to do me justice," Sievwright had stated.[2]

Before La Trobe had replied to this letter, he had gratefully received word from Sydney that Gipps had endorsed the way he'd handled the matter.[3] The Superintendent would also receive a letter from Edward Addis and Alfred Eyre,

Supplement to Geelong Advertiser

SATURDAY, FEBRUARY 1, 1845.

Over two days in February 1845, the Geelong Advertiser would publish four broadsheet pages of full transcripts of correspondence outlining some of Sievwright's experiences during his time as an Assistant Protector, and following his suspension. On the first day, the Advertiser brought out a special supplement containing the correspondence, with linking remarks from Sievwright. "We cannot see a man crushed, as Mr Sievwright has been, without crying 'shame'," declared the Advertiser, explaining why it had devoted such an unprecedented amount of space to his plight.

who'd been asked by Sievwright to have a third look at the claim in what he said was a "simplified" form. However, Addis and Eyre had reiterated that they were unable to reach a conclusion -- again pointing out that only Robinson could have figures showing whether there was any large discrepancy between the supplies sent for the use of the Western District Aborigines, those issued, and those still on hand.[4] La Trobe had told Sievwright he could only remark that Addis and Eyre had confirmed his opinion that the claim was "totally unsupported" by "straight-forward and conclusive evidence". Without such evidence, an officer in Sievwright's position should never have made such a claim.[5]

It was time, Sievwright had decided, to hold his tongue no longer. In another lengthy letter to La Trobe, published in its entirety in the *Advertiser*, Sievwright made the serious accusation that Robinson had withheld important documents from Addis and Eyre when they'd been called upon to re-examine his claim. These documents, the former Protector alleged, included the Mt Rouse accounts which he'd carefully prepared with the help of the accountant, Archibald McLachlan. If Robinson had not been so obstructive, Sievwright argued, Addis and Eyre would have been able to conclude that his claim was valid. Furthermore, the board had stated to him that if in the first instance he'd submitted the claim in its current simplified form, instead of encumbering it with unnecessary -- but conclusive -- evidence, the justness of the claim could have been decided immediately.

Not all of the material from Sievwright published in the *Advertiser* related to financial matters. Much of it also covered Sievwright's views on the maladministration of the Protectorate. Through other correspondence, he was able to demonstrate how he'd dissented from the outset with the Chief Protector's scheme of collecting members of different tribes in the one spot and expecting them to live in harmony. One published letter, written back in 1839 from Geelong, showed how Sievwright had recommended a system of reserves allowing each tribe to remain in its own territory. But Robinson of course had ignored this advice, instructing him to try to gather as many Aborigines as possible in one spot, regardless of tribe or tribal boundaries. Other letters showed how the Chief Protector had continued to insist on this plan without giving any detailed instructions on how he believed it could or should operate.

Ample proof that the system could not work, Sievwright remarked, had come after Robinson arrived at Keilambete and ordered him to move to Terang, at the same time suspending the system of supplies for work performed. "We accordingly moved the camp, upon which the Chief Protector left me, in the midst of 300 of the wildest of the human race, in the dilemma of having broken my portion of our original contract, from their supplies being stopped from the working party, and 'twas then the evil passions and uncontrollable ferocity of the savage became apparent. Deadly conflicts between the tribes were a matter of daily occurence; midnight murders of the most horrid description upon helpless females were perpetrated, accompanied by the most foul and disgusting acts of cannibalism, converting the picturesque shores of Terang into a hideous pandemonium."

"Sufficient proof has been subsequently obtained at Mt Rouse, where the system of the Chief Protector was persevered in, to show its total impracticability," Sievwright wrote in a closing commentary on his correspondence. "But when to their own hereditary feuds and murderous rites, which demand a victim for every evil, real or imaginary, they may individually sustain, were added their just complaint of being brought from their own ground, under a promise and compact which they had strictly observed, and I had failed to fulfil: the mutiny in the camp may be imagined, but can scarcely be described. The imbecility (I can use no fitter term) of the Chief Protector in throwing my party into this position, and then leaving us for nearly 12 months, to combat as best we could with its difficulties, was only equalled by his utter and unpardonable neglect of the numerous representations I made to him of the daily losses sustained by the settler, and of the fatal consequences likely to ensue to the natives."

The response from Robinson had been to ignore the responsibility, by instead falsely reporting that his assistant had collected a great number of strange tribes together, without the means of supplying their wants, and over whom he had insufficient control. This false report appeared to have been "readily selected for transmission to the Secretary of State, preparatory to the premeditated step, that was to rid the government of a troublesome officer, whose unflinching discharge of the onerous duties committed to his charge, and unfettered expression of dissent from measures which were but a mockery of the benevolent designs of the home government, had thus rendered it expedient to remove". Through this misrepresentation, he'd earned the censure of the Secretary of State for the result of a system over which he'd certainly had no control -- and from which he had from the beginning dissented. It was now for his own vindication, that he felt obliged to bring these matters before the public.

He would have abstained from such a measure, had it not been for Robinson's provocation in having accused him of embezzlement. In having attempted to impeach him with this "base and vulgar crime", the Chief Protector had "displayed to the world the bent and capability of a disposition still unemancipated from its original leaven". It had also shown the risk taken by the government in having allowed its respectability to be judged by the actions of such a man. Sievwright again stressed he'd been prepared to meet, and rebut, the false charges which had been made against him by Robinson. As he'd outlined in his correspondence printed in the *Advertiser*, no investigation into them -- other than those into the accounts -- had been held. But that was not to be the end of the matter, he warned, and he was planning present his case in London. "The Chief Protector well knew, that so long as he could retain me in this country, by the sure means he adopted of instituting unworthy charges against me, and prolonging their investigation, he could put off the hour, when his machinations would be brought before the higher tribunal to which they have not as yet been referred".

In his professional career, Sievwright suggested, the editor of the *Advertiser* must have had ample opportunity to observe what appeared to be "the besetting sin of the penal colonies, namely calumny in its most virulent form, and aspersion of character in its widest application". In winding up his letter, Sievwright would offer a philosophical explanation of this "morbid condition". In the great Alembic of society, as in that of the alchymist, the "foex populi" (dregs of the people), like the baser metals, were intransmutable "into fine gold". The knowledge of this painful truth had engendered that rabid malevolence "through which the lower orders would seek to obtain a temporal equality, by deterioration of the purer standard, to the mean level of the baser coin". Sievwright would end with a Shakespearean flourish: "Alas for Caesar! through the impress of whose image such currency is upheld."

The *Advertiser* offered no apology for having devoted so much space to Sievwright's disclosures, offering to publish any "counter statements" from Robinson or other sources. "If an individual be oppressed, and he be denied a hearing by the government, and prevented from appealing to the law; where else can he look for redress than to public opinion, through the medium of the press?" the *Advertiser* asked. "And how disgraceful would it be to that press to deny him this last chance of self-vindication. Viewing these disclosures as they appear in the columns of our last number, we have no hesitation in denouncing the conduct of his Excellency the Governor, his Honour the Superintendent, and the Chief Protector, as being mean and tyrannical. Whatever may have been their real opinions of Mr Sievwright's proceedings, they had no right to refuse him a full and fair investigation. It was unjust (and that is the strongest word we can employ, using it, as we do, most emphatically) to listen to ex parte statements *against* Mr Sievwright; to pass judgement on them without even telling him the nature of his imputed offence; to refuse any inquiry except into matter of accounts; and when that paltry boon was granted, to reject his claim on the ground that his evidence was of an *ex parte* nature. But why was it *ex parte*? It was in the power of the government alone to meet his statements, and why were they not met?"

"We know not whether most to reprobate the meanness or the tyranny of the government throughout the whole proceedings," the *Advertiser* commented.

"Of course we principally allude to the treatment Mr Sievwright has received *since* his suspension from office; for so long as the documentary evidence is withheld by the government it is impossible to pass a correct judgement with any degree of certainty. It is only by inference that we can judge of the nature of the evidence withheld: an inference only corroborated by the animus of the parties withholding such evidence. The disposition displayed by his Excellency the Governor in the affair is precisely that of an Eastern despot; and if he had sent the 'bowstring' instead of the order of suspension, his conduct could not have been more arbitrary and unjust. The conduct of the Superintendent and the Chief Protector must be weighed in other scales; for they would not have had courage to perform the greater crime without the Sultan's firman. Their conduct is principally characterised by the absence of all manliness and candour."

"We are conscious of having gone to the extreme verge of prudence in apply-ing these epithets to the 'powers that be'; but when indignation is an honest feel-ing, it should not be suppressed," the article continued. "We cannot see a man crushed, as Mr Sievwright has been, without crying 'shame'. We confess that until these disclosures were made, we always entertained a strong prejudice against Mr Sievwright, and did not scruple to express it, and we are therefore glad of the opportunity to make reparation."[6] It was an undreamed of triumph for Sievwright! The voice of the Western District squatters, which had so often condemned him, was admitting it had been wrong, albeit belatedly! But it was only one victory in the long fight to try to clear his name, and much remained to be done.

When he'd gone to the *Advertiser*, Sievwright did not realise that his still out-standing claim for 58 pounds had been the subject of more correspondence between Robinson, La Trobe, and the board of inquiry comprising Addis and Eyre. It would end up with the board stating yet again that Robinson was the only one who might have evidence to substantiate Sievwright's claim.[7] A shocked La Trobe had already demanded an explanation from Robinson about Sievwright's allegation that he'd withheld vital documents from the board.[8] In reply, Robinson would raise doubt that such documents had ever existed. He'd looked in his office for them, he alleged, but they couldn't be found. Unfortunately, his clerk at the time had gone off to Ireland, so could not be ques-tioned about them. Nevertheless, he assured La Trobe, the clerk had been "par-ticularly careful in matters of business" and would have kept them on file had Sievwright provided them. Robinson added that as far as he was concerned, his former assistant had been given "every facility" by himself -- and Addis and Eyre -- to prove his claim. Robinson claimed that no mention had been previ-ously made of the documents to which Sievwright was now alluding. "Mr Sievwright's proceedings are to me, to say the least, inexplicable," Robinson wrote, "and I believe to every other person who has had anything to do with the matter".

Furthermore, Robinson added, Watton had stated that he knew nothing about any private supplies of Sievwright's being left at Mt Rouse. In a statement before the Portland Police Magistrate, former overseer Davidson had also sworn that he believed all the stores at hand belonged to the government. Davidson's journal was the only valid document available for examination. But this comprised only gross amounts written on a few loose, dirty leaves of paper. No details at all were given of the way in which supplies had been received or allocated. It was ludicrous, Robinson commented, for Sievwright to claim that he'd contributed to the necessities of the reserve, in full faith of the supplies being reimbursed. Plenty of supplies had been provided, and there had been no need for Sievwright to make any such contributions. Addis and Eyre had confirmed his belief that his former Assistant did not have the slightest claim against the government. "In conclusion, I would briefly remark that as I could not possibly have any sinister object to serve, I think Mr Sievwright's subterfuge and attack on myself puerile and unwarrantable, especially as I have always evinced on account of his *family* a disposition to assist rather than otherwise," he declared.[9]

It had been almost 17 months since Sievwright had written to La Trobe to inform him that he'd sent the documents to the Chief Protector's office which Robinson was now claiming to know nothing about.[10] Beyond reference to this letter, Sievwright couldn't do anything to prove that the documents had existed. Indeed, it was quite possible that the Chief Protector had mislaid, discarded or even destroyed them. All he had to do was adhere to his story. Judging by his stonewalling to date, La Trobe hardly had any intention of ordering a search! After being provided with copies of the latest correspondence, and of the report of the second board of inquiry into his claim, Sievwright was faced with an obvious conclusion. In line with his military training, it was time to stage a tactical withdrawal, sometimes necessary to achieve ultimate victory.

In a final letter to La Trobe on the subject, Sievwright would point out that Addis and Eyre had been misled by La Trobe. The Superintendent had wrongly quoted him as having said that the board had expressed a view to him different from that which appeared in its second report. He'd merely remarked that the board had indicated a different opinion to La Trobe about one aspect of the inquiry -- the way he'd presented himself and his evidence. The remark could not have related to the board's overall findings, because at that time he'd not been told what they were. "As to my opinion of the Report, and correspondence of the Board, now that I am enabled to judge of them, I would avail myself of this opportunity to express my sense of the independent and upright conduct, manifested by the members, throughout these investigations, and at the same time would thus publicly offer my acknowledgement of the gentlemanly demeanour that has invariably marked their proceedings," Sievwright wrote. By implication, he was admitting that without assistance from Robinson, Addis and Eyre had reached the only conclusion they could.[11]

So it was that the old Fusilier ended one stage of his efforts to retrieve his 58 pounds. But that didn't mean he was about to give up trying to retrieve the money, and his reputation. In fact, it would not be long at all before Sievwright would find a new means of gaining publicity for his cause -- this time closer to the seat of the colonial government in Sydney. He would approach the fiery Scottish Presbyterian clergyman who'd been elected as a representative of Port Phillip on the New South Wales Legislative Council, John Dunmore Lang. Although he spent much of his time in Sydney, Lang of course read the Port Phillip papers, including the *Geelong Advertiser*, and had seen Sievwright's lengthy letter to the editor. Like James Harrison, Lang was impressed with the case of unfair treatment made out by the former Protector, and promised to take it up before the next session of the Legislative Council, using copies of official correspondence provided by him.

About the same time, the Sievwrights would receive letters from friends back in Britain saying they'd heard that Christina had been the cause of her husband's downfall. The alarming news that the family's scandalous situation was now the subject of gossip on the other side of the world would prompt a decision for Sievwright to immediately go back to London to try to explain to their friends in person what had occurred -- and to seek redress direct from the Colonial Office. As he prepared to leave, Christina sought a letter from La Trobe stating that complaints from her had not been the reason for her husband being suspended and then dismissed.[12] The letter had still not been provided when the time came a few weeks later for Sievwright to sail out of Melbourne aboard the barque, the *Cygnet*, late in May 1845, leaving behind his impoverished wife, seven children, and a reputation somewhat repaired, but still severely tarnished.

As the *Cygnet* crossed Port Phillip Bay its hold reeked with the combined smells of 746 bales of wool, 129 casks of tallow, 21 uncut eucalypt logs, and 35 tonnes of black wattle bark, the latter being taken to England for its tannin.[13] But Sievwright didn't notice. He was far too deep in thought about his arrival in the bay almost six-and-a-half years earlier to take up his new position as an Aboriginal Protector, and the fate which had since befallen him and his family. He thought again, too, of the Aborigines who'd been under his charge, and what might become of them. Ironically, even as the barque came within view of a tip of Barrabool territory as it passed through the heads and out of the bay, a letter was on its way to Melbourne from the man who'd been appointed to replace Sievwright -- suggesting that the government provide protection *from* the

Aborigines to the white settlers in one area not far from Mt Rouse. The Gunditjmara Aborigines in this area, John Watton told La Trobe, had been "very troublesome" for some time. They were reportedly being led in their attacks by the former prisoners, Jupiter and Cocknose.[14]

On August 7, 1845 -- 10 weeks after leaving Melbourne -- the *Cygnet* was in the final stages of its battle through the freezing and treacherous waters of the Drake Passage, dodging ice floes as it sailed below the South American continent out of the Pacific and into the Atlantic. On that day, in Sydney, the issue of Sievwright's dismissal was to take up a good deal of the time of the members of the New South Wales Legislative Council, when it was finally raised as promised by John Dunmore Lang. He would table in the Council a petition from Sievwright, along with many letters and other documents which the former Assistant Protector had laboriously copied, so he could take all the originals with him back to London.

The respectfully-worded petition from Sievwright was so lengthy, Lang remarked, that he could not even attempt to give an extract of it. Even more difficult would be any attempt to summarise the appendix, which comprised at least 40 papers. Still, he was able to say that Sievwright was complaining that he had not been given either from the head of his department, or from the government

By permission of the National Library of Australia
"Port Phillip Heads, Victoria" by S. T. Gill

generally, the support he'd needed to satisfactorily carry out his duties as a Protector. As well, he stated, Sievwright believed he was still owed 58 pounds in half salary which should have been paid between the date of his suspension and the date of receipt of confirmation from the Secretary of State that the suspension would not be lifted. Obviously, Lang had mistakenly become confused over Sievwright's claim for the 58 pounds he believed was still owed by the government. There was a separate claim for payment of half-salary during the 14-month period of his suspension, which should have amounted to about 165 pounds, but had never been paid.

Lang told the Council that the circumstances set forward appeared to present a prima facie case that Sievwright had been subjected to harsh treatment. The politician then spoke of the case as another example of the hardships being inflicted on the people of Port Phillip in being governed at such a distance. They could not clearly show their wants and grievances, except by incurring the expense of sending advocates to present their cases in Sydney. Here the Speaker interrupted Lang, suggesting that he return to the specific purport of Sievwright's petition. The member responded by saying that he would now present the petition, and move that it be read. This having been done, Lang told the Council that he could not pledge himself to the correctness of everything which Sievwright had claimed. But, he reiterated, it was clear that an inquiry into the former Assistant Protector's allegations was justified. He moved that the petition be received, and this was accepted -- but to Sievwright's misfortune, the Council moved on to other business without making any formal request for an inquiry.[15]

CHAPTER 32
Return to London

OR centuries, one of the most splendid pageants in London would be the Lord Mayor's Show, involving an annual procession to mark the swearing in of a new Lord Mayor. In 1845, it was the turn of John Johnson to replace the highly unpopular Michael Gibbs, who was greeted with "loud hisses and expressions of disrespect" as he passed through some of the streets of London, and then on barges along part of the River Thames, in his final hours in office. Among the banners that would flutter in the gentle breeze in the procession that accompanied him on that fine day was one bearing the arms adopted by sections of the Sievwright family. It was the banner used by John, one of the two cousins of Charles who were "freemen" of the City of London, and who had been fellow lottery agents with his father. John was now an office bearer in the Worshipful Company of Spectacle Makers -- one of the livery companies which elected the Lord Mayor.

It so happened that on Lord Mayor's Day in November 1845, the barque carrying Charles Sievwright back from Australia would finally sail into the Thames Estuary and drop anchor at Gravesend, about 45 kilometres downstream. That night, as Charles Sievwright awaited customs clearance aboard the *Cygnet*, looking forward to an end to five-and-a-half months of ship food, his cousin was certainly dining in grand style. The fare for the Lord Mayor's inauguration dinner included 250 tureens containing a total of about 700 litres of "real turtle" soup, 200 bottles of sherbet, 60 pigeon pies, and six dishes of "Captain White's Selim's true India curries". There were even 60 dishes in various forms of potato, the supply of which was about to be hit by a devastating outbreak of blight, causing a famine which would claim tens-of-thousands of European lives -- most of them Irish.[1]

Arriving back in London in debt and disgrace, as he'd done more than nine years earlier, Sievwright had no choice but to again seek financial support from his friends, and relatives. When he'd returned to London in 1836 after selling his army commission to pay off his gambling debts, his main supporter had been Viscount Falkland -- at that time, a member of the House of Lords. This time, Falkland was not available to lend a hand, being across the Atlantic in Nova Scotia, as that colony's Governor. Falkland was due to return to London soon to become captain of Queen Victoria's bodyguard, the Yeomen of the Guard. But

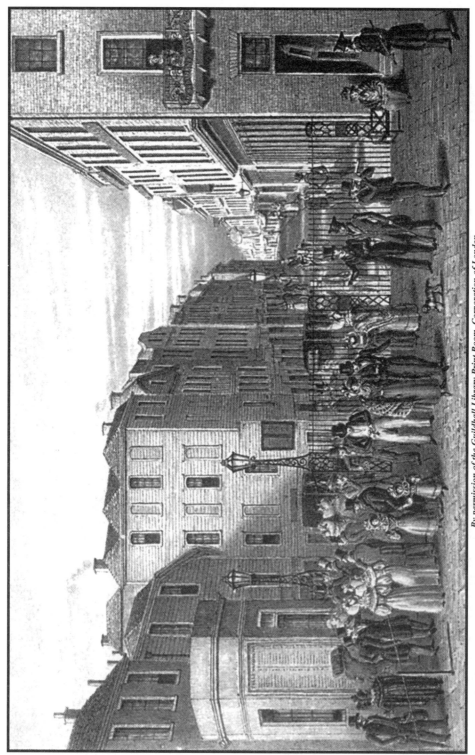

By permission of the Guildhall Library Print Room, Corporation of London
"View of the High Street of Gravesend, in Kent, from the pier" by H. Harris (engraver). It was here that Charles Sievwright arrived on his return to England aboard the "Cygnet" in November, 1845. It had been more than seven years since he'd left London to take up his new posting in Australia.

until then, Sievwright had to again appeal to the generosity of other friends, such as the Queen's cousin, Lord Frederick Fitzclarence -- as well as his own cousins.

Before he started his efforts to clear his name, Sievwright needed to travel to Edinburgh to visit his widowed mother. But the answer to his financial woes was certainly not there. His father had died while Sievwright was in Australia, leaving enough for his mother's support, but little more. Nor could he expect any financial aid from the rest of his immediate family. His unmarried sister, Lillias, who still lived with his mother, made only a humble income from teaching music. His brother John had returned to England after unsuccessfully trying to find someone willing to provide the capital for a squatting venture in Port Phillip. He'd resumed his previous job as a brewer's agent, but his spending pattern was taking him along the road to London's Court for Relief of Insolvent Debtors. Charles Sievwright's only other surviving brother, Francis, was also not in a position to help. He'd recently bought himself a commission as a lieutenant in the 9th infantry regiment in India, which was about to take part in the British army's first war against the Sikhs in Punjab. To raise the necessary amount for his commission, Francis had borrowed one-thousand rupees each from two fellow officers, and the debt had not been repaid.[2]

In London, Sievwright's friends with political influence -- and who'd helped him through his earlier period of unemployment -- had been Liberals, formerly Whigs. Thanks to the lobbying of Viscount Falkland and others, he'd been appointed in 1837 by the reformist Liberal government of William Lamb, the second Viscount Melbourne, after whom Port Phillip's capital took its name. While Sievwright was in Australia, it had been replaced by the Conservative Party government of Sir Robert Peel. The Secretary of State for the Colonies in Peel's government, Lord Stanley, had quickly agreed to Sievwright's dismissal, without calling for any inquiry. To get justice from Stanley now would require at least an admission that he'd acted with undue haste, if not unfairly. But by the time Sievwright had been to Edinburgh to visit his mother, and returned to London, Stanley would no longer be in the Peel Ministry.

Peel's new Secretary of State for the Colonies was William Ewart Gladstone, to whom Sievwright would write in March 1846, seeking an inquiry into his case. Ten days later, Gladstone would reply that it was impossible, at such a distance from the scene of the allegations, for the Colonial Office to directly investigate. If Sievwright wanted an inquiry, Gladstone decided, he would have to go back to Melbourne, to make himself available for questioning by a panel appointed there. At the same time, the Secretary of State pointed out to Sievwright that according to correspondence from Gipps, the main reason for his removal from office had been his "general unfitness for the performance of its duties" -- not the graver charges against his moral character.[3] Having just made the long journey back from Melbourne, Sievwright was exasperated by Gladstone's suggestion that he would need to go back for the inquiry he'd so long sought there. But he would become even more perturbed after the Colonial Secretary allowed him access to the documents received from Sydney relating to his suspension.

It would come as no surprise to Sievwright that George Robinson had played a major role in his downfall. But he was only just starting to learn to what extent. In the correspondence shown to him by Gladstone, Sievwright would see for the first time how it was a deceptive letter from the Chief Protector, written more than five years earlier, which had sparked Gipps' request to La Trobe to report on whether the Assistant Protector's services should be dispensed with. This was the letter in which Robinson had misleadingly accused Sievwright of *proposing* that rations be issued "indiscriminately" to the Western District Aborigines. Sievwright of course had made no such proposal, having suggested only that he be allowed to continue the food-for-work system at Lake Terang which had all but ceased on Robinson's orders. The Chief Protector's deceit had been made all the more damaging when an angry Gipps -- his mind freshly poisoned against Sievwright by one of the Bolden brothers -- had misinterpreted it to be a description of what Sievwright was *already doing*. When Sievwright got to see only Gipps' reply, he would not realise this had occurred, and would wrongly blame Robinson entirely for the deception.[4]

While Sievwright contemplated what to do next, there would be a development which would raise his hopes of obtaining justice: in June 1846, Peel's Conservative government would fall. A new Liberal government would be led by Lord John Russell -- who'd been Home Secretary and leader of the House of Commons back in 1837 when Falkland had unsuccessfully appealed to him for help in finding Sievwright a job. He'd later been Secretary of State for the Colonies for much of the time in which Sievwright had been employed in Australia. Russell's Colonial Secretary would be Henry George Grey, the third Earl Grey, to whom Sievwright would write initially in February 1847.

But even before he would receive a reply from the Colonial Office, Sievwright's case would receive a major setback. Not long back in England from Australia, George Gipps would die from a heart attack -- leaving only La Trobe and Robinson to answer for his suspension. Then a little over a fortnight later, Sievwright's campaign for reinstatement would be interrupted by news of another death -- that of his mother. After quickly returning to Edinburgh to attend the funeral, Sievwright left his sister, Lillias, to clear up matters relating to their mother's estate and went back to London. Their mother would leave about 70 pounds worth of furniture and silver cutlery, mainly to Lillias, who still lived in the family house and had been caring for her since their father's death.[5]

The day his mother's estate was being valued in Edinburgh, Sievwright would sit down in London to make what would end up being his main appeal for justice, in a letter to Earl Grey in May 1847. Until recently, he told the new Secretary of State, he'd believed his dismissal was because of the charges against his moral character. But after reading the letter sent by Gipps to La Trobe in February 1842, he'd realised that there was more to the matter. Gipps had also referred to having *officially* received "repeated reports of Mr Sievwright's inefficiency". The Assistant Protector took this to mean that the reports had come from La Trobe. He believed he was therefore obliged to draw Grey's attention to the "extraordinary measures" which the Colonial government had found it expedient to adopt in order to rid itself of a public servant who had had the misfortune to both incur La Trobe's displeasure, and to "render himself obnoxious to the squatter" by having "diligently and fearlessly" performed the duties set for him by one of Grey's predecessors, Lord Glenelg.

As a magistrate, Sievwright told Grey, he had with no hesitation and strict impartiality tried to bring before the proper tribunals those white men who had unfortunately clashed with the Aborigines while defending their property -- as well as those "lawless and depraved" whites who had committed wilful murder. "In fulfilling those duties, I was necessarily exposed on the one hand to the enmity and vituperation of the squatter and his agents, whose murderous acts were then for the first time brought to light, while on the other it appears that I became troublesome to the Government, through the incessant and pressing representations, which I deemed it my duty to make regarding the inert measures taken by the authorities who, in declining to bring the implicated parties to trial even for their justification, thus naturally excited a feeling of hostility against the officer whose duty was primarily to detect and report upon the cases of homicide and murder that came under his knowledge," Sievwright wrote.

Just one case out of many would illustrate his point, the Assistant Protector argued: the massacre by the Whyte brothers and their men in 1840. Relating the lowest estimate of the death tolls which had been given to him, Sievwright told Grey that according to the deposition of one of the whites involved, between 30 and 40 men had been shot dead on this occasion. Yet no trial or inquiry had taken place into this "outrageous transaction" beyond that originally conducted by him. He'd stopped giving his own opinion of the case, forwarding his depositions to the Government for expected action. But instead, the Crown Prosecutor had ruled that the blacks appeared to have been the aggressors -- and that their conduct would make the conviction of the whites involved "very uncertain". Purely because of this *doubt* about a successful prosecution, the matter had been allowed to lapse.

From the time he and his colleagues had arrived in Sydney, Sievwright went on, the creation of the Protectorate was regarded even in the highest quarter "as a tacit though unequivocal reproach to Colonial philanthrophy, and as an implied censure upon the vigilance of the Government". The cool reception which the Assistant Protectors had received had been "materially increased" when George Robinson had joined them in Melbourne to take over as Chief Protector. Having arrived as an emigrant in Van Diemen's Land "in the humble sphere of a brick-layer", he'd been selected by Sir George Arthur as a fit person to instruct Sievwright and his colleagues in "how to acquire the confidence of the natives". This was because Arthur believed that after having "facilitated the removal" of the last Van Diemen's Land Aborigines to an island in Bass Strait, Robinson had acquired a suitable knowledge of Aboriginal behaviour. "But, as it will be shown in the sequel, neither co-operation nor assistance of any kind, even in the shape of instructions to his colleagues, were rendered on his part -- while the periodic transmission of letters and reports to and from the Government which passed through his hands, were much retarded by Mr Robinson, who by his edu-cation was not well qualified for the duties that devolved upon him, even as a correspondent," Sievwright wrote.

The "supineness and negligence" of the Chief Protector, Sievwright told Grey, had thrown him and those who worked under him into a "hopeless position". Exaggerating slightly, he claimed that during the first three years of the exis-tence of the Protectorate, Robinson could not be prevailed upon even to visit the Western District. The Chief Protector had told the Colonial Government that the "serious evils and losses" which had occurred in the District had resulted from his Assistant's "imprudence and inability". This in turn had been reported to Lord Stanley after his suspension. But, Sievwright stated, the settlers' com-plaints about severe losses in attacks on their flocks and herds, as well as his own representations about them, had been received with "apparent apathy", as Robinson and his superiors displayed a "deplorable state of inaction". In the midst of the turmoil, Robinson had made the remark which had resulted in the unfounded allegation that he'd been issuing rations "indiscriminately" to the blacks under his care. At the same time, he'd been accused of having paid no attention to the instructions of the Chief Protector or of the Government.

It was remarkable, Sievwright wrote, that the only instructions he ever received from the Chief Protector, and for which he had so long and frequently applied, were precisely those upon which he was then acting. These required him "to endeavour to collect at one central station as many of the natives of his district as could be induced to congregate" -- notwithstanding the fact that he had dis-sented *in toto* from the practicability of such a scheme, as being "more wild than the elements it had to contend with". For Grey's information, Sievwright appended the letter he'd written to Robinson back in 1839, questioning the

George Augustus Robinson.

proposal to try to unite tribes, and suggesting instead that each tribe should be allowed to remain in its own territory. This letter should be enough to show his opinion of the "hopeless experiment" which Robinson had implemented, and which had "signally failed" in each of the districts allotted to his assistants.

Although he and his colleagues all had to cope with the consequences of Robinson's failed plan, Sievwright added, he'd had some additional difficulties. La Trobe had decided to "prejudge and condemn" his conduct and character on the basis of the statement of a "secret enemy" -- despite the fact that he was then, and remained, "incapable of countenancing or participating in any behaviour unbecoming of a gentleman". As well, Sievwright told Grey, the other districts had been gradually settled by the whites, and the differences between the races "as to right of occupancy" had "long been adjusted". The Western District, however, was the most extensive, and was then being occupied for the first time by squatters. In the course of his duties, he'd been obliged to repeatedly call for action by the colonial government to try "to check the appalling loss of life" which was occurring as the District was being taken over. He'd also drawn the attention of the New South Wales Governor to the "most arbitrary and unjust measures" taken by La Trobe towards the Aborigines. It was these factors combined, he had no doubt, which had led to the foundation of a scheme to remove him from office.

It had not been his intention to embarrass the colonial government by either "the inordinate display of a distempered zeal" or by becoming "the puling champion of a barbarous though suffering people", Sievwright wrote. "But I had been pledged to lend my energies to the national experiment that was being made for the amelioration and for the protection of the Aborigines, and my mind and capabilities were accordingly given to the task," he declared. In doing so, he had not only incurred the displeasure of the executive officers of the colonial government, but he and his family had made major sacrifices. While they'd lived in the bush with the Aborigines, his children had been denied access to schooling and, frequently, "the commonest necessities of life" had been totally unattainable. After undergoing these hardships, the family had been subjected to the "overwhelming and ruinous" experience of his arbitrary, unjust and unconstitutional suspension.

The decision to get rid of him could not be implemented, Sievwright told Grey, by finding fault with the way he'd performed any of his public duties -- even though he'd been left to perform them in his own way. Rather, a "series of the most foul and malignant calumnies" had been adopted and used as the grounds for his dismissal. Soon after La Trobe had become Port Phillip's Superintendent, he'd told Sievwright that the reason why he was being "discourteous" was because of undisclosed rumours about his character from undisclosed sources.

When he'd appealed to La Trobe for a thorough investigation, he'd been told that this should have been done by Robinson at the time the accusations were first made. Grey would undoubtedly be astonished to learn, Sievwright remarked, that almost three years later he'd been notified that Gipps had decided to suspend him, more on account of charges against his moral character than from "any want of capacity or perverseness". Thus, La Trobe had not been prepared to investigate the rumours when they came to his notice. But the Superintendent's attitude had changed after Sievwright had "fearlessly" investigated and proclaimed the "dark deeds" which were blotting his administration. It distinctly appeared that La Trobe had been prepared to revive the "extinct and forgotten calumnies", to have an apparently legitimate reason for Sievwright's removal, and to ensure the services of a more discreet successor.

"In full confidence of the supreme ascendancy of truth, I earnestly and I may say joyously demanded the investigation of the strictest tribunal in order that I and my family might at once and for ever be delivered from such degrading and truly indecent fabrications," Sievwright wrote. "But such were not the intentions of His Honour the Superintendent, who on finding that by the production of documents I was prepared to falsify the evidence which had been prematurely remitted to Sydney, as that 'in which entire confidence was to be placed, and that consequently there might be some difficulty in determining the precise points to be investigated'. Or, in other words, that he dare not approach a scrutiny which might terminate in the confusion of my calumniators, it appears that His Honour availed himself of all that sophistry and the most jesuistical application of distorted facts could effect, to give complexion and character to those orbate and anonymous defamations."

When the "truly colonial" accusations against him had first been made, Sievwright reminded Grey, he had immediately demanded a commission of inquiry into them. "I begged for the severest scrutiny into my past and present conduct, my moral and domestic character, and the *discharge of my official duties*, and stated that every facility would be given by myself and family towards arriving at the truth on these subjects," he wrote. "Your Lordship is aware how these my reiterated demands were for months evaded, and ultimately refused upon the pleas 'that my case was then in the hands of the Secretary of State'. The time and opportunity for these inquiries being then denied has now passed away. The scrutiny involved, when my calumniators and their agents might have been convened, would now be as useless to me as it would then have been fatal to their views."

As to the repeated reports supposedly made to the government of his inefficiency, Sievwright went on, it seemed to him surprising that no intimation was at any time given to him of the "slightest disapproval" of his official conduct.

The Governor's dispatches which he'd read at the Colonial Office made no mention of any act or omissions indicating "unfitness". In the correspondence appended, La Trobe and Robinson had both avoided making any specific complaint about the way in which he'd performed his duties. The closest the Superintendent had got was when he'd stated that unlike the other Assistant Protectors, Sievwright could not claim to have at least earned a degree of respect for having "a fair moral name and an evident desire to effect good, however limited the success". Nor could Sievwright claim to have the approbation of the government "as to the general tenor of his proceedings". At this point, La Trobe had again fallen back on the claims against his moral character as the reason why he should be dismissed. In a vain search for some other ground for his dismissal, Sievwright pointed out, La Trobe had, at considerable expense to the government, even appointed the special commission of inquiry -- comprising Charles Griffith and Frederick Powlett -- to investigate the Protector's report on the Muston's Creek murders. They'd found that their fellow magistrate's report had been "a correct and unexaggerated statement of the circumstances as they occurred".

The vague charge of "general unfitness" which had been made against him was a term easily applied against any individual. If such a charge could be held to justify removal from office, no public servant would be safe for a day -- and no-one would be willing to break their connections in Britain to take up employment in the colonies, Sievwright argued. Gipps had specified no actions showing "unfitness", so refutation was precluded. And the former Governor's death, Sievwright added, had deprived him the opportunity of testimony of vital importance to his case. "He was as it now appears very unfit for his office himself; and his death and that of others imposes great difficulties on me for which in justice allowance should be made."

And it was not just Gipps' death which had deprived Sievwright the opportunity of testimony of vital importance to his case. Two other people had also since died whom he would have liked to have been questioned by a board of inquiry about his behaviour. One was former fellow Protector James Dredge, who'd told Robinson that he'd been paying undue attention to Mary Parker, the wife of Protector Edward Parker. The other was Mary Parker herself. Other potential witnesses at the inquiry he'd unsuccessfully sought were now dispersed across the world. "Still," Sievwright concluded, "I am sustained by the hope that my claim for simple justice will yet be responded to by Your Lordship, upon that broad principle of equity, which is at once the shield of the oppressed and the glory or dishonour, by whomsoever it is granted or withheld."

Acknowledging Sievwright's letter, Grey would reiterate that any inquiry into the charges against his private character would be "futile and destitute of any satisfactory result" unless he returned to New South Wales for it to be conducted there. Nevertheless, the Secretary of State was prepared to call for a report from the authorities in the colony on the allegations Sievwright had made. Both the New South Wales authorities and Sievwright deserved such an investigation.[6] It was well short of the full inquiry the suspended Protector had been seeking for so long. But at least, after so many disappointments, some action was finally being taken to address his complaints.

CHAPTER 33
The inquiry

IN all bureaucracies, those with ultimate power need to delegate authority to a chain of underlings entrusted with implementation of decisions. Even the best conceived plans can be easily brought undone by incompetence in any link in the chain. Whenever there is a breakdown in smooth operation of the bureaucracy, it is generally easier and safer for functionaries to blame a subordinate. It is often difficult enough for senior administrators to detect when blame is being unfairly apportioned. Even more difficult for them, however, is to acknowledge when they have undeservedly maintained faith in the capabilities of particular individuals who have been blaming others. When the necessary combination of astuteness, courage and integrity is lacking to make such a realisation and address it, incompetence is allowed to perpetuate. Such was obviously the case with the Port Phillip Protectorate. La Trobe would express strong reservations about Robinson's organisational abilities, and the Protectorate's prospects of achieving its goals. But both La Trobe and Gipps would be unwilling to conclude that not only had they placed too much faith in Robinson's abilities, he was also unjustly blaming his assistants for his department's failings.

It was not as if Gipps and La Trobe were unaware of any public dissatisfaction with the Chief Protector. La Trobe in particular was well aware of numerous articles in the Melbourne press critical of the operations of the Protectorate since its inception. And many of these articles would question Robinson's abilities. One of the most vicious attacks on the Chief Protector -- and on La Trobe as his superior -- would appear in the *Patriot* in October 1846, as Gipps was on his way back to London. Over several editions, the *Patriot* would publish the full text of a lengthy petition to the Legislative Council in Sydney from William Le Souef, who had replaced James Dredge in 1840 as the Assistant Protector with responsibility for the Goulburn region. Le Souef had already sent one petition in 1844 to the Council complaining of his dismissal the previous year. But it would be in his 1846 petition in which he would give full vent to his anger.

Not long after he'd taken over from Dredge, the petition explained, he'd written to La Trobe, telling him of threats against the lives of all the white men and even a white child at the Goulburn reserve. The blacks of his area had been displaying feelings of "insubordination and revenge" -- largely provoked by the operation against them led by Major Lettsom, and the imprisonment of many of them in Melbourne. Lettsom's operation and the subsequent actions of the police and the Mackay brothers had left four of their number dead -- and at least six others had at least been wounded, if not killed, while trying to escape from custody. As might be expected, Le Souef said, the last Goulburn blacks to escape -- the ones who'd been sentenced to transportation and who'd jumped from the boat in the Yarra -- had "poisoned the minds of their brethren against the whites". A large number of Aborigines had visited the Goulburn reserve and Le Souef believed they'd had "hostile intentions". They'd left after hearing that a mounted policeman was in the area, but he still believed he was in a precarious situation, and wanted advice from Robinson or La Trobe on what to do. The Superintendent had referred the matter to Robinson, but Le Souef had waited in vain for guidance.

Lack of instructions would be one of the main complaints from Le Souef about administration of the Protectorate which bore a striking resemblance to those Sievwright had made. He, too, had constantly asked for instructions -- only to be subsequently accused of having neglected them! Almost without exception, Le Souef lamented, the Chief Protector had failed to answer "every momentous communication addressed to him" -- with the evident purpose of avoiding all official responsibility. Then, after being forced to use his own discretion, Robinson would unjustly complain. And it was not just the Chief Protector who'd been at fault, Le Souef told the Council. During the three years he'd been officially employed, both Robinson and La Trobe had displayed "the same inattention to the discharge of their duties" in relation to the welfare of the Aborigines. "No efficient effort was made, nor has any really judicious attempt since been made by the Protectorate, to effect any improvement in the religious or moral condition of the benighted natives, or to introduce among them those wholesome civil regulations that are indispensable to their own welfare, and to the tranquillity and security of the settlers," Le Souef complained.

As he'd done with Sievwright, Robinson had coupled notification of Le Souef's dismissal with an accusation of misappropriation of government property for personal use. This claim, Le Souef remarked, had been proven groundless after an investigation by "seven of the most respectable and influential inhabitants of Port Phillip", who had certified that his accounts were correct. But that was not all. Le Souef alleged that by accusing him of misappropriation, Robinson had been maliciously trying to shift the blame for his own "acts of peculation and irregularity". He could prove that Robinson had illegally requisitioned for supplies for his own use. Requisitions for any of the Aboriginal reserves could only be made by the Assistant Protectors -- and then counter-signed by the Chief Protector. But soon before Sievwright had left to return to England, Le Souef claimed, they'd been told by one of the government contractors, Alexander Broadfoot, that Robinson had been drawing requisitions with only his own signature. The Clerk of Works had confirmed the same practice. An inquiry by the Legislative Council, Le Souef suggested, would show that the deficiencies in accounts which the Chief Protector had falsely blamed on his assistants were in fact a result of his own illegal actions.

Le Souef would also refer to a matter concerning fellow Assistant Protector William Thomas, whom he described as a "highly deserving and honourable man". Back in 1842, Le Souef noted, Thomas had reported to Robinson that he had more whites than blacks at the reserve assigned to him in the Westernport District. Fearful that the report would reflect badly on his management, the Chief Protector had ordered Thomas to alter this statement. When his assistant had refused, Le Souef alleged, Robinson had illegally suspended his pay and allowances. Not long after this, Thomas' papers had been stolen in a very mysterious manner -- articles of value having been left untouched by the robber or robbers. Although Thomas' pay had been restored after three months, his allowances had remained suspended, Le Souef stated. La Trobe should have ascertained the reason for the action taken against Thomas. And if he knew the reason, and had done nothing about it, he was an accomplice in Robinson's illegal actions.

Again making very similar claims to those Sievwright had made, Le Souef would tell the Council he'd been "counteracted and undermined" by Robinson throughout his three years as a Protector. Rather than support him and the other assistants, the Chief Protector had pursued his own "erroneous and chimerical" system, which had resulted in the blacks of Port Phillip being in a much worse position than when he'd arrived in the District. The blacks were "perceptably degenerating" as they acquired European vices, and their numbers were rapidly diminishing. Many valuable lives might have been saved, and more than 50,000 pounds of public money would not have been utterly wasted, if the Legislative Council had paid due attention to a warning it had received about the Chief Protector more than six years earlier. In a speech to the Council, the Anglican Bishop of Australia, William Broughton, had denounced Robinson as "a mere visionary". Le Souef remarked he now had the experience to know that the Chief Protector was a visionary "without one spark or ray of genius".

Le Seouf's petition, the *Patriot* commented, proved what the public already believed: that instead of the department being an institution of benefit to the European and Aboriginal populations of Port Phillip, it was "an active injury to both". Le Souef had provided facts which traced the causes of the "mischievous results" of the government's "great scheme of philanthropy" to the failings of the individual to whom the government had entrusted its administration. "We repeat," the *Patriot* declared, "that whilst the arbitrary control of the Protectorate is vested in the hands of Mr Robinson, the government can hope for no better result than that concatenation of capricious ignorance, and gross incapacity, which have proceeded from this man's superintendence." The Chief Protector possessed an authority which was "more irresponsible and imperious" than was prudent to confer on any individual. This had been made worse by the "extremely injudicious" choice of Robinson as that person. He'd shown a total want of system, or even common order or common industry, to carry out the task assigned to him.

"That this unhappy issue is solely attributable to Mr Robinson is, we think, probable from the state of dependency in which his subordinates are sunk," the *Patriot* added. "They have not forgotten the lesson taught to them by the dismissal of Messrs Le Souef and Sievwright -- men who in point of character, birth and education, must have been degraded by having been the co-operators, much less the servants, of a mechanic, who has not even the ordinary intelligence of his class to recommend him. The Assistant Protectors, have in the instances above named, an example of the consequences of departing from the track of their Chief's blundering. They have witnessed the speedy punishment of those who, prompted by the will and the ability, burst through the impediments which ignorance and envy threw up to impede their exertions to be useful, to run the risk of sharing the same fate. Such has been, is and will be the Protectorate of Port Phillip until Mr Protector Robinson be translated to some occupation more appropriate to his genius."[1]

The attack on Robinson by the *Patriot* came as Christina Sievwright pursued attempts in Melbourne to help her husband clear his name, for example by seeking a character reference from William Thomas.[2] Christina would send copies of the *Patriot* article to Sievwright in London, and he would be delighted to receive them just in time to include one with his letter to Earl Grey making yet another request for an inquiry into the circumstances of his dismissal. The comments by the *Patriot*, he told the Secretary of State, showed "the opinion entertained by the public of Port Phillip of my official proceedings and also of the estimation in which the private character I left behind me is held".[3] To Grey, the article must have appeared to be strong independent evidence that Sievwright might not have exaggerated too much about his treatment -- and it could have been the factor which made him decide to investigate the suspended Protector's allegations.[4]

By an odd coincidence, the request for a report on the validity of the grounds for terminating Sievwright's employment would initially be referred to a son of the man who had authorised the application for his first job 31 years earlier. Lieutenant-General Charles FitzRoy had been commanding officer of The

King's Own Borderers when he'd signed the recommendation for Sievwright to be allowed to buy his commission as an ensign in the regiment for 400 pounds back in 1816.[5] The general's son, Charles Augustus FitzRoy, also a former army officer as well as a former Member of the House of Commons, had taken over as Governor of New South Wales three weeks after Gipps left for England. The new Governor would of course direct the request for a report on Sievwright's case to La Trobe, still Superintendent of Port Phillip.[6]

It had only been a year since publication in the *Patriot* of Le Souef's petition, and the accompanying remarks about the unfairness of the treatment both he and Sievwright had received. But La Trobe would claim to be nonplussed at being asked to comment on the suspended Protector's letter to Earl Grey. "I confess...that I scarcely know how I am to discharge the duty imposed upon me or deal with the paper referred to," he wrote. Nevertheless, he deigned to try. After perusal of the correspondence, La Trobe remarked, it seemed that Sievwright no longer believed that he'd been suspended because of the charges existing against his moral character. Instead, he'd concluded for the first time that his suspension had been mainly on the ground of "general unfitness" for his duties. The Superintendent admitted he didn't know what Gipps had stated in his initial report to London of Sievwright's suspension. He therefore didn't know whether the Assistant Protector's conclusion was accurate. But he was prepared to support the contention that Sievwright had been unsuitable -- partly with information he'd just requested from George Robinson and James Croke.

"To the statements made by these gentlemen, in explanation or controversion of Mr Sievwright's assertions, I consider it my duty to add that under no possible point of view can Mr Sievwright lay claim to the character which he arrogates to himself," La Trobe told FitzRoy. "He never distinguished himself in this district in the discharge of either ordinary official or magisterial duty. That he, in common with the other Assistant Protectors, had difficulties to contend with -- not only in consequence of original unfitness for the performance of the duties undertaken by them, the extraordinary character of the circumstances in which he and they were placed, and in plain truth from the peculiar character of the chief of their department -- I have always been ready to acknowledge. It is however, undoubted, that the actions of no individual of the number at the time entailed so much embarrassment upon the Government as those of Mr Sievwright, and that the facts upon which the general charge of unfitness was founded are undeniable."

It was certainly true, La Trobe agreed, that Sievwright had failed to conciliate the squatters. But it did not appear, as the Protector had claimed, that he'd made himself "obnoxious to the squatter" as a result of faithful discharge of duty. Rather, the ill will and hostility he'd provoked was more a result of "the contempt with which his private character was regarded" by many of the squatters -- coupled with "a want of common prudence and justice in his dealing with them". La Trobe was also dismissive of Sievwright's claim to have become "troublesome" to the government by merely performing his duties. And it was wrong for the Protector to claim that the executive and judicial authorities had been indisposed to help him discharge his magisterial functions. Such an attitude, La Trobe claimed, "never could exist".

As well, La Trobe would explicitly deny Sievwright's statement that in the course of his duties, he'd been obliged to call attention to "the arbitrary measures" adopted by the Superintendent towards the Aborigines. This, La Trobe claimed, was news to him. He'd been unaware until now, he told FitzRoy, of any such allegations by the Assistant Protector. Yet Sievwright had used the words "arbitrary" and "unwarrantable", for instance, when complaining back in 1840 about La Trobe's order banning the Barrabool blacks from Geelong. La Trobe's ban, Sievwright had argued, amounted to "oppression" and "injustice" -- from which he was supposed to be protecting the Aborigines -- and had been partly responsible for renewing "a spirit of antipathy and hostility to the Aborigines" in his district.

After seven years, La Trobe could be expected to have forgotten details of just one of the reports by one of the Assistant Protectors. But the language of that particular report by Sievwright had been remarkably strong in its criticism of La Trobe and other senior officials. It had been the same report in which Sievwright had attacked Crown Prosecutor Croke, Attorney-General Plunkett, and Foster Fyans -- criticism which resulted in the suspension of the Assistant Protector's salary. And there was no doubt that La Trobe had carefully read the contents. Before posting it on to Gipps, the Superintendent had written *two* covering letters -- one of them specifically mentioning Sievwright's complaint about "the arbitrary line of conduct pursued by the authorities in seeking to prevent visits by the natives to the townships".[7] So there were plenty of reasons for La Trobe to remember.

Predictably, in his statement in support of the justness of Sievwright's suspension, George Robinson would argue that his assistant had had ample instructions, and means to carry them into effect. "Mr Sievwright's want of success is to be attributed to want of judgement and to his own inefficiency," Robinson declared. Indeed, the Chief Protector claimed, Sievwright's "exceedingly unpopular" and "vexatious" actions had provoked "repeated complaints" to Gipps from the settlers. These had become so bad by late 1840 that the Governor had found it "necessary to interfere" -- ordering him to make a special trip to the Western District to "open a friendly communication" with some of its Aborigines. This was, typically, a gross exaggeration. It had been La Trobe who'd ordered Robinson on the trip -- and not as a result of any complaints about Sievwright, but rather in response to the large number of recent inter-racial clashes, involving significant loss of life. In giving instructions for the journey, La Trobe had certainly mentioned that the Chief Protector should try to gather information which he'd been unable to obtain from Sievwright about the tribes which had been involved in the clashes. But this had been the only reference made to the Assistant Protector.[8]

When he'd visited Keilambete in April 1841, Robinson remarked, the "greatest disorder and confusion" had prevailed. Sievwright had collected a large group of blacks from far and wide, over whom he had no control. His assistant had proceeded without any previous notice to dislodge John Thomson from the spot, ploughing up his folding ground, and commencing the formation of a homestead close to Thomson's huts "in the middle of his flocks". Sievwright had been ignorant of what the Chief Protector regarded as the single language being spoken by his charges -- yet Robinson claimed he'd been able to compile a vocabulary for his future use in just the few days he was at the camp. Then, when he'd asked his assistant to accompany him on his journey further west, he'd "begged to be excused" because his cart was out of repair. "The truth was Mr Sievwright as I have been told and as I have reason to believe did not like any mode of travelling," Robinson wrote. "He thought the risk too great to travel without firearms and with so small a party and I had to proceed alone."

Through the severe winter of 1841, Robinson boasted, he'd travelled about 4000 kilometres through the Western District, "dissecting it in every possible direction" and "communicating with *all* the Aborigines in general". He'd even gone to the Great Swamp near Mt Napier, which was "said to be the very hotbed of the worst natives". The blacks there had been friendly, and he'd parted from them "with the best understanding". The Chief Protector alleged he'd returned to Melbourne after a five month trip "without the slightest accident" happening to himself or the blacks from various tribes who'd accompanied him. "I had accomplished a duty which certainly ought to have been done 18 months previous by the Assistant Protector," he boasted. Without any other responsibilities, Robinson had certainly managed to visit a few parts of the district which Sievwright hadn't seen. But he'd greatly exaggerated his alleged success. Even his claim that none of his party had met with any injury was a blatant lie. Eurodap, the Jarcoort who'd been his main interpreter for more than half of the journey, had been killed in a clash after Robinson took him into Bunganditj territory -- and another Jarcoort in the party, Inergerook, had vowed to come back with his people to settle the score. Albeit inadvert, he had thus on at least one occasion contributed to inter-tribal strife.[9]

Except in Sievwright's case, Robinson also told La Trobe, he totally denied that the Protectorate had failed "in any particular". James Dredge had resigned, sure enough, but not because of dissatisfaction with the way the department was being run, Robinson claimed. Dredge had not complained of "want of instructions or want of means". Yet such complaints had comprised a major part of Dredge's resignation letter![10] Robinson's willingness to exaggerate was shameless. Except at the Western District reserves, he alleged, large numbers of Aborigines had been congregated "without the slightest irregularity or inconvenience". At the reserves set up by Sievwright at Keilambete and then Lake Terang, the "greatest confusion" had prevailed. Yet Robinson knew there had been much "irregularity and inconvenience" at the other reserves as well. Le Souef, for instance, had complained that the Goulburns were threatening to kill him and the other white men at his reserve. And soon after its establishment, the Westernport reserve under William Thomas had been virtually abandoned.

The Chief Protector would also allege that employing Sievwright had been unnecessarily expensive. Gross expenditure incurred by him as an Assistant Protector in the year of his suspension, 1842, amounted to more than 1800 pounds. His replacement, John Watton, had spent a total of only about 1200 pounds over the previous four years. By suspending Sievwright, Robinson calculated, there had been a "saving to the government" of more than 6000 pounds. This, too, was very misleading. Certainly, it had been less expensive for the government to employ Watton instead of Sievwright because his salary had been fixed lower. But the rest of the spending supposedly incurred by Sievwright had all been authorised by Robinson. If there had been any over-spending, it had only been with the Chief Protector's authority! And spending under Watton had only gone down because much less was now being provided at Mt Rouse -- to far fewer Aborigines.

There had also been "abundant reason" to be dissatisfied with the way in which Sievwright had exercised his magisterial functions, Robinson wrote. Notwithstanding the numerous atrocities perpetrated upon the Aborigines of his district, not a single conviction of a "white delinquent" had resulted. Sievwright's inquiries into the atrocities had been made "valueless" to the government because of his "unnecessary delay and mismanagement" -- for instance by the the way in which he'd taken the evidence of principals on oath. The Chief Protector cited the Mt Elephant massacre and the Henty poisoning as cases which Sievwright had mishandled -- not mentioning the reasons given for delays in launching investigations into them. In the case of the murders of the women and child at Muston's Creek, Robinson stated, Sievwright had failed to follow the tracks of the horses of the murderers, which "would have led to their haunts" -- and probably their conviction. Again, the fact that Sievwright at the time was trying to save the life of a seriously wounded black woman was ignored. And

Great Western Aborigine Station

	Flour	Meat	Tea	Sugar	Tobac	Soap	Salt	Rice	Oat meal	£	s	d
From 1st Febr to 31st Jan	12600	4000	86	600	56		1000			229	9	2
1 do 30 April	12000	6000					100			240	2	1
1 do 30 June		6000								98	6	9
1 do 31 July		6000	96	500	112					120	2	1
1 do 30 Septr		6000					005	005		113	0	5
doctor of October			96							11	0	0
1 to the 31 Octr	2000	6000		005			005			133	17	1
1 do 30 Nov		8000					005			136	9	2
										1082	8	9

		£	s	d
Flour	26000	2/0	284	7	6
Meat	42000	3/0	689	-	?
Tea	198	3/10½	33	0	0
Sugar	1600	3/4	26	13	4
Soap			3	10	0
Rice	168	2/2	36	9	2
Oatmeal	500	4/2	9	7	6
			1082	8	9

Reproduced courtesy of the Public Record Office of Victoria

Supplies approved for the "Great Western Aborigine Station" for 1842 (at Mt Rouse from mid-February). Across the table are listed quantities (measured in pound weights) of flour, meat, tea, sugar, tobacco, soap, salt, rice, and oat meal issued during the year. On the right of the table, the cost of these items is calculated, in pounds, shillings and pence. Throughout the year, meat was the most regularly distributed item — a total of 42,000 pounds (19,295 kg). It was also by far the most expensive item, accounting for more than half the total expenditure on the Station for the year of 1082 pounds, eight shillings, and nine pence.

Robinson, who had had exactly the same magisterial powers as his assistants, failed to mention that he'd personally never either initiated or even followed through any prosecutions over atrocities.[11]

James Croke, still Crown Prosecutor in Port Phillip, would also criticise Sievwright's actions as a magistrate. He would deny the suspended Protector's claim of "supineness" among the legal authorities in either Melbourne or Sydney in relation to cases involving clashes between the races. And he would gloss over the fact that Sievwright had constantly asked for more instructions on the proper manner to take depositions, virtually claiming instead that the suspended Protector had proceeded in defiance of the instructions he'd been given. "Public prosecutions were defeated not because the Authorities were inert but because Mr Sievwright uniformly in the performance of his duty as a Magistrate took the examination of the persons implicated on oath, thereby rendering the depositions taken by him illegal and nugatory," Croke wrote. "I must add that though the Attorney-General at Sydney and I myself as Public Prosecutor in this District frequently reprobated such a practice, yet Mr Sievwright preferred his own way of taking depositions to that recommended to him for adoption."

Croke told La Trobe he could recall only one case in which Sievwright had taken the depositions properly: the one involving Sandford Bolden. This had resulted in the squatter being put on trial for feloniously shooting, with intent to kill. In the case of the massacre by the Whyte brothers, cited by Sievwright as a prime example of the inertness of the authorities, Croke defended his decision not to prosecute. According to the depositions taken by Sievwright, Croke remarked, the Aborigines involved had been "the first to commence the battle". The Whytes and their men had therefore been acting in self-defence, and could not be put on trial "with the least hope of a successful result" -- notwithstanding the "legal infirmity" that Sievwright had taken their statements on oath. It was a significant hardening of Croke's stated position at the time that a successful prosecution would be "very uncertain" -- but not hopeless. More than seven-and-a-half years after the event, and again ignoring the fact that the Protector had sought guidance from the colonial authorities on how to proceed with legal action over the massacre, Croke would then boldly add: "If Mr Sievwright was of opinion that the homicides alluded to were inexcusable, or not perpetrated in self-defence, or unjustifiable, it is strange he did not commit the offenders."[12]

The remarks by Croke and Robinson would be allowed to pass on by La Trobe with little comment. But he was quite prepared to admit that when asked back in March 1842 whether Sievwright should be dismissed, it was not a belief in the "general unfitness" for his duties which had most influenced his reply. "It was the moral disadvantage under which he had all along most undeniably laboured, in consequence of the want of personal character, far more than the proofs under my hand of the existence of ignorance, or incapacity in the discharge of official duty, which weighed with me in recommending his suspension." Furthermore, almost six years later he still regarded the view he'd taken to be correct. When he'd been directed by Gipps to make an inquiry into the claims against Sievwright's moral character, he believed the evidence gathered had fully vindicated the conclusion he'd reached. And he believed this conclusion had been endorsed by the Governor, and later by Stanley when Sievwright's removal from office was confirmed. "He neither brought character, nor did he gain, or maintain it here," La Trobe told FitzRoy.

The only way to deal with Sievwright's claim of a conspiracy to get rid of him, La Trobe told FitzRoy, was by plain denial. If Sievwright was inferring that such a conspiracy had originated in Melbourne, he was mistaken. The Superintendent had the strongest reason to believe that the question of the expediency of Sievwright's removal from office had originated solely with FitzRoy's

From "The Chronicles of Early Melbourne"
William Lonsdale

predecessor. The question had been impressed upon Gipps' mind "by the proofs of Mr Sievwright's incapacity and the knowledge that injurious reports, affecting his moral character, had all along existed". La Trobe said he'd been "fully cognisant" of the "prevalence" of these reports. But he had certainly not been the one who had directed Gipps' attention to them.

"Mr Sievwright is in error, when he leaves it to be inferred that because no steps were taken to investigate the charges at an earlier date, they would be scouted as false by those who were acquainted with their nature, and with the character of the evidence on which they rested," the Superintendent added. "The position and circumstances of Mr Sievwright's family during a considerable portion of the intervening period had been such as to keep them in the public mind. It must be recollected that the graver charges brought against Mr Sievwright, either by members of his own family or his colleagues, were of a character to deter if not defy any investigation, and that no satisfactory result could follow its institution; and that there were many reasons why unnecessary allusion to them even, would be deprecated. But whatever may have been my opinion in the interval, as to the inefficiency of Mr Sievwright's official proceedings, the conviction that he was morally disabled from advancing the cause which he, with his family, had been appointed to promote, had never wavered."

Proof of the way in which Sievwright had neglected his family, La Trobe noted, rested to some degree "on the common observation of all who were in a position to mark the actual state of the family while in Melbourne, and some time after his arrival at Geelong". Still further evidence of "the improper or immoral character of both his previous and present habits" had been provided, both verbally and in voluntary written statements, by Sievwright's wife and daughter. No statements which Christina and Fanny Sievwright subsequently offered to give "upon oath" could set that evidence aside. The "elopement" of Christina and Fanny from Geelong to Melbourne in 1839 was, in La Trobe's view, obviously provoked by Sievwright's behaviour. The causes then assigned by them for it to Lonsdale and others could neither have been denied, nor otherwise explained.

Besides the accusations brought against him by his own family, La Trobe continued, Sievwright had arrived in Melbourne under the charge of "gross immorality" in having carried on "an improper intercourse" with Edward Parker's first wife, Mary. This had been reported to Robinson by James Dredge -- whose death Sievwright was now deploring as having deprived him of evidence to substantiate his claims about his character! He was also deploring the death of Mary Parker. But according to La Trobe, it could "scarcely be doubted" that the "assiduous attention" which Sievwright had paid to Mary Parker had amounted to attempted seduction. And to back this claim, the Superintendent would append a letter he'd obtained from her former husband. Still operating as a Protector on the Loddon River, north-west of Melbourne, Parker would start his reply by expressing appreciation for "the considerate manner" in which he'd been asked to comment on the accusation against Sievwright.

"Deeply afflicted as I now am in my person and family, the revival of this painful subject would have otherwise aggravated sufferings already hard to bear," he wrote. "However repulsive it is to me to enter into any detail, the nefarious conduct of Mr Sievwright in presuming to allude to the death of Mrs Parker as depriving him of 'testimony of vital importance' compels me explicitly to say what that 'testimony' must have been. An intimacy existed between myself and deceased wife, and Mr Sievwright during the brief period of our voyage in the same vessel from Sydney to Port Phillip -- and for a very few weeks after our arrival. In that period, Mr Sievwright induced us both to believe that he was unhappy and deeply injured by the conduct of his wife, stating that he had brought her out at the instance of her friends and for the sake of her children, but with the resolution of never living with her as a husband. This statement seemed to be confirmed by the very loose principles in reference to the obligations of a married life, openly avowed by Mrs Sievwright. Regarding him therefore at first as an object of pity, we were less suspicious of the efforts which he made to cultivate our acquaintance."

Then, Parker stated he and Mary were compelled to witness "a disgraceful scene of recrimination and violence" between Charles and Christina Sievwright. This had elicited from Mary such "a strong expression of abhorrence" for Charles Sievwright's character and conduct that he'd become suspicious. In reply to his inquiries, she had "exposed a tissue of artful villainy to which she had been for a short time subject" from him. "He had in fact endeavoured by every means in his power to effect her seduction," Parker told La Trobe. "Her unsophisticated character and ignorance of the world from her secluded education as a Clergyman's daughter, made her at first unsuspicious of his intentions and nothing but fear and a feeling of shame in having been made the object of such guilty attentions prevented her from exposing him when she became aware of his purpose. Justice to her memory compels me to acknowledge that I blame myself more than her for unguardedly suffering such an incongruous intimacy to be formed. Immediately the disclosure was made, I charged him in a note with his villainous conduct, and interdicted all further acquaintance. He wrote me an insulting letter in reply, affecting to be surprised, and indignant at the charge, and threatening the interference of his friends, and public exposure. I deemed no reply necessary from me, and I need scarcely add that he never dared to put his threats in execution."[13]

Serious aspersions about Edward Parker had been made only the previous year by former fellow Assistant Protector, William Le Souef. In his 1846 petition to the Legislative Council, Le Souef had suggested an investigation into financial dealings which he claimed had taken up so much of Parker's time in Melbourne when he was supposed to have been attending to the Aborigines under his care. Parker, Le Souef claimed, had been involved in land speculation in conjunction with two businessmen, as well as "bill transactions" with John Wyberg Shaw -- one of the Melbourne merchants who'd filed Supreme Court summonses against Sievwright over unpaid bills. Furthermore, Le Souef alleged, certain of the Protectorate's transactions had apparently involved "gross and illegal jobbing". He'd discovered that on Robinson's instructions, cattle had been purchased for the colonial government *from* Parker, through John Shaw. And Le Souef had imputed that these dubious transactions could even have involved La Trobe. The Superintendent, he claimed, was "commonly reputed to be connected with three or four different individuals in cattle and sheep dealing". At the very least, he must have been aware of the purchases, because he would have had to have signed the documents authorising payment.[14]

Parker and La Trobe both knew that Sievwright had worked with Le Souef to investigate dubious financial transactions relating to the Protectorate. Even if there was no basis to Le Souef's allegations, it was still in their interests to co-operate in helping to destroy Sievwright's credibility, in case he started making similar allegations. If instead Parker's credibility had been investigated, La Trobe could have found factors raising considerable suspicion about the accuracy of the account he'd given of Sievwright's alleged attempt to seduce his wife. According to Parker, the violent incident between the Sievwrights which led to Mary's "disclosure" occurred about five weeks after the Protectors and their families arrived in Melbourne. This was when pious James Dredge was expressing horror in his journal at Parker's "abominable" drunken behaviour after spending evenings in the military officers' mess. On at least one of these evenings, Parker had been accompanied by his supposedly "unsophisticated" wife. In the unlikely event that her upbringing as a clergyman's daughter had made her ignorant of worldly matters, her education would soon have been completed! Evenings in the mess were hardly tame affairs, as Dredge would discover when he received a report about how Parker had behaved at one of them -- in the presence of both his wife, and Sievwright. "Ensign Cormack, an avowedly ungodly young man, stated next day at our place that the 'parson', as he called him, spent the evening with them, drank brandy and water before preaching, and drank brandy and water after preaching, and smoked his pipe with the best of them," Dredge recorded.[15]

Had Dredge had his way, all the members of white society would have joined one of a number of groups set up in the early years of white settlement of Melbourne to promote restraint in the consumption of alcohol. One which would develop a large following, particularly among Roman Catholics, was a branch of the society formed by a friar from Cork in Ireland named Theobald Matthew. The Father Matthew Society would choose New Year's Eve in 1847 as an auspicious time to use its brass band to attract crowds of potential converts to temperance as it paraded through the streets of the town. Sounds of members of the band preparing their instruments for the performance would drift across Melbourne as La Trobe wrote the final lines of what he hoped would be his final report on the man chosen a decade earlier to look after the Aborigines in the south-western part of his dominion.

Parker's statement on the alleged seduction attempt, the Superintendent told FitzRoy, only added to the accumulated evidence which clearly showed that Sievwright's further connection with the government would have been a discredit to it. "Whatever might be the causes of disunion, past or present, in Mr Sievwright's family -- the exact truth of the statement made to his prejudice by its members or others, Mr Sievwright lay under a moral disability which never could be removed, and was really unfitted for this reason, if for no other, for the performance of the duties which he had taken upon him," La Trobe concluded.[16] Well over five years after he'd backed Sievwright's dismissal, the Superintendent had for the first time given detailed reasons for doing so. But long before Sievwright's suspension, La Trobe had been reminded in a letter from London that the British government regarded the protection of the Aborigines as a "sacred purpose".[17] If La Trobe had really thought Sievwright had been so unsuitable, the question remained why he'd allowed Sievwright to hold onto such a sensitive post for so long.

CHAPTER 34
Judgement

FROM time to time in the colonial press of New South Wales, publicity would be given to purported Aboriginal "poetry", provided by colonists who claimed to have overcome the language barrier. Early in 1848, the *Geelong Advertiser* would publish what it described as evidence of the "poetic talent of the Aborigines of Australia". An anonymous contributor stated: "As I have after some years' inauguration acquired sufficient knowledge of some of the dialects of the Australian natives of the Geelong District, to understand the import of their songs of war and love, I have translated a few as samples of their genius, and to prove that poetry is the spontaneous child of nature, which flourishes and grows amid the beautiful ranges in the wild woods." The Barrabool "poetry", uncannily British-like in its style, included two "war songs" which the contributor claimed were sung by "an approved chief" at a corroboree. Also provided was a verse describing the feelings of a Barrabool girl who'd been in love with a youth, but had been given away in marriage to "an old chief of another tribe". Finally, there was a wife's lament over the death of her husband, who'd been pierced with poisoned spears.[1]

Later that month, the Barrabool "poetry" in the *Advertiser* would catch the eye of John Fairfax or Charles Kemp, the English proprietors of the *Sydney Morning Herald*. They would decide the verses were of sufficient interest to warrant republication. As a compositor went through the laborious process of hand typesetting each character in the page containing them, elsewhere in Sydney that same day the next crucial step would be taken in the case of the Scotsman who'd had considerable experience of Barrabool and other Aboriginal widows mourning the deaths of their husbands. Governor FitzRoy would sit down to write a covering note to the Secretary of State in London to accompany La Trobe's report on Sievwright's claims of unfair dismissal. The Governor felt no need to be expansive. La Trobe's report, and its lengthy appendices, FitzRoy told Earl Grey, had shown that Sievwright's allegations had not been borne out by facts. Furthermore, he declared, Sievwright's conduct while in the service of the colonial government "fully justified" his removal from it -- and rendered him "totally unworthy" of the Earl's further notice.[2]

It would be another five months before a senior group of politicians and Colonial Office officials would be called upon to consider La Trobe's report.

Members included Earl Grey, and Grey's predecessor as Secretary of State, William Gladstone, still a Member of the House of Commons. Others would be the Permanent Undersecretary of the Colonial Office, Herman Merivale, and his assistant, Thomas Frederick Elliot, along with the Parliamentary Undersecretary, Sir Benjamin Hawes. In other words, the group included the two top politicians and the two top public servants with responsibility for colonial affairs. It was hardly the inquiry Sievwright had so long demanded. But at least he wasn't being fobbed off with a low-level committee. Except for the Prime Minister or Cabinet, Sievwright could hardly have had a higher-level British government group to determine his fate. Summarising the case, Earl Grey would state that FitzRoy had been asked to inquire into Sievwright's allegation that the charge against him of incompetency resulted from the vindictive feelings towards him prompted by "his too great zeal in the discharge of his duties". First, the group had to decide whether the New South Wales authorities had successfully vindicated themselves in the report provided by FitzRoy. Second, a decision had to be made whether to give Sievwright an opportunity to read the report.

Oddly enough, it would not be the damaging material written by Christina back in 1839 which would sway the group. Rather, it was Parker's fanciful letter about Sievwright having allegedly attempted to seduce his wife. Both the Undersecretaries, Merivale and Hawes, would consider Parker's letter to be critical evidence against the former Assistant Protector. In Merivale's opinion, La Trobe had left the case "in the somewhat unsatisfactory position" in which it was before it was referred to him. "I cannot collect from him whether or not he considers that independent of all moral guilt, the insufficiency of Mr Sievwright was such as to render his dismissal proper," Merivale wrote. "My own inference would be, that he would not have been suspended for mere insufficiency, but that he was so far from being useful or efficient, that they were glad to get rid of him on other grounds. But the *moral* case against Mr Sievwright is strengthened to a very serious degree by Mr Parker's letter. I can conceive no reason for distrusting it, and it shows how little credit is due to the boldest and apparently openest denials of such charges. I think therefore it may be sufficient, without farther distinguishing between the two sets of charges, to inform Mr Sievwright that on the Report now before him, the Secretary of State cannot annul the suspension."

The peculiar circumstances of the case, Merivale noted, involved Sievwright having had claims made about his personal character, against which he'd not been able to defend himself. He therefore believed Sievwright should be allowed to have a copy of FitzRoy's report. Benjamin Hawes would agree with Merivale's sentiments, but suggested it might be prudent for Sievwright merely be told that the report confirmed and justified his suspension. He, too, regarded Parker's letter as critical evidence. "Mr Parker's letter can hardly be doubted, and if not, some such remark should accompany the communication," Hawes proposed.³ Earl Grey would accept the advice of the Undersecretaries to tell Sievwright his dismissal would stand. But the Secretary of State believed Sievwright should be allowed to see La Trobe's report. He directed Hawes to inform the former Protector that by calling at the Colonial Office in Downing Street, he would be able to inspect it and its appendices. No mention would be made of how important Parker's letter had been regarded.⁴

After seeing La Trobe's report on his dismissal in London late in August 1848, Sievwright would angrily renew his campaign to clear his name. At least as late as mid 1849 -- seven years after his suspension -- he'd still be in London, the campaign still underway. "After many years' perseverance, he does not yet despair of ultimately succeeding," Christina would record on the other side of the world, as she struggled on trying to raise the children alone, suffering much from "the chilling winds of adversity". At one stage, she would approach Niel Black, as "an esteemed friend of Mr Sievwright", asking for a loan of up to five pounds to tide her over for a few months. She was embarrassed to learn from Black that her husband was already "deeply" in his debt. Black would "generously exonerate him from the intention of having incurred that which he afterwards could not defray". But Christina didn't attempt to enlarge the debt, cancelling her request for a further loan.⁵

Christina's husband, however, would never get the chance to pay back the money he owed Black. In fact, a year or so after she learned of the outstanding debt, Sievwright's fight for justice was over. It was not because he'd lost the will to continue the struggle. Rather, his body finally robbed him of the ability to keep going. To compound the tragedy, at the same time his desire to rejoin his family -- if ever he could afford the fare -- would be rendered virtually pointless. After arriving in Australia to take up his duties as an Aboriginal Protector, Sievwright had been described by one observer as "a fine, soldierlike man, muscular and strong, straight as a ramrod".⁶ But just 12 years later, no amount of physical fitness had been able to prevent Sievwright going both blind and deaf.

In his dark and silent misery, friends Sievwright had made during his days as a Fusilier were able to help by ensuring servants were on hand to feed and otherwise assist him. The friend who'd been the most helpful in winning his appointment as an Aboriginal Protector, Viscount Falkland, had long since gone to India as Governor of Bombay. But for some time, his former Fusilier commander, Lord Frederick Fitzclarence, was able to visit Sievwright in central London, where he continued to live. Before Fitzclarence would join Falkland in Bombay as commander-in-chief of the British military in western India, the

"View of Downing Street, Westminster" by T. C. Dibdin. The Secretary of State for the Colonies, Earl Grey, would allow Sievwright to call at the Colonial Office in Downing Street in August 1848 to inspect the report by La Trobe on his dismissal.

By permission of the Guildhall Library Print Room, Corporation of London former Protector would be told through simple embossed messages that one of his sons had died from an accident in the Western District of Port Phillip. Later, after the former Protector's physical condition had worsened with development of a serious heart disorder, he would learn that other friends still serving as Fusiliers were going off with other British and French forces to fight in the pro-longed and costly conflict against Russia which would become known as the Crimean War. He would learn, too, of the birth of two more grand-children in Van Diemen's Land -- and then of the death of his wife in Melbourne, where he'd farewelled her nine years earlier. Christina, aged 53, had had no assets which warranted leaving a will. A little over a year later, Sievwright would die from a combination of his bad heart and dropsy, aged 55, also intestate.

From a little room in the south-west London suburb of Pimlico -- in part of a five-storey building called Eccleston Terrace which would be demolished by a German bomb 85 years later -- Sievwright's body would be taken for burial in Brompton Cemetery, later described as a "biography in stone of West London in the heyday of the Empire".[7] Its many grand monuments and tombstones would not, however, include one for the only man to have served the Empire as an army officer and a Protector of the Australian Aborigines. Rather, Sievwright's coffin would be placed three metres down in a common, unmarked grave which would eventually be shared with two women unrelated to him who would die in equal obscurity, one eight years later, one 80 years later. Someone paid just over two pounds for Sievwright's burial. Someone also recorded his passing in a notice on the front page of *The Times*. "Deeply regretted", the notice blandly stated. By whom, and for how long, it did not say. The notice added that Sievwright had been "late of the Royal Fusiliers", though it had been 19 years since he'd left the regiment. Even when his death was recorded in the General Register Office in London, his occupation was given as "formerly captain in the Royal Fusiliers". There was no mention in the *Times*, or the GRO, of him having been an Aboriginal Protector.[8]

Almost four months after Sievwright's death, his eldest daughter would go back into mourning when she heard of it -- just two days after she'd ended a long mourning period after the death of her beloved mother.[9] The scandalous allega-tions in Port Phillip about Fanny and her father had not prevented her from being on the way to becoming a prominent member of "respectable" society in Hobart in Van Diemen's Land. At the time of her father's death, Fanny was married to an Anglican priest, and already the mother of four young children herself. She'd initially gone to Van Diemen's Land to work as governess to Lady Pedder, wife of its first Chief Justice, Sir John Lewes Pedder. Through visitors to the Pedders, Fanny had met her London-born husband, Arthur Davenport, who had sailed to Australia with five others to do missionary work. They'd been married at Richmond, near Hobart, in 1848, two-and-a-half years after Sievwright had returned to London. After working in Richmond and one other rural parish, Fanny's husband would be sent as the last government chaplain to Norfolk Island while it was still a convict settlement. On his return from the island, where Foster Fyans had earned his nickname "Flogger", Arthur Davenport was attached to the Holy Trinity church in Hobart, where he would remain for 23 years and become Archdeacon.

Charles and Christina Sievwright's second-eldest child, Marcus, would stay in the Port Phillip District. He would train as a lawyer, taking his articles initially in Geelong with English solicitor Charles Sladen, later a Premier of the State of Victoria, as Port Phillip would become. Marcus would finish his articles in Melbourne with another English solicitor, Henry Moor, second mayor of the town, and later a Member of the British House of Commons. Two years after being admitted to practise in the New South Wales Supreme Court in 1850, Marcus would marry Josephine Cornelia Lahon, a "tall and elegant" French woman who could only speak in broken English even years later. Marcus would later become a successful solicitor in Melbourne, where he would spend the rest of his long life.

For several years, Charles Sievwright the Second would work as a station manager for Charles and Peter Manifold -- two of the Western District squatters whose actions against the blacks had been subject to inquiry by his father. Among the stock he would manage would be some of the prize-winning cattle sold off after the deaths of two of the Bolden brothers.[10] Sandford Bolden, the only squatter ever prosecuted as a result of the actions of Charles Sievwright senior, would live for only 16 months after his acquittal on the charge of feloniously shooting with intent to kill at the Aborigine named Tatkier, who had still remained missing long after the shooting.[11] Sandford would die from injuries received when he fell from a horse near Melbourne, aged just 24. Less than three months later, his brother Armyne, only two years his elder, died of apoplexy after dining at the Melbourne Club.[12]

By a bizarre coincidence, Charles Sievwright junior would suffer the same fate as Sandford Bolden -- death after falling from a horse -- at almost the same age. Still scraping together a living working for the Manifold brothers, aged just 23, he was near Mt Leura on February 25, 1851 when a young horse threw him, then gave him a fatal kick in the breast bone. "Mr Sievwright was one of the finest young men in the colony, and a most dutiful son and brother," remarked the *Victoria Colonist*, reporting the accident. "He was to have started on Saturday for Melbourne to see his mother and sisters, whom he had not seen for two years."[13] Another Melbourne-based publication would also record young Charles' passing. "His early death is deeply regretted by those to whom his rare qualities have endeared him," it reported.[14]

Both of the twin daughters of Charles and Christina Sievwright, Frederica Christina and Melita Ysobel, would marry in Hobart. Frederica would marry George Matson, a New Zealand-born branch manager of the Bank of Australasia. Melita would marry Henry Hill, later Superintendent of Police in the Victorian gold-mining town of Ballarat. Ada Georgina would marry a solicitor, Stephen Clissold, and reside for a time in Melbourne, but she would return to England. Finally, Charles and Christina's youngest child, Adolphus Falkland, would start work in 1850 as a clerk in the Melbourne Post Office at the age of 15 -- almost five years after his father returned to London to fight to clear his name. After only 18 months in the job, Adolphus would receive a promotion to a salary of 100 pounds a year -- on the day the Port Phillip District officially became the separate colony of Victoria. Adolphus would later marry Mary Augusta Campbell, daughter of an English doctor, and would become Superintendent of Mails before his death from consumption at the age of only 33, leaving behind a wife and two infant children.

The two children of Adolphus Sievwright were among 20 grand-children of Charles and Christina born in Victoria or Tasmania. Eight of the grand-children would be produced by Fanny and her husband, Arthur Davenport. The first, Fanny Maria Davenport, would be born in Hobart in March 1849. She would follow her mother's example in marrying an Anglican clergyman -- the Reverend George Wood Shoobridge, a member of a leading family of hop-growers in Van Diemen's Land, and later Canon of St David's Cathedral in Hobart. Fanny Sievwright and Arthur Davenport's second child, Amy Clarisse, would marry John Fletcher Walker, who would become a very extensive landowner, and an active member of the Southern Tasmanian Agricultural and Pastoral Society.

Another grandson, Charles Francis Sievwright, would end up changing his name to Mohammed Abdul Hakk, after converting to Islam in Melbourne in 1896. He would spend several years travelling in India as a representative of the British and Indian Empire League of Australia. He would also spend some time in north Queensland, and would leave behind an unpublished novel entitled: *The Bride of a savage, or Thirty years' captivity amongst the blacks: an Australian aboriginal romance.* With the novel was a collection of photographs, including some of the author, and others of Aboriginal people hunting, and putting on paint in preparation for a fight. There was also one called "My Mirambeen".

Most of the other grand-children of Charles and Christina Sievwright would remain in Victoria or Tasmania, helping to ensure that there would still be descendants living in the two states a century-and-a-half after Charles left for London in 1845 to defend himself. But a few grand-children, like Lilian Davenport, would migrate to England. Lilian would marry the Reverend Arthur

Lucas, chaplain at a school in Kent, and later Canon of Rochester Cathedral. Another of the Davenport children, Katherine, would end up going to London to marry Charles John Plowden, an armorial Englishman whose father had been a colonel in the Bengal Native Infantry, and his grandfather Sheriff of Calcutta. That remarkable city would later be home for a while for one of Charles and Christina's great-grand-children. Amy Frances Shoobridge would continue the tradition started by her grandmother, marrying the Reverend Ormonde Birch, who would serve as Archdeacon of Calcutta.

At least one of the descendants of Charles Sievwright would follow his example in taking on a career in the British military. Charles George Matson would become an officer in the Royal Marines. He was a lieutenant when he married Nellie Collins, daughter of a Calcutta businessman, in England in 1885, and had been promoted to major by his retirement in 1903, having served the Empire in Egypt and elsewhere. Although Charles Sievwright's military career had not involved any actual battlefield experiences, at least two of his great-great-grand-children would die in battle -- both as Australian soldiers during World War One. As a lieutenant in an artillery division, Guy Kennedy Davenport would be killed by a German artillery shell, near Lagnicourt in France. A year later, Arthur Allan Orme Davenport, would also be killed in action in France. Their aunt, Lilian Lucas, would receive a telegram from King George V and Queen Mary expressing their "heartfelt sympathy" at the family's double loss.[15]

Like Charles Sievwright, George Robinson would never again see most of the seven children he'd left behind in Australia once he returned to England. But the rest of the former Chief Protector's life had little else in common with that of his former assistant. When Robinson sailed to London in 1852, he had a special annual pension of 220 pounds. Since the abolition of the Protectorate three years earlier, he'd also successfully speculated in gold from the newly-discovered fields near Melbourne, amassing four-thousand pounds worth, in addition to other valuable assets. His first wife had died in Melbourne in 1848, and less than a year after arriving in London he married for the second time. He and his new wife, Rose, almost 40 years his junior, would spend several years living on the Continent, much of it in Paris and Rome, as he devoted himself to learning French, Italian, drawing, painting, photography and piano-playing. With Rose, Robinson would have a further five children. The couple would return to England in 1858, and settle in Bath, where Robinson died in 1866, aged 75.[16]

Among the other major players in the downfall of Charles Sievwright, other than those in his own family, only Flogger Fyans would spend the rest of his life in the Port Phillip District. From 1849, Fyans would serve another term as Geelong's Police Magistrate before becoming its first mayor. He would die in Geelong, aged 80, in 1870.[17] Charles La Trobe would remain Port Phillip's

Superintendent until 1851, when he became Victoria's first Lieutenant-Governor. It was just before the discovery of gold near Melbourne, and the turbulent period which followed would stretch La Trobe's administrative skills to their limit. He would return late in 1854 to England, with an annual pension of 333 pounds. La Trobe would die in Sussex 21 years later, aged 74 -- failing eyesight having prevented him from writing a planned book relating his colonial experiences. He would leave a personal estate worth almost 16,000 pounds -- most of it in the form of former Aboriginal land in Melbourne.[18]

CHAPTER 35
And what remains

W HEN Charles Sievwright had taken up his duties in Port Phillip's Western District in 1839, the Aborigines for whom he was responsible far outnumbered the Europeans who had so far ventured into their territory. A decline in Aboriginal numbers, combined with an increase in white migration, meant that by the time of Sievwright's dismissal three-and-a-half years later, the Aborigines were already in a minority. Though their situation would become ever more precarious, no Protector would ever be appointed to replace him in the Western District. John Watton would remain in charge of the Mt Rouse reserve until 1850, unsuccessfully seeking a pay rise for taking on some of the tasks which had been performed there by Sievwright and his overseer.[1] But Watton would never concern himself much with the blacks elsewhere in the district. And even in his limited area of responsibility, Watton would be severely hampered by some of the same difficulties which Sievwright had experienced, and the number of blacks willing to live with him would soon drop.

Lack of food at Mt Rouse -- and the means to enhance the reserve's agricultural potential -- would become a regular theme of Watton's correspondence with George Robinson. Less than nine months after taking over from Sievwright, Watton was expressing similar frustration over the Chief Protector's lack of assistance. "I am wholly at a loss to know what to do respecting procuring supplies," he told Robinson. "I have again and again forwarded requisitions to Melbourne, but nothing has arrived at Port Fairy, nor have I received any instructions from you on the subject." He'd been obliged to procure a few articles off John Cox, and to borrow others from his own son-in-law, Acheson French -- "very much to his inconvenience and annoyance."[2] More than three years later, Watton would report that attendance at the reserve during 1846 had been "exceedingly desultory", averaging only 33. This he attributed to the very small quantity of provisions which he'd been able to issue, and to the "very great objection" which the Aborigines had to having to grind their own flour from the poor quality wheat allocated to them. This wheat was "so scruffy as to be totally valueless". No cultivation at all had taken place during the year. It was pointless trying cultivation with only a brush fence to protect the crops, and the request he'd made for money to make a proper post and rail fence had been rejected.

In the same report, Watton noted he'd heard of very few cases of aggression on the part of the blacks against the whites during the year. "Where collisions have occurred, they have been almost exclusively confined to the newly occupied localities," he wrote. And the number of clashes was only likely to further decline. "I am decidedly of opinion that the number of Aborigines in this District is very much on the decrease and I have been struck with the small number of young children amongst them. Unless the means of conducting this station be augmented during the ensuing years, it will be quite impossible that I can conduct it with credit to myself, satisfaction to the government, or essential benefit to the Aborigines."[3]

A year later, Watton would still be complaining that attendance at the reserve had been poor because of his lack of supplies. A little cultivation had taken place, but nothing extensive could be undertaken. For want of "a very trifling expenditure", the buildings on the station were "rapidly hastening to decay". Despite this, Watton would claim one positive development. Although some regrettable clashes had taken place between the whites and the Western District Aborigines during 1847, none had involved loss of life, he reported. "On the whole, I consider that the feeling existing between the two is daily becoming less unfriendly and that the civilisation of the Aborigines of this district is progressing even more rapidly than might be expected from the very small means allowed by the government for the amelioration of their condition."[4]

For some reason or other, however, Watton was lying. He knew full well that in May 1847, a shepherd employed on a station of George Wyndham Elms, west of Mt Rouse, had been murdered by some blacks. Watton himself had only recently given one version of what had occurred after the murder in a letter to Robinson. Without issuing any arrest warrants, John Cox had used his status as a magistrate to order the police stationed at The Grange in pursuit of the alleged murderers. The party had come across a party of blacks, spears had been thrown, and shots fired in return. "Two natives were killed, on one of whom the clothes and other property of the murdered shepherd were found," Watton had written. He believed that papers relating to the case had been forwarded by Cox to the Crown Prosecutor.[5]

It could have been that Watton had decided it was best to cover up when he subsequently learned of the real extent of the operation against the Gunditjmaras provoked by the murder of Elms' shepherd. According to one report recorded later by government official James Bonwick, the posse assembled for revenge was relatively small, but "mustered in rifles and pistols about fifty shots". The whites were guided into The Rocks by "a half civilised native" and "a stray wild Blackfellow". The party would find a party of Gunditjmara blacks having a morning meal. "Without a word of warning, the bullets of destruction were poured in among them," one of the whites involved would tell Bonwick. "Some fell at the first discharge, others snatched up their children and tried to fly, and some warriors turned round in desperation and seized their spears to defend their families. But all resistance was in vain. The Christians were too quick and too formidably armed for their heathen antagonists. Mothers, husbands, babes lay about the stones shrieking in maddening pain, moaning in dying struggle, or still in the sleep of death. More than thirty are said to have been thus laid low."

"But the part taken in the affray by the two guides is too important to be omitted in this narrative," Bonwick added. "The wild one was seen at the first fire to raise his waddy to strike an Englishman. Before his blow could fall a musket ball reached him. The other, the civilised one, having begged for a gun, had been presented with one loaded with powder only. The foremost in the work of slaughter, he rushed up to a native child and fired. With a curse upon the piece

Reproduced courtesy of the La Trobe Manuscripts Collection, State Library of Victoria
Assistant Protector William Thomas recorded that Warrie, "a fine black fellow" was captured by the Native Police in the Grampians and brought to Melbourne "after a great slaughter of the blacks". According to other Aborigines with him, the Native Police had killed 38 in the operation. After "some months" Thomas managed to have Warrie released into his care. The sketch of Warrie is by Thomas.

that would do no mischief, he grasped a stone, and smashed the head of the infant. When the battle was over, and our valorous countrymen were smoking their pipes, this wretch requested a weapon with which he might finish any still alive. The broken piece of a pair of shears was obtained, and with the grin of a demon the fellow is said to have ripped up the dying and the dead."[6]

There were other cases as well in which the whites would reduce Aboriginal numbers in the Western District by using their own race against them -- notably through use of the Native Police. They would be used in a number of operations in the District in the 1840s. One major operation would be prompted by the abduction and murder in August 1843 of the two-year-old daughter of a hotel licensee, Abraham Ward, also in Gunditjmara territory west of Mt Rouse. The *Portland Guardian* would report that as a result of the efforts of the Native Police and their white commanding officer, Henry Dana, the infant's bones had been "recovered and decently interred". According to information obtained by the troopers, the baby girl's brains had been "dashed out" with a waddy by one of the abductors because she'd been sick and crying for her mother.

At the same time, in the same area, squatter Christopher Bassett had been "barbarously murdered" and his body "shockingly mutilated", the *Guardian* told its readers. Bassett had been "a most industrious and steady settler", who through diligence and frugality had managed to obtain a small flock -- which had now been driven away and destroyed. "Such deeds occurring at the same instant is enough to rouse the settlers to annihilate the bloodthirsty tribe, and indeed little more is wanted to excite the inhabitants of the district to avenge these cold-blooded murders by a general massacre of the perpetrators," the *Guardian* suggested. The black police had already set an example. During the search for the abducted baby, they'd come across Bassett's alleged murderers. "A smart conflict ensued, in which the Native Police, though in considerable peril, evinced the greatest presence of mind and obedience of orders," the *Guardian* recorded. "But in self-defence, and in attempting to take some of the savages prisoners, we hear that nine or ten of the tribe were either killed or wounded."[7]

The Native Police, too, would eventually be responsible for killing the Gunditjmara resistance leaders, Jupiter and Cocknose -- several years after their release from prison in Melbourne. The squatter Thomas Browne recorded that the Native Police had had a "regular engagement" with a group of Gunditjmara blacks caught with portions of a freshly-slaughtered heifer and a calf. It was hoped that the action taken would be decisive in what had become the urgent task of crushing the "unprovoked" uprising among the blacks of the area. Browne learned from one of the Native Police, a young man named Buckup, that the "wild blacks" had been given "a scouring", although he was reluctant to provide much detail. From others involved, he learned that "plenty" of Gunditjmara people had been killed by the black troopers, among them Jupiter and Cocknose.[8]

The use of the Native Police to help to suppress resistance by fellow Aborigines would not last long. In just a few years, the Western District war was over. In 1858 -- three years after Sievwright's death -- a wide-ranging inquiry would hear that although the blacks of what had been the Port Phillip District still fought among themselves, they had long since ceased to be a danger to the whites. The committee of the Victorian Parliament which conducted the inquiry would conclude that when white settlement had begun in 1836, six to seven thousand Aborigines had been living in what was now Victoria. So great had the mortality rate been that in just 22 years, their numbers had dropped to only a few hundred. Most of these were "in a state of abject want" -- receiving almost no government help since the winding up of the Protectorate nine years earlier. "Indeed, the Blacks have been in a worse position than if the Protectorate had never been called into existence," the committee concluded, "for under that establishment they received assistance and protection, but were left to their own resources again, when it was abolished."

"The great and almost unprecedented reduction in the number of the Aborigines is to be attributed to the general occupation of the country by the white population; to vices acquired by contact with a civilised race, more particularly the indulgence in ardent spirits; and hunger, in consequence of the scarcity of game since the settlement of the Colony; and, also in some cases, to cruelty and ill-treatment," the committee reported. "The great cause, however, is apparently the inveterate propensity of the race to excessive indulgence in spirits, which it seems utterly impossible to eradicate. This vice is not only fatal, but leads to other causes which tend to shorten life." The evidence given to the committee about the devastation which alcohol had caused was overwhelming. Although the white men who gave evidence contradicted each other on many matters, there was no disagreement about the alcohol issue -- and many had emphasised it.

"The Aborigines are much addicted to drink, and have frequent quarrels from the effects of it," reported the squatter brother-in-law of the Winter brothers, Cecil Cooke. In his opinion, though, there was no point in excluding the blacks from the towns, because there were numerous public houses in the countryside, and they thought nothing of walking 20 or so kilometres "to get grog".[9] The committee was told that a law designed to stop the Aborigines being supplied with alcoholic drinks other than beer was not preventing them obtaining supplies. John McLeod, squatting in Gunditjmara territory on Darlot's Creek, near Port Fairy, said the five pound fine for publicans caught breaking the law was not enough to dissuade them.[10] Others remarked it was easy for the blacks to find a white man willing to buy for them.

The widely-travelled English historian, educationist and clerk of the Legislative Council, George William Rusden, believed the blacks' eagerness for alcohol was not surprising. "How could it be otherwise?" he asked. "Their hunting grounds are taken up by the whites; they themselves become interlopers in their native places; their presence in large bodies is incompatible with the occupation of their country by the whites; they have usually only the lowest classes (in point of morality) of the whites to associate with. They have no intellectual pursuits, no room for manly exercise in providing themselves with game, as was their wont; and they speedily adopt the vicious habits with which they are made acquainted by their invaders. They have no moral checks to appeal to, and the craving for the excitement of drink becomes a physical disease, controlling their wills as it does in many cases the civilised man, who has had better advantages, less excuse for yielding, and less temptation."[11]

Former Assistant Protector William Thomas, now Victoria's official Guardian of Aborigines, told the committee that the Aborigines could be as healthy as Europeans if they stayed in the bush, or if they worked on the station of "respectable" white settlers. "It is only when they stop for a week or two near a public inn, or with low characters, that their enervated constitutions are materially affected, which I have known so rapid that a few days have ended their career," Thomas reported. "Pulmonary disorders are what they are most liable to, and when drinking to excess, and not able to reach the encampment, down they lay, perhaps on a cold wet night, and throw themselves literally into the arms of death."[12] On one occasion, he'd found four or five drunken blacks at daybreak stuck in the mud of a creek. They'd been still alive, but would not be for long. "Cold comes on, and as soon as disease touches a black's chest you cannot save him," he'd remarked.[13] Thomas would also tell the committee that there'd been "awful drunkenness" among the Native Police. Though most had been young men when they joined the force, by 1858 all were dead. Some had not even reached the age of 35.[14]

Thomas would also tell the committee there was one key reason for the Protectorate having broken down: the insistence of the colonial authorities that only blacks who had performed some labour could receive rations. The Aborigines, he asserted, needed to be "decoyed feelingly into European labour". Their habit was not to work daily, but only when necessary to take advantage of what, before the arrival of the whites, had been available in abundance through "kind providence".[15] Another former Assistant Protector, Edward Parker, would state that throughout his term in office, he'd had "no benefit whatever" from any instructions from the Chief Protector, or from the Sydney government. From the outset, what he regarded as his limited success had been the result of his own initiative.[16] With complaints from Dredge, Sievwright, and Le Souef, it meant that every one of the former Protectors -- and Watton, as officer-in-charge at Mt Rouse -- had complained about the way in which the Protectorate had been run. Yet by 1858, the former Chief Protector had long been comfortably retired back in Europe on his special pension, with a favourable reputation still intact.

Foster Fyans -- who back in 1842 had declared that the Aborigines had suffered a "trifling disadvantage" by the arrival of the white men -- would tell the 1858 inquiry that the number of Barrabool people who used to live within 50 kilometres of Geelong had dropped from 297 to fewer than 20.[17] However, like when Sievwright had been unable to procure supplies from Robinson, some of the Barrabool blacks had obviously moved away from the town to fend for themselves in other parts of their territory. John Lang Currie, a Scottish squatter in Barrabool territory not far from where the Mt Elephant massacre had occurred in 1839, for instance, reported there were between 12 and 20 blacks in his area.[18] Former merchant navy captain Francis Ormond believed there were 40 Barrabool people in his part of their territory.[19]

To the west, a larger number of the Tjapwurong blacks and others for whom

Reproduced courtesy of the La Trobe Picture Collection, State Library of Victoria
A group of Aborigines at Geelong, in 1852. These are probably Barrabool people. The older ones, at least, would have lived for a time with Sievwright.

Sievwright had been responsible at Mt Rouse had been able to survive -- even though their mortality rate over the previous 10 years had been "very great". Patrick Mitchell, who ran a station near Mt Rouse, told the inquiry there 120 to 150 blacks still living in his area. "They consist of the Mt Rouse tribe, together with a few others whose former tribal distinctions are now obliterated," he wrote. Since the abolition of the Protectorate, the blacks in the Mt Rouse area had received no assistance whatsoever from the government. Many were "very robust in appearance and capable of considerable exertion" but they were of "generally enfeebled constitution" and easily succumbed to "attacks of those disorders incident to their exposed, unsettled, and improvident way of life". They were surviving partly by working for himself and other settlers. "Their former means of support -- hunting, fishing etc. -- are still open to them, but they have almost abandoned them."[20]

Cecil Cooke told the committee he believed Aboriginal numbers had dropped by three-quarters since he'd arrived in the colony 20 years earlier. He knew of three Gunditjmara clans, known to him as the Darlot Creek, Lake Condah and Eumeralla tribes. There were no more than 40 in each -- that is, fewer than 120 in total. Of the 40 or so blacks at Lake Condah, about 15 were children. All of them, he believed, were half-castes. He and other squatters were employing many of the Gunditjmara people, paying them in cash, food and clothing. Some hunting was also continuing, and Cooke believed the animals the blacks sought had been breeding at a much greater rate, in the much smaller area available as natural habitat. Possums, bandicoots and kangaroos, he claimed, were now "more numerous than when the white men first came to the country".[21] John McLeod also reported that there was "an abundance" of fish and kangaroo available for the Gunditjmara Aborigines. "But they will sooner beg about the stations for flour than catch them," he told the committee.[22] Francis Ormond believed the Barrabool people in his area were catching birds and fish, but selling them to white men for money to buy rum.[23]

Hugh Murray, still squatting in Colijon territory, was one of a group of leading colonists who had recommended back in 1849 that "the separation of the Aborigines from their native haunts" was "the only efficacious means of arresting the downward progress of the race". The idea had been to collect all the remaining blacks in one spot where they could be "civilised and evangelised" in the English language.[24] But by 1858, Murray believed there were only 19 Colijon blacks left -- mainly, he claimed, as a result of inter-tribal fighting, rather than white occupation of their land.[25] Murray thought it was probably too late to prevent the "total extinction" of the Colijon and other Victorian tribes. In areas highly-populated by whites, the birth-rate among the blacks had fallen to virtually zero.[26]

Marcus Sievwright would tell the 1858 committee that infanticide had for some time been "very prevalent" among the Aborigines. "The habit of destroying children arose generally from hunger, which eventually was perpetuated into a custom, and caused female children to be destroyed as soon as they were born, allowing the males to survive, the male children being a greater acquisition to a family than females," Marcus wrote.[27] Other white men would also give evidence about infanticide, but they would contradict Marcus. The victims, they stated, were usually half-caste *boys*. George Rusden would submit a report by a Church of England committee which he'd chaired in 1856, referring to the matter. Half-caste males were "almost invariably destroyed by the Aborigines", it alleged.[28] According to Charles Strutt, Police Magistrate at Echuca in northern Victoria, the frequency of the practice in his area stemmed from a fear that half-castes would "prove superior" to the full-blood Aborigines if they'd been allowed to live.[29]

The son of the former Assistant Protector in the Western District was one of the few white witnesses to tell the committee that the extinction of the Victorian Aborigines was not inevitable. Marcus suggested that large reserves should be formed, in locations chosen by the blacks. An "intelligent European family" chosen to run each reserve should try to prevent any contact with any other whites. Daily allowances of food should be issued, in return for the males performing duties such as fencing and grubbing. "The natives should be also induced to erect small huts to live in, and they should be well clothed in winter with woollen clothing, and supplied with good medical attendance to keep down prevailing diseases among them," Marcus wrote.[30] John Allan, whose station was near the southern border between Kirrae and Gunditjmara territory, told the committee he had a "voluminous" plan to help the blacks on special reserves -- if it could be properly funded and administered. Through "kindness and judicious treatment", the Aborigines could be induced to adopt "more civilised and fixed habits", Allan remarked. "I do not believe that God, in creating man, intended them to live and die like brutes."[31]

Almost all other witnesses, including William Thomas, would state that the Victorian Aborigines were doomed. Nevertheless, the committee would decide to recommend special reserves in an attempt to prevent their extinction. Proper provision should have been made for the Aborigines when their hunting grounds and means of living had first been taken from them, the committee stated. "Had they been a strong race, like the New Zealanders, they would have forced the new occupiers of their country to provide for them; but being weak and ignorant, even for savages, they have been treated with almost utter neglect," it reported to the Legislative Council. "With the exception of the Protectorate, which was an emanation of the Imperial Government, and which seemed to have been only partly successful, little or nothing has been done for the black denizens of the country. Victoria is now entirely occupied by a superior race, and there is scarcely a spot, excepting in the remote mountain ranges, or dense scrubs, on which the Aborigine can rest his weary feet. To allow this to continue would be to tolerate and perpetuate a great moral wrong; and your Committee are of opinion that, even at this late period, a vigorous effort should be made to provide for the remnants of the various tribes, so that they may be maintained in comparative plenty."[32]

The only way in which this could be done, the committee concluded, was by setting up reserves for each tribe, in its own territory. Run by Christian missionaries, these reserves should be large enough to enable the Aborigines to combine "agricultural and gardening operations with the depasturing of a moderate number of cattle and sheep". Efforts should also be made to induce the Aborigines "to take an interest in the occupations of civilised life and give their aid in carrying out the various branches of industry". Until they became self-supporting, the reserves should be given "ample supplies of provisions and blankets". The committee had hoped that all of the remaining Aborigines could be settled at a single locality, where they could be "civilised and Christianised". But it had been convinced by evidence that each tribe should have its own reserve. "The blacks would not leave their own hunting grounds, and would pine away at once if removed from them," it concluded.[33] In essence, the committee's recommendations were the same as those made almost 20 years earlier by Charles Sievwright, when the destruction of the Victorian Aborigines had just begun.

The committee's suggestion of reserves for each tribe would be regarded as far too radical, and would never be taken up by the Victorian government. The 1858 inquiry would lead, however, to the establishment of a reserve at a place the whites called Framlingham, on the Hopkins River outside Warrnambool, near the boundary between Gunditjmara and Kirrae territory. With an adjoining forest which allowed some traditional hunting to continue, it would be established as a Church of England mission. Then another Anglican mission would be established in 1867 in Gunditjmara territory at Lake Condah, on the edge of The Rocks near Mt Eccles. It was in this vicinity that Sievwright and Robinson had met and fed Jupiter and other resistance leaders, and had seen the "large-scale" systems the tribe had devised for catching fish, birds and kangaroos, a quarter of a century earlier. The Anglican missionaries at Framlingham and Lake Condah would do their best to promote Christianity and European values. But given the history of the area, it was an uphill battle. There was still much anger, anguish and distrust to overcome. One story which would be handed down through the generations among the blacks at the Lake Condah mission told of a massacre spot nearby where so much Aboriginal blood had been shed that no vegetation would ever grow there again.[34]

A Scotsman named James Dawson, who settled in the Western District in 1844, not long before, and not far from, the operation in which Jupiter and Cocknose died, would later make detailed studies of the remnants of the Western District Aborigines. Dawson lived first in Gunditjmara, and then in Kirrae the territory. In championing the Aboriginal cause throughout the latter half of the 19th Century, he would advocate many ideas similar to those which his compatriot, Charles Sievwright, had tried to promote years earlier. Largely, he would come across the same opposition among his fellow whites. Dawson would even be named a Guardian of the local Aborigines by the Victorian government, and eventually the results of much of his research into the languages and customs of several tribes would be published in Melbourne. It would become a primary reference work for future generations.

Based on information from Aboriginal informants, Dawson estimated that more than 2500 blacks could have once attended the great meetings of the Western District tribes, such as those held at a large marsh called Mirraewuae, near part of the border between Tjapwurong and Gunditjmara territory. He identified 10 distinct Western District Aboriginal languages. But by the time he wrote his book in 1880, Dawson thought there were only 14 Aborigines left who

Reproduced courtesy of the La Trobe Picture Collection, State Library of Victoria
"Lake Condah Aboriginal Station" (detail). This station was established in 1867 by the Anglican Church in Gunditjmara territory, on the edge of The Rocks. In the scene above, three children are playing cricket. The first cricket team from Australia to tour England, in 1868, would comprise Aborigines from the Western District.

spoke the Tjapwurong and two other languages. He believed that the Kirrae people, with whom Sievwright had spent so much time at Keilambete, Terang and Mt Rouse, were among the tribes already extinct. As a sad reminder that they had once existed, Dawson would organise the erection of a granite obelisk in a cemetery in the town of Camperdown -- dedicated to all the Western District Aborigines. Buried under the monument were the relocated remains of Wombeetch Puyuun, also known as Camperdown George, whom he regarded as a chief of the Kirrae people, and the last member of "the local tribes".[35]

It was not, however, the end of the Western District Aborigines. There were still many living in particular to the west at Lake Condah, and some at Framlingham. The proportion of full-bloods had greatly declined. But regardless of the actual ethnic composition of individuals, most of them felt and lived like Aborigines -- and were treated as such by the whites. The question of mixed race would cause much heartache with a development in the late 1880s when the population at the Lake Condah mission was at its highest. The Victorian government would introduce an Aborigines Protection Law Amendment Act, obliging many people of mixed blood to leave the mission -- with the hope that they would assimilate into the white community. It was a short-sighted and cruel policy, and the beginning of the end for the mission. Only those with lighter skin were forced to leave, splitting families. As the number of Aborigines living there gradually dropped, some of the land allocated for it was sold off, and it was officially closed in 1919.

Back in 1858, Marcus Sievwright had told the Legislative Council inquiry that he'd witnessed members of different tribes playing a variety of athletic sports and games, when they'd been assembled at Keilambete in 1841, and then Mt Rouse in 1842. At Keilambete, for instance, the younger men had held wrestling matches before the day's work assigned to them by Marcus' father.[36] Many of the Western District blacks would later win the grudging respect of the white community by their prowess in playing the white men's sports. The first cricket team from Australia to tour England, in 1868, would comprise Aborigines from the Western District -- and it would perform creditably. In local competition, too, Western District Aboriginal men would prove formidable opponents in cricket and later in Australian Rules football. Sometimes, the Gunditjmara men would receive a little cunning off-field support from their women. If a black football team was being outplayed, or a white batsman was scoring too well against black bowlers, the women would light a fire on the windward side of the ground and stack green eucalypt leaves onto it. The Gunditjmara men would often then be able to turn their fortunes around, using the advantage of being able to better cope with the resulting smoke![37]

Times would also come when Western District Aborigines would go off to fight in faraway battles as comrades-in-arms of Australian-born whites. Along with great-great-grandchildren of Charles Sievwright, some would fight and die in World War One in Europe as Australian soldiers.[38] One Gunditjmara man born and educated at Framlingham, Chris Saunders, would find plenty of use for the fighting spirit he'd inherited from his ancestors, as a member of an advance machine-gun unit. He would return to the Western District not believing in ghosts, but haunted by scenes of hundreds of mutilated bodies on European battlefields.[39] Just over 20 years later, two of his sons, Reginald and Harry, would be destined to witness many more battlefield casualties -- some after the Australian continent had been attacked for the first time since the arrival of the British invaders.

Reg Saunders, born near Framlingham and educated at Lake Condah, would serve in Palestine, Egypt, Libya, Greece, Crete and New Guinea, returning home at the end of World War Two as a lieutenant -- having become the first Aborigine to be commissioned as an Australian army officer. Later, during the Korean War, Reg would be promoted to captain. Before his death in 1990, he would work as a liaison officer for the Department of Aboriginal Affairs in the Australian capital. He would also serve for several years as a council member of the Australian War Memorial in Canberra, and would receive a Member of the British Empire award for his services to the Aboriginal community.[40] Reg's brother, Harry, would also enlist in the Australian army in World War Two. But he would never come home.

When Harry's company had been based on the Barid River in northern Lebanon, he would set an important personal hygiene standard at a time when his infantry battalion was suffering declining health. The second-in-command of his infantry battalion would later recall: "With the cooler weather coming on, A Company used to say that only the example of Harry Saunders, that excellent aborigine soldier, kept them up to the daily bath in the icy waters of the river. It was ten minutes down and forty minutes back up the steep bank." In Syria, Harry would be wounded by a grenade, but would go on to further action in New Guinea. Harry would display "the unflinching and steadfastness of the aborigine" before he became one of 25 Australians killed in three days of fierce fighting which resulted in the capture of a village near Gona, the first of the Japanese strongholds on the northern coast of New Guinea to fall to allied forces. Most of the dead Australians, including Harry, would be buried at a specially-prepared cemetery at Gona, in "the saddest and most solemn ceremony in the history of the battalion".[41]

After World War Two, there was strong support from the Council of the Shire of Portland for people like Reg Saunders and others with Aboriginal blood to be given priority in allocation of former mission land at Lake Condah being subdivided to resettle returning servicemen.[42] But the decision was not up to the Council and it would end up taking more than another 40 years before a sizeable portion of the land would finally be returned to the Gunditjmara people by the Victorian government. By then, the former mission site at Framlingham and its adjoining forest had also been returned to similar claimants. So after almost a century-and-a-half of white control, there would be two small portions of the Western District back under the control of descendants of those who had occupied it for thousands of years before white settlement.

The Aborigines of the Western District had come close to being exterminated, with the last full-blood probably dying towards the end of the 19th Century. But the fact remained that after many generations, there would still be some people with Aboriginal blood in their veins, living where their Aboriginal ancestors had lived. If a Scotsman called Charles Wightman Sievwright hadn't been the Protector of those ancestors through the crucial first years of contact with his fellow Europeans, encouraging and emboldening the blacks to resist aggression, there might not have been any at all. Certainly, even though it never occurred, the belief had become widespread among the Western District Aborigines, and at least some of the whites, that Sievwright could arrange the hanging of any white who dared to commit violence against them. It could therefore be argued, at least by those proud of the continent's Aboriginal heritage, that although Sievwright may have died in indignity -- and far from having received any acclamation for his efforts on behalf of the Aborigines -- he may not have lived in vain. And every year, when they're not in hibernation, the London squirrels scamper happily through the grass on top of his unmarked grave.

CHAPTER NOTES:

ADB = Australian Dictionary of Biography
AOT = Archives Office of Tasmania
Col Sec = Colonial Secretary
CSIL = Colonial Secretary's Inward Letters
Dixson = Dixson Library (State Library of New South Wales)
Fyans = Foster Fyans
GA = Geelong Advertiser
Gipps = George Gipps
HRA = *Historical Records of Australia*
HRV = *Historical Records of Victoria*
La Trobe = Charles Joseph La Trobe
Mitchell = Mitchell Library (State Library of New South Wales)
NAS = National Archives of Scotland
PGuard = Portland Guardian
PMerc = Portland Mercury
PPG = Port Phillip Gazette
PPH = Port Phillip Herald
PPP = Port Phillip Patriot
PRO = Public Record Office
Robinson = George Augustus Robinson
SG = Sydney Gazette
SH = Sydney Herald
Sievwright = Charles Wightman Sievwright
SM = Sydney Monitor
SMH = Sydney Morning Herald
SRNSW = State Records Authority of New South Wales
Times = The Times (London)
V & P = Votes & Proceedings
VPRS = Victorian Public Record Series (at PRO, Victoria)

CHAPTER 1:

1 Glenelg to Gipps 31 Jan 1838, HRV vol 2B pp. 373-5
2 Report of Proceedings of C. W. Sievwright from 1 March 1839 to 31 Aug 1839. Add Ms 86, Dixson
3 *PPP* 27 March 1839
4 Journal of James Dredge 28 March 1839, HRV vol 2B pp. 450-1; Journal of W. Thomas, 28 March 1839, HRV vol 2B p. 442; W. Thomas (junior), Reminiscences, Uncat Ms 214, Item 27, ML pp. 44-5
5 Report of Proceedings of C. W. Sievwright from 1 March 1839 to 31 Aug 1839. Add Ms 86, Dixson
6 Glenelg to Gipps 31 Jan 1838, HRV vol 2B pp. 373-5
7 Gipps to Col Sec April 1839, HRV vol 2B p. 458; Col Sec to La Trobe 24 April 1840, British House of Commons, Sessional Papers, 1844, vol. 34, pp. 55-6
8 Sievwright to Robinson 21 Aug 1839, Add Ms 86, Dixson (abridged transcript in *GA* 5 Feb 1845)
9 J. Clerke to Sievwright 19 August 1839, HRV vol 2B p. 649
10 Robinson to W. Thomas 3 Sept 1839, HRV vol 2B pp. 577-82; Auditor-General to Col Sec 19 Sept 1839, HRV vol 2B p. 419; J. Dredge to G. Robinson 30 Oct 1839, HRV vol 2B p. 713
11 ADB vol 1 pp. 174-5
12 Various letters between Fyans, A. Thomson, J. Clerke and Col Sec, Oct to Nov 1838, HRV vol2B pp. 740-2; G. Presland (ed.), *Journals of George Augustus Robinson Jan-March 1840*, p. 45
13 Report of Proceedings of C. W. Sievwright from 1 March 1839 to 31 Aug 1839. Add MS 86, Dixson
14 *SH* 14 & 19 Nov 1838
15 *SH* 14 Nov 1838
16 *SM* 19 Nov 1838

17 *The Australian*, 8 Dec 1838
18 *SG* 20 Nov 1838
19 *SH* 26 Nov 1838
20 *SH* 10 Dec 1838; *SM* 19 Dec 1838
21 Sievwright to Robinson 22 April 1839, Add Ms 86, Dixson
22 Report of Proceedings of C. W. Sievwright from 1 March 1839 to 31 Aug 1839, Add Ms 86, Dixson
23 Ibid.
24 W. Lonsdale to La Trobe 23 June 1842; Fyans to La Trobe 24 June 1842; W. Meeke to Fyans 16 July 1842, all
    with Gipps to Sec of State 20 Dec 1842, NSW Governor's Despatches Outwards, vol 41, Despatch No 238,
    Mitchell Ms A1230 (Papers 12 & 13)
25 Sievwright to Lord Glenelg 13 March 1838; Sir G. Grey to Sievwright 27 March 1838. HRV vol 2B pp. 381-3
26 Christina Sievwright to Robinson 11 March 1839, in Gipps to Sec of State 20 Dec 1842, NSW Governor's
    Despatches Outwards, vol 41, Despatch No 238, Mitchell Ms A1230 (Paper 11); G. Robinson to M. Robinson 16
    March 1839, Robinson Papers, Vol 54, Ms A7075, Mitchell (transcript in HRV vol 2B p. 445)
27 Fyans to Col Sec 5 July 1839, Add Ms 87, Dixson

CHAPTER 2:

1 Notice from Col Sec's Office 21 May 1839. Copy in British House of Commons, Sessional Papers, 1844, vol. 34,
   pp. 20-1
2 Notice from Col Sec's Office 18 Sept 1837. Ibid., p. 21
3 Report of Proceedings of C. W. Sievwright from 1 March 1839 to 31 Aug 1839. Add Ms 86, Dixson
4 HRV vol 2B pp. 652-3
5 HRV vol 2B pp. 646-7
6 Geelong Police Office Deposition Book 26 July 1839, VPRS 109
7 C. Roderick, *John Knatchbull* , pp. 91-2; R. Hughes, *The Fatal Shore*, p. 476
8 Petition to Governor Bourke from Western District squatters 8 June 1837, HRV vol 1 pp. 219-20
9 Col Sec to Fyans 12 Sept 1837; Bourke to Col Sec Sept 1837, HRV vol 1 pp. 221-2 & 225-7
10 Fyans to Col Sec 3 July 1839 Add Ms 87, Dixson
11 Ibid.
12 Geelong Court Register 3 July 1839, HRV vol 2B p. 645; Fyans to Sievwright 8 July 1839; Sievwright to Robinson
    13 July 1839; Robinson to Sievwright 22 July 1839; Sievwright to Robinson 21 Aug 1839, All in Add Ms 86,
    Dixson; Fyans to Col Sec 9 July 1839, HRV vol 2B p. 646; Col Sec to Fyans, 22 Aug 1839, HRV vol 2B p. 650
13 Geelong Court Register 20 Aug 1839, HRV vol 2B p. 649-50; Statement by Blackney to Fyans, encl. with
    Sievwright to Fyans 21 Aug 1839 (2 letters), Add Ms 86, Dixson
14 Fyans to Sievwright 21 Aug 1839, Add Ms 86, Dixson; Fyans to Col Sec 23 Aug 1839, CSIL 4/2471, SRNSW.
    (transcript in HRV vol 2B p. 651); Sievwright to Robinson 26 Aug 1839, Add Ms 86, Dixson; Minute of Journies
    made, cases inquired into, March to Aug 1839 by C. W. Sievwright, Add Ms 86, Dixson; Col Sec to La Trobe 3
    October 1839, HRV vol 2B p. 658
15 *PPG* 21 Sept 1839; G. Presland (ed.), *Journals of George Augustus Robinson Jan-March 1840*, p. 79; Journal of
    W. Thomas, April 1839, HRV vol 2B p. 520; *PPH* 21 June 1844
16 Report by Sievwright 17 April 1839, quoted in Journal of Rev. J. Orton, entry for 12 Jan 1841, Ms A1715, Mitchell
17 Robinson to Sievwright 1 April 1839, Add Ms 86, Dixson; Sievwright to Robinson 2 April 1839, Add Ms 86,
    Dixson; Journal of W. Thomas April 1839, HRV vol 2B p. 520; Report by Sievwright 17 April 1839, quoted in
    Journal of Rev. J. Orton, entry for 12 Jan 1841, Ms A1715, Mitchell
18 J. H. Plunkett to Col Sec 25 May 1839, HRV vol 2B pp. 642-3
19 Lonsdale to Attorney-General 2 July 1839, HRV vol 2B p. 643
20 *PPP* 5 Aug 1839
21 G. Arden, *Latest information with regard to Australia Felix*, pp. 95-6
22 *PPG* 7 Aug 1839.
23 Minute of Journies made, cases inquired into, March to August 1839 by C. W. Sievwright, Add Ms 86, Dixson;
    Lonsdale to Att-Gen 2 Jul 1839, HRV vol 2B p. 643; *PPP* 8 Aug 1839; *PPG* 14 Aug 1839
24 *PPP* 8 Aug 1839
25 Glenelg to Bourke 26 May 1837, HRA vol xix pp. 187 & 461; NSW Govt Notice 18 Nov 1837, HRA vol xix p.
    800
26 *PPG* 14 Aug 1839
27 *PPG* 17 Aug 1839
28 *PPG* 2 Oct 1839
29 Presland (ed.), *Journals of George Augustus Robinson Jan-March 1840*, p. 68

30 E. Finn, *The Chronicles of Early Melbourne*, pp. 602-3

CHAPTER 3:

1 *PPG* 14 Aug 1839
2 *PPP* 15 Aug 1839
3 *PPG* 17 Aug 1839
4 *PPG* 14 Aug 1839
5 *PPG* 7 Sept 1839
6 D H Wilsone to G R Wilsone 18 April & 9 Sept 1839, D H Wilsone letters, La Trobe Library Ms 9825 File 267/2a
7 Various documents, HRV vol 2B pp. 55-61; P. L. Browne (ed.), *Memoirs (of) Captain Foster Fyans*, p. 209
8 Robinson to La Trobe Dec 11 1841, British House of Commons, Sessional Papers, 1844, vol. 34, p. 170
9 Depositions taken by Sievwright 21 Jan 1840, quoted in Journal of Rev J Orton, entry for 12 Jan 1841, Ms A1715, Mitchell; J. Dawson, *Australian Aborigines*, p. lxxxiii; J. Bonwick, Western Victoria, p28
10 Sievwright to Robinson 21 Nov 1839, HRV vol 2B, pp. 658-9.
11 Sievwright to Robinson 13 Nov 1839; Robinson to La Trobe 14 Nov 1839; La Trobe to Robinson 20 Nov 1839; La Trobe to H F Gisborne 20 Nov 1839. HRV vol 2B pp. 660-2
12 Robinson to La Trobe 23 Nov 1839; La Trobe to Robinson 23 Nov 1839; Robinson to La Trobe 9 Jan 1840; Sievwright to Robinson 22 Jan 1839. HRV vol 2B pp. 498-9, 662 & 666; Sievwright to Robinson 30 Nov 1840. Transcript in *GA* 5 Feb 1845
13 Sievwright to Robinson 7 Dec 1839; La Trobe to Robinson 12 Dec 1839; H F Gisborne to La Trobe 29 Dec 1839. HRV vol 2B pp. 663-6
14 H F Gisborne to La Trobe 29 Dec 1839; Sievwright to Robinson 22 Jan 1839. HRV vol 2B pp665-8
15 Robinson to La Trobe 11 Dec 1841, British House of Commons, Sessional Papers, 1844, vol. 34, p. 170
16 Journal of Niel Black, Entries for 9 & 25 Dec 1839 & 18 Jan 1840, Ms 11519, La Trobe Manuscript Collection

CHAPTER 4:

1 D. Walker, *Principles of Scottish Private Law*, pp. 1170-83; J. Erskine, *An institute of the law of Scotland*, p. 326; Tack agreement between Trustees of Francis Sievwright & T. Scott 3 March 1805, Register of Deeds, March to April 1805, NAS RD3/306 pp. 458-464
2 HRV vol 2B Ch 1; ADB vol 2 pp. 522-523; T. F. Bride, *Letters from Victorian Pioneers*, pp. 129-135
3 G. Arden, *Latest information with regard to Australia Felix*, p. 97
4 Bride, *Letters from Victorian Pioneers*, pp. 41, 46, 94, 142-3; ADB vol 2 pp. 146-9 & 365-6
5 *PPG* 12 Feb 1840
6 T. L. Mitchell, *Three Expeditions into the Interior of Eastern Australia*, entry for 30 June 1836
7 J. H. Wedge to Lord Glenelg 22 April 22 1839, HRV vol 2B pp. 752-4; Russell to Gipps 24 Jan 1840 & J. H. Wedge to Russell 18 Jan 1840, British House of Commons, Sessional Papers, 1844, vol. 34, pp. 119-21
8 Statement by P. Codd 6 March 1840, transcript in British House of Commons, Sessional Papers, 1844, vol. 34, p. 142
9 Report of Sievwright on massacre, quoted in Journal of Rev J Orton, entry for 12 Jan 1841, Ms A1715, Mitchell; J. Croke to Robinson 15 & 17 June 1840, British House of Commons, Sessional Papers, 1844, vol. 34, pp. 142-3; Journal of Niel Black, entry for 23 March 1840, La Trobe Library Manuscript Ms 11519; J. G. Robertson to La Trobe 26 Sept 1853, Bride, Letters from Victorian Pioneers, p. 164; Statement by G. Winter 3 Jan 1842, British House of Commons, Sessional Papers, 1844, vol. 34, p. 187; J. Croke to La Trobe 28 Nov 1847, Ms A1267-23, Mitchell pp. 3606-11
10 *PPG* 4 & 7 March 1840
11 Memorial of Geelong District squatters to Gipps, forwarded 23 March 1840 by Alexander Thomson, VPRS 19/4 No 40/333; *PPG* 25 March 1840
12 J. Croke to Robinson 23 March 1840, VPRS 21
13 Sievwright to Robinson 21 March 1840 & encl. statements, VPRS 21; Diary of Charles Tyers, entry for 2 Feb 1840, HRV vol 6 p. 361
14 Journal of Rev. J. Orton, entry for 12 Jan 1841, Ms A1715, Mitchell; Croke to Robinson 15 June 1840, , British House of Commons, Sessional Papers, 1844, vol. 34, p. 143; La Trobe to Gipps 28 Aug 1841, Ibid. p. 136
15 Sievwright to Robinson 14 April 1840 & encl. statement, VPRS 21
16 *PPG* 7 & 25 March 1840

CHAPTER 5:

1 N. R. Cheyne, Accounts & receipts 1792-97, Steuart papers, Mss 5037, 5038, 5039; Notes, accounts & discharges 1790-92 & 1798. Advocates Ms, NLS, Ms 82.3.9, 82.3.10, 82.6.1, National Library of Scotland; C. Watson, Roll of Edinburgh Burgesses

2 Feu contract between Elizabeth Anne Hay, John Turnbull, Andrew Sievwright and Anne Robertson 27 May 1802, Midlothian Sheriff Court Register of Deeds July to Dec 1802, NAS SC 39/76/207

3 Letter of acknowledgement from Francis Sievwright to Andrew Sievwright 20 Sept 1797, Register of Deeds Nov to Dec 1805, NAS RD 3/309/2 pp306-308

4 PRO London WO 31/435; I. Scobie, The Scottish Regiments, p. 53

5 PRO London WO 25/786; P. Groves, *Historical Records of the 7th or Royal Regiment of Fusiliers*, pp. 163-6

6 J. Waugh to E. Waugh 1838, Waugh Family letters, Ms A-827, Mitchell p. 30; Sievwright to George Grey 31 Jan 1838 & Sir Frederick Hankey to Glenelg 1 Feb 1838. HRV vol 2B pp. 369-372; Sievwright to La Trobe 13 Aug 1842 & attached letters, all in Gipps to Sec of State 20 Dec 1842, NSW Governor's Despatches Outwards, vol 41, Despatch No 238, Mitchell Ms A1230 (Paper 20)

7 Report of Select Committee on Aborigines (British Settlements); House of Commons 26 June 1837, extracts in HRV vol 2A pp. 66-67

8 G. Arthur to Lord Glenelg 22 July 1837, HRV vol 2A p. 24; Col Office to Arthur 2 Nov 1837, HRV vol 2A p. 30

9 HRV vol 2A p. 33

10 HRV vol 2B pp. 368 & 383

11 HRV vol 2B pp. 369-373 &383

12 Journal of Niel Black 30 Sept 1839-8 May 1840 Entry for 25 Feb La Trobe Library Ms 11519

13 *PPG* 14 March 1840

14 Fyans to La Trobe 24 June 1842, in Gipps to Sec of State 20 Dec 1842, NSW Governor's Despatches Outwards, vol 41, Despatch No 238, Mitchell Ms A1230 (Paper 13)

15 J. Waugh to E. Waugh 1838, Waugh Family Letters, Mitchell Ms A-827, p. 30; John Sievwright to G. Robinson 30 March 1842, in Gipps to Sec of State 20 Dec 1842, NSW Governor's Despatches Outwards, vol 41, Despatch No 238, Mitchell Ms A1230 (Paper 11)

16 G. Gipps to Memorialists 18 April 1840, in *PPH* 22 May 1840 (also in British House of Commons, Sessional Papers, 1844, vol. 34, pp. 52-3)

17 Sievwright to Robinson 19 Aug 1842, in Gipps to Sec of State 20 Dec 1842, NSW Governor's Despatches Outwards, vol 41, Despatch No 238, Mitchell Ms A1230, Paper 24; Minute by La Trobe 29 Aug 1842, in Mitchell Ms A1230 (Paper No 25); Sievwright to Earl Grey 8 May 1847, HRA vol xxvi p. 588

18 J. Dawson, *Australian Aborigines*, pp. 58-9

19 Report of Proceedings of C. W. Sievwright from 1 June to 31 Oct 1840, encl. In La Trobe to Col Sec., 7 Dec 1841, in CSIL 4/2549 No 41/1328, SRNSW

20 J. Brock to La Trobe & Statement by Brock and others 20 May 1840, British House of Commons, Sessional Papers, 1844, vol. 34, pp. 123-4 &127 ; P. L. Browne (ed.), *Memoirs (of) Captain Foster Fyans*, p. 249; Report of R. Martin on condition of P. Rooney 4 June 1840 & Sievwright to Robinson 28 May 1840, encl. in Col Sec to La Trobe 13 Aug 1842, VPRS 19/34 No 42/1545

21 J. Brock to La Trobe 20 May 1840, British House of Commons, Sessional Papers, 1844, vol. 34, pp. 123-4 & 127

22 La Trobe to Sievwright 1 June 1840, Ibid. p. 141

23 J. H. Wedge to Russell 8 Feb 1841, HRA vol xxi p. 242 (also in British House of Commons, Sessional Papers, 1844, vol. 34, p. 125); G. Presland (ed.), *Journals of George Augustus Robinson 20 March to 15 May 1841*, entry for 29 April 1841

24 La Trobe to F. B. Russell 1 June 1840 & Sievwright to Robinson 10 June 1840 , British House of Commons, Sessional Papers, 1844, vol. 34, p. 141

25 Report of Proceedings of C. W. Sievwright from 1 December 1840 to 28 February 1841, Add Ms 86, Dixson; Col Sec to La Trobe 28 April 1840, VPRS 10 No 40/395

26 Sievwright to Robinson 27 Sept 1839, transcript in *GA* 5 Feb 5 1845

27 Report of Proceedings of C. W. Sievwright from 1 December 1840 to 28 February 1841, Add Ms 86, Dixson; Sievwright to Robinson 11 July 1840, VPRS 19/19 No 41/1374

28 Report of Proceedings of C. W. Sievwright from 1 December 1840 to 28 February 1841, Add Ms 86, Dixson

29 Sievwright to Robinson 24 July 1840; Statements by James Abbott 29 July & 1 Aug 1840 & Statement by Abbott 5 Sept 1840, encl. in La Trobe to Col Sec 7 Dec 1841, CSIL 4/2549 No 41/1328, SRNSW

30 Petitition to La Trobe from Western District squatters, 24 July 1840, encl. in La Trobe to Col Sec 15 Aug 1840, CSIL 4/2511 No 40/700, SRNSW; Statement of J. Thomson 29 Aug 1840, VPRS 24/476 No 1403

31 Fyans to La Trobe 7 Nov 1841, encl. in La Trobe to Col Sec 7 Dec 1841, CSIL 4/2549 No41/1328, SRNSW

32 Statements by W. Brack, J. Abbott & E. Pickering 23 Aug 1840 & 5 Sept 1840; Sievwright to Robinson 27 Sept 1841; Fyans to La Trobe 7 Nov 1841; Statement by Abbott to Fyans 1 Aug 1840, encl. in La Trobe to Col Sec 7 Dec 1841, CSIL 4/2549 No 41/1328, SRNSW

33 Report of Proceedings of C. W. Sievwright from 1 June to 31 Oct 1840, encl. In La Trobe to Col Sec 7 Dec 1841, in CSIL 4/2549 No 41/1328, SRNSW; Robinson to La Trobe 4 Dec 1841; Sievwright to Robinson 27 Sept 1841; Statement by William Brack 23 Aug 1840; encl. in La Trobe to Col Sec 7 Dec 1841, CSIL 4/2549 No 41/1328, SRNSW

34 G. Presland (ed.), *Journals of George Augustus Robinson 20 March to 15 May 1841*, entries for 29 March & 9 April 1841

CHAPTER 6:

1 Statement by Aborigines Protection Society 30 July 1839, HRA vol xx pp. 302-3

2 W. W. Burton to H. Labouchere 16 & 17 Aug 1839, HRA vol xx pp. 303-5

3 Normanby to Gipps 17 July 1839, HRA vol xx p. 243; Normanby to Gipps 31 Aug 1839, HRA vol xx pp. 302-3

4 Copy of Act passed by Leg. Council on 8 Oct 1839, British House of Commons, Sessional Papers, 1844, vol. 34, p. 26; Gipps to Normanby 14 Oct 1839 HRA vol xx p. 368 (also in HRV vol 2B pp. 760-761 with comments by James Stephen & Normanby)

5 J. Campbell & T. Wilde to Russell 27 July 1840; Russell to Gipps 11 Aug 1840, HRA vol xx p. 756

6 Croke to Robinson 15 &17 June 1840, British House of Commons, Sessional Papers, 1844, vol. 34, pp.142-3; La Trobe to Gipps 26 Nov 1840, ibid., pp.140-1; La Trobe to Gipps 28 Aug 1841, ibid., pp.135-7

7 Croke to La Trobe 23 April 1840, VPRS 19/4 No 40/305; Sievwright to Robinson 11 July 1840 & Robinson to Croke 17 July 1840, VPRS 21; Sievwright to Robinson 8 Aug 1840, VPRS 10 No 40/813; La Trobe to Col Sec 26 Nov 26 1840, British House of Commons, Sessional Papers, 1844, vol. 34, pp. 140-1

8 Sievwright to Robinson 8 Aug 1840, VPRS 10 No 40/813

9 Report of Proceedings of C. W. Sievwright from 1 June to 31 Oct 1840, encl. In La Trobe to Col Sec., 7 Dec 1841, in CSIL 4/2549 No 41/1328, SRNSW

10 La Trobe to Robinson 17 July 1840, CSIL 4/2511 No 40/7540, SRNSW

11 Report of Proceedings of C. W. Sievwright from 1 June to 31 Oct 1840, encl. In La Trobe to Col Sec., 7 Dec 1841, in CSIL 4/2549 No 41/1328, SRNSW

12 Sievwright to Robinson 6 July 1840, CSIL 4/2511 No 40/7540, SRNSW

13 La Trobe to Robinson 17 July 1840; Robinson to La Trobe 18 July 1840; Gipps' minute on La Trobe to Col Sec 24 July 1840, all in CSIL 4/2511 No 40/7540, SRNSW; Lonsdale to G. M. Langhorne 29 June 1839, VPRS 2140

14 Report of Proceedings of C. W. Sievwright from 1 June to 31 Oct 1840, encl. In La Trobe to Col Sec., 7 Dec 1841, in CSIL 4/2549 No 41/1328, SRNSW

15 La Trobe to Col Sec 5 Nov 1840, CSIL 4/2511 No 40/11571, SRNSW; G. Presland (ed.), *Journals of George Augustus Robinson 16 May to 15 Aug 1841*, entry for 27 June 1841; Statement by R. W. Tulloh 30 Dec 1841, British House of Commons, Sessional Papers, 1844, vol. 34, p.186

16 La Trobe to Col Sec 22 Oct 1840 & enclosures, CSIL 4/2511 No 40/11571, SRNSW; *PPP* 14 March 1842

17 La Trobe to Col Sec 22 Oct 1840 & enclosures, CSIL 4/2511 No 40/11571 SRNSW; Report of Sievwright Quoted in Journal of Rev. J. Orton, entry for 12 Jan 1841, Ms A1715, Mitchell; Sievwright to Croke 17 & 19 Oct 1840 & Croke to Sievwright 21 Oct 1840, VPRS 21

18 G. Presland (ed.), *Journals of George Augustus Robinson 16 May to 15 Aug 1841*, entries for 12, 15, 23, 25 & 29 July; ADB vol 1 pp. 605-6

19 Statement by R. Savage 14 Jan 1842, British House of Commons, Sessional Papers, 1844, vol. 34, p. 191

20 T. W. McCulloch to La Trobe 21 July 1840, encl. in La Trobe to Col Sec 22 Oct 1840, CSIL 4/2511 No 40/11108, SRNSW; J. G. Robertson to La Trobe 26 Sept 1853, T. F. Bride, *Letters from Victorian Pioneers*, p. 165

21 Report of Sievwright, quoted in Journal of Rev. J. Orton, entry for 12 Jan 1841, Ms A1715, Mitchell; Statements by H. Gibb & W. Brack 19 Oct & 24 Aug 1840, with Sievwright to Robinson 27 Sept 1841, encl. in La Trobe to Col Sec 7 Dec 1841, CSIL 4/2549 No 41/1328, SRNSW

22 Fenwick to La Trobe 12 Sept1840, CSIL 4/2511 No 40/897, SRNSW

23 Learmonth Station Diary, La Trobe Library Ms H15788 Box 102/9, Entries for 3 & 4 Sept 1840

24 D. H. Wilsone to G. R. Wilsone 30 Aug 1840, La Trobe Library Ms 9825, File 267/2(b)

25 Account of provisions issued by Sievwright, 1 Aug-30 Sept 1840, VPRS 12, Units 1 & 2.

26 La Trobe to Robinson 7 Sept 1840, VPRS 16 No 40/676

27 La Trobe to Col Sec 15 Aug 1840, CSIL 4/2511 No 40/8470, SRNSW; Fenwick to La Trobe 15 Aug 1840 & C. F. H. Smith to La Trobe 19 Aug 1840, VPRS 19/7 No 40/869

28 La Trobe to Robinson 7 Sept 1840, VPRS 16 No 40/676

29 La Trobe to Fyans 17 Sept 1840, VPRS 16 No 40/718
30 Fyans to La Trobe 20 Sept 1840, *British House of Commons, Sessional Papers*, 1844, vol. 34, pp. 88-9
31 Ibid.
32 Geelong Court Register 9 April & 7 June 1838, HRV vol 2A pp. 288-90; *SH* 31 May 1839; Principal Gaoler to W. Lonsdale 10 Sept 1839, HRV vol 2A p. 304; Journal of W. Thomas, Entry for 30 Sept 1839, HRV vol 2B p. 548
33 Fyans to La Trobe 20 Sept 1840, British House of Commons, Sessional Papers, 1844, vol. 34, pp. 88-9
34 Ibid.
35 Sievwright to Croke 16 Sept 1840, VPRS 21
36 Fyans to La Trobe 20 Sept 1840, British House of Commons, Sessional Papers, 1844, vol. 34, pp. 88-9
37 Croke to La Trobe 9 Sept 1840; Croke to Geelong Magistrates 16 Sept 1840; Croke to Plunkett 29 Sept 1840, VPRS 21
38 Fenwick to Croke 15 Sept 1840 & Croke to Plunkett 29 Sept 1840, VPRS 21
39 Sievwright to Croke 16 Sept 1840, VPRS 21
40 Croke to Sievwright 17 Sept 1840, VPRS 21

CHAPTER 7:

1 F. A. Powlett to La Trobe 18 Sept 1840, British House of Commons, Sessional Papers, 1844, vol. 34, p. 88
2 Gipps to Lettsom 28 Aug 1840, British House of Commons, Sessional Papers, 1844, vol. 34, p. 92; Gipps to La Trobe 29 Aug 1840, A. G. L. Shaw, *Gipps-La Trobe Correspondence*, p. 45; Gipps to Russell 3 Feb 1841, British House of Commons, Sessional Papers, 1844, vol. 34, p. 85
3 G. E. Mackay to La Trobe 30 Aug 1853, T. F. Bride, Letters from Victorian Pioneers, p. 212; Statement of J. S. A. Mackay 14 Feb 1841, British House of Commons, Sessional Papers, 1844, vol. 34, pp. 111-3
4 Glenelg to Bourke 26 July 1837, HRA vol xix p. 48; Gipps to Lettsom 28 Aug 1840, British House of Commons, Sessional Papers, 1844, vol. 34, p. 92
5 Gipps to La Trobe 29 Aug1840, Shaw, *Gipps-La Trobe Correspondence*, p. 45
6 La Trobe to Robinson 28 Sept 1840, VPRS 16 No 40/739
7 Thomas to Lettsom 28 Sept 1840, VPRS 11 Nos 40/332; Thomas to Robinson 28 Sept 1840, VPRS 11 No 40/333
8 Lettsom to Thomas 27 Sept 1840 & Thomas to Robinson 29 Sept 1840, VPRS 11 No 40/334
9 Thomas to Robinson 6 Oct 1840 VPRS 11 No 40/335; Thomas notes with sketch of "Windberry" (Winberri), R. B. Smyth Papers, Print No 20
10 La Trobe to Lettsom 10 Oct 1840, VPRS 16 No 40/773
11 Ibid.
12 Statements by C. H. Smith, W. P. Monk, S. Lettsom, R. Brennan, F. D. Vignolles, G. Fry 12 Oct 1840, VPRS 21/1; *PPP* 15 Oct 1840; *PPH* 13, 16 & 20 Oct 1840; Lettsom to Col Sec 23 Oct 1840, British House of Commons, Sessional Papers, 1844, vol. 34, pp. 93-4
13 Statements by S. Mann, S. Jennings, P. Cussen, W. Holland, B. Barker, J. Kelly, W. Wright, J. Rattenbury, P. Sheridan 14 & 15 Oct 1840, VPRS 21/1; La Trobe to Col Sec 14 Oct 1840, VPRS 16 No 40/775; Parker to Robinson 18 Oct 1840, VPRS 11 No 40/140; Robinson to La Trobe 5 Nov 1840, VPRS 21/1.
14 *PPP* 15 Oct 1840; *PPH* 20 Oct 1840
15 *PPH* 16 Oct 1840
16 Lettsom to Col Sec 23 Oct 1840, British House of Commons, Sessional Papers, 1844, vol. 34, pp. 93-4
17 Gipps to La Trobe 24 Oct 1840, Shaw, *Gipps-La Trobe Correspondence*, p. 48
18 La Trobe to Robinson 15 Oct 1840, VPRS 16 No 40/716; Parker to Robinson 18 Oct 1840, VPRS 11 No 40/140; Robinson to La Trobe 5 Nov 1840, VPRS 21/1.
19 La Trobe to Col Sec 19 Nov 1840, VPRS 16 No 40/864; La Trobe to Croke 7 Nov 1840, VPRS 16 No 40/821
20 La Trobe to Col Sec 5 Nov 1840, VPRS 16 No 40/813
21 La Trobe to Robinson 6 Nov 1840, VPRS16 No 40/817
22 La Trobe to Croke 7 Nov 1840, VPRS 16 No 40/821
23 La Trobe to Simpson 16 Nov 1840, VPRS 16 No 40/860
24 Statements by F. MacKerrick, S. Dayton, O. Nowlan & D. Douglas 13, 17 & 26 Oct 1840, VPRS 21/1.
25 Report of Proceedings of C. W. Sievwright from 1 June to 31 Oct 1840, encl. In La Trobe to Col Sec., 7 Dec 1841, in CSIL 4/2549 No 41/1328, SRNSW
26 Fyans to La Trobe 23 June 1840, VPRS 19/5 No 40/578
27 Report of Proceedings of C. W. Sievwright from 1 June to 31 Oct 1840, encl. In La Trobe to Col Sec., 7 Dec 1841, in CSIL 4/2549 No 41/1328, SRNSW
28 Ibid.
29 Croke to Sievwright 21 Oct 1840, VPRS 21
30 Sievwright to Croke 21 Oct 1840; Croke to Sievwright 2 Nov 1840; Croke to Plunkett 7 Nov 1840, all VPRS 21

31 Plunkett to Croke 30 Nov 1840 VPRS 21/1
32 A. Barton to La Trobe 24 Nov 1840 & other enclosures in VPRS 19/42 No 43/330

CHAPTER 8:

1 *PPG* 7 March 1840
2 Grey to Assistant Protectors 6 Feb 1838, HRV vol 2B pp. 377-8; Assistant Protectors to Col Sec 26 Oct 1838, HRV vol 2B pp. 385-6
3 Gipps to Col Sec April 1839, HRV vol 2B p. 457
4 Glenelg to Gipps 31 Jan 1838, HRV vol 2B pp. 373-5
5 La Trobe to Gipps 15 Jan 1840, CSIL 4/2511 No 40/66, SRNSW
6 Gipps to Col Sec April 1839, HRV vol 2B pp. 457-8
7 Col Sec to La Trobe 21 Oct 1839 & La Trobe to Robinson 6 Nov 1839, HRV vol 2B pp. 481-4
8 La Trobe to Gipps 15 Jan 15 1840, CSIL 4/2511 No 40/66, SRNSW
9 J. Dredge to Robinson 17 Feb 1840, British House of Commons, Sessional Papers, 1844, vol. 34, pp. 53-5
10 La Trobe to Gipps 4 April 1840, A. G. L. Shaw, *Gipps-La Trobe Correspondence*, p. 22
11 Col Sec to La Trobe 24 April 1840, British House of Commons, Sessional Papers, 1844, vol. 34, pp. 55-6
12 Ibid.
13 Dredge to Robinson 22 June 1840, British House of Commons, Sessional Papers, 1844, vol. 34, pp. 306-7
14 *PPG* 19 Aug 1840
15 Dredge to Robinson 22 June 1840, British House of Commons, Sessional Papers, 1844, vol. 34, pp. 306-7
16 Glenelg to Gipps 31 Jan 1838, HRV vol 2B pp. 373-5
17 Statement of Aborigines fallen in with by Sievwright in Sept 1840, VPRS 12/4467
18 Sievwright to Robinson 30 Nov 1840, CSIL 4/2547, SRNSW (transcript in *GA* 5 Feb 1845)
19 Report of Proceedings of C. W. Sievwright from 1 Sept to 30 Nov 1840, encl. In La Trobe to Col Sec 24 Dec 1840, in CSIL 4/2547 No 41/246, SRNSW
20 Robinson to Sievwright 8 Dec 1840, with La Trobe to Col Sec 24 Dec 1840, CSIL 4/2547, SRNSW (transcript in *GA* 5 Feb 1845); Robinson to Sievwright 28 Dec 1840, transcript in *GA* 5 Feb 1845
21 Sievwright to Robinson 21 Dec 1840 & 1 Jan 1841, transcripts in *GA* 5 Feb 1845
22 *PPP* 21 Dec 1840

CHAPTER 9:

1 NSW Government Notice 18 Nov 1837, in HRA vol xix p. 800
2 Report of Select Committee on Transportation pp. xx-xxi
3 Colonial Gazette 13 May 1840
4 Petition to La Trobe from Western District squatters, 24 July 24, encl. in La Trobe to Col Sec 15 Aug 1840, CSIL 4/2511, SRNSW; Fyans to La Trobe 20 Sept 1840, British House of Commons, Sessional Papers, 1844, vol. 34, pp. 88-9; W. H. Pettit to La Trobe 2 Sept 1840, VPRS 10 No 40/903
5 *PPH* 9 Oct, 10 Nov & 18 Dec 1840; *PPP* 21, 24 & 31 Dec 1840 & 1 Feb 1841; *PPH* 8 Jan 1841
6 Bourke to Glenelg 8 Sept 1837, HRA vol xix pp. 83-4; Glenelg to Gipps 14 Dec 1837, HRA vol xix pp. 202-3; Gipps to Glenelg 1 May 1838, HRA vol xix p. 401; Gipps to Glenelg 28 Aug 1838, HRA vol xix p. 550
7 *SH* 28 Aug 1840
8 *PPG* 26 Sept 1840; *PPH* 9 & 13 Oct 9 1840; *PPP* 1 & 8 1841; Col Sec to La Trobe 31 Oct 1840, VPRS 19/8 No 40/1130; La Trobe to Committee for the Importation of Coolies 19 Nov 1840, VPRS 16 No 40/866
9 *PPP* 21 Dec 1840; *PPH* 25 Dec 1840
10 Robinson to Sievwright 19 Dec 1840, encl. in CSIL 4/2549 No 41/10718, SRNSW
11 Fenwick to Croke 5 Sept 1840 & Croke to La Trobe 9 Sept 1840, VPRS 21; *PPH* 30 April 1841; Sievwright to Robinson 27 Sept 1841, encl. in CSIL 4/2549 No 41/10718, SRNSW
12 *PPP* 5 Oct 1840
13 La Trobe to Col Sec 9 Sept 1841 & attached papers, CSIL 4/2548 No 41/8359, SRNSW
14 Thomas to Robinson 29 Sept 1840, VPRS 11 No 40/333.
15 *PPH* 18 May 1841; *PPP* 20 May 1841
16 W. Thomas (junior), Reminiscences, 1841-3, entry for 4 Jan 1841, uncat Ms, Set 214, Item 27, Mitchell
17 Croke to Montgomery 1 Jan 1841, VPRS 21; *PPP* 7 Jan 1841; *PPH* 8 Jan 1841; *PPG* 9 Jan 1841
18 *PPP* 7 Jan 1841; Journal of Rev. J. Orton, entry for 6 Jan 1841, Ms A1715, Mitchell
19 Journal of Rev. J. Orton, entry for 6 Jan 1841, Ms A1715, Mitchell
20 *PPP* 7 Jan 1841; *PPH* 8 Jan 1841; *PPP* 9 Jan 1841; Journal of Rev. J. Orton, entry for 6 Jan 1841, Ms A1715, Mitchell

21 Journal of Rev. J. Orton, entry for 6 Jan 1841, Ms A1715, Mitchell
22 *PPP* 7 Jan 1841; *PPH* 8 Jan 1841
23 Journal of Rev. J. Orton, entry for 15 Jan 1841, Ms A1715, Mitchell; W. Thomas (junior), Reminiscences, 1841-3, entries for 19 Jan & 1 Feb 1841, uncat Ms Set 214 Item 27, Mitchell; Statements by G. Wintle, J. Robinson, W. Allingham, F. Hyde, W. Collett to Board of Inquiry 14 & 15 Jan 1841, CSIL 4/2547 No 41/1750, SRNSW
24 La Trobe to H. W. Parker 27 Aug 1840, VPRS 16 No 40/660; *PPP* 7 Jan 1841
25 Sievwright to Robinson 7 April 1841; Sievwright to La Trobe 27 May 1841, VPRS 19/19 No 41/1374; *GA* 5 Feb 1845

CHAPTER 10:

1 Land sale figures to Sept 1840, HRV vol 6, p. 249
2 Russell to Gipps 31 May 1840, HRA vol xx, pp. 641-8; Notices from Col Sec's Office 5 Dec 1840 & 21 Jan 1841 (in *SG* 16 March 1841)
3 *PPP* 31 Dec 1840
4 Gipps to La Trobe 12 Dec 1840, A. G. L. Shaw, *Gipps-La Trobe Correspondence*, p. 52
5 Gipps to Normanby, 10 Dec 1839, HRA vol xx, p. 431
6 *PPH* 9 Feb 1841; *PPP* 11 Feb 1841
7 *PPH* 12 Feb 1841; *PPP* 15 Feb 1841
8 Gipps to La Trobe 20 Feb 1840, Shaw, *Gipps-La Trobe Correspondence*, pp. 63-64
9 E. Parker to W. H. Dutton & J. M. Darlot, 18 Nov 1840. Transcript in *PPH* 8 Jan 1841; Parker to Editor of *PPH* 9 Jan 1841, in *PPH* 15 Jan 1841
10 *PPH* 4, 8 & 11 Dec 1840
11 *PPH* 8 Jan 1841
12 Parker to Editor of *PPH* 9 Jan 1841, *PPH* 15 Jan 1841
13 *PPH* 15 Jan 1841
14 Parker to Robinson 5 Jan 1841, VPRS 11 No 41/159
15 J. D. Lyon Campbell to La Trobe 31 Dec 1840, VPRS 19/9 No 40/1349; La Trobe to Lachlan Mackinnon 8 Jan 1841, VPRS 16 No 41/13
16 Col Sec to La Trobe 23 Jan 1841, VPRS 10 No 41/151
17 La Trobe to Robinson 9 Jan 1841, VPRS 16 No 41/20; La Trobe to Powlett 18 Jan 1841, VPRS 16 No 41/60; Powlett to La Trobe 26 Jan 1841, VPRS 10 No 41/400; Col Sec to La Trobe 6 March 1841, VPRS 10 No 41/400
18 Report of Proceedings of C. W. Sievwright from 1 Dec 1840 to 28 Feb 1841, Add Ms 86, Dixson
19 Report of Proceedings of C. W. Sievwright from 1 Sept to 30 Nov 1840, encl. In La Trobe to Col Sec 24 Dec 1840, in CSIL 4/2547 No 41/246, SRNSW
20 Report of Proceedings of C. W. Sievwright from 1 Dec 1840 to 28 Feb 1841, Add Ms 86, Dixson

CHAPTER 11:

1 Robinson to Assistant Protectors, 8 July 1839, HRV vol 2B pp. 724-5
2 Fyans to Col Sec, 1 Aug 1839, HRV vol 2B p. 729
3 Sievwright to Robinson 17 July 1839, HRV vol 2B pp. 727-8
4 Parker to Robinson 24 July 1839, HRV vol 2B p. 728; Robinson to Col Sec 30 July 1839, HRV vol 2B p. 729
5 Robinson to Col Sec 30 July 1839, HRV vol 2B p. 729
6 NSW Govt. Gazette No 442, 21 Aug 1839
7 La Trobe to Robinson 28 Oct 1839, HRV vol 2B p. 598
8 Journal of W. Thomas, entry for 18 Nov 1839, HRV vol 2B p. 562; Thomas to Robinson 29 Feb 1840, HRV vol 2B pp. 617-21
9 La Trobe to Col Sec 8 May 1840, VPRS 16 No 40/221
10 Col Sec to La Trobe 6 June 1840, HRV vol 2B p. 734; NSW Govt. Gazette 26 Aug 1840
11 La Trobe to Robinson 12 Sept 1840, VPRS 12 No 40/706
12 La Trobe to Robinson and Police Magistrates 28 Sept 1840, HRV vol 2B p. 734
13 La Trobe to Lettsom 10 Oct 1840, VPRS 16 No 40/773; *PPH* 13 Oct 1840
14 Sievwright to La Trobe 27 Jan 1841, VPRS 10 No 41/180
15 Ibid. La Trobe's minute 29 Jan 1841
16 Statements by W. Beatson, D. Matheson, E. Molloy & D. Fisher, 8 Feb 1841, VPRS 109; *GA* 13 Feb 1841
17 *GA* 13 Feb 1841

18 *GA* 12 Dec 1840
19 Fenwick to La Trobe 12 Feb 1841, VPRS 19/11 No 41/237; Robinson to Croke 26 Feb 1841, VPRS 21
20 Thomas to La Trobe 23 Sept 1839 & Thomas to Plunkett 30 Sept 1839, HRV vol2B pp. 587-90; Application for warrants by Sievwright 28 Jan 1841, VPRS 109
21 Sievwright to Robinson July 17 1839, HRV vol2B p. 727
22 Report of Proceedings of C. W. Sievwright from 1 Dec 1840 to 28 Feb 1841, Add Ms 86, Dixson; Marcus Sievwright in Report of Select Committee of Victorian Legislative Council on Aborigines, 1858-59, p. 74

CHAPTER 12:

1 Col Sec's minute on Robinson to Col Sec 8 July 1839, HRV vol 2B p. 727; La Trobe to Gipps 19 Oct 1839, A. G. L. Shaw, *Gipps-La Trobe Correspondence*, pp. 4-6
2 Parker in Report of Select Committee of Victorian Legislative Council on Aborigines, 1858-59, p. 23
3 Robinson to La Trobe 9 Nov 1840, enclosed with No 41/10718, CSIL 4/2549, SRNSW
4 La Trobe to Col Sec 19 Nov 1840, enclosed with No 41/10718, CSIL 4/2549, SRNSW
5 La Trobe to Col Sec 26 Nov 1840, British House of Commons, Sessional Papers, 1844, vol. 34, pp. 140-1
6 Col Sec to La Trobe 31 Oct 1840, Ibid. p. 91
7 La Trobe to Col Sec 19 Nov 1840 & Gipps' marginal note 12 Dec 1840, enclosed with CSIL 4/2549 No 41/10718, SRNSW
8 Gipps to La Trobe 12 Dec 1840, Shaw, *Gipps-La Trobe Correspondence*, pp. 51-2
9 Report of Proceedings of C. W. Sievwright from 1 June to 31 Oct 1840, encl. In La Trobe to Col Sec., 7 Dec 1841, in CSIL 4/2549 No 41/1328, SRNSW
10 Col Sec to La Trobe 16 Jan 1841, VPRS 10 No 41/164
11 J. Docker to Gipps 31 Dec 1840, British House of Commons, Sessional Papers, 1844, vol. 34, pp. 107-8 (also in CSIL 4/2547 No 41/770, SRNSW)
12 La Trobe to Col Sec 23 Dec 1840, VPRS 16 No 40/969
13 Gipps to La Trobe 16 Jan 1841, Shaw, *Gipps-La Trobe Correspondence*, pp. 54-5
14 La Trobe to Col Sec 16 Jan 1841, encl. in CSIL 4/2547 No 41/2367, SRNSW
15 La Trobe to Croke 23 Jan 1841, VPRS 16 No 41/79
16 La Trobe to Robinson 2 Feb 1841, VPRS 16 No 41/110
17 Robinson to La Trobe 3 Feb 1841, VPRS 10 No 41/189
18 Simpson to La Trobe 6 Feb 1841, encl. in CSIL 4/2547 No 41/2767, SRNSW
19 Plunkett to Simpson 30 Nov 1840, Ibid.
20 Gipps to Lettsom Aug 28 1840, British House of Commons, Sessional Papers, 1844, vol. 34, p. 92
21 Powlett to La Trobe 10 Feb 1841, encl. in CSIL 4/2547 No 41/2367, SRNSW
22 La Trobe to Powlett 11 Feb 1841, Ibid.
23 Col Sec to La Trobe 26 Feb 1841, VPRS 10 No 41/370
24 Croke to La Trobe 12 Feb 1841, VPRS 19/11 No 41/232
25 La Trobe to Col Sec 23 Feb 1841, CSIL 4/2547 No 41/2767, SRNSW
26 Robinson to La Trobe 27 Feb 1841; Statement by J. Docker 12 Feb 1841; Statement by J. S. A. Mackay 14 Feb 1841, British House of Commons, Sessional Papers, 1844, vol. 34, pp. 107-11
27 La Trobe to Robinson 4 Feb 1841, VPRS 16 No 41/226
28 Robinson to Sievwright 3 March 1841, mentioned in Robinson to La Trobe 14 Oct 1841, CSIL 4/2549 No 41/1576, SRNSW
29 Robinson to Sievwright 3 March 1841, mentioned in Sievwright to Robinson 21 March 1841, encl. in VPRS 19/19 No 41/1374
30 La Trobe to Robinson 2 March 1841, VPRS 16 No 41/241
31 Report of Proceedings of C. W. Sievwright from 1 Dec 1840 to 28 Feb 1841, Add Ms 86, Dixson
32 Report of Proceedings of C. W. Sievwright from 1 March 1839 to 31 Aug 1839, Add Ms 86, Dixson
33 Report of Proceedings of C. W. Sievwright from 1 Dec 1840 to 28 Feb 1841, Add Ms 86, Dixson
34 La Trobe to Gipps 15 Feb 1841 & Gipps' marginal note 28 Feb 1841, CSIL 4/2547 No 41/2491, SRNSW
35 La Trobe to Robinson 21 Dec 1841, VPRS 16 No 41/1438
36 *GA* 13 March 1841
37 Fenwick to La Trobe 19 March 1841, VPRS 19/12 No 41/434
38 G. Presland (ed.), *Journals of George Augustus Robinson 20 March to 15 May 1841*, entry for 22 March 1841; *PPH* 23 March 1841; *GA* 27 March & 10 April 1841; *PPG* 10 April 1841
39 *GA* 27 March 1841
40 Gipps to Russell 3 Feb 1841, British House of Commons, Sessional Papers, 1844, vol. 34, pp. 85-7

CHAPTER 13:

1 Robinson to La Trobe 11 March 1841, encl. in CSIL 4/2548 No 41/3690, SRNSW; G. Presland (ed.), *Journals of George Augustus Robinson 20 March to 15 May 1841*, entry for 12 April
2 La Trobe to Robinson 27 Nov 1840, encl. in CSIL 4/2548 No 41/3690, SRNSW
3 Sievwright to Robinson 21 March 1841, encl. in VPRS 19/19 No 41/1374
4 Fyans to J. Thomson 23 March 1841; Robinson to Thomson 23 March 1841; Thomson to Fyans 24 March 1841; Fyans to Robinson 24 March 1841, all encl. in VPRS 19/19 No 41/1374; G. Presland (ed.), *Journals of George Augustus Robinson 20 March to 15 May 1841*, entry for 23 March
5 G. Presland (ed.), *Journals of George Augustus Robinson 20 March to 15 May 1841*, entries for 23-27 March
6 Ibid., entries for 27-28 March & 1-3 April
7 Ibid., entries for 3-6 April
8 Ibid., entry for 6 April; Sievwright to Robinson 21 March 1841 & Sievwright to Robinson 7 April 1841, both encl. in VPRS 19/19 No 41/1374
9 Sievwright to Robinson 7 April 1841, encl. in VPRS 19/19 No 41/1374
10 G. Presland (ed.), *Journals of George Augustus Robinson 20 March to 15 May 1841*, entry for 8 April 1841; Sievwright to Robinson 9 April 1841, VPRS 19/19 No 41/1374
11 G. Presland (ed.), *Journals of George Augustus Robinson 20 March to 15 May 1841*, entry for 9 April 1841; Sievwright to Robinson 9 April 1841, VPRS 19/19 No 41/1374
12 La Trobe to Robinson 21 July 1840, VPRS 16 No 40/560
13 G. Presland (ed.), *Journals of George Augustus Robinson 20 March to 15 May 1841*, entry for 11 April 1841; Robinson to La Trobe 12 April 1841, encl. in VPRS 19/19 No 41/1374
14 G. Presland (ed.), *Journals of George Augustus Robinson 20 March to 15 May 1841*, entry for 13 April 1841
15 Ibid., entries for 8, 11 & 13 April 1841
16 Ibid., entry for 14 April 1841; Sievwright to Robinson 14 April 1841, encl. in VPRS 19/19 No 41/1374
17 G. Presland (ed.), *Journals of George Augustus Robinson 20 March to 15 May 1841*, entries for 14 & 16 April 1841 Ibid., entry for 17 April 1841; Robinson to Sievwright 15 April 1841, encl. in VPRS 19/19 No 41/1374
18 G. Presland (ed.), *Journals of George Augustus Robinson 20 March to 15 May 1841*, entry for 17 April 1841
19 Ibid., entry for 19 April 1841
20 J. Thomson to La Trobe 20 April 1841, encl. in VPRS 19/19 No 41/1374
21 La Trobe to Sievwright April 22 1841, encl. in VPRS 19/19 No 41/1374
22 La Trobe to J. Thomson 22 April 1841, VPRS 16 No 41/417; La Trobe to Col Sec 24 April 1841, VPRS 16 No
23 41/424; Col Sec to La Trobe 12 May 1841, encl. in VPRS 19/19 No 41/1374; Gipps to La Trobe 15 May 1841, A. G. L. Shaw, *Gipps-La Trobe Correspondence*, p. 78
GA 5 Feb 1845
24 G. Presland (ed.), *Journals of George Augustus Robinson 20 March to 15 May 1841*, entries for 21 & 22 April 1841
25 Sievwright to La Trobe 25 April 1841 & Sievwright to Robinson 25 April 1841, VPRS 19/15 No 41/878 (extract in British House of Commons, Sessional Papers, 1844, vol. 34, pp. 240-2)
26

CHAPTER 14:

1 Plunkett to Col Sec 13 June 1837, HRV vol1 pp. 274-6
2 *PPP* 15 Oct 1840 & 15 April 1841; *PPH* 13 April 1841; *PPG* 14 April 1841
3 Willis to Gipps 30 March 1839, Gipps to Glenelg 19 April 1839, HRA vol xx pp. 118-25
4 Gipps to Russell 3 Jan 1841, HRA vol xxi pp. 160-5
5 *PPP* 15 Oct 1840; Gipps to Russell 3 Jan 1841, HRA vol xxi pp. 160-5
6 *PPH* 13 & 30 April 1841; *PPG* 14 April 1841; *PPP* 15 & 29 April 1841; *GA* 1 May 1841
7 Croke to Geelong Magistrates 16 Sept 1840, VPRS 21; Croke to Sievwright 17 Sept 1840, VPRS 21; La Trobe to Cussen 25 Feb 1841, VPRS 16 No 41/228; *PPP* 29 April 1841; *PPH* 30 April 1841
8 *PPH* 4 & 7 May 1841; *PPP* 6 May 1841; W. Thomas in Report of Select Committee of Victorian Legislative Council on Aborigines, 1858-59, p. 72
9 La Trobe to Col Sec 23 Feb 1841, CSIL 4/2547 No 41/2767 & enclosures, SRNSW; *PPG* 19 May 1841
10 *PPH* 18 May 1841; *PPG* 19 May 1841; *PPP* 20 May 1841
11 *PPP* 17 & 20 May 1841; *PPH* 18 & 21 May 1841; *PPG* 19 May 1841
12 *PPH* 21 May 1841
13 *PPP* 24 May 1841; *PPH* 25 May 1841; *PPG* 26 May 1841; La Trobe to Col Sec 23 April 1841, VPRS 16 No 41/420

14 *PPP* 24 May 1841

15 G. Presland (ed.), *Journals of George Augustus Robinson 20 March to 15 May 1841*, entries for 13 & 14 May 1841; G. Presland (ed.), *Journals of George Augustus Robinson 16 May to 15 Aug 1841*, entries for 27 May & 15 June 1841; Blair to La Trobe 8 June 1841, VPRS 10 No 41/874; J. G. Robertson to La Trobe 26 Sept 1853, T. F. Bride, *Letters from Victorian Pioneers*, pp. 161-4

16 J. G. Robertson to La Trobe 26 Sept1853, Bride, *Letters from*, pp. 161-4

17 *PPP* 3 June 1841; *PPG* 6 June 1841

18 Statement of T. Grant, 26 May 1841, VPRS 24/1, 1841/No 41

19 G. Presland (ed.), *Journals of George Augustus Robinson 16 May to 15 Aug 1841*, entries for 20 May and 3 June 1841; Blair to La Trobe 1 June 1841, encl. in VPRS 10 No 41/830

20 La Trobe to Blair 27 Nov 1840, VPRS 16 No 40/886

21 Blair to La Trobe 8 Dec 1840, VPRS 19/9 No 40/1275

22 La Trobe to Col Sec 24 Dec 1840, VPRS 19/10 No 41/147; T. C. Harrington to La Trobe 22 Jan 1841, CSIL 4/2547 No 40/968, SRNSW

23 La Trobe to Col Sec 30 March 1841, VPRS 16 No 41/335

24 Col Sec to La Trobe 6 May 1841, VPRS 19/14 No 41/690

25 Blair to La Trobe 28 May 1841, VPRS 19/15 No 41/827

26 Blair to La Trobe 1 June 1841, encl. in VPRS 10 No 41/830

27 G. Presland (ed.), *Journals of George Augustus Robinson 16 May to 15 Aug 1841*, entries for 20 & 22 May 1841; Supplement to *PPP* 12 June 1841

28 Sievwright to La Trobe 27 May 1841, encl. in VPRS 19/19 No 41/1374

29 Report of Proceedings of C. W. Sievwright from March to May 1841. Extract in *GA*, 5 Feb 1845; Precis of Quarterly Reports of C. W. Sievwright from 1 June to 31 Aug 1841, Add Ms 86, Dixson; Return of Deaths & Births of the Aboriginal Natives of Central Station, Western District, from 1 March to 31 Aug 1841, VPRS 12

CHAPTER 15:

1 *PPP* 12 July 1841

2 *PPP* 27 May 1841

3 *SH* 8 June 1841

4 *PPP* 12 July 1841

5 *SH* 2, 3 & 7 June 1841

6 Gipps to Russell 17 July 1841, HRA vol xxi p. 435

7 *SH* 9 June 1841; *PPH* 18 June 1841

8 Report on the Best Means of Promoting the Civilisation of the Aboriginal Inhabitants of Australia by G. Grey, British House of Commons, Sessional Papers, 1844, vol. 34, pp. 100-4; *PPP* 15 & 19 July 1841

9 J. H. Wedge to Russell 18 Jan 1840, British House of Commons, Sessional Papers, 1844, vol. 34, pp. 119-21

10 Russell to Gipps 24 Jan 1840, Ibid., p. 119

11 Russell to Gipps 21 Feb 1841, Ibid., p. 124

12 Gipps to La Trobe 24 July 1841, A. G. L. Shaw, *Gipps-La Trobe Correspondence*, pp. 91-2

13 Gipps to Russell 29 July 1841, British House of Commons, Sessional Papers, 1844, vol. 34, p. 126

14 Russell to Gipps 8 Oct 1840, Ibid., pp. 99-100

15 Gipps to Russell 7 April 1841, Ibid., pp. 104-6 (also in HRA vol xxi pp. 312-5)

16 Hurst to La Trobe 22 July 1841, VPRS 19/17 No 41/1145

17 Report of Proceedings of C. W. Sievwright from 1 June to 31 Aug 1841, Add Ms 86, Dixson

18 J. Dawson, *Australian Aborigines*, pp. 72-4

19 Report of Proceedings of C. W. Sievwright from 1 June to 31 Aug 1841, Add Ms 86, Dixson

20 Ibid.

21 *GA* 17 July 1841

22 Ibid.

23 G. Presland (ed.), *Journals of George Augustus Robinson 16 May to 15 Aug 1841*, entry for 9 July 1841

CHAPTER 16:

1 La Trobe to Robinson 27 Nov 1840, VPRS 16 No 40/885

2 Robinson to La Trobe 11 March 1841, VPRS 19/12 No 41/4039

3 La Trobe to Robinson 27 Nov 1840, VPRS 16 No 40/885

4 G. Presland (ed.), *Journals of George Augustus Robinson 20 March to 15 May 1841* & G. Presland (ed.), *Journals of George Augustus Robinson 16 May to 15 Aug 1841*, numerous entries

5 Report of Robinson's journey March to Aug 1841 in A. S. Kenyon, *The Aboriginal Protectorate of Port Phillip*, pp. 138-67

6 G. Presland (ed.), *Journals of George Augustus Robinson 16 May to 15 Aug 1841*, entry for 23 June 1841

7 Kenyon, *The Aboriginal Protectorate*, p. 167

8 G. Presland (ed.), *Journals of George Augustus Robinson 16 May to 15 Aug 1841*, entry for 27 July 1841

9 Kenyon, *The Aboriginal Protectorate*, p. 154

10 G. Presland (ed.), *Journals of George Augustus Robinson 20 March to 15 May 1841*, entries for 15 April and 10 May 1841

11 G. Presland (ed.), *Journals of George Augustus Robinson 20 March to 15 May 1841*, entries for 24, 29 & 30 April 1841; G. Presland (ed.), *Journals of George Augustus Robinson 16 May to 15 Aug 1841*, entries for 8 & 9 July 1841

G. Presland (ed.), *Journals of George Augustus Robinson 20 March to 15 May 1841*, entries for 29 April, 2 & 10

12 May 1841; G. Presland (ed.), *Journals of George Augustus Robinson 16 May to 15 Aug 1841*, entry for 28 July 1841

G. Presland (ed.), *Journals of George Augustus Robinson 16 May to 15 Aug 1841*, entry for 30 May 1841

13 Ibid., entries for 31 May; 8 & 26 June; 11 July 1841

14 Ibid., entries for 27 June & 2 July 1841

15 G. Presland (ed.), *Journals of George Augustus Robinson 20 March to 15 May 1841*, entries for 27 April & 9 May

16 1841; G. Presland (ed.), *Journals of George Augustus Robinson 16 May to 15 Aug 1841*, entries for 27 May; 2 & 3 June; 27 July; 8, 9 & 10 Aug 1841

Report of Proceedings of C. W. Sievwright from 1 June to 31 Aug 1841, Add Ms 86, Dixson; Sievwright replies

17 to NSW Leg Council, Committee on Immigration, circular on the Aborigines, 24 Sept 1841, Ms A611, Mitchell pp. 75-84

GA 4 Oct 1841

18 J. Webster to La Trobe 28 Aug 1841, VPRS 19/18 No 41/1335

19 La Trobe to Fyans 3 Sept 1841, VPRS 16 No 41/980

20 La Trobe to Col Sec 1 Sept 1841, VPRS 16 No 41/968; Sievwright to Robinson 27 Sept 1841, CSIL 4/2549 No

21 41/10718, SRNSW

Sievwright to Robinson 27 Sept 1841 & enclosures, CSIL 4/2549 No 41/10718, SRNSW

22 La Trobe to Robinson 5 Oct 1841, VPRS 16 No 41/1108; Robinson to La Trobe 14 Oct 1841 & La Trobe to Fyans

23 15 Oct 1841, CSIL 4/2549 No 41/10718, SRNSW

CHAPTER 17:

1 *PPP* 11 June 1840; E. Finn, *The Chronicles of Early Melbourne*, pp. 906-7

2 *PPH* 14 & 17 Sept; *PPP* 18 Oct 18,1841

3 Gipps to LaTrobe 14 Aug 1841, A. G. L. Shaw, *Gipps-La Trobe Correspondence*, p. 98

4 Gipps to La Trobe 28 Aug 1841, Shaw, *Gipps-La Trobe Correspondence*, p. 101

5 *GA* 18 Oct1841

6 *GA* 15 Oct 1841

7 *PPG* 30 Oct & *GA* 1 & 8 Nov

8 La Trobe to Hurst 1 Feb1 1842, British House of Commons, Sessional Papers, 1844, vol. 34, p. 192

9 *Launceston Advertiser* 11 Nov 1841

10 *PPP* 18 Nov & 6 & 20 Dec; *PPG* 8 & 29 Dec; *PPH* 31 Dec

11 R. V. Billis & A. S. Kenyon, *Pastures New*, pp. 141-6

12 *PPH* 3 Dec 1841; *PPG* 4 Dec 1841; *PPP* 6 Dec1841; Sievwright to Robinson 5 Nov 1841 & Statements by G. Bolden, L. Bolden, P. Carney and W. Kearnan, with trial papers, Queen vs Sandford George Bolden, VPRS 30/185 NCR11

13 *PPH* 3 & 10 Dec 1841

14 *PPH* 7 Dec 1841

15 *PPH* 7 Dec1841

16 La Trobe to Col Sec 9 Sept 1841 & enclosures, CSIL 4/2548 No 41/8359, SRNSW; Gipps to Russell 28 Sept 1841, HRA vol xxi, pp. 525-6

17 *PPP* 6 Dec 1841; *GA* 13 Dec 1841

18 *PPH* 10 Dec 1841

19 *GA* 13 Dec 1841

20 La Trobe to Col Sec 7 Dec 1841 CSIL 4/2549 No 41/10718, SRNSW

21 Ibid., Gipps' marginal note 19 Dec 1841

22 Gipps to La Trobe 18 Dec 1841, Shaw, *Gipps-La Trobe Correspondence*, pp. 111-2

23 Report of Proceedings of C. W. Sievwright from 1 Dec 1841 to 28 Feb 1842, in CSIL/11 No 42/5708, Dixson
La Trobe to Col Sec 19 Jan 19 1842, VPRS 16 No 42/132

CHAPTER 18:

1 Grey to Russell 3 Aug 1841, HRA vol xxi pp. 695-9
2 Gipps to La Trobe 3 July 1841, A. G. L. Shaw, *Gipps-La Trobe Correspondence*, p. 86
3 Gipps to Stanley 11 Aug 1842, HRA vol xxii pp. 197-9
4 C. Sturt, *Two Expeditions Into the Interior of Southern Australia*; *PPG* 30 Oct 1841; ADB vol 1 p. 362
5 La Trobe to Blair 3 Dec 1841 VPRS 16 No 41/1345
6 G. Presland (ed.), *Journals of George Augustus Robinson 16 May to 15 Aug 1841*, entries for 31 May & 6 June
1841
7 G. Presland (ed.), *Journals of George Augustus Robinson 16 May to 15 Aug 1841*, entry for 27 June 1841;
Statements by R. W. Tulloh 30 Dec 1841 & 1 Jan 1842, British House of Commons, Sessional Papers, 1844, vol.
34, pp.185-6
8 Statements by T. Norris, G. Winter, S. Henty, J. Henty, D. Edgar, T. McCulloch, E. Barnett, R. Savage & J. Allison
1-14 Jan 1842, British House of Commons, Sessional Papers, 1844, vol. 34, pp. 186-191; A. Barton to La Trobe
24 Nov 1840 & other enclosures in VPRS 19/42 No 43/330
9 G. Presland (ed.), *Journals of George Augustus Robinson 16 May to 15 Aug 1841*, entry for May 27 1841
10 Statement by A. Pilleau 10 Jan 1842, British House of Commons, Sessional Papers, 1844, vol. 34, p.188
11 Statement by T. McCulloch 14 Jan 1842, Ibid., p. 190
12 Blair to La Trobe 15 Jan 1842, Ibid., pp. 184-185
13 G. Presland (ed.), *Journals of George Augustus Robinson 16 May to 15 Aug 1841*, entry for 31 May 1841, Robinson
to La Trobe 11 Dec 1841, British House of Commons, Sessional Papers, 1844, vol. 34, p.169
14 Statement by T. Norris 1 Jan 1842, British House of Commons, Sessional Papers, 1844, vol. 34, pp.186-7;
Statement by S. Henty 12 Jan 1842, Ibid., p. 189
15 Memorial to La Trobe from Buninyong stockholders and residents February 1841, VPRS 19/13 No 41/535
16 *PPH* 5 May 1840
17 La Trobe to Col Sec 13 Aug 1841, VPRS 16 No 41/711
18 G. Presland (ed.), *Journals of George Augustus Robinson 16 May to 15 Aug 1841*, entries for 15-22 & 25 July &
1 & 6 August 1841
19 Gipps to La Trobe 12 Dec 1840, Shaw, *Gipps-La Trobe Correspondence*, pp. 51-2
20 La Trobe to Col Sec 1 Feb 1842, British House of Commons, Sessional Papers, 1844, vol. 34, pp. 183-4
21 Blair to La Trobe 8 Dec 1840, VPRS 19/9 No 40/1275; Blair to La Trobe 28 May 1841, VPRS 19/15 No 41/827
22 La Trobe to Col Sec 15 June 1841, VPRS 16 No 41/604; La Trobe to Col Sec 7 Oct 1841, VPRS 16 No 41/1120;
Lieut. A. W. Riley to La Trobe 28 Oct 1841, VPRS 19/21, No 41/1786
23 J. Webster to La Trobe 28 Aug 1841, VPRS 19/18 No 41/335
24 La Trobe to Col Sec 15 June 1841 No & 24 August 1841, VPRS 16 No 41/609
25 La Trobe to Hurst 1 Feb 1842, British House of Commons, Sessional Papers, 1844, vol. 34, pp. 192-3
26 Col Sec to La Trobe 14 Feb 1842, VPRS 19/27 No 42/469
27 B. Hurst to H. Murray & other settlers 22 Dec 1841, in *PPG* 29 Dec 1841; *PPG* 11 Dec 1841
28 *PPH* 4 Jan 1842
29 Deposition of J. Guthrie 7 Jan 1842, VPRS 24 Unit 1, 1842/No 32
30 Blair to La Trobe 29 Jan 1842, VPRS 19/25 No 42/295 (also in British House of Commons, Sessional Papers, 1844,
vol. 34, p. 202)

CHAPTER 19:

1 *Caledonian Mercury*, in *Times* 4 Jan 1842
2 La Trobe to Col Sec 13 Sept 1841, VPRS 16 No 41/1035; La Trobe to Robinson 13 Oct 1841, VPRS 16 No.
41/1145
3 R. Boldrewood, *Old Melbourne Memories*, p. 119; P. L. Browne (ed.), *Memoirs (of) Captain Foster Fyans*, p. 243
4 Robinson to La Trobe 24 Dec 1841 & enclosure, VPRS 10 1841/2614
5 Ibid.; La Trobe to Col Sec 27 Dec 1841, VPRS 16 No 41/1479; Col Sec to La Trobe 5 Jan 1842, VPRS 10 No
42/92
6 La Trobe to Robinson 2 March 1841, VPRS 16 No 41/241
7 La Trobe to Robinson 21 Dec 1841, VPRS 16 No 41/1438; La Trobe to Col Sec 27 Dec 1841, VPRS 16 No 41/1480
8 *PPG* 22 Dec 1841; *PPP* 23 Dec 1841
9 *PPH* 24 Dec 1841

10 Willis to La Trobe, 23 Dec 1841, VPRS 19/22 No 41/1835

11 La Trobe to Col Sec circa 23 Dec 1841, VPRS 16 vol 12, p. 244; Col Sec to La Trobe 5 Jan 1842, VPRS 19/24 No 42/96; La Trobe to Deputy Sheriff 13 Jan 1842, VPRS 16 No 42/44

12 La Trobe to Robinson 1 Jan 1842, VPRS 16 No 42/1

13 Robinson to La Trobe 4 Jan 1842, encl. in VPRS 19/42 No 43/330

14 Sievwright to Robinson 19 Oct 1841, in FitzRoy to Sec of State 14 March 1848, Transcripts of Despatches from NSW Governor, 1846-48, Despatch No 58, Mitchell Ms A1267-23 , pp. 3600-3601

15 Robinson to La Trobe 4 Jan 1842, encl. in VPRS 19/42 No 43/330

16 Report of Proceedings of C. W. Sievwright from 1 Dec 1841 to 28 Feb 1842, in CSIL/11 No 42/5708, Dixson

17 A. Barton to La Trobe 24 Nov 1840, encl. in VPRS 19/42 No 43/330

18 G. Presland (ed.), *Journals of George Augustus Robinson 16 May to 15 Aug 1841*, entry for 3 June1841

19 Sievwright to Robinson 15 Jan 1842, VPRS 19/42 No 43/330

20 Stephen Henty to Sievwright 9 Feb 1842, encl. in Sievwright to Robinson 15 Jan 1842, VPRS 19/42 No 43/330

21 Statements by T. Connell & J. Daley 14 Jan 1842, encl. in Sievwright to Robinson 15 Jan 1842, VPRS 19/42 No 43/330

22 Sievwright to Robinson 15 Jan 1842, VPRS 19/42 No 43/330

23 Report of Proceedings of C. W. Sievwright from 1 Dec 1841 to 28 Feb 1842, in CSIL/11 No 42/5708, Dixson

24 E. Finn, *The Chronicles of Early Melbourne*, pp. 394-6; I. MacFarlane, *1842 The Public Executions at Melbourne*, pp. 11-16 & 59-60; *PPH* 21 Jan 1842; *PPG* 22 Jan 1842; *PPP* 24 Jan 1842; La Trobe to Deputy Sheriff 26 Jan 1842, VPRS 16 No 42/105

CHAPTER 20:

1 V. Savill, *Drumborg-Greenvale*, p. 1

2 Smith, *The Boandik Tribe*, pp. 14-16

3 R. Boldrewood, *Old Melbourne Memories*, p. 54

4 Boldrewood, *Old Melbourne Memories*, p. 42

5 ADB vol 1 p. 555, HRV vol 6 pp. 383, 385, 392, 394, 400

6 ADB vol 1 p. 573; Boldrewood, *Old Melbourne Memories*, p. 44; *GA* 10 Jan 1842

7 Deposition of J. Guthrie 7 Jan 1842, VPRS 24, Unit 1, 1842/No 32

8 Boldrewood, *Old Melbourne Memories*, p. 55

9 French to La Trobe Jan (n.d.) 1842, VPRS 19/25 No 42/194; Croke to La Trobe 11 July 1842, VPRS 19/39 encl. with No 42/2364; *GA* 10 Jan 1842; Boldrewood, *Old Melbourne Memories*, p. 55; P. L. Browne (ed.), *Memoirs (of) Captain Foster Fyans*, pp. 246-248

10 *GA* 13 Dec 1841

11 Fyans to La Trobe 24 Jan 1842, VPRS 19/39 No 42/2364; *GA* 10 Jan 1842; Browne (ed.), *Memoirs (of) Captain Foster Fyans*, p. 248

12 *GA* 31 Jan 1842

13 Blair to La Trobe 29 Jan 1842, British House of Commons, Sessional Papers, 1844, vol. 34, p. 202; Statement of J. Salvage 11 Feb 1842, VPRS 24/1, 1842/No 7; W. D. Bernard to Fyans 16 Feb 1842 & La Trobe to Col Sec 2 March 1842, British House of Commons, Sessional Papers, 1844, vol. 34, pp. 207-8; Boldrewood, *Old Melbourne Memories*, p. 17; I. Clark (ed.), *Journal of G. A. Robinson from 8 March to 7 April 1842*, entry for 22 March 1842; Robinson to La Trobe 9 April 1842, British House of Commons, Sessional Papers, 1844, vol. 34, p. 211

14 Statements by J. Salvage and J. Wilson, 11 Feb 1842, VPRS 24/1, 1842/No 7

15 G. Presland (ed.), *Journals of George Augustus Robinson 20 March to 15 May 1841*, entry for 2 May 1841; Bernard to Fyans 16 Feb 1842, British House of Commons, Sessional Papers, 1844, vol. 34, p. 206; Robinson to La Trobe 9 April 1842, Ibid., p. 211; Journal of the Proceedings of C. W. Sievwright from 1 March to 31 May 1842, in CSIL/11 No 42/5708, Dixson

16 Report of the Proceedings of C. W. Sievwright from 1 Dec 1841 to 28 Feb 1842, in CSIL/11 No 42/5708, Dixson; I. Clark (ed.), *Journal of G. A. Robinson from 8 March to 7 April 1842*, entries for 15 & 18 March 1842

17 La Trobe to Fenwick 24 June 1842, VPRS 16 No 42/839; La Trobe to Robinson 1 July 1842, VPRS 16 No 42/860; La Trobe to Fenwick 8 Aug 1842, VPRS 16 No 42/1003; Col Sec to La Trobe 31 Aug 1842, VPRS 19/35 No 42/1700

CHAPTER 21:

1 Notebook of W. H. Hovell, entry for 17 Dec, 1824, in E. Scott (Ed.), *Australian Discovery* Vol Two, p.105

2 J. Dawson, *Australian Aborigines*, pp. 105-6

3 G. Presland (ed.), *Journals of George Augustus Robinson 20 March to 15 May 1841*, entries for 30 April and 1 May, 1841;Bernard to Fyans 16 Feb 1842, British House of Commons, Sessional Papers, 1844, vol. 34 pp. 205-6

4 Bernard to Fyans 16 Feb 1842, British House of Commons, Sessional Papers, 1844, vol. 34 pp. 205-7
5 Robinson to La Trobe 9 April 1842, British House of Commons, Sessional Papers, 1844, vol. 34, p. 210; *PPG* 22 Dec 1841 & *PPP* 23 Dec 1841
6 *GA* 21 Feb 1842
7 Fyans to La Trobe 1 Jan 1842, VPRS 19/24 No 42/15 (also in British House of Commons, Sessional Papers, 1844, vol. 34 pp. 180-1)
8 Fyans to La Trobe 16 Feb 1842, VPRS 19/39, encl. with No 42/2364 (also in British House of Commons, Sessional Papers, 1844, vol. 34 p. 205)
9 Fyans to La Trobe 16 Feb 1842, British House of Commons, Sessional Papers, 1844, vol. 34, p. 205; G. Presland (ed.), *Journals of George Augustus Robinson 16 May to 15 Aug 1841*, entries for 2 & 6 July 1841
10 La Trobe to Blair 12 Feb 1842, British House of Commons, Sessional Papers, 1844, vol. 34, p. 204; Petition of Portland Bay Settlers to La Trobe 22 Jan 1842 & La Trobe's reply to petition 4 Feb 1842, Ibid., pp. 203-4
11 La Trobe to Fyans and La Trobe to OIC, Detachment of 80th Regiment at Portland, 18 Feb 1842, Ibid., p. 207
12 La Trobe to Robinson 18 Feb 1842, British House of Commons, Sessional Papers, 1844, vol. 34, pp. 207-8; Robinson to La Trobe 21 Jan 1842, VPRS 10 No 1842/139
13 Sievwright's report from 1 Sept to 30 Nov 1841, extract in *GA* 5 Feb 1845

CHAPTER 22:

1 Letter from the Aborigines Protection Society to Port Phillip colonists (n.d.), *PPG* 16 Feb 1842
2 La Trobe to Hurst 1 Feb 1842, British House of Commons, Sessional Papers, 1844, vol. 34, pp. 192-3; La Trobe to Portland Bay settlers 4 Feb 1842, Ibid., pp. 203-4
3 Sievwright to Croke 26 Feb 1842, British House of Commons, Sessional Papers, 1844, vol. 34, pp. 218-9; Report of trial of R. G. Hill, J. Betts & J. Beswicke, 31 July & 1 Aug 1843, Ibid., pp. 263-72; La Trobe to Col Sec & encl. statement by T. Osbrey 29 May 1843, Ibid., p. 272; S. Smith to Claud Farie and Niel Black 26 July 1842, encl. with La Trobe to Col Sec 22 Aug 1842, CSIL 4/2626 No 42/7033, SRNSW
4 Gipps to La Trobe 18 Dec 1841, A. G. L. Shaw, *Gipps-La Trobe Correspondence*, pp. 111-112; Robinson to La Trobe 21 Jan 1842, VPRS 10 No 1842/139; Col Sec to La Trobe 25 Feb 1842, VPRS 10 No 1842/491
5 I. Clark (ed.), *Journal of G. A. Robinson from 8 March to 7 April 1842*, entries for 15-20 March, 1842
6 Ibid., entry for 21 March, 1842; Journal of the Proceedings of C. W. Sievwright from 1 March to 31 May 1842, in CSIL/11 No 42/5708, Dixson; Statement by R. Manifold 16 April 1842, VPRS 19/33 No 42/1492
7 G. Presland (ed.), *Journals of George Augustus Robinson 20 March to 15 May 1841*, entries for 27 April, 1841; I. Clark (ed.), *Journal of G. A. Robinson from 8 March to 7 April 1842*, entries for 22 & 23 March 1842; Journal of the Proceedings of C. W. Sievwright from 1 March to 31 May 1842, in CSIL/11 No 42/5708, Dixson
8 G. Presland (ed.), *Journals of George Augustus Robinson 20 March to 15 May 1841*, entry for 27 April 1841; Journal of the Proceedings of C. W. Sievwright from 1 March to 31 May 1842, in CSIL/11 No 42/5708, Dixson
9 I. Clark (ed.), *Journal of G. A. Robinson from 8 March to 7 April 1842*, entry for 28 March 1842; Journal of the Proceedings of C. W. Sievwright from 1 March to 31 May 1842, in CSIL/11 No 42/5708, Dixson; Blair to La Trobe 7 March 1842, VPRS 19/29 No 42/753
10 Robinson to La Trobe 9 April 1842, British House of Commons, Sessional Papers, 1844, vol. 34, pp. 208-211; J. Bonwick, *Western Victoria*, p. 66
11 *GA* 25 Oct 1841
12 S. Evans to S. Henty 24 Aug 1841 & Blair to La Trobe 28 Aug 1841, VPRS 10 No 41/1395
13 Blair to La Trobe 22 March 1842, VPRS 19/29 No 42/751
14 Petition to La Trobe from J. Kilgour & other Portland Bay settlers (n.d.), British House of Commons, Sessional Papers, 1844, vol. 34, pp. 213-4 & *PPG* 30 March 1842
15 La Trobe to J. Kilgour & others 26 March 1842, British House of Commons, Sessional Papers, 1844, vol. 34, pp. 214-215
16 H. Wills to La Trobe, March (n.d.) 1842, British House of Commons, Sessional Papers, 1844, vol. 34, pp. 215-6; G. Presland (ed.), *Journals of George Augustus Robinson 16 May to 15 Aug 1841*, entries for 12, 15, 23, 25 & 29 July 1841
17 Gipps to La Trobe 14 March 1842, Shaw, *Gipps-La Trobe Correspondence*, p. 122; La Trobe to Col Sec 29 March 1842, VPRS 16 No 42/434 (also in British House of Commons, Sessional Papers, 1844, vol. 34, pp. 212-3)

CHAPTER 23:

1 J. Dowling to Gipps 8 Jan 1842, British House of Commons, Sessional Papers, 1844, vol. 34, pp. 145-6; *GA* 27 Sept 1841

2 Statements by D. Fisher, J. W. Oldman, P. Connolly & T. Wright 7 & 13 Aug 1841, VPRS 24, Unit 1, 1841/No 44; Statement of Foster Fyans to court & other details of trial of Bonjon 16 Sept 1841, British House of Commons, Sessional Papers, 1844, vol. 34, pp. 146-155; *PPP* 20 Sept 1841

3 Willis to Gipps 22 Sept 1841; Col Sec to Dowling 4 Jan 1842; Dowling to Gipps 8 Jan 1842; Gipps to Stanley 24 Jan 1842; Account of trial of Bonjon, all in British House of Commons, Sessional Papers, 1844, vol. 34, pp. 143-155

4 Sievwright to Robinson 25 April 1841 VPRS 19/15 No.41/878

5 Report of Robinson's journey March to Aug 1841 in A. S. Kenyon, *The Aboriginal Protectorate of Port Phillip*, p. 165; Gipps to Stanley 28 Dec 1842, British House of Commons, Sessional Papers, 1844, vol. 34, p. 239

6 Sievwright to Robinson 24 Jan 1842, encl. in VPRS 19/27 No 42/500

7 Robinson to La Trobe 7 March 1842, VPRS 19/27 No 42/500; Croke to La Trobe 14 March 1842, VPRS 19/27 No 42/527

8 Journal of the Proceedings of C. W. Sievwright from 1 March to 31 May 1842, in CSIL/11 No 42/5708 Dixson

9 La Trobe to Col Sec 1 April 1842, VPRS 16 No 42/441

10 Journal of the Proceedings of C. W. Sievwright from 1 March to 31 May 1842, in CSIL/11 No 42/5708 Dixson

11 Fyans to La Trobe 8 April 1842, VPRS 19/39 No 42/2364

12 Fyans to La Trobe 10 April 1842, VPRS 19/39 No 42/2364; P. L. Browne (ed.), *Memoirs (of) Captain Foster Fyans*, pp. 246 & 259-62

13 Fyans to La Trobe 14 April 1842, VPRS 19/39 No 42/2364; Browne (ed.), *Memoirs (of) Captain Foster Fyans*, pp. 246-7

14 Fyans to La Trobe 16 April & 9 Oct 1842, VPRS 19/39 No 42/2364

15 C. Codd to La Trobe 15 March 1842 & marginal note by La Trobe 15 March 1842, VPRS 19/34 No 42/537

16 Fyans to La Trobe 22 April 1842, VPRS 19/39 No 42/2364; Browne (ed.), *Memoirs (of) Captain Foster Fyans*, pp. 249-50

17 Sievwright to Robinson 21 April 1842, with Robinson to La Trobe 6 June 1842, VPRS 19/31 No 42/1091

18 Fyans to La Trobe 1 May 1842, VPRS 19/39 No 42/2364; Browne (ed.), *Memoirs (of) Captain Foster Fyans*, p. 251; *Hobart Courier* 13 May 1842; *PPP* 19 May 1842; Sievwright to Robinson 23 June 1842, VPRS 21

19 A. Cameron to Editor, *PPP* 9 May 1842

20 Sievwright to Robinson 21 April 1842; Robinson to La Trobe 6 June 1842, VPRS 19/31 No 42/1091

21 Sievwright to Robinson 25 April 1842, VPRS 19/31 No 42/1104

22 *GA* 13 June 1842

CHAPTER 24:

1 *PPG* 20 May 1840; 30 May, 1841 & 6 Feb 1841

2 Col Sec to La Trobe 14 Feb 1842, VPRS 19/26 No 42/397

3 La Trobe to Robinson 28 Feb 1842, VPRS 16 No 42/293; Robinson to La Trobe 4 March 1842, VPRS 19/27 No 42/501

4 La Trobe to Col Sec 4 March 1842, British House of Commons, Sessional Papers, 1844, vol. 34, p. 217

5 Russell to Gipps 11 Aug 1841, British House of Commons, Sessional Papers, 1844, vol. 34, p. 96; *GA* 7 March 1842; *PPG* 9 March 1842

6 Letter from 12 squatters to La Trobe 23 April 1842, in *PPP* 10 May 1842

7 *GA* 16 May & *PPP* 16 May 1842

8 La Trobe to Fyans, Blair & French 26 March 1842, VPRS 16 No 42/407; La Trobe to Col Sec 29 March 1842, British House of Commons, Sessional Papers, 1844, vol. 34, p. 218; Notice of Reward e.g. in *PPH* 1 April 1842

9 Sievwright to Robinson 21 April 1842, encl. with La Trobe to Col Sec 1 June 1842, CSIL 4/2626, No 42/4263, SRNSW

10 *GA* 6 June 1842

11 Col Sec to La Trobe 21 April 1842, British House of Commons, Sessional Papers, 1844, vol. 34, p. 219

12 La Trobe to Fyans, Powlett & Griffith 10 June 1842, VPRS 16 No 42/756

13 Statement by Sievwright at Melbourne Police Office 3 June 1843, *PPP* 5 June & *PPG* 7 June 1843

14 Statement by D. O'Neill 21 May 1842, VPRS 24/1, 1842/ No 8; French to Croke 22 May 1842, VPRS 21 No 28/42; French to La Trobe 23 May 1842, VPRS 19/30 No 42/1020; La Trobe to Gipps 6 June 1842, VPRS 16 No 42/739; Statements by J. L. Wheatley & D. O'Neill 6 & 8 Nov 1844, Queen vs Koort Kirrup, VPRS 30 Unit 188

15 *PPG* 25 May & *PPP* 26 May 1842

16 Journal of the Proceedings of C. W. Sievwright from 1 March to 31 May 1842, in CSIL/11 No 42/5708 Dixson

17 Robinson to La Trobe 9 April 1842; La Trobe to Col Sec 26 April 1842, British House of Commons, Sessional Papers, 1844, vol. 34, pp. 208-211

18 Robinson to La Trobe 26 April 1842, VPRS 10 No 42/794

19 La Trobe to Col Sec 7 May 1842, VPRS 16 No 42/588

20 Gipps to Stanley 16 May 1842, British House of Commons, Sessional Papers, 1844, vol. 34, pp. 212 & 216

21 La Trobe to Robinson 7 May 1842, VPRS 16 No 42/591

22 Robinson to Sievwright 28 May 1842, *GA* 5 Feb 1845

23 Summonses against Sievwright, 1842. Entries 683, 782, & 917, Supreme Court Prothonotary's Index to Action Books, VPRS 5327; Judgement against Sievwright 25 May 25, 1842, Supreme Court Prothonotary's Judgement Book, Trinity Term 1842, VPRS 5331 Unit 1 p. 45 No 5

24 Sievwright to Robinson 11 June 1842, VPRS 10 No 1842/1168 (also in *GA* 5 Feb 1845)

25 Col Sec to La Trobe 3 June 1842, VPRS 10 No 42/1123

26 La Trobe to Lonsdale 17 June 1842, VPRS 16 No 42/794; La Trobe to Fyans 23 June 1842, VPRS 16 No 42/830

27 La Trobe to Robinson 17 June 1842, VPRS 16 No 42/801 & No 42/802

28 La Trobe to Powlett and Griffiths 10 June 1842, VPRS 16 No 42/756; *PPH* 9 June 1843

29 La Trobe to Fyans 13 June 1842, VPRS 16 No 42/761 & No 42/762

30 e.g. *PPH* 1 April 1842

31 Robinson to La Trobe 9 April 1842, British House of Commons, Sessional Papers, 1844, vol. 34, p. 210

32 G. Presland (ed.), *Journals of George Augustus Robinson 16 May to 15 Aug 1841*, entry for 6 June, 1841

33 I. Clark (ed.), *Journal of G. A. Robinson from 8 March to 7 April 1842*, entry for 24 March 1842

34 Blair to La Trobe 13 May 1842, VPRS 19/30 No 42/917

35 Statement by Corporal H. Graham 6 Nov 1844, encl. with papers relating to trial of Koort Kirrup, VPRS 30 Unit 188

CHAPTER 25:

1 A. Massola, *Bunjil's Cave*, pp. 1-2

2 J. Dawson, *Australian Aborigines*, pp. 49, 53-4

3 Ibid., p. 76

4 Ibid., pp. 63 & 68-71

5 Ibid., pp. 55 & 58-9

6 Robinson to La Trobe 9 Jan 1843, VPRS 19/40 No 43/55

7 Sievwright to Col Sec 1 Dec 1838, HRV vol 2B pp. 388-9

8 Sievwright to Robinson 5 May 1839; P. Cussen to Robinson 6 May 1839, HRV vol 2B pp. 460-61; Journal of W. Thomas, entry for 13 May 1839, HRV vol 2B p. 524

9 Sievwright to Robinson 11 July 1842, VPRS 11 No 1842/287

10 Robinson to La Trobe 28 June & 6 July 1842, VPRS 10 No 1842/1208

11 Lonsdale to La Trobe 23 June 1842, with Gipps to Sec of State 20 Dec 1842, NSW Governor's Despatches Outwards, vol 41, Despatch No 238, Mitchell Ms A1230 (Paper No 12)

12 Fyans to La Trobe 24 June 1842, Ibid. (Paper No 13)

13 William Meek to Fyans 16 July 1842, Ibid. (Paper No 13)

14 Christina Sievwright to Fyans (circa June 1839), Ibid. (Paper No 13)

15 Robinson to La Trobe 9 July 1842, Ibid. (Paper No 11)

16 List of immigrants aboard the *Hope* 16 December 1838, HRV vol 4 pp. 281-3; *SMH* 19 Dec 1838; W. Thomas (junior), Reminiscences, Mitchell Ms 214/27 p. 35

17 Journal of J. Dredge, entries for 3 & 11 Feb 1839, HRV vol 2B pp. 422-423

18 Journal of W. Thomas, entry for April, 1839, HRV vol 2B p. 520

19 Christina Sievwright to Robinson 11 March 1839, with Gipps to Sec of State 20 Dec 1842, NSW Governor's Despatches Outwards, vol 41, Despatch No 238, Mitchell Ms A1230 (Paper No 11)

20 Robinson to Maria Robinson 16 March 1839, HRV vol 2B p. 445

21 John Sievwright to Robinson 30 March 1842, with Gipps to Sec of State 20 Dec 1842, NSW Governor's Despatches Outwards, vol 41, Despatch No 238, Mitchell Ms A1230 (Paper No 11)

22 John Sievwright to Robinson 11 May 1842, VPRS 11 Item No 286

23 *PPP* 18 July; *PPH* 19 July; *PPG* 20 July 1842

24 *PPG* 20 July; *PPP* 21 July; *PPH* 22 July; *GA* 25 July1842

25 Sievwright to Robinson 21 April 1842, VPRS 19/31 No 42/1091

26 *PPG* July 20; *PPH* July 22, 1842

27 La Trobe to Col Sec 25 Nov 1839 & Gipps' minute 5 December 1839, HRV vol 2B p. 682

28 Sievwright to Robinson 21 April 1842 & Robinson to La Trobe 6 June 1842, VPRS 19/31 No 42/1091

29 La Trobe to Gipps 26 July 1842, Shaw, *Gipps-La Trobe Correspondence*, pp. 149-50

30 Col Sec to La Trobe 13 Aug 1842 & enclosures, VPRS 19/34 No 42/1545

31 Willis to La Trobe 19 July 1842, VPRS 19/34 No 42/1328)
32 La Trobe to Col Sec 19 July 1842, VPRS 16 No 42/952
33 C. Griffith, *The Present State and Prospects*, p. 195
34 *PMerc* 31 August 1842
35 *PGuard* 17 Sept 1842
36 *PMerc* 5 Oct 1842

CHAPTER 26:

1 Sievwright to La Trobe 3 Aug 1842, VPRS 10 No 42/1493
2 La Trobe to Robinson 17 June 1842, VPRS 16 No 42/803
3 *PPP* 21 July 1842
4 *PPG* 30 July 1842
5 La Trobe to Robinson 12 Aug 1842, with Gipps to Sec of State 20 Dec 1842, NSW Governor's Despatches Outwards, vol 41, Despatch No 238, Mitchell Ms A1230 (Paper No 16)
6 Christina Sievwright to La Trobe 13 Aug 1842, Ibid. (Paper No 16)
7 Sievwright to La Trobe 13 Aug 1842 & enclosures: Palmerston to Falkland 22 June 1837; Morpeth to Falkland 10 May 1836; Falkland to Sievwright 6 Nov 1836; 14 Jan 1837; 11 June 1837; Vivian to Falkland 28 April 1837; Russell to Falkland 1 Sept 1837; A. Ponsonby to Sievwright 1 Dec 1837; Ibid. (Paper No 20)
8 Robinson to La Trobe 28 June & 6 July 1842, VPRS 10 No 42/1208; Sievwright to La Trobe 15 Aug 1842, with Gipps to Sec of State 20 Dec 1842, NSW Governor's Despatches Outwards, vol 41, Despatch No 238, Mitchell Ms A1230 (Paper No 21); La Trobe's margin note 24 Aug 1842 on Sievwright to La Trobe 13 Aug 1842, VPRS 10 No 42/1510
9 Sievwright to Robinson 19 Aug 1842, with Gipps to Sec of State 20 Dec 1842, NSW Governor's Despatches Outwards, vol 41, Despatch No 238, Mitchell Ms A1230 (Paper No 24)
10 Robinson to La Trobe 30 Aug 1842, Ibid. (Paper No 26)
11 Croke to Court Sheriff 29 June 1842, VPRS 21; Croke to La Trobe 11 July 1842, VPRS 19/39 No 42/2364
12 French to La Trobe 9 Aug 1842, VPRS 19/34 No 42/1526
13 James Hunter to La Trobe 1 Sept 1842, VPRS 19/34 No 42/1618 (also in British House of Commons, Sessional Papers, 1844, vol 34, p. 234); S. MacGregor to French 22 Aug 1842; Hunter to La Trobe 6 Sept 1842; Fyans to La Trobe 6 Sept 1842; VPRS 19/35 No 42/1664; MacGregor to French 8 Aug 1842 & French to La Trobe 22 Sept 1842, VPRS 19/36 No 42/1822; Statements by MacGregor, S. Gorrie, W. Brice, & R. Cochrane 21 Sept 1842; Sievwright to Croke 22 Sept 1842; French to La Trobe 22 Sept 1842, VPRS 21, Unit 1; R. Boldrewood, *Old Melbourne Memories*, pp. 44-5
14 *PMerc* 31 Aug 1842
15 Statement of F. W. Desailly 29 Aug 1842, VPRS 24, Unit 476, No 1404.; Blair to La Trobe 8 Sept 1842, British House of Commons, Sessional Papers, 1844, vol 34, p. 236
16 La Trobe to Col Sec 22 Aug 1842, Ibid., p. 231
17 French to La Trobe 28 July 1842, Ibid., p. 232
18 La Trobe to French 22 Aug 1842, VPRS 16 No 42/1088; La Trobe to Dana 22 Aug 1842, VPRS 16 No 42/1090; Instructions for Dana's guidance on mission to Western District with Native Police 22 Aug 1842, VPRS 16 pp. 134-136
19 Native Police Standing Orders & H. E. P. Dana to La Trobe 19 Jan 1843, in British House of Commons, Sessional Papers, 1844, vol 34, pp. 289-90
20 Return of Native Police for 1842, Ibid., pp. 291-2

CHAPTER 27:

1 E. Finn, *The Chronicles of Early Melbourne*, pp. 394-8
2 Col Sec to La Trobe 13 Aug 1842 & enclosed minutes of Executive Council meeting, VPRS 19/34 No 42/1545
3 *PPH* 26 Aug 1842
4 Robinson's Journal, 24 June-3 Nov 1842, Mitchell Ms A7039, entry for 26 Aug 1842
5 *PPG* 7 Sept 1842; Finn, *The Chronicles of Early Melbourne*, pp. 398-400
6 *PPP* 9 Sept 1842
7 La Trobe to Col Sec 30 Aug 1842, VPRS 16 No. 42/1157
8 *PGuard* 10 Sept 1842
9 La Trobe to Fyans 2 & 5 Sept 1842, VPRS 16 Nos 42/1177 & 42/1191; La Trobe to French 3 & 5 Sept 1842, VPRS 16 Nos 42/1188 & 42/1195; La Trobe to Blair 5 Sept 1842 VPRS 16 No 42/1192; French to La Trobe 30 Aug 1842, VPRS 19/35 Nos 1661 & 1662

10 Fyans to La Trobe 6 Sept 1842, VPRS 19/35 No 42/1664
11 La Trobe to French, Blair, Fyans, Dana & Watton 3 Sept 1842, VPRS 16 No 42/1189
12 La Trobe to Col Sec 18 July 1842, VPRS 16 Nos 42/934 & 42/938
13 Christina Sievwright to La Trobe 17 Sept 1842, VPRS 10 No 42/1923
14 Frances Anna Sievwright to La Trobe 17 Sept 1842, VPRS 10 No 42/1923
15 Depositions of S. MacGregor, S. Gorrie, W. Brice & R. Cochrane 21 Sept 1842, encl. with La Trobe to Croke 10 Oct 1842, VPRS 21, Unit 1
16 *PPH* 16 Sept 1842
17 *PPH* 20 & 30 Sept 1842
18 *PPH* 7 Oct 1842

CHAPTER 28:

1 *PPP* 5 Sept 1842
2 NSW Leg. Council V&P 1843, Return to an address by Dr Thomson, p. 477
3 *Proposed Plan for the Better Treatment of the Aborigines of Australia Felix* by J. H. Patterson 7 June 1842, VPRS 2599, Unit 11 (also in *PPH* 21 June 1842)
4 Journal of the Proceedings of C. W. Sievwright from 1 March to 31 May 1842, in CSIL/11 No 42/5708, Dixson
5 Parker to Robinson 5 Oct 1842 & Robinson to La Trobe 6 Oct 1842, VPRS 19/36 No 42/1867
6 Stanley to Gipps 30 Nov 1842, HRA vol xxii p. 379
7 *PMerc* 31 Aug 1842; T. F. Bride, Letters from Victorian Pioneers, p. 152
8 Blair to La Trobe 16 May 1842, VPRS 19/30 No 42/962; Deposition of J. Ellis 21 May 1842, The Queen vs Cold Morning VPRS 30/185 NCR 42
9 G. Presland (ed.), *Journals of George Augustus Robinson 16 May to 15 Aug 1841*, entries for 16 & 17 May 1841
10 I. Clark (ed.), *Journal of G. A. Robinson from 8 March to 7 April 1842*, entry for 23 March 1842
11 Blair to La Trobe 16 May 1842 VPRS 19/30 No 42/962
12 Fyans to La Trobe 24 Jan 1842, VPRS 19/39 No 42/2364
13 Blair to La Trobe 19 May 1842, VPRS 19/30 No 42/923
14 Col Sec to La Trobe 26 July 26 1842, VPRS 19/33 No 42/1470; La Trobe to Blair 12 Aug 1842, VPRS 16 No 42/1053
15 Queen vs Cold Morning, trial papers, VPRS 30/185 NCR 42
16 Blair to H. F. Gurner 7 July 1845, with Queen vs. Koort Kirrup, VPRS 30/188
17 Croke to Robinson 6 July 1842, VPRS 21
18 Sievwright to Croke 1 Aug 1842, VPRS 21
19 *PPH* 19 July 1842; Croke to La Trobe 24 Aug 1842, VPRS 19/34 No 42/1566
20 Robinson to La Trobe 9 Sept 1842 with notes by La Trobe 26 Sept & J. D. Pinnock (n.d.), VPRS 19/35 No 42/1789; *PPH* 6 Sept 1842
21 *PGuard* 10 Sept 1842 & *PMerc* 21 Sept 1842
22 Fyans to La Trobe 9 Oct 1842, British House of Commons, Sessional Papers, 1844, vol 34, p. 235; *PMerc* 31 Aug & 7 Sept 1842; *PGuard* 10 Sept & 8 Oct 1842; Statement by T. Winter 3 Sept 1842, encl. with French to La Trobe 15 Oct 1842, VPRS 19/37 No 42/2045
23 Fyans to La Trobe 26 Dec 1842, British House of Commons, Sessional Papers, 1844, vol 34, pp. 259-60
24 *PGuard* 10 Sept 10 & 22 Oct 1842 & Return of prisoners apprehended by Native Mounted Police Oct 1842, British House of Commons, Sessional Papers, 1844, vol 34, p. 293
25 French to La Trobe 12 Nov 1842, VPRS 19/38 No 42/2116; Dana to La Trobe 22 Nov 1842, VPRS 19/38 No 42/2153
26 L. MacKinnon to La Trobe 29 March 1843, VPRS 19/43 No 43/554
27 *PPH* 6 Sept 1842; *PGuard* 29 Oct 1842
28 *PGuard* 5 Nov 1842
29 *PGuard* 26 Nov 1842
30 *PGuard* 3 Dec 1842; French to La Trobe 5 Dec 1842, VPRS 19/39 No 42/2280; Blair to La Trobe 10 Dec 1842, VPRS 19/39 No 42/2329; French to La Trobe 30 Dec 1842, VPRS 19/40 No 43/19; G. Presland (ed.), *Journals of George Augustus Robinson 16 May to 15 Aug 1841*, entry for 27 May 1841
31 La Trobe to Col Sec 13 Oct 1842, encl. with Gipps to Sec of State 20 Dec 1842, NSW Governor's Despatches Outwards, vol 41, Despatch No 238, Mitchell Ms A1230
32 La Trobe to Col Sec 2 Aug 1842, VPRS 16 No 42/990; Gipps to Stanley 9 Sept 1842, despatch No 161, HRA vol xxii pp. 258-259
33 Gipps to Stanley 9 Sept 1842, despatch No 161 HRA Vol xxii pp. 258-259
34 La Trobe to Robinson, Fyans & Lonsdale 27 Aug 1842, VPRS 16 No 42/1145
35 La Trobe to Col Sec 6 Aug 1842, VPRS 16 No 42/1006

CHAPTER 29:

1 Col Sec to La Trobe 17 July 1842, in CSIL 4/2626 No 42/4263, SRNSW
2 La Trobe to Col Sec 18 July 1842, in CSIL 4/2626 No 42/5716, SRNSW
3 *SG* 20 & 25 Aug 1842; *SMH* 24 Aug 1842
4 *SMH* 30 Aug & 1 Sept 1842
5 La Trobe to Col Sec 1 Feb 1842, VPRS 16 No 42/161; Col Sec to La Trobe 14 Feb 1842, VPRS 19/27 No 42/469
6 R. W. Tulloh to La Trobe 3 March 1842, VPRS 19/27 No 42/469; La Trobe to R. W. Tulloh 4 March 1842, VPRS 16 No 42/304; Gipps to Stanley 11 March 1842, British House of Commons, Sessional Papers, 1844, vol 34, p. 183 (also in HRA vol xxi p. 746)
7 Fyans to La Trobe 13 May 1842, VPRS 19/32 No 42/1294
8 La Trobe to Blair 30 May 30 1842, VPRS 16 No 42/675; La Trobe to Fyans 4 June 1842, VPRS 16 No 42/720; La Trobe to Col Sec 6 June 1842, VPRS 16 No 42/726; Col Sec to La Trobe 2 July 1842, VPRS 19/32 No 42/1294
9 La Trobe to Fyans 4 June 1842, VPRS 16 No 42/721
10 La Trobe to Col Sec 23 Aug 1842, VPRS 16 No 42/1094
11 Gipps to La Trobe 6 Sept 1842; A. G. L. Shaw, *Gipps-La Trobe Correspondence*, p. 165
12 Watton to Robinson 10 Dec 1843 & Robinson to La Trobe 20 Feb 1843, VPRS 19/43 No 43/330
13 Sievwright to La Trobe 27 Jan 1843, VPRS 10 No 1843/194 (transcript in *GA* 5 Feb 1845)
14 Sievwright to La Trobe 2 Feb 1843, VPRS 10 No 43/235
15 Robinson to La Trobe 4 Feb 1843, with enclosures, VPRS 10 No 43/234
16 Col Sec to La Trobe 13 Feb 1843, VPRS 10 No 43/365
17 Col Sec to La Trobe 20 Feb 1843, VPRS 10 No 43/385
18 Sievwright to La Trobe 2 March 1843 & La Trobe's marginal note, VPRS 10 No 43/460
19 T. F. Bride, *Letters from Victorian Pioneers*, pp. 307-311 (first edtn only)

CHAPTER 30:

1 La Trobe to Col Sec 29 March 1842, British House of Commons, Sessional Papers, 1844, vol 34, pp. 212-3
2 Gipps to Stanley 16 May 1842, Ibid., p. 216; Stanley to Gipps 20 Dec 1842, HRA vol xxii pp. 436-39)
3 Stanley to Gipps 25 March 1843, HRA vol xxii pp. 592-3
4 Gipps to Sec of State 20 Dec 1842 & enclosures, NSW Governor's Despatches Outwards, vol 41, Despatch No 238, Mitchell Ms A1230 (Gipps' covering letter also in VPRS 10 43/2599)
5 Stanley to Gipps 5 June 1843, HRA vol xxii p. 769
6 F. Nesbitt to La Trobe April 1843, CSIL 4/2627 No 43/3823, SRNSW
7 Fenwick to La Trobe 1 May 1843, CSIL 4/2627 No 43/3823, SRNSW
8 La Trobe to Col Sec 9 May 1843, CSIL 4/2627 No 43/3823, SRNSW
9 Gipps' marginal notes of 20 & 31 May 1843 on La Trobe to Col Sec 9 May 1843, CSIL 4/2627 No 43/3823, SRNSW; Gipps to La Trobe 20 May 1843, A. G. L. Shaw, *Gipps-La Trobe Correspondence*, pp. 209-210
10 D. H. Wilson to G. R. Wilsone 9 Sept 1839, D. H. Wilsone letters Ms 9825 File 267/2a La Trobe Library; Statement by W. Kearnan at trial of S. G. Bolden, *PPH* 3 Dec; *PPG* 4 Dec & *PPP* 6 Dec1841; Fyans to La Trobe 1 Jan 1842, British House of Commons, Sessional Papers, 1844, vol 34 p. 180; Blair to La Trobe 29 Jan 1842, British House of Commons, Sessional Papers, 1844, vol 34 p. 202; Fyans report for March-June 1842, P. L. Browne (ed.), *Memoirs (of) Captain Foster Fyans*, p. 245; W. D. Bernard to Fyans 12 Feb 1842, British House of Commons, Sessional Papers, 1844, vol 34 p. 206
11 *PPP* 1 & 5 Jun 1843; *PPG* 6 June 1843; *PPH* 9 June 1843; Jeffcott to La Trobe 18 Aug 1843, British House of Commons, Sessional Papers, 1844, vol 34 pp. 270-272
12 Statement by T. Osbrey 29 May 1843, Ibid. p. 272
13 Gipps to Stanley 13 October 1843, HRA vol xxi, p. 320
14 Gipps to Stanley 2 July 1843, HRA vol xxiii pp. 3-4
15 Robinson to La Trobe 17 June 1843, encl. with La Trobe to Col Sec 18 July 1842, CSIL 4/2626 No 42/5716, SRNSW
16 Report of trial of R. G. Hill, J. Betts & J. Beswicke 31 July & 1 August 1843; Jeffcott to La Trobe 18 Aug 1843, British House of Commons, Sessional Papers, 1844, vol 34 pp. 263-272; Robinson to La Trobe 9 Aug 1843; La Trobe to Col Sec 9 Aug 1843 & Gipps' marginal notes 20 Aug 1843, all in CSIL 4/2626 No 43/6086, SRNSW
17 Robinson to La Trobe 27 June 1843, VPRS 10 No 43/1795 with La Trobe's marginal note 3 July 1843; Robinson to La Trobe 5 July 1843, VPRS 10 No 43/1846; H. F. Gurner to Sievwright 7 July 1843, VPRS 10 No 43/1863; Gurner to La Trobe 8 Aug 1843, VPRS 10 No 43/2031; Sievwright to La Trobe 29 Sept 1843, VPRS 10 No 43/2348
18 Sievwright to La Trobe 7 Sept 1843, VPRS 10 No 43/2216

19 Sievwright to La Trobe 21 Sept 1843, VPRS 10 No 43/2287
20 Sievwright to La Trobe 29 Sept 1843, VPRS 10 No 43/2348
21 *GA* 5 Feb 1845
22 Sievwright to La Trobe 28 Oct 1843, VPRS 10 No 43/2501
23 Col Sec to La Trobe 8 Nov 1843, VPRS 10 No 43/2599
24 Sievwright to La Trobe 21 Nov, VPRS 10 No 43/2632; La Trobe's marginal notes with Christina Sievwright to La Trobe 23 Nov 1843, VPRS 10 No 43/2640
25 Christina Sievwright to La Trobe 23 Nov 1843, VPRS 10 No 43/2640
26 Sievwright to La Trobe 25 Nov 1843, VPRS 10 No 43/2650
27 Board to La Trobe 5 March 1844, VPRS 10 No 44/453
28 Sievwright to La Trobe 24 Jan 1844, VPRS 10 No 44/187
29 Col Sec to La Trobe 22 Feb 1844, VPRS 10 No 44/386
30 Board to La Trobe 5 March 1844, VPRS 10 No 44/453; Sievwright comments *GA* 5 Feb 1845
31 Robinson to La Trobe 13 March 1844, VPRS 10 No 44/485; *GA* 5 Feb 1845
32 Col Sec to La Trobe 28 March 1844, VPRS 10 No 44/588
33 Sievwright to La Trobe 10 April 1844, VPRS 10 No 44/657
34 Sievwright to La Trobe 2 Nov 1844 , VPRS 10 No 44/1966
35 Addis & Eyre to La Trobe 19 Nov 1844, VPRS 10 No 44/2009
36 Robinson to La Trobe 2 Dec 1844 ,VPRS 10 No 44/2131; Return of expenditure on "Great Western Aboriginal Station" for 1842, VPRS 12, Unit 2, No 9
37 Col Sec to La Trobe 18 Dec 1844 , VPRS 10 No 44/2268

CHAPTER 31:

1 *GA* 30 Jan & 6 Feb 1841
2 Sievwright to La Trobe 6 Dec 1844, VPRS 10 No 44/2166
3 Col Sec to La Trobe 18 Dec 1844, VPRS 10 No 44/2268
4 Addis & Eyre to La Trobe 26 Dec 1844 & Sievwright to Addis & Eyre 18 Dec 1844, VPRS 10 No 44/2280
5 La Trobe to Sievwright 30 Dec 1844, transcript in *GA* 5 Feb 1845
6 *GA* 5 & 8 Feb 1845
7 Addis & Eyre to La Trobe 30 Jan 1845, VPRS10 No 45/230
8 Marginal notes by La Trobe 27 Jan 1845, VPRS 10 No 45/160
9 Robinson to La Trobe 27 Jan 1845, VPRS 10 No 45/194
10 Sievwright to La Trobe 7 Sept 1843, VPRS 10 No 43/2216
11 Sievwright to La Trobe 8 Feb 1845, VPRS10 No 45/294
12 Christina Sievwright to La Trobe 15 March 1845, VPRS 19/69 No 45/510
13 *GA* 28 May, 11 June; *PPP* 28 May; *PPH* 28 May, 29 May & 26 June 1845
14 Watton to La Trobe 27 May 1845, VPRS 11 Unit 9 No 45/497
15 *PPP* 18 Aug 1845

CHAPTER 32:

1 *Times* 11 Nov 1845
2 Will of Francis Sievwright, Kasauli, India, 16 April 1845, Register of Deeds, NAS, RD5/814 pp. 396-397)
3 Gladstone to Sievwright 27 March 1846. Summarised by Earl Grey 14 Aug 1848, encl. with FitzRoy to Sec of State 14 March 1848, Transcripts of Despatches from NSW Governor, 1846-48, Despatch No 58, Mitchell Ms A1267-23 (also mentioned in Sievwright to Earl Grey, May 8, 1847, HRA vol xxv p. 584)
4   Sievwright to Earl Grey May 8, 1847 HRA vol xxv pp. 584-86)
5 Ann Sievwright to Lillias Sievwright 3 Nov 1841, SC 70/4/3 pp. 925-926, NAS & Deposition of Lillias Sievwright 8 May 1847, SC 70/1/67 p.717, NAS
6 Sievwright to Earl Grey 8 May 1847; B. Hawes to Sievwright 22 May 1847; Grey to FitzRoy 24 May 1847, HRA vol xxv pp. 583- 591

CHAPTER 33:

1 Petition of W. Le Souef to NSW Leg. Council, in *PPP* 15, 16, 19, 20, & 21 Oct 1846
2 Robinson's Journal 18 Sept 1846-Feb 1848, entry for 27 Oct, Mitchell Ms A7041 p. 547
3 Sievwright to Earl Grey 8 May 1847, HRA vol xxv p. 590
4 Grey to FitzRoy 24 May 1847, HRA vol xxvi p. 583
5 Sievwright to Charles FitzRoy 10 Jan 1816, WO31/435, PRO London

6 Col Sec to La Trobe 5 Oct 1847, VPRS 10 No 47/1864
7 La Trobe to Col Sec 19 Nov 1840, CSIL 4/2549 No 41/1071, SRNSW
8 La Trobe to Robinson 27 Nov 1840, VPRS 16 No 40/885
9 see Chapter 16
10 see Chapter 8
11 Robinson to La Trobe Nov (n.d.) 1847, with FitzRoy to Sec of State 14 March 1848, Transcripts of Despatches from NSW Governor, 1846-48, Despatch No 58, Mitchell Ms A1267-23 pp. 3581-3592
12 Croke to La Trobe 28 Nov 1847, Ibid. pp. 3606-3611
13 La Trobe to FitzRoy 31 Dec 1847, Ibid. pp. 3569-3580; Robinson to La Trobe Nov (n.d.) 1847, Ibid. pp. 3581-3592; E. Parker to La Trobe 7 Dec 1847, Ibid. pp. 3611-3613
14 Petition of W. Le Souef to NSW Leg. Council, extract in *PPP* 20 Oct 1846
15 Journal of James Dredge Entries for 3 & 10 Feb 1839, HRV vol 2B pp. 422-423
16 La Trobe to FitzRoy 31 Dec 1847, with FitzRoy to Sec of State 14 March 1848, Transcripts of Despatches from NSW Governor, 1846-48, Despatch No 58, Mitchell Ms A1267-23 pp. 3569-3580;
17 Russell to Gipps, La Trobe etc. 25 Aug 1840 HRA vol xx pp. 774-6

CHAPTER 34:

1 *GA* 3 March 1848
2 FitzRoy to Earl Grey 14 March 1848, HRA vol xxvi pp. 272-273; *SMH* 15 March 1848
3 Comments by Earl Grey, H. Merivale, & B. Hawes on FitzRoy despatch August 1848, with FitzRoy to Sec of State 14 March 1848, Transcripts of Despatches from NSW Governor, 1846-48, Despatch No 58, Mitchell Ms A1267-23 pp. 3614-16
4 B. Hawes to Sievwright 26 Aug 1848, Secretary of State's NSW Domestic Entry Book: Offices & Individuals, CO 202/55 p.308, PRO London
5 Christina Sievwright to Niel Black, 4 Sept & 22 Oct 1849, Niel Black Papers, Box 3, La Trobe Library Ms 8996
6 W. Thomas (junior), Reminiscences, Mitchell Ms 214/27 p.31
7 Brompton Cemetery pamphlet, 1993
8 *Times* 19 Sept 1855
9 Diary of Frances Anna Davenport, Entries for 1-3 Jan 1856, Davenport Papers, NS144/2/2, Archives Office of Tasmania
10 R. V. Billis & A. S. Kenyon, *Pastures New*, p. 157
11 I. Clark (ed.), *Journal of G. A. Robinson from 8 March to 7 April 1842*, entry for 13 March 1842
12 ADB, vol 1 p.124; E. Finn, *The Chronicles of Early Melbourne*, pp. 896-897
13 *The Colonist*, quoted in Argus 4 March 1851
14 *Argus* 4 March 4 1851
15 Telegram to Lilian Lucas 5 April 1918, Davenport Papers, NS144/1/3, Archives Office of Tasmania
16 ADB vol 2, p. 387; V. Rae-Ellis, *Black Robinson*, pp. 255-260
17 ADB vol 2, p. 423
   Ibid, pp. 90-93

CHAPTER 35:

1 Watton to La Trobe 12 Jan 1848, VPRS 11 No 544
2 Watton to Robinson 5 June 1843, VPRS 11 No 476
3 Watton annual report for 1846, VPRS 11 No521
4 Watton annual report for 1847, VPRS 11 No 542
5 Watton to Robinson 7 October 1847, VPRS 11 No 540
6 J. Bonwick, *Western Victoria*, pp. 170-171
7 *PGuard* 26 Aug & 2, 9,16 Sept 1843
8 R. Boldrewood, *Old Melbourne Memories*, pp. 69-72
9 Report of Vic. Leg. Council Committee on Aborigines, 1858-59, pp. iii-vi; C. P. Cooke to committee p. 34 of report
10 Ibid. p. 32
11 Ibid. p. 32
12 Ibid. p. 27
13 Ibid. p. 1
14 Ibid. p. 4
15 Ibid. p. 41

16 (16) Ibid. p. 23
17 (17) Foster Fyans to La Trobe 1 Jan 1842, British House of Commons, Sessional Papers, 1844, vol. 34, p. 180; Fyans' evidence to Vic. Leg. Council Committee on Aborigines, 1858-59 (n.d.), VPRS 2599 Unit 11
18 (18) Report of Vic. Leg. Council Committee on Aborigines, 1858-59, p. 26
19 (19) Ibid. p. 26
20 (20) Ibid. pp. 26, 27 & 30
21 (21) Ibid. pp. 25, 30 & 36; C. P. Cooke, evidence to Vic. Leg. Council Committee on Aborigines, 1858-59, VPRS 2599 Unit 11
22 (22) Report of Vic. Leg. Council Committee on Aborigines, 1858-59, p. 30
23 (23) Ibid. p. 30
24 (24) Ibid. p. 41
25 (25) Ibid. p. 26.; H. Murray, evidence to Vic. Leg. Council Committee on Aborigines, 1858-59, VPRS 2599 Unit 11
26 (26) Report of Vic. Leg. Council Committee on Aborigines, 1858-59, pp. 43-44
27 (27) Ibid. p. 73
28 (28) Ibid. p. 43
29 (29) Ibid. p. 51
30 (30) Ibid. pp. 72-3
31 (31) Ibid pp. 43-4
32 (32) Ibid. p. iv
33 (33) Ibid. p. v
34 (34) V. Savill, *Dear Friends, Lake Condah Mission*, p. 136
35 (35) J. Dawson, *Australian Aborigines*, pp. 3-4
36 (36) Report of Vic. Leg. Council Committee on Aborigines, 1858-59, p. 74
37 (37) Savill, *Dear Friends, Lake Condah Mission*, p. 63
38 (38) Ibid. p. 90
39 (39) Ibid. p. 94
40 (40) Ibid. pp. 92-3
41 (41) Ibid. pp. 114-115; W. B. Russell, *The Second Fourteenth Battalion*, pp. 93 & 191-194
42 (42) Savill, *Dear Friends, Lake Condah Mission*, pp. 69-70

SELECT BIBLIOGRAPHY:

OFFICIAL PRINTED SOURCES:

Britain:
British House of Commons, Sessional Papers, 1844, vol. 34. Aborigines (Australian Colonies). Return to an address…asking for extracts from the Despatches of the Governors of the Australian Colonies, with the Reports of the Protectors of Aborigines, and…other correspondence…

Report of the Select Committee on Transportation, Parliamentary Papers 1837-38, xxii

New South Wales:
Government Gazettes
Legislative Council, Votes & Proceedings, Report from the Committee on Immigration,with Minutes of Evidence & Replies to Circular Letter on the Aborigines, 1841 (see Mitchell Library MsA611)
Legislative Council, Votes & Proceedings, Return to an address by Dr Thomson on 29 August 1843, comprising the expenditure on Aborigines 1823-43, the results of trials of Aborigines 1837-43, etc.

Victoria:
Report of the Select Committee of the Legislative Council on the Aborigines, together with the proceedings of the committee, minutes of evidence, and appendices. 1858-59.

OFFICIAL MANUSCRIPT SOURCES:

Public Record Office of Victoria, Melbourne:

VPRS 10: Registered Inward Correspondence to the Superintendent of Port Phillip District Relating to Aboriginal Affairs, 1839-51
VPRS 11: Unregistered Inward Correspondence to the Chief Protector of Aborigines, 1839-51
VPRS 12/4467: Aboriginal Protectorate Returns, 1840-49
VPRS 16/2142: Superintendent, Port Phillip District. Registered Outward Correspondence, 1839-51
VPRS 18/2139: Registers of Inward Correspondence
VPRS 19: Superintendent of Port Phillip District. Registered Inward Correspondence, 1840-51 (includes drafts of outward correspondence)
VPRS 24: Inquest Deposition Files, 1840-51
VPRS 30: Criminal Trial Briefs, 1841-51
VPRS 109: Geelong Police Office Deposition Book
VPRS 2139: (see VPRS 18)
VPRS 2140: Port Phillip Police Magistrate's Letter Book. Letters Outward, 1836-40
VPRS 2599: Original papers tabled in Victorian Legislative Council (restricted access)
VPRS 4397: Unregistered Correspondence Relating to the Suspension of C.W. Sievwright from the Office of Assistant Protector
VPRS 4410: Aboriginal Protectorate. Weekly, Monthly, Quarterly and Annual Reports and Journals, 1836-49
VPRS 4467: (see VPRS 12)
VPRS 4729: Port Phillip Magistrate Inward Registered Correspondence, 1836-39
VPRS 5327: Supreme Court Prothonotary's Index to Action Books
VPRS 5331: Supreme Court Prothonotary's Judgement Book, 1841-53
VPRS 6929: Attorney-General's Office, Inward Unregistered Correspondence, 1840-50

Public Record Office, London:
Army Lists
WO 25: Services of Officers on the Active List, 1829-1919
WO 31/435: Commander-in-Chief's Memoranda, 1816
CO 202/55: Secretary of State's NSW Domestic Entry Book: Offices & Individuals, 1848
Census details for 1841 and 1851

State Records New South Wales, Sydney:
New South Wales Colonial Secretary's Inward Correspondence, Port Phillip Papers, 1840-47

Archives Office of Tasmania, Hobart:
Davenport Papers. NS 144, Series 1-6. Various Papers, photographs etc. deposited by Mary Cecily Shoobridge, great-great-grand-daughter of C. W. Sievwright

La Trobe Library, Melbourne (Manuscripts Collection):
Black, Niel. Journal of. Ms 11519
Learmonth Station Diary. Ms H15788, Box 102/9
Smyth, R.B. Papers. Ms 8781, Box 1176/7a & 1176/7b
Wilsone, D.H. Lettters. Ms 9825, File 267/2a & 267/2b

Mitchell Library, Sydney:
Australian Aborigines: reports etc. on employment and civilisation, 1832-41, Ms A611: includes Minutes of Evidence & Replies to Circular Letter on the Aborigines, for NSW Legislative Council Committee on Immigration, 1841
NSW Governor's Despatches Outwards, Mss A1230 &1267-23
Orton, J., Journal of: Ms A1715
Robinson, G. A: Journals, Letterbooks, correspondence and other papers, 1823-72, Mss A7022-A7092
Thomas, W., Reminiscences: 1841-43, uncat ms, set 214, item 27
Waugh Family Letters: Ms A827

Dixson Library, Sydney:
Manuscripts, letters, depositions etc., relating to Aborigines in Port Phillip District, Add Mss 86 & 87
Archival estrays: Colonial Secretary's Inward Letters, CSIL/11

General Register Office, London:
Birth, Death and Marriage records

Guildhall Library, London:
Register of Freedom Admissions
Spectacle Makers' Company, Record of Freedom Admissions 1694-1873, Ms 6031/1-6

Brompton Cemetery, London:
Burial records

General Register Office for Scotland, Edinburgh:
Birth, Death and Marriage Records
Census records, 1841

National Archives of Scotland, Edinburgh:

Register of Deeds
Sheriff Court, Midlothian: Minute Book Register of Deeds

National Library of Scotland, Edinburgh:

Steuart Papers: Ms5037-5039
Advocates Mss.

Episcopal Church of Scotland, Stirling:

Marriage Register, 1822

NEWSPAPERS:

Argus, The
Australian, The
Caledonian Mercury (Edinburgh)
Colonial Gazette
Colonist, The
Edinburgh Magazine & Literary Miscellany
Geelong Advertiser
Hobart Courier
Hobart Mercury
Launceston Advertiser
Port Phillip Gazette
Port Phillip Herald
Port Phillip Patriot
Portland Guardian & Normanby General Advertiser
Portland Mercury
Sydney Gazette
Sydney Herald (*Sydney Morning Herald* after July 1842)
Sydney Monitor
Times, The (London)

PUBLISHED SOURCES:

Arden, George. *Latest information with regard to Australia Felix, the finest province of the great territory of New South Wales....* Facsimile edtn. Queensberry Hill Press, Melbourne 1977.

Australian Dictionary of Biography, vols 1-6, edited by Douglas Pike, Bede Nairn and others. Melbourne University Press 1966-76.

Barnes, Major R. Money. *A History of the Regiments and Uniforms of the British Army.* Fifth edtn. Seeley Service & Co, London 1962.

Bassett, Marnie. *The Hentys: An Australian Colonial Tapestry.* Oxford University Press, London 1954.

Billis, R. V. & Kenyon, A. S. *Pastures New.* 2nd edition. Stockland Press, Melbourne 1974.

------ *Pastoral Pioneers of Port Phillip.* 2nd edition. Stockland Press, Melbourne 1974.

Boldrewood, Rolf. *Old Melbourne Memories*. First published George Robertson and Company, Melbourne, 1884. Republished William Heinemann Limited 1969.

Bonwick, James. *Western Victoria: Its Geography, Geology and Social Condition*. First published Thomas Brown, Geelong, 1858. Republished William Heinemann Australia 1970.

Bride, Thomas Francis (ed.). *Letters from Victorian Pioneers*. Government Printer, Melbourne 1898.

Browne, Thomas Alexander. See Boldrewood, Rolf.

Brown, P. L. (ed.). *Memoirs recorded at Geelong, Victoria, Australia by Captain Foster Fyans*. Geelong Advertiser Pty Ltd, Geelong 1986.

Cannon, Michael. *Who killed the Koories?*. William Heinemann, Melbourne 1990.

------ (general ed.) *Historical Records of Victoria* vols 1-6. Government Printer, Melbourne 1981-91.

Christie, Michael F. *Aborigines in Colonial Victoria* 1835-86. Sydney University Press 1979.

Clark, Ian. *Scars in the Landscape: A Register of Massacre Sites in Western Victoria, 1803-1859*. Aboriginal Studies Press, Canberra 1995.

Clarke, Anne. *Lake Condah Project Aboriginal Archaelogy: Resource Inventory*. Victorian Archaelogical Survey, Occasional Reports Series No 36, Department of Conservation & Environment, Melbourne 1991.

Cope, Sir William H. *The History of the Rifle Brigade*. Chatto and Windus, London 1877.

Coutts, P. J. F. *The Victorian Aboriginals 1800 to 1860*. Readings in Victorian Prehistory, vol. 2. Victorian Archaelogical Survey, Ministry for Conservation, Melbourne 1981.

Coutts, P. J. F & Lorblanchet, M. *Aboriginals and Rock Art in the Grampians, Victoria, Australia*. Records of the Victorian Archaelogical Survey No 12, Ministry for Conservation, Melbourne 1982.

Coutts, P. J. F, Frank, R. K. & Hughes, P. *Aboriginal Engineers of the Western District, Victoria*. Records of the Victorian Archaelogical Survey No 7, Ministry for Conservation, Melbourne 1978.

Critchett, Jan. *A 'distant field of murder': Western District frontiers 1834-1848*. Melbourne University Press, Melbourne 1990.

Dawson, James. *Australian Aborigines: The languages and customs of several tribes of Aborigines in the Western District of Victoria, Australia*. Facsimile edtn. Australian Institute of Aboriginal Studies, Canberra 1981.

de Serville, Paul. *Port Phillip gentlemen and good society before the gold rushes*. Oxford University Press Melbourne, 1980.

Erskine, John. *An Institute of the Law of Scotland*. Butterworths, Edinburgh 1871.

Finn, Edmund (Garryowen). *The Chronicles of Early Melbourne 1835 to 1852*. Facsimile edtn. Heritage Publications, Melbourne 1976.

Forsyth, Robert. *The Beauties of Scotland containing a clear and full Account of the Agriculture, Commerce, Mines and Manufactures of the Population, Cities, Towns, Villages etc of Each County*. Vols

1-5. Vernor and Hood, Edinburgh 1805-1808.

Goldie, Frederick. *A Short History of the Episcopal Church in Scotland.* Second Edition. The Saint Andrew Press, Edinburgh 1976.

Griffith, Charles. *The Present State and Prospects of the Port Phillip District of New South Wales.* William Curry, Junior and Company, Dublin 1845.

Groves, Lieut.-Colonel Percy. *Historical Records of the 7th or Royal Regiment of Fusiliers now known as The Royal Fusiliers (The City of London Regiment) 1685-1903.* Frederick B. Guerin, Guernsey, 1903.

Gunn, R. G. *Bunjil's Cave: Aboriginal Rock Art Site.* Victorian Archaelogical Survey, Occasional Reports Series No 13, Ministry for Conservation, Melbourne 1983.

------ *The Prehistoric Rock Art Sites of Victoria: A Catalogue.* Victorian Archaelogical Survey, Occasional Reports Series No 5, Ministry for Conservation, Melbourne 1981.

Hazzard, Margaret. *Punishment Short of Death.* Hyland House Publishing, Melbourne 1984.

Hughes, Robert. *The Fatal Shore: a history of the transportation of convicts to Australia, 1787-1868.* Collins Harvill, London 1987.

Kenyon, A. S. *The Aboriginal Protectorate of Port Phillip.* The Victorian Historical Magazine, Vol xxii, No 3, March 1928, pp. 134-71.

Kerr, William. *Kerr's Melbourne Almanac and Port Phillip Directory for 1841: a compendium of useful and accurate information connected with Port Phillip.* First published by William Kerr, Melbourne, 1841. Facsimile edition. Landsdown Slattery, Mona Vale, New South Wales 1978.

Kiddle, Margaret. *Men of Yesterday: A social history of the Western District of Victoria 1834-1890.* Melbourne University Press, Melbourne 1961.

MacFarlane, Ian (compiler). *1842 The Public Executions at Melbourne.* Victorian Government Printing Office, Melbourne 1984.

Massola, Aldo. *The Aborigines of South-Eastern Australia As They Were.* Heinemann, Melbourne 1971.

------ *Bibliography of Victorian Aborigines.* Hawthorn Press, Melbourne 1971.

------ *Bunjil's Cave: Myths, Legends & Superstitions of the Aborigines of South-eastern Australia.* Lansdowne Press, Melbourne 1968.

Mitchell, Thomas. *Three Expeditions into the Interior of Eastern Australia: with a description of the recently explored region of Australia Felix and of the present colony of New South Wales.* 2nd edtn. Boone, London 1839.

Post Office Annual Directory...in...Edinburgh and Leith. 1813-44

Rae-Ellis, Vivienne. *Black Robinson: Protector of Aborigines.* Melbourne University Press, 1988.

Reichl, Phyllis. *Volcanic Plains of Western Victoria.* Thomas Nelson (Australia) Limited. 1968.

Roderick, Colin. *John Knatchbull: From Quarterdeck to Gallows.* Angus & Robertson, Sydney 1963.

Russell, W. B. *The Second Fourteenth Battalion: A History of An Australian Infantry Battalion in the Second World War.* Angus & Robertson, Sydney & Melb 1948.

Savill, Vanda. *Dear Friends, Lake Condah Mission etc.* Kalprint Graphics, Hamilton 1976.

------ *Drumborg-Greenvale, Heart of the Shire of Portland.* Osborn Mannett, Hamilton 1977.
Scobie, Major Ian H. Mackay (Ed.). *The Scottish Regiments of the British Army.* Oliver and Boyd Limited, Edinburgh 1943.

Scott, Ernest (Ed.). *Australian Discovery, Vol. Two -- By Land.* J. M. Dent & Sons, London 1929.

Shaw, A. G. L. (Ed.). *Gipps-La Trobe Correspondence 1839-1846.* Melbourne University Press at the Miegunyah Press, Melbourne 1989.

Sinclair, Sir John. *The Statistical Account of Scotland: drawn up from the communications of the Ministers of the different parishes.* First published by William Creech, Edinburgh, 1791-1799. Microfiche edition. State Library of Victoria 1992.

Smith, Mrs. James. *The Booandik Tribe of South Australian Aborigines: A Sketch of Their Habits, Customs, Legends and Language.* Government Printer, Adelaide 1880.

Sturt, Charles. *Two Expeditions Into the Interior of Southern Australia during the years 1828, 1829, 1830 and 1831 with observations on the soil, climate and general resources of the colony of New South Wales.* First published Smith, Elder and Co, London, 1833. Facsimile edtn. Doubleday Australia 1982.

Tindale, Norman B. *Aboriginal Tribes of Australia: their terrain, environmental controls, distribution, limits, and proper names.* ANU Press, Canberra 1974.

Walker, David M. *Principles of Scottish Private Law.* Clarendon Press, Oxford 1970.

Watson, Charles B Boog. *Roll of Edinburgh Burgesses and Guild Brethren 1761-1841.* FRSE, Edinburgh 1933.

Watson, Frederick (ed.). *Historical Records of Australia.* Series 1. Commonwealth Parliament, Canberra 1914-25.

Williams, M.A.J; De Decker, P.; Kershaw, A.P. *The Cainozoic in Australia: A Re-appraisal of the Evidence.* Special Publication of the Geological Society of Australia No 18. Sydney 1991.

INDEX